The army that carved out Japan's land empire is examined in depth in two volumes. Drawn from WW 2 period and modern Japanese and American sources the Imperial Army's corps are arranged as they were deployed in the field, each with its history and order of battle. Divisions and brigades follow in detail. In addition an index of individual units, arranged by code number, is provided to make searching easy. Over 6.000 units are identified and are represented in the two books.

Today the Japanese Army remains mysterious, in part because it was secretive by nature. These books are wide ranging and informative, but of special interest is their ability to draw back the curtain on one of the Imperial Japanese Army's most coveted secrets, the intelligence camouflage it called Tsushogo.

To Tina, who made all this possible.

"War is a series of catastrophes which result in victory." (ed: or defeat)
Albert Pike (American 1809-91)

Special thanks to: Laura Onischuk and Elizabeth Rooney for guidance and assistance, Mr. Tadashi Yoda for kind assistance with the impenetrable organization of Japan's home defense units, Guy H. Pierce (US Army Ret.) for his infectious Japanese language skills, Joan Pinyol for his wonderful book *The Rising Sun in Arms*. Minerva Hui for trusting me with her late husband's camera, Teri Bryant for sharp eyes and deep knowledge and Harvey Low for being an oasis in a Pacific War desert.

The Imperial Japanese Army
Volume 1
Japan, the Annexed Territories and Manchuria

Roderick S. Grigor

This publication's sole aim is to inform for historical purposes. It has been produced without any intention of glorifying, excusing or ignoring the many horrific war crimes and atrocities the Imperial Japanese Army committed throughout the war.

Period artifacts are from the author's collection, except where indicated. The black and white artwork was created using war time photographs, some of which originate with Japanese print media in the 1930s and 40s but most are from soldiers' personal photo albums. In the present day, with one exception, the reference photographs used are in the author's possession.

Copyright © Roderick S. Grigor 2020
Cover design, artwork and map illustrations © Roderick S. Grigor 2020
All rights reserved. No part of this publication may be reproduced or transmitted by any means electronic or mechanical including scanning or any electronic storage and retrieval system without prior permission in writing from the publisher.

December 2020

Copy editor: Elizabeth Rooney

Print ISBN: 978-1-7772728-0-7
eBook ISBN: 978-1-7772728-1-2

Address: P.O. Box 98064
970 Queen St. East
Toronto, Ontario
Canada
M4M9L9
Email: paperblossombooks@gmail.com

The typeface throughout is 10 point, Times New Roman PS MT, except photos are in 8 pt and Japanese Kanji which are 12 and 10 point MS PMincho.

The Imperial Japanese Army
Japan, the Annexed Territories and Manchuria

Contents:	Page
Introduction:	8
Chapter 1. **Winds of Change 1920 to 1941**	11
1920 to 1941, unit types, identity discs and the army lists	
Chapter 2. **Japan and the Territories**	19
Notes on chapter	
Chart: Armies in Japan and the Territories showing parent-subordinate relationships and stationed or occupied location.	20
Imperial Headquarters	22
Formosa: 10th Area Army	30
Formosa Army District	33
Ryukyu Islands: 32nd Army	36
8th Air Division	43
Mainland Japan: Hokkaido, Karafuto, Kurile Islands 5th Area Army	47
Hokubu Army District	53
Hokkaido: 1st Air Division	56
North and Central Honshu: 1st General Army	59
Northern Honshu: 11th Area Army, 50th Army	60, 61
Tohoku Army District	62
Eastern Japan: 12th Area Army	67
Kanto Plain: 36th Army	69
Northeast of Tokyo: 51st army	70
Bōsō Peninsula: 52nd Army	71
South of Tokyo: 53rd Army	72
Tokyo Defense Army	73
Tokyo Bay Fortress Group	74
Tobu Army District	75
Central Honshu: 13th Area Army	84
Central Honshu Coast: 54th Army	86
Tokai Army District	86
Western Honshu, Shikoku and Kyushu: 2nd General Army	93
Central Japan: 15th Area Army	96
Chubu Army District	97
Western Honshu: 59th Army	103
Chugoku Army District	104
Shikoku: 55th Army	108
Shikoku Army District	109
Kyushu: 16th Area Army,	113
Kagoshima: 40th Army	115
Northern Kyushu: 56th Army	116
Southern Kyushu: 57th Army	117

Contents: Chapter 2 continued	Page
Seibu Army District	119
Mainland Japan: Air General Army	126
Central Japan: 1st Air Army	131
Southern Japan: 6th Air Army	135
Homeland Railway	139
Shipping Transport Command	142
<u>Manchuria and Korea</u>	149
Manchuria: Kwantung (Kanto) Army	150
34th Army	156
4th Army	158
2nd Air Army	160
Continental Railway	164
Eastern Manchuria: 1st Area Army	167
3rd Army	170
5th Army	172
South and West Manchuria: 3rd Area Army	174
30th Army	177
44th Army	178
Korea: 17th Area Army	180
Cheju Island: 58th Army	184
Korean Army District	186
5th Air Army	192
Chapter 3. **Divisions and Brigades**:	197
Divisions	
Infantry brigades transition to infantry groups	197
From square to triangular divisions	198
Divisional infantry group headquarters	
Independent brigades	199
<u>On Conscription and Replacement Personnel</u>:	
Conscription into the Army	
<u>Depot Divisions / Divisional Districts</u>:	200
Hoju: Replacement Units	
Depot Divisions	
Home Stations of Units Activated Outside Japan	
Home Designations	
Army District Units and Replacements	
1940 Territorial Recruiting Reorganization	
Chart: Evolving Home Depot Designations	201
Replacement System Reorganized	
Divisions:	202
Imperial Guard	203
Regular Infantry Divisions	204
Armored Divisions	253
Anti Aircraft Artillery Divisions	254

Contents:	Page
Brigades:	257
Independent Mixed Brigades	258
Cavalry Brigade	278
Independent Armored Brigades	278
Air Raiding Brigade (Paratroop/Glider)	281
Amphibious Brigades	282
Mobile Brigade	283
Guard Brigades (Tokyo)	283
Fortress Units	284
Locale Defense Unit	285
Chapter 4. **Unit Code Numbers**:	287
Rules and Regulations for Unit Codes	287
Index of Sequential Unit Code Numbers	292
Abbreviations (in parentheses) Identifying Parent Organization(s)	293
Sequential code names and numbers list	294
Appendix:	376
Chart 1: Imperial Army ca. 1945: In numerical sequence	376
General Armies	
Area Armies	
Armies	377
Air Armies	378
Shipping and Rail	
Chart 2: Army Activations and Movement from 1940 to 1945	379
Bibliography:	384
Maps:	
Imperial Japanese General Armies Map	20
Imperial General HQ armies under its direct control Map	22
Formosa and the Ryukyu Islands, 10th Area Army Map	30
Mainland Japan, Imperial HQ direct control, 1st and 2nd Armies	47
Hokkaido and the northern territories, 5th Area Army Map	48
Honshu 1st General Army Map	58
Northern Honshu, 11th Area Army/Tohoku Army District Map	60
Eastern Honshu, 12th Area Army/Tobu Army District Map	67
East-central Honshu, 13th Area Army/Tokai Army District Map	84
Honshu, Kyushu and Shikoku, 2nd General Army Map	93
Honshu, Shikoku, 15th Area Army/Chugoku and Shikoku Map	95
Kyushu, 16th Area Army Map	112
Manchuria, Kwantung Army	149
4th and 34th Armies Map	157
2nd Air Army Map	160
Manchuria Railroad Map	164
1st Area Army Map	167
3rd Area Army Map	174
Korea, 17th Area Army Map	180

Introduction

It's engaging to read about the South Pacific in World War 2 and how remote islands were transformed into small corners of hell. Many written accounts make the Japanese seem archaic, suicidal, anonymous. Long ago I became curious about the men who were Japan's soldiers and their paths to the battlefields of Asia and beyond.

The Internet is without doubt one of man's great steps forward. It's opened many doors during its short existence, including the ones traversed to research these pages.

JACAR, the Japan Center for Asian Historical Records is at the top of my list of sources. The Center opened Japan's incredible history archives to the world-wide public and is a wonderful example of preserving the past for the future. Another resource I drew on heavily is the 185 volume set *Japanese Monographs*. In this case, it arrived in the mail on 2 CDs containing Library of Congress microfilm impressions. They were purchased from the late Jim Lansdale of Florida. Also, my special thanks to Tadashi Yoda for educating me on the relationship between the Area Armies and Army Districts in Japan, no small matter.

In both *Monograph* and JACAR documents the occasional error appears. They can be mistakes, assumptions or misprints and are in both English and Japanese. Each suspect entry was checked against two independent sources where these were available. Very occasionally the inclusion or deletion of bits of information result from a judgement call, one or two of which may well come back to bite me later. Sometimes a chance find filled an important gap in the big picture; where these finds appear indisputable they were often exciting revelations. On the other hand, a piece of information with enough doubt attached would be cut, even where it was tempting to fill a gap with it.

At this point I wish to offer thanks to the authors, all former soldiers, responsible for committing their history to paper, much of which remains in hand-written form only.

Space saving measures

Overall, the design of *The Imperial Japanese Army* is consistent throughout both volumes based on the idea that once a reader has been through it they will be able to find what they desire. It is intended for anyone possessing one or both to use them to identify artifacts that fall within its purview on the spot and with minimum effort, as much as for any other purpose.

Given the amount of information in each volume, the histories have been abbreviated to save space and preserve detail. Putting dates to events is a priority here as these are first and foremost reference works. As a rule assume the end date for one army posting is also the start date for its next posting. If a month/day date appears without a year then the previous entry's year applies. Sometimes only the unit's activation year appears indicating it didn't survive more than that year before being demobilized or destroyed.

Research and collecting

Collecting anything seriously requires knowledge to prevent reckless purchases. In that respect these two books may be game-changers for Pacific War history buffs drawn to researching and/or collecting Japanese army memorabilia.

This work centers around the Tsushogo system of code names and numbers that hide unit names. Not finding a code number in the list doesn't mean it didn't exist. Many code numbers were lost during and since the war for many reasons: unit reorganizations, destruction of documents in battle, etc. By some accounts it's possible the lists in these two volumes contain slightly more than 25% of all the code numbers issued. Even if that doesn't sound like a comprehensive listing it's probably as good as it gets. Nonetheless at least 75% of the unit code numbers that matter to history and almost all those associated with the army's divisions and brigades are included.

Seventy-five years on

VJ Day took place 75 years ago this month yet Japanese militaria remains the least recognizable of that of all the armies that fought in World War 2. Common civilian address books sometimes appear as unit rosters and luggage tags as dog tags, etc. Fake Japanese dog tags are known to have been manufactured in China, artificially aged and sold in the West, so *caveat emptor*. Fakes are still not that common but it's a good practice to examine prospective acquisitions closely, ask questions and compare to known examples. It's also true that genuine Japanese Army dog tags continue to appear with unidentified stampings whose meanings have been forgotten, the most common of these being a number over 12 in the center column.

Drawing back the curtain

By November 1945 the Imperial Japanese Army had ceased to exist. Notwithstanding, in the West it is still most often remembered for heinous criminal acts committed by brutal soldiers. For many decades after discussion of it has remained a delicate subject, although by now there is almost no one alive who can provide a first-hand account of events. All that remains is the retelling of it and these two volumes contain a significant part of that story.

Toronto
August 2020

A *sea duty company* unloading Daihatsu landing barges in China (author)

Chapter 1

Winds of Change 1920 to 1941

In the teens and early 1920s Japan began feeling its way towards a progressive society. The best expression of this came from the national election of 1924 when the newly elected government passed a Universal Manhood Suffrage Act. For the first time males 25 years and older who had an income were given the right to vote. On May 1 1925, under government orders to cut expenditures, the Army disbanded four temporary divisions throwing thousands of soldiers into the streets. Economic expansion gave way to the Great Depression in 1929 and liberal pretensions crumbled under the weight of an entrenched aristocracy and fascist and communist agitation, falling exports and rising prices. Adding to discontent, between 1931 and 1933 Japan exited the gold standard causing the yen to fall forty-five percent in value.

On September 18, 1931, Kwantung Army officers engineered the Mukden Incident and the reinforcement of Manchuria began. At the same time guerilla activity became so widespread, military operations were extended throughout the territory. On February 18, 1932, Manchuria proclaimed itself an independent state with the Emperor Pu Yi on its throne and placed itself under Japan's protection. Installing China's last Emperor as its head of state was a crude attempt to legitimize a Japanese coup. Between April and December 1932 the Kwantung Army doubled in size to four divisions, one mixed brigade and two cavalry brigades. The following year one division was permanently withdrawn.

Manchuria Incident Medal, for participation in Manchuria 1931-1934 (author)

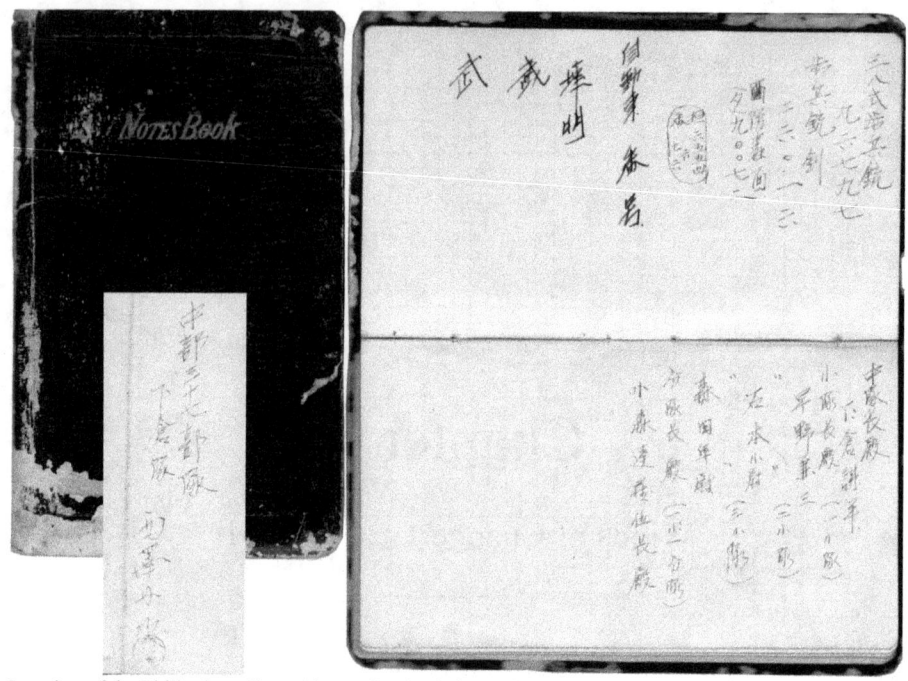

Invasion of the Philippines diary: Above: Service information on cover and first page, (inset) back cover has his training/replacement unit information. 'Chubu' 37 = 128th I.R. Replacement Unit (author)

Under pretext of the recent *China Incident*, at midnight on Nov 20, 1937 Imperial General Headquarters deactivated and reactivated itself under new rules that rid it of civilian oversight. The Army General Staff now exercised control over all military matters. It immediately doubled the size of the Kwantung Army to six divisions. Six days later Shanghai fell and the march on Nanking began. The escalating war in China went hand in hand with enhanced security precautions. On Sept 1, 1937, the names and sizes of units in the field were to be made vague by giving them their commander's surname and adding *group* or *unit* in place of regiment, battalion or company.

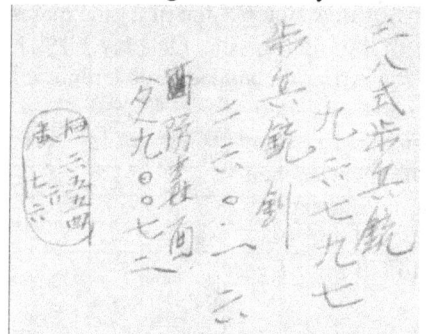

Enlarged detail: R to L: His Type 38 rifle serial # 96797 and bayonet serial # 26016. His dog tag info is inside the oval, 'Kaki' 6554, 6th Company, 9th Inf. Regt., 16th Div. 1941-2 (author)

At the outbreak of the China Incident Japan's army easily destroyed a poorly led and equipped enemy but was still small and in need of modernization. Sept 5, 1937 Japan's national defense and munitions industries were placed under military control and in March 1938 the National Mobilization Law was passed. These measures helped to greatly accelerate military industrial production. In Dec 1937 the army had just 24 divisions and 54 air squadrons. With hostilities ramping up and spreading the Army began to agitate for expansion, but it was not until Changkufeng in 1938 and Nomohan in 1939 that the need to modernize also hit home. On Sept 10, 1940 the Army adopted a measure called Tsushogo that replaced commander's names with code names and numbers as outlined in the *1941 Detailed Rules for Army Mobilization Plan.*

By Dec 1941 there were 51 divisions, 59 brigades and close to 40 air regiments. Training in mobile combat tactics, encirclement, night attacks and hand-to-hand combat was updated. Combat conditions the army had never faced such as amphibious landings under fire and jungle warfare were studied. Initially the new training was directed at units stationed on Formosa, in south China and in French Indochina. These were ostensibly nucleus formations for the Southern Expeditionary Army, which planners earmarked for the invasions of Malaya, Burma, Java, Sumatra, Borneo, Celebes, Guam, Bismarck Archipelago, Dutch Timor and the Philippines. While the 38th Division, nicknamed *Swampers*, in south China was assigned the task of taking Hong Kong from Britain.

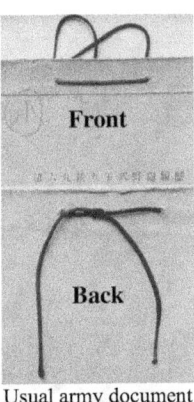

Usual army document binding for adding pages as needed.

Japan's most pressing need, the ability to produce synthetic oil, would have been solved if Germany had been able to share the secret and ship equipment to manufacture it but the war in Europe intervened. By 1940 Japan's munitions industry had developed to the point where it could keep pace with mobilization requirements and battle losses.

On July 28, 1941, the United States, Britain and the Netherlands placed a trade embargo on Japan as punishment for the military occupation of French Indochina, which threatened Allied interests in the region. This effectively cut off Japan's access to oil. Based on reserves the nation had six months to a year to replace what had been lost. On Aug 5 Japan attempted to open negotiations but met with America's outright rejection. The Japanese Government and Imperial Headquarters held a liaison conference in early September to decide future national policy. With diplomacy's failure war was inevitable. On Nov 5 Tojo proclaimed Japan ready for a war that would "ensure self-preservation and establish a new order in Greater East Asia."

On Dec 1, 1941, Japan declared itself at war with America, Britain and the Netherlands appointing Dec 8 as *X-Day*, which military planners considered to be the last good day to launch attacks. By evening on the 8th, Pearl Harbor had been bombed, Malaya invaded, Hong Kong, Midway, Wake and Guam attacked, the Philippines bombed and Bangkok occupied by the Imperial Guard Division. In order to escalate the attack on Malaya, Japan had decided to invade its Thai ally without prior notification. Thereby Dec 8 marked the beginning of that which Japan referred to as *The Greater East Asia War*. On Dec 10 British battleship Prince of Wales and cruiser Repulse were sunk by the Japanese Navy's land-based 22nd Air Flotilla in Saigon.

"Constructing East Asian New Order" Flags of Japan, China and Manchuria appear on a propoganda pin promoting a phony alliance

Within days the balance of power in southern Asia and the Pacific had shifted from West to East. The opportunity to create its much-touted new social order in East Asia, which Japan called the *Greater East Asia Co-Prosperity Sphere*, had arrived. Apart from

China Incident Medal Established 1939, abolished 1946. For participation in China 1937-45 (photos this page, author)

employing a few bureaucrats the Co-Prosperity Sphere amounted to nothing more than propaganda for an army of occupation.

Unit types

Until 1937 Japan's small army was very capable within its limitations. Infantry served as the primary arm of service with field divisions and brigades designed around providing it with support for sustained operations.

The largest mobile formation in the army was the division, these were by nature small towns with their own communications, medical, veterinary, transport, repair etc. facilities.

Overall command and control in the field was provided by an army headquarters, which usually directed operations from a fixed position in the rear. When an army headquarters had a permanent location (i.e., it was a garrison), purpose-activated communications, intelligence and/or depot units were often permanently attached. Most requirements however were provided for by specialized independent units dedicated to transport, construction, labor, etc.

Army unit types were also divided into categories unrelated to function; these were Field, Independent, Specially Established, Temporarily Formed, Replacement and Line of Communications. Field and independent units were regular army units of all types. Independent units were created to deploy under the control of an army headquarters. Today, if a code name from one of these has survived then some its history has too.

Private purchase Wire Company pen case for a communications unit officer (author)

Memorabilia mainly from a Japanese soldier's wartime service in China: Conscription notice, service record booklet, two diaries, photos of himself, a comfort bag sent from Korea and his service bag (author)

Chapter 1

Infantry parade through the streets of Kanazawa, ca. 1920s (anonymous photo)

<u>Specially Established Units</u> were created as cost effective gap fillers for regular army shortcomings. Specially established construction, land or sea duty units had a permanent establishment of 61 officers and men. Up to 604 local and transient workers were conscripted for an average of 665. These units provided personnel for road clearing, loading and unloading cargo, building infrastructure, etc.

<u>Specially Established Machine Cannon Units</u> had an authorized strength of 85 men. Armed with Type 98 (1938) 20mm machine cannon, these units were created to compensate for the army's lack of automatic weapons, something the United States had in abundance.

<u>Specially Established Guard Units</u> were mostly older semi-regular or time-expired part-time soldiers who provided security throughout Japan and the territories. Battalions varied in size, but generally averaged around 500 poorly armed men, while companies were fixed at about 126.

<u>Temporarily Formed Units</u> absorbed displaced and surplus personnel in the field.

<u>Replacement Units</u> were common and usually associated with a particular regiment. They were intended to replace time-expired soldiers or fill in for casualties taken in the field. Once in theater, these

Superior private, 3rd Field Artillery Regiment with a borrowed sword, ca. 1938. He wears a Type 5 tunic with newer Type 98 insignia. A transitional look that was not uncommon in China at the time (anonymous photo)

troops could also be reassigned to act independently or attached to another unit with similar training and depleted by circumstances.

Line of Communications Units operated behind front lines to manage movement, provide security or hospital care or facilitate the movement of supplies to the front and casualties to the rear.

Rapid Firing Gun Units were anti-tank gun units, originally armed with the inadequate Type 94 (1936) 37mm cannon and later upgraded to Type 1 (1941) 37mm and Type 1 (1942) 47mm cannon. Both fired armor-piercing and high-explosive shells.

Mountain Artillery Units were armed with Type 41 (1908) and Type 94 (1934) 75mm mountain guns, weapons designed to be broken down and transported/manhandled through mountain or jungle terrain and deployed as infantry support.

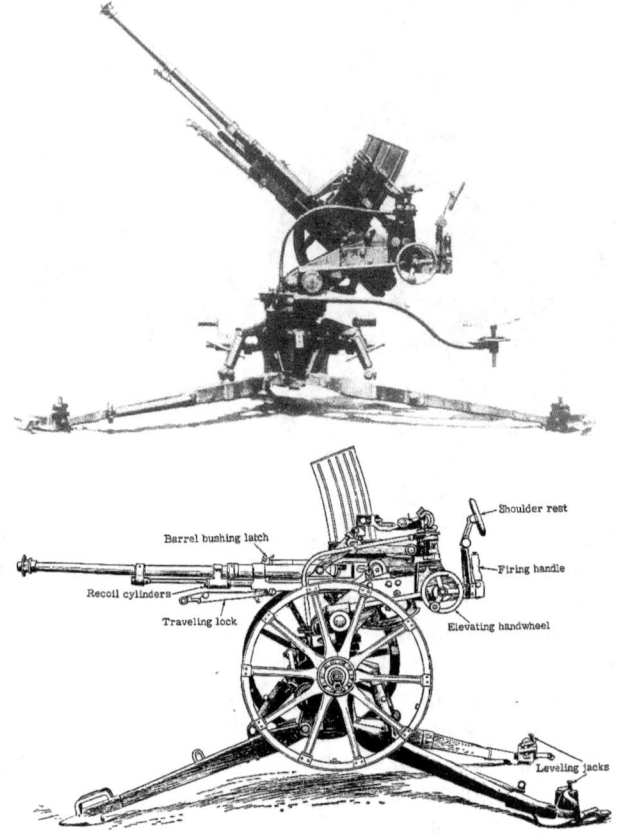

Type 98 Machine Cannon. This weapon was issued to 'Specially Established Machine Cannon Units' and others to compensate for Japan's overall lack of large caliber automatic weapons. (images: upper: Taki's Type 98 page. lower: Handbook on Japanese Military Forces)

The organization of an infantry regiment
Headquarters unit
3 rifle battalions
Signal unit
Artillery company
Anti-tank company
Infantry battalion:
HQ unit, 4 rifle companies, 1 machine gun company, 1 battalion gun platoon
Rifle company: 3 platoons, each 4 squads.
Machine gun company: 4 MG platoons each with 2 squads, ammo platoon 3 squads.
Numbering of units within an infantry regiment:
Rifle companies were numbered according to their place in the regiment not battalion: 1st Battalion = 1st to 4th Companies, 2nd Battalion = 5th to 8th: 3rd Battalion = 9th to 12th. An infantry battalion had one machine gun company numbered for the battalion. Each regiment had 3, the 1st, 2nd and 3rd Machine Gun Companies.

Identity discs (dog tags)
Tags are oval in shape, measure about 1 ¾" x 1 ¼" and read from right to left. The Japanese on these oft-found war souvenirs is a mystery to most. The number on a tag's left side identifies an individual soldier. His ID number is also found on a page in his

Company's personnel roster as well as in a duplicate roster held by the regiment's home duty unit. Unfortunately many rosters were destroyed, especially those carried into the field. Nowadays any attempt to locate a soldier through his identification tag is, to say the least, unrealistic.

A tag's right side number showed an abbreviated unit name until the introduction of code names and numbers (Tsushogo) in 1940. Thereafter unit names were hidden behind code numbers. Threat of transfer or reorganization usually precluded small independent units from *crowning* their code numbers with a code name under the new naming rules. These crowns usually appear on the tags of units within permanent organizations such as divisions, brigades, sometimes armies.

Code names and numbers were as much part of a unit's permanant identity as its unit name and home station were.

Tag: 9942, 6th Air Signal Regiment, 3rd Co. It was a wire company posted to Silay, the P.I. early 1945

Demobilization and army unit lists

The army had 6,983,000 men in arms, 3,655,000 in Japan alone at the time of surrender. The War Ministry issued a general demobilization outline Aug 18, 1945 and by Aug 30th 1,500,000 Japanese soldiers had been discharged.

Occupation forces arrived aboard the US 3rd Fleet, which entered Sagami Bay on Aug 27. Local commanders were ordered to report to senior US Army commanders in their areas as their staff worked on demobilization status numbers, unit tables of organization and personnel strengths. US authorities checked this information against Imperial Japanese Headquarters files or with on-the-spot checkups.

By the end of October the Imperial Army had nine army unit lists in English with notes to assist occupation forces.

On Dec 1st the Ministries of the Army and Navy were rechristened the 1st and 2nd Demobilization Ministries respectively.

Tag: 12936, the 26th Independent Mixed Regiment, 6th Company (front and back). Part of the Shimbu Army Group for the defense of Manila, later became the Bicol Detachment

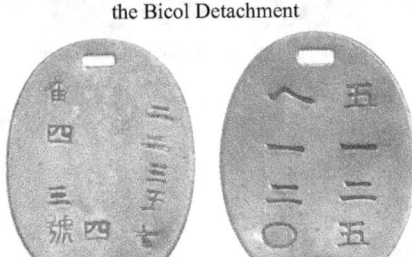

Left side tag: 22357, 145th Division Rapid Firing Gun Unit (anti tank). Division activated in Feb 1945.
Right side: 5125, 5th Ind. Mixed Regiment, 1st Battalion on Wake Island, became 13th Ind. Mixed Regt. The 2nd Battalion was sunk off Truk and the 3rd Battalion was on Marcus Is.

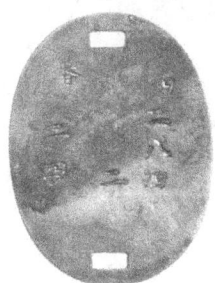

Left Tag: 4284, the 23rd Independent Infantry Battalion, 62nd Division. Part of the 6th Ind. Mixed Brigade in China, absorbed into the 62nd Div.and sent to Shuri, Okinawa where it was destroyed.
Right Tag: 9948, 3rd Air Raiding Regt. (paratroopers), Rofu Company; participated in the Dec. 6, 1944 attack on the Burauen Airfields, Luzon.
(photos this page; author)

Japanese soldiers reconnoitering suspected enemy positions

A patrol on the move in China (author)

Chapter 2

Japan and the Territories

It's not only important to have true-to-life, detailed representations of individual armies and major units, it's also desirable to create an accurate picture of the Imperial Army as a whole. In Japan proper, the Army arranged itself geographically, starting with Hokkaido in the north and ending at Kyushu in the south. Two general armies and five area armies were created on April 8, 1945 under the *Army Mobilization Plan for Early 1945*. The area armies ran in sequence from the 11th to 16th (absent the 14th) north to south beginning on northern Honshu.

As an annexed territory Taiwan should appear after Japan but because Imperial General Headquarters maintained direct control over it via the 10th Area Army, it appears early. Also annexed to Japan, Korea is out of place as it is found after Manchuria, which was ostensibly an independent state. The reason for this is the 17th Area Army became subordinate to the Kwantung Army in Manchuria on Aug 10, 1945, immediately after the Russian invasion to provide for a unified command and coordinated defense.

The chart on the next page, *Armies in Japan and the Territories*, provides headquarters locations for the army groups in Japan, Taiwan, Korea and Manchuria. It serves as a visual guide for locating an army within its grouping. Excepting air armies, rail and shipping commands, which are found under their superiors' organization following the land forces, individual armies throughout this chapter follow each other in the same order as is shown on the chart.

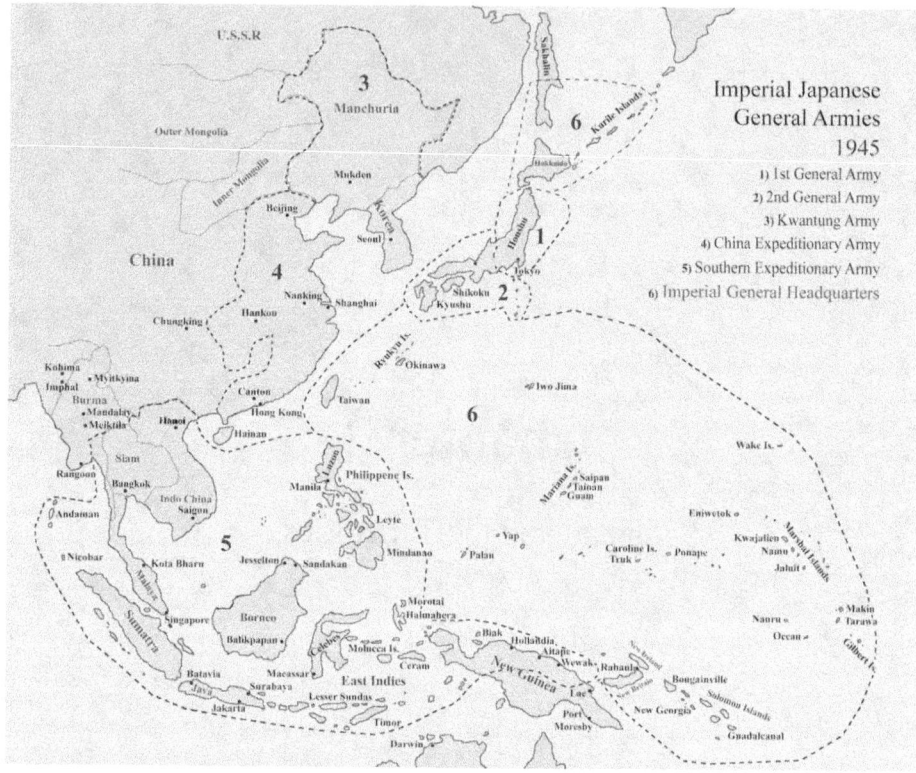

Armies in Japan and the Territories:
1. Imperial General Headquarters: Tokyo
a. under direct control: 5th Area Army - Hokkaido and the islands north of Japan
a. 27th Army - Kurile Islands (deactivated Jan. 22, 1945)
b. 10th Area Army - Taipei, Formosa
b. 32nd Army - Okinawa; 8th Air Division - Formosa
c. Shipping Transport Command - Ujina

2. 1st General Army: Tokyo, Honshu's northeast, east and north coast districts
a. 11th Area Army - Sendai
a. 50th Army - Aomori
b. 12th Area Army - Tokyo
b. 36th Army - Urawa, 51st Army - Mito; 52nd Army - Susui; 53rd Army - Tamagawa; Tokyo Defense Army - Tokyo; Tokyo Bay Army Corp - Tateyama
c. 13th Area Army - Nagoya
c. 54th Army - Shinshiromachi
d. 6th Air Army - Fukuoka

3. 2nd General Army: Hiroshima, western Honshu, Shikoku and Kyushu Districts
a. 15th Area Army - Osaka
a. 55th Army - Kochi; 59th Army - Hiroshima
b. 16th Area Army - Fukuoka

b. 40ᵗʰ Army - Kagoshima; 56ᵗʰ Army -Iizuka; 57ᵗʰ Army - Takanabe

4. Kwantung Army: - Hsinking, Manchuria
a. under direct control: 4ᵗʰ Army - Tsitsihar, Manchuria
a. 34ᵗʰ Army - Hamhung, Korea
b. 2ⁿᵈ Air Army - southern Manchuria
c. 1ˢᵗ Area Army - Mutanchiang, Manchuria
c. 3ʳᵈ Army - Yenchi; 5ᵗʰ Army - Yehho
d. 3ʳᵈ Area Army - Mukden, Manchuria
d. 30ᵗʰ Army - Meihokou; 44ʰ Army - Liaoyuan
e. 17ᵗʰ Area Army - Seoul, Korea
e. 58ᵗʰ Army - Cheju Island
f. 5ᵗʰ Air Army - Seoul, Korea
g. Continental Railway System - Manchuria

5. Air General Army: Air Command - Tokyo
1ˢᵗ Air Army - Tokyo
6ᵗʰ Air Army - Fukuoka

6. Imperial GHQ Command: Tokyo
Homeland Railway Command - Tokyo
Army Ministry – Ichigaya Heights, Shinjuku, Tokyo
Inspector General of M.T.

Notes on army units lists
Column 1 heading: Name of the army, Column 2 heading: Code name
Column 1 below: Unit names   Column 2 below: Code numbers
Parethesis (123) is the number of men authorized to serve in the unit. Please note occasionally the **actual** number of men present at the time the record was created is shown instead of the authorized number, depending on the available source.
Column 2 heading and body combine to form the unit's code name and number (called its *Tsushogo* in Japanese).
Example: 10ᵗʰ Area Army Air Intelligence Unit is *Wan* 湾4570 (2,037) with a complimnent of 2,037 men.

Imperial General Headquarters

The Imperial Japanese Army
Taiwan, Ryukyus and Hokkaido Regions

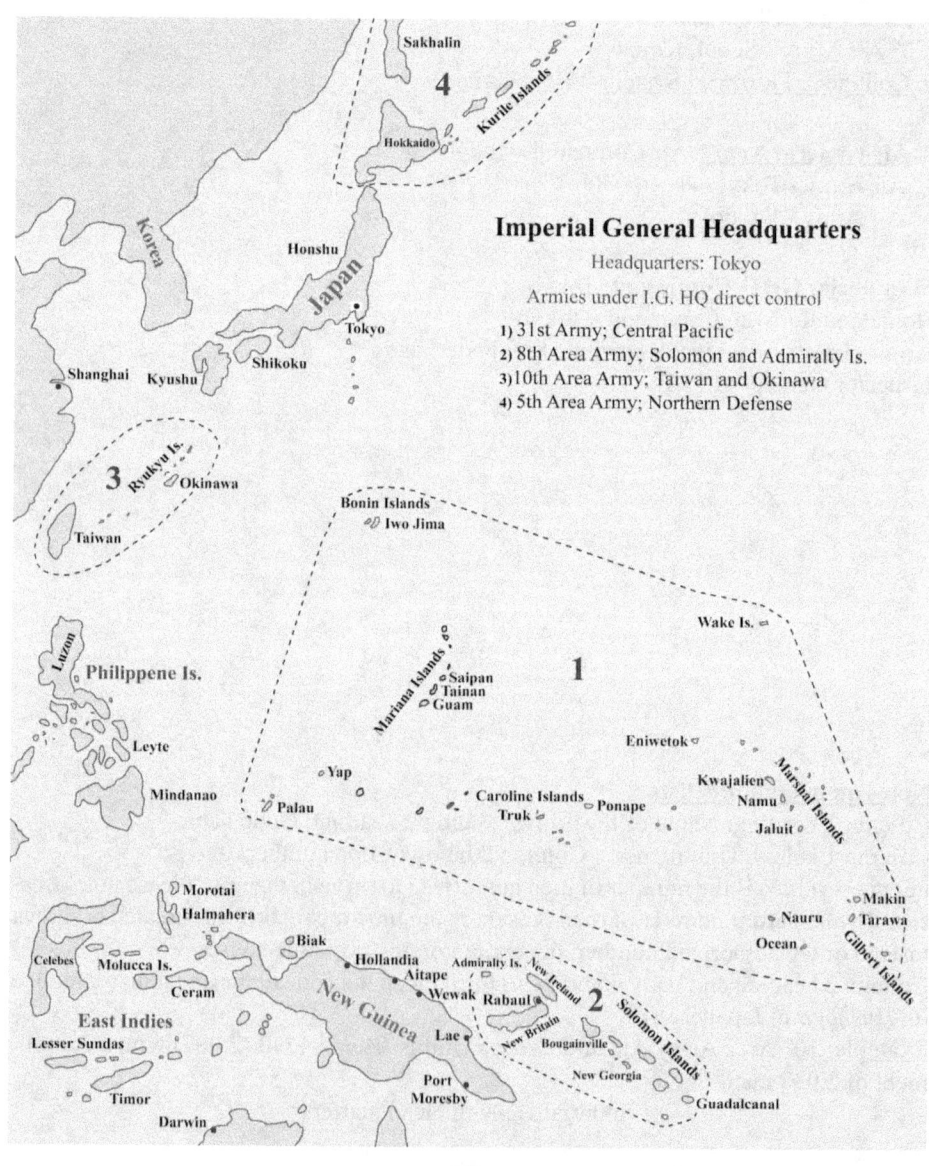

Chapter 2

Imperial General Headquarters:

Imperial General Headquarters served at the pleasure of the Emperor. At midnight Nov. 20, 1937, Military Decree #1 abolished Imperial General Headquarters, removed civilian oversight and immediately re-established it as the exclusive authority on all military matters. A founding ordinance defined it as the "highest body of the Supreme Command". Within Imperial Headquarters the Army and Navy remained as ever independent from each other. Where joint Army/Navy action was required, staff studies served as the basis for *central agreements*, which outlined the agreed to terms of mutual cooperation. A new central agreement was required every time the Army and Navy committed themselves to a joint operation.

The Ministry of the Army building was located in Miyakezaka, central Tokyo but moved to Ichigaya Heights Shinjuku later in the war (date unknown). After the war, on December 1, 1945 the Ministry of the Army became the 1st Demobilization Ministry.

Note: *Imperial General Headquarters never had its own kanji code name.*

The Liaison Conference System: Liaison Conferences coordinated action between the Government and Imperial Headquarters on matters of importance. The Liaison Committee existed to avoid any conflict created by having the Premier become a member of Imperial Headquarters. Its mission in that respect was to keep Cabinet informed. It was comprised of the Ministers for War (Army) and the Navy and the Chiefs of Staff for the Army and Navy. From 1940 a Liaison Conference could also be called upon to act as a Supreme War Council.

Cabinet Council: Constitutionally, certain issues had to be referred to and approved by the Cabinet Council. Legislative bills, budgets, foreign treaties, civil laws, etc.

Army Governance: Headed by the Chief and Deputy Chief of Army General Staff
General Affairs Bureau – mobilization and training,
1st Bureau – operations
2nd Bureau – intelligence
3rd Bureau – transport and communications
4th Bureau – historical
18th Group – radio intelligence deciphering (reported directly to the Chief of A.G.S.).
Reorganized in 1943 into: 1st Bureau – operations, 2nd Bureau – intelligence, 3rd Bureau – transport and communications.

Army General Staff was responsible for homeland defense through General Defense Command. As well it provided strategic planning for the Kwantung Army, China Expeditionary Army, Southern Expeditionary Army and, in cooperation with the navy, Pacific islands defense. Central agreements gave either the Army or Navy jurisdiction over isolated island chains throughout the Pacific and Indian Oceans regions.

Imperial General Headquarters could issue two types of orders:
a. An Imperial Decree whereby Chief of General Staff relayed the Emperor's wishes.
b. By Direction of Imperial General Headquarters. Chief of the General Staff issued *instructions* which were to be regarded as orders.

Divisions and brigades were sometimes taken under I.G.HQ's direct control to facilitate reassignment or for missions that required Army/Navy cooperation.

Subordinate armies / duty dates:
Kwantung Army from Apr 12, 1919 until Aug 19, 1945
Korea Army from 1910 until Jan 22, 1945   became 17th Area Army

North China Area Army from Nov 17, 1937 until Sept 23, 1939   to China Exp.Army
China Expeditionary Army from Sept 23, 1939 until Sept 2, 1945
South China Area Army from July 25, 1940 until July 5, 1941   became 23rd Army
General Defense Army from July 12, 1941 until Apr 8, 1945   bec. General Armies
23rd Army from July 5, 1941 until Aug 15, 1941
25th Army from July 5, 1941 until Nov 6, 1941
Southern Expeditionary Army from Nov 6, 1941 until Sept 12, 1945
17th Army from May 18, 1942 until Nov 15, 1942
14th Army from June 29, 1942 until Mar 27, 1944
8th Area Army from Nov 15, 1942 until Sept 7, 1945
Northern Defense Army from Feb 5, 1943 until Mar 6, 1944   became 5th Area Army
2nd Area Army from Oct 30, 1943 until Mar 27, 1944
31st Army from Feb 25, 1944 until the war ended   Pacific Islands
5th Area Army from Mar 16, 1944 until Sept 22, 1945
Formosa Army from Mar 22, 1944 until Sept 22, 1944   became 10th Area Army
General Defense HQ from May 5, 1944 until Mar 31, 1945
10th Area Army from Sept 22, 1944 until Oct 25, 1945
1st General Army from Apr 8, 1945 until Nov 30, 1945
2nd General Army from Apr 8, 1945 until Oct 15, 1945
Air General Army from Apr 8, 1945 until Aug 15, 1945
17th Area Army from Jan 22, 1945 until Aug 10, 1945

Service History:

1941: On Apr 13th the *Soviet Japanese Neutrality Pact* was signed in Moscow, it was to expire on Apr 25, 1946 ○ June 22nd, Germany invaded Russia ○ On July 5th, the 25th Army became active in French Indochina ○ On Jul 24th Vichy France signed a mutual defense agreement with Japan allowing it to occupy southern Indochina ○ In Aug Manchuria received its largest ever troop reinforcement disguised as a training exercise. The Kwantung Army increased to 700,000 men and 600 airplanes ○ On Oct 23rd the Tojo Government came to power ○ On Nov 5th Japan resolved to force the U.S. to sue for peace and block Britain from Australia and India by taking control of the Indian Ocean. Japan already had bases in Indochina, Hainan Is., Southern China, Taiwan, Palau, Bonin Is. The Southern Expeditionary Army was organizing ○ Dec 1st Japan declares hostilities to begin against the US, Britain and Netherlands to preserve the Empire. The China Expeditionary Army, Southern Expeditionary Army and Kwantung Army receive orders for their roles on Dec 8th, X Day (for details see China and Southern ExpeditionaryArmies) ○ Dec 7th, the Pearl Harbor attack ○

1942: Jan 19th, the Dept. of Governor General of Hong Kong was created ○ Jan 23rd, the South Seas Detachment takes Rabaul ○ IGHQ looked into occupying Australia in early 42 but the ten divisions and ships needed were not available. Instead they planned to cut sea routes to America by occupying Fiji, Samoa, New Caledonia and Port Moresby ○ Apr 18th, Doolittle Raiders bombed Tokyo, in retaliation Japan destroyed all enemy airbases in Chekiang, China ○ On May 3rd the occupation of the Solomon Islands was completed ○ June 10th, Imperial Headquarters began withdrawing units from the Southern Expeditionary Army and returning them to Manchuria and China ○ May 5th, IGHQ announced the invasion of Midway for June 7th and placed the Ichiki Detach. (Midway) and North Seas Detach (Aleutian Is.) under Navy control ○ On May 18th the 17th Army became active in the Solomon Islands. Four aircraft carriers were lost at Midway scuttling the invasion. The occupations of New Caledonia, Port Moresby, Samoa and Fiji were also abandoned ○ June 6th and 7th Attu and Kiska were occupied without opposition ○ June 22nd the India Independence League was formed with Japanese Govt. support ○ On June 29th the 14th Army was transferred from Southern Army to IGHQ control to facilitate a military administration in the Philippines ○ On July 10th the 3rd Air Army was created ○ In October IGHQ reviewed the potential for counterattacks from China, Indian Ocean, Southwest Pacific, Southeast Pacific, and Northeast ○ On Nov 10th the Indochina Garrison Army became active in Saigon to oversee negotiations with the Indochina Govt. ○ Nov 16th the 8th Area Army became active, it controlled the 17th Army in the Solomon Is., the new 18th Army on New Guinea and the 2nd Air Brigade. ○ In Nov/Dec 18th Army re-supply and reinforcement efforts became critical ○ On Dec 10th the Chungking Szechuan operations were canceled to replace losses in the Pacific, which had become a priority. Resources were too thin to deliver a crippling blow in China ○ In Dec Rabaul, main operating base in the Southeast Pacific became a major enemy target ○ Army General Staff recommend expropriating 300,000 tons of shipping for military use but the Minister of War refused ○ On Dec 31st IGHQ cancelled the offensive in the Solomons and postponed the occupation of eastern New Guinea ○

1943: Jan 4th, the 8th Area Army was ordered to withdraw from Guadalcanal on Feb 1st and establish a more favorable position on New Guinea ○ On Jan 9th the 1st Air Division was activated and on Feb 11th transferred from 1st Air Army to the Northern Army ○ Dire circumstances in the southeast Pacific prevented Army General Staff from publishing a plan for the southwest area until the end of February ○ Mar 25th the Army took control of the northern Solomons and Navy the central Solomons ○ In mid April as conditions were deteriorating in the southeast Pacific the Army and Navy agreed to reinforce small island garrisons. 1st and 2nd South Seas Garrison Units were activated ○ May 29th the US recaptured Attu in the Kuriles, by Aug 1st the Kiska garrison had evacuated safely ○ Jul 28th, the 4th Air Army organized and was attached to the 8th Area Army ○ On Sept 8th Italy surrendered releasing Allied troops and equipment to fight in the East ○ In Sept Ministry of Munitions is established in Tokyo ○ Sept 15th, due to the collapsing New Guinea, Solomons, Marshalls line Army General Staff went on the defensive, effectively isolating about 300,000 troops ○ By mid September, with so many transport ships sunk it had become impossible to replace the losses. The Army and Navy were given orders for a joint study on ways to protect sea-going transport ○ On Sept 30th operational guidance for the southeast and central Pacific reiterated fortifying and counter attacking the enemy ○ In Sept a Philippine Republic puppet state was established for Oct 14th (dissolved 17/8/45) ○ Oct 21st the Free India Provisional Government was created in Burma. Its military wing, the India National Army, was allied with Japan ○ In October IGHQ began to plan operation *Ichi-Go*, a rail corridor stretching from Manchuria to French Indochina ○ Nov 1st, U.S. troops landed near Torokina, Bougainville Island and on the 21st at Makin and Tarawa in the Gilbert Islands ○ Nov 22nd to the 26th, the Cairo Conference resulted in a Dec 1st communiqué announcing the Pacific War would only end with Japan's unconditional surrender ○ In late 1943 Army General Staff had the Southern Army build a base on Halmahera. New shipping routes were established and in the Philippines harbors became relay hubs for the Southeast area ○

1944: Jan 7th, IGHQ approved *U-Go*. 15th Army in Burma was to destroy British forces in the Imphal Basin ○ Jan 24th, the China Expeditionary Army was ordered to start *Ko-go* in April, the North China phase of *Ichi-go* along Beijing-Hankou Railway ○ On Feb 1st the U.S. landed on Kwajalein and Roi in the Marshall Islands, taking both by the 6th ○ Feb 10th, Army General Staff published a plan to reorganize railway units as attacks on shipping had increased dependence on other transport ○ Feb 15th, Army General Staff orders the Southern Army, 2nd Area Army and Northern Army to supply strategically placed sea bases in Bay of Bengal, Southwest Pacific and Kurile Is. with small boat maintenance units, signal installations, anti aircraft units and stockpiles of munitions and fuel ○ Feb 17th, Truk Island bombed with many ships at anchor sunk ○ Feb 20th General Tojo appoints himself Chief of Army General Staff (resigns Jul 18th after Saipan falls) and Admiral Shimada Chief of the Navy General Staff ○ Feb 29th U.S. troops land in the Admiralty Is. ○ Mar 14th, as the 8th Area Army was isolated in Rabaul Army General Staff ordered the 18th Army and 4th Air Army to join the 2nd Area Army. Japan's strategy in the Central Pacific was to deny island bases to the US ○ At the end of March the Japanese Army had 3,650,000 troops, I.G.HQ estimated the need for an additional 1,000,000 men to win the war ○ On Mar 25th an Army/Navy agreement was reached on Central Pacific operations. Fighting on Kiska, Attu and Guadalcanal had made them realize they needed a unified command in the Pacific. Army units were placed under Naval control in the Carolines, Marianas and Ogasawaras. The 31st Army now answered to the Central Pacific Fleet but was in charge of land operations in the Carolines, Marianas and Ogasawaras. Regardless of arm of service the most senior officer on an island would assume command in combat ○ On April 15th Army General Staff placed the 2nd Area Army under Southern Expeditionary Army control ○ On Apr 19th *Ichi-go* began in China. Divided in two parts: *Ko-go* (North) ran along the Beijing-Wuhan railway sector mainly in Henan Province and *To-go* (South) in Hunan Province ○ July 4th Army General Staff ordered the Southern Army to terminate *U-go* in Burma ○ Late April, aware their enemy in the Pacific was superior and growing stronger Army General Staff began planning A-go to draw American forces into a naval battle off the Marianas ○ In May an attack was expected on the Philippines. Southern Expeditionary Army HQ redeployed to the P.I. to oversee the 14th Area Army, 4th Air Army and Naval preparations but it proved difficult to direct operations elsewhere when situations became critical ○ May 27th the US landed on Biak ○ On June 15th the US landed on Saipan ○ June 19th and 20th *A-go, The Great Marianas Turkey Shoot*, occured ○ In June all air army training schools converted to Air Training Divisions ○ On July 18th the Japanese public is finally informed of Saipan, Tojo is defeated by a cabinet vote of no confidence and replaced with the Koiso Cabinet ○ July 21st, US troops invade Guam ○ On July 24th *Sho-go*, plans for the decisive battle, were published in 4 parts ○ In early Aug the Southern Army requested permission to move its headquarters to Singapore or Saigon. To compensate for US firepower independent machine cannon units were organized and attached to various combat organizations ○ On Sept 10th the 6th Area Army was activated in central China ○ On Sept 15th the US invades Morotai and Peleliu ○ Oct 18th Imperial General Headquarters orders *Sho-go*, defense of the Philippines, to begin immediately ○ On Oct 20th Americans land on Leyte, P.I. ○ Oct 24th and 25th, the naval battles of Suriago Strait and Samar. Suriago Strait proved critical to US domination of the sea-lane ○ At the end of October there were about 6,390,000 reservists in Japan, with 4,690,000 ready for active duty. IGHQ estimated it needed 40 more divisions plus rear area service units to complete Japan's defenses. There were not enough trained personnel, especially engineers and signalmen. About 87% of Japanese adults worked in food and munitions ○ On Nov 17th the Southern Expeditionary Army's headquarters finally received permission to move to Saigon ○ On Nov 24th Saipan based US B-29's bombed Tokyo ○ Dec 15th the US landed on Mindoro, the Philippines and the Kwantung Army Railway renamed the Continental Railway ○ Beginning in Dec the continental railway replaced sea transport to various areas ○ As Germany was near collapse there were concerns over Soviet aggression in Japan ○

1945: In January three divisions of replacement troops were organized in Japan and shipped to China ○ In January four fully equipped divisions and a third of the Kwantung Army's equipment and war materiel was sent from Manchuria to Japan. Key personnel required by General Defense Command also returned. I.G.HQ ordered 40 divisions and 20 mixed brigades mobilized for homeland defense ○ Jan 9th, American troops land in the Lingayen Gulf, P.I. ○ Jan 16th, an emergency mobilization of eight divisions and four mixed brigades begins in Manchuria ○ On Feb 1st US troops attack Batangas and Lingayen ○ Feb 3rd, the 10th Area Army on Formosa receives orders to prevent the Americans from creating air and sea bases threatening Formosa and the Nansei Is. ○ On Feb 6th the homeland defense districts reorganize. The three army districts become five area armies and five military districts. Commanders and staff of area armies are given the equivalent rank in their military district administration. A tentative Army Navy agreement on air operations in the East China Sea is reached ○ From Feb 6th onward the Korea Army's orders were to protect the railway system and build defenses along the Yalu and Toukou rivers ○ On Feb. 11th the 17th Area Army was activated in Korea ○ Feb 16th, the US sent 1,200 sorties from aircraft carriers into Japan's Kanto district. Flying in at low altitude to avoid radar they hit airfields all over the district ○ On Feb 19th US troops land on Iwo Jima ○ Beginning late-Feb and running until Apr 8th under the 1st Group Army Mobilization Plan divisions raised to defend the homeland were mobilized. Due to limited manpower and equipment this was the first of three group mobilizations. Depot division troops became nuclei for the new divisions. 13 in mainland Japan, 1 each in Hokkaido, Karafuto, the Kuriles and 2 in Korea. They were guard divisions to defend coastlines and fight holding actions but their initial task was to build fortifications ○ In March the 11th, 25th, 57th and 1st Tank Divisions shipped from Manchuria to Japan. ○ On Mar 9th B29's dropped incendiary bombs on Tokyo causing fires and heavy casualties ○ Mar 14th, Japanese troops took control of central and south Indochina marking the end of a shaky alliance with the French colony ○ By mid-March Kyushu, Shikoku and Kinki were subjected to daily air attacks ○ Mar 19th, the 6th Air Army was placed under Navy control to coordinate all air units in the Nansei Islands ○ Mar 20th, planning for *Ketsu-go* (the final battle) began ○ Mar 25th the US lands on Kerama Is. exposing Okinawa as its next target ○ On Apr 1st the US lands troops on Okinawa ○ Apr 5th, in Moscow the Soviet Foreign Minister told Japan's ambassador the Soviets would not renew the 1941 Nonaggression Pact. ○ On Apr 8th the 1st General Army, 2nd General Army and Air General Army's orders of battle bulletins were published ○ In April the Army and Navy signed an agreement that divided responsibilities for the decisive battle in Japan and the surrounding seas ○ Mid April, Soviets renounce the *Soviet-Japanese Neutrality Pact* indicating they planned to go to war against Japan ○ On April 15th the 1st and 2nd General Armies are activated. To avoid disruption subordinate units were gradually transferred over. The

1st General Army was responsible for North, Northeastern and East Coast Military Districts, the 2nd General Army for the Central and Western Military Districts. General Defense Command was simultaneously deactivated ○ In mid-April enemy fighter planes began operating out of Iwo Jima ○ The 2nd Group Army Mobilization began in early April, with the best personnel conscripted into 8 well-equipped mobile divisions, the 201st, 202nd, 205th, 206th, 209th, 212th, 214th and 216th Divisions ○ On Apr 6th an order for 6 independent tank brigades and 5 tank regiments was issued ○ On May 23rd the 3rd Group Army Mobilization Plan started and ran through June. 18 divisions were mobilized for homeland defense; 221st, 222nd, 224th, 225th, 229th, 230th, 231st, 303rd, 308th, 312th, 316th, 321st, 322nd, 344th, 351st and 354th Divisions. The 234th and 355th Divisions were activated later under the same scheme ○ Army General Staff wanted all units in position for Ketsu-go, transfers were made to fill gaps in the defenses ○ The 40th Army's headquarters in Formosa and the 77th Division in the Northern District were redeployed to Kyushu ○ On May 8th the 5th Area Army received new operational orders reflecting its recently reduced strength ○ On May 30th the Kwantung Army was reorganized to conform to *Operating Plan Against the Soviets in Manchuria and Korea Outline*. It called for the China Exp Army to send 4 divisions to Manchuria and prepare for war with the Soviet Union ○ In June, under the 3rd Group Army Mobilization Plan, new army headquarters were organized; the 50th Army under the 11th Area Army, 54th Army under the 13th Area Army and 59th Army under the 15th Area Army ○ On June 20th Army General Staff issued ordered the 10th Area Army take the offensive around Sakijima and Formosa ○ A new operational boundary between the 10th Area Army and 2nd General Army ran between Kagoshima and Okinawa ○ On June 23rd the Tokyo Defense Army was activated to strengthen Tokyo's defenses and protect the Imperial Palace ○ At the end of June air units were redeployed from southern Japan to Formosa and air-training units in Japan were reorganized into combat units and placed under the Air General Army's command ○ All air units on Formosa were scheduled to redeploy to Japan in August but the war ended ○ On July 1st control of the 10th, 11th and 12th Air Divisions passed from the 1st and 2nd General Armies to the Air General Army, which now had tactical control over Japan's airspace ○ Operation *Sei-go* concentrated Japan's fighter aircraft to intercept bombing raids but the plan fell short due to the numbers of American land and carrier based fighter escorts ○ Operation *Nichi-go* targeted enemy submarines in the Soya, Tsushima and Tsugaru Straits with a patrol system and tightened defenses ○ *Ketsu-go* anticipated the invasion of western Japan and focused on the destruction of US transport ships prior to landing ○ On Aug 6th the US dropped the atomic bomb on Hiroshima ○ On Aug 8th Russia declared the Soviet-Japanese Neutrality Pact void, Japan's ambassador in Moscow was informed but phone lines from the embassy were cut to prevent Japan finding out ○ Aug 9th, the Soviet Union declared war on Japan but hostilities had already begun at midnight on Aug 8th ○ The morning of Aug 9th Supreme War Council met at the Imperial Palace and while it was in session a second atomic bomb was dropped at 11:30 am on Nagasaki ○ On Aug 9th the 17th Area Army was placed under Kwantung Army control for 0600 on Aug 10th ○ On Aug. 14th the Minister of War and the Chief of Army General Staff informed all the armies under IGHQ control of the approaching end to hostilities ○ Emperor Hirohito broadcast Japan's surrender on Aug 15th. IGHQ immediately issued orders to suspend active operations ○ On Aug 16th direct talks began over the radio with General MacArthur's headquarters in Manila ○

Chapter 2

On Aug 16th at 4:00 pm Imperial Headquarters issued the order for all Japanese Army and Navy Forces to surrender unconditionally ○ Officially, the war against the US Britain and the Netherlands lasted a little over 3 yrs and 8 months ○

Emperor Hirohito attending a military review and exercise (author)

Formosa and the Ryukyu Islands

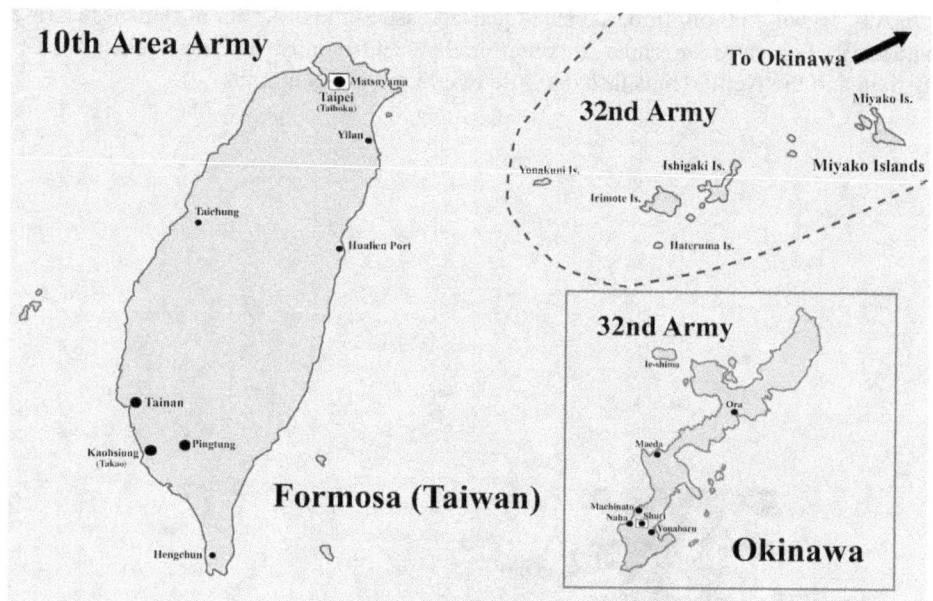

10th Area Army 湾 *Wan*

The 10th Area Army became active on September 22, 1944, to replace the Formosa Army. Its headquarters remained in Taipei and the former Formosa Army's commander, Lt General Ando Rikichi, was appointed its commander. The 10th Area Army was deactivated on October 25, 1945.

Subordinate armies / duty dates:
32nd Army from Sept 22, 1944, until June 24, 1945
40th Army from Jan 16, 1945, until May 14, 1945

Service History:
1944: Mar 22nd the Formosa Army was activated in Taihoku (Taipei) to replace the Formosa District Army, and was placed under IGHQ control the same day ○ Jul 11th, the 32nd Army joined the Formosa Army's order of battle ○ Sept 22nd the 10th Area Army was activated in Taihoku, Formosa replacing the Formosa Army and placed under IGHQ control the same day. The 10th Area Army was responsible for Formosa and Ryuku Islands, including Okinawa ○ Formosa served Japan's military as a transit waypoint south. Until the war threatened Japan and its immediate surroundings Imperial Headquarters paid little attention to defending the area.

1945: On Jan 16th Imperial HQ reorganized Formosa and activated the 40th Army HQ. By the end of February Formosa hosted five divisions and six brigades ○ Feb 3rd, end of war orders for the 10th Area Army were to prevent enemy sea and air base construction near Formosa and the Nansei Islands. Formosa and Okinawa were to be held at all costs to preserve air bases in the East China Sea area. Sink enemy convoys and provide the China Expeditionary Army with support if an enemy landing on China's southeast coast appeared likely. Air operations would be coordinated with air units from Kyushu, southern Korea and the lower reaches of the Yangtze River ○ On Feb 6th Formosa Army District was part of the reorganization of area armies and army districts. 10th Area Army HQ gained control of the Formosa Army District, its commanders and staff officers holding the equivalent rank in both organizations ○

On Feb 13th the 4th Air Army was deactivated in the Philippines and its HQ flown to Formosa ○ May 14th, the 40th Army HQ was removed from the 10th Area Army's order of battle and transferred to the 16th Area Army in Kyushu to fill a tactical gap ○ June 24th the 10th Area Army took direct control of remaining 32nd Army units that were by-passed by US forces in the Ryuku Islands, except Amami Jima which was placed under the 57th Army and Okinawa which was under US control ○ The 10th Area Army had 202,000 men in arms, 43,600 of those in the Ryukyu Is. when the war ended ○

Major Units: See division / brigade page for order of battle

9th Division Kanazawa 1898 武 *Take* – Taipei	204-5
12th Division Kureme 1898 劍 *Ken* – Tainan	206
50th Division Taiwan 1944 蓬 *Hoo* – Pingtung County	210
66th Division Taiwan 1944 敢 *Kan* – Yilan	212-3
71st Division Asahikawa 1942 命 *Mei* – Tainan	213
61st Independent Mixed Brigade 1944 鎧 *Yoroi* – Babuyan Islands, P.I.	In Vol. 2
75th Independent Mixed Brigade 1945 興 *Kyou* – Hokoto (Pescadores)	263
76th Independent Mixed Brigade 1945 律 *Ritsu* – Hoping Island	264
100th Independent Mixed Brigade 1945 磐石 *Banjaku* – Kaohsiung	267
102nd Independent Mixed Brigade 1945 八幡 *Hachiman* – Hualien Port	267-8
103rd Independent Mixed Brigade 1945 破竹 *Hachikoe* – Takao	268
112th Independent Mixed Brigade 1945 雷神 *Raijin* – Yilan	269

Units under the control of the 10th Area Army: 湾 *Wan*

10th Area Army Headquarters	No # (2,183)	Matsuyama
10th Area Army Air Intelligence Unit	4570 (2,037)	
10th Area Army Field Ordinance Depot	10800	
10th Area Army Freight Depot	12806	
10th Area Army Motor Vehicle Depot	21141	
10th Area Army Signal Unit	1791	
Formosa Army Ordinance Depot	12800 (171)	
Formosa Army Freight Depot	12805 (161)	
Formosa Provisional Epidemic Prevention Dept.	21136	
31st Field Disease Prevention / Water Supply Dept.	13360 (220)	
33rd Signal Regiment	21301 (1,719)	
34th Signal Regiment	12877 (1,716)	
10th Area Army Sector Headquarters	12892	
10th Raiding Unit Headquarters	12875 (90)	
1st Takasago Raiding Unit	12831	
2nd Takasago Raiding Unit	12832	
5th Field Artillery Battalion	14605	
7th Independent Machinegun Battalion	1796 (334)	
8th Independent Machinegun Battalion	1797 (334)	
24th Independent Machinegun Battalion	14202 (334)	
4th Independent Rapid Firing Gun Battalion	4600 (353)	
16th Independent Rapid Firing Gun Battalion	1798 (403)	
29th Independent Rapid Firing Gun Company	14602 (118)	
30th Independent Rapid Firing Gun Company	14603 (118)	
161st Field Anti-Aircraft Regiment	4550 (1,351)	

10th Area Army: continued　　　　　　　　　　　　湾 *Wan*

Unit	Code	Location
162nd Field Anti-Aircraft Regiment	4587 (1,411)	
82nd Field Anti-Aircraft Battalion	12426 (521)	
83rd Field Anti-Aircraft Battalion	12524 (521)	
56th Field Machine Cannon Company	2181 (105)	
57th Field Machine Cannon Company	2182 (105)	Takao
58th Field Machine Cannon Company	12428 (105)	
59th Field Machine Cannon Company	12429 (105)	
60th Field Machine Cannon Company	12430 (105)	
61st Field Machine Cannon Company	12431 (105)	
86th Field Machine Cannon Company	12871 (105)	
87th Field Machine Cannon Company	12872 (105)	
88th Field Machine Cannon Company	12873 (105)	
89th Field Machine Cannon Company	12874 (105)	
90th Field Machine Cannon Company	12876 (105)	
91st Field Machine Cannon Company	12898 (105)	
92nd Field Machine Cannon Company	21117 (105)	
93rd Field Machine Cannon Company	21118 (105)	
56th Specially Established Machine Cannon Unit	12544 (85)	
25th Tank Regiment	5307	
42nd Independent Engineer Battalion	12883 (894)	
64th Independent Engineer Battalion	5265 (894)	
1st Field Fortification Unit	5735 (374)	
50th Field Duty Unit Headquarters	12826 / 13826 (17)	
6th Independent Railway Regiment	12896	
9th Independent Railway Battalion	unknown (1,034)	
213th Independent Motor Transport Company	3877	
214th Independent Motor Transport Company	3874	
305th Independent Motor Transport Company	1743 (183)	
308th Independent Motor Transport Company	1746 (183)	
354th Independent Motor Transport Company	12893 (134)	
91st Land Duty Company	8221	
8th Field Well Drilling Company	7051 (119)	
9th Field Well Drilling Company	7052 (119)	
111th Specially Established Land Duty Company	1761 (61)	
112th Specially Established Land Duty Company	1762 (61)	
113th Specially Established Land Duty Company	1763 (61)	
114th Specially Established Land Duty Company	1764 (61)	
115th Specially Established Land Duty Company	1765 (61)	
116th Specially Established Land Duty Company	1766 (61)	
117th Specially Established Land Duty Company	1767 (61)	
112th Specially Established Sea Duty Company	1769 (61)	
113th Specially Established Sea Duty Company	1770 (61)	
114th Specially Established Sea Duty Company	1771 (61)	
115th Specially Established Sea Duty Company	1772 (61)	
116th Specially Established Sea Duty Company	1773 (61)	

10th Area Army: continued

Unit	Code
117th Specially Established Sea Duty Company	1774 (61)
106th Specially Est. Construction Duty Company	1777 (61)
Penghu Island Army Hospital	21128
Keelung Island Army Hospital	21124
Taipei Army Hospital	21123
Taichung Army Hospital	21131
Tainan Army Hospital	21125
Taitung Army Hospital	21130 (40)
Hualien Army Hospital	21129 (204)
Chiayi Army Hospital	21132
Kaohsiung (Takao) Army Hospital	21126 (253)
Pingtung Army Hospital	21127
Hoko Island Army Hospital	unknown
221st Line of Communications Hospital	21138
222nd Line of Communications Hospital	21133
500th Specially Est. Casualty Transport Unit	13850
501st Specially Est. Casualty Transport Unit	13851
22nd Line of Communications Veterinary Depot	13827 (177)
Penghu Island Fortress Headquarters	No #
Penghu Island Fortress Heavy Artillery Regiment	unknown
Penghu Island Fortress Army Hospital	unknown
Keelung Island Fortress Headquarters	unknown
Keelung Island Fortress Heavy Artillery Regiment	4512
10th Area Army Training Unit	unknown
10th Area Army Judiciary Corp	No #
Taiwan POW Camp	No #

10th Area Army Shipping and Sea Raiding Units: 湾 Wan

Unit	Code
4th Sea Raiding Base Unit Headquarters	19772 (42)
20th Sea Raiding Squadron	19759 (107)
21st Sea Raiding Squadron	19760 (107)
22nd Sea Raiding Squadron	19761 (107)
23rd Sea Raiding Squadron	19762 (107)
24th Sea Raiding Squadron	19763 (107)
25th Sea Raiding Squadron	19764 (107)
21st Sea Raiding Base Battalion	5768 (900)
22nd Sea Raiding Base Battalion	5769 (900)
23rd Sea Raiding Base Battalion	14164 (900)
24th Sea Raiding Base Battalion	14165 (900)
25th Sea Raiding Base Battalion	16275 (900)
137th Specially Established Sea Duty Company	19787 (61)
138th Specially Established Sea Duty Company	19788 (61)
15th Sea Transport Battalion	19817 (1,165)
7th Field Shipping Depot	19808 (815)
14th Sea Raiding Base Unit	16791

Formosa Army District 湾 *Wan*

Formosa (Taiwan) Island

50th Depot Division:

Unit	Location	Barracks # (Personnel)
50th Depot Division Headquarters	Tainan	湾
301st Infantry Regiment	Taipei	湾 3
302nd Infantry Regiment	Tainan	湾 4
303rd Infantry Regiment	Fengshan	湾 7
50th Cavalry Regiment	unknown	湾
50th Mountain Artillery Regiment	Taihoku	湾 5
50th Engineer Regiment	Takao	湾 6
50th Division Signal Unit	Taihoku	湾 9
50th Transp. Regiment	Hozan	湾 10

Major units supplied by the 50th Depot Division include:
48th Div., 50th Div., 23rd I.M.B.

10th Area Army: Formosa home defense units		湾 *Wan*
500th Specially Est. Guard Motor Transport Unit		13800 (67)
501st Specially Est. Guard Motor Transport Unit		13801 (67)
502nd Specially Est. Guard Motor Transport Unit		13802 (67)
503rd Specially Est. Guard Motor Transport Unit		13803 (67)
504th Specially Est. Guard Motor Transport Unit		13804 (67)
500th Specially Established Guard Transport Unit		13810 (951)
501st Specially Established Guard Transport Unit		13811 (951)
502nd Specially Established Guard Transport Unit		13812 (951)
503rd Specially Established Guard Transport Unit		13813 (951)
504th Specially Established Guard Transport Unit		13814 (951)
505th Specially Established Guard Transport Unit		13815 (155)
506th Specially Established Guard Transport Unit		13816 (155)
507th Specially Established Guard Transport Unit		13817 (155)
508th Specially Established Guard Transport Unit		13818 (155)
509th Specially Established Guard Transport Unit		13819 (155)
510th Specially Established Guard Transport Unit		13820 (155)
511th Specially Established Guard Transport Unit		13821 (155)
512th Specially Established Guard Transport Unit		13822 (155)
513th Specially Established Guard Transport Unit		13823 (155)
514th Specially Established Guard Transport Unit		13824 (155)
50th Field Transport Headquarters		13825
50th Field Duty Headquarters Unit		13826 / 12826 (17)
500th Specially Established Guard Land Duty Unit		13830 (61)
501st Specially Established Guard Land Duty Unit		13831 (61)
502nd Specially Established Guard Land Duty Unit		13832 (61)
503rd Specially Established Guard Land Duty Unit		13833 (61)
504th Specially Established Guard Land Duty Unit		13834 (61)
500th Specially Established Guard Sea Duty Unit		13840 (61)

Unit	Number
501st Specially Established Guard Sea Duty Unit	13841 (61)
502nd Specially Established Guard Sea Duty Unit	13842 (61)
503rd Specially Established Guard Sea Duty Unit	13843 (61)
504th Specially Established Guard Sea Duty Unit	13844 (61)
505th Specially Established Guard Sea Duty Unit	13845 (61)
504th Specially Established Garrison Battalion	13861 (550)
505th Specially Established Garrison Battalion	13862 (550)
506th Specially Established Garrison Battalion	13863 (550)
535th Specially Established Garrison Battalion	13864 (550)
536th Specially Established Garrison Battalion	13865 (550)
519th Specially Established Garrison Company	13866 (126)
509th Specially Established Garrison Battalion	13867 (550)
520th Specially Established Garrison Company	13868 (126)
507th Specially Established Garrison Battalion	13869 (550)
510th Specially Established Garrison Battalion	13870 (550)
511th Specially Established Garrison Battalion	13871 (550)
508th Specially Established Garrison Battalion	13872 (550)
512th Specially Established Garrison Battalion	13873 (550)
537th Specially Established Garrison Battalion	13874 (550)
538th Specially Established Garrison Battalion	13875 (550)
539th Specially Established Garrison Battalion	13876 (550)
540th Specially Established Garrison Battalion	13878 (550)
522nd Specially Established Garrison Company	13879 (126)
523rd Specially Established Garrison Company	13880 (126)
521st Specially Established Garrison Company	13882 (126)
524th Specially Established Garrison Company	13883 (126)
504th Specially Established Garrison Company	13886 (126)
513th Specially Established Garrison Battalion	13887 (550)
514th Specially Established Garrison Battalion	13888 (550)
515th Specially Established Garrison Battalion	13889 (550)
516th Specially Established Garrison Battalion	13890 (550)
517th Specially Established Garrison Battalion	13891 (550)
551st Specially Established Garrison Battalion	4586 (550)
560th Specially Established Garrison Battalion	4594 (550)
561st Specially Established Garrison Battalion	4591 (550)
562nd Specially Established Garrison Battalion	4596 (550)
563rd Specially Established Garrison Battalion	4597 (550)
564th Specially Established Garrison Battalion	4598 (550)
565th Specially Established Garrison Battalion	4599 (550)
566th Specially Established Garrison Battalion	4593 (550)
501st Specially Established Garrison Battalion	unknown (420)
502nd Specially Established Garrison Battalion	unknown (420)
506th Specially Established Garrison Company	unknown (126)
504th Specially Established Garrison Company	unknown (126)
507th Specially Established Garrison Engineer Unit	unknown (930)
508th Specially Established Garrison Engineer Unit	unknown (930)

10ᵗʰ Area Army: Home defense units continued   湾 *Wan*

509ᵗʰ Specially Established Garrison Engineer Unit	unknown (930)
510ᵗʰ Specially Established Garrison Engineer Unit	unknown (930)
511ᵗʰ Specially Established Garrison Engineer Unit	unknown (930
512ᵗʰ Specially Established Garrison Engineer Unit	unknown (930)
513ᵗʰ Specially Established Garrison Engineer Unit	unknown (930)
514ᵗʰ Specially Established Garrison Engineer Unit	unknown (930)
515ᵗʰ Specially Established Garrison Engineer Unit	unknown (930)
516ᵗʰ Specially Established Garrison Engineer Unit	unknown (930)
517ᵗʰ Specially Established Garrison Engineer Unit	unknown (930)
518ᵗʰ Specially Established Garrison Engineer Unit	unknown (930)

Okinawa

32ⁿᵈ Army 球 *Kyu*

The 32ⁿᵈ Army was activated Mar 22, 1944, in Naha Okinawa and placed under the Western District Army on May 10ᵗʰ. After the battle of Okinawa the 32ⁿᵈ Army was placed under Formosa Army (later renamed 10ᵗʰ Area Army) command on July 11ᵗʰ. The 32ⁿᵈ Army was commanded by Lt Gen Masao Watanabe from Apr 1, 1944 until Aug 8ᵗʰ and Lt Gen Mitsuru Ushijima until he committed suicide on Okinawa June 23ʳᵈ. With no date available for its deactivation the 32ⁿᵈ Army was effectively ended on June 24, 1945, when the 10ᵗʰ Area Army absorbed its bypassed remnants.

Service History: *Until Feb 1944 Formosa and Ryuku Islands were lightly defended.*
1944: In mid March *Tei-go* operation (to defend the Ryukus) began. On Mar 15ᵗʰ the 32ⁿᵈ Army was activated and placed under Western District Army control ○ June 29ᵗʰ, *Toyama Maru* bound for Okinawa with the 44ᵗʰ and 45ᵗʰ I.M.B. aboard was torpedoed with the loss of 3,627 lives ○ July 11ᵗʰ, the 32ⁿᵈ Army is attached to the Formosa Army ○ Mid-July, the 9ᵗʰ, 24ᵗʰ and 62ⁿᵈ Divisions had arrived on Okinawa. Reinforcements continued to arrive until September ○ On Nov 17ᵗʰ the 9ᵗʰ Division was dropped from the 32ⁿᵈ Army and shipped to the Philippines ○ Ieshima and Okinawa became stopover waypoints on air routes to the Philippines ○
1945: On Jan 3ʳᵈ and 4ᵗʰ major air raids hit Okinawa ○ On Jan 15ᵗʰ the 32ⁿᵈ Army's HQ moved from Anri to Shuri and Mt. Tsukazan ○ Jan 21ˢᵗ and 22ⁿᵈ major air raids again hit Okinawa ○ In February contact between Japan, the Ryukus and Formosa had almost been severed ○ Mar 1ˢᵗ saw a major air raid on Okinawa ○ Mar 10ᵗʰ, unusable and indefensible airfields in the Ryukus were destroyed ○ Mar. 23ʳᵈ another large air raid ○ On Mar 24ᵗʰ ten US battleships and ten cruisers shelled Okinawa as they circumnavigated it ○ On Mar 29ᵗʰ the last suicide missions from Okinawa's airfields were flown ○ On April 1ˢᵗ American forces land on Okinawa ○ Apr 3ʳᵈ, two south bound US Divisions contacted the Gaya Detachment ○ On April 5ᵗʰ Gaya Detachment withdrew to Kochi ○ Apr 6ᵗʰ, Imperial Navy operation *Ten-go* ends in failure ○ Apr 7ᵗʰ, Army General Staff order an offensive, US troops land near Nago and encounter

the Kunigami Detachment ○ Apr 8th a 62nd Div night attack failed to achieve results ○ April 12th to 18th, the 273rd Ind Inf Btn, 44th I.M.B. was destroyed and the 23rd Ind Inf Btn, 62nd Div. lost half its strength ○ Apr 16th Ieshima garrison sent word US troops had landed then contact was lost ○ Apr 19th new front lines were established between Hill 141 and Kaniku. The 23rd Ind Inf Btn withdrew from Kakasu to Awacha ○ Around Machinato fighting intensified and the situation became critical. 24th Div and 44th I.M.B. pulled back to the northern defense zone to avoid an amphibious attack from the rear ○ Apr 24th the situation around Machinato became critical so two btns were temporarily added to the 62nd Div's command ○ Apr 27th the 24th Div completed redeployment ○ April 29th, the 32nd Army decided to abandon the holding action for an offensive on May 4th ○ On Apr 30th Gusukuma fell isolating part of the 62nd Div as fighting along the Maeda Escarpment continued ○ May 4th, on X Day the 32nd Army offensive began at 0450 with a half hour artillery barrage but was stalled by noon ○ On May 5th the offensive ended ○ On the 9th Uchima fell ○ After 20 days on the front lines the 23rd Ind Inf Btn and 14th Ind Machinegun Btn were withdrawn from Awacha to Keizuka and Dakeshi ○ May 12th in and around Keizuka, Dakeshi and Amike Hill the fighting intensified ○ May 14th, the 64th Inf Bgde, 62nd Div withdrew to Shuri ○ May 15th the 44th I.M.B. was in Naha ○ On May 19th the fighting eased but the 7th Hvy Artillery Regt in ruined Ozato Castle was destroyed by U.S. artillery ○ By May 22nd the Army was exhausted. Most of its best troops were casualties although 50,000 remained ○ May 23rd the order to withdraw to Kiyamu Peninsula was issued. 3,000 troops from the 62nd Div advanced from Shuri to southeast of Tsukasan to cover the withdrawal ○ May 26th, near Taira the 62nd Div began launching attacks after dark. The 24th Div and 44th I.M.B. continued to lose ground ○ On May 29th the 24th Division's movement began and on the 30th a pause in the fighting allowed the army to pull back in good order ○ June 31st, the rearguards for the 24th Division and 44th I.M.B. pulled back ○ June 1st the 64th Inf Bgde, 32nd Inf Regt and Naval Base Force halted the advancing enemy ○ June 2nd, the 64th Inf Bgde and 32nd Inf Regt pulled back to new positions around Kiyamu ○ The 32nd Army has about 30,000 men left and a fifth of their automatic weapons, tenth of their heavy infantry weapons and half their field guns ○ From June 6th into the next day the 1st Btn, 15th Ind Mixed Regt fought near Gushichan ○ On June 11th at 2330 the Naval Base Force in Oroku sent its last message as it fought to delay an attack on the left flank of the 24th Div ○ June 12th the 24th Div was attacked on Kuniyoshi Hill, a section of the 44th I.M.B. was overrun threatening the Division's rear and flank. Six units of service troops filled the gaps but were slaughtered ○ June 13th the brigade was unable to contact its left flank. The 13th and 15th I.I.B. (62nd Div) were sent to keep its flank from collapsing ○ June 14th the 13th I.I.B. arrived at the shoreline losing most of its men to a lack of cover. The 15th I.I.B. commander was ill so it barely moved ○ June 15th, the 44th I.M.B. front line was thrown into confusion, pockets became isolated in the center and on the left. The entire 62nd Div was sent to save it ○ June 16th, the 15th I.I.B. on Hill 108 lost contact with friendly forces. After dark the 62nd Div moved east hoping to re-establish contact ○ The next day with Hill 108 still in its grasp the 62nd Div went to aid the 24th Division. The 24th Div was close to collapse. Gaps appeared in the 89th IR's line and another between the 32nd IR and 22nd IR The entire 22nd I.R. HQ had died on Hill 73 ○ June 18th the 62nd Division completed deployment and the 44th I.M.B. HQ left for Mabuni after dark. The 89th IR slowly collapsed as U.S. tanks cut the 32nd IR lines and advanced to northwest of Medeera, splitting the front lines in two. The 32nd Army HQ and 62nd Div HQ were near Mabuni and the 24th Div HQ in Medeera ○ On June 19th with the 32nd Army's fate sealed, its final orders were to continue with a guerilla war ○ On June 20th as the fighting began dying away the 10th Area Army commander issued a citation honoring the 32nd Army ○ On June 21st the Americans declared Okinawa secure. The 24th Div sent a last message. Mabuni was lost but recaptured by the 32nd Army's HQ guard platoon. ○ On June 23rd at dawn L. Gen Ushijima committed suicide and the 62nd Div HQ, 4th I.M.B. HQ, Army Artillery Unit HQ were destroyed near Mabuni. The fighting died away at 1200 hours. ○ On June 28th the 24th Div HQ was destroyed near Medeera ○

Major Units: See division / brigade page for order of battle

24th Division Harbin 1939 山 *Yama* – Okinawa		206
62nd Division Kyoto 1943 石 *Ishi* – Okinawa		211
44th Independent Mixed Brigade 1944 球 *Kyu* – Okinawa		259

Units attached to the 24th Division: 山 *Yama*

3rd Independent Machinegun Battalion	6090 球 (334)
17th Independent Machinegun Battalion	5247 (334)
3rd Independent Rapid Firing Gun Battalion	6403 (353)

Units attached to the 62nd Division   石 *Ishi*

4th Independent Machinegun Battalion	10290 (334)
14th Independent Machinegun Battalion	18809 (334)
32nd Independent Rapid Firing Gun Company	14739 (118)
27th Tank Regiment (minus 3rd Coy; on Miyako)	12102 (700)
223rd Specially Established Guard Company	7078 (126)
224th Specially Established Guard Company	7079 (126)
14th Field Well Drilling Company	4649 (119)

Units attached to the 44th IMB   球 *Kyu*

272nd Independent Infantry Battalion	14212 (683)	from 45th IMB
273rd Independent Infantry Battalion	14213 (683)	from 45th IMB
7th Medium Artillery Regiment	4152 (268)	
23rd Shipping Engineer Regiment (minus 3rd Co.)	16741 (770)	

Under control of the 32nd Army: Shuri, Okinawa   球 *Kyu*

32nd Army Headquarters	1616 (1,344)	Shuri Castle
32nd Army Fortification Defense Unit	1616	(incl. in HQ)
32nd Army 4th Independent Company	1616	(incl. in HQ)
32nd Army 5th Independent Company	1616	(incl. in HQ)
32nd Army Air Intelligence Unit (11 radar stations)	19564 (2,024)	
2nd Ordinance Duty Unit	12365 (237)	
32nd Army Field Ordinance Depot	18812 (937)	
32nd Army Field Freight Depot	18811 (508)	
27th Field Disease Prev. and Water Supply Dept.	5753 (239)	
32nd Army Ordinance Duty Unit	12518 (199)	
5th Artillery Command	9700 (119)	
1st Field Medium Artillery Regt, minus 1st Battalion	6523 (1,300)	

Unit	Code (Number)
23rd Field Medium Artillery Regiment	3109 (1,773)
22nd Independent Rapid Firing Gun Battalion	13222 (604)
23rd Independent Rapid Firing Gun Battalion	13223 (604)
21st Field Anti-Aircraft Headquarters	12545 (71)
36th Signal Regiment	18830 (1,801)
27th Signal Regiment, 5th Company	2527
106th Independent Wire Company	12909 (310)
126th Independent Wire Company	12973 (310)
127th Independent Wire Company	12974 (310)
100th Independent Radio Platoon	12918 (57)
113th Independent Radio Platoon	12538 (57)
114th Independent Radio Platoon	12539 (57)
115th Independent Radio Platoon	12540 (57)
116th Independent Radio Platoon	12541 (57)
66th Independent Engineer Battalion	10279 (821)
501st Specially Established Guard Engineer Unit	18815 (930)
502nd Specially Established Guard Engineer Unit	18816 (930)
503rd Specially Established Guard Engineer Unit	18817 (930)
504th Specially Established Guard Engineer Unit	18818 (930)
Okinawa Army Hospital	18803 (254)
49th Line of Communications Sector Command	5896 (203)
49th Line of Communications Duty Unit	5896 (511)
49th Line of Communications Guard Unit	5896 (1,035)
215th Independent Motor Transport Company	5879
259th Independent Motor Transport Company	6058 *
2nd Field Fortification Construction Unit	10158 (368)
6th Fortification Construction Duty Company	2774 (339)
7th Fortification Construction Duty Company	2775 (339)
20th Field Well Drilling Company	18810 (81)
72nd Land Duty Company	4832 (511)
83rd Land Duty Company	5807 (511)
102nd Specially Established Sea Duty Company	8885 (61)
103rd Specially Established Sea Duty Company	8886 (61)
104th Specially Established Sea Duty Company	8887 (61)
11th Sea Transport Battalion	16798 (548)
1st Independent Survey Company	1221
Okinawa Military Police	No #
100th Independent Heavy Artillery Battalion	18804 (499)
1st Independent Mortar Regiment	3666 (400)
3rd Independent Trench Mortar Company	12396 (326)
4th Independent Trench Mortar Company	12397 (326)
5th Independent Trench Mortar Company	12398 (326)
6th Independent Trench Mortar Company	12439 (326)

*259th Ind. Motor Transport Co. w/Sakaguchi Det. for 16th Army invasion of Java.

The Ryukyu Islands

On June 24, 1945, following Okinawa a number of 32nd Army units became stranded on islands by-passed by the US. These were absorbed into the 10th Area Army, except the Amami Jima Detachment, which was placed under the 57th Army in Kyushu.
Note: For the division and brigades orders of battle see page...

Miyako Jima Detachment — 球 *Kyu* (24,845) — page

28th Division 1940 豊 *Toyo*	*	207-8
59th Independent Mixed Brigade 1944 碧 *Heki*	*	260
60th Independent Mixed Brigade 1944 駒 *Koma*	*	261

Attached to the 28th Division: 豊 *Toyo*

27th Tank Regiment, 3rd Company	撃12102 (70) from Okinawa
1st Field Medium Artillery Regiment, 1st Battalion	6523 (606)
5th Ind. Rapid Firing Gun Battalion (anti-tank)	6250 (491)
47th Specially Established Machine Cannon Unit	12444 (85)
505th Specially Est. Garrison Engineer Company	18819 (930)
4th Sea Raiding Squadron	16780 (110)
4th Sea Raiding Base Battalion	16791 (900)
30th Sea Raiding Base Battalion	unknown (900)
205th Airfield Battalion	8360 (372)
129th Field Airfield Construction Unit	15393 (175)
284th Independent Motor Transport Company	7030 1 pln on Ishigaki
109th Land Duty Company	6443 (351)
16th Field Well Drilling Company	6601 (119)
8th Fortification Construction Duty Company	2776 (339) 1 pln on Ishigaki
18th Independent Machinegun Battalion	5248 (334)
32nd Army Air Intelligence Unit (2 radar stations)	19564 (101) (103)
2nd Mobile Ordinance Repair Unit	12365 (237)
Miyako Jima Army Hospital	6071 (40)

Ishigaki Jima Detachment — 球 *Kyu* (5,484) — page

45th Independent Mixed Brigade 1944 球 *Kyu*	*	260

Attached units:

28th Division, 3rd Field Hospital	5681 (287)
19th Independent Machinegun Battalion	3323 (334)
8th Medium Artillery Regiment	4154 (320)
48th Specially Established Machine Cannon Unit	12445 (85)
209th Specially Established Guard Company	7094 (126)
210th Specially Established Guard Company	7095 (126)
226th Specially Established Guard Company	7081 (126)
227th Specially Established Guard Company	7082 (126)
506th Specially Established Guard Engineer Unit	18820 (930)

Ishigaki Jima Detachment continued

32nd Army Air Intelligence Unit (1 radar station)	19564 (102)	Type 4 mobile
69th Airfield Battalion	9192 (372)	
128th Field Airfield Construction Unit	15392 (175)	
8th Fortress Construction Company, 1 platoon	2776	from Miyako Jima
284th Independent Motor Transport Co., 1 platoon	7030	from Miyako Jima
Funauki Army Hospital	4173	

Daito Jima Detachment　　　　　　　　　　　　球 *Kyu* (4,609)

Daito Island Detachment Headquarters	9760 **	
36th Infantry Regiment (28th Div.)	5629 (3,100)	
32nd Army Air Intelligence Unit (2 radar stations)	19564 (99) (97)	field type
22nd Independent Mixed Regiment (minus 3rd Btn)	7166 (2,230) ***	
49th Specially Established Machine Cannon Unit	12446 (85)	
50th Specially Established Machine Cannon Unit	12447 (85)	
211th Specially Established Guard Company	7096 (126)	
101st Specially Established Sea Duty Company	8884 (61)	
69th Airfield Battalion	9192 (372)	

Kunigami Detachment:　　　　　　　　　　　　　球 *Kyu*

3rd Raiding Unit	18813 (400)
4th Raiding Unit	18814 (400)
225th Specially Established Garrison Company	7080 (126)

** Former 85th Line of Communications Guard Unit Headquarters
*** 3rd Battalion on Kikaigashima

32nd Army Shipping and Sea Raiding Units:　　暁 *Akatsuki*

7th Shipping Transport HQ, Okinawa Branch	4500	
5th Shipping Engineer Regiment	6147 (1,099)	
9th Shipping Engineer Regiment	9421 (1,099)	
23rd Shipping Engineer Regiment	16741 (1,099)	
26th Shipping Engineer Regiment, minus 3rd Coy	16744 (1,099)	
28th Shipping Engineer Regiment	16757 (1,099)	
30th Shipping Engineer Regiment	16759 (1,099)	
1st Sea Raiding Squadron	16777 (110)	
2nd Sea Raiding Squadron	16778 (110)	
3rd Sea Raiding Squadron	16779 (110)	
5th Sea Raiding Squadron	16781 (110)	
26th Sea Raiding Squadron	19765 (107)	
27th Sea Raiding Squadron	19766 (107)	
28th Sea Raiding Squadron	19767 (107)	
29th Sea Raiding Squadron	19768 (107)	
30th Sea Raiding Squadron	19769 (104)	Kaida City

32nd Army Shipping and Sea Raiding Units continued

5th Sea Raiding Base Headquarters	19773 (42)
1st Sea Raiding Base Battalion	16788 (900)
2nd Sea Raiding Base Battalion	16789 (900)
3rd Sea Raiding Base Battalion	16790 (900)
26th Sea Raiding Base Battalion	10172 (900)
27th Sea Raiding Base Battalion	10173 (900)
28th Sea Raiding Base Battalion	6477 (900)
29th Sea Raiding Base Battalion	15066 (900)
11th Shipping Group Headquarters	2952 (70)
3rd Independent Sea Transport Company	16752 (84)

32nd Army Air Units

19th Air Sector Command	2569 (43)
44th Airfield Battalion	16644 (372)
50th Airfield Battalion	16650 (372)
56th Airfield Battalion	9173 (372)
29th Field Airfield Construction Unit	15385 (702)
118th Independent Maintenance Unit (Ki-43 Oscar)	18983 (233)
10th Field Meteorological Unit, 3rd Company	19565 (227)

8ᵗʰ Air Division 誠 *Makoto* 18900

The 8ᵗʰ Air Division was activated in Tokyo June 10, 1944 and placed under Formosa Army control. From June 15ᵗʰ the Air Division's headquarters were in Taihoku, Formosa with Maj Gen Kenji Yamamoto its commander from June 10ᵗʰ until the war ended. **Note**: Sei 18900 are *kamikaze units*. In this air division's case these units were sent out as soon they joined and so identified only by the division's code number.

Service History:
1944: June 10ᵗʰ, the 8ᵗʰ Air Division was attached to the Formosa Army ○ July 22ⁿᵈ, the Air Div. transferred to the Navy's 2ⁿᵈ Air Fleet ○ Oct 23ʳᵈ, to the 10ᵗʰ Area Army ○
1945: On Jan 15ᵗʰ the 9ᵗʰ Air Brigade joined the 8ᵗʰ Air Division ○ Feb 16ᵗʰ the 22ⁿᵈ Air Brigade, training brigade for air to surface special attack unit replacement pilots was placed under the air division's control ○ Mar 16ᵗʰ Staff Officer Nishi was appointed commander of special attack unit *Sei* ○ Mar 25ᵗʰ preparations to deploy began ○ Mar 26ᵗʰ recon unit the 10ᵗʰ Air Regt makes contact with three enemy task forces and the Air Division attacks US ships around Kerama Island ○ Mar 27ᵗʰ 9 planes from the 32ⁿᵈ *Sei* Air Unit flew a dawn suicide attack on US ships ○ Mar 28ᵗʰ and 29ᵗʰ 7 planes of the 41ˢᵗ *Sei* Air Unit flew in the last two suicide attacks from Okinawa ○ Mar 29ᵗʰ the 19ᵗʰ Air Regiment joined the 22ⁿᵈ Air Brigade ○ On Mar 31ˢᵗ Staff Officer Fukuzawa replaced Nishi as the 22ⁿᵈ Air Brigade commander ○ Apr 1ˢᵗ making repeated sorties the 10ᵗʰ Air Regiment reconnoitered the US landing on Okinawa ○ Apr 1ˢᵗ the 42ⁿᵈ Ind. Air Squadron joined the 8ᵗʰ Air Division ○ Apr. 5ᵗʰ the 19ᵗʰ Air Regiment was transferred to the 9ᵗʰ Air Brigade ○ On Apr 6ᵗʰ the Navy's *Ten-go* operation ends in failure ○ On Apr 10ᵗʰ all special attack units in Kyushu transferred to the 6ᵗʰ Air Army. The 117ᵗʰ *Sei* Air Unit in Taito and 118ᵗʰ *Sei* Air Unit in Choshu join the 22ⁿᵈ Air Brigade ○ Enemy air attacks make it increasingly difficult to use the Miyako and Ishigaki airfields ○ From Apr 12ᵗʰ to 30ᵗʰ the 8ᵗʰ Air Division goes after enemy shipping ○ The 32ⁿᵈ Army requests air support for its offensive on Okinawa, X Day was to be May 4ᵗʰ ○ The 8ᵗʰ Air Division devotes the first half of May to rebuilding, repairing and reorganizing its depleted air units. The 9ᵗʰ Air Brigade returns to Formosa and the 22ⁿᵈ Air Brigade receives new special attack units ○ May 21ˢᵗ to 30ᵗʰ bad weather prevents flying ○ By the end of May Okinawa is lost ○ On June 6ᵗʰ the 8ᵗʰ Air Division resumed targeting enemy shipping around Okinawa but air strikes in support of ground troops on Okinawa are terminated ○ June 21ˢᵗ, the US declares Okinawa secure. In less than two months the war will end ○

<u>8ᵗʰ Air Division</u>: Formosa 1944   誠 *Makoto* 18900

8ᵗʰ Air Division Headquarters	18901 (721)	Taihoku
• 46ᵗʰ Ind/ Air Squadron (Ki-51 recon)	19107 (117)	
• 47ᵗʰ Independent Air Squadron	9910 (117)	
• 48ᵗʰ Ind. Air Squadron (Ki-51 recon)	9911 (117)	joined 5/13/45
• 49ᵗʰ Ind. Air Squadron (Ki-51 recon)	9912 (117)	
• 10ᵗʰ Air Regiment (Ki-46 Recon)	9640 (172)	
• 29ᵗʰ Air Regiment (Ki-84 special attack)	9163 (275)	
• 108ᵗʰ Air Regiment	19103 (233)	
<u>9ᵗʰ Air Brigade</u>	誠 *Makoto*	
9ᵗʰ Air Brigade Headquarters	9601 (49)	

9th Air Brigade continued   誠 *Makoto*
- 23rd Ind. Air Squadron (Ki-61 fighters)   41 (158)   joined 5/13/45
- 20th Air Regiment (Ki-43 fighters)   18968 (323)
- 19th Air Regiment (Ki-61 sp. attack unit)   15352 (249)
- 24th Air Regiment (Ki-43 fighters)   9602 (322)
- 105th Air Regiment (Ki-61 sp. attack unit)   19102 (161)

25th Independent Air Brigade   誠 *Makoto*
25th Independent Air Brigade Headquarters   18966 (121)
- 8th Air Regiment (Ki-84, Ki-27 fighters)   9913 / 31 (453)
- 12th Air Regiment (light bomber)   9122
- 13th Air Regiment (fighter)   11703 (542)
- 21st Air Regiment (fighter)   11050 (185)
- 27th Air Regiment (light bomber)   9123
- 50th Air Regiment (fighter)   9914 (269)
- 58th Air Regiment (heavy bomber)   9145 (279)
- 61st Air Regiment (heavy bomber)   9604 (295)
- 67th Air Regiment   18969

22nd Air Brigade   誠 *Makoto*
22nd Air Brigade Headquarters   10652 (96)
- 17th Air Regiment (Ki-61 fighters)   15351 (249)   joined 5/13/45

Units that joined the 8th Air Division Apr. 14, 1945
- 41st Independent Air Squadron (Recon)   16683 (123)
- 42nd Independent Air Squadron   19104 (117)
- 43rd Independent Air Squadron   19108 (117)
- Sei 114th Air Unit (Ki-45 2 seat fighters)   18900
- Sei 115th Air Unit (Ki-79 training planes)   18900

Units destroyed in Kamikaze special attack operations by mid-April '45
- Sei 32nd Air Unit (recon)   18900
- Sei 36th Air Unit (Ki-36 recon)   18900
- Sei 37th Air Unit (Ki-36 recon)   18900
- Sei 38th Air Unit (Ki-36 recon)   18900
- Sei 39th Air Unit (Ki-43 fighter)   18900
- Sei 40th Air Unit   18900
- Sei 41st Air Unit (Ki-27 fighters)   18900

Joined after mid-April 1945
- Sei 26th Air Regiment (Ki-43 fighter)   8339 (183)
- Sei 204th Air Regiment (Ki-43 fighter)   11071 (275)

Newly attached from 5th Air Army in mid-May '45
- Sei 25th Air Unit (Ki-48 twin engine bomber)   18900
- Sei 28th Air Unit (Ki-51 assault plane)   18900
- Sei 71st Air Unit (Ki-51 assault plane)   18900
- 24th Independent Air Squadron   16500
- 71st Independent Air Squadron   9180

104th Independent Air Training Brigade:

Unit	Number
104th Ind. Air Training Brigade Headquarters	35
20th Secondary Air Training Unit	42
21st Secondary Air Training Unit	43
22nd Secondary Air Training Unit	44
3rd Advanced Air Training Squadron (Ki-54, Ki-79)	522
Makoto Air Replacement Unit	19122
38th Air Sector Command	9916 (44)
39th Air Sector Command	18928 (44)
42nd Air Sector Command	19101 (44)
52nd Air Sector Command	19113 (44)
53rd Air Sector Command	19114 (44)
112th Airfield Battalion	18937 (372)
138th Airfield Battalion	18457 (372)
139th Airfield Battalion	18458 (372)
156th Airfield Battalion	18495 (372)
157th Airfield Battalion	18496 (372)
158th Airfield Battalion	18497 (372)
187th Airfield Battalion	19032 (372)
188th Airfield Battalion	19033 (372)
3rd Airfield Company	8349 (231)
59th Airfield Company	18468 (226)
60th Airfield Company	18469 (226)
61st Airfield Company	18470 (225)
62nd Airfield Company	18471 (225)
63rd Airfield Company	18472 (225)
64th Airfield Company	18473 (225)
73rd Airfield Company	18480 (226)
74th Airfield Company	18481 (226)
133rd Field Airfield Construction Unit	15397 (175)
146th Field Airfield Construction Unit	18410 (175)
16th Air Signal Regiment	18499 (1,670)
21st Air Signal Unit	19159 (450)
8th Air Special Signal Unit	19157 (259)
7th Wireless Radio Unit	18955 (212)
26th Wireless Radio Unit	16626 (244)
62nd Wireless Radio Unit	18903 (196)
10th Field Meteorology Unit minus 3rd Company	19565 (1,008)
9th Air Intelligence Unit	19161 (805)
5th Field Air Freight Depot	19024 (442)
5th Field Air Repair Depot	19023 (1,506)
113th Ind. Maintenance Unit (Ki-67 Peggy)	18978 (275)
115th Independent Maintenance Unit (Ki-67)	18980 (275)
125th Independent Maintenance Unit (Ki-44 Tojo)	18990 (233)
134th Independent Maintenance Unit (Ki-61 Tony)	19006 (233)
142nd Independent Maintenance Unit (Ki-48 Lily)	19014 (275)

104th Independent Air Training Brigade continued

145th Independent Maintenance Unit (Ki-48)	19017 (275)
149th Independent Maintenance Unit (Ki-21 Sally)	19021 (275)
151st Independent Maintenance Unit (Ki-43 Oscar)	19115 (233)
158th Ind. Maintenance Unit (Ki-84 Frank)	19116 (233)
159th Independent Maintenance Unit (Ki-84)	19117 (233)
192nd Ind. Maintenance Unit (Ki-102B Randy)	19118 (336)
193rd Independent Maintenance Unit (Ki-67)	19119 (275)
307th Ind. Maintenance Unit (Ki-46 Dinah)	19120 (167)

Above: Juggler touring with the Japanese version of a USO show
Below: The audience (author)

Chapter 2

Mainland Japan

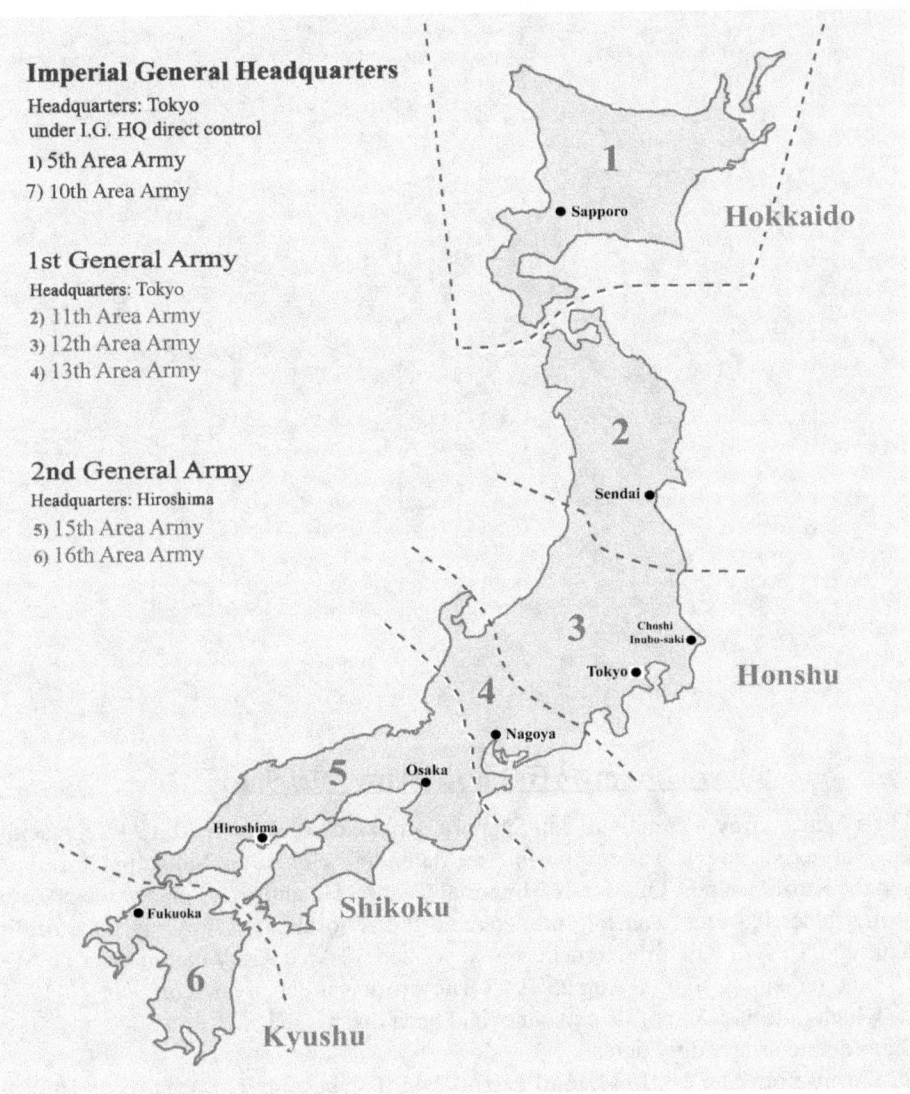

Imperial General Headquarters
Headquarters: Tokyo
under I.G. HQ direct control
1) 5th Area Army
7) 10th Area Army

1st General Army
Headquarters: Tokyo
2) 11th Area Army
3) 12th Area Army
4) 13th Area Army

2nd General Army
Headquarters: Hiroshima
5) 15th Area Army
6) 16th Area Army

Northern Japan, Karafuto and the Kuriles

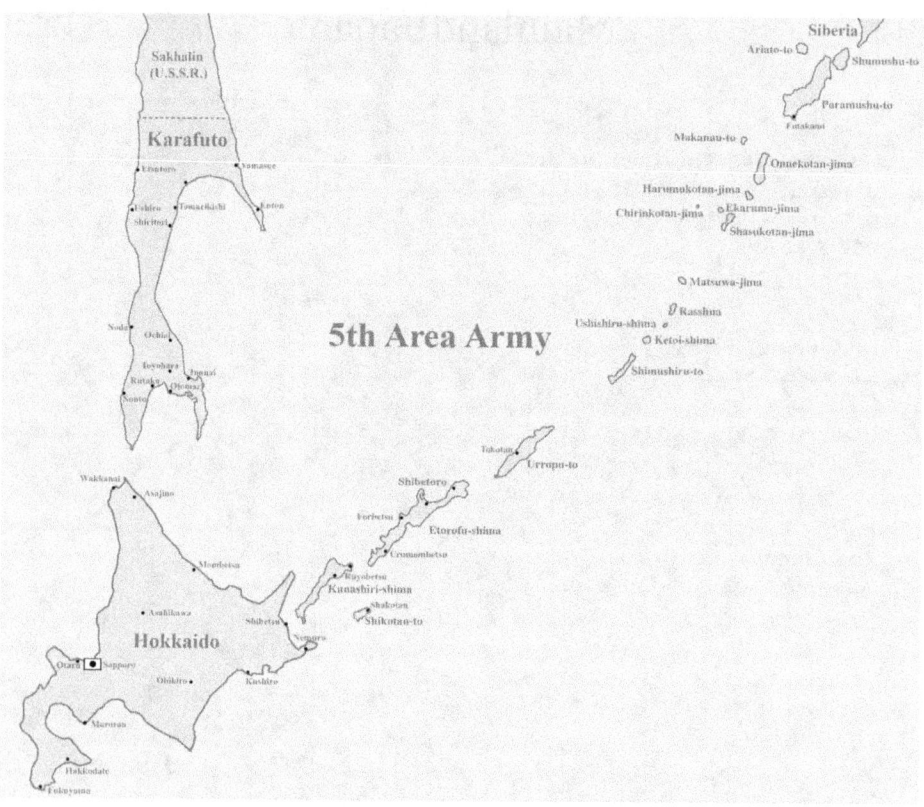

5th Area Army / Hokubu Army District 達 *Tatsu*

The 5th Area Army was activated in Sapporo, Hokkaido on March 10, 1944, replacing the Northern Army. It was responsible for defending Hokkaido, Sakhalin (Karafuto) and the Kurile Islands. On Mar 16th Imperial General Headquarters placed the 5th Area Army under its direct control and activated the subordinate 27th Army on Etorofu, Kurile Is. Lt Gen Kiichiro Higuchi was appointed 5th Area Army commander on Mar 10th and remaining so until Aug 25 1945. The Army was deactivated on Sept 22, 1945, by which time 125,300 of its personnel had been discharged.

Subordinate army / duty dates:
27th Army from Mar 16, 1944, until Feb 6, 1945 (HQ became 11th Area Army HQ)
Service History:
Northern District Army: Dec 2, 1940
1940: Dec. 2nd the Northern District Army became active in Sapporo to defend northern Japan. It included the 57th Div, Karafuto Mixed Brigade & Tsugaru Fortress ○
1941: Mar 1st the 67th Infantry Group joined the Northern District Army ○ Aug 15th, handed control of Soya Fortress ○ Oct 24th, given control of Kitachishima Fortress ○ On Dec. 2nd the 7th Division joined the Northern District Army ○
1942: On June 6th and 7th the North Seas Detachment landed unopposed on Kiska and Attu Islands in the Kuriles ○ Oct 20th part of the Kuril Fortress Infantry Unit was sent to Attu Island under Navy control ○ Oct 24th, North Sea Detachment became the North

Sea Garrison, it had three infantry battalions and a fortress unit under the Navy's 5th Fleet ○ Nov 5th the Northern District Army was made responsible for northern Japan, the Kuriles and Aleutians, which had previously been under General Defense Army control ○

Northern Army: Feb 11, 1943
1943: On Feb 11th the Northern District Army became the Northern Army in Sapporo. It included the North Seas Garrison, 1st Air Division and Northern Shipping Unit. ○ May 12th the US landed on Attu, approximately 2,000 defenders were annihilated ○ May 20th because it was believed the US planned further activity in the area the 7th Division was placed into the Northern Army's order of battle ○ On Aug 1st the 5,000 troops on Kiska were evacuated ○ Sept 22nd, 1st Kurile Garrison Unit is sent to northern Kuriles, 2nd Kurile Garrison Unit to Matsuwa Island, and 3rd Kurile Garrison Unit to Urrupu and Etorofu ○

1944: In January the Northern Army and Northeastern Area Fleet planned the defense for the Northeast Area, in Chitose, Hokkaido ○ On Feb 18th orders arrived to reorganize the Northern Army into the 5th Area Army and 27th Army ○ In mid-February 1st Air Division units arrived in Kushiro, Nemuro, Muroman and the Tsugaru and Soya Straits to provide air protection for shipping, surveillance and against enemy infiltration ○

5th Area Army: Mar 27, 1944
Mar 27th, the 5th Area Army headquarters was activated along side its subordinate, the 27th Army. Its headquarters were in Sapporo and 27th Army's were on Etorofu Is. ○ Apr 18th the 7th Division deployed to Obihiro, Hokkaido ○ On May 11th the 5th Area Army reorganized; the 91st Division built up was with units already stationed on Chishima and in the northern Kuriles ○ In the southern Kuriles troops were organized into the 43rd I.M.B. and 8th Ind Mixed Regt ○ In July the 69th I.M.B. organized on Kunashiri and Shikotan close to Hokkaido, the main island ○ In July the 7th and 77th Divisions had been completed and, with the 7th Depot Division, were placed under 5th Area Army control ○ In Aug the 69th I.M.B. was assigned to the 27th Army ○ In September the 1st Air Division's 1st Air Brigade, minus 54th Air Regt, transferred south forcing the 5th Area Army to reorganize ○ In late October the 54th Air Regt in the northern Kuriles redeployed to Hokkaido ○ On Nov 1st the 47th Division, previously committed to Hokkaido was instead sent to central China. The 27th Army headquarters in the Kuriles, without planes or ships could not obtain supplies or construction materials and served no real purpose ○

1945: On Jan 23rd Imperial Headquarters ordered the 27th Army headquarters be sent to the Hokkaido mainland ○ On Feb 2nd the 27th Army headquarters was relocated to Sendai and reorganized into the 11th Area Army headquarters. The 5th Area Army took control of 27th Army units ○ Feb 6th, Japan's three army commands were deactivated, five area army headquarters (operational) and five military district headquarters (administrative) replaced them. The 5th Area Army's headquarters continued to oversee the Northern District ○ Feb 21st the 43rd and 69th I.M.B. in Sapporo received two Ind. Inf. Btns and became the 89th Division, the Karafuto Mixed Brigade received one inf. regt. and became the 88th Division and the 31st and 32nd Guard Units on Hokkaido combined to become the 101st I.M.B. ○ On Mar 27th the 5th Area Army reorganization was completed ○ Apr 7th, during mobilization the 147th Division, earmarked for the 5th Area Army, was transferred to the 52nd Army in Chiba ○ Apr 15th the 91st Division became responsible for Paramushiro Straight and Shumushu Island ○ On Hokkaido in

April new troops arrived, there was also a plan to organize civilians. The 101st I.M.B. replaced the 77th Div. in eastern Hokkaido, it was sent one Ind Inf Btn from the 1st Kurile Group. The 42nd Div went to Wakkanai to take command of the Soya Fortress garrison, including one battalion from the 89th Div, 1st Ind Inf Battalion from the 1st Kurile Group, two Field Artillery Companies from the 91st Division and one trench mortar battery. The Tsugaru Fortress Garrison was sent two Inf Btns, two Field Art Companies and two trench mortar batteries from the 91st Div to defend Tsugaru Strait, Mori City, Uchiura Bay and Tsugaru Fortress from on the bay side and entrance to the bay. The last stand area on Hokkaido was to be the Asahigawa Plain 〇 The 5th Area Army's mission was to prevent the Americans from building sea and air bases. Prevent enemy attempts to land on Hokkaido and secure the coasts of Tsugaru and Soya straights. If the Soviets attacked the 5th Area Army was responsible for securing southern Sakhalin 〇 On June 10th a ship was torpedoed off Otaru in waters previously considered safe. From that day IGHQ ordered all convoys to the Kuriles stopped until the seas were clear of enemy submarines. On June 25th the first B-29's were seen reconnoitering Hakodate. At this point Japan as a whole recognized the war was entering its final phase 〇 June 26th, Matsuwa Island was placed under 41st Ind Mixed Regt and Urrupu Island under the 129th I.M.B. 42nd Div units the 1st Ind Inf Garrison Btn, field artillery and mortar units under the 101st I.M.B.'s control were encouraged to form a division capable of mobile land maneuvers. The Soya Fortress Garrison, an Ind Inf Btn and two Fortification Btns were under the 42nd Division commander's control. The Nemuro Defense Unit was formed around an Ind. Inf. Btn. from the 89th Division 〇 On Jul 7th evidence was obtained that a US submarine had passed through Soya Strait, the same day communications with Sakhalin Is. were cut 〇 On Jul 14th 320 planes attacked Hokkaido 〇 Jul 15th 450 planes hit Nemuro, Kushiro, Obihiro, Urakawa, Muroran, Hakodate, Otaru and a task force of 4 battleships, 2 cruisers and 8 destroyers fired 300 to 400 shells on Muroran. It was thought perhaps 80 US planes had been shot down in the attacks. Japanese losses for the two days were about 20,000 tons of shipping plus railway damage. The Muroran Iron and Steel Works was hit by about 30 shells, part of a gun barrel factory and an entire electricity generating plant were destroyed. The Japan Iron and Steel Works plant had to stop production for about ten days 〇 On Aug 9th the USSR invaded Manchuria. At 0800 Sakhalin Is. telegraph wire was cut near Handa and the outposts between Handa and Kamishikuka had to withdraw. 10 km south in the Happo Mountains main position the Isumisawa Platoon of the 125th Inf Regt was destroyed in a 5-hour fight 〇 On Aug 12th the Red Army landed troops at Ambetsu on Sakhalin's west coast and on the 13th at Etsutoru 〇 The 88th Division dug in south of the central military road between Handa and Kamishikuka. Soviet troops attacked on the 14th and fighting around Etsutoru became heavy until news that the war had ended arrived 〇 The order to surrender came the next day but if it was unavoidable men were allowed to defend themselves. Up till Aug 18th officers in the central military road area had a hard time enforcing the cease-fire 〇 The 5th Area Army was made to take its surrender orders from the Kwantung Army. 〇 Fighting in the Kuriles ceased on the 19th except in Maoka on Sakhalin where the fighting ended on August 23rd 〇

<u>Major Units</u>: See division / brigade page for order of battle
7th Division Sapporo 1888 熊 *Kuma* – Obihiro　　　　　　　　　　　　　　204
42nd Division Sendai 1943 勲 *Isao* – Shinshiru (Niijirishima) Island　　　208-9

88th Division Asahikawa 1945 要 *Kaname* – Toyohara, Sakhalin Is. (Karafuto)	217	
89th Division Asahikawa 1945 摧 *Sai* – Etorofu Is.	218	
91st Division Asahikawa 1944 先 *Saki* – Shumushu Is.	218-9	
101st Independent Mixed Brigade 達 *Tatsu* – Tomakomia, Hokkaido	267	
129th Independent Mixed Brigade 高嶺 *Takane* – Uruppu	275	
Muroran Guards Unit 1945 達 *Tatsu* – Hokkaido	286	

Units under direct control of the 5th Area Army   達 *Tatsu*

Unit	Code	Location
5th Area Army Headquarters	8150 (230)	Sapporo
5th Area Army Headquarters Intelligence Dept.	8150 (40)	
5th Area Army Headquarters Signal Section	8150 (33)	
5th Area Army Signal Unit	12613 (248)	
5th Area Army Intelligence Unit	9899	
5th Area Army Air Intelligence Unit	9574 (2,046)	
25th Signal Regiment	12612 (1,322)	Tomawaka
41st Independent Mixed Regiment	13611 (2,380)	Matsuwa Is
22nd Tank Regiment	12614 (1,041)	Obihiro
13th Independent Rapid Firing Gun Company	14400 (145)	Shasukotan
14th Independent Rapid Firing Gun Company	14401 (145)	
17th Independent Rapid Firing Gun Company	14457 (145)	
31st Independent Rapid Firing Gun Company	14721 (145)	Sorai
7th Independent Heavy Artillery Company	28800 (90)	
8th Independent Heavy Artillery Company	28801 (90)	
15th Independent Mortar Battalion	12304 (648)	
16th Independent Mortar Battalion	12305 (619)	
18th Independent Mortar Battalion	12400 (648)	
19th Independent Mortar Battalion	12401 (648)	
6th Independent Machinegun Battalion	17406 (334)	
23rd Independent Machinegun Battalion	14201 (334)	
37th Independent Field Artillery Battalion	28799 (541)	Soya
33rd Independent Rapid Firing Gun Battalion	28791 (350)	Wakkanai
5th Anti Aircraft Unit Headquarters	28796 (70)	
24th Anti Aircraft Regiment	5686 (1,094)	Obihiro
67th Independent Anti-Aircraft Battalion	28792 (605)	
68th Independent Anti-Aircraft Battalion	28793 (605)	Takigawa
66th Independent Field Anti-Aircraft Company	28794 (437)	Wakkanai
67th Independent Field Anti-Aircraft Company	28795 (397)	Hakodate
23rd Independent Field Anti-Aircraft Company	1027 (179)	
19th Independent Field Searchlight Company	28797 (186)	
62nd Field Machine Cannon Company	12432 (105)	Uruppu
67th Field Machine Cannon Company	12531 (105)	
21st Sea Transport Battalion	27401 (548)	
29th Sea Transport Battalion	28775 (541)	Hakodate
76th Independent Signal Labor Unit	28776 (302)	
77th Independent Signal Labor Unit	28777 (302)	
78th Independent Signal Labor Unit	28778 (302)	
79th Independent Signal Labor Unit	28779 (302)	

Unit	Code	Location
80th Independent Signal Labor Unit	28780 (302)	
81st Independent Signal Labor Unit	28781 (302)	
82nd Independent Signal Labor Unit	28782 (302)	
83rd Independent Signal Labor Unit	28783 (302)	
84th Independent Signal Work Unit	28784 (302)	
85th Independent Signal Labor Unit	28785 (302)	
Soya Fortress Headquarters	9506 (104)	Soya
Soya Army Hospital	9507 (11)	Soya
Soya Fortress Heavy Artillery Regiment	9503 (530)	Soya
1st Soya Fortress Infantry Unit	9533 (204)	Soya
2nd Soya Fortress Infantry Unit	9534 (204)	Soya
3rd Soya Fortress Infantry Unit	9531 (204)	Soya
4th Soya Fortress Infantry Unit	9532 (204)	Soya
649th Independent Infantry Battalion	28789 (1,000)	Soya
Tsugaru Fortress Headquarters	No # (119)	Hakodate
Tsugaru Fortress Heavy Artillery Regiment	71 (677)	Hakodate
1st Tsugaru Infantry Unit	7533	Hakodate
2nd Tsugaru Infantry Unit	7534	Hakodate
36th Independent Field Artillery Battalion	28798 (820)	Hakodate
31st Independent Anti-Aircraft Battalion	9562 (438)	Hakodate
356th Specially Established Guard Battalion	2200 (550)	Hakodate
Nemuro Defense Unit Headquarters	28790 (26)	Nemuro
66th Field Machine Cannon Company	12530 (101)	Nemuro
306th Specially Established Engineer Unit	13636 (930)	Nemuro
Nemuro Army Hospital	unknown (12)	Nemuro
460th Independent Infantry Battalion	23011 (1,125)	Nemuro Def U
307th Specially Established Guard Company	2219 (126)	Karafuto
309th Specially Established Guard Company	2261 (126)	
310th Specially Established Guard Company	2262 (126)	
327th Specially Established Guard Company	15565 (126)	
302nd Specially Established Guard Battalion	15564 (420)	
304th Specially Established Engineer Unit	13634 (930)	
280th Independent Infantry Battalion	8648 (1,348)	from 129th Div
290th Independent Infantry Battalion	12690 (1,150)	Hakodate
11th Field Horse Replacement Depot	28714 (697)	Senbiri

Army Units on Karafuto/Sakhalin Is.   要 *Kaname* (88th Division)

Unit	Code
302nd Specially Established Guard Company	2214 (126)
354th Specially Established Guard Battalion	unknown (550)
357th Specially Established Guard Battalion	15563 (550)
330th Specially Established Guard Company	15569 (126)
331st Specially Established Guard Company	15570 (126)
305th Specially Established Guard Engineer Unit	13635 (930)

Chapter 2

Hokubu Army District
Sakhalin and Hokkaido Areas

Hokubu Army District Headquarters   Sapporo   北部 (864)

Asahikawa Divisional District

Asahikawa Divisional District HQ   Asahikawa   北部 (271)

Recruiting and home defense units
7ᵗʰ Depot Division / Asahikawa Divisional District

Unit	Location	Barracks # (Personnel)
7ᵗʰ Depot Division Headquarters	Asahikawa	*Hokubu*
26ᵗʰ Infantry Regt Replacement Unit	Asahikawa	北部 2
27ᵗʰ Infantry Regt Replacement Unit	Asahikawa	北部 3
28ᵗʰ Infantry Regt Replacement Unit	Asahikawa	北部 4
7ᵗʰ Cavalry Regt Replacement Unit	Asahikawa	北部 5
7ᵗʰ Mountain Art. Regt Repl Unit	Asahikawa	北部 6
7ᵗʰ Engineer Regiment Repl. Unit	Asahikawa	北部 7
7ᵗʰ Transport Regiment Repl. Unit	Asahikawa	北部 8
7ᵗʰ Div. Signal Unit Repl. Unit	Asahikawa	北部 8
Reorganized on Feb 6, 1945		
Asahikawa 1ˢᵗ Inf. Replacement Unit	Asahikawa	北部 178 (3,202)
Asahikawa 2ⁿᵈ Inf. Replacement Unit	Asahikawa	北部 179 (3,202)
Asahikawa 3ʳᵈ Inf. Replacement Unit	Asahikawa	北部 180 (3,202)
Asahikawa Artillery Repl. Unit	Asahikawa	北部 181 (759)
Asahikawa Engineer Repl. Unit	Asahikawa	北部 182 (705)
Asahikawa Signal Replacement Unit	Asahikawa	北部 183 (345)
Asahikawa Transport Repl. Unit	Asahikawa	北部 184 (659)

Major units supplied by the Asahikawa Divisional District include: 7ᵗʰ Division, 24ᵗʰ Division, 71ˢᵗ Division, 77ᵗʰ Division, 91ˢᵗ Division, 115ᵗʰ Division, Karafuto Mixed Brigade, 3ʳᵈ Amphibious Brigade and 4ᵗʰ Amphibious Brigade.

Toyohara Regimental District: Karafuto (Sakhalin) Prefecture Admin. District

Toyohara Regimental District Headquarters	No # (79)	
Karafuto (Sakhalin Is.) District:	陽 *Yo*	
Karafuto District 1ˢᵗ Specially Est. Garrison Unit	30126 (308)	Toyohira City
Karafuto District 2ⁿᵈ Specially Est. Garrison Unit	30127 (308)	Toyohira City
352ⁿᵈ Specially Established Garrison Battalion	2211 (550)	Toyohira City
353ʳᵈ Specially Established Garrison Battalion	2212 (550)	Toyohira City
303ʳᵈ Specially Established Engineer Unit	13633 (930)	Toyohira City
Karafuto District 3ʳᵈ Specially Est. Garrison Unit	30128 (308)	Honto-cho
306ᵗʰ Specially Established Garrison Company	2218 (126)	Honto-cho
Karafuto District 4ᵗʰ Specially Est. Garrison Unit	30129 (308)	Maoka-cho
305ᵗʰ Specially Established Garrison Company	2217 (126)	Maoka-cho
Karafuto District 5ᵗʰ Specially Est. Garrison Unit	30130 (308)	Otomari-cho

351st Specially Established Garrison Battalion	2210 (550)	Otomari-cho
Karafuto District 6th Specially Est. Garrison Unit	30131 (308)	Chitori-cho
Karafuto District 7th Specially Est. Garrison Unit	30132 (308)	Shikuka-cho
Karafuto District 8th Specially Est. Garrison Unit	30133 (308)	Etsutoru-cho
303rd Specially Established Garrison Company	2215 (126)	Tomari-cho
301st Specially Established Garrison Company	2213 (126)	Manui-mura
304th Specially Established Garrison Company	2216 (126)	Kushumai-cho
307th Specially Established Garrison Company	2219 (126)	Nishinotoro-mura
308th Specially Established Garrison Company	2260 (126)	Kaiba-to
301st Specially Established Engineer Unit	13631 (930)	Nairo-cho
302nd Specially Established Engineer Unit	13632 (930)	Ochiai-cho

宰 *Sai*

322nd Specially Established Garrison Company	2291 (126)	Etrouto
323rd Specially Established Garrison Company	2292 (126)	Kunijirito
324th Specially Established Garrison Company	2299 (126)	Irokotanto

Asahikawa Regimental District: Asahikawa City Administrative District
Administrative District Branch offices: Kamikawa, Soya, Rumoi
Asahikawa Regimental District Headquarters   No # (79)

Asahikawa District: 北部 *Hokubu*

Asahikawa District 1st Specially Est. Garrison Unit	30101 (308)	Asahikawa City
Asahikawa District 2nd Specially Est. Garrison Unit	30102 (308)	Asahikawa City
Asahikawa District 3rd Specially Est. Garrison Unit	30103 (308)	Rumoi-cho

達 *Tatsu*

355th Specially Established Garrison Company   2276 (126)

北部 *Hokubu*

Asahikawa District 4th Specially Est. Garrison Unit   30104 (308)   Wakkanai

達 *Tatsu*

311th Specially Established Garrison Company	2269 (126)	Yokijiri-mura
312th Specially Established Garrison Company	2270 (126)	Youri-mura
313th Specially Established Garrison Company	2274 (126)	Rumoi-cho
354th Specially Established Garrison Company	2275 (126)	
304th Specially Established Engineer Unit	13634 (930)	Asajino-mura

Sapporo Regt. District: Sapporo, Muroran, Iwamisawa, Yubari City Admin. Dist.
Admin District Branch offices: Ishikari, Iburi, Hidata, Sorachi
Sapporo Regimental district Headquarters   No # (79)

Sapporo District: 北部 *Hokubu*

Sapporo District 1st Specially Est. Garrison Unit   30105 (308)   Sapporo City

達 *Tatsu*

375th Specially Established Garrison Battalion	15562 (550)	Sapporo City
308th Specially Established Engineer Unit	13638 (930)	Sapporo City

Sapporo District continues

	北部 *Hokubu*	
Sapporo District 2nd Specially Est. Garrison Unit	30106 (308)	Muroran City
Sapporo District 3rd Specially Est. Garrison Unit	30107 (308)	Iwamizawa City
Sapporo District 4th Specially Est. Garrison Unit	30108 (308)	Yubari City
	達 *Tatsu*	
330th Specially Established Garrison Company	15569 (126)	Yubari City
	北部 *Hokubu*	
Sapporo District 5th Specially Est. Garrison Unit	30109 (308)	Tokigawa-cho
Sapporo District 6th Specially Est. Garrison Unit	30110 (308)	Ebitsu-cho
Sapporo District 7th Specially Est. Garrison Unit	30111 (308)	Tomakomi-cho
Sapporo District 8th Specially Est. Garrison Unit	30112 (308)	Urakawa-cho
	達 *Tatsu*	
321st Specially Established Garrison Company	2289 (126)	Cape Erimo
309th Specially Established Engineer Unit	13639 (930)	Numansha-mura
310th Specially Established Engineer Unit	13640 (930)	Shiraoi-mura

Hakodate Regimental District: Hakodate City, Otaru City Administrative Districts
Administrative District Branch offices: Oshima, Hiyama, Shiribeshi

Hakodate Regimental District Headquarters	No # (79)	

Hakodate District

	北部 *Hokubu*	
Hakodate District 1st Specially Est. Garrison Unit	30113 (308)	Hakodate City
Hakodate District 2nd Specially Est. Garrison Unit	30114 (308)	Hakodate City
	達 *Tatsu*	
356th Specially Established Garrison Battalion	2200 (550)	Hakodate City
314th Specially Established Garrison Company	2277 (126)	Okujiri-mura
	北部 *Hokubu*	
Hakodate District 3rd Specially Est. Garrison Unit	30115 (308)	Kotara City
Hakodate District 4th Specially Est. Garrison Unit	30116 (308)	Egashi-cho
Hakodate District 5th Specially Est. Garrison Unit	30117 (308)	Kuchian-cho

Kushiro Regimental District: Koshiro, Obihiro, Kitami City Admin. Districts
Administrative District Branch offices: Kitami, Tokaichi, Abashiri, Nemuro

Kushiro Regimental District Headquarters	No # (79)	

Kushiro District:

	北部 *Hokubu*	
Kushiro District 1st Specially Est. Garrison Unit	30118 (308)	Kushiro City
Kushiro District 2nd Specially Est. Garrison Unit	30119 (308)	Kushiro City
320th Specially Established Garrison Company	2288 (126)	Kushiro City
Kushiro District 3rd Specially Est. Garrison Unit	30120 (308)	Kitami City
Kushiro District 4th Specially Est. Garrison Unit	30121 (308)	Obihiro City
Kushiro District 5th Specially Est. Garrison Unit	30122 (308)	Obihiro City
307th Specially Established Engineer Unit	13637 (930)	Obihiro City

Kushiro District: continued

Kushiro District 6th Specially Est. Garrison Unit	30123 (308)	Nemuro City
302nd Specially Established Garrison Battalion	15564 (430)	Nemuro City
306th Specially Established Engineer Unit	13636 (930)	Nemuro City
Kushiro District 7th Specially Est. Garrison Unit	30124 (308)	Abashiri-cho
318th Specially Established Garrison Company	2286 (126)	Abashiri-cho
Kushiro District 8th Specially Est. Garrison Unit	30125 (308)	Tohokaru-cho
315th Specially Established Garrison Company	2278 (126)	Kobe-mura
316th Specially Established Garrison Company	2284 (126)	Monbetsu
317th Specially Established Garrison Company	2285 (126)	Kamiwakibetsu
331st Specially Established Garrison Company	15570 (126)	Kiritafu-mura

Air Unit attached to the 5th Area Army:

1st Air Division: 1943 Otaru, Hokkaido   鏑 *Kabura* 1045 / 北部200

1st Air Division Headquarters	1046 (243)	Otaru
20th Air Brigade Headquarters	19270 (65)	Muroran
• 54th Air Regiment (fighter)	19272 (322)	Sapporo
• 32nd Air Regiment (light bomber)	9143 (235)	Kenebetu
• 38th Air Regiment	19342 / 北部142 (144)	
20th Air Sector Command	19335 / 北部135 (50)	
21st Air Sector Command	19252 / 北部152 (50)	
27th Air Sector Command	18435 (50)	Obihiro
1st Airfield Battalion	19274 (406)	Ochiai
2nd Airfield Battalion	19257 (406)	Numanohata
49th Airfield Battalion	19336 / 北部136 (414)	
55th Airfield Battalion	19337 / 北部137 (414)	
63rd Airfield Battalion	19338 / 北部138 (414)	
73rd Airfield Battalion	19320 (406)	Kenebetsu
77th Airfield Battalion	19345 (414)	Yakumo
80th Airfield Battalion	19346 (414)	Kenebetsu
83rd Airfield Battalion	19347 (414)	Obihiro
178th Airfield Battalion	18950 (406)	Hokkaido
12th Field Airfield Construction Unit	15306 (670)	Numanohata
21st Field Airfield Construction Unit	19266 (648)	
10th Air Signal Regiment	19275 (1,122)	Obihiro
6th Air Special Signal Unit	12906 (259)	
1st Fixed Signal Unit	19253 (265)	
11th Wireless Radio Unit	19254 (199)	Ochiai
12th Wireless Radio Unit	19255 (199)	
20th Air Intelligence Unit	19276 / 北部76 (821)	Ochiai
20th Air Navigation Aid Unit	19277 (578)	Sapporo
11th Field Meteorological Unit	19349 (713)	Obihiro
6th Field Air Repair Depot	19250 (566)	Obihiro / Ochiai
6th Field Air Freight Depot	19251 (289)	Obihiro

1st Air Division continued

119th Independent Maintenance Unit (Ki-43, Oscar)	18984 (172)	Sapporo
139th Ind. Maintenance Unit (Ki-46, Dinah)	19011 (172)	Obihiro
150th Ind. Maintenance Unit (Ki-49, Helen)	19022 (172)	Obihiro

1st Air Division: Activated in Sapporo, Japan January 9, 1943. Based in Otaru, Hokkaido, it was attached to the 1st Air Army from Jan 9th until Feb 11th, the Northern Army until Mar 16, 1944, 5th Area Army until May 8, 1945 and Air General Army until the war ended. The 1st Air Division's headquarters was organized on May 5 1942.

Foraging for hay (author)

End: Imperial Headquarters direct control

The Imperial Japanese Army

Northern and Central Honshu

1st General Army

1) 11th Area Army
50th Army

2) 12th Area Army
36th Army
51st Armt
52nd Army
53rd Army

3) 13th Area Army
54th Army

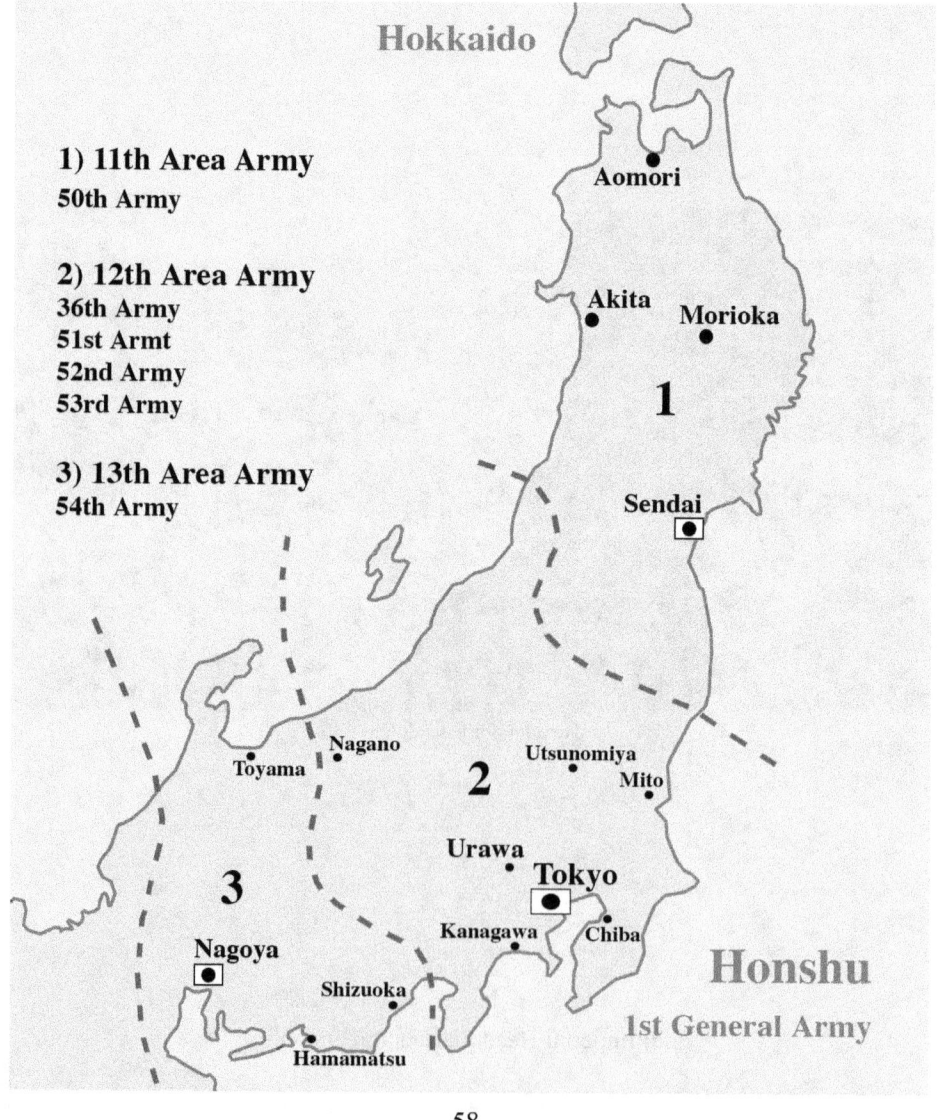

Chapter 2

1st General Army 東方 *Toho*

The 1st General Army was created under the *Army Mobilization Plan for Early 1945* to replace the northern half of General Defense Command, which had overseen all Japan. It was activated on April 8, 1945. Units from the old command were shifted to the new one a few at a time to avoid any disruptions within the two organizations. From April 8th until Sept 12th the 1st General Army's Headquarters was located in Tokyo under Field Marshal Hajime Sugiyama. It was responsible for defending the north, east and northeast coast from the Tsugaru Straits to Osaka. On Aug 18th the 1st General Army had 851,500 active duty members. It was deactivated on Nov 30th.

Subordinate armies / duty dates:
11th Area Army from Apr 8, 1945 until Sept 13, 1945
12th Area Army from Apr 8, 1945 until Oct 18, 1945
13th Area Army from Apr 8, 1945 until Nov 15, 1945

Service History:
1944: On July 28th the 36th Army became active in the Kanto District of Japan and the 32nd Army was transferred from the Western Army to the Formosa Army ○
1945: On Feb 6th the Homeland Defense Districts were reorganized. The three army command headquarters were deactivated and simultaneously replaced by five area army headquarters for field operations and five army district headquarters to administrate the army districts. ○ On Apr 13th, during a conference of 1st General Army commanders, its Tokyo HQs in the Ichigaya neighborhood were destroyed in an air raid ○ End of June, the 1st General Army received permission to relocate its headquarters to a less vulnerable area. After examining communications and transportation facilities Takasaki was determined as best suited. The move was tentatively set to take place in September ○ Also in September the 12th Area Army was scheduled to move its HQ from Tokyo to Matsuyama ○ On Aug 15th Japan surrendered ○ Sept 2nd surrender documents were signed aboard the battleship Missouri ○ The 1st General Army provided security units for several months after the ceremony, only to disestablish them when the army of occupation was in place ○ On Sept 12th General. Sugiyama committed suicide ○ The 1st General Army was deactivated on November 30th ○

Units under control of the 1st General Army:	東方 *Toho*	
1st General Army Headquarters	8151 (554)	Tokyo
1st General Army Headquarters Signal Section	8151 (87)	
1st General Army Headquarters Flight Section	8151 (16)	

Northern Honshu

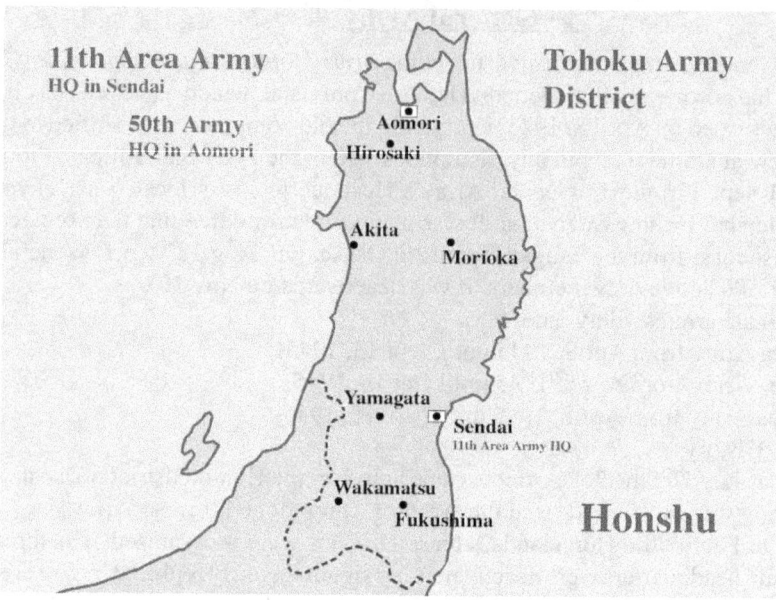

11th Area Army / Tohoku Army District 進 *Susumu*

The 11th Area Army headquarters was activated in Sendai on February 6, 1945, from former 27th Army headquarters personnel. It served under General Defense Command until April 8th and the 1st General Army until Sept 13th. Based in Sendai, Miyagi Prefecture its commander was Lt Gen Teiichi Yoshimoto from Feb 6th until June 22nd and General Keisuke Fujie until Sept 13th. On Aug 15th the 11th Area Army had 117,271 active duty members.

Subordinate army / duty dates:
50th Army from June 19, 1945 until Sept 11, 1945

Service History:
1945: On Jan 22nd the 27th Army HQ in the Kurile Islands was deactivated with orders to relocate to Sendai ○ On Feb 6th the Homeland Defense Districts were reorganized and the former 27th Army headquarters became the 11th Area Army headquarters. Its mission was to oversee the new Northeast Army District, which had previously been the Northeast District Army's responsibility ○ On June 19th the 50th Army was placed under 11th Area Army command ○ The 11th Area Army was deactivated in Sendai on Sept 13th ○

Major Units: See division / brigade page for order of battle
72nd Division Sendai 1944 伝 *Den* – Fukushima   213-4
142nd Division Sendai 1945 護仙 *Gosen* – Yoshioka, Miyagi   233
222nd Division Hirosaki 1945 八甲 *Hakko* – Hasedō, Yamagata   246
322nd Division Sendai 1945 磐梯 *Bandai* - Iwanuma, Miyagi   252
113th Independent Mixed Brigade 1945 瑞光 *Zuihikari* – Fukushima   270

Units under control of the 11th Area Army: Sendai   進 *Susumu*

11th Army Headquarters   12300 (233)   Sendai
12th Independent Mountain Artillery Regiment   27385 (2,970)   Nanakitada
34th Independent Heavy Artillery Battalion   13363 (116)   Shiogama

11th Area Army continued

Unit	Number	Location
21st Independent Rapid Firing Gun Battalion	15575 (480)	Fujita
2nd Trench Mortar Battalion	27445 (507)	Hirosaki
3rd Trench Mortar Battalion	27446 (1,407)	
44th Independent Tank Regiment	21409 (608)	Morioka
48th Independent Anti Aircraft Battalion	1064 (353)	Sakata
34th Independent Anti Aircraft Company	9566 (90)	Kamanishi
18th Independent Machine Cannon Company	13339 (90)	Okuma
19th Independent Machine Cannon Company	13340 (90)	Ueda
38th Signals Regiment	21401 (1,817)	Morioka
4th Independent Signal Labor Unit	27393 (53)	Miyagi
5th Independent Signal Labor Unit	27394 (53)	Yamagata
6th Independent Signal Labor Unit	27395 (53)	Miyagi
7th Independent Signal Labor Unit	27396 (53)	Sendai
8th to 10th Independent Signal Labor Unit	27397-9 (303 each)	
17th Field Transport Headquarters	21442 (37)	Sendai
69th Line of Communications Sector Command	30203 (203)	Sendai
69th Line of Communications Duty Unit	30204 (511)	Aomori
8th Engineers Headquarters	21412 (93)	Okido
85th Independent Engineer Battalion	27406 (185)	Murata
86th Independent Engineer Battalion	27407 (184)	Hirosaki
7th Field Horse Remount Depot	21446 (300)	Sanbongi
33rd Garrison Headquarters	5220 (28)	Kamaishi
325th Specially Established Garrison Company	5225 (126)	Kamaishi
324th Specially Established Garrison Company	5234 (126)	Kamaishi
30th Specially Established Garrison Company	3316 (126)	Shinzukawa-m.
31st Specially Established Garrison Company	3317 (126)	Ishinomaki City
32nd Specially Established Garrison Company	3318 (126)	Haruno-machi
33rd Specially Established Garrison Company	3319 (126)	Tomoka-machi
34th Specially Established Garrison Company	3320 (126)	Onahama-machi
326th Specially Established Garrison Company	5226 (126)	Akumi-gun

Northern Honshu, Tsugaru Strait Region

50th Army 俊 *Shun*

The 50th Army was activated in Aomori, Japan on June 10, 1945, under the army mobilization plan third group mobilization, in preparation for the decisive battle. Placed under 11th Area Army control on June 19th, its headquarters were in Aomori under Lt Gen Toshimoto Hoshino from June 15th until deactivation on Sept 11th.

Service History:
1945: On June 10th the 50th Army was activated in Aomori ○ June 15th Lt. Gen.

50th Army continued

Hoshino was appointed 50th Army commander ○ June 19th, the 50th Army was placed under 11th Area Army control with the mission of defending Japan's northeast coast ○ On June 19th the 157th and 308th Div and 95th I.M.B. were placed into the 50th Army's order of battle ○ On Sept 11th the 50th Army was deactivated in Aomori ○

Major Units: See division / brigade page for order of battle

157th Division Hirosaki 1945 護弘 *Goro* – Sanbongi, Miyagi		239-40
308th Division Hirosaki 1945 岩木 *Yuwaki* – Shimokita, Aomori		250
95th Independent Mixed Brigade 1945 俊 *Shun* – Hachinohe, Aomori		266

Units under control of the 50th Army: Aomori　　俊 *Shun* 27500

Unit	Barracks # (Personnel)	Location
50th Army Headquarters	21413 (352)	Aomori
15th Independent Machinegun Battalion	15573 (680)	Akita
1st Trench Mortar Battalion	27444 (550)	Nobeji
24th Independent Mortar Battalion	27402 (680)	Sanbongi
84th Independent Engineer Battalion	27405 (188)	Komaki
49th Signals Regiment	27449 (1,120)	Aomori
332nd Specially Established Garrison Company	5232 (126)	Hachinohe
333rd Specially Established Garrison Company	5233 (126)	Kunohe

Tohoku Army District:
Tohoku Area

Tohoku Army District Headquarters　　Sendai　　東北 (596)

Hirosaki Divisional District:

Hirosaki Divisional District HQ　　Hirosaki　　東部 (260)

Recruiting and home defense units
57th Depot Division / Hirosaki Divisional District:

Unit	Location	Barracks # (Personnel)
57th Depot Division Headquarters	Hirosaki	*Tobu*
52nd Infantry Regiment Repl. Unit	Hirosaki	東部 57
117th Infantry Regt Replacement Unit	Akita	東部 58
132nd Infantry Regiment Repl.Unit	Yamagata	東部 59
57th Cavalry Regt Replacement Unit	Hirosaki	東部 60
57th Field Art. Regiment Repl. Unit	Hirosaki	東部 69
57th Engineer Regt Replacement Unit	Morioka	東部 78
57th Div. Signal Unit Repl. Unit	Hirosaki	東部 79
57th Transp. Regt Replacement Unit	Hirosaki	東部 80
Reorganized into 東北 *Feb 6, 1945*		*Tohoku*
Hirosaki 1st Infantry Repl. Unit	Hirosaki	東北 57 (3,202)
Hirosaki 2nd Infantry Repl. Unit	Akita	東北 58 (3,202)
Hirosaki Artillery Replacement Unit	Hirosaki	東北 69 (576)
Hirosaki Engineer Replacement Unit	Morioka	東北 78 (705)
Hirosaki Signal Replacement Unit	Hirosaki	東北 79 (345)
Hirosaki Transport Replacement Unit	Hirosaki	東北 84 (659)

4ᵗʰ Signal Regiment Repl. Unit　　　Aomori　　　東北 81 (511)
22ⁿᵈ Tank Regiment Repl. Unit　　　Morioka　　　東北 45

Major units supplied by the Hirosaki Divisional District include:
8ᵗʰ Div., 36ᵗʰ Div., 47ᵗʰ Div., 57ᵗʰ Div., 69ᵗʰ Div., 107ᵗʰ Div., 108ᵗʰ Div., 26ᵗʰ I.M.B., 28ᵗʰ I.M.B., 55ᵗʰ I.M.B., 58ᵗʰ I.M.B., 3ʳᵈ Cav. Bgde.

Aomori Regimental District: Aomori Prefecture Administrative District
Aomori District:　　　　　　　　　　　　　　　　東北 *Tohoku*

Unit	Code	Location
Aomori District 1ˢᵗ Specially Est. Garrison Unit	20750 (471)	Aomori City
Aomori District 2ⁿᵈ Specially Est. Garrison Unit	20751 (473)	Yukawa-machi
Aomori District 3ʳᵈ Specially Est. Garrison Unit	20752 (324)	Nakazato-machi
Aomori District 4ᵗʰ Specially Est. Garrison Unit	20753 (324)	Goshogawara .
Aomori District 5ᵗʰ Specially Est. Garrison Unit	20754 (324)	Kizukuri-machi
Aomori District 6ᵗʰ Specially Est. Garrison Unit	20755 (324)	Ajigasawara-m.
Aomori District 7ᵗʰ Specially Est. Garrison Unit	20756 (325)	Hirosaki City
Aomori District 8ᵗʰ Specially Est. Garrison Unit	20757 (324)	Fujishiro-mura
Aomori District 9ᵗʰ Specially Est. Garrison Unit	20758 (471)	Kuroishi-machi
Aomori District 10ᵗʰ Specially Est. Garrison Unit	20759 (503)	Shimokita-gun
Aomori District 11ᵗʰ Specially Est. Garrison Unit	20760 (471)	Koji-mura
Aomori District 12ᵗʰ Specially Est. Garrison Unit	20761 (324)	Sanbonji-machi
Aomori District 13ᵗʰ Specially Est. Garrison Unit	20762 (324)	Gonohe-machi
Aomori District 14ᵗʰ Specially Est. Garrison Unit	20763 (325)	Hachinohe City

Morioka Regimental District: Iwate Prefecture Administrative District
Morioka District　　　　　　　　　　　　　　東北 *Tohoku*

Unit	Code	Location
Morioka District 4ᵗʰ Specially Est. Garrison Unit	20767 (324)	Kamaishi
11ᵗʰ Specially Established Engineer Unit	13316 (930)	Morioka
Morioka District 8ᵗʰ Specially Est. Garrison Unit	20771 (325)	Morioka
Morioka District 1ˢᵗ Specially Est. Garrison Unit	20764 (473)	Kunohe
Morioka District 2ⁿᵈ Specially Est. Garrison Unit	20765 (324)	Shimohei-gun
Morioka District 3ʳᵈ Specially Est. Garrison Unit	20766 (324)	Miyako City
Morioka District 5ᵗʰ Specially Est. Garrison Unit	20768 (471)	Sukuri-machi
Morioka District 6ᵗʰ Specially Est. Garrison Unit	20769 (324)	Hukuoka-machi
Morioka District 7ᵗʰ Specially Est. Garrison Unit	20770 (324)	Mukibori-mura
Morioka District 9ᵗʰ Specially Est. Garrison Unit	20772 (325)	Senpoku-machi
Morioka District 10ᵗʰ Specially Est. Garrison Unit	20773 (325)	Hizume-machi
Morioka District 11ᵗʰ Specially Est. Garrison Unit	20774 (324)	Hunumaki-m.
Morioka District 12ᵗʰ Specially Est. Garrison Unit	20775 (324)	Kurasawajiri-m.
Morioka District 13ᵗʰ Specially Est. Garrison Unit	20776 (325)	Tono-machi
Morioka District 14ᵗʰ Specially Est. Garrison Unit	20777 (324)	Iwatani-do-m.
Morioka District 15ᵗʰ Specially Est. Garrison Unit	20778 (325)	Mizusawa-m.
Morioka District 16ᵗʰ Specially Est. Garrison Unit	20779 (324)	Ichinoseki-m
Morioka District 17ᵗʰ Specially Est. Garrison Unit	20780 (324)	Senmaya-cho

Akita Regimental District: Akita Prefecture Administrative District
Akita District　　　　　　　　　　　　東北 *Tohoku*

Akita District 1st Specially Est. Garrison Unit	20781 (473)	Odate-machi
Akita District 2nd Specially Est. Garrison Unit	20782 (471)	Hanayu-machi
Akita District 3rd Specially Est. Garrison Unit	20783 (326)	Hututsui-machi
Akita District 4th Specially Est. Garrison Unit	20784 (471)	Noshiro City
Akita District 5th Specially Est. Garrison Unit	20785 (473)	Funakawako-m.
Akita District 6th Specially Est. Garrison Unit	20786 (325)	Akita City
Akita District 7th Specially Est. Garrison Unit	20787 (324)	Akita City
Akita District 8th Specially Est. Garrison Unit	20788 (324)	Honso-machi
Akita District 9th Specially Est. Garrison Unit	20789 (326)	Shirogate-machi
Akita District 10th Specially Est. Garrison Unit	20790 (477)	Okuma-machi
Akita District 11th Specially Est. Garrison Unit	20791 (471)	Yokote-machi
Akita District 12th Specially Est. Garrison Unit	20792 (471)	Yuzawa-machi

Sendai Divisional District:

Sendai Divisional District HQ　　Sendai　　東北 (292)

Recruiting and home defense units
2nd Depot Division / Sendai Divisional District:

Unit	Location	Barracks # (Personnel)
2nd Depot Division Headquarters	Sendai	*Tobu*
4th Infantry Regt Replacement Unit	Sendai	東部 22
16th Infantry Regt Replacement Unit	Shibata	東部 23
29th Infantry Regt Replacement Unit	Wakamatsu	東部 24
2nd Recon Regt Replacement Unit	Sendai	東部 25
2nd Fld. Art. Regt Replacement Unit	Sendai	東部 27
2nd Engineer Regt Replacement Unit	Sendai	東部 29
2nd Transport Regt Replacement Unit	Sendai	東部 30
2nd Div. Signal Unit Repl. Unit	Sendai	東部 31
Reorganized into 東北 *Feb 6, 1945*		*Tohoku*
Sendai Divisional District HQ	Sendai	東北 (264)
Sendai 1st Infantry Replacement Unit	Sendai	東北 122 (1,933)
Sendai 2nd Infantry Replacement Unit	Wakamatsu	東北 124 (1,933)
Sendai 3rd Infantry Replacement Unit	Yamagata	東北 138 (1,933)
Sendai Artillery Replacement Unit	Sendai	東北 127 (576)
Sendai Engineer Replacement Unit	Sendai	東北 129 (705)
Sendai Signal Unit Repl. Unit	Sendai	東北 130 (345)
Sendai Transport Replacement Unit	Sendai	東北 131 (659)

Major units supplied by the Sendai Divisional District include:
2nd Div., 13th Div., 22nd Div., 42nd Div., 72nd Div., 3rd I.M.B., 24th I.M.B., 43rd I.M.B., 54th I.M.B., 8th Ind. Inf. Bgde, 1st Amphibious Bgde.

Sendai Regimental District: Miyagi Prefecture Administrative District

Sendai District

63rd Specially Established Garrison Battalion

	進 *Susumu*	
	3315 (550)	Sendai
	東北 *Tohoku*	

12th Specially Established Engineer Unit — 13317 (933) Sendai
13th Specially Established Engineer Unit — 13318 (933) Harano-machi
Sendai District 3rd Specially Est. Garrison Unit — 1356 (300) Sendai
Sendai District 4th Specially Est. Garrison Unit — 1358 (300) Sendai

進 *Susumu*

Sendai District 1st Specially Est. Garrison Unit — 1354 (300) Yamashita-mura
Sendai District 2nd Specially Est. Garrison Unit — 1355 (300) Masuda-mura
Sendai District 5th Specially Est. Garrison Unit — 1359 (300) Tohu-mura
Sendai District 6th Specially Est. Garrison Unit — 1360 (300) Shiogama City
Sendai District 7th Specially Est. Garrison Unit — 1361 (300) Hirose-mura
Sendai District 8th Specially Est. Garrison Unit — 1367 (300) Inogawa-machi

東北 *Tohoku*

Sendai District 9th Specially Est. Garrison Unit — 1368 (300) Ishinomaki City
Sendai District 10th Specially Est. Garrison Unit — 1369 (300) Watanami-machi
Sendai District 11th Specially Est. Garrison Unit — 1370 (300) Yokoyama-mura
Sendai District 12th Specially Est. Garrison Unit — 1371 (300) Kesenuma-machi
Sendai District 13th Specially Est. Garrison Unit — 1372 (300) Shiroishi-machi
Sendai District 14th Specially Est. Garrison Unit — 1375 (300) Kakuda-machi
Sendai District 15th Specially Est. Garrison Unit — 1376 (300) Okawara-machi
Sendai District 16th Specially Est. Garrison Unit — 1377 (300) Yoshioka-machi
Sendai District 17th Specially Est. Garrison Unit — 1378 (300) Nakanitta-machi
Sendai District 18th Specially Est. Garrison Unit — 1379 (300) Hurakawa-machi
Sendai District 19th Specially Est. Garrison Unit — 1383 (300) Iwadeyama-m.
Sendai District 20th Specially Est. Garrison Unit — 1384 (300) Wakuya-machi
Sendai District 21st Specially Est. Garrison Unit — 1385 (300) Sunami-machi
Sendai District 22nd Specially Est. Garrison Unit — 1386 (300) Wakanayagi-m.
Sendai District 23rd Specially Est. Garrison Unit — 1390 (300) Kesenuma-machi

Fukushima Regimental District: Fukushima Prefecture Administrative District
Fukushima District: 東北 *Tohoku*

Fukushima District 1st Specially Est. Garrison Unit — 3333 (300) Nakoso-machi
Fukushima District 2nd Specially Est. Garrison Unit — 3334 (250) Onahama-machi
Fukushima District 3rd Specially Est. Garrison Unit — 3335 (300) Oura-mura
Fukushima District 4th Specially Est. Garrison Unit — 3336 (300) Taira City
Fukushima District 5th Specially Est. Garrison Unit — 3337 (300) Namie-machi
Fukushima District 6th Specially Est. Garrison Unit — 3338 (300) Kashima-machi
Fukushima District 7th Specially Est. Garrison Unit — 3339 (300) Tanakura-machi
Fukushima District 8th Specially Est. Garrison Unit — 3340 (330) Ishikawa-machi
Fukushima District 9th Specially Est. Garrison Unit — 3341 (400) Miharu-machi

Fukushima District: continued   東北 *Tohoku*

Fukushima District 10th Sp. Est. Garrison Unit	3342 (350)	Nihonmatsu-m.
Fukushima District 11th Sp. Est. Garrison Unit	3343 (350)	Yaki-machi
Fukushima District 12th Sp. Est. Garrison Unit	3344 (300)	Kawamata-machi
Fukushima District 13th Sp. Est. Garrison Unit	3345 (300)	Shirakawa-machi
Fukushima District 14th Sp. Est. Garrison Unit	3346 (300)	Sugogawa-machi
Fukushima District 15th Sp. Est. Garrison Unit	3347 (300)	Koriyama City
Fukushima District 16th Sp. Est. Garrison Unit	3348 (300)	Fukuyama-machi
Fukushima District 17th Sp. Est. Garrison Unit	3349 (300)	Fukushima City
Fukushima District 18th Sp. Est. Garrison Unit	3350 (350)	Noda-mura
Fukushima District 19th Sp. Est. Garrison Unit	3351 (200)	Tajima-machi
Fukushima District 20th Sp. Est. Garrison Unit	3352 (200)	Omiya-machi
Fukushima District 21st Sp. Est. Garrison Unit	3353 (300)	Wakamatsu City
Fukushima District 22nd Sp. Est. Garrison Unit	3354 (300)	Kitaaizu-gun
Fukushima District 23rd Sp. Est. Garrison Unit	3355 (300)	Inuwashiro-m.
Fukushima District 24th Sp. Est. Garrison Unit	3356 (300)	Kitakata-machi
Fukushima District 25th Sp. Est. Garrison Unit	3357 (300)	Takata-machi
Fukushima District 26th Sp. Est. Garrison Unit	3358 (300)	Sakashita-machi

Yamagata Regimental District: Yamagata Prefecture Administrative District
Yamagata District   東北 *Tohoku*

Yamagata District 1st Specially Est. Garrison Unit	3364 (350)	Yonezawa City
Yamagata District 2nd Specially Est. Garrison Unit	3365 (350)	Yonezawa City
Yamagata District 3rd Specially Est. Garrison Unit	3366 (350)	Akayu-machi
Yamagata District 4th Specially Est. Garrison Unit	3367 (300)	Nagai-machi
Yamagata District 5th Specially Est. Garrison Unit	3368 (300)	Kaminoyama-m.
Yamagata District 6th Specially Est. Garrison Unit	3369 (300)	Yamagata City
Yamagata District 7th Specially Est. Garrison Unit	3390 (300)	Tendō-machi
Yamagata District 8th Specially Est. Garrison Unit	3391 (300)	Yamanobe-machi
Yamagata District 9th Specially Est. Garrison Unit	3392 (300)	Nishimurayama
Yamagata District 10th Specially Est. Garrison Unit	3393 (300)	Tateoka-machi
Yamagata District 11th Specially Est. Garrison Unit	3394 (300)	Shinjō-machi
Yamagata District 12th Specially Est.Garrison Unit	3395 (300)	Oyama-machi
Yamagata District 13th Specially Est. Garrison Unit	3396 (300)	Tsuruoka City
Yamagata District 14th Specially Est. Garrison Unit	3397 (300)	Fujishima-machi
Yamagata District 15th Specially Est. Garrison Unit	3398 (300)	Sakata City
Yamagata District 16th Specially Est. Garrison Unit	3399 (300)	Motodate-machi

Tokyo, East Coast and the Kanto Plain

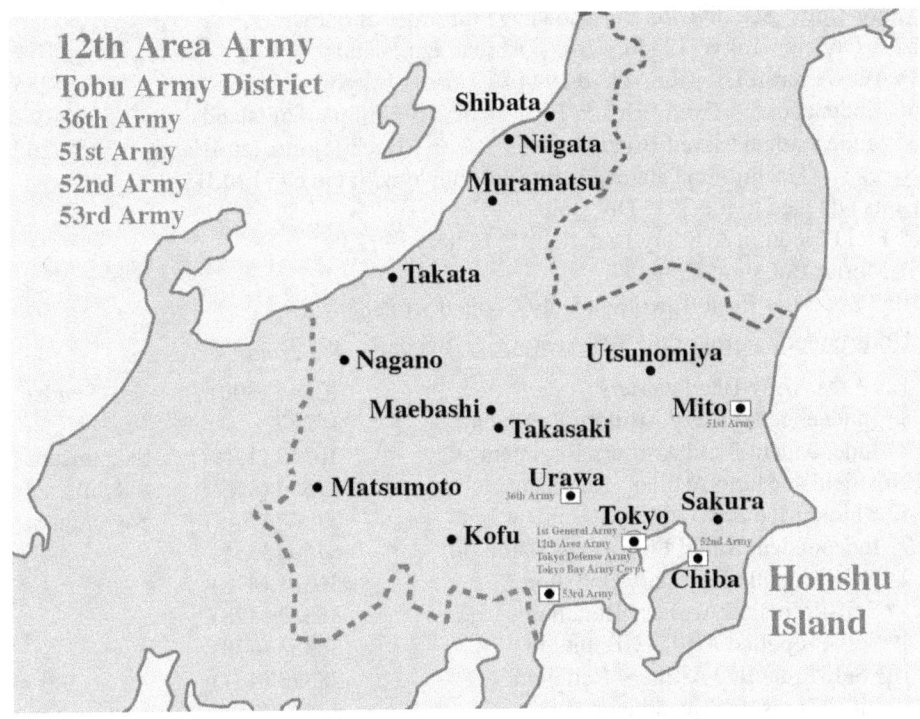

12th Area Army / Tobu Army District: 幡 Hata

The 12th Area Army was activated on Jan 22, 1945 in Tokyo from former Eastern District Army HQ personnel. With headquarters in Tokyo it served under General Defense Headquarters from Feb 6th until Apr 8th and 1st General Army until Oct 10th. Its commander was General Keisuke Fujie from Feb. 6th until Mar. 9th, General Shizuichi Tanaka until Aug 24th and Lt Gen Kenzō Kitano from Sept 23rd until it was deactivated on October 18th.

Subordinate armies / duty dates:
36th Army from Apr 8, 1945 until Oct 10, 1945
51st Army from Apr 8, 1945 until Oct 10, 1945
52nd Army from Apr 8, 1945 until Oct 10, 1945
53rd Army from Apr 8, 1945 until Oct 10, 1945
Tokyo Defense Army from June 23, 1945 until Oct 10, 1945
Tokyo Bay Fortress Group June 19, 1945 until Sept 11, 1945

Service History:
1945: On Jan 22nd the 12th Area Army HQ was activated, it was responsible for defending the Eastern Army District, including Tokyo ○ Feb 6th, the 12th Area Army HQ was in Tokyo, same day as the Homeland Defense reorganization ○ On Apr 8th the 36th, 51st, 52nd and 53rd Armies were placed under 12th Area Army command ○ On June 19th Tokyo Bay Fortress was placed under the 12th Area Army ○ June 23rd the Tokyo Defense Army was activated and placed under 12th Area Army command. 30 enemy divisions were expected to land in the Tokyo area but not until Mar-Apr '46. It was thought Kyushu would be attacked first ○ On Aug 15th Japan surrendered ○ Aug 24th, Gen. Tanaka committed suicide ○ On Oct 18th the 12th Area Army was deactivated ○

The Imperial Japanese Army

Major Units: See division / brigade page for order of battle
321st Division Tokyo 1945 磯 *Iso* – Oshima, Izu Islands	251-2
1st Anti-Aircraft Division Tokyo 1944 晴 *Hare* – Tokyo	255
66th Independent Mixed Brigade 1944 境 *Saki* – Niijima, Izu Islands	261-2
67th Independent Mixed Brigade 1944 浦 *Ura* – Hachijojima, Izu Islands	262

Note: The Hachijojima attached units are shown with the 67th I.M.B.

Units attached to the 321st Division:
6th Field Medium Artillery Battalion, 1st Battery 磯12380
5th Mortar Battalion 磯36373
105th Specially Established Sea Duty Company 磯8888

Units under control of the 12th Area Army: Sendai 幡 *Hata*

Unit	Code	Location
12th Area Army Headquarters	12345 (300)	Sendai
3rd Independent Heavy Artillery Regiment	14237	
8th Independent Field Artillery Regiment	36369 (1,941)	Sakaimachi
26th Field Medium Artillery Regiment	13369 (1,773)	Ichikawa
52nd Field Medium Artillery Regiment	3794 (1,742)	Sagamihara
7th Independent Rapid Firing Gun Battalion	6750 (353)	
2nd Self-Propelled Artillery Battalion	36381 (478)	
3rd Self-Propelled Artillery Battalion	36382 (478)	
4th Self-Propelled Artillery Battalion	36383 (478)	
10th Self-Propelled Artillery Battalion	28373 (481)	
8th Field Transport Headquarters	3862 (37)	
44th Independent Motor Transport Battalion	5704 (808)	Kawagoe
47th Independent Motor Transport Battalion	6052 (808)	Kawagoe
53rd Independent Motor Transport Battalion	7014 / 7104 (808)	Kakioka
66th Independent Motor Transport Battalion	3604 (808)	Umawatshi
67th Independent Motor Transport Battalion	3620 (808)	Toshigi
3rd Motor Transport Unit	8124 (155)	
65th Line of Communications Hospital	7864 (359)	Omiya
1st Signals Unit Headquarters	36405 (82)	Tokyo
30th Signal Regiment	12616 (636)	Kawagoe
51st Signal Regiment	36408 (1,093)	Saitama
2nd Signals Unit Headquarters	36406 (82)	Saitama
1st Short Wave Signal Company	36409 (159)	Saitama
12th to 35th Independent Signal Labor Units	36412 to 36334 (302 ea)	
136th Independent Wire Company	13933 (310)	Chiba
151st Independent Radio Platoon	13742 (57)	Chiba
152nd Independent Radio Platoon	13743 (57)	Chiba
103rd Independent Engineer Battalion	36404 (870)	
117th Independent Engineer Battalion	28375 (871)	Hiroshima
118th Independent Engineer Battalion	28376 (885)	
3rd Garrison Unit Headquarters	3310 (28)	Niigata City
2nd Specially Established Garrison Battalion	3311 (403)	Sado-gun
3rd Specially Established Garrison Battalion	3312 (403)	Niigata City
21st Specially Established Garrison Company	3313 (126)	Kashiwazaki City
22nd Specially Established Garrison Company	3314 (126)	Nishikubiki-gun

12th Area Army continued

Unit	Number	Location
190th Land Duty Company	36437 (501)	Tokyo
191st Land Duty Company	36438 (501)	Naoetsu
192nd Land Duty Company	36439 (501)	Niigata
193rd Land Duty Company	36440 (501)	Nagano
194th Land Duty Company	36441 (501)	Nagano
22nd Sea Transport Battalion	36435 (637)	
17th Field Service Unit Headquarters	2618 (17)	
13th Tractor Company	2611 (808)	Ibaraki
14th Tractor Company	2612 (808)	Yachimata
24th Bridging Materials Company	4618 (680)	
25th Bridging Materials Company	4619 (680)	
31st Bridging Materials Company	6415 (680)	
2nd Field Construction Unit Headquarters	8230 (78)	Tokyo
5th Field Construction Unit Headquarters	2619 (78)	Urawa
6th Field Construction Unit Headquarters	2620 (78)	Meguro
39th Construction Duty Company	4639 (511)	Nagano
1st Fortification Construction Duty Company	2116 (339)	Saitama
2nd Fortification Construction Duty Company	2117 (339)	
3rd Fortification Construction Duty Company	4164 (339)	Ibaraki

Kanto Region

36th Army 富士 *Fuji*

The 36th Army was activated in Tokyo on July 15, 1944. It served directly under Imperial General Headquarters from July 21st until Oct 27th, General Defense Command until Apr 8th 1945 and 12th Area Army until Oct 10th. The 36th Army was a reserve army with its HQ in Urawa, Saitama Prefecture. Its commander was Lt Gen Toshimichi Uemura from July 18th until the 36th Army was deactivated on Oct 10th. Its code name 'Fuji' was for Mount Fuji, the foot of which lay within its deployment area.

Service History:

1944: Jul 15th the 36th Army was activated in Tokyo and assigned to Urawa, Saitama as a reserve force for the Kanto District ○ July 18th, Lt Gen Toshimichi Uemura was appointed 36th Army commander ○ On July 21st the 81st and 93rd Div and 4th Armored Div join its order of battle ○ On Oct 21st, the 36th Army was attached to IGHQ ○ On Oct 27th the 36th Army was placed under Defense General HQ control ○

1945: Mar 15th the 1st Armored Div joined the 36th Army's order of battle ○ On Apr 8th the 36th Army joined the 12th Area Army ○ June 1st, 4th Amphibious Bgde joined the 36th Army ○ The 36th Army was deactivated in Saitama on October 10th ○

Major Units: See division / brigade page for order of battle

Unit	Page
81st Division Utsunomiya 1942 納 *Nou* – Yuki-cho, Ibaraki	215-6
93rd Division Kanazawa 1944 決 *Ketsu* – Matsudo	219-20
201st Division Tokyo 1945 武蔵 *Musasi* – Tokyo	241
202nd Division Sendai 1945 青葉 *Aoba* – Maebashi, Gunma	241-2

209th Division Kanazawa 1945 加越 *Kaetsu* – Ishikawa　　　　243-4
214th Division Utsunomiya 1945 常盤 *Tokina* –Tochigi　　　　244-5
1st Armored Division Fukuoka 1942 拓 *Taku* – Sano, Tochigi　　254
4th Armored Division Chiba 1944 鋼 *Hagane* – Sakura, Chiba　　254
4th Amphibious Brigade 1944 払 *Harai* – Saitama　　　　　　　283

<u>Units under control of the 36th Army</u>: Urawa　　富士 *Fuji*

Unit	Strength	Location
36th Army Headquarters	18100 (809)	Urawa
8th Independent Mountain Artillery Regiment	22462 (2,496)	Tochigi
17th Independent Mountain Artillery Regiment	28320 (2,983)	
27th Independent Rapid Firing Gun Battalion	14204 (403)	Chibaasahi
21st Independent Machinegun Battalion	3325 (334)	Sukuyama-machi
7th Trench Mortar Battalion	36375 (1,465)	Chiba
8th Trench Mortar Battalion	36376 (1,465)	
9th Trench Mortar Battalion	36377 (1,465)	
10th Trench Mortar Battalion	36378 (1,465)	
11th Trench Mortar Battalion	36379 (1,465)	
23rd Trench Mortar Battalion	28382 (1,414)	Kashiwa
32nd Trench Mortar Battalion	28383 (1,414)	
6th Signal Regiment	3618 (1,825)	Saitama
62nd Independent Engineer Battalion	14203 (894)	Matsudo
88th Independent Engineer Battalion	27409 (884)	
101st Independent Engineer Battalion	36402 (870)	
102nd Independent Engineer Battalion	36403 (870)	

Coastline Northeast of Tokyo

51st Army 建 *Ken*

The 51st Army was activated in Mito, Ibaraki Prefecture on March 31, 1945. Lt Gen Kengo Noda, was appointed 51st Army commander on Apr 7th and its headquarters became operational in Mito on Apr 8th. It was deactivated October 10th.

<u>Service History</u>:
<u>1945</u>: Mar 31st, the 51st Army was activated in Mito, Ibaraki to guard the east coast north of Tokyo ○ On Apr 7th Lt Gen Kengo Noda became the 51st Army commander ○ Apr 8th, the 51st Army in Mito was placed under the 12th Area Army's command and the 44th Div, 151st Div and 7th Armored Div became 51st Army subordinates ○ On June 19th the 221st Div joined the 51st Army ○ June 21st the 116th I.M.B. joined ○ On July 25th the 115th I.M.B. joined ○ On Oct 10th the 51st Army was deactivated ○

<u>Major Units</u>: See division / brigade page for order of battle
44th Division Osaka 1944 橘 *Tachibana* – Takahagi, Ibaraki　　　209
151st Division Utsunomiya 1945 護宇 *Gou* – E. of Kasumigaura　　237
221st Division Nagano 1945 天龍 *Tenryuu* – Ota　　　　　　　　246
115th Independent Mixed Brigade 1945 建 *Ken* – Kashima　　　　270-1

116th Independent Mixed Brigade 1945 建 *Ken* – Tamatsukuri		271
7th Independent Armored Brigade 1945 琢 *Ei Toshi* – Mito		281

Units under control of the 51st Army: Mito	建 *Ken*	
51st Army Headquarters	21410 (516)	Mito
7th Artillery Headquarters	1210 (119)	Urawa
13th Independent Mountain Artillery Regiment	36670 (2,901)	Ibaraki
9th Field Medium Artillery Regiment	8737 (2,234)	Kiharamura
16th Field Medium Artillery Battalion	36384	
12th Independent Heavy Artillery Battalion	3103 (620)	Iwamanachi
35th Independent Heavy Artillery Battalion	13364 (701)	Kuju-mura
37th Independent Machine Cannon Company	13343 (150)	Katta-machi
3rd Artillery Intelligence Regiment	12307 (637)	Kawawada
91st Independent Engineer Battalion	36392 (870)	Edosaki-machi
92nd Independent Engineer Battalion	36393 (870)	Mito
93rd Independent Engineer Battalion	36394 (870)	Hokata
8th Signal Regiment	7590 (1,068)	Iwamachi
45th Line of Communications Sector Command	4818 (203)	Tsuchiura
45th Line of Communications Duty Unit	4818 (511)	Mt Fuji
45th Line of Communications Guard Unit	4818 (1,035)	

Bōsō Peninsula

52nd Army 捷 *Sho*

The 52nd Army was activated in Shisui, Chiba on Mar 31, 1945, where it remained. Lt Gen Tokumatsu Shigeta was appointed commander Apr 7th and it came under 12th Area Army control on April 8th. The 52nd Army was deactivated in Shisui on Oct 10th.

Service History:

1945: On Mar 31st the 52nd Army was activated in Chiba ○ Apr 7th Lt Gen Tokumatsu Shigeta became 52nd Army commander ○ Apr 8th the 52nd Army was placed under the 12th Area Army and the 3rd Imperial Guard Division, 152nd Div and 3rd Independent Armored Bgde were placed under its control ○ On Oct 10th the 52nd Army was deactivated ○

Major Units: See division / brigade page for order of battle

3rd Imperial Guard Division Tokyo 1944 範 *Han* – Koto, Tokyo		203
147th Division Asahikawa 1945 護北 *Gokita* – Mobaru, Chiba		235
152nd Division Kanazawa 1945 護沢 *Gotaku* – Chōshi, Chiba		137-8
234th Division Tokyo 1945 利根 *Tone* – Yokaichiba		249
3rd Independent Armored Brigade 1945 徹 *Tooru* – Sarashina, Chiba		280

Units under control of the 52nd Army: Shisui	捷 *Sho*	
52nd Army Headquarters	13333 (623)	Susui

52nd Army: continued   捷 Sho

Unit	Code (Strength)	Location
48th Independent Tank Regiment	12358 (400)	Yachimata
8th Artillery Headquarters	1211 (119)	Yachimata-machi
14th Independent Mountain Artillery Regiment	36371 (2,000)	Sarutamura
14th Heavy Artillery Regiment	13361 (850)	Asahimachi
27th Field Medium Artillery Regiment	13370 (1,810)	Yachimata
7th Field Medium Artillery Battalion	12381 (695)	Chiba
18th Field Medium Artillery Battalion	36386 (755)	Ichikawa
11th Independent Heavy Artillery Battalion	3102 (620)	Chiba
42nd Independent Heavy Artillery Battalion	36389 (498)	Asahi-Omachi
24th Independent Rapid Firing Gun Battalion	3226 (480)	Togane-machi
40th Trench Mortar Battalion	22463 (868)	Chiba
35th Independent Machine Cannon Company	13341 (138)	Katori-gun
36th Independent Machine Cannon Company	13342 (138)	Fuse-machi
2nd Artillery Intelligence Regiment	3609 (625)	Yachimata
67th Independent Engineer Battalion	3364 (821)	
69th Independent Engineer Battalion	No # (850)	Oto-machi
94th Independent Engineer Battalion	36395 (870)	Nagano
95th Independent Engineer Battalion	36396 (870)	Chiba
96th Independent Engineer Battalion	36397 (870)	
97th Independent Engineer Battalion	36398 (870)	
39th Signal Regiment	13373 (1,400)	Shimizumachi
150th Line of Communications Sector Command	5897 (203)	Chiba
150th Line of Communications Duty Unit	5897 (511)	Tsuchiura
150th Line of Communications Guard Unit	5897 (1,035)	
19th Field Duty Headquarters	3872 (17)	
1st/19th Field Duty Unit	3872	

Coastline South of Tokyo

53rd Army 断 Dan

The 53rd Army was activated in Odawara, Kanagawa on March 31, 1945. Its commander, Lt Gen Yaezō Akashiba, was appointed on April 7th and April 8th the 53rd Army was placed under 12th Area Army control. It was deactivated between August 30th and October 10th.

Service History:
1945: On March 31st the 53rd Army was activated in Kanagawa ○ April 7th, Lt Gen Yaezō Akashiba was appointed 53rd Army commander ○ April 8th, the 53rd Army in Odawara, Kanagawa was made subordinate to the 12th Area Army and the 84th, 140th Div and 2nd Armored Bgde were placed under its command ○ On June 19th the 316th Div was attached to the 53rd Army ○ June 23rd the 117th I.M.B. was attached ○ Between August 30th and Oct. 10th the 53rd Army was deactivated ○

Major Units: See division / brigade page for order of battle
84th Division Himeji 1944 突 *Totsu* – Matsuda 216
140th Division Tokyo 1945 護東 *Goto* – Fujisawa 232
316th Division Kyoto 1945 山城 *Yamashiro* – Kōzu 251
117th Independent Mixed Brigade 1945 東部 *Tobu* – Kumazu 271
2nd Independent Armored Brigade 1945 顕 *Ken* – Odawara 279

Units under control of the 53rd Army: Odawara 断 *Dan*

Unit	Number	Location
53rd Army Headquarters	21601 (530)	Odawara
36th Independent Mixed Regiment	36366 (3,046)	Mishima
37th Independent Mixed Regiment	36367 (3,046)	Kashiwa
11th Artillery Headquarters	36368 (125)	Kyodo
2nd Field Medium Artillery Regiment	3765 (2,284)	Ofuna
13th Independent Heavy Artillery Battalion	3104 (620)	Kyodo
36th Independent Heavy Artillery Battalion	13365 (498)	
16th Trench Mortar Battalion	3156 (829)	
5th Artillery Intelligence Regiment	1020 (640)	Oiso
74th Independent Engineer Battalion	22464 (850)	Tokyo
98th Independent Engineer Battalion	36399 (870)	
99th Independent Engineer Battalion	36400 (870)	
50th Signal Regiment	36407 (1,080)	Koayu mura
101st Specially Established Guard Company	5746 (126)	Atami
151st Line of Communications Sector Command	5700 (203)	Kanagawa
151st Line of Communications Duty Unit	5700 (511)	Kanagawa
151st Line of Communications Guard Unit	5700 (1,035)	Kanagawa
20th Field Duty Headquarters	3873 (17)	Kanegawa

Tokyo City

Tokyo Defense Army 幡 *Hata*

The Tokyo Defense Army was activated in Tokyo on June 22, 1945, its headquarters located within the Imperial Palace compound. On June 23rd the TDA was placed under 12th Area Army control. The TDA's commander was Lt Gen Jō Īmura from June 22nd until Aug 20th and Lt Gen Shōzō Terakura until it was deactivated on October 10th.
Service History:
1945: On June 22nd the Tokyo Defense Army HQ was activated on the Imperial Palace grounds. Its was created to improve and strengthen Tokyo's defenses, protect the Palace and environs and construct fortifications to prevent an enemy from entering the city ○ June 23rd the 1st, 2nd and 3rd Guard Brigades were attached to the Tokyo Defense Army. If Tokyo were invaded two or three divisions would be called on to reinforce the Tokyo Defense Army ○ It was deactivated in Tokyo on October 10th ○
Major Units: See division / brigade page for order of battle
1st Guard Brigade 1945 幡 *Hata* – Tokyo 284

Tokyo Defense Army continued
2nd Guard Brigade 1945 幡 *Hata* – Tokyo   284-5
3rd Guard Brigade 1945 幡 *Hata* – Tokyo   285

Units under the Tokyo Defense Army: Tokyo	幡 *Hata*	
Tokyo Defense Headquarters	No # (190)	Tokyo
2nd Artillery Headquarters	12311 (110)	Ichikawa
8th Field Medium Artillery Regiment	12301 (1,252)	Tokyo
11th Field Medium Artillery Regiment	3769 (2,286)	Chiba
19th Field Medium Artillery Regiment	12303 (1,252)	Matsudo
6th Engineer Unit Headquarters	12325 (147)	Tokyo
7th Engineer Unit Headquarters	12326 (147)	Urawa
25th Independent Engineer Regiment	12315 (568)	
27th Independent Engineer Regiment	13001 (1,153)	
83rd Independent Engineer Battalion	27404 (870)	Tokyo
116th Independent Engineer Battalion	28374 (472)	Hiroshima

Tokyo Bay Army Corps 房 *Bō*

The Tokyo Bay Army Corps was activated in Tokyo on June 15, 1945, its headquarters in Fumagata under Lt Gen Shihei Oba. The TBAC was attached to the 12th Area Army on June 19th and deactivated between Sept 3rd to 11th.

Service History:
1945: On June 15th the Tokyo Bay Army Corps was activated in Tokyo under Lt Gen Shihei Oba ○ On June 19th the Tokyo Bay Army Corps was placed under 12th Area Army control and the 354th Div, 96th and 114th I.M.B. were made subordinate ○ Between Sept 3rd and 11th the TBAC was deactivated ○

Major Units: See division / brigade page for order of battle
354th Division Tokyo 1945 武甲 *Buko* – Maruyama Cho   255
96th Independent Mixed Brigade 1945 幡 *Hata* – Tateyama, Tokyo   266
114th Independent Mixed Brigade 1945 房 *Husa* – Yokosuka   270

Units under control of Tokyo Bay Army Corps:	房 *Bō*	
Tokyo Bay Fortress Headquarters	13300 (203)	Fumagata
Tokyo Bay Fortress Artillery Regiment	2112 (1,825)	Yokosuka
1st Tokyo Bay Fortress Artillery Unit	13367 (603)	Chiba
2nd Tokyo Bay Fortress Artillery Unit	13368 (483)	Shizouka
Tokyo Bay Fortress Signal Unit	2121 (473)	Chiba
Attached Units	房 *Bō*	
6th Field Heavy Artillery Battalion, minus 1st Bty	12380 (500)	
6th Trench Mortar Battalion	36374 (1,465)	Chiba
1st Tokyo Bay Fortress Engineer Unit	4104 (264)	Chiba
2nd Tokyo Bay Fortress Engineer Unit	4105 (264)	Chiba
100th Independent Engineer Battalion	36401 (870)	

Chapter 2

Tobu Army District:
Kanto-Koshinetsu area

Tobu Army District Headquarters	Tokyo	東部 *Tobu*
1st Imperial Guards Division	Tokyo 1943	隅 *Gū* (15,297)
9th Ind. Mountain Artillery Regiment		22612

Utsunomiya Divisional District:

Utsunomiya Divisional District HQ	Utsunomiya	東部 (288)

Recruiting and home defense units
51st Depot Division / Utsunomiya Divisional District:

Unit	Location	Barracks # (Personnel)
51st Depot Division Headquarters	Utsunomiya	*Tobu*
66th Infantry Regt Replacement Unit	Utsunomiya	東部 36
102nd Infantry Regiment Repl. Unit	Mito	東部 37
115th Infantry Regt Replacement Unit	Takasaki	東部 38
51st Cavalry Regt Replacement Unit	Utsunomiya	東部 39
14th Field Art. Regiment Repl. Unit	Utsunomiya	東部 40
51st Engineer Regt Replacement Unit	Utsunomiya	東部 42
51st Div. Signal Unit Repl. Unit	Utsunomiya	東部 43
51st Transport Regiment Repl. Unit	Utsunomiya	東部 44
Reorganized on Feb 6, 1945		*Tobu*
Utsunomiya 1st Inf. Repl. Unit	Utsunomiya	東部 36 (1,933)
Utsunomiya 2nd Inf. Repl. Unit	Mito	東部 37 (1,933)
Utsunomiya 3rd Inf. Repl. Unit	Takasaki	東部 38 (1,933)
Utsunomiya Artillery Repl. Unit	Utsunomiya	東部 40 (576)
Utsunomiya Engineer Repl. Unit	Mito	東部 42 (705)
Utsunomiya Signal Repl. Unit	Utsunomiya	東部 43 (345)
Utsunomiya Transport Repl. Unit	Utsunomiya	東部 44 (659)

Major units supplied by the Utsunomiya Divisional District include:
14th Div., 33rd Div., 41st Div., 51st Div., 63rd Div., 81st Div., 5th I.M.B., 60th I.M.B., 68th Bgde., 1st Fld. Repl Unit.

Mito Regimental District: Ibaraki Prefecture Administrative District
Mito District   東部 *Tobu*

Unit	Barracks #	Location
4th Specially Established Garrison Battalion	2869 (420)	Hidachi City
16th Specially Established Engineer Unit	13321 (930)	Yashida-mura
17th Specially Established Engineer Unit	13322 (930)	Hokota-machi
Mito District 1st Specially Est. Garrison Unit	30801 (407)	Tokuhagi-machi
Mito District 2nd Specially Est. Garrison Unit	30802 (407)	Okomachi
Mito District 3rd Specially Est. Garrison Unit	30803 (407)	Tenkano-mura
Mito District 4th Specially Est. Garrison Unit	30804 (297)	Omiya-machi
Mito District 5th Specially Est. Garrison Unit	30805 (297)	Ishizuka-machi
Mito District 6th Specially Est. Garrison Unit	30806 (407)	Mito City
Mito District 7th Specially Est. Garrison Unit	30807 (407)	Nishiibaraki

Mito District continue   東部 *Tobu*

Mito District 8th Specially Est. Garrison Unit	30808 (297)	Nagaoka-mura
Mito District 9th Specially Est. Garrison Unit	30809 (205)	Shimodate-ma
Mito District 10th Specially Est. Garrison Unit	30810 (407)	Ishioka-machi
Mito District 11th Specially Est. Garrison Unit	30811 (407)	Tsuchiura City
Mito District 12th Specially Est. Garrison Unit	30812 (205)	Tanitabe-machi
Mito District 13th Specially Est. Garrison Unit	30813 (205)	Ishishita-machi
Mito District 14th Specially Est. Garrison Unit	30814 (297)	Sakai-machi
Mito District 15th Specially Est. Garrison Unit	30815 (205)	Hokoto-machi
Mito District 16th Specially Est. Garrison Unit	30816 (297)	Asahu-mach
Mito District 17th Specially Est. Garrison Unit	30817 (297)	Edosaki-machi
Mito District 18th Specially Est. Garrison Unit	30818 (297)	Kyugasaki-ma
Mito District 19th Specially Est. Garrison Unit	30819 (297)	Toride-machi

Utsunomiya Regimental District: Tochigi Prefecture Administrative District
Utsunomiya District   東部 *Tobu*

14th Specially Established Engineer Unit	13319 (930)	Kuroiso-machi
15th Specially Established Engineer Unit	13320 (930)	Kiyohara-machi
Utsunomiya District 1st Spe. Est. Garrison Unit	30820 (407)	Kuroiso-machi
Utsunomiya District 2nd Spe. Est. Garrison Unit	30821 (407)	Otahara-machi
Utsunomiya District 3rd Spe. Est. Garrison Unit	30822 (297)	Yaita-machi
Utsunomiya District 4th Spe. Est. Garrison Unit	30823 (297)	Nikkō-machi
Utsunomiya District 5th Spe. Est. Garrison Unit	30824 (297)	Ashio-machi
Utsunomiya District 6th Spe. Est. Garrison Unit	30825 (297)	Kurasuyama-ma
Utsunomiya District 7th Spe. Est. Garrison Unit	30826 (297)	Ujiie-chō
Utsunomiya District 8th Spe. Est. Garrison Unit	30827 (407)	Utsuno-miya
Utsunomiya District 9th Spe. Est. Garrison Unit	30828 (297)	Kanuma-machi
Utsunomiya District 10th Spe. Est. Garrison Unit	30829 (297)	Maoka-machi
Utsunomiya District 11th Spe. Est. Garrison Unit	30830 (297)	Tochigi City
Utsunomiya District 12th Spe. Est. Garrison Unit	30831 (297)	Koyama-machi
Utsunomiya District 13th Spe. Est. Garrison Unit	30832 (297)	Sano City
Utsunomiya District 14th Spe. Est. Garrison Unit	30833 (297)	Ashikaka City

Maebashi Regimental District: Gunma Prefecture Administrative District
Maebashi District   東部 *Tobu*

Maebashi District 1st Specially Est. Garrison Unit	30834 (297)	Mizukami-mura
Maebashi District 2nd Specially Est. Garrison Unit	30835 (297)	Numata-machi
Maebashi District 3rd Specially Est. Garrison Unit	30836 (297)	Nakanojo-machi
Maebashi District 4th Specially Est. Garrison Unit	30837 (297)	Naganohara-ma
Maebashi District 5th Specially Est. Garrison Unit	30838 (297)	Shibukawa-ma
Maebashi District 6th Specially Est. Garrison Unit	30839 (297)	Kiryu City
Maebashi District 7th Specially Est. Garrison Unit	30840 (297)	Yamada-gun
Maebashi District 8th Specially Est. Garrison Unit	30841 (297)	
Maebashi District 9th Specially Est. Garrison Unit	30842 (297)	Maebashi City

Maebashi District 10th Specially Est. Garrison Unit 30843 (297) Tatebayashi-ma
Maebashi District 11th Specially Est. Garrison Unit 30844 (297) Namashina-mu
Maebashi District 12th Specially Est. Garrison Unit 30845 (407) Isesaki City
Maebashi District 13th Specially Est. Garrison Unit 30846 (297) Takasaki City
Maebashi District 14th Specially Est. Garrison Unit 30847 (297) Annaka-machi
Maebashi District 15th Specially Est. Garrison Unit 30848 (297) Unui-gun
Maebashi District 16th Specially Est. Garrison Unit 30849 (297) Fujioka-machi
Maebashi District 17th Specially Est. Garrison Unit 30850 (297) Tomioka-machi
13th Specially Established Garrison Company 2871 (126)
18th Specially Established Engineer Unit 13323 (930)

Tokyo Divisional District

Tokyo Divisional District HQ Tokyo 東部 (385)

Recruiting and home defense units
2nd Imperial Guards Depot Division / Tokyo Divisional District:

Unit	Location	Barracks # (Personnel)
2nd Guards Depot Division HQ	Tokyo	*Tobu*
Konoe 3rd Inf. Regt Repl. Unit	Tokyo	東部 6
Konoe 4th Inf. Regt Repl. Unit	Kofu	東部 63
Konoe 5th Inf. Regt Repl. Unit	Sakura	東部 64
Konoe 2nd Cav. Regt Repl. Unit	Tokyo	東部 10
Konoe 2nd Field Art. Regt Repl. Unit	Tokyo	東部 12
Konoe 2nd Engr. Regt Repl. Unit	Kashiwa	東部 14
Konoe 2nd Signal Unit Repl. Unit	Tokyo	東部 16
Konoe 2nd Transp. Regt Repl. Unit	Tokyo	東部 17
1st Inf. Replacement Unit	Mizonokuchi	東部 62
2nd Inf. Replacement Unit	Kashiwa	東部 83
Reorganized on Feb 6, 1945		*Tobu*
Tokyo 1st Infantry Replacement Unit	Mizonokuchi	東部 62 (1,597)
Tokyo 2nd Infantry Replacement Unit	Kashiwa	東部 83 (1,597)
Tokyo 3rd Infantry Replacement Unit	Tokyo	東部 6 (3,202)
Tokyo 4th Infantry Replacement Unit	Kohu	東部 63 (3,202)
Tokyo 5th Infantry Replacement Unit	Sakura	東部 64 (3,202)
Tokyo Artillery Replacement Unit	Tokyo	東部 12 (576)
Tokyo Engineer Replacement Unit	Kashiwa	東部 14 (705)
Tokyo Signal Replacement Unit	Tokyo	東部 16 (345)
Tokyo Transport Replacement Unit	Tokyo	東部 17 (659)

Major units supplied by the Tokyo Divisional District:

1st Trench Mortar Regt Repl. Unit	Numata	東部 unknown (585)
21st Independent Engineer Regiment	Kounodai	東部 15 (399)
25th Independent Engineer Regiment		東部 15 (568)
1st Signal Regiment Repl. Unit	Haramachida	東部 88 (511)
8th Fld Med. Arty Regt Repl. Unit	Tokyo	東部 72 (762)
17th Fld Med. Arty Regt Repl Unit	Kounodai	東部 73 (893)

Major units supplied by the Tokyo Divisional District continued

18th Fld Med. Arty Regt Repl Unit	Kounodai	東部 74 (787)
Yokosuka Arty Regiment Repl. Unit	Yokosuka	東部 75 (1024)
Arty Intelligence Regt Repl. Unit	Yokosuka	東部 89 (515)
Balloon Regiment Replacement Unit	Chiba	東部 unknown (587)

Other major units supplied by the Tokyo Divisional District:
1st Gd. Div., 2nd Gd. Div., 3rd Gd. Div., 1st. Div., 27th Div., 28th Div., 31st Div., 32nd Div., 35th Div., 59th Div., 60th Div., 61st Div., 109th Div., 114th Div., 117th Div., 8th I.M.B., 9th I.M.B., 17th I.M.B., 22nd I.M.B., 34th I.M.B., 35th I.M.B., 36th I.M.B., 50th I.M.B., 53rd I.M.B., 70th I.M.B., 72nd I.M.B., 1st Ind. Inf. Bgde, 9th Fld. Rep. Unit, 1st Railway Regt.

Tokyo Regimental District: Tokyo Metropolitan Police Administrative District

Tokyo District　　　　　　　　　　　　　　　　　　東部 *Tobu*

59th Specially Established Garrison Battalion	7874 (550)	Toyoshima-ku
60th Specially Established Garrison Battalion	7875 (550)	Suginami-ku
61st Specially Established Garrison Battalion	7876 (550)	Ebara-ku
62nd Specially Established Garrison Battalion	7877 (550)	Katsushika-ku
55th Specially Established Garrison Battalion	7855 (550)	Kojimachi-ku
56th Specially Established Garrison Battalion	7856 (550)	Shitaya-ku
57th Specially Established Garrison Battalion	7857 (550)	Yotsuya-ku
58th Specially Established Garrison Battalion	7858 (550)	Shiba-ku
64th Specially Established Garrison Battalion	13308 (550)	Adachi-ku
65th Specially Established Garrison Battalion	13309 (550)	Setagaya-ku
66th Specially Established Garrison Battalion	13310 (550)	Omori-ku
67th Specially Established Garrison Battalion	13311 (550)	Honjo-ku
68th Specially Established Garrison Battalion	13312 (550)	Kitatama-gun
69th Specially Established Garrison Battalion	13313 (550)	Tachikawa City
1st Specially Established Engineer Unit	2161 (930)	Kojimachi-ku
2nd Specially Established Engineer Unit	2162 (930)	Ōji-ku
3rd Specially Established Engineer Unit	2163 (930)	Ōji-ku
4th Specially Established Engineer Unit	2164 (930)	Shinagawa-ku
6th Specially Established Engineer Unit	2166 (930)	Nakano-ku
23rd Specially Established Engineer Unit	13328 (930)	Itabashi-ku
25th Specially Established Engineer Unit	13330 (930)	Kitatama-ku
26th Specially Established Engineer Unit	13331 (930)	Tachikawa-ku
Tokyo District 1st Specially Est. Garrison Unit	30641 (570)	Adachi-ku
Tokyo District 2nd Specially Est. Garrison Unit	30642 (570)	Itabashi-ku
Tokyo District 3rd Specially Est. Garrison Unit	30643 (570)	Itabashi-ku
Tokyo District 4th Specially Est. Garrison Unit	30644 (570)	Suginami-ku
Tokyo District 5th Specially Est. Garrison Unit	30645 (570)	Suginami-ku
Tokyo District 6th Specially Est. Garrison Unit	30646 (420)	Setagaya-ku
Tokyo District 7th Specially Est. Garrison Unit	30647 (420)	Setagaya-ku
Tokyo District 8th Specially Est. Garrison Unit	30648 (570)	Kitatama-ku
Tokyo District 9th Specially Est. Garrison Unit	30649 (570)	Kitatama-ku

Tokyo District 10th Specially Est. Garrison Unit　　30650 (570)　　Kitatama-ku
Tokyo District 11th Specially Est. Garrison Unit　　30651 (570)　　Kitatama-ku
Tokyo District 12th Specially Est. Garrison Unit　　30652 (570)　　Kitatama-ku
Tokyo District 13th Specially Est. Garrison Unit　　30653 (570)　　Kitatama-ku
Tokyo District 14th Specially Est. Garrison Unit　　30654 (420)　　Minamitama-g
Tokyo District 15th Specially Est. Garrison Unit　　30655 (420)　　Minamitama-g
Tokyo District 16th Specially Est. Garrison Unit　　30656 (570)　　Hachōij City
Tokyo District 17th Specially Est. Garrison Unit　　30657 (420)　　Minamitama-g
Tokyo District 18th Specially Est. Garrison Unit　　30658 (420)　　Nishitama-gun
Tokyo District 19th Specially Est. Garrison Unit　　30659 (570)　　Nishitama-gun
Tokyo District 20th Specially Est. Garrison Unit　　30660 (570)　　Nishitama-gun

Yokohama Regimental District: Kanagawa Prefecture Administrative District
Yokohama District　　　　　　　　　　　　　　東部 *Tobu*
51st Specially Established Garrison Battalion　　7887 (550)　　Kawasaki City
52nd Specially Established Garrison Battalion　　7888 (550)　　Kawasaki City
53rd Specially Established Garrison Battalion　　7889 (550)　　Yokohama City
54th Specially Established Garrison Battalion　　7890 (550)　　Yokohama City
14th Specially Established Garrison Company　　7891 (126)　　Odawara City
7th Specially Established Engineer Unit　　　　2167 (930)　　Kawasaki City
8th Specially Established Engineer Unit　　　　2168 (930)　　Yokohama City
27th Specially Established Engineer Unit　　　　13332 (930)　　Akiō-gun
Yokohama District 1st Specially Est. Garrison Unit　　30721 (400)　　Kawasaki City
Yokohama District 2nd Specially Est. Garrison Unit　　30722 (400)　　Yokohama City
Yokohama District 3rd Specially Est. Garrison Unit　　30723 (400)　　Yokohama City
Yokohama District 4th Specially Est. Garrison Unit　　30724 (320)　　Yokohama City
Yokohama District 5th Specially Est. Garrison Unit　　30725 (400)　　Yokohama City
Yokohama District 6th Specially Est. Garrison Unit　　30726 (320)　　Yokohama City
Yokohama District 7th Specially Est. Garrison Unit　　30727 (520)　　Yokosuka City
Yokohama District 8th Specially Est. Garrison Unit　　30728 (400)　　Yokosuka City
Yokohama District 9th Specially Est. Garrison Unit　　30729 (520)　　Kamakura City
Yokohama District 10th Sp. Est. Garrison Unit　　30730 (520)　　Fujisawa City
Yokohama District 11th Sp. Est. Garrison Unit　　30731 (400)　　Kōza-gun
Yokohama District 12th Sp. Est. Garrison Unit　　30732 (400)　　Kōza-gun
Yokohama District 13th Sp. Est. Garrison Unit　　30733 (400)　　Kōza-gun
Yokohama District 14th Sp. Est. Garrison Unit　　30734 (400)　　Tsukui-gun
Yokohama District 15th Sp. Est. Garrison Unit　　30735 (400)　　Akiō-gun
Yokohama District 16th Sp. Est. Garrison Unit　　30736 (520)　　Nakahara
Yokohama District 17th Sp. Est. Garrison Unit　　30737 (320)　　Nakahara
Yokohama District 18th Sp. Est. Garrison Unit　　30738 (320)　　Ashigarakami-g
Yokohama District 19th Sp. Est. Garrison Unit　　30739 (400)　　Ashigarashimo
Yokohama District 20th Sp. Est. Garrison Unit　　30740 (320)　　Ashigarashimo
Yokohama District 21st Sp. Est. Garrison Unit　　30741 (320)　　Ashigarashimo
Yokohama District 22nd Sp. Est. Garrison Unit　　30742 (320)　　Ashigarashimo
Yokohama District 23rd Sp. Est. Garrison Unit　　30743 (320)　　Yokohama City

Yokohama District continued

Yokohama District 24th Sp. Est. Garrison Unit	30744 (320)	Yokohama City
Yokohama District 25th Sp. Est. Garrison Unit	30745 (320)	Yokohama City
Yokohama District 26th Sp. Est. Garrison Unit	30746 (320)	Yokohama City

Urawa Regimental District: Saitama Prefecture Administrative District
Urawa District   東部 *Tobu*

25th Specially Established Garrison Company	7878 (126)	Omiya City
19th Specially Established Engineer Unit	13324 (930)	Kumagaya City
24th Specially Established Engineer Unit	13329 (930)	Iruma-gun
Urawa District 1st Specially Est. Garrison Unit	30681 (520)	Urawa City
Urawa District 2nd Specially Est. Garrison Unit	30682 (520)	Kawaguchi City
Urawa District 3rd Specially Est. Garrison Unit	30683 (400)	Koshitani-machi
Urawa District 4th Specially Est. Garrison Unit	30684 (520)	Kasugabe-machi
Urawa District 5th Specially Est. Garrison Unit	30685 (520)	Hisaku-machi
Urawa District 6th Specially Est. Garrison Unit	30686 (520)	Kasu-machi
Urawa District 7th Specially Est. Garrison Unit	30687 (520)	Omiya City
Urawa District 8th Specially Est. Garrison Unit	30688 (520)	Kōnosu-machi
Urawa District 9th Specially Est. Garrison Unit	30689 (520)	Kawagoe City
Urawa District 10th Specially Est. Garrison Unit	30690 (400)	Tokorozawa-ma
Urawa District 11th Specially Est. Garrison Unit	30691 (400)	Hannō-machi
Urawa District 12th Specially Est. Garrison Unit	30692 (400)	Sukato-machi
Urawa District 13th Specially Est. Garrison Unit	30693 (520)	Matsuyama-ma
Urawa District 14th Specially Est. Garrison Unit	30694 (520)	Kumagaya-ma
Urawa District 15th Specially Est. Garrison Unit	30695 (520)	Yorii-machi
Urawa District 16th Specially Est. Garrison Unit	30696 (520)	Honjō-machi
Urawa District 17th Specially Est. Garrison Unit	30697 (520)	Chichiba-machi

Chiba Regimental District: Chiba Prefecture Administrative District
Chiba District   東部 *Tobu*

26th Specially Established Garrison Company	7879 (126)	Chōshi City
28th Specially Established Garrison Company	7897 (126)	Katsuara-cho
29th Specially Established Garrison Company	7898 (126)	Tateyama City
5th Specially Established Engineer Unit	2165 (930)	Ishikawa City
20th Specially Established Engineer Unit	13325 (930)	Inuba-gun
21st Specially Established Engineer Unit	13326 (930)	Inuba-gun
22nd Specially Established Engineer Unit	13327 (930)	East Katsushika
Chiba District 1st Specially Est. Garrison Unit	30601 (530)	Kaijo-gun
Chiba District 2nd Specially Est. Garrison Unit	30602 (530)	Katori-gun
Chiba District 3rd Specially Est. Garrison Unit	30603 (530)	Katori-gun
Chiba District 4th Specially Est. Garrison Unit	30604 (530)	Katori-gun
Chiba District 5th Specially Est. Garrison Unit	30605 (530)	Sōsa-gun
Chiba District 6th Specially Est. Garrison Unit	30606 (530)	Inba-gun
Chiba District 7th Specially Est. Garrison Unit	30607 (530)	Inba-gun

Chiba District continued

Unit	Barracks #	Location
Chiba District 8th Specially Est. Garrison Unit	30608 (530)	Inba-gun
Chiba District 9th Specially Est. Garrison Unit	30609 (530)	Yamatake-gun
Chiba District 10th Specially Est. Garrison Unit	30610 (530)	Chiba City
Chiba District 11th Specially Est. Garrison Unit	30615 (530)	East Katsushika
Chiba District 12th Specially Est. Garrison Unit	30616 (530)	Chōsei-gun
Chiba District 13th Specially Est. Garrison Unit	30617 (530)	Ichihara-gun
Chiba District 14th Specially Est. Garrison Unit	30618 (300)	Ichihara-gun
Chiba District 15th Specially Est. Garrison Unit	30619 (530)	
Chiba District 16th Specially Est. Garrison Unit	30620 (300)	Ichihara-gun
Chiba District 17th Specially Est. Garrison Unit	30621 (300)	Kimitsu-gun
Chiba District 18th Specially Est. Garrison Unit	30622 (530)	Kimitsu-gun
Chiba District 19th Specially Est. Garrison Unit	30623 (420)	Kimitsu-gun
Chiba District 20th Specially Est. Garrison Unit	30624 (420)	
Chiba District 21st Specially Est. Garrison Unit	30625 (530)	Awa-gun
Chiba District 22nd Specially Est. Garrison Unit	30626 (420)	Awa-gun
Chiba District 23rd Specially Est. Garrison Unit	30611 (530)	Chiba-gun
Chiba District 24th Specially Est. Garrison Unit	30612 (530)	Ichikawa City
Chiba District 25th Specially Est. Garrison Unit	30613 (530)	Matsudo City
Chiba District 26th Specially Est. Garrison Unit	30614 (420)	East Katsushika

Kofu Regimental District: Yamanashi Prefecture Administrative District

Kōfu District　　　　　　　　　　　　　東部 *Tobu*

Unit	Barracks #	Location
Kōfu District 1st Specially Est. Garrison U.	30761 (400)	N. Miyakodome-gun
Kōfu District 2nd Specially Est. Garrison Unit	30762 (400)	N. Miyakodome
Kōfu District 3rd Specially Est. Garrison Unit	30763 (520)	S. Mayakodome
Kōfu District 4th Specially Est. Garrison Unit	30764 (520)	Higashiyaskiro
Kōfu District 5th Specially Est. Garrison Unit	30765 (520)	E. Yamanashiro
Kōfu District 6th Specially Est. Garrison Unit	30766 (520)	Kōfu City
Kōfu District 7th Specially Est. Garrison Unit	30767 (520)	Kitakoma-gun
Kōfu District 8th Specially Est. Garrison Unit	30768 (520)	Kitakoma-gun
Kōfu District 9th Specially Est. Garrison Unit	30769 (520)	Nakakoma-gun
Kōfu District 10th Specially Est. Garrison Unit	30770 (320)	Minamikoma-g
Kōfu District 11th Specially Est. Garrison Unit	30771 (320)	Nishiyasuhiro-g
Kōfu District 12th Specially Est. Garrison Unit	30772 (320)	Minamikoma-g

Nagano Divisional District:

Unit	Location	Barracks #
Nagano Divisional District HQ	Nagano	東部 (366)

Recruiting and home defense units

54th Depot Division / Nagano Divisional District:

Unit	Location	Barracks # (Personnel)
54th Depot Division Headquarters	Himeji	*Chubu*
111th Infantry Regt Replacement Unit	Himeji	中部 46

Nagano Divisional District continued

Unit	Location	Barracks # (Personnel)
121st Infantry Regt Replacement Unit	Tottori	中部 47
154th Infantry Regiment Repl. Unit	Okayama	中部 48
54th Cavalry Regiment Repl. Unit	Himeji	中部 50
54th Field Art. Regt Repl. Unit	Himeji	中部 51
54th Engineer Regt Replacement Unit	Okayama	中部 52
54th Div. Signal Unit Repl. Unit	Himeji	中部 53
54th Transport Regt Repl. Unit	Himeji	中部 54
Reorganized into 東部 *Feb 6, 1945*		*Tobu*
Nagano 1st Inf. Replacement Unit	Nagano	東部 11 (1,933)
Nagano 2nd Inf. Replacement Unit	Matsumoto	東部 50 (1,933)
Nagano 3rd Inf. Replacement Unit	Shibata	東部 56 (1,933)
Nagano Artillery Replacement Unit	Nobeyama	東部 51 (576)
Nagano Engineer Replacement Unit	Ojiya	東部 52 (705)
Nagano Signal Replacement Unit	Nagano	東部 53 (345)
Nagano Transport Replacement Unit	Nagano	東部 54 (659)

Formerly Kanazawa Divisional District and Niigata Regimental District

<u>Major units supplied by the Nagano Divisional District include:</u>

19th Tank Regiment	Kawanishi	東部 49

<u>Other major units supplied by the Tokyo Divisional District include:</u>
10th Div., 17th Div., 54th Div., 84th Div., 110th Div., 38th I.M.B., 56th I.M.B., 7th Field Replacement Unit

Nagano Regimental District: Nagano Prefecture Administrative District
Nagano District   東部 *Tobu*

Nagano District 1st Specially Est. Garrison Unit	31001 (427)	Minamisaku-g
Nagano District 2nd Specially Est. Garrison Unit	31002 (509)	Kitasaku-gun
Nagano District 3rd Specially Est. Garrison Unit	31003 (414)	Ueda City
Nagano District 4th Specially Est. Garrison Unit	31004 (210)	Ueda City
Nagano District 5th Specially Est. Garrison Unit	31005 (263)	Matsushiro-ma
Nagano District 6th Specially Est. Garrison Unit	31006 (466)	Fuji-machi
Nagano District 7th Specially Est. Garrison Unit	31007 (343)	Susaka-machi
Nagano District 8th Specially Est. Garrison Unit	31008 (344)	Uno-machi
Nagano District 9th Specially Est. Garrison Unit	31009 (267)	Iiyama-machi
Nagano District 10th Specially Est. Garrison Unit	31010 (531)	Yoshida-machi
Nagano District 11th Specially Est. Garrison Unit	31011 (327)	Nagano City
Nagano District 12th Specially Est. Garrison Unit	31012 (303)	Omachi
Nagano District 13th Specially Est. Garrison Unit	31013 (257)	Toyoshima-ma
Nagano District 14th Specially Est. Garrison Unit	31014 (303)	Matsumoto City
Nagano District 15th Specially Est. Garrison Unit	31015 (674)	Hongo-mura
Nagano District 16th Specially Est. Garrison Unit	31016 (350)	Fukushima-ma
Nagano District 17th Specially Est. Garrison Unit	31017 (235)	Okaya City
Nagano District 18th Specially Est. Garrison Unit	31018 (260)	Suwa City

Nagano District continued

Nagano District 19th Specially Est. Garrison Unit	31019 (444)	Suwa-gun
Nagano District 20th Specially Est. Garrison Unit	31020 (485)	Kamiina-gun
Nagano District 21st Specially Est. Garrison Unit	31021 (230)	Iida City
Nagano District 22nd Specially Est. Garrison Unit	31022 (636)	Kamisato-mura

Niigata Regimental District: Niigata Prefecture Administrative District
Niigata District   東部 *Tobu*

Niigata District 1st Specially Est. Garrison Unit	31101 (440)	Murakami-ma
Niigata District 2nd Specially Est. Garrison Unit	31102 (376)	Shibata-machi
Niigata District 3rd Specially Est. Garrison Unit	31103 (372)	Mizuhara-machi
Niigata District 4th Specially Est. Garrison Unit	31104 (91)	Tongawa-machi
Niigata District 5th Specially Est. Garrison Unit	31105 (260)	Nizu-machi
Niigata District 6th Specially Est. Garrison Unit	31106 (297)	Matsumura-ma
Niigata District 7th Specially Est. Garrison Unit	31107 (499)	Makimura
Niigata District 8th Specially Est. Garrison Unit	31108 (390)	Sanjo City
Niigata District 9th Specially Est. Garrison Unit	31109 (257)	Teradomari-ma
Niigata District 10th Specially Est. Garrison Unit	31110 (239)	Sekihara-machi
Niigata District 11th Specially Est. Garrison Unit	31111 (388)	Nagaoka City
Niigata District 12th Specially Est. Garrison Unit	31112 (356)	Kitauonuma-gun
Niigata District 13th Specially Est. Garrison Unit	31113 (372)	Kashiwazaki
Niigata District 14th Specially Est. Garrison Unit	31114 (289)	Toraichi
Niigata District 15th Specially Est. Garrison Unit	31115 (265)	Muikaichi
Niigata District 16th Specially Est. Garrison Unit	31116 (95)	Ōshima-mura
Niigata District 17th Specially Est. Garrison Unit	31117 (297)	Saki-machi
Niigata District 18th Specially Est. Garrison Unit	31118 (356)	Nakakubiki-gun
Niigata District 19th Specially Est. Garrison Unit	31119 (356)	Takata City
Niigata District 21st Specially Est. Garrison Unit	31121 (316)	Nishikubiki-gun
Niigata District 22nd Specially Est. Garrison Unit	31122 (482)	Sado-gun

Division on parade, an infantry regiment passes in review (author)

Central Honshu

13th Area Army / Tokai Army District 秀 *Shuu*

The 13th Area Army was activated in Nagoya on January 22, 1945, from former East-Central District Army personnel. Appointed Feb 2nd its commander was Lt Gen Tasuke Okada and its HQ was in Nagoya, Aichi Prefecture. The 13th Area Army served under the General Defense Command from Feb 6th until Apr 8th and 1st General Army from Feb 4th until it was deactivated in Nagoya on September 13th.

Subordinate army / duty dates:
54th Army from June 19, 1945, until Sept 22, 1945

Service History:
1945: On Jan 22nd Japan's Homeland Defense Districts were reorganized and the 13th Area Army activated to defend the East Sea Military District ○ Feb 2nd, the 13th Area Army setup headquarters in Nagoya, Aichi Prefecture ○ On Feb 4th Lt Gen Tasuke Okada became the 13th Area Army commander ○ Feb 6th, the 13th Area Army was made subordinate to Defense General HQ, and the 73rd Div joined its order of battle ○ Feb 18th the 97th I.M.B. joined the 13th Area Army ○ Apr 8th the 1st General Army replaced Defense General HQ. The 143rd and 153rd Div were placed under the 13th Area Army's command ○ On May 10th the 209th Div joined the 13th Area Army ○ June 19th, the 54th Army was activated and placed under the 13th Area Army's command along

with the 229th Div. The same day the 143rd, 209th Div and 97th I.M.B. were removed ○
On Nov 15th the 13th Area Army was deactivated ○

Major Units: See division / brigade page for order of battle

73rd Division Hiroshima 1944 怒 *Ikari* – Toyohashi	214
153rd Division Kyoto 1945 護京 *Gokyu* – Ujiyamada, Mie Prefecture,	238
229th Division Kanazawa 1945 北越 *Kitaetsu* – Iida, Nagano Prefecture	247-8
8th Independent Armored Brigade 1945 鋭敏 *Eibin* – Aichi	280
2nd Anti-Aircraft Division 1945 逐 *Chiku* – Nagoya	256

Units under control of the 13th Area Army: Nagoya 秀 *Shuu*

Unit	Code	Location
13th Area Army Headquarters	12480 (496)	Nagoya
4th Artillery Intelligence Regiment	12308 (664)	Toyokawa
Nagoya Anti-Aircraft Artillery Headquarters	4167	
15th Independent Mountain Artillery Regiment	21769 (2,981)	Matto-machi
6th Self-Propelled Artillery Battalion	21791 (481)	
38th Independent Heavy Artillery Battalion	4152 (406)	Irako
41st Independent Heavy Artillery Battalion	36387 (498)	Irako
15th Trench Mortar Battalion	21766 (904)	Kanazawa
22nd Trench Mortar Battalion	28291 (1,414)	
9th Engineer Unit Headquarters	21603 (92)	Nagoya
70th Independent Engineer Battalion	14320 (479)	Takahashi
108th Independent Engineer Battalion	21739 (885)	
115th Independent Engineer Battalion	28324 (885)	
40th Signal Regiment	13374 (1,831)	Inuyama
53rd Signal Regiment	13513 (1,097)	Yoro
4th Short Wave Signal Company	28387 (159)	Osaka
152nd Line of Communications Unit Headquarters	20800 (196)	Shinjo
152nd Line of Communications Duty Company	20801 (210)	Kuruchino
19th Field Transport Headquarters	21646 (37)	Nagoya
36th Independent Signal Engineer Unit	27820 (302)	Hukori
37th Independent Signal Engineer Unit	27821 (302)	Nishikasugai
38th Independent Signal Engineer Unit	27822 (302)	Fukori
39th Independent Signal Engineer Unit	27823 (302)	Miyoshi
40th Independent Signal Engineer Unit	27824 (302)	Nagara
41st Independent Signal Engineer Unit	27825 (302)	Ichinomiya
42nd Independent Signal Engineer Unit	27826 (302)	Ichinomiya
43rd Independent Signal Engineer Unit	27827 (302)	Hirawa
44th Independent Signal Engineer Unit	27828 (302)	Kamo
45th Independent Signal Engineer Unit	27829 (302)	Kamazawa
2nd Electric Company	36456 (147)	Nagoya
195th Land Duty Company	36442 (201)	Takaoka
196th Land Duty Company	36443 (201)	Takaoka
197th Land Duty Company	36444 (200)	Nanao
198th Land Duty Company	36445 (201)	Takasha
199th Land Duty Company	36446 (201)	Toyama
24th Sea Transport Battalion	21795 (547)	
9th Field Horse Remount Depot	21733 (237)	Yamata

Central Honshu, East Coast

54th Army 颯 *Satsu* 21640

The 54th Army was activated in Shinshirō, Aichi on June 19, 1945, with its headquarters in Shinshirō. On June 15th Lt Gen Nobuo Kobayashi became the 54th Army commander. On June 19th it was assigned to the 13th Area Army and deactivated on Sept 22nd.

Service History:
1945: June 15th Lt Gen Nobuo Kobayashi was appointed to command the 54th Army ○ June 19th, the 54th Army was activated in Shinshirō, Aichi Prefecture on Japan's east coast, south of Tokyo and placed under 13th Area Army control ○ On June 19th the 143rd, 209th 224th and 355th Div and 97th, 119th and 120th I.M.B. were attached ○ On Sept 22nd the 54th Army HQ was deactivated in Shinshirō ○

Major Units: See division / brigade page for order of battle
143rd Division Nagoya 1945 護古 *Goko* – Kiga, Shizuoka	233
224th Division Hiroshima 1945 赤穂 *Akao* – In transit when the war ended	246-7
355th Division Himeji 1945 那智 *Nashi* – In transit when the war ended	253
97th Independent Mixed Brigade 1945 東明 *Tomei* – Toyohashi	266
119th Independent Mixed Brigade 1945 東旭 *Tokyoku* – Asahina,	272
120th Independent Mixed Brigade 1945 東天 *Joten* – Shimizu	272

Units under the 54th Army: Shinshiromachi   颯 *Satsu* 21640

54th Army Headquarters	21641 (387)	Shinjō
3rd Artillery Headquarters	21642 (119)	Kiga
33rd Independent Field Artillery Battalion	21767 (412)	Gamagori
34th Independent Field Artillery Battalion	21768 (411)	Horinouchi
53rd Field Medium Artillery Regiment	12582 (1,783)	Mikatagahara
37th Independent Heavy Artillery Battalion	4151 (383)	Arai
13th Trench Mortar Battalion	3107/21764 (906)	Anbara
14th Trench Mortar Battalion	3108/21765 (926)	Kasamatsu
105th Independent Engineer Battalion	21736 (481)	Toyohashi
106th Independent Engineer Battalion	21737 (479)	Kosakai
107th Independent Engineer Battalion	21738 (480)	Wato
48th Signal Regiment	27448 (1,110)	Shinjō

Tokai Army District:
Tokai Hokuriko Area

Tokai Army District Headquarters	Nagoya	東海 *Tokai* (1,318)

Kanazawa Divisional District:

Kanazawa Divisional District HQ	Kanazawa	東海 *Tokai* (333)

Recruiting and home defense units
52nd Depot Division / Kanazawa Divisional District

Unit	Location	Barracks # (Personnel)
52nd Depot Division Headquarters	Kanazawa	*Tobu*

52nd Depot Division / Kanazawa Divisional District continued

Unit	Location	Barracks # (Personnel)
		Tobu
52nd Depot Division Headquarters	Kanazawa	東部 48
69th Infantry Regt Replacement Unit	Toyama	東部 48
107th Infantry Regiment Repl.Unit	Kanazawa	東部 49
150th Infantry Regiment Repl. Unit	Matsumoto	東部 50
52nd Cavalry Regit Replacement Unit	Kanazawa	東部 51
52nd Mtn Arty Regiment Repl. Unit	Kanazawa	東部 52
52nd Engineer Regiment Repl. Unit	Kanazawa	東部 53
52nd Div. Signal Unit Repl. Unit	Kanazawa	東部 54
52nd. Transport Regiment Repl. Unit	Kanazawa	東部 55

Reorganized into 東海 Feb 6, 1945 — *Tokai*

Unit	Location	Barracks # (Personnel)
Kanazawa 1st Inf. Replacement Unit	Kanazawa	東海 94 (1,933)
Kanazawa 2nd Inf. Replacement Unit	Toyama	東海 96 (1,933)
Kanazawa Artillery Repl. Unit	Kanazawa	東海 97 (576)
Kanazawa Engineer Repl. Unit	Kanazawa	東海 98 (705)
Kanazawa Signal Replacement Unit	Kanazawa	東海 99 (345)
Kanazawa Transport Repl. Unit	Kanazawa	東海 101 (659)

Major units supplied by the Kanazawa Divisional District include:

Unit	Location	Barracks # (Personnel)
2nd Fld Med Arty Regt. Repl. Unit	Nagoya	東海 9 (1,716)
3rd Fld Med Arty Regt Repl. Unit	Nagoya	東海 70 (893)

Other major units supplied by the Tokyo Divisional District:
9th Div., 21st Div., 52nd Div., 93rd Div., 1st I.M.B., 57th I.M.B., 59th I.M.B., 7th Ind. Inf. Bgde, 2nd Field Replacement Unit, 10th Field Repl. Unit, 5th Border Guard Unit.

Kanazawa Regimental District: Ishikawa Prefecture Administrative District

Kanazawa District   東海 *Tokai*

Unit	Barracks (Pers.)	Location
Kanazawa District 1st Specially Est. Garrison Unit	31201 (282)	Iida-machi
Kanazawa District 2nd Specially Est. Garrison Unit	31202 (282)	Washima-machi
Kanazawa District 3rd Specially Est. Garrison Unit	31203 (417)	Notobe-machi
Kanazawa District 4th Specially Est. Garrison Unit	31204 (407)	Nanao City
Kanazawa District 5th Specially Est. Garrison Unit	31205 (282)	Hasaku-machi
Kanazawa District 6th Specially Est. Garrison Unit	31206 (282)	Tsuhata-machi
Kanazawa District 7th Specially Est. Garrison Unit	31207 (282)	Kanazawa City
Kanazawa District 8th Specially Est. Garrison Unit	31208 (282)	Kanazawa City
Kanazawa District 9th Specially Est. Garrison Unit	31209 (273)	Matsuzumi-ma
Kanazawa District 10th Specially Est.Garrison Unit	31210 (282)	Terai-machi
Kanazawa District 11th Specially Est. Garrison Unit	31211 (282)	Kawatsu City
Kanazawa District 12th Specially Est.Garrison Unit	31212 (407)	Enuma-gun
27th Specially Established Garrison Company	6614 (134)	Washima-machi

Toyama Regimental District: Toyama Prefecture Administrative District

Toyama District   東海 *Tokai*

Toyama District: continued   東海 *Tokai*

Unit	Barracks # (Personnel)	Location
Toyama District 1st Specially Est. Garrison Unit	31213 (282)	Tomari-machi
Toyama District 2nd Specially Est. Garrison Unit	31214 (282)	Aozu-machi
Toyama District 3rd Specially Est. Garrison Unit	31215 (282)	Namekawa-ma
Toyama District 4th Specially Est. Garrison Unit	31216 (282)	Toyama City
Toyama District 5th Specially Est. Garrison Unit	31217 (282)	Toyama City
Toyama District 6th Specially Est. Garrison Unit	31218 (282)	Osawano-machi
Toyama District 7th Specially Est. Garrison Unit	31219 (282)	Takata-machi
Toyama District 8th Specially Est. Garrison Unit	31220 (282)	Imizu-gun
Toyama District 9th Specially Est. Garrison Unit	31221 (282)	Takaoka City
Toyama District 10th Specially Est. Garrison Unit	31222 (282)	Ide-machi
Toyama District 11th Specially Est. Garrison Unit	31223 (282)	Ishido-machi
Toyama District 12th Specially Est. Garrison Unit	31224 (407)	Himi-gun
23rd Specially Established Garrison Company	6611 (134)	Fushiki-machi
24th Specially Established Garrison Company	6612 (134)	S hiraineto-machi

Nagoya Divisional District:

Nagoya Divisional District HQ   Nagoya   東海 (280)

Recruiting and home defense units
3rd Depot Division / Nagoya Divisional District

Unit	Location	Barracks # (Personnel)
3rd Depot Division Headquarters	Nagoya	*Tobu* (139)
6th Infantry Regt Replacement Unit	Nagoya	中部 2
34th Infantry Regiment Repl. Unit	Shizuoka	中部 3
68th Infantry Regiment Repl. Unit	Gifu	中部 4
3rd Cavalry Regt Replacement Unit	Nagoya	中部 6
3rd Artillery Corps Headquarters	Mishima	中部 7
3rd Field Art. Regt Replacement Unit	Nagoya	中部 8
3rd Engineer Regt Replacement Unit	Toyohashi	中部 11
3rd Div. Signal Unit Repl. Unit	Nagoya	中部 12
3rd Transport Regt Replacement Unit	Nagoya	中部 13
Reorganized into 東北 *Feb 6, 1945*		*Tokai*
Nagoya 1st Inf. Replacement Unit	Nagoya	東海 5 (1,933)
Nagoya 2nd Inf. Replacement Unit	Shizuoka	東海 25 (1,933)
Nagoya 3rd Inf. Replacement Unit	Gifu	東海 26 (1,933)
Nagoya 4th Inf. Replacement Unit	Tsu	東海 59 (1,933)
Nagoya Artillery Replacement Unit	Nagoya	東海 28 (576)
Nagoya Engineer Replacement Unit	Toyohashi	東海 31 (705)
Nagoya Signal Replacement Unit	Nagoya	東海 32 (345)
Nagoya Transport Replacement Unit	Nagoya	東海 35 (659)

Major units supplied by the Nagoya Divisional District:

2nd Field Arty. Regiment Repl. Unit	Mishima	東海 9
3rd Field Arty. Regiment Repl. Unit	Mishima	東海 10

Other major units supplied by the Nagoya Divisional District:
3rd Div., 26th Div., 29th Div., 38th Div., 43rd Div., 100th Div., 104th Div., 5th Ind. Inf. Bgde., 6th Ind. Inf. Bgde., 4th Cav. Bgde., 4th Field Repl. Unit

Nagoya Regimental District: Aichi Prefecture Administrative District

Nagoya District　　　　　　　　　　　　　東海 *Tokai*

Unit	Code	Location
162nd Specially Established Garrison Battalion	4134 (550)	Nagoya City
164th Specially Established Garrison Battalion	4136 (550)	Nagoya City
105th Specially Established Engineer Unit	4146 (550)	Nagoya City
106th Specially Established Engineer Unit	4147 (930)	Nagoya City
110th Specially Established Engineer Unit	4178 (930)	Okazaki City
111th Specially Established Engineer Unit	4179 (930)	Nagoya City
Nagoya District 1st Specially Est. Garrison Unit	31401 (300)	Kitasetsu-gun
Nagoya District 2nd Specially Est. Garrison Unit	31402 (300)	Ono-machi
Nagoya District 3rd Specially Est. Garrison Unit	31403 (750)	Tawara-machi
Nagoya District 4th Specially Est. Garrison Unit	31404 (300)	Minamisetsu-g
Nagoya District 5th Specially Est. Garrison Unit	31405 (750)	Toyokawa City
Nagoya District 6th Specially Est. Garrison Unit	31406 (750)	Toyohashi City
Nagoya District 7th Specially Est. Garrison Unit	31407 (750)	Ochisuke-machi
Nagoya District 8th Specially Est. Garrison Unit	31408 (500)	Honjuku-mura
Nagoya District 9th Specially Est. Garrison Unit	31409 (500)	
Nagoya District 10th Specially Est. Garrison Unit	31410 (500)	Okazaki City
Nagoya District 11th Specially Est. Garrison Unit	31411 (300)	
Nagoya District 12th Specially Est. Garrison Unit	31412 (600)	
Nagoya District 13th Specially Est. Garrison Unit	31413 (500)	Nishio-machi
Nagoya District 14th Specially Est. Garrison Unit	31414 (750)	Seto City
Nagoya District 15th Specially Est. Garrison Unit	31415 (300)	Nishin-mura
Nagoya District 16th Specially Est. Garrison Unit	31416 (500)	Chita-gun
Nagoya District 17th Specially Est. Garrison Unit	31417 (500)	
Nagoya District 18th Specially Est. Garrison Unit	31418 (300)	Higashikasugai
Nagoya District 19th Specially Est. Garrison Unit	31419 (750)	Kasugai City
Nagoya District 20th Specially Est. Garrison Unit	31420 (750)	Nagoya City
Nagoya District 21st Specially Est. Garrison Unit	31421 (300)	Nishikasugai-g
Nagoya District 22nd Specially Est. Garrison Unit	31422 (500)	Niwa-gun
Nagoya District 23rd Specially Est. Garrison Unit	31423 (300)	Isa-machi
Nagoya District 24th Specially Est. Garrison Unit	31424 (300)	Ishinomiya City
Nagoya District 25th Specially Est. Garrison Unit	31425 (500)	
Nagoya District 26th Specially Est. Garrison Unit	31426 (750)	Tsushima-machi

Gifu Regimental District: Gifu Prefecture Administrative District

Gifu District:　　　　　　　　　　　　　東海 *Tokai*

Unit	Code	Location
163rd Specially Established Garrison Battalion	4135 (550)	Gifu City
104th Specially Established Engineer Unit	4145 (930)	Akasaka-machi

Gifu Regimental District continued   東海 *Tokai*

Unit	Code	Location
112th Specially Established Engineer Unit	4180 (930)	Nako-machi
Gifu District 1st Specially Est. Garrison Unit	31461 (450)	Furukawa-ma
Gifu District 2nd Specially Est. Garrison Unit	31462 (300)	Takayama City
Gifu District 3rd Specially Est. Garrison Unit	31463 (450)	Miya-mura
Gifu District 4th Specially Est. Garrison Unit	31464 (300)	Masuda-gun
Gifu District 5th Specially Est. Garrison Unit	31465 (300)	Hachiman-ma
Gifu District 6th Specially Est. Garrison Unit	31466 (450)	Nakatsu-machi
Gifu District 7th Specially Est. Garrison Unit	31467 (300)	Toki-gun
Gifu District 8th Specially Est. Garrison Unit	31468 (300)	Tajimi City
Gifu District 9th Specially Est. Garrison Unit	31469 (450)	Kani-gun
Gifu District 10th Specially Est. Garrison Unit	31470 (300)	Ota-machi
Gifu District 11th Specially Est. Garrison Unit	31471 (450)	Mino-machi
Gifu District 12th Specially Est. Garrison Unit	31472 (300)	Yamagata-gun
Gifu District 13th Specially Est. Garrison Unit	31473 (300)	Gifu City
Gifu District 14th Specially Est. Garrison Unit	31474 (600)	Gifu City
Gifu District 15th Specially Est. Garrison Unit	31475 (300)	Kasamatsu-ma
Gifu District 16th Specially Est. Garrison Unit	31476 (300)	Kitagata-machi
Gifu District 17th Specially Est. Garrison Unit	31477 (300)	
Gifu District 18th Specially Est. Garrison Unit	31478 (300)	Namori-mura
Gifu District 19th Specially Est. Garrison Unit	31479 (450)	Ogaki City
Gifu District 20th Specially Est. Garrison Unit	31480 (300)	Kiyashiro-machi
Gifu District 21st Specially Est. Garrison Unit	31481 (300)	Takata-machi
Gifu District 22nd Specially Est. Garrison Unit	31482 (300)	Takasu-machi

Shizuoka Regimental District: Shizuoka Prefecture Administrative District
Shizuoka District: 東海 *Tokai*

Unit	Code	Location
109th Specially Established Engineer Unit	4177 (930)	Hamamatsu City
Shizuoka District 1st Specially Est. Garrison Unit	31431 (450)	Shimoda-machi
Shizuoka District 2nd Specially Est. Garrison Unit	31432 (300)	Matsuzaki-ma
Shizuoka District 3rd Specially Est. Garrison Unit	31433 (300)	Ito-machi
Shizuoka District 4th Specially Est. Garrison Unit	31434 (450)	Daigin-machi
Shizuoka District 5th Specially Est. Garrison Unit	31435 (450)	Atama City
Shizuoka District 6th Specially Est. Garrison Unit	31436 (300)	Mishima City
Shizuoka District 7th Specially Est. Garrison Unit	31437 (450)	Numazu City
Shizuoka District 8th Specially Est. Garrison Unit	31438 (450)	Nagaizumi-mu
Shizuoka District 9th Specially Est. Garrison Unit	31439 (450)	Yoshihara-machi
Shizuoka District 10th Specially Est. Garrison Unit	31440 (300)	Funomiya City
Shizuoka District 11th Specially Est. Garrison Unit	31441 (450)	Okitsu-machi
Shizuoka District 12th Specially Est. Garrison Unit	31442 (450)	Shimizu City
Shizuoka District 13th Specially Est. Garrison Unit	31443 (600)	Shizuoka City
Shizuoka District 14th Specially Est. Garrison Unit	31444 (300)	Miwa-mura
Shizuoka District 15th Specially Est. Garrison Unit	31445 (600)	Shita-gun
Shizuoka District 16th Specially Est. Garrison Unit	31446 (300)	Shimada-machi
Shizuoka District 17th Specially Est. Garrison Unit	31447 (450)	Kawasaki-machi

Shizuoka Regimental District continued

Shizuoka District 18th Specially Est. Garrison Unit	31448 (300)	Haibara-gun
Shizuoka District 19th Specially Est. Garrison Unit	31449 (600)	Kikugawa-ma
Shizuoka District 20th Specially Est. Garrison Unit	31450 (450)	Mori-machi
Shizuoka District 21st Specially Est. Garrison Unit	31451 (600)	Banda-gun
Shizuoka District 22nd Specially Est. Garrison Unit	31452 (300)	Banda-gun
Shizuoka District 23rd Specially Est. Garrison Unit	31453 (450)	Hikisa-gun
Shizuoka District 24th Specially Est. Garrison Unit	31454 (600)	Hamamtsu City
Shizuoka District 25th Specially Est. Garrison Unit	31455 (600)	Yūtō-mura
Shizuoka District 26th Specially Est. Garrison Unit	31456 (300)	Hamana-gun
108th Specially Established Garrison Company	4139 (126)	Kumahara-machi
102nd Specially Established Garrison Company	5747 (126)	Omasaki-mura
103rd Specially Established Garrison Company	5748 (126)	Maisaka
101st Specially Established Garrison Company	4756 (126)	Atami City
107th Specially Established Garrison Company	4138 (126)	Kamo-gun

Tsu Regimental District: Mei Prefecture Administrative District
Tsu District   東海 *Tokai*

114th Specially Established Engineer Unit	4182 (930)	Komata-machi
Tsu District 1st Specially Est. Garrison Unit	31501 (450)	Kuwana City
Tsu District 2nd Specially Est. Garrison Unit	31502 (300)	Zaira-mura
Tsu District 3rd Specially Est. Garrison Unit	31503 (300)	Inben-machi
Tsu District 4th Specially Est. Garrison Unit	31504 (600)	Yokkaichi City
Tsu District 5th Specially Est. Garrison Unit	31505 (450)	Mie-gun
Tsu District 6th Specially Est. Garrison Unit	31506 (300)	Suzuka City
Tsu District 7th Specially Est. Garrison Unit	31507 (450)	Kamiyama-ma
Tsu District 8th Specially Est. Garrison Unit	31508 (300)	Ichinada-machi
Tsu District 9th Specially Est. Garrison Unit	31509 (600)	Tan City
Tsu District 10th Specially Est. Garrison Unit	31510 (300)	Muramushi-mu
Tsu District 11th Specially Est. Garrison Unit	31511 (450)	Fuchu-mura
Tsu District 12th Specially Est. Garrison Unit	31512 (450)	Ueno City
Tsu District 13th Specially Est. Garrison Unit	31513 (450)	Nebari-machi
Tsu District 14th Specially Est. Garrison Unit	31514 (450)	Kui-machi
Tsu District 15th Specially Est. Garrison Unit	31515 (450)	Yachi-mura
Tsu District 16th Specially Est. Garrison Unit	31516 (450)	Matsusaka City
Tsu District 17th Specially Est. Garrison Unit	31517 (450)	Hanaoka-machi
Tsu District 18th Specially Est. Garrison Unit	31518 (450)	Soka-machi
Tsu District 19th Specially Est. Garrison Unit	31519 (600)	Toba-machi
Tsu District 20th Specially Est. Garrison Unit	31520 (450)	Isobe-mura
Tsu District 21st Specially Est. Garrison Unit	31521 (450)	Ugiyamada City
Tsu District 22nd Specially Est. Garrison Unit	31522 (450)	Ugiyamada City
Tsu District 23rd Specially Est. Garrison Unit	31523 (300)	Yoshizu-mura
Tsu District 24th Specially Est. Garrison Unit	31524 (450)	Nagashima-ma
Tsu District 25th Specially Est. Garrison Unit	31525 (450)	Otaka-machi
Tsu District 26th Specially Est. Garrison Unit	31526 (600)	Kitamuro-gun

Tsu District continues   東海 *Tokai*
105th Specially Established Garrison Company   4122 (126)   Ugiyamada City
109th Specially Established Garrison Company   4140 (126)   Yokkaichi City
104th Specially Established Garrison Company   4121 (126)   Toba-machi

Emperor Hirohito on white horse attending a military parade (author)

Infantry passing in review (author)

Chapter 2

Western Honshu, Shikoku and Kyushu

2nd General Army

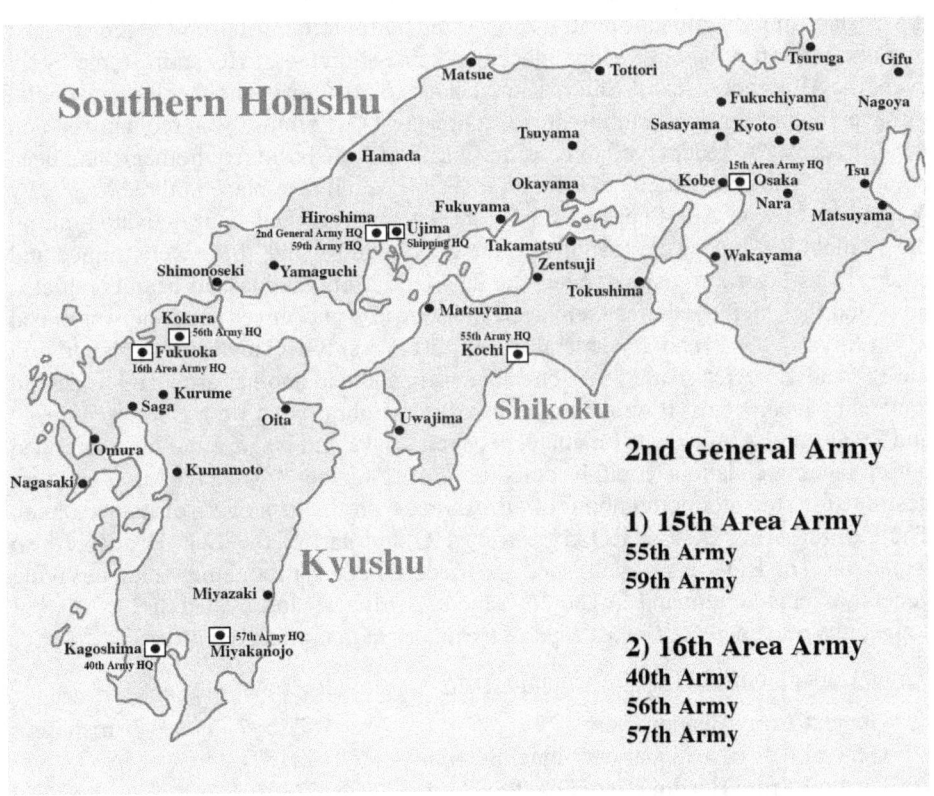

2nd General Army 西方 *Seiho*

The 2nd General Army headquarters began to organize on April 8, 1945 and became active April 15th, with the mission of defending Western Honshu, Shikoku and Kyushu. Its HQ were located in Hiroshima. The 2nd General Army reported directly to Chief of the Army General Staff. Field Marshal Hata Shunroku was its commander in chief from Apr 7th until it was deactivated on October 15th. The 2nd General Army had 700,600 members as of August 1945.

Subordinate armies / duty dates:
15th Area Army from Apr 8, 1945 until Sept 13, 1945.
16th Area Army from Apr 8, 1945 until Oct 15, 1945

Service History:
1945: On Mar 31st, the code name and number *Seiho* 8152 were assigned to the 2nd General Army. The Defense General Command reorganized Japan into two areas under the *Army Mobilization Plan for early 1945* ○ On April 8th the 2nd General Army was placed under I.G.HQ control and its order of battle was published ○ On Apr 15th the headquarters staff met in Osaka and the 2nd General Army was activated to defend Kyushu, Western Honshu and Shikoku. As major changes from one command to another can easily result in confusion and disruption the changeover preceded slowly a few units at a time ○ On Apr 17th army staff left Osaka for the permanent 2nd General Army Headquarters in Hiroshima ○ On Apr 18th the 2nd General Army became active. Every effort was to be made to impede the Allies on Kyushu, which is next in importance to the Kanto Plain with Tokyo and the Imperial Palace ○ In April during the 2nd stage mobilization the central and western anti-aircraft groups were reorganized into anti aircraft divisions ○ Japan faced an acute shortage of HQ staff. In the likely event the Allies cut Kyushu, Shikoku and Chugoku off from each other it seemed vital to have another army HQ in the area ○ On May 14th Formosa was reorganized and the 40th Army HQ redeployed to Kyushu ○ End of June basic requirements had been completed. The preparations to meet an invasion would take place in three stages, by the end of July, in Aug-Sept and finally in Oct ○ Of 12 Divisions activated during the 1st mobilization 5 were assigned to the 2nd General Army, these were trained and equipped as coastal divisions. After the 3rd Stage Mobilization had been completed units and their deployed areas remained more or less unchanged until the war ended ○ On July 21st the 1st and 2nd General Army staff met at IGHQ to discuss a plan to fold the 13th and 15th Area Armies into one area army and add another army HQ to defend the Sea of Japan coast. It was thought the Allies might drive a wedge between the 1st and 2nd General Armies with an attack between Osaka and Nagoya but the war ended before recommendations could be acted on ○ Aug 6th the 2nd General Army HQ was destroyed by the atomic bombing of Hiroshima with the loss of 80 of its personnel. The Central Army District HQ, 59th Army HQ and part of the 224th Div were also wiped out. The HQ was re-established at a predetermined site and the senior surviving general assumed command ○ The 2nd General Army was deactivated on Oct 13th but some units remained active past Japan's surrender to maintain civil order ○

Units Under Control of the 2nd General Army:	西方 *Seiho*	
2nd General Army Headquarters	8152 (597)	Hiroshima
2nd General Army Headquarters Signal Section	8152 (87)	
2nd General Army Headquarters Flight Section	8152 (16)	

Chapter 2

Western Honshu and Shikoku

Central Japan

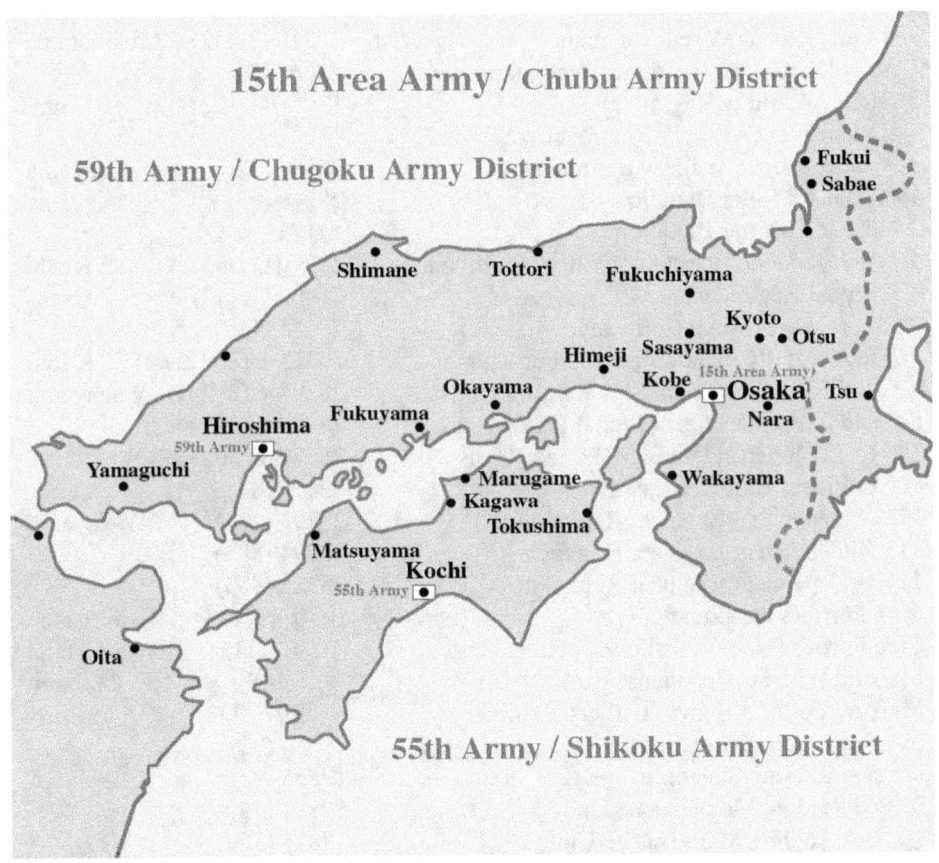

15th Area Army / Chubu Army District 楠 *Kusunoki*

The 15th Area Army was activated in Osaka Jan 22, 1945, from former Central Army District personnel. Headquarters in Osaka under General Defense Command from Feb 6th to Apr 8th and 2nd General Army until Sept 13th. Lt Gen Masamitsu Kawabe was its commander from Feb 6th to Apr 7th and Lt Gen Eitarō Uchiyama until deactivation.
Subordinate armies / duty dates:
55th Army from Apr 8, 1945 until Sept 20, 1945
59th Army from June 19,1945, until Sept 14, 1945
Service History:
1945: Jan 22nd, the 15th Area Army was activated ○ On Feb 6th it became responsible for defending the Central Army District under Defense General Army control ○ Apr 8th, it was placed under 2nd General Army control ○ Aug 15th Japan surrendered, at the time it had 222,531 members ○ The 15th Area Army was deactivated Sept 13th ○
Major Units: See division / brigade page for order of battle

Unit		Page
144th Division Osaka 1945 護阪 *Gohan* – Wakayama		233-4
225th Division Osaka 1945 金剛 *Kongo* – Kobe		247
123rd Independent Mixed Brigade 1945 紀伊 *Kii* – Gobo		273-4
3rd Anti-Aircraft Division 1945 炸 *Saku* – Osaka		256

Units under control of the 15th Area Army: Osaka   楠 *Kusunoki*

Unit	Code	Location
15th Area Army Headquarters	12490 (405)	Osaka
38th Independent Mixed Regiment	28319 (3,442)	Amaji-shima
Central District Anti-Aircraft Headquarters	4166	
5th Heavy Artillery Regiment	中部 75 (422)	Miyama
4th Independent Artillery Regiment	中部 1437	
32nd Independent Artillery Battalion	27384 (326)	Wakayama
19th Trench Mortar Battalion	28248 (852)	Wakayama
35th Trench Mortar Battalion	14172	
16th Independent Mountain Artillery Regiment	28290 (2,983)	Kochi
45th Signal Regiment	21402 (1,797)	Osaka
3rd Short Wave Signal Company	28386 (159)	
46th to 48th Independent Signal Labor Units	28253-5 (302 each)	Kyoto
49th and 50th Independent Signal Labor Units	28295-6 (302 ea.)	Wakayama
51st and 52nd Independent Signal Labor Units	28325-6 (302 each)	
53rd to 55th Independent Signal Labor Units	28377-9 (302 each)	
10th Engineer Unit Headquarters	12476 (87)	Osaka
112th Independent Engineer Regiment	28293 (471)	Wakayama
113th Independent Engineer Regiment	28294 (885)	
114th Independent Engineer Regiment	28323 (885)	
Yura Fortress Headquarters	中部 75 (103)	Awaji Island
Yura Fortress Heavy Artillery Regiment	4150 (1,112)	Awaji Island
Maizuru Fortress Headquarters	中部 145	Maizuru
Maizuru Fortress Heavy Artillery Regiment	中部 71 (223)	Maizuru
39th Sea Raiding Squadron	19854 (92)	
40th Sea Raiding Squadron	19855 (92)	
9th Sea Raiding Maintenance Unit	19874 (399)	
10th Sea Raiding Maintenance Unit	19875 (399)	

15th Area Army continued

23rd Sea Transport Battalion	36436 (537)	
25th Sea Transport Battalion	28327 (548)	
26th Sea Transport Battalion	28380 (548)	
215th Land Duty Company	29146 (500)	
216th Land Duty Company	29147 (500)	
217th Land Duty Company	29148 (235)	Yamaguchi
218th Land Duty Company	29149 (197)	Yamaguchi
219th Land Duty Company	29150 (250)	Yamaguchi
201st Specially Established Garrison Battalion	7159 (550)	
106th Specially Established Garrison Company	4137 (126)	Shirahama-machi
111th Specially Established Garrison Company	4176 (126)	Kushimoto-machi

Chubu Army District:
Kinki Area

Chubu Army District Headquarters   Osaka   中部 (762)

Kyoto Divisional District:

Recruiting and home defense units

53rd Depot Division / Kyoto Divisional District:

Unit	Location	Barracks # (Personnel)
53rd Depot Division Headquarter	Kyoto	*Chubu*
119th Infantry Regt Replacement Unit	Tsuruga	中部 36
128th Infantry Regiment Repl. Unit	Kyoto	中部 37
151st Infantry Regt Replacement Unit	Tsu	中部 38
53rd Cavalry Regiment Repl. Unit	Kyoto	中部 39
53rd Field Art. Regiment Repl. Unit	Kyoto	中部 40
53rd Engineer Regt Replacement Unit	Kyoto	中部 41
53rd Div. Signal Unit Repl. Unit	Kyoto	中部 42
53rd Transport Regiment Repl. Unit	Kyoto	中部 43
Reorganized Feb 6, 1945		*Chubu*
Kyoto 1st Infantry Replacement Unit	Kyoto	中部 137 (1,933)
Kyoto 2nd Infantry Replacement Unit	Tsuruga	中部 136 (1,933)
Kyoto Artillery Replacement Unit	Kyoto	中部 140 (576)
Kyoto Engineer Replacement Unit	Kyoto	中部 141 (705)
Kyoto Signal Replacement Unit	Kyoto	中部 142 (345)
Kyoto Transport Replacement Unit	Kyoto	中部 143 (659)

Major units supplied by the Kyoto Divisional District include:

Maizuru Fortress Headquarters	Maizuru	中部 (6)
Maizuru Fortress Hvy Artillery Regt	Maizuru	中部 71 (231)
5th Heavy Artillery Regiment	Miyama	中部 75 (422)
3rd Trench Mortar Regt Repl. Unit	Sabae	中部 80 (535)
1st Radio Signal Replacement Unit	Shinodayama	中部 (887)

Other major units supplied by the Kyoto Divisional District:
15th Div., 16th Div., 53rd Div., 62nd Div., 116th Div., 118th Div., 29th I.M.B., 61st I.M.B.

Kyoto Regimental District: Kyoto Prefecture Administrative District
Kyoto Regimental District HQ:　　Kyoto　　　中部 (118)
Kyoto District:　　　　　　　　　　　　　中部 *Chubu*

Unit	Number	Location
160th Specially Established Garrison Battalion	4132 (527)	Sakyou-ku
161st Specially Established Garrison Battalion	7635 (527)	Higashiyama-ku
Kyoto District Headquarters	No # (45)	Fushimi-ku
Kyoto District 5th Specially Est. Garrison Unit	7639 (306)	Fushimi-ku
Kyoto District 6th Specially Est. Garrison Unit	7640 (306)	Higashiyama-ku
Kyoto District 7th Specially Est. Garrison Unit	7641 (306)	Shimogyou-ku
Kyoto District 8th Specially Est. Garrison Unit	7642 (306)	Sakyou-ku
Kyoto District 9th Specially Est. Garrison Unit	7643 (306)	Nakagyou-ku
Kyoto District 10th Specially Est. Garrison Unit	7644 (306)	Kamigyou-ku
Kyoto District 11th Specially Est. Garrison Unit	7645 (306)	Ukyou-ku
Kyoto District 1st Specially Est. Garrison Unit	7635 (306	Kozu-machi
Kyoto District 2nd Specially Est. Garrison Unit	7636 (306)	Tanabe-machi
Kyoto District 3rd Specially Est. Garrison Unit	7637 (306)	Kuse-gun
Kyoto District 4th Specially Est. Garrison Unit	7638 (306)	Otokuni-gun
Kyoto District 12th Specially Est. Garrison Unit	7646 (306)	Kameoka-machi
Kyoto District 13th Specially Est. Garrison Unit	7647 (306)	Shuuzan-machi
Kyoto District 14th Specially Est. Garrison Unit	7652 (306)	Sonobe-machi
Kyoto District 15th Specially Est. Garrison Unit	7653 (306)	Ayabe-machi
Kyoto District 16th Specially Est. Garrison Unit	7654 (306)	Fukushiyama
Kyoto District 17th Specially Est. Garrison Unit	7655 (306)	Miyazu-machi
Kyoto District 18th Specially Est. Garrison Unit	7656 (306)	Yoshizu-machi
Kyoto District 20th Specially Est. Garrison Unit	7658 (306)	Tsunano-machi
Kyoto District 21st Specially Est. Garrison Unit	7659 (306)	Kamino-mura
Kyoto District 22nd Specially Est. Garrison Unit	7648 (306)	Maijuru City
Kyoto District 19th Specially Est. Garrison Unit	7657 (306)	Mineyama-machi

Otsu Regimental District: Shiga Prefecture Administrative District
Otsu District:　　　　　　　　　　　　　中部 *Chubu*

Unit	Number	Location
Otsu District 11th Specially Est. Garrison Unit	7670 (406)	Sakata-mura
Otsu District 3rd Specially Est. Garrison Unit	7662 (304)	Kusatsu-machi
Otsu District 4th Specially Est. Garrison Unit	7663 (406)	Mizukuchi-machi
Otsu District 5th Specially Est. Garrison Unit	7664 (304)	Yasu-machi
Otsu District 6th Specially Est. Garrison Unit	7665 (406)	Kamo-gun
Otsu District 8th Specially Est. Garrison Unit	7667 (304)	Aichigawa-machi
Otsu District 9th Specially Est. Garrison Unit	7668 (304)	Takamiya-machi
Otsu District 10th Specially Est. Garrison Unit	7669 (304)	Hikone City
Otsu District 12th Specially Est. Garrison Unit	7671 (304)	Nagahama City

Otsu District: continued

Unit	Barracks # (Personnel)	Location
Otsu District 13th Specially Est. Garrison Unit	7672 (304)	Higashiasai-gun
Otsu District 14th Specially Est. Garrison Unit	7673 (406)	Ika-gun
Otsu District 15th Specially Est. Garrison Unit	7674 (408)	Takashima-gun
Otsu District 16th Specially Est. Garrison Unit	7675 (304)	Katada-machi
Otsu District Headquarters	No # (32)	Otsu City
Otsu District 1st Specially Est. Garrison Unit	7660 (304)	Otsu City
Otsu District 2nd Specially Est. Garrison Unit	7661 (304)	Otsu City
113th Specially Established Engineer Unit	4181 (939)	Yokaichi-machi
Otsu District 7th Specially Est. Garrison Unit	7666 (304)	Yokaichi-machi
110th Specially Established Garrison Company	4141 (126)	Maibara-machi

Fukui Regimental District: Fukui Prefecture Administrative District
Fukui District　　　　　　　　　　　　　中部 *Chubu*

Unit	Barracks # (Personnel)	Location
Fukui District 1st Specially Est. Garrison Unit	7676 (406)	Mikuni-machi
Fukui District 2nd Specially Est. Garrison Unit	7677 (406)	Maruoka-machi
Fukui District 3rd Specially Est. Garrison Unit	7678 (306)	Morita-machi
Fukui District 4th Specially Est. Garrison Unit	7679 (306)	Ono-mura
Fukui District Headquarters	No # (32)	Huku City
Fukui District 5th Specially Est. Garrison Unit	7680 (306)	Huku City
Fukui District 6th Specially Est. Garrison Unit	7681 (306)	Shimomonju-mu
Fukui District 7th Specially Est. Garrison Unit	7682 (312)	Asahi-mura
Fukui District 8th Specially Est. Garrison Unit	7683 (306)	Subae-machi
Fukui District 9th Specially Est. Garrison Unit	7684 (306)	Kamiyama-mura
Fukui District 10th Specially Est. Garrison Unit	7685 (309)	Konjo-mura
Fukui District 11th Specially Est. Garrison Unit	7686 (412)	Isuruga City
Fukui District 12th Specially Est. Garrison Unit	7687 (306)	Mikata-mura
Fukui District 13th Specially Est. Garrison Unit	7688 (309)	Kohama-machi
Fukui District 14th Specially Est. Garrison Unit	7689 (306)	Takahama-machi

Osaka Divisional District:

Osaka Divisional District HQ	Osaka	中部 (272)

Recruiting and home defense units
4th Depot Division / Osaka Divisional District

Unit	Location	Barracks # (Personnel)
4th Depot Division Headquarters	Osaka	*Chubu*
8th Infantry Regt Replacement Unit	Osaka	中部 22
37th Infantry Regt Replacement Unit	Sakai	中部 23
61st Infantry Regt Replacement Unit	Wakayama	中部 24
4th Cavalry Regt Replacement Unit	Sakai	中部 25
4th Field Art. Regt Replacement Unit	Shinodayama	中部 27
4th Engineer Regt Replacement Unit	Takatsuki	中部 29
4th Div. Signal Unit Repl. Unit	Osaka	中部 30

4th Depot Division / Osaka Divisional District continue

Unit	Location	Barracks # (Personnel)
4th Transport Regt Replacement Unit *Reorganized Feb 6, 1945*	Sakai	中部 31 *Chubu*
Osaka 1st Infantry Replacement Unit	Osaka	中部 22 (1,933)
Osaka 2nd Infantry Replacement Unit	Osaka	中部 23 (1,933)
Osaka 3rd Infantry Replacement Unit	Wakayama	中部 24 (1,933)
Osaka 4th Infantry Replacement Unit	Himeji	中部 46 (1,933)
Osaka Artillery Replacement Unit	Shinodayama	中部 27 (576)
Osaka Engineer Replacement Unit	Takatsuki	中部 29 (705)
Osaka Signal Replacement Unit	Osaka	中部 68 (345)
Osaka Transport Replacement Unit	Sakai	中部 55 (659)

Major units supplied by the Osaka Divisional District include

4th Div., 25th Div., 34th Div., 44th Div., 68th Div., 2nd I.M.B., 25th I.M.B., 37th I.M.B., 2nd Ind. Inf. Bgde., 11th Ind. Inf. Bgde., Hong Kong Defense Unit, 5th Field Repl. Unit

Osaka Regimental District: Osaka Prefecture Administrative District
Osaka District   中部 *Chubu*

Unit	Barracks # (Personnel)	Location
155th Specially Established Garrison Battalion	4120 (550)	Osaka City 56A
156th Specially Established Garrison Battalion	4128 (550)	Osaka City 56A
157th Specially Established Garrison Battalion	4129 (550)	Osaka City 56A
158th Specially Established Garrison Battalion	4130 (550)	Osaka City
159th Specially Established Garrison Battalion	4131 (550)	Osaka City
Osaka District 1st Specially Est. Garrison Unit	7690 (349)	Osaka City
Osaka District 2nd Specially Est. Garrison Unit	7691 (344)	Osaka City
Osaka District 3rd Specially Est. Garrison Unit	7692 (354)	Osaka City
Osaka District 4th Specially Est. Garrison Unit	7693 (349)	Osaka City
Osaka District 5th Specially Est. Garrison Unit	7694 (356)	Osaka City
Osaka District 6th Specially Est. Garrison Unit	7695 (358)	Osaka City
Osaka District 7th Specially Est. Garrison Unit	7696 (347)	Osaka City
Osaka District 8th Specially Est. Garrison Unit	7697 (350)	Osaka City
Osaka District 9th Specially Est. Garrison Unit	7698 (350)	Osaka City
Osaka District 10th Specially Est. Garrison Unit	7699 (337)	Osaka City
Osaka District 11th Specially Est. Garrison Unit	13400 (358)	Osaka City
Osaka District 12th Specially Est. Garrison Unit	13401 (346)	Osaka City
Osaka District 13th Specially Est. Garrison Unit	13402 (354)	Osaka City
Osaka District 14th Specially Est. Garrison Unit	13403 (375)	Osaka City
Osaka District 15th Specially Est. Garrison Unit	13404 (370)	Osaka City
Osaka District 16th Specially Est. Garrison Unit	13405 (382)	Osaka City
Osaka District 17th Specially Est. Garrison Unit	13406 (356)	Osaka City
Osaka District 18th Specially Est. Garrison Unit	13407 (343)	Osaka City
101st Specially Established Engineer Unit	4142 (930)	Huse City
Osaka District 22nd Specially Est. Garrison Unit	13411 (347)	Huse City
102nd Specially Established Engineer Unit	4143 (930)	Sakai City

Osaka Regimental District continued

Osaka District 19th Specially Est. Garrison Unit	13408 (447)	Sakai City
103rd Specially Established Engineer Unit	4144 (930)	Toyonaka City
Osaka District 21st Specially Est. Garrison Unit	13410 (239)	Toyonaka City
115th Specially Established Engineer Unit	4183 (930)	Yao-machi
Osaka District 35th Specially Est. Garrison Unit	13424 (579)	Yao-machi
118th Specially Established Engineer Unit	4186 (930)	Sano-machi
Osaka District 31st Specially Est. Garrison Unit	13420 (562)	Sano-machi
Osaka District 20th Specially Est. Garrison Unit	13409 (449)	Kishiwada City
Osaka District 23rd Specially Est. Garrison Unit	13412 (239)	Ikeda City
Osaka District 24th Specially Est. Garrison Unit	13413 (293)	Suita City
Osaka District 25th Specially Est. Garrison Unit	13414 (243)	Izumiōtsu City
Osaka District 26th Specially Est. Garrison Unit	13415 (243)	Kaizuka City
Osaka District 27th Specially Est. Garrison Unit	13416 (239)	Takatsuki City
Osaka District 28th Specially Est. Garrison Unit	13417 (347)	Toyono-gun
Osaka District 29th Specially Est. Garrison Unit	13418 (349)	Mishima-gun
Osaka District 30th Specially Est. Garrison Unit	13419 (570)	Izumikita-gun
Osaka District 32nd Specially Est. Garrison Unit	13421 (561)	Oyaki-machi
Osaka District 33rd Specially Est. Garrison Unit	13422 (358)	Minamikōchi-g
Osaka District 34th Specially Est. Garrison Unit	13423 (518)	Tendabayashi
Osaka District 36th Specially Est. Garrison Unit	13425 (472)	Hirakata-machi

Nara Regimental District: Nara Prefecture Administrative District
Nara District　　　　　　　　　　　　　　　　中部 *Chubu*

Nara District 1st Specially Est. Garrison Unit	13430 (405)	Nara City
Nara District 2nd Specially Est. Garrison Unit	13431 (455)	Ikoma-gun
Nara District 3rd Specially Est. Garrison Unit	13432 (435)	Tengyo-gun
Nara District 4th Specially Est. Garrison Unit	13433 (355)	Namiishi-machi
Nara District 5th Specially Est. Garrison Unit	13434 (475)	Sakurai-machi
Nara District 6th Specially Est. Garrison Unit	13435 (445)	Takata-machi
Nara District 7th Specially Est. Garrison Unit	13436 (316)	
Nara District 8th Specially Est. Garrison Unit	13437 (325)	Takaishi-gun
Nara District 9th Specially Est. Garrison Unit	13438 (345)	Uda-gun
Nara District 10th Specially Est. Garrison Unit	13439 (325)	Gojo-machi
Nara District 11th Specially Est. Garrison Unit	13440 (375)	Shimoichi-ma
Nara District 12th Specially Est. Garrison Unit	13441 (405)	Kamiichi-machi
Nara District 13th Specially Est. Garrison Unit	13442 (205)	Totsukawa-mura

Wakayama Regimental District: Wakayama Prefecture Administrative District
Wakayama District　　　　　　　　　　　　　中部 *Chubu*

Wakayama District 1st Specially Est. Garrison Unit	13443 (485)	Wakayama City
Wakayama District 5th Specially Est. Garrison Unit	13447 (459)	Wakayama City
Wakayama District 2nd Specially Est. Garrison Unit	13444 (452)	Kainan City

Wakayama District continued   中部 *Chubu*

Wakayama District 3rd Specially Est. Garrison Unit	13445 (324)	Tanabe City
Wakayama District 4th Specially Est. Garrison Unit	13446 (245)	Nimiya City
Wakayama District 6th Specially Est. Garrison Unit	13448 (427)	
Wakayama District 7th Specially Est. Garrison Unit	13449 (426)	Hashimoto-ma
Wakayama District 8th Specially Est. Garrison Unit	13450 (315)	Arida-gun
Wakayama District 9th Specially Est. Garrison Unit	13451 (384)	Gobō-machi
Wakayama District 10th Sp. Est. Garrison Unit	13452 (479)	Nishimuro-gun
Wakayama District 11th Sp. Est. Garrison Unit	13453 (324)	Nachi-machi

Kobe Regimental District: Hyogo Prefecture Administrative District
Kobe District   中部 *Chubu*

11th Garrison Headquarters	4117 (55)	Kobe City
151st Specially Established Garrison Battalion	4123 (550)	Kobe City
152nd Specially Established Garrison Battalion	4124 (550)	Kobe City
153rd Specially Established Garrison Battalion	4125 (550)	Kobe City
107th Specially Established Engineer Unit	4148 (930)	Kobe City
108th Specially Established Engineer Unit	4149 (930)	Kobe City
Kobe District 1st Specially Est. Garrison Unit	13454 (456)	Kobe City
Kobe District 2nd Specially Est. Garrison Unit	13455	Kobe City
Kobe District 3rd Specially Est. Garrison Unit	13456	Kobe City
Kobe District 4th Specially Est. Garrison Unit	13457 (205)	Kobe City
Kobe District 5th Specially Est. Garrison Unit	13458 (159)	Kobe City
Kobe District 6th Specially Est. Garrison Unit	13459 (411)	Kobe City
Kobe District 7th Specially Est. Garrison Unit	13460 (154)	Ashiya City
Kobe District 8th Specially Est. Garrison Unit	13461 (413)	Nishinomiya
Kobe District 9th Specially Est. Garrison Unit	13462 (?)	Amagasaki City
154th Specially Established Garrison Battalion	4126 (550)	Amagasaki City
116th Specially Established Engineer Unit	4184 (930)	Itami City
Kobe District 10th Specially Est. Garrison Unit	13463 (154)	Itami City
Kobe District 11th Specially Est. Garrison Unit	13464 (305)	Sumoto City
Kobe District 12th Specially Est. Garrison Unit	13465 (311)	Akashi City
Kobe District 13th Specially Est. Garrison Unit	13466 (108)	Aioi City
Kobe District 14th Specially Est. Garrison Unit	13467 (425)	Himegi City
Kobe District 28th Specially Est. Garrison Unit	13481 (392)	Himegi City
Kobe District 15th Specially Est. Garrison Unit	13468 (168)	Harima City
Kobe District 16th Specially Est. Garrison Unit	13469 (352)	Sumiyoshi-mura
Kobe District 17th Specially Est. Garrison Unit	13470 (364)	Kawanishi-ma
Kobe District 18th Specially Est. Garrison Unit	13471 (330)	Mita-machi
Kobe District 19th Specially Est. Garrison Unit	13472 (356)	Okubo-machi
Kobe District 20th Specially Est. Garrison Unit	13473 (310)	Miki-machi
Kobe District 21st Specially Est. Garrison Unit	13474 (311)	Yashiro-machi
Kobe District 22nd Specially Est. Garrison Unit	13475 (310)	Hojo-machi
Kobe District 23rd Specially Est. Garrison Unit	13476 (309)	Naka-machi
117th Specially Established Engineer Unit	4185 (930)	Kakogawa-machi

Kobe District continued

Unit	Number	Location
Kobe District 25th Specially Est. Garrison Unit	13478 (543)	Kakogawa-ma
Kobe District 24th Specially Est. Garrison Unit	13477 (206)	Seishi-machi
Kobe District 26th Specially Est. Garrison Unit	13479 (360)	
Kobe District 27th Specially Est. Garrison Unit	13480 (260)	Tuwara-machi
Kobe District 29th Specially Est. Garrison Unit	13482 (310)	Aboshi-machi
Kobe District 30th Specially Est. Garrison Unit	13483 (176)	Sako-gun
Kobe District 31st Specially Est. Garrison Unit	13484 (227)	Akao-gun
Kobe District 32nd Specially Est. Garrison Unit	13485 (294)	
Kobe District 33rd Specially Est. Garrison Unit	13486 (457)	Shishiku-machi
Kobe District 34th Specially Est. Garrison Unit	13487 (427)	Mihara-gun
Kobe District 35th Specially Est. Garrison Unit	13488 (302)	Shinoyama-ma
Kobe District 36th Specially Est. Garrison Unit	13489 (311)	Kashuwabara
Kobe District 37th Specially Est. Garrison Unit	13490 (203)	Takeda-machi
Kobe District 38th Specially Est. Garrison Unit	13491 (308)	Yatsushika-ma
Kobe District 39th Specially Est. Garrison Unit	13492 (262)	Toyooka-machi
Kobe District 40th Specially Est. Garrison Unit	13493 (201)	Shirozaki-gun
Kobe District 41st Specially Est. Garrison Unit	13494 (204)	Hamasaka-ma

Western Honshu

59th Army / Chugoku Army District 山陽 Sanyo

The 59th Army was activated in Hiroshima on June 12, 1945, from former Hiroshima Army District personnel. On June 19th it was placed into the 15th Area Army's order of battle. The 59th Army's headquarters were located in Hiroshima City under the command of Lt Gen Yōji Fujii from June 15th until Aug. 6th when he was killed in the atomic bombing of Hiroshima. Lt Gen Teiki Nakanishi until Aug 12th and Lt Gen Hisao Tani until it was deactivated on September 14th.

Service History:
1945: May-June, as part of the 3rd group, army mobilization plan for the decisive battle, the Western Army District's sub-district of Hiroshima became Chugoku Army District ○ On June 12th the 59th Army was activated in Hiroshima, with the mission of defending south central Japan ○ On June 15th Lt Gen Yoji Fujii became 59th Army commander ○ June 19th, the 59th Army was placed under the 15th Area Army's control. The 230th, 231st Div and 124th I.M.B. were placed under 59th Army control ○ On Aug 6th the atomic bomb fell on Hiroshima and 59th Army's headquarters killing Lt Gen Fujii amongst others ○ On Aug 6th Lt Gen Teiki Nakanishi temporarily became 59th Army commander ○

Major Units: See division / brigade page for order of battle
230th Division Tokyo 1945 総武 Sobu – Okayama   248
231st Division Hiroshima 1945 大國 Okuni – Yamaguchi   248-9
124th Independent Mixed Brigade 1945 鬼城 Onishiro – Yamaguchi   274

Units Under Control of the 59th Army: Hiroshima   山陽 Sanyo

Unit	Barracks #	Location
59th Army Headquarters	32200 (231)	Hiroshima
21st Guard Company	7163 (215)	Kaitaichi
251st Specially Established Garrison Battalion	7161 (6)	Hiroshima
212th Specially Established Guard Company	7162 (126)	Ube
207th Specially Established Guard Engineer Unit	2786 (930)	Shimonoseki
Hiroshima Line of Comm. Sector Unit HQ	No # (7)	Hiroshima
103rd Specially Established Land Duty Company	8876 (165)	Kaita
122nd Specially Established Sea Duty Company	11170 (138)	Kaita

Chugoku Army District Area:
Chugoku Area

Chugoku Army District HQ   Hiroshima   中国 (396)

Hiroshima Divisional District:

Hiroshima Divisional District HQ   Hiroshima   中国 Chugoku

Recruiting and home defense units
5th Depot Division / Hiroshima Divisional District

Unit	Location	Barracks # (Personnel)
5th Depot Division Headquarters	Hiroshima	Chubu
11th Infantry Regt Replacement Unit	Hiroshima	中部 2
21st Infantry Regt Replacement Unit	Hamada	中部 3
42nd Infantry Regt Replacement Unit	Yamaguchi	中部 4
5th Cavalry Regt Replacement Unit	Hiroshima	中部 5
5th Field Artillery Regt Repl Unit	Hiroshima	中部 6
5th Engineer Regt Replacement Unit	Hiroshima	中部 7
5th Div. Signal Unit Repl Unit	Hiroshima	中部 9
5th Transport Regt Replacement Unit	Hiroshima	中部 10
Reorganized on Feb 6, 1945		*Chubu*
Hiroshima Divisional District		
Renamed to Chugoku	*Jun 20, 1945*	*Chugoku*
Chugoku 1st Inf Replacement Unit	Hiroshima	中国 104 (1,933)
Chugoku 2nd Inf Replacement Unit	Hamada	中国 106 (1,933)
Chugoku 3rd Inf Replacement Unit	Yamaguchi	中国 110 (1,933)
Chugoku 4th Inf Replacement Unit	Tottori	中国 47 (1,933)
Chugoku 5th Inf Replacement Unit	Okayama	中国 48 (1,933)
Chugoku Artillery Replacement Unit	Hiroshima	中国 111 (576)
Chugoku Engineer Replacement Unit	Hiroshima	中国 114 (705)
Chugoku Signal Replacement Unit	Hiroshima	中国 121 (345)
Chugoku Transport Repl Unit	Hiroshima	中国 139 (659)

Other Hiroshima Stationed Replacement Units

Shimonoseki Hvy Artillery Repl Unit	Shimonoseki	中国 74
6th Shipping Engineer Repl Unit	Yanai	中国 8
Shipping Signal Regt Repl Unit	Ujina	中国 87
Sea Pursuit Unit Replacement Unit	Kushigahama	中国

Major units supplied by the Hiroshima Divisional District

5th Div., 39th Div., 64th Div., 70th Div., 105th Div., 27th I.M.B., 64th I.M.B., 65th Bgde., 12th Ind. Inf. Bgde

Okayama Regimental District: Okayama Prefecture Administrative District
Okayama District　　　　　　　　　　　　　　中国 *Chugoku*

Okayama District 1st Specially Est. Garrison Unit	32001 (305)	Okayama City
Okayama District 2nd Specially Est. Garrison Unit	32002 (172)	Okayama City
Okayama District 3rd Specially Est. Garrison Unit	32003 (207)	Kurashiki City
Okayama District 4th Specially Est. Garrison Unit	32004 (305)	Tokubo-gun
Okayama District 5th Specially Est. Garrison Unit	32005 (207)	Tsuyama City
Okayama District 6th Specially Est. Garrison Unit	32006 (305)	Tsuyama City
Okayama District 7th Specially Est. Garrison Unit	32007 (207)	Tamano City
Okayama District 8th Specially Est. Garrison Unit	32008 (172)	Tamano City
Okayama District 9th Specially Est. Garrison Unit	32009 (172)	Konakawa-chō
Okayama District 10th Specially Est. Garrison Unit	32010 (305)	Seto-chō
Okayama District 11th Specially Est. Garrison Unit	32011 (305)	Katagami-chō
Okayama District 12th Specially Est. Garrison Unit	32012 (305)	邑久-chō
Okayama District 13th Specially Est. Garrison Unit	32013 (172)	Saidaji-chō
Okayama District 14th Specially Est. Garrison Unit	32014 (305)	Kojima-gun
Okayama District 15th Specially Est. Garrison Unit	32015 (305)	Kibi-gun
Okayama District 16th Specially Est. Garrison Unit	32016 (207)	Tamashima-chō
Okayama District 17th Specially Est. Garrison Unit	32017 (305)	Kasaoka-chō
Okayama District 18th Specially Est. Garrison Unit	32018 (172)	Oda-gun
Okayama District 19th Specially Est. Garrison Unit	32019 (172)	Shoro-chō
Okayama District 20th Specially Est. Garrison Unit	32020 (207)	Kamifusa-gun
Okayama District 21st Specially Est. Garrison Unit	32021 (207)	Naruhane-chō
Okayama District 22nd Specially Est. Garrison Unit	32022 (305)	Atetsu-gun
Okayama District 23rd Specially Est. Garrison Unit	32023 (305)	Katsuyama-chō
Okayama District 24th Specially Est. Garrison Unit	32024 (305)	Katsumada-chō
Okayama District 25th Specially Est. Garrison Unit	32025 (207)	Hayashino-chō
Okayama District 26th Specially Est. Garrison Unit	32026 (305)	Kume-gun

Tottori Regimental District: Tottori Prefecture Administrative District
Tottori District　　　　　　　　　　　　　　中国 *Chugoku*

Tottori District 1st Specially Est. Garrison Unit	32027 (305)	Imai-chō
Tottori District 2nd Specially Est. Garrison Unit	32028 (305)	Tottori City

Tottori District continued   中国 *Chugoku*

Tottori District 3rd Specially Est. Garrison Unit	32029 (305)	Komo-mura
Tottori District 4th Specially Est. Garrison Unit	32030 (305)	Hodai-mura
Tottori District 5th Specially Est. Garrison Unit	32031 (305)	Kurayoshi-chō
Tottori District 6th Specially Est. Garrison Unit	32032 (305)	Akasaki-chō
Tottori District 7th Specially Est. Garrison Unit	32033 (305)	Seihe-gun
Tottori District 8th Specially Est. Garrison Unit	32034 (305)	Sakai-chō
Tottori District 9th Specially Est. Garrison Unit	32035 (305)	Yonago City
Tottori District 10th Specially Est. Garrison Unit	32036 (305)	Mizoguchi-chō

Hiroshima Regimental District: Hiroshima Prefecture Administrative District
Hiroshima District   中国 *Chugoku*

Hiroshima District 11th Sp. Est. Garrison Unit	32047 (305)	Abe-chō
Hiroshima District 12th Sp. Est. Garrison Unit	32048 (305)	Kabei-chō
Hiroshima District 13th Sp. Est. Garrison Unit	32049 (305)	Yashida-chō
Hiroshima District 14th Sp. Est. Garrison Unit	32050 (305)	Saiji-chō
Hiroshima District 15th Sp. Est. Garrison Unit	32051 (207)	Yasuura-chō
Hiroshima District 16th Sp. Est. Garrison Unit	32052 (207)	Takehara-chō
Hiroshima District 17th Sp. Est. Garrison Unit	32053 (305)	Kawauchi-chō
Hiroshima District 18th Sp. Est. Garrison Unit	32054 (207)	Kozaki-chō
Hiroshima District 19th Sp. Est. Garrison Unit	32055 (207)	Kie-chō
Hiroshima District 20th Sp. Est. Garrison Unit	32056 (305)	Tsuchio-chō
Hiroshima District 21st Sp. Est. Garrison Unit	32057 (305)	Ota-mura
Hiroshima District 22nd Sp. Est. Garrison Unit	32058 (305)	Matsunaga-chō
Hiroshima District 23rd Sp. Est. Garrison Unit	32059 (305)	Hirotani-chō
Hiroshima District 24th Sp. Est. Garrison Unit	32060 (305)	Kamishimo-chō
Hiroshima District 25th Sp. Est. Garrison Unit	32061 (305)	Sanji-chō
Hiroshima District 26th Sp. Est. Garrison Unit	32062 (305)	Shohara-chō
251st Specially Established Garrison Battalion	7161 (550)	Hiroshima City
205th Specially Established Engineer Unit	2784 (705)	Hiroshima City
Hiroshima District 1st Specially Est. Garrison Unit	32037 (305)	Hiroshima City
Hiroshima District 2nd Specially Est. Garrison Unit	32038 (305)	Hiroshima City
Hiroshima District 3rd Specially Est. Garrison Unit	32039 (305)	Kure City
Hiroshima District 4th Specially Est. Garrison Unit	32040 (305)	Onomichi City
Hiroshima District 5th Specially Est. Garrison Unit	32041 (305)	Fukuyama City
Hiroshima District 6th Specially Est. Garrison Unit	32042 (305)	Mihara City
Hiroshima District 7th Specially Est. Garrison Unit	32043 (207)	Edaichi-chō
Hiroshima District 8th Specially Est. Garrison Unit	32044 (207)	Nakamura
Hiroshima District 9th Specially Est. Garrison Unit	32045 (305)	Saiki-gun
Hiroshima District 10th Sp. Est. Garrison Unit	32046 (305)	Tsuda-chō

Matsue Regimental District: Shimane Prefecture Administrative District
Matsue District: 樟 *Kusu*

201st Specially Established Garrison Battalion　　7159 (497)　　Saigo-chō

中国 *Chugoku*

Matsue District 17th Specially Est. Garrison Unit	32079 (172)	Saigo-chō
Matsue District 1st Specially Est. Garrison Unit	32063 (207)	Matsue City
Matsue District 17th Specially Est. Garrison Unit	32079 (172)	Saigo-chō
Matsue District 1st Specially Est. Garrison Unit	32063 (207)	Matsue City
Matsue District 4th Specially Est. Garrison Unit	32066 (207)	Matsue City
Matsue District 2nd Specially Est. Garrison Unit	32064 (207)	Izumu City
Matsue District 3rd Specially Est. Garrison Unit	32065 (207)	Hamada City
Matsue District 5th Specially Est. Garrison Unit	32067 (172)	Yasuku-chō
Matsue District 6th Specially Est. Garrison Unit	32068 (172)	Yokota-chō
Matsue District 7th Specially Est. Garrison Unit	32069 (172)	Kitsugi-chō
Matsue District 8th Specially Est. Garrison Unit	32070 (207)	Kakeai-chō
Matsue District 9th Specially Est. Garrison Unit	32071 (207)	Hirata-chō
Matsue District 10th Specially Est. Garrison Unit	32072 (207)	Taisha-chō
Matsue District 11th Specially Est. Garrison Unit	32073 (172)	Ota-chō
Matsue District 12th Specially Est. Garrison Unit	32074 (172)	Nima-gun
Matsue District 13th Specially Est. Garrison Unit	32075 (207)	Kawamoto-chō
Matsue District 14th Specially Est. Garrison Unit	32076 (207)	Naka-gun
Matsue District 15th Specially Est. Garrison Unit	32077 (207)	Mino-gun
Matsue District 16th Specially Est. Garrison Unit	32078 (172)	Tsuwano-chō
Matsue District 18th Specially Est. Garrison Unit	32080 (172)	Chibu-gun

Yamaguchi Regimental District: Yamaguchi Prefecture Administrative District
Yamaguchi District:　　　　　　　　中国 *Chugoku*

Yamaguchi District 4th Specially Est. Est. Unit	32084 (305)	Ootsu-gun
Yamaguchi District 5th Specially Est. Garrison Unit	32085 (305)	Abu-gun
Yamaguchi District 6th Specially Est. Garrison Unit	32086 (305)	Isa-chō
Yamaguchi District 7th Specially Est. Garrison Unit	32087 (305)	Nishiichi-chō
Yamaguchi District 8th Specially Est. Garrison Unit	32088 (305)	Ogashi-chō
Yamaguchi District 9th Specially Est. Garrison Unit	32089 (172)	Hongō-mura
Yamaguchi District 10th Sp. Est. Garrison Unit	32090 (172)	Kano-chō
Yamaguchi District 11th Sp. Est. Garrison Unit	32091 (172)	Izumo-mura
Yamaguchi District 14th Sp. Est. Garrison Unit	32094 (172)	Funaki-chō
Yamaguchi District 17th Sp. Est. Garrison Unit	32097 (305)	Fujikawa-mura
Yamaguchi District 18th Sp. Est. Garrison Unit	32098 (172)	Takamori-chō
Yamaguchi District 19th Sp. Est. Garrison Unit	32099 (207)	Kudamatsu City
Yamaguchi District 20th Sp. Est. Garrison Unit	32100 (207)	Tokuyama City
Yamaguchi District 23rd Sp. Est. Garrison Unit	32103 (172)	Onoda City
Yamaguchi District 24th Sp. Est. Garrison Unit	32104 (207)	Ōshima-gun
Yamaguchi District 25th Sp. Est. Garrison Unit	32105 (172)	Yanai-chō
Yamaguchi District 26th Sp. Est. Garrison Unit	32106 (207)	Hirao-chō
Yamaguchi District 12th Sp. Est. Garrison Unit	32092 (305)	Yamaguchi City
Yamaguchi District 13th Sp. Est. Garrison Unit	32093 (172)	Yamaguchi City

Yamaguchi District continued   中国 *Chugoku*

212th Specially Established Garrison Company	7162 (158)	Ube City 59A
Yamaguchi District 22nd Sp. Est. Garrison Unit	32102 (307)	Ube City
206th Specially Established Engineer Unit	2785 (1,199)	Hōfu City
Yamaguchi District 21st Sp. Est. Garrison Unit	32101 (207)	Hōfu City
254th Specially Established Garrison Battalion	2741 (550)	Shimonoseki City
201st Specially Established Engineer Unit	2761 (930)	Shimonoseki City
Yamaguchi District 15th Sp. Est. Garrison Unit	32095 (305)	Shimonoseki C.
Yamaguchi District 16th Sp. Est. Garrison Unit	32096 (305)	Shimonoseki C.
Yamaguchi District 1st Specially Est. Garrison Unit	32081 (305)	Abu-gun
Yamaguchi District 2nd Specially Est. Garrison Unit	32082 (305)	Hagi City
Yamaguchi District 3rd Specially Est. Garrison Unit	32083 (305)	

Shikoku

55th Army / Shikoku Army District 偕 *Kai*

The 55th Army was activated in Kōchi, Kōchi Prefecture on Mar 31, 1945, from former Zentsuji Army sub-District personnel. On Apr 8th it was placed under 15th Area Army control. Its headquarters were in Shinkai, Kōchi Prefecture under Lt Gen Kumakichi Harada from Apr. 7th until deactivation in Kōchi on September 20, 1945.

Service History:
1945: On Mar 31st the 5th Army's headquarters activated in Kōchi with former Zentsuji Divisional District personnel ○ On Apr 7th Lt Gen Kumakichi Harada was appointed 55th Army commander ○ Apr 8th, the 55th Army was placed into the 15th Area Army's order of battle, its headquarters in Shinkai, a northern suburb of Kōchi ○ On Apr 8th the 11th and 155th Div transferred into the 55th Army's order of battle ○ In June the military sub-district of Zentsuji was re-designated Shikoku Military District. The 55th Army's staff became responsible for its administration under the homeland defense district reorganization plan, which saw the commander of the 55th Army and certain of his staff serve at the equivalent rank as staff for Chugoku Military District as well ○ On June 19th the 344th Div. joined the 55th Army ○ June 23rd the 121st I.M.B. joined the 55th Army ○ The Army was deactivated on September 20th ○

Major Units: See division / brigade page for order of battle

11th Division Zentsuji 1898 錦 *Nishiki* – Shikoku, in transit to Kochi	205
155th Division Zentsuji 1945 護土 *Godo* – Kōchi	239
205th Division Hiroshima 1945 安芸 *Aki* – Kōchi	242

Chapter 2

344th Division Zentsuji 1945 剣山 *Kenzan* – Shukuge   252
121st Independent Mixed Brigade 1945 菊水 *Kikumei* – Tokushima   273

Units Under Control of the 55th Army: Kōchi   偕 *Kai*

Unit	Code	Location
55th Army Headquarters	12475 (300)	Kōchi
45th Tank Regiment	12357 (400)	Zentsuji
47th Tank Regiment	21411 (400)	Tokushima
10th Artillery Headquarters	27400 (59)	Kochi
6th Independent Mountain Artillery Regiment	6482 (3,791)	Kochi
31st Independent Field Artillery Battalion	27383 (529)	Shimoda
17th Independent Heavy Artillery Battalion	36385 (691)	Kochi
39th Independent Heavy Artillery Battalion	4153 (384)	Wakayama
5th Independent Heavy Artillery Company	4154 (138)	Kochi
9th Mortar Battalion	28322 (481)	
22nd Independent Mortar Battalion	12435 (473)	Kochi
25th Independent Mortar Battalion	28384 (447)	Kochi
26th Independent Mortar Battalion	28385 (340)	Kochi
16th Trench Mortar Battalion	28247 (903)	Tokushima
17th Trench Mortar Battalion	28381 (995)	Kochi
18th Trench Mortar Battalion	28341 (1,414)	
37th Trench Mortar Battalion	6483 (482)	Kochi
79th Independent Engineer Battalion	6484 (689)	Amatsubo
37th Signal Regiment	12938 (1,446)	Tadotsu
118th Independent Wire Company	12389 (310)	
109th Independent Engineer Battalion	28250 (733)	Watsuyama
110th Independent Engineer Battalion	28251 (731)	Shishibuki
111th Independent Engineer Battalion	28252 (735)	Takamatsu
20th Field Transport Headquarters	unknown (37)	
149th Line of Communications Duty Company	14262 (511)	

Shikoku Army District:
Shikoku Area

Shikoku Army District Headquarters   Zentsuji   四国 (421)

Zentsuji Divisional District:

Zentsuji Divisional District HQ   Zentsuji   西部 *Seibu*

Recruiting and home defense units
55th Depot Division / Zentsuji Divisional District

Unit	Location	Barracks # (Personnel)
55th Depot Division Headquarters	Zentsuji	*Chubu*
112th Infantry Regt Replacement Unit	Marugame	中部 82
143rd Infantry Regiment Repl. Unit	Tokushima	中部 83
144th Infantry Regiment Repl. Unit	Kochi	中部 84
55th Cavalry Regt Replacement Unit	Zentsuji	中部 85

55th Depot Division / Zentsuji Divisional District continued

Unit	Location	Barracks # (Personnel)
55th Mtn Arty Regt Replacement Unit	Zentsuji	中部 86
55th Engineer Regt Replacement Unit	Zentsuji	中部 87
55th Div. Signal Unit Repl. Unit	Marugame	中部 88
55th Transport Regiment Repl. Unit	Zentsuji	中部 89

Reorganized on Feb 6, 1945

Zentsuji Divisional District HQ	Zentsuji	

Renamed on Jun 12 1945   Seibu

Unit	Location	Barracks # (Personnel)
Shikoku 1st Inf. Replacement Unit	Marugame	西部 149 (3,202)
Shikoku 2nd Inf. Replacement Unit	Tokushima	西部 150 (3,202)
Shikoku 3rd Inf. Replacement Unit	Kochi	西部 155 (3,202)
Shikoku Artillery Replacement Unit	Zentsuji	西部 156 (759)
Shikoku Engineer Replacement Unit	Zentsuji	西部 157 (705)
Shikoku Signal Replacement Unit	Marugame	西部 158 (345)
Shikoku Transport Replacement Unit	Zentsuji	西部 159 (659)

Major units supplied by the Zentsuji Divisional District include:
11th Div., 40th Div., 55th Div., 45th I.M.B., 62nd I.M.B., 13th Ind. Inf. Bgde

Takamatsu Regimental District: Kagawa Prefecture Administrative District
Takamatsu District   四国 *Shikoku*

Unit	Barracks # (Personnel)	Location
Takamatsu District 1st Specially Est. Garrison Unit	6485 (300)	Takamatsu City
Takamatsu District 2nd Specially Est. Garrison Unit	6486 (300)	Takamatsu City
Takamatsu District 3rd Specially Est. Garrison Unit	6487 (300)	Sakaide City
Takamatsu District 4th Specially Est. Garrison Unit	6488 (300)	Marugame City
Takamatsu District 5th Specially Est. Garrison Unit	6489 (300)	Okawa-gun
Takamatsu District 6th Specially Est. Garrison Unit	6490 (300)	Hirai-machi
Takamatsu District 7th Specially Est. Garrison Unit	6491 (300)	Anzukawa-gun
Takamatsu District 8th Specially Est. Garrison Unit	6492 (300)	Takinomiya-mura
Takamatsu District 9th Specially Est. Garrison Unit	6493 (300)	Kotohira-machi
Takamatsu District 10th Sp. Est. Garrison Unit	6494 (300)	Kamitakase-mura
Takamatsu District 11th Sp. Est. Garrison Unit	6495 (300)	Mitoyo-gun
Takamatsu District 12th Sp. Est. Garrison Unit	6496 (300)	Mitoyo-gun
Takamatsu District 13th Sp. Est. Garrison Unit	32325 (92)	Tawa-mura
Takamatsu District 14th Sp. Est. Garrison Unit	32326 (92)	Yasuhara-mura
Takamatsu District 15th Sp. Est. Garrison Unit	32327 (92)	Mitoyo-gun

Tokushima Regimental District: Tokushima Prefecture Administrative District
Tokushima District: 四国 *Shikoku*

Unit	Barracks # (Personnel)	Location
Tokushima District 1st Specially Est. Garrison Unit	6540 (300)	Tokushima City
Tokushima District 2nd Specially Est. Garrison Unit	6541 (300)	Itano-gun
Tokushima District 3rd Specially Est. Garrison Unit	6542 (300)	Ishii-machi

Tokushima District 4th Specially Est. Garrison Unit	6543 (300)	Kawashima-ma
Tokushima District 5th Specially Est. Garrison Unit	6544 (300)	Awa-gun
Tokushima District 6th Specially Est. Garrison Unit	6545 (300)	Waki-machi
Tokushima District 7th Specially Est. Garrison Unit	6546 (300)	Shinko-machi
Tokushima District 8th Specially Est. Garrison Unit	6547 (300)	Ikeda-machi
Tokushima District 9th Specially Est. Garrison Unit	6548 (300)	Hanenowa-machi
Tokushima District 10th Sp. Est. Garrison Unit	6549 (300)	Tomioka-machi
Tokushima District 11th Sp. Est. Garrison Unit	6550 (300)	Kaifu-gun
Tokushima District 12th Sp. Est. Garrison Unit	6551 (300)	Kaifu-gun

Matsuyama Regimental District: Ehime Prefecture Administrative District
Matsuyama District　　　　　　　　　　　四国 *Shikoku*

Matsuyama District 1st Specially Est. Garrison Unit	6510 (300)	Araihama City
Matsuyama District 2nd Sp. Est. Garrison Unit	6511 (300)	Saijo City
Matsuyama District 3rd Sp. Est. Garrison Unit	6512 (300)	Imabari City
Matsuyama District 4th Sp. Est. Garrison Unit	6513 (300)	Matsuyama City
Matsuyama District 5th Sp. Est. Garrison Unit	6514 (300)	Yawatahama City
Matsuyama District 6th Sp. Est. Garrison Unit	6515 (300)	Uwajima City
Matsuyama District 7th Sp. Est. Garrison Unit	6516 (300)	Uma-gun
Matsuyama District 8th Sp. Est. Garrison Unit	6517 (300)	Izumikawa-machi
Matsuyama District 9th Sp. Est. Garrison Unit	6518 (300)	Tanbara-machi
Matsuyama District 10th Sp. Est. Garrison Unit	6519 (300)	Onsen-gun
Matsuyama District 11th Sp. Est. Garrison Unit	6520 (300)	Kuninaka-machi
Matsuyama District 12th Sp. Est. Garrison Unit	6521 (300)	Hisakata-machi
Matsuyama District 13th Sp. Est. Garrison Unit	6522 (300)	Oosu-machi
Matsuyama District 14th Sp. Est. Garrison Unit	6523 (300)	Higashiuwa-gun
Matsuyama District 15th Sp. Est. Garrison Unit	6524 (300)	Nishiuwa-gun
Matsuyama District 16th Sp. Est. Garrison Unit	6525 (300)	Kitauwa-gun
Matsuyama District 17th Sp. Est. Garrison Unit	6526 (300)	Kitauwa-gun
Matsuyama District 18th Sp. Est. Garrison Unit	6527 (300)	Minamiuwa-gun
Matsuyama District 19th Sp. Est. Garrison Unit	6528 (300)	Tsukawa-machi
Matsuyama District 20th Sp. Est. Garrison Unit	32330 (300)	Kawakami-mura

Kochi Regimental District: Kochi Prefecture Administrative District
Kochi District　　　　　　　　　　　智 *Tomo*

228th Specially Established Garrison Company	6460 (126)	Aki-gun
229th Specially Established Garrison Company	6466 (126)	Shimizu-chō

四国 *Shikoku*

Kochi District 1st Specially Est. Garrison Unit	6560 (300)	Kochi City
Kochi District 2nd Specially Est. Garrison Unit	6561 (300)	Aki-chō
Kochi District 3rd Specially Est. Garrison Unit	6562 (300)	Noichi-chō
Kochi District 4th Specially Est. Garrison Unit	6563 (300)	Motoyama-chō
Kochi District 5th Specially Est. Garrison Unit	6564 (300)	Takaoka-gun

Kochi District continued   四国 *Shikoku*

Kochi District 6th Specially Est. Garrison Unit	6565 (300)	Suzaki-chō
Kochi District 10th Specially Est. Garrison Unit	6569 (300)	Aki-gun
Kochi District 11th Specially Est. Garrison Unit	32335 (300)	Tosa-gun
Kochi District 12th Specially Est. Garrison Unit	32336 (300)	Gokawa-gun
Kochi District 7th Specially Est. Garrison Unit	6566 (300)	Kubokawa-chō
Kochi District 8th Specially Est. Garrison Unit	6567 (300)	Nakamura-chō
Kochi District 9th Specially Est. Garrison Unit	6568 (300)	Sukumo-chō

Kyushu

Chapter 2

16th Area Army / Seibu Army District 睦 *Mutsumi*

The 16th Area Army headquarters was activated in Fukuoka on January 22, 1945, from former Western District Army personnel. It served under Defense General Headquarters from Feb 6th until Apr 8th and 2nd General Army until the war ended. 16th Area Army headquarters were located in Fukuoka under Lt Gen Isamu Yokoyama from February. 2nd until it was deactivated on October 15th.

Subordinate armies / duty dates:
57th Army from Apr 8, 1945, until Oct 16, 1945
56th Army from Apr 21, 1945, until Oct 15, 1945
40th Army from May 14, 1945, until Sept 29, 1945

Service History:
1945: On Jan 22nd the 16th Area Army was activated in Fukuoka to replace the Western District Army ○ Feb 2nd, Lt Gen Isamu Yokoyama became 16th Area Army commander ○ On Feb 6th the three command HQ were deactivated and replaced by five area armies for operations and five administrative military districts. The 16th Area Army was made responsible for the Western Army District (Kyushu) and placed under the Defense General Army ○ On Apr 8th the 16th Area Army was placed under 2nd General Army command and the 57th Army placed under its control ○ Apr 21st the 56th Army was placed into the 16th Area Army's order of battle ○ On May 14th the 40th Army HQ in Formosa joined the 16th Area Army's order of battle ○ On Aug 15th Japan surrendered. The 16th Area Army on Kyushu, with the subordinate 57th, 56th and 40th Armies had a total of 478,192 members ○ On Oct 15th the 16th Area Army was deactivated in Fukuoka ○

Major Units: See division / brigade page for order of battle

Unit	Page
25th Division Tonei 1940 国 *Kuni* – In transit to Kobayashi	207
57th Division Hirosaki 1940 奥 *Oku* –Fukuoka, in transit to 1st General Army	210
77th Division Asahikawa 1944 稔 *Minoru* – Kajiki	214-5
206th Division Kumamoto 1945 阿蘇 *Aso* – South Kyoto	243
216th Division Kyoto 1945 比叡 *Hiei* – Fukuoka	245
107th Independent Mixed Brigade 1945 堡 *Ho* – Yamaguchi	268
118th Independent Mixed Brigade 1945 堅塁 *Kenrui* – Saganoseki	272
122nd Independent Mixed Brigade 1945 堅城 *Kenjō* – Nagasaki	273
126th Independent Mixed Brigade 1945 敬忠 *Keichu* – Amakusa	275
4th Anti-Aircraft Division 1945 彗 *Sui* – Kokura	257

Units under the 16th Area Army: Fukuoka   睦 *Mutsumi*

Unit	Code	Location
16th Area Army Headquarters	13500 (525)	Fukuoka
18th Independent Mountain Artillery Regiment	15117 (2,981)	Takase
9th Independent Heavy Artillery Battalion	1023 (538)	Jitogun
433rd Independent Infantry Battalion	42346 (1,036)	Amakusa
434th Independent Infantry Battalion	42347 (1,036)	Amakusa
435th Independent Infantry Battalion	42348 (1,036)	Hitoyoshi-ma
3rd Signal Unit Headquarters	13378 (72)	Tashiro-machi
7th Signal Regiment	5091 / 4362 (1,098)	Tashiro
52nd Signal Regiment	13512 (1,098)	Hitoyoshi
5th Short Wave Signal Company	13514 (159)	Fukuoka
1st Independent Signal Labor Unit	27390 (302)	

16th Area Army: continued   睦 *Mutsumi*

Unit	Code	Location
2nd Independent Signal Labor Unit	27391 (302)	
3rd Independent Signal Labor Unit	27392 (302)	
11th Independent Signal Labor Unit	36410 (302)	
12th Independent Signal Labor Unit	36411 (302)	
56th to 60th Independent Signal Labor Units	15124-8 (302 each)	
61st to 65th Independent Signal Labor Units	42355-9 (302 each)	
66th and 67th Independent Signal Labor Units	15129-30 (302 each)	
71st to 75th Independent Signal Labor Units	42360-4 (302 each)	
11th Engineer Unit Headquarters	13511 (93)	Tamana-gun
89th Independent Engineer Battalion	36390 (870)	Kumamoto City
123rd Independent Engineer Battalion	15123 (891)	Yamagun
124th Independent Engineer Battalion	42354 (891)	Kumamoto
59th Line of Communications Sector Command	7070 (203)	Hitoyoshi-machi
59th Line of Communications Duty Unit	7171 (511)	Hitoyoshi-machi
59th Line of Communications Guard Unit	7170 (1,035)	
9th Field Transport Headquarters	3646 (37)	Kumamoto
56th Independent Motor Transport Battalion	6420 (750)	Shonai-machi
84th Independent Motor Transport Battalion	7574 (750)	Shonai-machi
27th Sea Transport Battalion	15140 (548)	Moji
28th Sea Transport Battalion	42365 (542)	
30th Sea Transport Battalion	29140 (548)	
26th Shipping Engineer Regiment, 3rd Company	16744 (329)	Anami Oshima
31st Sea Raiding Squadron	19846 (92)	
32nd Sea Raiding Squadron	19847 (92)	
33rd Sea Raiding Squadron	19848 (92)	
34th Sea Raiding Squadron	19849 (92)	
35th Sea Raiding Squadron	19850 (92)	
36th Sea Raiding Squadron	19851 (92)	
37th Sea Raiding Squadron	19852 (92)	
38th Sea Raiding Squadron	19853 (92)	
1st Sea Raiding Maintenance Unit	19866 (399)	
2nd Sea Raiding Maintenance Unit	19867 (399)	
3rd Sea Raiding Maintenance Unit	19868 (399)	
4th Sea Raiding Maintenance Unit	19869 (399)	
5th Sea Raiding Maintenance Unit	19870 (399)	
6th Sea Raiding Maintenance Unit	19871 (399)	
7th Sea Raiding Maintenance Unit	19872 (399)	
8th Sea Raiding Maintenance Unit	19873 (399)	
16th Field Duty Headquarters	8866 (17)	Yoshimatsu
50th Field Road Construction Unit	5530 (304)	Sueyoshi-machi
119th Line of Communications Hospital	2206 (359)	Takasaki
Tsushima Fortress Headquarters	No # (182)	Tsushima
Tsushima Fortress Heavy Artillery Regiment	2736 (1,658)	Tsushima
1st Tsushima Fortress Infantry Battalion	2730 (826)	Kaichi
2nd Tsushima Fortress Infantry Battalion	2731 (826)	Kaichi

3rd Tsushima Fortress Infantry Battalion	2732 (826)	Kaichi
4th Tsushima Fortress Infantry Battalion	15134 (826)	Kaichi
5th Tsushima Fortress Infantry Battalion	15135 (826)	Kaichi
6th Tsushima Fortress Infantry Battalion	15136 (826)	Kaichi
216th Specially Established Garrison Company	9765 (126)	Nitta-chō
217th Specially Established Garrison Company	9766 (126)	Kamiagata-gun
202nd Specially Established Garrison Battalion	6790 (550)	Huke

Kagoshima

40th Army 陽 *Yo*

The 40th Army was activated in southern Formosa Jan 8, 1945. On Jan 12th Lt Gen Mitsuo Nakazawa was appointed 40th Army commander. Headquarters in Taihoku, Formosa with the 10th Area Army from Jan 16th until May 14th, redeployed to Ijūin, Kagoshima in Kyushu under the 16th Area Army until it was deactivated on Sept 29th.

Service History:
1945: Jan 8th the 40th Army HQ was activated in southern Formosa ○ On Jan 16th the 40th Army, with its headquarters deployed to Taihoku, became subordinate to the 10th Area Army ○ On Jan 12th Lt Gen Mitsuo Nakazawa became commander of the 40th Army ○ May 14th, the 40th Army HQ redeployed from Formosa to Ijūin, Kyushu (to fill a tactical gap) and placed under the 16th Area Army's control ○ On June 19th the 146th, 303rd Div and 125th I.M.B. were subordinated to the 40th Army ○ On Sept 29th the 40th Army was deactivated ○

Major Units: See division / brigade page for order of battle
146th Division Kumamoto 1945 護南 *Gonan* – Oguchi, Kagoshima		234-5
303rd Division Nagoya 1945 高師 *Takashi* – Kagoshima		249-50
125th Independent Mixed Brigade 1945 敬天 *Keiten* – Ibusuki, Kagoshima		274

Units under control of the 40th Army: Ijūin	陽 *Yo*	
40th Army Headquarters	21300 (264)	Ijuin
40th Army Headquarters Signal Section	21300 (33)	Iijuin
13th Independent Tank Company	12635 (66)	
4th Artillery Headquarters	21643 (113)	Kawauchi
44th Independent Heavy Artillery Battalion	12588 (453)	Kajiyada-gun
28th Field Medium Artillery Regiment	14318 (2,283)	Oguchi
20th Field Medium Artillery Battalion	21794 (700)	Ijuin
8th Self-Propelled Artillery Battalion	2829 (481)	Kawachi City
21st Trench Mortar Battalion	28321 (1,361)	Shikoku
24th Trench Mortar Battalion	15118 (1,361)	Kawabe-gun
25th Trench Mortar Battalion	42350 (1,361)	Kawabe-gun
61st Independent Machine Cannon Company	12504 (71)	Hitoyoshi-machi
43rd Signal Regiment	13379 (1,825)	Miyamojo
104th Independent Engineer Battalion	21735 (891)	
122nd Independent Engineer Battalion	42353 (891)	Kogoshima
9th Independent Field Artillery Regiment	15116 (1,859)	Takase
206th Specially Established Garrison Company	7091 (126)	Satsuma-gun

Northern Kyushu

56th Army 宗 *Shuu*

The 56th Army was activated in Iizuka, Fukuoka on March 31, 1945. Its headquarters in Iizuka on April 21st the 56th Army was subordinated to the 16th Area Army. It's commander, Lt. Gen. Ichirō Shichida, was appointed on Apr 15th and retired when the army was deactivated on Oct 15th.

Service History:
1945: Mar 31st, the 56th Army HQ was activated in Iizuka, Fukuoka ○ On Apr 15th Lt. Gen. Ichiro Shichida was made the 56th Army's commander ○ Apr 21st, 56th Army headquarters in Iizuka was placed into the 16th Area Army's order of battle. The 145th Div., 4th Ind Armored Bgde, Iki and Shimonoseki Fortresses were placed under the 56th Army's command ○ June 19th, the 312th and 351st Div were placed under the 56th Army's command ○ On Oct 15th the 56th Army was deactivated in Iizuka ○

Major Units: See division / brigade page for order of battle

Unit		Code	Location	Page
145th Division Hiroshima 1945 護州	*Gosyu*	– Ashiya, Fukuoka		234
312th Division Kureme 1945 千歳	*Chitose*	– Imari, Saga		250
351st Division Utsunomiya 1945 赤城	*Akagi*	– Koga, Fukuoka		252-3
4th Independent Armored Brigade 1945 鑿	*Saku*	– Fukumaru, Fukuoka		283

Units under control of the 56th Army: Iizuka   宗 *Shuu*

Unit	Code	Location
56th Army Headquarters	13580 (222)	Iizuka
46th Independent Tank Regiment	12546 (368)	Fukushima
6th Artillery Headquarters	28401 (119)	Katsuyagun
10th Field Medium Artillery Regiment	1014 (1,649)	Sue
29th Field Medium Artillery Regiment	13505 (2,263)	Ebitsu
19th Field Medium Artillery Battalion	21793 (700)	Higashimatsura
1st Self-Propelled Artillery Battalion	36380 (478)	Iizuka City
12th Trench Mortar Battalion	21763 (1,407)	Sozogun
27th Trench Mortar Battalion	15120 (1,407)	Sozogun
1st Artillery Intelligence Regiment	1221 (570)	Chojahara
44th Signal Regiment	13557 (1,803)	Iitsuka
71st Independent Engineer Battalion	14173 (814)	Sozogun
90th Independent Engineer Battalion	36391 (870)	Sozogun
119th Independent Engineer Battalion	15121 (891)	Higashimatsura
11th Tractor Company	2609 (145)	Kokura
60th Line of Comm. Sector Command	5124 (203)	Iizuka
60th Line of Communications Duty Unit	5124 (511)	Iizuka
60th Line of Communications Guard Unit	5124 (1,035)	
68th Independent Motor Transport Battalion	4464 (808)	Orio-machi
31st Field Duty Unit Command	13540 (17)	North Kyushu
137th Land Duty Unit	13541 (511)	Himenohama
138th Land Duty Unit	13542 (511)	Enohara
139th Land Duty Unit	13543 (511)	Shimogata
140th Land Duty Unit	13544 (511)	Karatsu
141st Land Duty Unit	13545 (511)	Karatsu
142nd Land Duty Unit	13546 (511)	Conoura

56th Army continued

Unit	Number	Location
143rd Land Duty Unit	13547 (511)	Hidakachi
33rd Construction Duty Company	7852 (511)	Keho
Iki Fortress Headquarters	No # (179)	Iki Island
Iki Fortress Heavy Artillery Regiment	2737 (1,371)	Iki Island
1st Iki Fortress Infantry Battalion	2745 (826)	Iki Island
2nd Iki Fortress Infantry Battalion	2746 (826)	Iki Island
3rd Iki Fortress Infantry Battalion	2747 (826)	Iki Island
4th Iki Fortress Infantry Battalion	2748 (826)	Iki Island
5th Iki Fortress Infantry Battalion	2749 (826)	Iki Island
6th Iki Fortress Infantry Battalion	2750 (826)	Iki Island
7th Iki Fortress Infantry Battalion	15137 (826)	Iki Island
8th Iki Fortress Infantry Battalion	15138 (826)	Iki Island
9th Iki Fortress Infantry Battalion	15139 (826)	Iki Island
219th Specially Established Garrison Company	9768 (126)	Takeumi
Shimonoseki Fortress Headquarters	No # (159)	Shimonoseki
Shimonoseki Heavy Artillery Regiment	2735 (883)	Shimonoseki
21st Security Battalion	7097 (853)	Kokura
254th Specially Established Garrison Battalion	2741 (550)	Shimonoseki
201st Specially Established Engineer Unit	2761 (930)	Shimonoseki

Southern Kyushu

57th Army 鋒 *Ho*

The 57th Army was activated in Takarabe, Kagoshima Prefecture on March 31, 1945 and placed under 16th Area Army command on Apr 8th. Headquarters in Takarabe, Kyushu under Lt Gen Kanji Nishihara who was appointed commander Apr 6th remaining until the 57th Army was deactivated on Oct 16th.

Service History:
1945: On Mar 31st the 57th Army was activated in Takarabe to defend Miyazake Prefecture and Osumi Peninsula ○ On Apr 6th Lt Gen Kanji Nishihara became the 57th Army's commander ○ On Apr 8th the 57th Army became subordinate to the 16th Area Army. The 86th, 146th, 154th 156th Div, 98th I.M.B. 5th and 6th Independent Armored Brigade. were placed into the 57th Army's order of battle ○ May 1st the 3rd Amphibious Brigade was attached to the 57th Army ○ May 14th the 109th I.M.B. joined the 57th Army ○ In June the headquarters for the 4th Anti Aircraft Division redeployed to Takarabe and was placed under 57th Army control ○ On Oct 16th the 57th Army was deactivated in Takarabe ○

Major Units: See division / brigade page for order of battle

Unit	Page
86th Division Kurume 1944 積 *Seki* – Miyakonojo, Shibushi	217
154th Division Hiroshima 1945 護路 *Goro* – south Kyushu	238
156th Division Kurume 1945 護西 *Gosei* – Miyazaki	239
212th Division Kurume 1945 菊池 *Kikuike* – Miyazaki	24
98th Independent Mixed Brigade 1945 堅志 *Kenoi* – Kumamoto	266-7
109th Independent Mixed Brigade 1945 劍閃 *Kensen* – Tanegashima	269

5th Independent Tank Brigade 1945 躍 *Yaku* – Honjo, Kagoshima 280
6th Independent Tank Brigade 1945 闘 *Tou* – Kirishima, Kagoshima 281

<u>Units under control of the 57th Army</u>: Takanabe   鋒 *Ho*

Unit	Code	Location
57th Army Headquarters	13590 (388)	Takarabe
23rd Independent Mixed Regiment	7074	Tanegashima (Is.)
1st Artillery Headquarters	3870 (117)	Miyazaki-gun
13th Field Medium Artillery Regiment	12581 (1,082)	Kakikihara
54th Field Medium Artillery Regiment	12583	
28th Independent Field Artillery Battalion	14235 (528)	Jitogun
40th Independent Heavy Artillery Battalion	13561 (392)	Jitogun
43rd Independent Heavy Artillery Battalion	28388 (453)	Umekitada
5th Self-Propelled Artillery Battalion	21790 (481)	Sumiyoshi-ma
7th Self-Propelled Artillery Regiment	28249 (481)	Sadohara-machi
2nd Rocket Launcher Battalion	12383 (845)	Miyazaki
4th Trench Mortar Battalion	36372 (1,465)	Miyazaki-gun
20th Trench Mortar Battalion	28372 (1,414)	Kitashoken-g
26th Trench Mortar Battalion	15119 (1,407)	Fukuoka City
28th Trench Mortar Battalion	42351 (1,407)	Miyazaki City
6th Artillery Intelligence Regiment	12402 (667)	Kubokami
54th Field Heavy Artillery Regiment	12583 (1,773)	Yasuhisa
19th Independent Mountain Artillery Regiment	42349 (2,981)	Takase
41st Signals Regiment	13556 (1,814)	Shonai
3rd Engineer Unit Headquarters	1271 (167)	Takarabe-machi
72nd Independent Engineer Battalion	15052 (814)	Takarabe-machi
82nd Independent Engineer Battalion	27403 (884)	Takarabe-machi
120th Independent Engineer Battalion	42352 (891)	Miyakonojo
121st Independent Engineer Battalion	15122 (891)	Kureme
12th Tractor Company	2610 (80)	Sadohara
7th Field Transport Headquarters	5071 (37)	Hitashoken
65th Line of Communications Sector Command	6711 (203)	Nishishoken
65th Line of Communications Duty Unit	6713 (511)	Nishishoken
65th Line of Communications Guard Unit	6712 (1,035)	
34th Independent Motor Transport Battalion	5864 (808)	Shonai-machi
4th Field Construction Command	5204 (40)	Shomai-machi
13th Field Construction Command	6916 (17)	Otobusa
44th Construction Duty Company	5727 (511)	
45th Construction Duty Company	5728 (511)	Shomai-machi
32nd Field Construction Command	13548 (17)	Okawa-machi
144th Land Duty Company	13549 (511)	Saga City
145th Land Duty Company	13550 (511)	Hirado-machi
146th Land Duty Company	13551 (511)	Okawa-machi
147th Land Duty Company	13552 (511)	Okawa-machi
148th Land Duty Company	13553 (511)	Hirado
149th Land Duty Company	13554 (511)	Imari
150th Land Duty Company	13555 (511)	Fukue
99th Line of Communications Hospital	6946 (359)	Kobayashi

57ᵗʰ Army continued

204ᵗʰ Specially Established Garrison Company	7089 (126)	Nobeoka City
205ᵗʰ Specially Established Garrison Company	7090 (126)	Yutsu-chō
207ᵗʰ Specially Established Garrison Company	7092 (126)	Kamiyaku-mura
208ᵗʰ Specially Established Garrison Company	7093 (126)	Shimoyaku-mura

Amami Oshima Detachment: 球 *Kyu*

Amami Oshima Island: (organized 3/24/44 in Omura, Japan)

6ᵗʰ Medium Artillery Regiment	2740 (997) detach 64ᵗʰ I.M.B.
220ᵗʰ Specially Established Garrison Company	7075 (126) Kasari-chō
221ˢᵗ Specially Established Garrison Company	7076 (126) Nase-chō
222ⁿᵈ Specially Established Garrison Company	7077 (126) Ōshima-gun
Amami Oshima Army Hospital	unknown (40)

Tokunoshima Island

64ᵗʰ Independent Mixed Brigade Tokunoshima	球 *Kyu* (7,643)
36ᵗʰ Signal Regiment, one wire and one radio pltn	18830 (110)
71ˢᵗ Land Duty Company	4831 (511)
75ᵗʰ Airfield Company	18482 (226)
26ᵗʰ Shipping Engineer Regiment, 3ʳᵈ Company	16744 (329)
Tokunoshima Army Hospital	unknown (40)

On June 24, 1945, following the destruction of the 32ⁿᵈ Army on Okinawa, the Amami Jima Detachment was placed under 57ᵗʰ Army control. Kikaigashima, Okino Erabu Jima and Yoron Jima also had small contingents of troops from the 64ᵗʰ I.M.B.

Seibu Army District:

Seibu Army District:
Kyushu Area

Seibu Army District Headquarters	Fukuoka	西部 (1,137)

Kurume Divisional District:

Kurume Divisional District HQ	Kurume	西部 (271)

Recruiting and home defense units

56ᵗʰ Depot Division / Kurume Divisional District

Unit	Location	Barracks # (Personnel)
56ᵗʰ Division Headquarters	Kurume	*Seibu*
113ᵗʰ Infantry Regt Replacement Unit	Fukuoka	西部 46
146ᵗʰ Infantry Regiment Repl Unit	Omura	西部 47
148ᵗʰ Infantry Regiment Repl Unit	Kurume	西部 48
56ᵗʰ Recon Regt Replacement Unit	Kurume	西部 50
56ᵗʰ Field Arty. Regiment Repl. Unit	Kurume	西部 51
56ᵗʰ Engineer Regt Replacement Unit	Kurume	西部 52
56ᵗʰ Div Signal Unit Repl. Unit	Kurume	西部 53

56th Depot Division / Kurume Divisional District continued

Unit	Location	Barracks # (Personnel)
56th Transport Regiment Repl. Unit	Kurume	西部 54
Reorganized		*Seibu*
Kurume 1st Inf Replacement Unit	Kurume	西部 148 (3,202)
Kurume 2nd Inf Replacement Unit	Fukuoka	西部 146 (3,202)
Kurume 3rd Inf Replacement Unit	Omura	西部 147 (3,202)
Kurume Artillery Replacement Unit	Kurume	西部 151 (759)
Kurume Engineer Replacement Unit	Kurume	西部 152 (705)
Kurume Signal Replacement Unit	Kurume	西部 153 (345)
Kurume Transport Replacement Unit	Kurume	西部 154 (659)

Major units supplied by the Kurume Divisional District:

Unit	Location	Barracks # (Personnel)
2nd Signal Regt Replacement Unit	Sarushi	西部 81 (511)
5th Fld Med Arty Regiment Repl Unit	Kokura	西部 72 (1,069)
6th Fld Med Arty Regiment Repl Unit	Kokura	西部 73 (1,067)
Sasebo Artillery Regiment Repl Unit	Sasebo	西部 75 (634)
Shimonoseki Artillery Regt Rep Unit	Kurume	西部 49
18th Tank Regt Replacement Unit	Shimonoseki	西部 (983)

Fukuoka Regimental District: Fukuoka Prefecture Administrative District

Fukuoka District Headquarters	No # (55)	Fukuoka City

Fukuoka District: 西部 *Seibu*

Unit	Barracks # (Personnel)	Location
Fukuoka District 1st Specially Est. Garrison Unit	15143 (300)	Hachiya-chō
Fukuoka District 2nd Specially Est. Garrison Unit	15144 (300)	Yakihashi-chō
Fukuoka District 3rd Specially Est. Garrison Unit	15145 (300)	Komorie, Moji
Fukuoka District 4th Specially Est. Garrison Unit	15146 (300)	Ogura City
Fukuoka District 5th Specially Est. Garrison Unit	15147 (300)	Tobata City
Fukuoka District 6th Specially Est. Garrison Unit	15148 (300)	Yahata City
Fukuoka District 7th Specially Est. Garrison Unit	15149 (300)	Wakamatsu City
Fukuoka District 8th Specially Est. Garrison Unit	20904 (300)	Yahata City
Fukuoka District 9th Specially Est. Garrison Unit	20905 (300)	Tōgo-chō
Fukuoka District 10th Specially Est. Garrison Unit	20906 (300)	Nogata City
Fukuoka District 11th Specially Est. Garrison Unit	20907 (300)	Wakamiya-chō
Fukuoka District 12th Specially Est. Garrison Unit	20908 (300)	Togawa City
Fukuoka District 13th Specially Est. Garrison Unit	20909 (300)	Ishizuka City
Fukuoka District 14th Specially Est. Garrison Unit	20910 (300)	Osamu-chō
Fukuoka District 15th Specially Est. Garrison Unit	20911 (300)	Kasuya-gun
Fukuoka District 16th Specially Est. Garrison Unit	20912 (300)	Futsukaichi-chō
Fukuoka District 17th Specially Est. Garrison Unit	20913 (300)	Fukuoka City
Fukuoka District 18th Specially Est. Garrison Unit	20914 (300)	Fukuoka City
Fukuoka District 19th Specially Est. Garrison Unit	20915 (300)	Maebara-chō
Fukuoka District 20th Specially Est. Garrison Unit	20916 (300)	Amaki-chō
Fukuoka District 21st Specially Est. Garrison Unit	20917 (300)	Yoshii-chō

Fukuoka District continued

Fukuoka District 22nd Specially Est. Garrison Unit	20918 (300)	Mitsu-gun
Fukuoka District 23rd Specially Est. Garrison Unit	20919 (300)	Kurume City
Fukuoka District 24th Specially Est. Garrison Unit	20920 (300)	Shirojima-chō
Fukuoka District 25th Specially Est. Garrison Unit	20921 (300)	Fukushima-chō
Fukuoka District 26th Specially Est. Garrison Unit	20922 (300)	Kuroki-chō
Fukuoka District 27th Specially Est. Garrison Unit	20923 (300)	Sanmon-gun
Fukuoka District 28th Specially Est. Garrison Unit	20924 (300)	Omuta City
22nd Specially Established Garrison Company	7164 (204)	Kasuya-gun
252nd Specially Established Garrison Battalion	6796 (550)	Fukuoka City
203rd Specially Established Garrison Company	6793 (126)	Omuta City
213th Specially Established Garrison Company	6797 (126)	Noogata City
214th Specially Established Garrison Company	6798 (126)	Iizuka City
215th Specially Established Garrison Company	6799 (126)	Saeda-chō
255th Specially Established Garrison Battalion	2742 (550)	Ogura City 56A
256th Specially Established Garrison Battalion	2743 (550)	Yahata City 56A
257th Specially Established Garrison Battalion	2744 (550)	Tobata City 56A
202nd Specially Established Engineer Unit	2762 (930)	Ogura City 56A
203rd Specially Established Engineer Unit	2763 (930)	Yahata City 56A
204th Specially Established Engineer Unit	2764 (930)	Tobata City 56A
208th Specially Established Engineer Unit	2787 (930)	Ashiya-chō
209th Specially Established Engineer Unit	2788 (930)	Fukuoka City
210th Specially Established Engineer Unit	2789 (930)	Mutsui-gun

Saga Regimental District: Saga Prefecture Administrative District

Saga District Headquarters	No # (32)	Saga City
Saga District:	西部 *Seibu*	
Saga District 1st Specially Est. Garrison Unit	20925 (300)	Tosa-chō
Saga District 2nd Specially Est. Garrison Unit	20926 (300)	Kanzaki-chō
Saga District 3rd Specially Est. Garrison Unit	20927 (300)	Saga City
Saga District 4th Specially Est. Garrison Unit	20928 (300)	Saga-gun
Saga District 5th Specially Est. Garrison Unit	20929 (300)	Ojiro-chō
Saga District 6th Specially Est. Garrison Unit	20930 (300)	Takeo-chō
Saga District 7th Specially Est. Garrison Unit	20931 (300)	Kajima-chō
Saga District 8th Specially Est. Garrison Unit	20932 (300)	Karatsu City
Saga District 9th Specially Est. Garrison Unit	20933 (300)	Higashimatsuura
Saga District 10th Specially Est. Garrison Unit	20934 (300)	Imari-chō
201st Specially Established Garrison Company	6791 (126)	Karatsu City 56A
202nd Specially Established Garrison Company	6792 (126)	Imari-chō 56A
211th Specially Established Engineer Unit	2790 (930)	Kanzaki-gun

Nagasaki Regimental District: Nagasaki Prefecture Administrative District
Nagasaki District: 西部 *Seibu*

Nagasaki District: continued　　　　　　　　西部 *Seibu*

Unit	Barracks # (Personnel)	Location
Nagasaki District 1st Specially Est. Garrison Unit	20935 (300)	
Nagasaki District 2nd Specially Est. Garrison Unit	20936 (300)	Hirado-chō
Nagasaki District 3rd Specially Est. Garrison Unit	20937 (300)	Emukai-chō
Nagasaki District 4th Specially Est. Garrison Unit	20938 (300)	Sasebo City
Nagasaki District 5th Specially Est. Garrison Unit	20939 (300)	Ōmura City
Nagasaki District 6th Specially Est. Garrison Unit	20940 (300)	Isahaya City
Nagasaki District 7th Specially Est. Garrison Unit	20941 (300)	Seti-chō
Nagasaki District 8th Specially Est. Garrison Unit	20942 (300)	Nagasaki City
Nagasaki District 9th Specially Est. Garrison Unit	20943 (300)	Shimabara City
Nagasaki District 10th Specially Est. Garrison Unit	20944 (300)	Minamitakago-g
Nagasaki District 11th Specially Est. Garrison Unit	20945 (300)	Iki-gun
Nagasaki District 12th Specially Est. Garrison Unit	20946 (300)	Sasuna-chō
Nagasaki District 13th Specially Est. Garrison Unit	20947 (300)	Shimogata-gun
Nagasaki District 14th Specially Est. Garrison Unit	20948 (300)	Fukue-chō
Nagasaki District 15th Specially Est. Garrison Unit	20949 (300)	Nakadoori-chō
202nd Specially Established Garrison Battalion	6790 (420)	Fukue-chō
253rd Specially Established Garrison Battalion	9764 (550)	Nagasaki C. 56A
Nagasaki District Headquarters	No # (38)	Nagasaki City
Nagasaki District 1st Specially Est. Garrison Unit	20935 (300)	Shisa-chō
216th Specially Established Garrison Company	9765 (126)	Nitta-chō
217th Specially Established Garrison Company	9766 (126)	Kamiagata-gun
218th Specially Established Garrison Company	9767 (126)	Shimokata-gun
219th Specially Established Garrison Company	9768 (126)	Iki-gun
Nagasaki Army Hospital	2781 (16)	Nagasaki

Kumamoto Divisional District:

Kumamoto Divisional District HQ　　Kumamoto　　西部 (281)

Recruiting and home defense units
6th Depot Division / Kumamoto Divisional District:

Unit	Location	Barracks # (Personnel)
6th Depot Division Headquarters	Kumamoto	*Seibu*
13th Infantry Regiment Repl. Unit	Kumamoto	西部 16
23rd Infantry Regiment Repl. Unit	Miyakonojo	西部 17
45th Inf. Regiment Replacement Unit	Kagoshima	西部 18
6th Cavalry Regiment Repl. Unit	Kumamoto	西部 19
6th Field Art. Regiment Repl. Unit	Kumamoto	西部 21
6th Engineer Regiment Repl. Unit	Kumamoto	西部 22
6th Div. Signal Unit Repl. Unit	Kumamoto	西部 23
6th Transport Regiment Repl. Unit	Kumamoto	西部 24
Reorganized on Feb 6, 1945		*Seibu*
Kumamoto 1st Inf. Replacement Unit	Kumamoto	西部 61 (3,202)
Kumamoto 2nd Inf. Replacement Unit	Kumamoto	西部 60 (3,202)
Kumamoto 3rd Inf. Replacement Unit	Kagoshima	西部 18 (3,202)

Kumamoto Divisiona District continued

Kumamoto Artillery Repl. Unit	Kumamoto	西部 21 (759)
Kumamoto Engineer Repl. Unit	Kumamoto	西部 65 (705)
Kumamoto Signal Replacement Unit	Kumamoto	西部 66 (345)
Kumamoto Transport Repl. Unit	Kumamoto	西部 67 (659)

Major units supplied by the Kumamoto Divisional District include:
6th Div., 23rd Div., 37th Div., 46th Div., 58th Div., 102nd Div., 103rd Div.

Kumamoto Regimental District: Kumamoto Prefecture Administrative District

Kumamoto District Headquarters	No # (31)	Kumamoto City

Kumamoto District 西 *Sei*

212th Specially Established Engineer Unit	2791 (930)	Kumamoto City
Kumamoto District 1st Specially Est. Garrison Unit	14353 (300)	Kumamoto City
Kumamoto District 2nd Specially Est. Garrison Unit	14354 (300)	Kawajiri-chō
Kumamoto District 3rd Specially Est. Garrison Unit	14355 (300)	Takase-chō
Kumamoto District 4th Specially Est. Garrison Unit	14356 (300)	Arao City
Kumamoto District 5th Specially Est. Garrison Unit	14357 (300)	Yamaga-chō
Kumamoto District 6th Specially Est. Garrison Unit	14358 (300)	Sumifu-chō
Kumamoto District 7th Specially Est. Garrison Unit	14359 (300)	Aso-gun
Kumamoto District 8th Specially Est. Garrison Unit	14360 (300)	Mifune-chō
Kumamoto District 9th Specially Est. Garrison Unit	14361 (300)	Matsuhashi-chō
Kumamoto District 10th Sp. Est. Garrison Unit	14362 (300)	Miyahara-chō
Kumamoto District 11th Sp. Est. Garrison Unit	14363 (300)	Yatsushiro City
Kumamoto District 12th Sp. Est. Garrison Unit	14364 (300)	Hitoyoshi City
Kumamoto District 13th Sp. Est. Garrison Unit	14365 (300)	Ashikita-gun
Kumamoto District 14th Sp. Est. Garrison Unit	14366 (300)	Misumi-chō
Kumamoto District 15th Sp. Est. Garrison Unit	14367 (300)	Amakusa-gun
Kumamoto District 16th Sp. Est. Garrison Unit	14368 (300)	Tomioka-chō
Kumamoto District 17th Sp. Est. Garrison Unit	14369 (300)	Amakusa-gun

Ōita Regimental District: Ōita Prefecture Administrative District

Ōita District Headquarters	No # (25)	Ōita City

Ōita District: 西 *Nishi*

Ōita District 1st Specially Est. Garrison Unit	14370 (300)	Nakatsu City
Ōita District 2nd Specially Est. Garrison Unit	14371 (300)	Shimoge-gun
Ōita District 3rd Specially Est. Garrison Unit	14372 (300)	Usa-gun
Ōita District 4th Specially Est. Garrison Unit	14373 (300)	Takada-chō
Ōita District 5th Specially Est. Garrison Unit	14374 (300)	Kunisaki-chō
Ōita District 6th Specially Est. Garrison Unit	14375 (300)	Hayami-gun
Ōita District 7th Specially Est. Garrison Unit	14376 (300)	Beppu City
Ōita District 8th Specially Est. Garrison Unit	14377 (300)	Ōita City
Ōita District 9th Specially Est. Garrison Unit	14378 (300)	Usuki-chō

Ōita District continued   西 *Nishi*

Ōita District 10th Specially Est. Garrison Unit	14379 (300)	Saiki City
Ōita District 11th Specially Est. Garrison Unit	14380 (300)	Kamae-chō
Ōita District 12th Specially Est. Garrison Unit	14381 (300)	Minamiamabe-g
Ōita District 13th Specially Est. Garrison Unit	14382 (300)	Mie-chō
Ōita District 14th Specially Est. Garrison Unit	14383 (300)	Taketa-chō
Ōita District 15th Specially Est. Garrison Unit	14384 (300)	Ōita-gun
Ōita District 16th Specially Est. Garrison Unit	14385 (300)	Mori-chō
Ōita District 17th Specially Est. Garrison Unit	14386 (300)	Hida City

Miyazaki Regimental District: Miyazaki Prefecture Administrative District

Miyazaki District Headquarters	No # (25)	Miyazaki City

Miyazaki District: 西 *Nishi*

213th Specially Established Engineer Unit	2792 (1,155)	Kotō-gun
214th Specially Established Engineer Unit	2793 (1,155)	Miyakonojo C
Miyazaki District 1st Specially Est. Garrison Unit	14387 (300)	Nobeoka City
Miyazaki District 2nd Specially Est. Garrison Unit	14388 (300)	Kadogawa-mura
Miyazaki District 3rd Specially Est. Garrison Unit	14389 (300)	Takachiho-chō
Miyazaki District 4th Specially Est. Garrison Unit	14390 (300)	Tomitaka-chō
Miyazaki District 5th Specially Est. Garrison Unit	14391 (300)	Takanabe-chō
Miyazaki District 6th Specially Est. Garrison Unit	14392 (300)	Tsumi-chō
Miyazaki District 7th Specially Est. Garrison Unit	14393 (300)	Miyazaki City
Miyazaki District 8th Specially Est. Garrison Unit	14394 (300)	Miyazaki-gun
Miyazaki District 9th Specially Est. Garrison Unit	14395 (300)	Takaoka-chō
Miyazaki District 10th Specially Est. Garrison Unit	14396 (300)	Kobayashi-chō
Miyazaki District 11th Specially Est. Garrison Unit	14397 (300)	Takashiro-chō
Miyazaki District 12th Specially Est. Garrison Unit	14398 (300)	Mayakonojo C
Miyazaki District 13th Specially Est. Garrison Unit	14399 (300)	Nanyō-chō

Kagoshima Regimental District: Kagoshima Prefecture Administrative District

Kagoshima District Headquarters	No # (31)	Kagoshima City

Kagoshima District: 西 *Nishi*

215th Specially Established Engineer Unit	2794 (130)	Kawanabe-gun
216th Specially Established Engineer Unit	2795 (130)	Chiran-chō
217th Specially Established Engineer Unit	2796 (130)	

剣閃 *Kensen*

257th Specially Established Garrison Battalion	2744 (420)	Kumage-gun

西 *Nishi*

Kagoshima District 1st Specially Est. Garrison Unit	9053 (300)	Demizu-chō
Kagoshima District 2nd Sp. Est. Garrison Unit	9054 (300)	Mizuhiki-chō
Kagoshima District 3rd Specially Est. Garrison Unit	9055 (300)	Sendai City

Kagoshima District continued

Kagoshima District 4th Specially Est. Garrison Unit	9056 (300)	Satsuma-gun
Kagoshima District 5th Specially Est. Garrison Unit	9057 (300)	Hiki-gun
Kagoshima District 6th Specially Est. Garrison Unit	9058 (300)	Hiki-gun
Kagoshima District 7th Specially Est. Garrison Unit	9059 (300)	Kase-chō
Kagoshima District 8th Specially Est. Garrison Unit	9060 (300)	Kawabe-gun
Kagoshima District 9th Specially Est. Garrison Unit	9061 (300)	Yamakawa-chō
Kagoshima District 10th Sp. Est. Garrison Unit	9062 (300)	Hirokawa-chō
Kagoshima District 11th Sp. Est. Garrison Unit	9063 (300)	Kagoshima City
Kagoshima District 12th Sp. Est. Garrison Unit	9064 (300)	Hayato-chō
Kagoshima District 13th Sp. Est. Garrison Unit	9065 (300)	Oguchi-chō
Kagoshima District 14th Sp. Est. Garrison Unit	9066 (300)	Shikaya-chō
Kagoshima District 15th Sp. Est. Garrison Unit	9067 (300)	Kanzoku-gun
Kagoshima District 16th Sp. Est. Garrison Unit	9068 (300)	Takayama-chō
Kagoshima District 17th Sp. Est. Garrison Unit	9069 (300)	Shibushi-chō
Kagoshima District 18th Sp. Est. Garrison Unit	9070 (300)	Kumage-gun
Kagoshima District 19th Sp. Est. Garrison Unit	9071 (300)	Kamiyoku-mura

Okinawa Regimental District: Okinawa Prefecture Administrative District
Okinawa District

220th Specially Established Garrison Company	unknown (126)
221st Specially Established Garrison Company	unknown (126)
222nd Specially Established Garrison Company	unknown (126)

Divisional cavalry / reconnaissance unit on parade (author)

End of 2nd General Army

Air Defense; Mainland Japan

Air General Army 師 Sui

By the end of March 1945 the loss of airplanes, pilots and flight crews had created severe shortages. Air General Army was created from former Inspectorate General of Army Aviation personnel on March 31st. April 7th General Masakazu Kawabe was appointed commander and on April 8th Air General Army was placed under Imperial General Headquarters direction. Headquarters were in Tokyo from April 7th until it had completed the demobilization of its personnel around November 1st.

Subordinate armies / duty dates:
1st Air Army from Apr 8, 1945, until the war ended – Tokyo
2nd Air Army from May 15, 1945, until the war ended – Manchuria
5th Air Army from May 15, 1945, until the war ended – Korea
6th Air Army from May 28, 1945, until the war ended – Fukuoka

Service History:
1944: July 15th the 11th and 12th Air Divisions were activated in Japan, the 11th in Osaka was formed around the 18th Air Brigade and the 12th in Ozuki around the 19th Air Brigade. These two plus the 10th Air Division comprised Japan's main air defense ○
1945: On Mar 31st, to coordinate all air army units in Japan, the Air General Army was formed from former Inspectorate General of Army Aviation personnel ○ From Apr 8th Air Army HQ personnel spent three days organizing. Its order of battle, which came from Imperial HQ, included the 1st Air Army, 6th Air Army, all air training divisions and supply and maintenance depots. All flying schools were closed and the students drafted into active duty units to finish training ○ In April the 6th Air Army was still attached to the Navy's Combined Fleet for Okinawa operations and the 10th and 11th Air Divisions were with the 1st and 2nd General Armies ○ May 2nd, revised plans. Operation *Ketsu-go* had originally been assigned to the 6th Air Army and later reassigned to the 53rd Air Division. The Giretsu Infantry Raiding Brigade was transferred from the 1st Air Army to the 6th to prepare for *Gi-go*, designed to help turn the tide on Okinawa but without success ○ On May 15th the Air Armies in Japan and Manchuria reorganized. The 2nd Air Army with the Kwantung Army, 5th Air Army with the China Expeditionary Army and 1st Air Div with the 5th Area Army came under Air General Army control ○ May 28th the 6th Air Army was released from Combined Fleet control to join the Air General Army. Shikoku was added to 6th Air Army responsibilities and the boundary

dividing it with the 1st Air Army was revised to conform to the boundary dividing the 1st and 2nd General Armies. The 51st Air Div and Akeno Air Instruction Division were placed under 6th Air Army control. The Akeno Division was sent to Shikoku ○ On July 1st Imperial HQ changed its policy of preserving the air force and ordered the interception of enemy bombers in strength. The 10th, 11th and 12th Air Divisions with the 1st and 2nd General Armies were transferred to the Air General Army. To conserve planes Air General Army laid down rules forbidding attacks on non-escort enemy fighters, except in situations that were especially advantageous or necessary ○ From July the Air General Army had full tactical control over Japan's airspace ○ In July the Japan Airways Company was conscripted into the Air General Army, to replace losses in shipping and rail transport, and renamed the Special Air Transport Service. An immediate benefit was the acquisition of Japan Airways experienced maintenance and service personnel ○ In mid-July *Sei-go* provided Japan with a coordinated response to air attacks by deploying mobile and permanent air defense units in strategic areas around the country ○ On July 14th the Army and Navy reached an agreement to cooperate on *Ketsu-go*. In early August there were about 800 fighters and bombers, 2,000 suicide planes and 13,200,000 gallons of aviation fuel available for *Ketsu-Go*.

Under Control of the Air General Army: Tokyo	師 *Sui*	
Air General Army Headquarters	500 (688)	Tokyo
32nd Air Intelligence Unit	1950 (6,825)	Tokyo
33rd Air Intelligence Unit	34216 (3,091)	Nagoya
35th Air Intelligence Unit	7437 (4,401)	Osaka
36th Air Intelligence Unit	8074 (5,596)	Fukuoka
37th Air Intelligence Unit	7440 (3,567)	Korea
8th Air Navigational Aid Unit	19160 (669)	Atsusa
Central Air Traffic Control Department	18918 (3,023)	Hachiogi
11th Underground Construction Unit	7261 (764)	Kurashiki
12th Underground Construction Unit	12359 (764)	Matsuyama
13th Underground Construction Unit	21604 (764)	Kashihara
14th Underground Construction Unit	12477 (764)	Miyagaki
15th Underground Construction Unit	13515 (764)	Kumamoto
16th Underground Construction Unit	12360 (766)	Nasu
17th Underground Construction Unit	12478 (764)	Kumamoto
18th Underground Construction Unit	19501 (764)	Inuyama
19th Underground Construction Unit	19502 (766)	Nara
20th Underground Construction Unit	19503 (764)	Gifu
2nd Ultra Short Wave Signal Company	21637 (159)	
1st Electric Wave Induction Unit	34217 (572)	Kodaira
• 1st Independent Air Unit	34219 (178)	Yachimata
• 4th Independent Air Unit (2nd Ind. A.U.)	19031 (135)	Kashihara
1st Photographic Work Unit	34224 (287)	Shimoshizu
• 28th Independent Air Unit	9160 (144)	Togane
Army Flying School	No # (734)	
102nd Ind. Maintenance Unit (Ki-84, Frank)	18960 (233)	
103rd Independent Maintenance Unit (Ki-84)	18961 (233)	
104th Independent Maintenance Unit (Ki-84)	18962 (233)	

Air General Army continued   師 *Sui*

105th Independent Maintenance Unit (Ki-84)	18963 (233)	
122nd Independent Maintenance Unit (Ki-44, Tojo)	18987 (233)	
123rd Independent Maintenance Unit (Ki-44)	18988 (233)	
127th Independent Maintenance Unit (Ki-45, Nick)	18992 (336)	
131st Independent Maintenance Unit (Ki-81, Tony)	19003 (233)	
135th Ind. Maintenance Unit (Ki-46, Dinah)	19007 (167)	
136th Independent Maintenance Unit (Ki-46)	19008 (167)	
Kamigahara Army Air Depot	34203 (4,463)	Kamigahara
106th Independent Maintenance Unit (Ki-84)	18964 (233)	
107th Independent Maintenance Unit (Ki-84)	18972 (233)	
108th Independent Maintenance Unit (Ki-84)	18973 (233)	
109th Independent Maintenance Unit (Ki-84)	18974 (233)	
128th Independent Maintenance Unit (Ki-45)	18993 (336)	
132nd Independent Maintenance Unit (Ki-81)	19004 (233)	
148th Independent Maintenance Unit (Ki-21, Sally)	19020 (275)	
Osaka Army Air Depot	34204 (2,138)	Osaka
Tachiarai Army Air Depot	34205 (2,792)	Tachiarai
110th Independent Maintenance Unit (Ki-84)	18975 (233)	
111th Independent Maintenance Unit (Ki-84)	18976 (233)	
112th Independent Maintenance Unit (Ki-84)	18977 (233)	
114th Independent Maintenance Unit (Ki-84)	18979 (233)	
124th Independent Maintenance Unit (Ki-44)	18989 (233)	
129th Independent Maintenance Unit (Ki-45)	19001 (336)	
133rd Independent Maintenance Unit (Ki-81)	19005 (233)	
137th Independent Maintenance Unit (Ki-46)	19009 (167)	
144th Independent Maintenance Unit (Ki-48, Lily)	19016 (275)	
147th Ind. Maintenance Unit (Ki-67, Peggy)	19019 (275)	
Utsunomiya Army Air Depot	34206 (2,409)	Utsunomiya
101st Independent Maintenance Unit (Ki-84, Frank)	18959 (233)	
116th Independent Maintenance Unit (Ki-43, Oscar)	18981 (233)	
121st Independent Maintenance Unit (Ki-44)	18986 (233)	
126th Independent Maintenance Unit (Ki-45)	18991 (336)	
130th Independent Maintenance Unit (Ki-81)	19002 (233)	
140th Independent Maintenance Unit (Ki-51, Sonia)	19012 (336)	
143rd Independent Maintenance Unit (Ki-48)	19015 (275)	
146th Independent Maintenance Unit (Ki-67)	19018 (275)	
Pyongyang Army Air Depot	34207 (1,463)	Pyongyang
Osaka Army Air Freight Depot	34209 (3,029)	Osaka
Tokyo Army Air Freight Depot	34208 (1,934)	Tokyo
Shibukawa Army Hospital	unknown (204)	Shibukawa

20th Fighter Brigade Komaki 1945   師 *Sui*

20th Fighter Brigade Headquarters	34220 (320)	Takamatsu
23rd Air Brigade Headquarters	18965 (150)	Komaki

20th Fighter Brigade continued   師 *Sui*
- 5th Air Regiment (fighter)   15310 (543)   Kiyosu
- 111th Air Regiment (fighter)   34217 (411)   Komaki
- 112th Air Regiment (fighter)   34218(411)   Nitta
- 2nd Independent Air Unit (HQ recon)   19029 (178)   Kashiwabara

20th Fighter Group: From the Akeno and Hitachi Air Instruction Divisions deployed in the Tokai area for air defense and as a mobile reserve for the Air General Army.

11th Air Division: Osaka 1944   天鷲 *Amawashi*

11th Air Division Headquarters	1041 (515)	Osaka
• 55th Air Regiment (fighter)	18427 (322)	Sano
• 56th Air Regiment (fighter)	18428 (322)	Itami
• 246th Air Regiment (fighter)	19196 (322)	Taisho
47th Air Sector Command	19351 (44)	Komaki
42nd Airfield Battalion	19197 (273)	Komaki
61st Airfield Battalion	18931 (372)	Hamamatsu
62nd Airfield Battalion	18932 (372)	Sano
143rd Airfield Battalion	18460 (372)	Itami
163rd Airfield Battalion	9930 (372)	Kiyosu
246th Airfield Battalion	19198 (273)	Taisho

11th Air Division: Activated in Osaka on July 15, 1944. Its headquarters in Osaka it was attached to General Defense Headquarters from July 17th until Dec 26th, 6th Air Army until Apr 8, 1945, 1st Air Army until July 18th and Air General Army until the war ended.

51st Air Division: reorganized Feb. 13, 1945, Gifu   空 *Sora*

51st Air Division Headquarters	501 (499)	Gifu
4th Air Training Brigade Headquarters	514 (75)	
1st Secondary Flight Training Unit (air crew)	530 (383)	Kakogawa
10th Secondary Flight Training Unit (air crew)	533 (307)	Gifu
40th Secondary Flight Training Unit (air crew)	538 (344)	Gifu
6th Advanced Flight Training Unit (air crew)	540 (995)	Miki
8th Advanced Flight Training Unit	523 (378)	
10th Advanced Flight Training Unit	524 (394)	North Ise
11th Advanced Flight Training Unit	525 (391)	Medachibaru
7th Primary Flight Training Unit (pilot)	18432	Kyoto
8th Primary Flight Training Unit (pilot)	18423	Tottori
3rd Flight Training Unit	571	
5th Flight Training Unit	573 (1,053)	Tachiarai
6th Flight Training Unit	574	
7th Flight Training Unit	575 (2,737)	
8th Flight Training Unit	576 (3,765)	Yokaichi
9th Flight Training Unit	577 (1,053)	Matsue
1st Gifu Flight Training Unit	563 (1,406)	Gifu

51ˢᵗ Air Division continued   空 *Sora*

2ⁿᵈ Gifu Flight Training Unit	564 (1,628)	Gifu
Nara Flight Training Unit	565 (887)	Nara
Hamamatsu Army Hospital	unknown (86)	
Kakamigahara Army Hospital	unknown (72)	
Matsuyama Army Hospital	unknown (56)	

51ˢᵗ Air Division: Activated in Gifu on Feb 13, 1945. Its headquarters were in Gifu it was attached to 1ˢᵗ Air Army from Feb 20ᵗʰ until Apr 8ᵗʰ and Air General Army until the war ended.

52ⁿᵈ Air Division: reorg. Feb. 13, 1945, Saitama   紺 *Kon*

52ⁿᵈ Air Division Headquarters	502 (395)	Kumagaya
3ʳᵈ Air Training Brigade Headquarters	513 (70)	Tokorozawa
4ᵗʰ Flight Training Unit	572 (339)	Kodama
12ᵗʰ Flight Training Unit	578 (303)	Koriyama
1ˢᵗ Advanced Flight Training Unit	520 (394)	Sagami
4ᵗʰ Secondary Flight Training Unit	531 (482)	Kashiwa
39ᵗʰ Secondary Flight Training Unit	537 (344)	Sayama
Tachikawa Secondary Flight Training Unit	561 (582)	Tashikawa
Tokorozawa Secondary Flight Training Unit	560 (517)	Tokorozawa
Hachinohe Secondary Flight Training Unit	562 (410)	Hachinohe
Tokorozawa Army Hospital	unknown (124)	Tokorozawa
Sendai 2ⁿᵈ Army Hospital	unknown (59)	
Hachinohe Army Hospital	unknown (53)	
Koriyama Army Hospital	unknown (24)	

52ⁿᵈ Air Division: Activated in Kumatani on Feb 13, 1945. Its headquarters were in Kumatani. It was attached to Air General Army from Apr 8ᵗʰ until the war ended.

2ⁿᵈ Air Training Brigade: 中部 *Chubu*

2ⁿᵈ Air Training Brigade Headquarters	512 (54)	Yokkaichi
31ˢᵗ Air Signals Regiment	551 (2,097)	Sasayama
1ˢᵗ Air Intelligence Regiment	552 (2,279)	Iwata
1ˢᵗ Air Navigation Regiment	554 (2,071)	Hino
1ˢᵗ Meteorological Regiment	555 (1,952)	Suzoka
13ᵗʰ Flight Education Unit	579 (2,947)	Takada
1ˢᵗ Army Air Education Unit	581 (1,067)	
Army Airfield Construction Training Department	100 (414)	Toyohashi

2ⁿᵈ Air Training Brigade: Activation date unknown. Attached to the Air General Army from Apr 8, 1945 until the war ended.

1st Air Army 燕 *Tsubame*

The 1st Air Army was activated in Gifu on April 13, 1942. Under General Defense Headquarters from Aug 10th until Apr 13, 1943, Imperial General Headquarters until Apr 8, 1945 and Air General Army until the war ended. 1st Air Army headquarters were located in Gifu from Apr 13th until Apr 7, 1945 then moved to Tokyo for the defence of the skies over northeastern Japan. It was commanded by Lt Gen Takeo Yasuda from June 1, 1942 until May 1, 1943, Lt Gen Kumaichi Teramoto until Jul. 20, 1943, Lt Gen Prince Yi Un until Apr 1, 1945 and Lt Gen Takeo Yasuda until the war ended.

Service History:
1942: April 13th the 1st Air Army was activated in Gifu ○ May 31st the 1st Air Division was activated and placed into the 1st Air Army's order of battle ○ Aug 10th the 1st Air Army was placed under General Defense Headquarters command ○
1943: Feb 5th the 1st Air Div was transferred to the Northern Army on Hokkaido ○
1944: In mid Feb 1st Air Army air units deploy to bases on southern Kyushu, southwest home islands and Formosa to protect shipping and guard against enemy incursions ○
1945: On Apr 8th the 1st Air Army was attached to the newly activated Air General Army in Tokyo and its headquarters relocated there ○ In April the 1st Air Army is Air General Army only front line organization but its main strength, the 10th Air Division, was still under the 1st General Army's control ○ July 1st, the Air General Army finally gained full control over the air space around Japan. The 10th Air Division was returned to the 1st Air Army ○ All personnel had been demobilized by Nov. 1st ○

Units under control of the 1st Air Army: Tokyo	燕 *Tsubame*	
1st Air Army Headquarters	30001 (260)	Tokyo
• 16th Independent Air Unit (HQ recon)	18999 (144)	Kodama
• 28th Independent Air Unit (HQ recon)	9160 (322)	Togane
• 74th Air Regiment (heavy bomber)	9132 (532)	Sakado
12th Air Brigade Headquarters	8320 (51)	Takahagi
• 1st Air Regiment (fighter)	8301 (208)	Takahagi
• 11th Air Regiment (fighter)	8311 (208)	Takahagi
26th Air Brigade Headquarters	34221 (73)	Nasuno
• 3rd Air Regiment (2 engine assault)	18967 (295)	Noshiro
• 45th Air Regiment (2 engine assault)	10654 (295)	Hokoda
16th Air Brigade Headquarters	18422 (28)	Shimodate
• 51st Air Regiment (fighter)	18424 (322)	Shimodate
• 52nd Air Regiment (fighter)	18425 (322)	Shimodate
4th Air Signal Headquarters	16640	Tokyo
7th Air Signal Regiment	19185 (3,501)	Chofu
13th Air Signal Regiment	550 師 (803 +*)	Chofu
2nd Air Special Signal Unit	19156	
1st Wireless Radio Unit	19187 (215)	Tokyo
2nd Wireless Radio Unit	19188 (199)	Tokyo
4th Wireless Radio Unit	18952 (212)	Shimodate
21st Wireless Radio Unit	16621 (196)	Saitama Ken
63rd Wireless Radio Unit	19550 (209)	Chofu
64th Wireless Radio Unit	19551 (209)	Gunma Ken
65th Wireless Radio Unit	19552 (209)	Irumagawa

1st Air Army continued

燕 *Tsubame*

Unit	Number	Location
66th Wireless Radio Unit	19553 (209)	Nasu
67th Wireless Radio Unit	19554 (209)	Kodama
17th Air Sector Command	18927 (50)	M.-Nagano
40th Air Sector Command	18929 (44)	Iwate
66th Airfield Battalion	18935 (372)	Hachinohe
74th Airfield Battalion	18936 (372)	Nishiro
95th Airfield Battalion	18436 (372)	Iwate
144th Airfield Battalion	18461 (372)	Kodama
164th Airfield Battalion	18938 (372)	Kanamaruhara
165th Airfield Battalion	18939 (372)	Nitta
166th Airfield Battalion	18940 (372)	Nitta
169th Airfield Battalion	18941 (372)	Nitta
170th Airfield Battalion	18942 (372)	Tatebayashi
175th Airfield Battalion	18947 (372)	Shimodate
176th Airfield Battalion	18948 (372)	Takamatsu
177th Airfield Battalion	18949 (372)	Nasuno
189th Airfield Battalion	19034 (372)	Miki
190th Airfield Battalion	19035 (372)	Yura
232nd Airfield Battalion	19531 (372)	Matsuyama
233rd Airfield Battalion	19532 (372)	Masuda
234th Airfield Battalion	19533 (372)	Sakato
237th Airfield Battalion	19536 (372)	Yokaichi
238th Airfield Battalion	19537 (372)	Chikugo
239th Airfield Battalion	19538 (372)	Ueki
62nd Air Sector Command	21813 (44)	Matsudo-Saitama
252nd Airfield Battalion	19364 (553)	Kofu
253rd Airfield Battalion	19365 (553)	T.-Shimonasuno
256th Airfield Battalion	21814 (553)	Ishigama
257th Airfield Battalion	21815 (553)	Sayama
258th Airfield Battalion	21816 (553)	T.-Kyohara
56th Airfield Company	18465 (226)	Mie Ken
58th Airfield Company	18467 (226)	Nakatsu
71st Airfield Company	18478 (226)	Izu Oshima
72nd Airfield Company	18479 (226)	Izu Niijima
76th Airfield Company	19539 (226)	Kofu
77th Airfield Company	19540 (226)	Niigata Ken
78th Airfield Company	19541 (226)	Nagano Ken
79th Airfield Company	19542 (226)	Niigata Ken
80th Airfield Company	19543 (226)	Gifu
81st Airfield Company	19544 (226)	Fukui
82nd Airfield Company	19545 (226)	
155th Ind. Maintenance Unit (Ki-43, Oscar)	19163 (233)	Yabuki
160th Ind. Maintenance Unit (Ki-84, Frank)	19164 (233)	Togane
164th Independent Maintenance Unit (Ki-84)	19393 (233)	Nasu
165th Independent Maintenance Unit (Ki-84)	19394 (233)	Nasu

1st Air Army continued

Unit	Number	Location
176th Independent Maintenance Unit (Ki-84)	19061 (233)	Taisho
177th Independent Maintenance Unit (Ki-84)	19062 (233)	Hotarugaike
178th Independent Maintenance Unit (Ki-84)	19063 (233)	Sakato
179th Independent Maintenance Unit (Ki-84)	19064 (233)	Sakato
183rd Ind. Maintenance Unit (Ki-102A, Randy)	19068 (336)	Ibaraki
184th Independent Maintenance Unit (Ki-102A)	19069 (336)	Togane
185th Independent Maintenance Unit (Ki-102A)	19070 (336)	Nasu
186th Independent Maintenance Unit (Ki-102A)	19071 (336)	Nasu
188th Independent Maintenance Unit (Ki-102B)	19073 (336)	Kashihara
190th Independent Maintenance Unit (Ki-102B)	19075 (336)	Nasu
195th Independent Maintenance Unit (Ki-102B)	19167 (336)	Sanoke
196th Ind. Maintenance Unit (Ki-67, Peggy)	19168 (275)	Matsumoto
197th Independent Maintenance Unit (Ki-67)	19077 (275)	Kumamoto
198th Independent Maintenance Unit (Ki-67)	19078 (275)	Yoshizawa
301st Independent Maintenance Unit (Ki-67)	19081 (275)	Ashihara
302nd Independent Maintenance Unit (Ki-21, Sally)	19082 (275)	Tokorozawa
306th Independent Maintenance Unit (Ki-21)	19086 (275)	Namashina
309th Ind. Maintenance Unit (Ki-46, Dinah)	19395 (167)	Kodama
310th Independent Maintenance Unit (Ki-46)	19087 (167)	Fukuoka
311th Independent Maintenance Unit (Ki-46)	19088 (167)	Chiran
314th Independent Maintenance Unit (unknown)	19370 (233)	Tashiarai
315th Independent Maintenance Unit (unknown)	21817 (233)	Togane
3rd Independent Machine Cannon Company	13334	
4th Independent Machine Cannon Company	13335 (138)	
5th Independent Machine Cannon Company	13336 (138)	
6th Independent Machine Cannon Company	13337 (138)	
17th Independent Machine Cannon Company	13338 (138)	
38th Independent Machine Cannon Company	13344 (144)	
39th Independent Machine Cannon Company	13345 (144)	
40th Independent Machine Cannon Company	13346 (144)	
41st Independent Machine Cannon Company	13347 (144)	
45th Independent Machine Cannon Company	21608 (144)	
46th Independent Machine Cannon Company	21609 (144)	
55th Independent Machine Cannon Company	28219 (144)	
56th Independent Machine Cannon Company	28220 (144)	
57th Independent Machine Cannon Company	28221 (144)	
58th Independent Machine Cannon Company	28222 (144)	
59th Independent Machine Cannon Company	28223 (144)	
60th Independent Machine Cannon Company	28224 (144)	
20th Field Airfield Construction Headquarters	15324 (648)	Inba
25th Field Airfield Construction Unit	2406 (702)	Sakato
26th Field Airfield Construction Unit	2407 (701)	Kashigaya
130th Field Airfield Construction Unit	15394 (175)	Kanagawa Ken
131st Field Airfield Construction Unit	15395 (175)	Saitama Ken
132nd Field Airfield Construction Unit	15396 (175)	Kakogawa

1st Air Army continued   燕 *Tsubame*

Unit	Number	Location
141st Field Airfield Construction Unit	18405 (175)	Osaka
147th Field Airfield Construction Unit	18411 (175)	Naruto
148th Field Airfield Construction Unit	18412 (175)	Yamaguchi Ken
149th Field Airfield Construction Unit	18413 (175)	Aichi Ken
150th Field Airfield Construction Unit	18414 (175)	Kiyosa
158th Field Airfield Construction Unit	14236 (356)	Tochigi Ken
159th Field Airfield Construction Unit	3359 (356)	Iwaki
160th Field Airfield Construction Unit	4850 (356)	Ibaraki Ken
162nd Field Airfield Construction Unit	7262 (356)	Mie Ken
168th Field Airfield Construction Unit	10265 (356)	Gifu
169th Field Airfield Construction Unit	10266 (356)	Kyoto
174th Field Airfield Construction Unit	15580 (356)	Ehime Ken

*Note: 13 Air Signal Regiment (803 + 1,200 trainees)

10th Air Division: 1944 Tokyo   天翔 *Tenshō*

Unit	Number	Location
10th Air Division Headquarters	1040 (459)	Tokyo
• 18th Air Regiment (fighter)	19190	Kashiwa
• 23rd Air Regiment (fighter)	19026 (322)	Inba
• 53rd Air Regiment (fighter)	18426 (322)	Matsudo
• 70th Air Regiment (fighter)	8370 (287)	Kashiwa
46th Air Sector Command	19350 (44)	Shimodate
3rd Airfield Battalion	19191 (273)	Kashiwa
6th Airfield Battalion	19192 (273)	Matsudo
7th Airfield Battalion	19193 (273)	Inba
43rd Airfield Battalion	19194 (273)	Narimasu
116th Airfield Battalion	18437 (372)	Fujigaya
140th Airfield Battalion	16638 (372)	Yachimata
141st Airfield Battalion	16639 (372)	Koshigaya
244th Airfield Battalion	19195 (273)	Chofu
65th Airfield Company	18474 (226)	Tokorozawa

10th Air Division: Activated in Tokyo on March 8, 1944. Its headquarters were located in Tokyo and it was attached to the 1st Air Army from Mar 8th until May 5th, Defense General Headquarters until Dec 26th, 6th Air Army until Apr 8, 1945 and 1st Air Army until the war ended.

6th Air Army 靖 *Yasu*

The 6th Air Army was activated in Fukuoka on December 26, 1944, from former Army Air Training personnel. Headquarters in Fukuoka, it was attached to General Defense Headquarters from Dec 26th until March 19, 1945, placed under control of the Navy's Combined Fleet until Apr 8th when it joined the Air General Army. It was returned to army control on May 26th. The 6th Air Army headquarters were in Fukuoka, Japan from December 20th. Lt Gen Michio Sugawara was appointed commander on Dec 26th and remained so until the war ended. All its personnel had demobilized by Nov. 1st.

Service History:
1944: On Dec 26th the 6th Air Army was activated in Fukuoka ○
1945: From Mar 19th the 6th Air Army was under Combined Fleet control to coordinate with Naval air units for operations around Okinawa ○ Mar 25th, the 6th Air Army took part in *Ten-go* operation, the air war against the US at the start Okinawa ○ In April the 6th Air Army continued to attack Americans on Okinawa under Combined Fleet control ○ On April 8th the 6th Air Army was placed into the Air General Army's order of battle, even though it remained under tactical command of the Combined Fleet ○ On May 2nd as Okinawa continued to worsen, Air General Army reinforced the 6th Air Army with 100 planes from Kamikaze units and a small number of fighter and bomber regiments ○ In May, in preparation for operation *Gi-go*, the Giretsu Raiding Brigade transferred over from the 1st Air Army ○ May 23rd, Operation *Gi-go*. Giretsu Raiders landed on Yontan Airfield, Okinawa destroying 9 planes and damaging more ○ On May 26th, with Okinawa lost Imperial HQ released the 6th Air Army from Combined Fleet control to join the Air General Army for the final battle ○ On July 1st the Air General Army finally gained full control over the air space around Japan. The 12th Air Division was returned to the 6th Air Army ○

Major Unit: See brigade's pages for order of battle

1st Infantry Raiding Brigade 1944 鷲 *Ran*		138 and 282
Units under the 6th Air Army: Fukuoka	靖 *Yasu*	
6th Air Army Headquarters	19500 (340)	Fukuoka
• 7th Air Regiment (heavy bomber)	21202 (532)	Itami
• 98th Air Regiment (heavy bomber)	21203 (532)	Kodama
• 14th Air Regiment (heavy bomber)	9906 (497)	Nitta
• 60th Air Regiment (heavy bomber)	2378 (497)	Kumamoto
• 106th Air Regiment (HQ Recon.)	18924	
• 107th Air Regiment (heavy bomber)	18925 (465)	
• 110th Air Regiment (heavy bomber)	19027 (218)	Kumano Sho
27th Air Brigade Headquarters	34222 (61)	Kodama
100th Air Brigade Headquarters	18919 (38)	Takamatsu
• 101st Air Regiment (fighter)	18920 (145)	Takamatsu
• 102nd Air Regiment (fighter)	18921 (145)	
• 103rd Air Regiment (fighter)	18922 (145)	Mihara
6th Air Brigade Headquarters	9115	Tachiarai
• 65th Air Regiment (light bomber)	9104 (197)	Chiran
• 66th Air Regiment (light bomber)	9150 (470)	Banse
206th Independent Air Unit Headquarters	21201 (54)	Kaiundai
• 3rd Independent Air Unit	19030	

6th Air Army continued   靖 *Yasu*

- 12th Independent Air Unit   11614 (144)
- 1st Ind. Air Squadron (anti submarine)   18926 (120)
- 66th Ind. Air Squadron (direct co-op)   9171 (121)   Gannosu
- 200th Air Regiment   19028 (513)

Unit	Number	Location
41st Air Sector Command	18930 (50)	Miyakonojo
45th Air Sector Command	16647 (44)	Taikyu
49th Air Sector Command	16641 (44)	Korea
60th Air Sector Command	19359 (44)	Takamatsu
61st Air Sector Command	19360 (44)	Kakogawa
142nd Airfield Battalion	18459 (372)	Mitabaru
145th Airfield Battalion	18462 (372)	Shisea
146th Airfield Battalion	18463 (372)	Itami
162nd Airfield Battalion	18498 (372)	Kumanosho
171st Airfield Battalion	18943 (372)	Gunzan
172nd Airfield Battalion	18944 (372)	Miyakonojo
173rd Airfield Battalion	18945 (372)	Mansei
174th Airfield Battalion	18946 (372)	Kumamoto
181st Airfield Battalion	16655 (372)	Kei
191st Airfield Battalion	19352 (372)	Taikyu
192nd Airfield Battalion	19353 (372)	Sentoku
195th Airfield Battalion	19354 (372)	Heijo
210th Airfield Battalion	17379 (372)	Saigen
211th Airfield Battalion	17380 (372)	Moppo
227th Airfield Battalion	19386 (372)	Chiran
228th Airfield Battalion	19387 (372)	Miyakonojo
229th Airfield Battalion	19388 (372)	Kikuchi
230th Airfield Battalion	19389 (372)	Okayama
231st Airfield Battalion	19390 (372)	Moppo
245th Airfield Battalion	8244 (372)	Kaishu
247th Airfield Battalion	8306 (372)	Saishu
249th Airfield Battalion	19361 (553)	Takamatsu
250th Airfield Battalion	19362 (553)	Miki
251st Airfield Battalion	19363 (553)	Takamatsu
254th Airfield Battalion	19366 (553)	Yokaichi
255th Airfield Battalion	19376 (553)	Miki
55th Airfield Company	18464 (437)	Kikushi
57th Airfield Company	18466 (226)	Saishu
83rd Airfield Company	19546 (226)	Yonago
84th Airfield Company	19547 (226)	Tachiarai
7th Field Air Repair Depot	8316 (1,823)	Taikyu
7th Field Air Repair Depot, 2nd Ind. Maint. Unit	8316 (113)	
154th Ind. Maintenance Unit (Ki-43, Oscar)	19162 (233)	Bofu
157th Independent Maintenance Unit (Ki-43)	19391 (233)	Metabara
163rd Ind. Maintenance Unit (Ki-84, Frank)	19392 (233)	Shimodate
169th Independent Maintenance Unit (Ki-48)	19054 (233)	Miyakonojo

6th Air Army continued

Unit	Number	Location
170th Independent Maintenance Unit (Ki-48)	19055 (233)	Gannasu
175th Independent Maintenance Unit (Ki-48)	19060 (233)	Bofu
189th Ind. Maintenance Unit (Ki-102B, Randy)	19074 (336)	Kaiundai
199th Ind. Maintenance Unit (Ki-67, Peggy)	19079 (275)	Kumamoto
200th Independent Maintenance Unit (Ki-67)	19080 (275)	Tachiarai
305th Independent Maintenance Unit (Ki-74, Patsy)	19085 (275)	Urusan
312th Independent Maintenance Unit (unknown)	19368 (233)	Kakogawa
313th Independent Maintenance Unit (unknown)	19369 (233)	Takamatsu
27th Field Airfield Construction Unit	2408 (702)	Oita
28th Field Airfield Construction Unit	2409 (702)	Kumamoto
30th Field Airfield Construction Unit	15386 (702)	Miyakonojo
142nd Field Airfield Construction Unit	18406 (477)	Takanabe
151st Field Airfield Construction Unit	18415 (175)	Kamibeppu
152nd Field Airfield Construction Unit	18416 (175)	Fukuoka
153rd Field Airfield Construction Unit	18417 (175)	Korea
154th Field Airfield Construction Unit	18418 (175)	Taikyu
163rd Field Airfield Construction Unit	7263 (356)	Ozuki
172nd Field Airfield Construction Unit	7057 (356)	Kumamoto
173rd Field Airfield Construction Unit	20903 (356)	Kurume
175th Field Airfield Construction Unit	15150 (356)	Tanyo
176th Field Airfield Construction Unit	8801 (356)	
177th Field Airfield Construction Unit	14100 (356)	
1st Air Signal Headquarters	19548 (118)	Fukuoka
18th Air Signal Regiment	19186 (1,699)	Taisho
19th Air Signal Regiment	21205 (2,313)	Fukuoka
21st Air Signal Unit	19159 (198)	
6th Wireless Radio Unit	18954 (212)	Takamatsu
13th Wireless Radio Unit	19189/122 中部 (212)	Taisho
14th Wireless Radio Unit	109 西部 (212)	Ozuki
68th Wireless Radio Unit	19555 (209)	Osaka
69th Wireless Radio Unit	19556 (209)	Takamatsu
70th Wireless Radio Unit	19557 (209)	Fukuoka
71st Wireless Radio Unit	19558 (209)	Kumamoto
72nd Wireless Radio Unit	19559 (209)	Banse
73rd Wireless Radio Unit	19560 (209)	Nittabara
74th Wireless Radio Unit	19561 (209)	Miyakonojo
75th Wireless Radio Unit	19562 (209)	Chiran
9th Special Air Signal Unit	19158 (259)	Fukuoka
7th Independent Machine Cannon Company	28207 (138)	
8th Independent Machine Cannon Company	28208 (138)	
9th Independent Machine Cannon Company	28209 (138)	
10th Independent Machine Cannon Company	28210 (138)	
22nd Independent Machine Cannon Company	2163 (144)	
29th Independent Machine Cannon Company	8049 (144)	
30th Independent Machine Cannon Company	8020 (144)	

6th Air Army continued	靖 *Yasu*	
52nd Independent Machine Cannon Company	28216 (144)
53rd Independent Machine Cannon Company	28217 (144)
54th Independent Machine Cannon Company	28218 (144)
10th Field Air Freight Depot	8394 (296)	Taikyu

	靖 *Yasu*	
7th Air Brigade:		
7th Air Brigade Headquarters (suicide attack unit)	9121 (49)	Tiran
21st Air Brigade Headquarters (suicide attack unit)	18423 (28)	Miyakonojou
• 72nd Air Regiment (fighter)	18430	
• 73rd Air Regiment (fighter)	18431	

	天風 *Tenpū*	
12th Air Division: 1944 Ozuki		
12th Air Division Headquarters	1042 (613)	Ozuki
• 4th Air Regiment (fighter)	35001 (322)	Ozuki
• 71st Air Regiment (fighter)	18429 (322)	Houfu
• 47th Air Regiment (fighter)	34212 (322)	Ozuki
• 19th Ind. Air Squadron (HQ recon)	21204	
51st Air Sector Command	19373 (44)	Ashiya
4th Airfield Battalion	35003 (273)	Ozuka
64th Airfield Battalion	18933 (372)	Fukuoka
65th Airfield Battalion	18934 (372)	Nakahara
193rd Airfield Battalion	19036 (372)	Kasuya
194th Airfield Battalion	19037 (372)	Tachiarai-South
235th Airfield Battalion	19534 (372)	Bofu
236th Airfield Battalion	19535 (372)	Mitsumata
248th Airfield Battalion	35004 (273)	Ashiya

12th Air Division: Activated in Ozuki, Japan on July 15, 1944. Its headquarters located in Ozuki, it was attached to General Defense Headquarters from July 17th until Dec 26th and 6th Air Army until the war ended.

	鸞 *Ran*	
1st Raiding Brigade: 1944		
1st Raiding Brigade Headquarters	unknown (63)	Miyazaki
1st Infantry Raiding Regiment	9945 (894)	Yokoshiba
2nd Infantry Raiding Regiment	9946 帥 (894)	Miyazaki
1st Tank Raiding Unit	19049 帥 (465)	Miyazaki
1st Raiding Maintenance Unit	19051 帥 (340)	Miyazaki
101st Airfield Company	19043 (174)	Takanabe
102nd Airfield Company	19152 (179)	Taigo
103rd Airfield Company	19053 (179)	Mitsuyo

1st Air Raiding Group: Activated Nov. 30, 1944, the bulk of the 1st Raiding Group was sent to Clark Field, the Philippines where its headquarters also became Kembu Group HQ, one of the four army groups defending the Philippines. The 1st Raiding Brigade remained in Japan with the 1st Air Army. In May 1945 it transferred to the 6th Air Army for *Gi-go*, the disruption of US air operations on Okinawa. *Gi-go* took place after dark on May 23rd. Twelve heavy bombers carrying 120 men landed on Yontan airfield in northern Okinawa. They destroyed nine planes and 70,000 gallons of aviation fuel.

Japan Railway

Homeland Railway Command 線 *Sen*

With the exception of the Army Railway Section, Japan's railways had been in civilian hands until the China Incident. In July 1937 the 1st Railway Sector Headquarters was created to manage an expected increase in troop movement. To further that effort in November Imperial Headquarters created the Transportation and Communications Bureau. In August 1939 the 1st Railway Sector HQ was deactivated and replaced, its personnel becoming the nucleus for the 1st Railway Command, 150 men under a Major General in Tokyo. Throughout the country Railway Station Commands were created to direct the movement of men, clothing, munitions and provisions. It was soon found that while large-scale movements were planned centrally the many local units operating independently interfered with overall operations.

After the Pacific War began in 1941 military rail transport increased steadily. Without making major changes best practices were relied on to provide functionality and the rail system remained unchanged until July 1944 and the fall of Saipan. Anticipating increasing American bombing raids and the battle for Japan, rail administration didn't believe that rail transport would hold up under normal operating procedures.

July 1944, 1st Railway Command was dissolved and the Homeland Railway Command created. Under evolving circumstances transportation became more and more difficult. In Mar 1945 railway branch offices became railway district commands and the entire rail organization went from an administrative body to becoming a field command. In June Imperial HQ created twenty-three new Railway Station HQ with the authority to direct and reorganize transport operations around air raids and other attacks.

Under the Imperial Railway Bureau: Tokyo	線 *Sen*	
Homeland Railroad Command Headquarters	No # (242)	Tokyo
Railway Training Group Headquarters	91 (325)	Tsudanuma
16th Railway Regiment	86 (2,747)	Chiba
17th Railway Regiment	87 (2,745)	Tsudanuma
Railway Bureau Training Center	No #	
Railway Bureau Research Department	No #	
Railway Bureau Cadet Training Corp	No #	

Imperial Railway Bureau continued
Tokyo District Railway Unit:

	線 Sen	
Tokyo District Railway Headquarters	No # (305)	Tokyo
119th Railroad Station Headquarters	33998 (17)	Abiko
127th Railroad Station Headquarters	34000 (17)	Ishioka
175th Railroad Station Headquarters	3857 (27)	Tokyo
178th Railroad Station Headquarters	Unknown (17)	Takasaki
8th Independent Railway Battalion	13358 (1,541)	Hisaki
8th Independent Railroad Engineer Unit	33958 (1,522)	Chigasaki
13th Independent Railroad Engineer Unit	33963 (1,522)	Kasama
16th Independent Railroad Engineer Unit	33966 (1,522)	Tokyo
19th Independent Railroad Engineer Unit	33969 (1,519)	Takasaki
24th Independent Railroad Engineer Unit	33974 (1,522)	Abika

Nagoya District Railway Unit:

	線 Sen	
Nagoya District Railway Headquarters	No # (252)	Nagoya
128th Railroad Station Headquarters	34001 (17)	Tsuruga
132nd Railroad Station Headquarters	15079 (17)	Shizuoka
134th Railroad Station Headquarters	34003 (17)	Nagoya
4th Independent Railroad Battalion	13354 (1,541)	Ichinomiya
6th Independent Railroad Engineer Unit	33956 (1,522)	Shizuoka
7th Independent Railroad Engineer Unit	33957 (1,522)	Toyohashi
20th Independent Railroad Engineer Unit	33970 (1,522)	Tsuruga

Osaka District Railway Unit:

	線 Sen	
Osaka District Railway Headquarters	No # (262)	Osaka
122nd Railroad Station Headquarters	33999 (17)	Kyoto
140th Railroad Station Headquarters	15080 (17)	Himeji
179th Railroad Station Headquarters	No # (27)	Hukuchiyama
3rd Independent Railroad Battalion	13353 (1,541)	Sohoda Mura
5th Independent Railroad Engineer Unit	33955 (1,522)	Himeji
11th Independent Railroad Engineer Unit	33961 (1,522)	Takatsuki

Hiroshima District Railway Unit:

	線 Sen	
Hiroshima District Railway Headquarters	No # (267)	Hiroshima
139th Railroad Station Headquarters	34004 (17)	Okayama
185th Railroad Station Headquarters	15078 (27)	Shomo-ichi
2nd Independent Railroad Battalion	13352 (1,541)	Hiroshima
10th Independent Railroad Engineer Unit	33960 (1,522)	Shimonoseki
18th Independent Railroad Engineer Unit	33968 (1,522)	Okayama

Shikoku District Railway Unit:

	線 Sen	
Shikoku District Railroad Headquarters	No # (38)	Takamatsu

Shikoku District Railway Unit continued
150th Railroad Station Headquarters   34007 (17)   Takamatsu
153rd Railroad Station Headquarters   34008 (17)   Kochi
4th Independent Railroad Engineer Unit 33954 (1,542)   Takamatsu

Moji District Railway Unit: 線 Sen
Moji District Railway Headquarters   No # (302)   Moji
144th Railroad Station Headquarters   32420 (27)   Nagoshima
149th Railroad Station Headquarters   34006/7035 (17)   Kumamoto
171st Railroad Station Headquarters   33992 (27)   Oita
191st Railroad Station Headquarters   9756 (27)   Oita
2nd Railroad Regiment   5801 (2,545)   Kumamoto
1st Independent Railroad Battalion   13351 (1,534)   Matsue
1st Independent Railroad Engineer Unit 33951 (1,519)   Kagoshima
2nd Independent Railroad Engineer Unit 33952 (1,522)   Mujazaki
3rd Independent Railroad Engineer Unit 33953 (1,522)   Naokata
9th Independent Railroad Engineer Unit 33959 (1,522)   Kumamoto
12th Independent Railroad Engineer Unit 33962 (1,524)   Oita
17th Independent Railroad Engineer Unit 33967 (1,522)   Tosu

Sendai District Railway Unit: 線 Sen
Sendai District Railway Headquarters   No # (193)   Sendai
103rd Railroad Station Headquarters   33997 (17)   Fukushima
166th Railroad Station Headquarters   34011 (17)   Aomori
6th Independent Railroad Battalion   13356 (1,545)   Fudodo
14th Independent Railroad Engineer Unit 33964 (1,522)   Aomori

Niigata District Railway Unit: 線 Sen
Niigata District Railway Headquarters No # (191)   Niigata
165th Railroad Station Headquarters   34010 (17)   Akita
177th Railroad Station Headquarters   34002 (17)   Nagano
5th Independent Railroad Battalion   13355 (1,544)   Sanjo
21st Independent Railroad Engineer Unit 33971 (1,522)   Naoetsu

Sapporo District Railway Unit: 線 Sen
Sapporo District Railway Headquarters No # (196)   Sapporo
7th Independent Railroad Battalion   13357 (1,542)   Iwamitsu
15th Independent Railroad Engineer Unit 33965 (1,522)   Hakodate
22nd Independent Railroad Engineer Unit 33972 (1,522)   Kitami
23rd Independent Railroad Engineer Unit 33973 (1,523)   Obihiro

Sakhalin District Railway Unit: 線 *Sen*
Sakhalin District Railway Headquarters   No # (196)
Note: Railway unit strengths are from Demobilization Bureau figures.

Army Shipping Units

Shipping Transport Command 暁 *Akatsuki*

From early Meiji times until the end of World War Two the army preferred to maintain control over shipping its soldiers abroad. In peace time the Army Transport Department organized the movement of troops by sea but after the war in China began the Transport Dept. reorganized into the Shipping Transport Command. It was guven responsibility for boarding and off loading troops, munitions and supplies as well as converting civilian ships into troop transports.

In Jul 1942 Shipping Transport Command became General Shipping Command under Imperial General Headquarters control, at the same time a number of new shipping units were created and the existing ones expanded.

Embarkation followed certain operational procedures. Ports and dates had to be chosen and time allotted to prepare transports and organize the troops. Railway capacity, harbor facilities and navigation routes had to be considered. Convoys of about 20,000 gross tons were preferred. An Anchorage Headquarters allocated ship board space according to unit type and the embarkation schedule. The General in command of his troops was responsible for ensuring loading ran on schedule and the Anchorage HQ was responsible for space allocation. Special attention was paid to off loading plans if combat was expected in the landing zone. The troops and their supplies were divided up so the loss of any one ship wouldn't seriously affect the entire operation's chance of success. Once in motion nothing was allowed to interfere with the completion of a shipping operation.

From the start off loading units evolved slowly with the first shipping engineers being organized in 1928. The Army Transport Department's Training Section was created in 1929 and reorganized into the Shipping Training Department in 1943.

Successful landings required the off loading units and their passengers to be prepared for an orderly and swift debarkation. Anchorage for transport ships was to be close to shore as possible. Occasionally an assault force would launch its first wave some distance from shore to speed up off loading, those ships weighing anchor and moving closer to the beach to meet the returning landing craft for the second wave.

Weak Allied air power and surprise attacks contributed much to Japan's early war amphibious landing successes. The Army soon learned it could quickly and efficiently off load lightly equipped troops but supplies and equipment were slow and vulnerable, especially under combat conditions. The clumsy old style barges continued to be used out of necessity but compared to an equivalent number of new type landing craft it required more barges and off loading personnel to land fewer troops and supplies.

The principle landing craft were called Daihatsu (large) and Shohatsu (small). The Army was looking for better solutions to the movement of men and materials in combat zones and planned to replace wooden landing craft new iron ones. In 1940 research was begun into freight carrying submarines, special barges, amphibious trucks and high-speed transport ships for use in forward areas. Pursuit boats to counter submarines, torpedo boats and high speed suicide craft called "special attack boats" were also being designed.

To fight off air attacks the army's transport ships had a few anti-aircraft guns and machine cannon installed but there were never enough. To compensate the Army commissioned dedicated anti-aircraft ships called "Bokusen" to escort the convoys. Each had between 5 and 10 AA guns and several artillery pieces for anti submarine protection, later on additional anti aircraft guns replaced the anti-submarine artillery.

Service History:

1941: Sept to Nov, in preparation for the Pacific War base ports were established in Ujina, Osaka, Kobe, Moji, Keelung, Pusan and Canton ○

1942: July 14th, to serve increased demand as the war escalated Shipping Transport Command was replaced by General Shipping Command ○

1943: In Sept units stationed in Ujina, Shanghai, Singapore, Rabaul, Halmahera and Otaru were reorganized and consolidated with units in other areas. A small craft fleet of landing barges and fishing boats for local transportation added capacity ○ Heavy shipping losses were occurring between Japan and the southern areas so I.G.HQ ordered a joint Army-Navy study on ways to protect sea-going transportation ○

Note: Mobile Transport Company: Crew for one SS assault landing transport ship.

Units under Army Transport Command: Ujina	暁 *Akatsuki* (101,277)	
General Shipping Command Headquarters	2940 (3,340)	Ujina
1st Shipping Headquarters	2943	
Shipping Training Department	6167 (2,343)	Hiroshima
Shipping Artillery Group Headquarters	6180 (1,135)	Hiroshima
16th Shipping Engineer Regiment	16700 (1,099)	Saipan
48th Shipping Engineer Regiment	19837 (1,099)	Tsuruga
49th Shipping Engineer Regiment	19838 (1,099)	Fushiki
50th Shipping Engineer Regiment	19839 (1,099)	Niigata
54th Shipping Engineer Regiment	19830 (1,099)	
58th Shipping Engineer Regiment	6175 (792)	Niigata
41st Sea Raiding Squadron	19856 (92)	
42nd Sea Raiding Squadron	19857 (92)	
43rd Sea Raiding Squadron	19858 (92)	
44th Sea Raiding Squadron	19859 (92)	
45th Sea Raiding Squadron	19860 (92)	
46th Sea Raiding Squadron	19861 (92)	
47th Sea Raiding Squadron	19862 (92)	
48th Sea Raiding Squadron	19863 (92)	
49th Sea Raiding Squadron	19864 (92)	

Army Shipping Transport Command continued   暁 *Akatsuki*

Unit	Number	Location
50th Sea Raiding Squadron	19865 (92)	
11th Sea Raiding Maintenance Unit	19876 (368)	Kaidaichi
12th Sea Raiding Maintenance Unit	19877 (368)	Kaidaichi
13th Sea Raiding Maintenance Unit	19878 (368)	Kaidaichi
14th Sea Raiding Maintenance Unit	19879 (368)	Kaidaichi
15th Sea Raiding Maintenance Unit	19880 (368)	Kaidaichi
16th Sea Raiding Maintenance Unit	19881 (368)	Kaidaichi
17th Sea Raiding Maintenance Unit	19882 (368)	Kaidaichi
18th Sea Raiding Maintenance Unit	19883 (368)	Kaidaichi
19th Sea Raiding Maintenance Unit	19884 (368)	Kaidaichi
20th Sea Raiding Maintenance Unit	19885 (368)	Kaidaichi
1st Shipping Artillery Regiment	2953 (9,709)	Hukuyama
1st Shipping Machine Cannon Regiment	6178 (4,983)	Hukuyama
2nd Shipping Machine Cannon Regiment	6179 (4,983)	Moji
Shipping Intelligence Regiment	19776 (6,083)	Nishinomiya
1st Mobile Transport Unit Headquarters	16706 (112)	Hakodate
2nd Mobile Transport Company	16726 (133)	Moji
3rd Mobile Transport Company	16727 (132)	Miyatsu
4th Mobile Transport Company	16728	sunk Nov 30, 1944
5th Mobile Transport Company	16729 (103)	Tsuruga
6th Mobile Transport Company	16730 (144)	Takekojima
7th Mobile Transport Company	16731 (105)	Hagi
10th Mobile Transport Company	16734 (93)	Senzaki
11th Mobile Transport Company	16735 (132)	Hagi
12th Sea Transport Battalion	19814	
13th Sea Transport Battalion	19815 (1,165)	Moji
14th Sea Transport Battalion	19816 (621)	Moji
15th Mobile Transport Company	16739	
2nd Mobile Transport Unit Headquarters	16761 (112)	Nanao
16th Sea Transport Battalion	19818 (512)	Shimonoseki
17th Sea Transport Battalion	19819 (1,165)	Moji
18th Sea Transport Battalion	19820 (1,165)	Shimonoseki
19th Sea Transport Battalion	19833 (1,165)	Tsueishi
20th Sea Transport Battalion	19834 (1,165)	Ube
29th Sea Transport Battalion	28775 (541)	Hakodate
21st Mobile Transport Company	16767 (103)	Moji
22nd Mobile Transport Company	16768 (103)	Shimonatsu
23rd Mobile Transport Company	16769 (103)	Nanao
24th Mobile Transport Company	16770 (103)	Nanao
25th Mobile Transport Company	16771 (103)	Miyatsu
26th Mobile Transport Company	16772 (103)	Inishima
27th Mobile Transport Company	16773 (103)	Miyatsu
28th Mobile Transport Company	16774 (103)	Miyatsu
29th Mobile Transport Company	16775 (103)	Nanao
30th Mobile Transport Company	16776 (103)	Nanao

Army Shipping Transport Command continued

Unit	Code (men)	Location
1st High Speed Transport Battalion	16707 (1,071)	Mimi
1st Sea Pursuit Battalion	16708 (799)	Karatsu
5th Shipping Signal Battalion	19775 (746)	Moji
6th Shipping Signal Battalion	19835 (746)	Niigata
7th Shipping Signal Battalion	19836 (746)	Tokyo
1st Transport Submarine Unit Headquarters	unknown (307)	Tokyo
1st to 6th Transport Submarines	unkn. (35 men each)	Tokyo
2nd Submarine Transport Unit Headquarters	unknown (300)	Moji
Plus 7th to 10th Transport Submarines	unknown (35 men each)	Moji
59th Anchorage Headquarters	16722 (135)	Niigata
60th Anchorage Headquarters	16723 (103)	
1st Shipping Engineer Replacement Unit	東部90 (2,199)	Ube
6th Shipping Engineer Replacement Unit	unknown (2,199)	Yonoi
9th Shipping Engineer Replacement Unit	16709 (2,969)	Onomichi
Shipping Signal Replacement Unit	16710 (1,339)	
Mobile Transport Replacement Unit	16711 (2,691)	
Sea Pursuit Battalion Replacement Unit	16712 (3,432)	
Shipping Artillery Training Unit	unknown (555)	
Shipping Maintenance Training Unit	unknown (969)	
Shipping Cadet Unit	unknown	
Shipping Special Cadet Unit	unknown (404)	
Field Shipping Main Depot	6140 (735)	Hiroshima
8th Field Shipping Depot	19821	
9th Field Shipping Depot, 1st and 2nd Branch Depot	6196 (649)	Niigata
10th Field Shipping Depot, 1st and 2nd Branch Depot	6197 (649)	
11th Field Shipping Depot	6198 (1,456)	Moji
30th Sea Raiding Base Battalion	9790 (900)	
200th Land Duty Company	19886 (502)	Hiroshima
201st Land Duty Company	19887 (502)	Fukuyama
202nd Land Duty Company	19888 (502)	Tsuruga
203rd Land Duty Company	19889 (502)	Makata
204th Land Duty Company	19890 (502)	Moji
205th Land Duty Company	19891 (502)	Goto
206th Land Duty Company	19892 (502)	Shimonoseki
207th Land Duty Company	19893 (502)	Moji
208th Land Duty Company	19894 (502)	Hiroshima
209th Land Duty Company	19895 (502)	Hiroshima
517th Construction Duty Company	28471 (511)	
35th Field Duty Unit Headquarters	12569 (547)	Niigata
67th Sea Duty Company	12570 (511)	Niigata
68th Sea Duty Company	12571 (511)	Niigata
69th Sea Duty Company	12572 (511)	Tsuruga
70th Sea Duty Company	12573 (511)	Tsuruga
71st Sea Duty Company	12753 (511)	Sakata
72nd Sea Duty Company	12754 (511)	Fushiki

Army Shipping Transport Command continued   暁 *Akatsuki*

Unit	Number	Location
73rd Sea Duty Company	12755 (511)	Fushiki
74th Sea Duty Company	12756 (511)	
75th Sea Duty Company	12757 (511)	
76th Sea Duty Company	12758 (511)	
Military Shipping Detention Depot	6182 (1)	
Shipping Judicial Corp	No #	
1st Shipping Transport Headquarters	6168 (211)	Moji
2nd Shipping Transport Headquarters	2941 (211)	
Tokyo Branch Office	No # (64)	Tokyo
Busan Branch Office	No #	Pusan, Korea
Kaohsiung Branch Office	No #	Taiwan
Hanshin Branch Office	No # (40)	Osaka
Hiroshima Branch Office	No # (69)	Ujina
Kobe Branch Office	No #	Hyōgo Pref., Japan
Keelung Branch Office	No #	Taiwan
Tsuruga Branch Office	No #	Fukui Pref., Japan
South Kyushu Branch Office	No # (124)	Kagoshima
Dalian Branch Office	No # (116)	Manchuria
131st Specially Established Sea Duty Company	19781 (61+*)	Tokyo
132nd Specially Established Sea Duty Company	19782 (61+)	Osaka
133rd Specially Established Sea Duty Company	19783 (61+)	Sakai
134th Specially Established Sea Duty Company	19784 (61+)	Moji
135th Specially Established Sea Duty Company	19785 (61+)	
136th Specially Established Sea Duty Company	19786 (61+)	Sakata
North Kyushu Branch Office	No # (76)	Moji
Hokuriku Branch Office	No # (160)	Niigata
Palau Branch Office	No #	
San'in Branch Office	No # (117)	Tsuruga
35th Shipping Engineer Regiment	19812 (1,099)	Hirato
36th Shipping Engineer Regiment	19813 (1,099)	Mokpo Korea
2nd Shipping Signal Battalion	16719 (746)	Hiroshima

<u>5th Shipping Transport Unit</u>:   暁 *Akatsuki*

Unit	Number	Location
5th Shipping Transport Headquarters	6160 (240)	Otaru
Otaru Branch Office	No # (57)	Otaru
Hakodate Branch Office	No # (1,121)	Hakodate
6th Shipping Engineer Regiment	6174 (1,099)	
27th Shipping Engineer Regiment	6151 (1,099)	
57th Shipping Engineer Regiment	6155 (1,542)	
Shipping Fixed Signal Regiment	2959	deactivated 3/3/45
6th Sea Transport Battalion	6193 (548)	Nemuro
30th Field Anchorage Headquarters	4826 (69)	
53rd Field Anchorage Headquarters	9259 (45)	

5th Shipping Transport Unit continued

152nd Specially Established Sea Duty Company	19802 (61+)	Kotaru
153rd Specially Established Sea Duty Company	19803 (61+)	
154th Specially Established Sea Duty Company	19804 (61+)	Shimobuji
155th Specially Established Sea Duty Company	19805 (61+)	Nemuro
6th Debarkation Unit	6186 (1,014)	
4th Field Shipping Depot	6195 (1,225)	
1st Shipping Signal Battalion	16718 (746)	Otaru

Shipping Headquarters Tokyo Branch:

暁 2940 (74) — Tokyo

13th Shipping Transport Unit:

暁 *Akatsuki*

13th Shipping Group Headquarters	2942 (81)	Tokyo
22nd Shipping Engineer Regiment	16740 (1,099)	Noda
39th Shipping Engineer Regiment	19824 (1,099)	Kisarazu
1st Independent Sea Transport Company	16751 (84)	Tokyo

14th Shipping Group:

暁 *Akatsuki*

14th Shipping Group Headquarters	2947 (58)	Hakata
37th Shipping Engineer Regiment	19822 (1,099)	Senzaki
38th Shipping Engineer Regiment	19823 (1,099)	Pusan

15th Shipping Group:

暁 *Akatsuki*

15th Shipping Group Headquarters	2950 (58)	Misumi
31st Shipping Engineer Regiment	16760 (1,099)	Sashiki
40th Shipping Engineer Regiment	19825 (1,099)	Shimabara
46th Shipping Engineer Regiment	19831 (1,099)	Shiroshima

16th Shipping Group:

暁 *Akatsuki*

16th Shipping Group Headquarters	2951 (58)	Tamano
41st Shipping Engineer Regiment	19826 (1,099)	Manao
42nd Shipping Engineer Regiment	19827 (1,099)	Ajino
43rd Shipping Engineer Regiment	19828 (1,099)	Moema
44th Shipping Engineer Regiment	19829 (1,099)	Niigata
45th Shipping Engineer Regiment	19830 (1,073)	Shiratori
47th Shipping Engineer Regiment	19832 (1,099)	Akita

Shipping Medical Unit: Nishima, Hiroshima

暁 *Akatsuki*

Shipping Medical Unit Headquarters	6177 (35)	Niijima
14th Hospital Shipping Medical Section	7140 (104)	Hiroshima
51st Hospital Shipping Medical Section	6163 (102)	Niigata

Shipping Medical Unit: Nishima, Hiroshima　　暁 *Akatsuki*
53rd Hospital Shipping Medical Section　　6775 (102)　　Niijima
55th Hospital Shipping Medical Section　　6777 (83)　　Kotara
56th Hospital Shipping Medical Section　　6779 (83)　　Moji

Note*: A Specially Established Sea Duty Company had an authorized strength of 61 officers and men + an additional +/- 604 local or foreign conscripted laborers.

Winter patrol in Manchuria (author)

Chapter 2

Manchuria and Korea

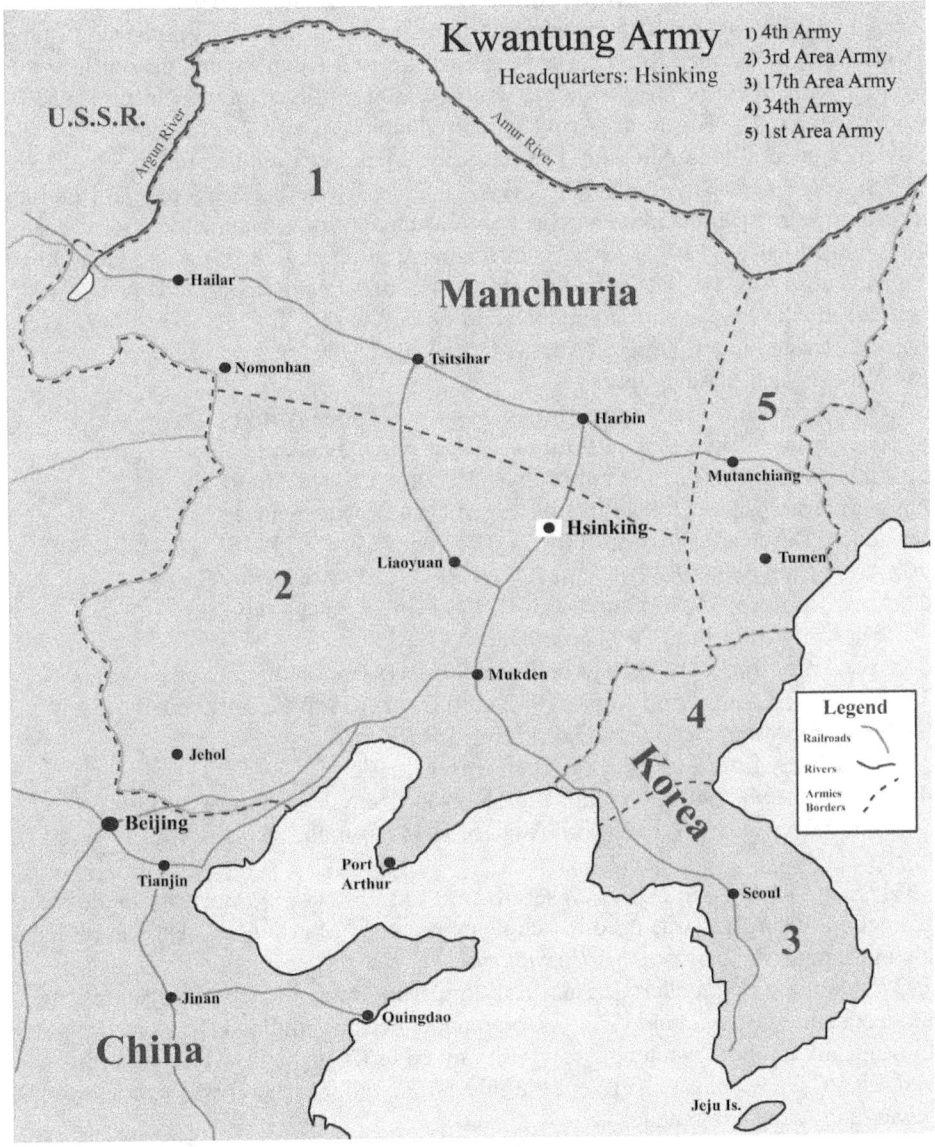

Manchuria

Kwantung Army 德 *Toku*

After the 1905 Russo-Japanese War, Russia ceded its leased territory on Manchuria's Lisotung Peninsula to Japan, subsequently the Kwantung Leased Territory Garrison was established in 1906. On April 12, 1919, Kwantung Army Headquarters became active in Tokyo and the Garrison reorganized into the Kwantung Army. This change in status eliminated civilian oversight in Manchuria and freed the army to govern itself without interference. Unshackling provided the opportunity for Gekokujō (lower rules the higher) to flourish as a kind of institutional insubordination, which paved the way for many excesses committed by the army later on. On July 7, 1937 the Kwantung Army moved its HQ to Hsinking where it remained for the duration of the war. In June 1941 Germany invaded Russia. The hostilities worried Japan enough that on July 11th *Special Maneuvers of the Kwantung Army*, the largest ever movement of Japanese troops, began. The Kwantung Army secretly doubled its size. In April Japan and the Soviets signed a non-aggression pact ensuring Manchuria relative peace for as long as Russia and Germany fought. On July 4, 1942 the Kwantung Army reorganized into a general army. Gen Kenkichi Ueda was Kwantung Army commander from Mar 6, 1936 until Sept 7, 1939, Lt Gen Yoshirō Umezu until July 18, 1944 and Gen Otozō Yamada until Aug 11, 1945. The Soviet invasion of Manchuria began on Aug 9, 1945 and ended when Japan surrendered unconditionally on the 15th. The Kwantung Army was deactivated in Hsinking on August 19th.

Subordinate armies / duty dates:
3rd Army from Jan 13, 1938 until July 4, 1942 (to 1st Area Army)
4th Army from Jul 15, 1938 until July 4, 1942 (to 2nd Area Army)
5th Army from May 19, 1938 until July 4, 1942 (to 1st Area Army)
6th Army from Aug 4, 1938 until July 4, 1942 (to 2nd Area Army)
Kwantung Defense Army from July 24, 1941 until May 30, 1945
20th Army from Sept 19, 1941 until July 4, 1942 (to 1st Area Army)
2nd Army from Apr 16, 1942 until July 4, 1942 (to 2nd Area Army)
1st Area Army from July 4, 1942 until Aug 15, 1945
2nd Area Army from July 4, 1942 until Oct 30, 1943 (to Southern Exped. Army)
1st Mechanized Army from July 4, 1942 until Oct 30, 1943 (deactivated Oct. 30th)
3rd Area Army from Oct 30, 1943 until Aug 15, 1945
17th Area Army from Aug 10, 1945 until Aug 15, 1945
4th Army from May 30, 1945 until Aug 15, 1945 (from the 3rd Area Army)
34th Army from June 18, 1945 until Aug 15, 1945 (from the 6th Area Army)

Service History:
1931: Sept 18th, a small explosion set off next to rail tracks by Japanese soldiers and blamed on insurgents was used to subjugate a part of Manchuria Japan had no legal claim to. Later dubbed the *Mukden Incident* ○

1932: On Feb 18th, under China's last Emperor, Puyi, Manchuria declared itself independent. The Kwantung Army's Commander became Ambassador Plenipotentiary to Manchukuo and Kwantung Army HQ moved to Changchun, which was renamed Hsinking (New Capital) ○ In Sept the title of Governor General was restored to the Kwantung Army commander ○

1937: From July 25th to 31st the *North China Incident* took place as a series of small battles around the Beijing-Tianjin area ○

1938: On Jan 13th the 3rd Army joined the Kwantung Army ○ July 15th the 4th Army joined the Kwantung Army ○ On July 29th the *Changkufeng Incident* took place. Soviet troops occupied the heights above Rajin Port in Korea ○ On Aug 11th a ceasefire was signed allowing the Soviets keep the heights ○

1939: May 11th a land dispute on the Manchu-Mongolia border began to escalate towards the *Nomonhan Incident* ○ On May 19th the 5th Army joined the Kwantung Army ○ On Aug 4th the 6th Army joined the Kwantung Army ○ In August Japan and Russia fought a "little war", called *Nomonhan* in Japan, *Khalkhin Gol* in Russia. Japan's 23rd Div was defeated badly ○ On Sept 15th a ceasefire was signed ○

1941: On Apr 13th the *Soviet-Japanese Neutrality Pact* was signed in Moscow (set to expire Apr 25, 1946) ○ On June 22nd Germany invaded Russia ○ In July *Special Maneuvers of the Kwantung Army* also called *The 100th Preparation* began under pretext of a large-scale training exercise. Reinforcements from Japan doubled the Kwantung Army's size ○ On Sep 19th the 20th Army joined the Kwantung Army's order of battle ○

1942: April 16th the 2nd Army joined the Kwantung Army's order of battle ○ On June 24th the 1st Mechanized Army was activated in Siping, Manchuria ○ On July 4th the Kwantung Army reorganized into a General Army. The 1st and 2nd Area Armies and the 1st Mechanized Army joined the Kwantung Army's order of battle. The 3rd, 5th and 20th Armies were attached to the 1st Area Army and the 2nd, 4th and 6th Armies were attached to the 2nd Area Army ○ On July 24th the Kwantung Defense Army was activated and placed under the Kwantung Army's control ○ In October, because Manchuria was an important base for stockpiling food and supplies to be sent outward to all areas, the Inspectorate of Supply for the Kwantung Army was created ○

1943: Manchuria remained quiet for another year ○ On Oct 30th the 3rd Area Army was attached to the Kwantung Army and the 2nd Area Army was removed and reorganized in Qiqihar for service in the Pacific ○ On Oct 5th IGHQ held a planning session in Tokyo, it was decided at least 23 divisions would be needed in a war with Russia ○ Oct 30th, the 1st Mechanized Army was deactivated as a failed experiment ○ On Oct 30th the 2nd Area Army HQ and 2nd Army HQ began the journey south ○ On Dec 26th IGHQ announced plans to counter a Soviet invasion along the northern border, but the Kwantung Army objected as it had spent years preparing to engage them along the eastern border. The new plan was adopted with the start of 1945 as the date for completing preparations ○

1944: In mid-January a senior operations officer submitted the new defense plan for Manchuria to IGHQ., it was adopted as temporary but never became official policy ○ In early February Kwantung Army HQ began defense preparations but with large numbers of troops preparing to deploy elsewhere most HQ staff were preoccupied ○ Feb 1st, the 27th Division was the first of many divisions to be shipped out of Manchuria, before this only small combat and service units were sent ○ Feb 10th, the 14th and 29th Div were ordered south ○ Between Feb 21st and Apr 4th I.G.HQ ordered the creation of 12 expeditionary units, along with the 2nd Amphibious Brigade (also former Kwantung Army personnel) resulting in the combined loss of another 50,000 men ○ By mid-April studies of those remaining in Manchuria showed they equaled just 9 full divisions. To compensate IGHQ authorized converting the Arshaan Garrison

Unit into the 107th Div and activating the 1st Mobile Brigade, Fushin Garrison Unit and 14th Border Garrison Unit ○ June 20th, reacting to Saipan, IGHQ ordered the 9th Div, 68th Brigade, 2nd Mobile Regt., 26th and 27th Tank Regt, 28th Engineer Regt and numerous other units to secretly assemble near Pusan for shipment south ○ In early July most had been sent to Okinawa, some to Formosa, the 36th Inf. Regt to the P.I. and the 26th Tank Regt to Iwo Jima. The 2nd Mobile Regt returned to the Mobile Bgde ○ July 12th, the 108th, 111th and 112th Div. were activated in Manchuria to replace those sent south but they were under strength and lacking equipment ○ Jul 13th, first US air raid on Manchuria ○ On July 24th the 1st, 8th, 10th Div and 2nd Armored Div were ordered to prepare to move ○ At night on July 29th the Soviets removed newly placed wire entanglements from Wuchiatsu ○ Sept 18th, IGHQ instructed the Kwantung Army to defend Manchuria, support the southern war and prepare for operations against the Soviets. Offensive plans were abandoned for the first time and holding operations adopted ○ Sept 21st, the Kwantung Defense Army moved its HQ to Mukden ○ Sept 26th, U.S. B-29s bombed Anshan, Dairen, Penchihu and Suichung ○ Sept 27th, the 23rd Div was transferred to the P.I. and replaced in the Hsingan Mtns by the 119th Div ○ On Sept 27th the 20th Army demobilized and its units sent to the 3rd and 5th Armies, its HQ transferred to the 6th Area Army in China ○ Dec 4th, the "Gembu" Kamikaze Unit (15 pilots), the first such unit raised in Manchuria, was dispatched from Hsinking to the Philippines ○ On Dec 11th IGHQ. ordered the Kwantung Army to disband the existing railway command structure and reorganize it into the Continental Railway, to provide for rail movement in an uninterrupted flow ○ By December Kwantung Army strength had dropped by nearly fifty-percent compared to December 1942 ○

1945: January, the Kwantung Army's plan was to fight delaying actions against the Soviets as the bulk of its strength redeployed to fortifications along the Manchuria-Korea border ○ Jan 16th, Army General Staff ordered the emergency mobilization of 121st through 128th Divisions and 77th through 80th Independent Mixed Brigades. The nuclei came from 3rd Cavalry Brigade and border garrison unit personnel, already active divisions were added to as well ○ Four fully equipped divisions were sent to Japan and two partially equipped divisions to Korea. Additionally a third of the military equipment and materiel in Manchuria was shipped to Japan along with key personnel ○ In late February the Soviets deployed a force thought to be 40 infantry divisions strong ○ April, intelligence revealed a slow build up of troops on the Manchurian border ○ Mid-April, hinting at its plans Russia renounced *The Soviet-Japanese Neutrality Pact*. Japan expected action by September ○ In April the 11th, 25th, 57th, 111th, 120th, 121st Div and 1st Tank Division were transferred from Manchuria to Japan and Korea for the final battle ○ May 30th, the 4th Army rejoined the Kwantung Army. The Kwantung Defense Army became the 44th Army under 3rd Area Army control ○ June 18th, the 34th Army HQ was transferred to Kwantung Army control in north Korea and deployed on the Korean/Russian border with utmost secrecy ○ In July the 4th Army received permission to manage the defense of northern Manchuria on its own terms ○ By July 10th about 250,000 of 400,000 eligible Japanese reservists living in Manchuria were conscripts in eight divisions, the 134th through 139th, 148th and 149th. The 158th Division was still pending ○ On July 13th the 34th Army received orders from Army General Staff to try to halt any Soviet advance toward Pyongyang while protecting Seoul ○ On July 28th the 30th Army mobilized in Yenchi under 3rd Area Army control and was responsible for constructing fortifications in the southeast border region ○ On August 8th Russia declared war on Japan ○ On Aug 9th the Soviet Far East Command invaded Manchuria, Inner Mongolia and south Sakhalin ○ Aug 9th, IGHQ placed the 17th Area Army under Kwantung Army control effective 0600 Aug 10th ○ The Kwantung Army fought delaying actions throughout Manchuria while attempting to concentrate forces in the fortified zone along the Korean border ○ On Aug 15th Emperor Hirohito broadcast Japan's surrender over the radio. IGHQ issued orders to immediately suspend all operations. The Soviet Far Eastern Army advanced to the Mutanchiang Plain in the east, Sunwu in the north, the Tahsinganling Mountains in the northwest and Taoan and Taonan in the west. The Kwantung Army officially deactivated in Hsinking on Aug 19th ○

Major Unit: See division page for order of battle

158th Division Manchuria 1945 不滅 *Fumetsu* – never completed mobilization   240

Units under the Kwantung Army: Hsinking	徳 *Toku*
Kwantung Army Inspectorate General of Supply	3100 (15501) 監 (680)
Kwantung Army Headquarters Signal Section	3100 監 (101)
Kwantung Army Military Police Headquarters	30 (3,319)
K. Army Chemical Department Training Unit	25231
Kwantung Army Intelligence Department	25241 (951)
K. Army Intelligence Department Signal Section	25241 (222)
Kwantung Army Special Intelligence Unit	25242 (1,744)
Kwantung Army Signal Intelligence Department	25244 (75)
Kwantung Army Water Purification Department	25201 to 25206 (1,378)
Kwantung Army Accounting Department	25208
K. Army NCO/Officer Candidate Intendance Unit	13923 (106)
K. Army NCO/Officer Candidate Medical Unit	13924 (69)
K. Army NCO/Officer Candidate Veterinary Unit	13925 (41)
Kwantung Army Education Section	13946
Kwantung Army Survey Department	13949 (464)
Kwantung 1st NCO/Officer Candidate Infantry Unit	13980 (193)
Kanto.2nd NCO/Officer Candidate Infantry Unit	13981 (170)
K. Army Staff Training Unit	13982
K. Army NCO/Officer Candidate Cavalry Unit	13983 (71)
K. Army NCO/Officer Candidate Artillery	13984 (232)
K. NCO/Officer Candidate Anti-Aircraft Unit	13985 (738)
K. Army NCO/Officer Candidate Engineer Unit	13986 (781)
K. Army NCO/Officer Candidate Transport Unit	13987 (108)
Kwantung Army Signals Training Unit	13988 (955)
Kwantung Army Fixed Signal Unit Headquarters	7580 (550)
11th Fixed Signals Unit	7586 (150)
12th Fixed Signals Unit	7585 (150)
13th Fixed Signals Unit	7584 (150)
14th Fixed Signals Unit	7583 (150)
Kwantung Army Signal Headquarters	37606 (550)
Kwantung Army 1st Signal Unit	37607 (1,021)
Kwantung Army 2nd Signal Unit	37608 (1,021)
Kwantung Army 3rd Signal Unit	37609 (1,021)

Kwantung Army: continued   徳 *Toku*

18th Signal Regiment	7588 (1,913)
57th Signal Regiment	37401 (1,913)
1st Independent Meteorological Company	13997 (336)
Kwantung Army Siping Fuel Depot	25211/25212
Kwantung Army Field Motor Transport Depot	15500 (2,163)
Kwantung Army Ordnance Manufacturing Depot	15503 (1,776)
K. Army Ordnance Manuf. Depot Guard Company	15503 (1,279)
Kwantung Army Field Ordinance Depot	15504 / 2648 (2,782)
Kanto Army Ordinance Depot Guard Company	15504 (852)
Kwantung Army Ordinance Replacement Depot	15505 (1,200)
Kwantung Army Field Freight Depot	2651 (2,291)
Kanto Army Field Freight Harbin Branch Depot	15507
Kwantung Army Field Clothing Depot	15508 (200)
Kwantung Army Clothing Depot Guard Company	15508 (385)
Kwantung Army Field Provisions Depot	15509 (160)
Kanto Army Provisions Depot Guard Company	15509 (515)
Kwantung Army Field Munitions Depot	15510 (120)
Kwantung Army Munitions Depot Guard Company	15510 (153)
Kwantung Army Medical Stores Depot	15511 (80)
Kwantung Medical Stores Depot Guard Company	15511 (153)
Kwantung Army Field Veterinary Depot	1290 / 25296 (912)
Kwantung Army Veterinary Stores Depot	15512 (100)
Kanto Veterinary Stores Depot Guard Company	15512 (153)
Kwantung Army Horse Remount Depot	15513 (524)
Kwantung Army 1st Field Horse Remount Depot	15514 (512)
Kwantung Army Horse Convalescence Depot	25207 (92)
Kwantung Army Special Intelligence Service	25233 (32)
Kwantung Army Construction Headquarters	13903 (180)
1st Kwantung Construction Unit	13904 (1,175)
2nd Kwantung Construction Unit	13905 (1,175)
3rd Kwantung Construction Unit	13906 (1,175)
Kwantung Army Construction Engineer Unit	13907 (294)
Kwantung Army Construction Materials Depot	13908 (163)
Kwantung Army Construction Inspectorate	13909 (50)
16th Field Anti-Aircraft Unit Headquarters	満州 3774
57th Independent Transport Battalion	6261 (1,028)
58th Independent Transport Battalion	6262 (1,028) Hsinking
64th Independent Transport Battalion	15502 / 2614 (808)
62nd Line of Communications Duty Company	7039 (511)
277th Independent Motor Transport Company	3989 (183)
68th Field Service Unit Headquarters	unknown (17)
65th Land Duty Company	7849 (511)
120th Specially Established Land Duty Company	3655 (61)
121st Specially Established Land Duty Company	3656 (61)
122nd Specially Established Land Duty Company	5046 (61)

Kwantung Army: continued

123rd Specially Established Land Duty Company	5047 (61)
Kwantung Army 1st Duty Unit	15538 (1,335)
Kwantung Army 2nd Duty Unit	15539 / 4374 (1,335)
Kwantung Army 3rd Duty Unit	13971 (2,146)
Kwantung Army 4th Duty Unit	13972 (809)
Kwantung Army 5th Duty Unit	15540 (1,072)
Kwantung Army 6th Duty Unit	15541 (538)
Kwantung Army 7th Duty Unit	15542 (538)
Kwantung Army 8th Duty Unit	15543 (538)
Kwantung Army 9th Duty Unit	15544 (538)
10th Kwantung Army Duty Unit	15545 (1,649)
Kwantung Army 1st Independent Duty Company	15546 (191)
Kwantung Army 2nd Independent Duty Company	15547 (191)
Kwantung Army 3rd Independent Duty Company	15548 (191)

Army hospitals under Kwantung Army control:　　監 *Kan* / 満州 *Manshu*

193rd Line of Communications Hospital	9482 (206)
1st Kanto Army Hospital	7551
Dairen Army Hospital	15518 / 900 (196)
Xingcheng (2nd Kanto) 1st Army Hospital	15534 / 869 (196)
Xingcheng (61st Kanto) 2nd Army Hospital	15535 / 2 (50)
Fengtian (3rd Kanto) Army Hospital	15525 / 145 (304)
Tieling (4th Kanto) Army Hospital	15526 / 248 (113)
Lushun (21st Kanto) Army Hospital	15517 / 79 (134)
Gōngzhǔlǐng (27th Kanto) Army Hospital	15528 / 248 (113)
Hsinking (5th Kanto) 1st Army Hospital	15529 / 875 (584)
Hsinking (7th Kanto) 2nd Army Hospital	15530
Port Arthur Army Hospital	15516 / 79
Jinzhou (6th Kanto) Army Hospital	15519 / 304 (50)
Siping (33rd Kanto) Army Hospital	15527 / 907 (113)
Mukden (39th Kanto) Army Hospital	15533 / 145
Ryujuton (51st Kanto) Army Hospital	15520 / 399 (50)
Yingkou (52nd Kanto) Army Hospital	15521 / 8 (50)
Haicheng (55th Kanto) Army Hospital	15522 / 232 (50)
Liaoyang (39th Kanto) 1st Army Hospital	15523 / 393 (113)
Liaoyang (58th Kanto) 2nd Army Hospital	15524 / 535 (50)
Jinzhou (54th Kanto) Army Hospital	15536 / 496 (304)
Harbin (56th Kanto) 1st Army Hospital	15531 / 7 (304)
Harbin (57th Kanto) 2nd Army Hospital	15532 / 40 (50)
Tieling (4th Kanto) Army Hospital	15526 / 89 (50)
Shinkyo (now Changchun) 1st Army Hospital	満州 875 (164)
Shinkyo (now Changchun) 2nd Army Hospital	満州 114 (167)
Ajō Army Hospital	満州 392 (50)

North Korean Border

34th Army 展 *Ten* (呂武 *Robu*)

The 34th Army was activated on July 3, 1944, from former Wuhan Defense Army personnel. The Wuhan Defense Army was an 11th Army subordinate comprised of rear echelon units who were to secure the area left vacant when the 11th Army went south for Ichi-go. The 34th Army's HQ were in Hankow, China under Lt Gen Tadayoshi Sano from July 5, 1944 until June 18th and Lt Gen Sen'ichi Kushibuchi until August 18, 1945. It served under the China Expeditionary Army from July 17th until Aug 26th, 6th Area Army until June 18, 1945 and Kwantung Army (new order of battle assigned June 17th) until Aug. 18th. The 34th Army was deactivated in Kanko, northern Korea on August 18th.

Service History:
1944: On July 3rd the 34th Army became active in China's Wuhan-Hankou area O
1945: From Mar 21st to Apr 8th the 34th Army participated with the 12th Army in its Laohokau operation. The Kucheng Detachment (39th Div blocking force) prevented enemy reinforcements from interfering freeing the rest of the Division to capture Nanchang, Hsiangyang and Fanchengchen O After Laohokao airfield fell the Kucheng Detachment rejoined the 39th Division on the offensive O Apr 8th, after the 12th Army captured Laohokao the 34th Army returned to its starting point O Mid April, a weak dispersed 110th Division bore the brunt of the Chinese 1st War Sector Army's offensive O On April 29th, with reinforcements of seven infantry battalions, the 110th Division went on the offensive O May 10th, the 110th Div suspended its attack after suffering severely O By June 18th Chinese activity had gradually slackened and the 34th Army re-established its lines O On June 18th the 34th Army HQ were placed under Kwantung Army control. Under the utmost secrecy it was redeployed to Hamhung in northern Korea while its other units remained in the Wuchang-Hankou area under 6th Area Army control. Its new mission was to free up the 17th Area Army from defending the Korean-Soviet border O On July 13th Army General Staff gave orders regarding the 34th Army if the Soviets attacked between the 34th Army and 17th Area Army. If destroying the Soviets in northern Korea proved impossible the 34th Army was to delay any enemy advance towards Pyongyang while protecting Seoul O

Major Units: See division / brigade page for order of battle
59th Division North China 1942 衣 *Koromo* – Hamhung   211
137th Division Manchuria 1945 扶翼 *unknown* – Chongping   230-1
133rd Independent Mixed Brigade 1945 福寿 *Fukuhisashi* – Tungning   277

Units under control of the 34th Army: Hamhung   展 *Ten*

Unit	
34th Army Headquarters	18000 (315)
56th Signal Regiment	14056 (1,913)
Yunghsing Bay Fortress Headquarters	No # (119)
Yunghsing Bay Fortress Guard/ 642nd Guard Btn.	7403 (831)
Yunghsing Bay Fortress Artillery 658 Unit	7403 (2,191)
Mutanchiang Heavy Artillery Regiment	4387 (2,191)
11th Independent Field Artillery Battalion	1484 (616)
15th Trench Mortar Battalion	3155 (866)
115th Independent Motor Transport Battalion	17051 (680)

34th Army continued
462nd Specially Established Guard Battalion	unknown (550)
107th Specially Est/ Construction Duty Company	5657 (61)
127th Specially Established Land Duty Company	14957 (61)
179th Line of Communications Hospital	9484 (333)

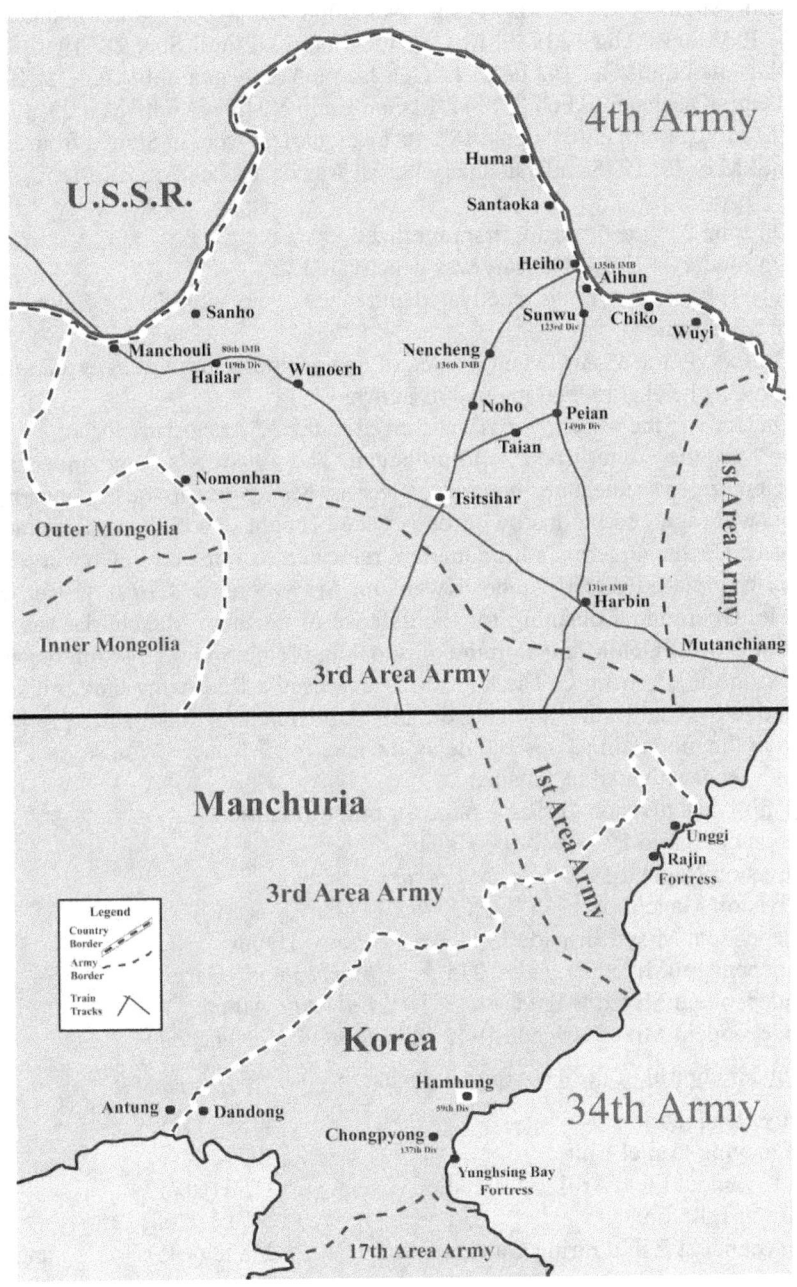

Northern Manchuria

4th Army 光 *Hikari* 4475

The 4th Army was activated on July 15, 1938 as a garrison for the Sunwu area in northern Manchuria. It served under Kwantung Army control from July 15th until July 4, 1942, 2nd Area Army until Oct 30, 1943, 3rd Area Army until May 30, 1945 and Kwantung Army until August 18th. Lt Gen Kesago Nakajima was appointed commander from July 15, 1938 until Aug 1, 1939, Lt Gen Jun Ushiroku until Sept 28, 1940, Lt Gen Kohei Washitsu until Oct 15, 1941, Lt Gen Isamu Yokoyama until Dec 21, 1942, Lt Gen Tatsumi Kusaba until Feb 7, 1944, Lt Gen Kanji Nishihara until Mar 23, 1945 and Lt Gen Mikio Uemura until August 18th. Its headquarters were in Sunwu from July 15, 1938 until May 15, 1945 and Tsitsihar where it was deactivated on Aug 18th.

Service History:
1904: On June 24th the 4th Army first mobilized O
1906: On January 17th the 4th Army was deactivated O
1938: July 15th the 4th Army is reactivated and made responsible for the Sunwu area in northern Manchuria O
1942: On July 4th the 4th Army and its area of responsibility were transferred to the 2nd Area Army, its headquarters remained in Sunwa O
1943: On Oct 30th the 4th Army was transferred to the 3rd Area Army O
1945: In May the Soviet troop build up began. The 4th Army's commander, Lt Gen Mikio Uemura, was the only general officer in Manchuria to raise concerns. His warnings were ignored but his own troops were brought to a high state of readiness. O On May 15th the 4th Army's headquarters relocated to Tsitsihar O On May 30th the 4th Army was placed directly under Kwantung Army control O In July war seemed inevitable. Operational planning for the defense of northern Manchuria was placed in the hands of Lt Gen Mikio Uemura O On Aug 9th the Soviet invasion began with an attack on the 4th Army O The 80th I.M.B. repulsed a Red Army tank brigade that attempted to overrun Hailar, allowing the 119th Division. to withdraw to a pre-planned position in the mountain passes and delay the enemy's advance O On August 18th the 4th Army was deactivated in Tsitsihar O

Major Units: See division / brigade page for order of battle

119th Division Tokyo 1944 宰 *Sai* – Hailar	223
123rd Division Nagoya 1945 松風 *Matzukaze* – Sunwa	225-6
149th Division Manchuria 1945 不撓 *Futou* – Peian	236
80th Independent Mixed Brigade 1945 銳鋒 *Eihou* – Hailar	265
131st Independent Mixed Brigade 1945 奮進 *Funsusumu* – Harbin	276
135th Independent Mixed Brigade 1945 不朽 *Fukyuu* – Aihun	278
136th Independent Mixed Brigade 1945 奮躍 *Funyaku* – Nencheng	278

Units under control of the 4th Army: Tsitsihar   光 *Hikari* 4475

4th Army Headquarters	4455 (311)	
Load Carrying Camel Unit	20702	
10th Independent Field Artillery Battalion	3150 (617)	
17th Mortar Battalion	20717 / 26817 (864)	
30th Independent Rapid Firing Gun Battalion	26830 (496)	anti tank

4th Army continued

42nd Signal Regiment	13928 (1,825)
29th Independent Engineer Regiment	1894 (1,846) road and bridge
1st Kwantung Army Special Guard Unit	unknown
12th Raiding Unit	26898 (3,789)
102nd Guard Headquarters	13112 (62)
654th Specially Established Guard Battalion	3164 (550)
602nd Specially Established Guard Battalion	3167 (420)
604th Specially Established Guard Company	2694 (126)
625th Specially Established Guard Company	No # (126)
626th Specially Established Guard Company	No # (126)
631st Specially Established Guard Company	No # (126)
632nd Specially Established Guard Company	No # (126)
633rd Specially Established Guard Company	No # (126)
634th Specially Established Guard Company	No # (126)
104th Guard Headquarters	13025 / 277 満州
635th Specially Established Guard Company	No # (126)
637th Specially Established Guard Company	No # (126)
645th Specially Established Guard Company	No # (126)
646th Specially Established Guard Company	No # (126)
647th Specially Established Guard Company	No # (126)
608th Specially Established Engineer Unit	No # (930)
614th Specially Established Engineer Unit	No # (930)
74th Line of Communications Duty Company	2600 / 14211 (511)
76th Line of Communications Duty Company	2602 (511)
46th Line of Communications Guard Unit	4621 (1,035)
27th Bridging Materials Company	6021 (410)
28th Bridging Materials Company	3963 (410)
1st Construction Unit	4410
34th Field Road Construction Unit	4840 (304)
46th Construction Duty Company	5729 (511)
49th Casualty Clearing Platoon	3763 (54)
18th Field Ordinance Depot	2635 (2,596)
18th Field Motor Vehicle Depot	2640 (2,889)
18th Field Freight Depot	2645 (2,079)
11th Army Veterinary Quarantine Depot	2630 (164)

4th Army Hospitals   光 Hikari / 満州 Manshu

Qiqihar (9th Kanto) Army Hospital	26854 / 54 (167)
Hailar (26th Kanto) 2nd Army Hospital	26855 / 321 (131)
Songo (35th Kanto) 1st Army Hospital	26850 / 582 (113)
Songo (87th Kanto) 2nd Army Hospital	13137 / 30
Fularji (81st Kanto) Army Hospital	26856 / 101 (50)
Heihe (83rd Kanto) Army Hospital	26851 / 389 (50)
Aigun (84th Kanto) Army Hospital	26853 / 372 (50)
Bei'an (85th Kanto) Army Hospital	26852 / 99 (50)

4th Army Hospitals continued
Nenjiang (86th Kanto) Army Hospital
免渡沟 (89th Kanto) Army Hospital
Jimmu Temple (39th Kanto) Army Hospital

光 *Hikari* / 満州 *Manshu*
26857 / 199 (77)
26858 / 915 (50)
13133 / 22

2nd Air Army 羽 *Hane*

The 2nd Air Army was activated on Hsinking Airfield in Manchuria on June 1, 1942, from former Kwantung Army Air Unit personnel. Its headquarters were on Hsinking Airfield under the Kwantung Army from June 1st until May 8, 1945 when it transferred to the Air General Army. Lt Gen Ritsudo Suzuki was 2nd Air Army commander from June 1st until May 19, 1943, Lt Gen Torashirō Kawabe until Aug 8, 1944, Lt Gen Giichi Itahana until June 1, 1945 and Lt Gen Uichirō Harada until the 2nd Air Army was deactivated on September 4th.

Service History:

1942: Prior to June and before transfers to the Pacific had begun the Kwantung Army Air Unit was at its largest ○ On Mar 20th the 15th Ind Air Unit and 60th Air Regt were transferred to the Pacific area ○ On June 1st Kwantung Army Air Unit Headquarters became the 2nd Air Army HQ on Hsinking Airfield ○ On June 10th the 10th Air Bgde was transferred to the 2nd Air Army from the Southern Army ○ July 1st, the 29th Ind. Air Unit was sent to the 2nd Air Army from China ○

1943: In January the 8th Air Bgde was transferred to the 3rd Air Army ○ The 5th Air Bgde and 74th Air Regt were activated and placed under 2nd Air Army control ○ During the summer nearly the entire air army was sent to the Philippines for the decisive battle and new replacement air units raised. ○ Concrete blast shelters were built for the aircraft on front line airfields. Training was modified to suit small sized air units and enhanced training began for air sector, repair, supply and communications units ○

1944: In the spring many 2nd Air Army units were sent to Japan ○ In April the obsolete Manchukuo Air Force was absorbed into the 2nd Air Army and the 104th Air Regiment, 25th and 81st Ind Squadrons flying Ki-45 Dragonslayers were added ○ On July 31st the 70th Air Regt (Type 02 fighters) was loaned to the 2nd Air Army to defend the Anshan area ○ On Aug 19th the 15th Ind Air Bgde HQ was set up in Anshan ○ On Aug 21st the 88th Anti Aircraft Battalion was organized and attached to the Kwantung Defense Army in Anshan ○

1945: In April the Kwantung Army determined a Russian invasion was due after October ○ In late June an airfield shortage in Korea had the 5th Air Army using Manchurian airfields in Hsingcheng, Hsiungyuehoheng, Suchung, Chou-Shuitsu and Houchiatun. It created congestion and hampered 2nd Air Army operations ○ In early Aug the 2nd Air Army had about 360 combat capable aircraft out of 1000, with most pilots were still in training ○ On Aug 6th Soviet heavy artillery began to deploy near Tungning ○ In July Soviet river crossing units were reported to be assembling near Hulin and Hutou. The 2nd Air Army was to be prepared for the defense of Manchuria by the end of August ○ On Aug 9th Russia declared war and crossed into Manchuria ○ On Aug 10th crossing the outer Mongolian border the Soviet army advanced to Horengoro. The 101st Air Training Brigade and 4th Advanced Air Training Unit began operating out of Tsitsihar ○ Aug 11th, the 15th Air Brigade relocated to Chinchow and Tsitsihar ○ By Aug 12th the Soviet had reached Hailar, Wuchakow, Tulieh, Maotu and Linhsi. The 101st Air Training Brigade attacked 50 km to the east of Lichuan ○ On Aug 13th Soviet troops were in Hsingan and Lichun 40 km southwest of Taonan. Bad weather forced the 15th Air Brigade to return to Anshan. The 101st Air Training Brigade struck 30 km to the west of Taonan. ○ On Aug 14th the Soviets attacked Muling in east Manchuria and continued their advance west. Planes from the 15th Air Brigade raided near Linhai and the 101st Air Training Brigade attacked 15 km west of Taonan. The 15th Air Bgde and 101st Air Training Brigade flew from bases in Anshan and Kungchuling, the 26th Air Training Unit and 4th Advanced Air Training Unit flew from a base in Fenchipo. The 1st Hane Special Attack Unit (5th Advanced Air Training Unit) prepared for suicide missions ○ On Aug 15th, last day of the war, the 15th Air Brigade attacked Taonan, the 101st Air Training Brigade relocated to Tsitsihar and the Hane Special Attack Unit struck Taonan from Hsinking then relocated to Tsitsihar. At noon the Emperor declared unconditional surrender ending the war ○ On Aug 16th reconnaissance continued in anticipation of a resumption of hostilities. The 2nd Air Army's Chief of Staff awaited orders at Kwantung Army Headquarters ○ On Aug 17th orders for the cessation of hostilities arrived ○ On Sept 4th the Soviets took three 2nd Air Army generals, including Harada, into custody and suspended the 2nd Air Army's headquarters ○

Units under control of the 2nd Air Army: Hsinking　　羽 Hane

Unit	Code
2nd Air Army Headquarters	8312 / 満州800 (261)
2nd Air Sector Command	9105 (67)
14th Air Sector Command	11612 (26)
28th Air Sector Command	11636 (42)
57th Air Sector Command	16677 (44)
58th Air Sector Command	16678 (44)
2nd Air Signal Regiment	8362 / 満州996 (1,749)
8th Air Signal Regiment	16608 (1,938)
2nd Air Special Signal Unit	5122
10th Air Navigation Unit	unknown (189)
4th Air Rout Office	unknown (318)
22nd Wireless Radio Unit	16622 (196)
27th Wireless Radio Unit	16627 (196)
28th Wireless Radio Unit	16628 (209)
29th Wireless Radio Unit	16629 (209)
2nd Air Army Temporary Airfield Construction Unit	16684　　Haicheng
2nd Air Army Temporary Signal Training Unit	16694　　Hsinking
3rd Air Intelligence Regiment	8365 / 満州767 (1,704)
11th Air Intelligence Regiment	16662 (1,763)
17th Air Intelligence Unit	16696 (995)
2nd Meteorological Regiment	8398 (1,624)
15th Air Brigade HQ (Ironworks defense unit)	11610 (124)　　Anshan
• 104th Air Regiment (fighter)	18923 (145)　　Anshan
• 25th Ind. Air Squadron (2-seat fighter)	16682 (129)　　Liaoyang
• 81st Ind. Air Squadron (2-seat fighter)	9162 (142)　　Anshan
101st Ind. Air Training Brigade Headquarters	15312 (36)　　Kungchuling
23rd Secondary Air Training Unit (light bomber)	15353 (400)　　Chingshanpao
24th Secondary Air Trning Unit (heavy bomber)	15354 (395)　　Tsitsihar
26th Secondary Air Training Unit (fighter)	16616 (395)　　Mengkuli
42nd Secondary Air Training Unit (HQ recon)	16642 (395)　　Yamentun
22nd Advanced Air Training Unit (assault)	16664　　Hsiungyuehcheng
4th Advanced Air Training Unit (fighter)	16634 (449)　　Mukden
13th Advanced Air Training Unit (fighter)	16663
14th Advanced Air Training Unit	unknown (434)　Kungchuling
9th Airfield Battalion	16609 (372)
10th Airfield Battalion	16607 (372)
11th Airfield Battalion	16616 (372)
13th Airfield Battalion	16617 (372)
16th Airfield Battalion	9116 (372)
29th Airfield Battalion	9199 (372)
30th Airfield Battalion	9107 (372)
36th Airfield Battalion	8336 (372)
39th Airfield Battalion	9164 (372)
40th Airfield Battalion	9626 (372)
45th Airfield Battalion	11618 (372)

2nd Air Army: continued

Unit	Number
53rd Airfield Battalion	9149 (372)
54th Airfield Battalion	16614 (372)
67th Airfield Battalion	9191 (372)
71st Airfield Battalion	8371 (372)
79th Airfield Battalion	9193 (372)
88th Airfield Battalion	8388 (372)
93rd Airfield Battalion	9129 (372)
97th Airfield Battalion	9628 (372)
201st Airfield Battalion	8358 (372)
212th Airfield Battalion	16632 (372)
213th Airfield Battalion	16633 (372)
214th Airfield Battalion	16674 (372)
215th Airfield Battalion	8335 (372)
216th Airfield Battalion	16676 (372)
240th Airfield Battalion	16670 (372)
241st Airfield Battalion	8304 (372)
242nd Airfield Battalion	8342 (372)
243rd Airfield Battalion	8343 (372)
170th Field Airfield Construction Unit	6481 (356)
171st Field Airfield Construction Unit	15073 (356)
42nd Construction Duty Company	3028 (511)
45th Independent Transport Battalion	1350 (1,028)
Kwantung Army Air Depot	16680
8th Field Air Repair Depot	8331 Lankang
9th Field Air Repair Depot	8341 (1,170) Yushutun
9th Field Air Repair Depot, 1st to 7th Ind. Maint. U.	8341 (113 men in each)
10th Field Air Repair Depot	8355 (1,057) Chiamussu
10th Field Air Repair Depot 3rd, 4th Ind. Maint. Unit.	8355 (113 men in each)
11th Field Air Repair Depot	8367 (1,741) Ssuping Depot
11th Ind. Air Repair Depot 3rd Ind. Maint. Unit	8367 (113)
12th Field Air Repair Depot	8372 (1,741) Pingfang
12th Field Air Repair Depot 3rd, 5th Ind. Maint. Units	8372 (113 men in each)
7th Field Air Freight Depot	8391 (489)
8th Field Air Freight Depot	8392 (489)
9th Field Air Freight Depot	8393 (489)
11th Field Air Freight Depot	8395 (313)
2nd Air Army 1st Education Unit	2571 (323)
2nd Air Army 1st Training Unit	16613
70th Land Duty Company	3308 (511)
89th Land Duty Company	4018 (511)
90th Land Duty Company	4019 (511)

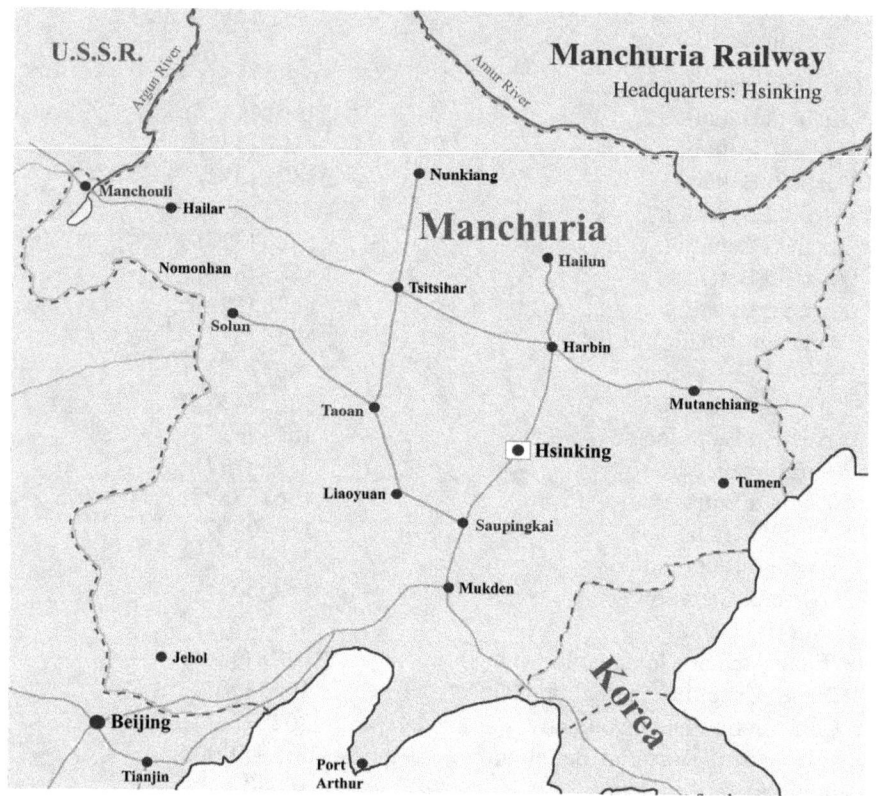

Continental Railway 路 Michi

After the Russo-Japanese War in 1906, Japan acquired the Kwantung Leased Territory and its Russian built railway. The South Manchuria Railway Company, created to operate it, was later replaced by the Kwantung Field Railway Command in Hsinking.
Service History:
1941: After *Special Maneuvers of the Kwantung Army* in July the Kwantung Army made upgrading the continental railway a priority ○
1942: In Korea improvements were made to the main rail line and to sea port connections for ship to train transfers. In Manchuria improvements to the Holungmen-Heishantou rail line, Tungan-Tungshihchen rail line and the conversion of Hsinking-Harbin and Harbin-Mutanchiang to double track lines were all completed by summer. Due to the danger of submarine attacks, which remained scarce until the spring of 1942, goods from China and Manchuria usually traveled down the Korean peninsula by train to Pusan and then by ship to Japan ○
1943: In addition to cereal, coal and steel from Manchuria, Japan annually imported 6 to 7 million tons of rice from Korea. China supplied salt, raw cotton, coal and aluminum. On the continent managing movement by rail presented many problems, there was never enough rolling stock and rail capacity was lacking on South Korea's trunk line ○ In the spring the *Continental Railway Wartime Transportation Conference* was held in Tokyo. To smooth overland transport the Kwantung Army requested the formation of a joint organization for the four separate continental railway systems ○ In May the

Continental Railway Transport Council began work in Changchun. With increasing rail shipments the Council's results were good. Land transport capacity increased, reaching its all time maximum of 3 million tons in the 1st quarter of 1944, although it was still short of a 5 million ton goal ○ After losing Saipan and the Philippines supply lines faced numerous disruptions so efforts to move goods were intensified. The rail system and sea ports in South Korea were vital assets until the US Navy began laying magnetic mines in the Korean Strait. After that sea routes to and from Japan shifted to North Korean ports and the Sea of Japan coast ○

Units under the Continental Railway System	路 *Michi*	
Continental Railway Headquarters	34200 (731)	Hsinking
Continental Railway Dept Education Unit	unknown (121)	
Kwantung Army Field Railway Depot	2650 (104)	
Kwantung Army Field Railway Depot Guard Co.	2650 (153)	
1st Railway Command	No #	
2nd Railway Regiment	5803	
2nd Railway Materials Depot	5807 (158)	
3rd Railway Command	1230 (66)	
4th Railway Regiment	1238 / 徳34102 (2,543)	
3rd Railway Materials Depot	5808 (158)	
22nd Independent Railway Battalion	34111 (1,270)	
23rd Independent Railway Battalion	34112 (934)	
6th Specially Est. Railway Construction Duty Unit	1242 (22)	
3rd Specially Est Railway Bridge Construction Unit	1241 (22)	
Korean Army Railway Headquarters	No # 線	
5th Railway Command	4350 (120)	
19th Railway Regiment	4351 朝 (3,500)	
20th Railway Regiment	4352 朝 (3,500)	
10th Independent Railway Battalion	1259 (1,034)	
11th Independent Railway Battalion	1266 (1,034)	
12th Independent Railway Battalion	1267 (1,034)	
18th Independent Railway Battalion	4354 (711)	
19th Independent Railway Battalion	4355 (841)	
20th Independent Railway Battalion	4356 (742)	
21st Independent Railway Battalion	4357 (853)	
1st Armored Train Unit	4370 (368)	
2nd Armored Train Unit	4371 (275)	
80th Railway Regiment, 1st Battalion	15763 (1,270)	
15th Independent Railway Battalion	1286 (1,034)	
17th Independent Railway Battalion	4353 (1,034)	
2nd Bridge Construction Battalion	2531 (575)	
Continental Railway Management Training Unit	No # (121)	
Kwantung Army 1st Railway Station Headquarters	7554 (106)	
105th Railway Station Command	4825 (27)	
107th Railway Station Command	4636 (27)	
111th Railway Station Command	5721 (27)	
112th Railway Station Command	5722 (27)	

Continental Railway System continued　　　路 *Michi*

Unit	Number
113th Railway Station Command	5723 (27)
116th Railway Station Command	4003 (27)
123rd Railway Station Command	8210 (27)
124th Railway Station Command	8011 (27)
129th Railway Station Command	6903 (27)
137th Railway Station Command	7111 (27)
146th Railway Station Command	7038 (27)
155th Railway Station Command	6432 (27)
156th Railway Station Command	9731 (27)
159th Railway Station Command	9734 (27)
160th Railroad Station Command	9730 (106)
172nd Railway Station Command	1233 (106)
173rd Railway Station Command	1234 (106)
174th Railway Station Command	1235 (106)
176th Railway Station Command	3858 満 (20)
186th Railway Station Command	7183 (106)
169th Railway Station Command	2004 (27)
170th Railway Station Command	2005 (27)
103rd Railway Station Command	33997
104th Railway Station Command	1395 (17)
119th Railway Station Command	33998 / 4000
126th Railway Station Command	10054
128th Railway Station Command	34001
134th Railway Station Command	34003
139th Railway Station Command	34004 / 7113
142nd Railway Station Command	7116 (17)
194th Railway Station Command	9758 (17)
143rd Railway Station Command	7117 (17)
148th Railway Station Command	7034
149th Railway Station Command	7035 / 34006
152nd Railway Station Command	6427
153rd Railway Station Command	34008 / 6428
164th Railway Station Command	unknown
207th Railway Station Command	2017 (17)
208th Railway Station Command	unknown (17)
209th Railway Station Command	7593 (17)
210th Railway Station Command	7594 (17)
211th Railway Station Command	7595 (17)
212th Railway Station Command	7596 (17)
3rd Railway Regiment	1231 / 34101
188th Railway Station Command	7181
189th Railway Station Command	7185

Chapter 2
Eastern Manchuria

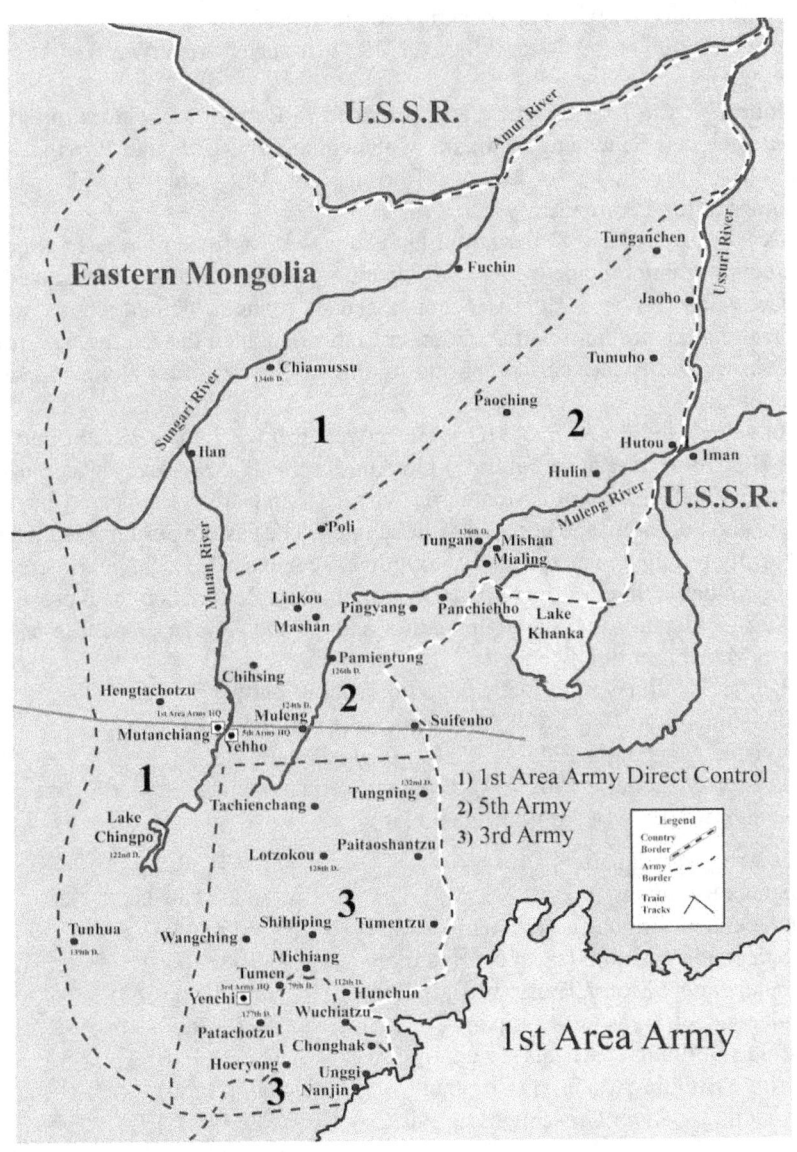

1st Area Army 鋭 *Ei* 1441

The 1st Area Army was activated on June 27, 1942 and placed under Kwantung Army control on July 4th. Its headquarters were in Mutanchiang and it was charged with defending eastern Manchuria against the Soviets. Lt Gen Tomoyuki Yamashita, 'The Tiger of Malaya', was appointed commander from July 1st until Sept 26, 1944 and Lt Gen Seiichi Kita until August 18th. When the Kwantung Army became a general army on July 4, 1942, the 1st and 2nd Area Armies were created to fill a void in the chain of command. The 1st Area Army was deactivated in Mutanchiang on Aug 18, 1945.

Subordinate armies / duty dates:
2nd Army from July 4, 1942, until Oct 30, 1943 (to the 2nd Area Army)
3rd Army from July 4, 1942, until deactivated on Aug 18, 1945
5th Army from July 4, 1942, until deactivated on Aug 18, 1945
20th Army from July 4, 1942, until Sept 27, 1944 (to the 6th Area Army)

Service History:
1942: June 27th, the 1st Area Army was activated in Eastern Manchuria to defend an area that included Sanchiang, Tungan, Mutanchiang and Chientao Provinces ○ On July 4th, after his conquest of Malaya, Tojo appointed Lt Gen Tomoyuki Yamashita commander of the 1st Area Army ○

1943: Oct 30th, the 1st and 2nd Armored Divisions were assigned to the 1st Area Army and the tank training brigade went to the Kwantung Army when the Mechanized Army was deactivated ○ Dec 26th, IGHQ announced its plans to defend against a Soviet invasion along the northern border. Counter to this new plan the Kwantung Army and 1st Area Army had spent years preparing to engage Soviet forces along Manchuria's eastern border ○

1945: In March the 3rd Army's HQ were moved from Yehho to Yenchi and the 5th Army's HQ from Tungan to Yehho ○ On Aug 9th the 1st Area Army was the first to report the Soviet invasion of Manchuria when Russian troops appeared in front of Tungning and Suifenho, and bombed Mutanchiang. The eastern border was hit hardest. The 5th Army put up an unexpectedly stout defense and stalled a Soviet pincer attack, providing valuable time for the retreat toward Tunghua Redoubt on the Korean border ○ On Aug 15th Japan surrendered unconditionally ○ On Aug 26th Japanese resistance in eastern Manchuria finally ended ○

Major Units: See division / brigade page for order of battle

122nd Division Tokyo 1945 舞鶴 *Maitsuru*– Lake Chingpo	225
134th Division Manchuria 1945 勾玉 *Unknown*– Chiamussu	229
139th Division Manchuria 1945 不屈 *Fukutsu* – Tunhua	232

Units under the 1st Area Army: Mutanchiang　　　鋭 *Ei* 1441

1st Area Army Headquarters	1448 (601)
17th Signals Regiment	7589 (1,913)
12th Independent Engineer Regiment	13000 (961)
114th Independent Motor Transport Battalion	13081 (680)
140th Independent Motor Transport Battalion	unknown (680)
80th Independent Transport Company	6478 (398)
29th Bridge Building Materials Company	7102 (410)
32nd Bridge Building Materials Company	6416 (680)
6th Division, 21st River Crossing Materials Coy.	9354 (605)

1st Area Army: continued

42nd Sea Duty Company	4012 (511)
Kwantung Army 2nd Field Horse Remount Depot	13028 (512)
16th Field Ordinance Depot	2633 (2,344)
2nd Specially Established Garrison Unit	No #
103rd Guard Headquarters	13027 (315)
655th Specially Established Guard Battalion	3165 (550)
603rd Specially Established Guard Battalion	1253 (420)
605th Specially Established Guard Battalion	2604 (420)
620th Specially Established Guard Company	No # (126)
621st Specially Established Guard Company	No # (126)
622nd Specially Established Guard Company	No # (126)
624th Specially Established Guard Company	No # (126)
627th Specially Established Guard Company	No # (126)
636th Specially Established Guard Company	No # (126)
613th Specially Established Guard Engineer Unit	No # (930)
1st Area Army Temporary Court-Martial	満 845 (20)
6th Kwantung Army Military Detention Camp	満 857 (9)

1st Area Army Hospitals

	鋭 Ei / 満州 Manshu
Hsinking (7th Kanto) 1st Army Hospital	13016
Hsinking (7th Kanto) 2nd Army Hospital	15530
Mudanjiang (8th Kanto) 1st Army Hospital	13011/664 (167)
Port Arthur (24th Kanto) 1st Army Hospital	21081/148 (131)
Linkou (25th Kanto) Army Hospital	21082/588 (131)
Jiamusi 1st (38th Kanto) Army Hospital	13012/791 (836)
Jiamusi 2nd (90th Kanto) Army Hospital	13021/696 (50)
60th Kanto Army Hospital	13022/961 (50)
Ning'an (62nd Kanto) Army Hospital	13013/10 (50)
69th Kanto Army Hospital	13014/2105
Suifenhe (76th Kanto) Army Hospital	13015/61 (50)
Hōsei (72nd Kanto) Army Hospital	13017/492 (50)
Boli (78th Kanto) Army Hospital	13018/233 (50)
76th Kanto Army Hospital	13020/13015
Xingshan (91st Kanto) Army Hospital	13023/931 (50)
Fujin (92nd Kanto) Army Hospital	13024/120 (50)
Mishan Army Hospital	13085/78 (50)
Mamorukami (69 Kanto) Army Hospital	21085/348 (50)
Baodong Army Hospital	21092

U.S.S.R./Eastern Manchuria Border

3rd Army 岩 *Iwa* 3692

The 3rd Army was activated Jan 13, 1938 to secure eastern Manchuria's border with the Soviet Union and the Hsinking-Tumen Rail line, which ran from east Manchuria into northern Korea. Its headquarters were in Mutanchiang under Kwantung Army control from Jan 13th until July 4, 1942, when it was transferred to the 1st Area Army and its HQ moved to Yehho. By Mar 15, 1945 with war imminent the 3rd Army's headquarters were moved to Yenchi. Lt Gen Otozō Yamada was 3rd Army's commander from Jan 13th until Dec 10th, Lt Gen Hayao Tada until Sept 12, 1939, Lt Gen Kamezō Suetaka until Mar 1, 1941, Lt Gen Masamitsu Kawabe until Aug 17, 1942, Lt Gen Eitarō Uchiyama until Feb 7, 1944, Lt Gen Hiroshi Nemoto until Nov 22nd and Lt Gen Keisaku Murakami until it was deactivated in Yenchi on August 18, 1945.

Service History:
1943: On Oct 30th the 2nd Army headquarters recieved orders to go south and the 3rd Army was assigned the 2nd Army's duties along with most of its units ○ On November 6th the 2nd Army headquarters departed Manchuria ○
1945: On March 15th the 3rd Army's headquarters redeployed from Yehho to Yenchi ○ On Aug 9th the Soviets invaded Manchuria, unable to stall them the army was either overrun or by-passed in the onslaught. The 3rd Army ended in the Korea fortified zone with some units holding out until Aug 25th ○

Major Units: See division / brigade page for order of battle

Unit	Page
79th Division Korea 1945 奏 *Kanade* – Tumen	215
112th Division Kureme 1944 公 *Kou* – Hunchun	222
127th Division Utsunomiya 1945 英邁 *Eimai* – Patachotzu	227-8
128th Division Kanazawa 1945 英武 *Eibu*– Lotzokou	228
132nd Independent Mixed Brigade 1945 奮戦 *Hunshen* – Tungning	276-7
1st Mobile Brigade 1945 速 *Soku* – Shihliping	284

Units under control of the 3rd Army: Yenchi   岩 *Iwa* 3692

Unit	Code	Location
3rd Army Headquarters	3600 (258)	Yenchi
43rd Independent Mixed Regiment	7181	
101st Independent Mixed Regiment	7481 (2,061)	Chonghak
Tungning Heavy Artillery Regiment	26709/4329 (2,209)	Tungning
2nd Heavy Artillery Regiment	1214 (1211)	Acheng
3rd Heavy Artillery Regiment	1215 (1208)	Hsiachengtsu
2nd Independent Heavy Artillery Company	3039 / 3339 (180)	Acheng
1st Independent Trench Mortar Company	12394 (326)	
55th Signal Regiment	26721 / 3680 (1,913)	
1st Independent Motor Transport Company	26722 (526)	
69th Independent Transport Company	6752 (398)	Laoheishan
Rajin Fortress Headquarters	6337 (151)	Rajin
Rajin Fortress Artillery Unit	7402 (590)	Rajin
460th Specially Established Guard Battalion	unknown (550)	
623rd Specially Established Guard Company	No # (126)	
651st Specially Established Guard Company	No # (126)	
113th Independent Motor Transport Battalion	27570 (680)	Chaoyangchuan
52nd Independent Transport Battalion (packhorse)	3752 (1,026)	Tatutzuchuan

3rd Army: continued

15th Veterinary Quarantine Depot	5737 (137)	Shantung
15th Field Ordinance Depot	2632 (2,344)	Yenchi
20th Field Ordinance Depot	2637 (805)	Hunchun
16th Field Motor Transport Depot	2638 (2,497)	Tatutzuchuan
20th Field Motor Transport Depot	2642 (708)	Hunchun
16th Field Freight Depot	2643 (1,593)	Chaoyangchuan
20th Field Freight Depot	2647 (660)	Hunchun
46th Field Road Construction Unit	3611 (304)	Tungning
84th Land Duty Company	5731/6531 (511)	Tuhuangtzu
95th Land Duty Company	6917 (511)	Laoheishan
32nd Construction Duty Company	7851 (511)	Yenchi
77th Line of Communications Guard Unit	2603 (511)	
77th Line of Communications Duty Company	5770 (511)	Chengtzukou
79th Line of Communications Duty Company	7041 (511)	Laoheishan
13th Line of Communications Medical Unit HQ	4631 (120)	Mutanchiang
97th Line of Communications Hospital	8204 (359)	Haicheng/Ningan
9th Patient Transport Unit Headquarters	7868 (117)	Agochi (N Korea)
36th Casualty Clearing Platoon	7870 (54)	

3rd Army Hospitals

岩 *Iwa*

Hunchun (blank) Army Hospital	26711/342 (131)	Yenchi
22nd Kanto Army Hospital	unknown	
Hailar (23rd Kanto) 1st Army Hospital	21080 (50)	
Yanji (28th Kanto) Army Hospital	26712/987 (113)	
Lao Heishan (30th Kanto) Army Hospital	26714/862 (50)	
Tungning (73rd Kanto) 1st Army Hospital	467 (191)	Yenchi
Tungning (66th Kanto) 2nd Army Hospital	21086/137 (50)	Langtungkou
Tungning (blank) 3rd Army Hospital	26717/332 (50)	Chengtzukou
64th Kanto Army Hospital	26718	
65th Kanto Army Hospital	unknown	
67th Kanto Army Hospital	unknown	
Baoqing (74th Kanto) Army Hospital	21085 (50)	
Pingyang (blank) Army Hospital	21079 (50)	

Mutanchiang to Manchu/Russia Border

5th Army 城 *Shiro* 5087

The 5th Army was activated first on December 7, 1937, as a garrison in south China under Imperial Headquarters direct control. General Mikio Furushō was 5th Army commander from Dec 8th (was deactivated on Feb 15th) until Feb 26, 1938.

The 5th Army was reactivated in Tungan, Manchuria on May 19, 1939 under Kwantung Army control. Based in Tungan, it was responsible for the area between the Mutanchiang plain and Tungan. On July 4, 1942 the 5th Army was transferred to the 1st Area Army and its headquarters moved to Ningan. Lt Gen Kenji Doihara was 5th Army commander from May 19th until Sept 28, 1940, Lt Gen Shigekazu Hada until Oct 10, 1941, Lt Gen Jō Imura until Oct 29, 1943, Lt Gen Toshimichi Uemura until June 27, 1944 and Lt Gen Tsunemori Shimuzu until the 5th Army was deactivated in Ningan on August 18, 1945.

Service History:
1943: On Nov 6th when the 2nd Army headquarters departed Manchuria for the South Pacific the 5th Army was assigned a number of its former units O
1945: At the end of March the 5th Army HQ moved from Tungan to Yehho O On Aug 9th during the Soviet invasion of Manchuria the 5th Army acquitted itself well. Between Aug. 12th and 16th, with less than 30 artillery pieces the 126th and 135th Div stalled two Soviet field armies at Mutanchiang O The 5th Army continued to resist until the war ended and orders arrived to disengage O

Major Units: See division / brigade page for order of battle

124th Division Sendai 1945 遠謀 *Enbou* – Muleng		226
126h Division Kumamoto 1945 英断 *Eidan* – Pamientung		227
135th Division Manchuria 1945 真心 *Magokoro* – Tungan		229
15th Border Garrison Unit 城 *Shiro* – Hutou		(not in book)

Units under control of the 5th Army: Yehho   城 *Shiro* 5087

Unit	Code
5th Army Headquarters	5033 (702)
20th Heavy Artillery Regiment	3492 / 21099 (1,773)
5th Independent Heavy Artillery Battalion	1219 (616)
8th Independent Heavy Artillery Battalion	1022 (616)
1st Independent Heavy Artillery Company	1261 (180)
31st Independent Rapid Firing Gun Unit (anti-tank)	17421 / 21076 (496)
1st Engineer Unit Headquarters	1226 / 358 (32)
18th Independent Engineer Regiment	1893 (1,846)
3rd Field Fortification Unit	4838 (374)
64th Land Duty Company	7848 (511)
92nd Land Duty Company	8222 (511)
9th Guerilla Unit	13080 (1,534)
46th Signal Regiment	13948 (1,913)
45th Field Road Construction Unit	5245 (304)
628th Specially Established Guard Company	No # (126)
629th Specially Established Guard Company	No # (126)
630th Specially Established Guard Company	No # (126)
641st Specially Established Guard Company	No # (126)
64th Independent Transport Battalion	7000 (2,440)
70th Independent Transport Company	6753 (398)

5th Army continued

71st Independent Transport Company	6754 (398)
46th Line of Communications Duty Unit	4620 (511)
80th Line of Communications Duty Company	2608 (511)
75th Line of Communications Guard Unit	1386 (1,035)
19th L. o. C. Medical Unit Headquarters	2623 (120)
47th Casualty Clearing Platoon	3755 (54)
20th Veterinary Quarantine Depot	2631 (137)
17th Field Ordinance Depot	2634 (2,740)
17th Field Motor Vehicle Depot	2639 (2,693)
17th Field Freight Depot	2644 (1,986)
25th Field Motor Vehicle Depot	9831 (1,010)
25th Field Motor Vehicle Depot Guard Unit	9831 (645)
25th Field Freight Depot	9832 (508)
25th Field Freight Depot 1st Mobile Repair Section	9832 (93)
25th Field Freight Depot Guard Unit	9832 (476)
25th Field Freight Depot 3rd Mobile Repair Section	9832 (93)
25th Field Freight Depot 2nd Mobile Repair Section	9832 (93)
Hulin (32nd Kanto) Army Hospital	21083 (113)
Suiyang (34th Kanto) Army Hospital	21087 (113)
Mudanjiang (37th Kanto) 2nd Army Hospital	21077 (113)
Mudanjiang (63rd Kanto) 3rd Army Hospital	21094 (50)
Hutou (68th Kanto) Army Hospital	21084 (77)
73rd Kanto Army Hospital	21088
Xingshu (78th Kanto) Army Hospital	21092 (50)
Jixi (79th Kanto) Army Hospital	21093 (692)
Bamiantongzhen (80th Kanto) Army Hospital	21089 (692)

End 1st Area Army

South and West Manchuria

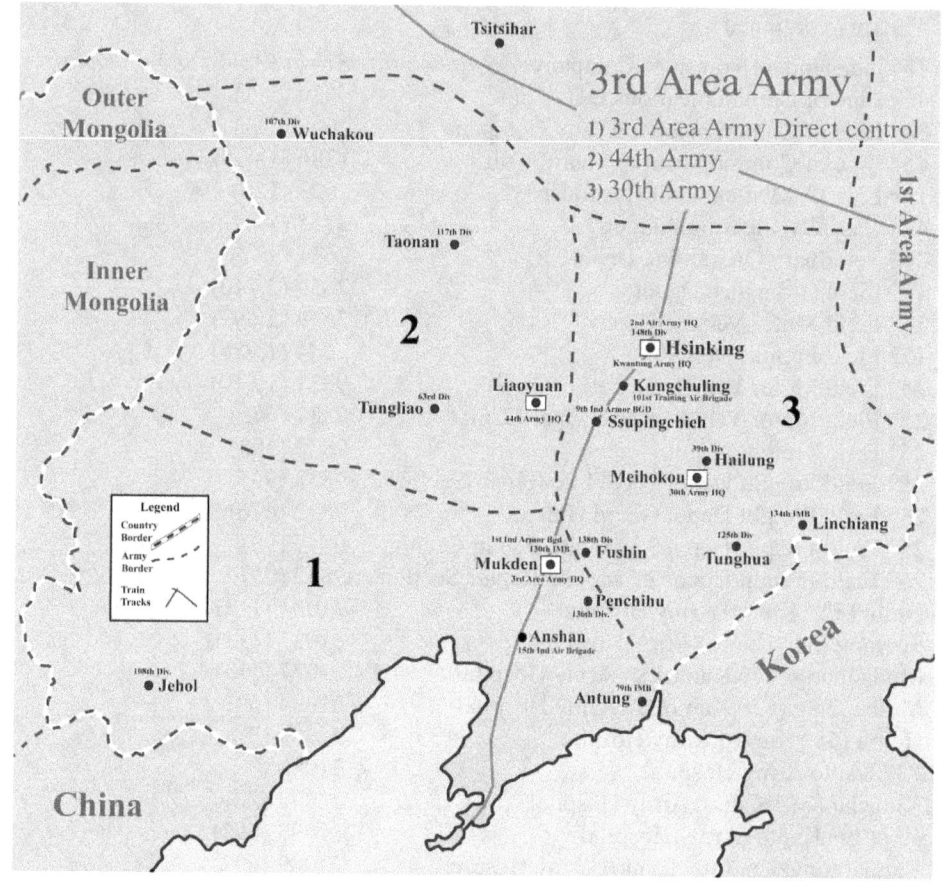

3ʳᵈ Area Army 強 *Kyou* 9331

The 3ʳᵈ Area Army was activated on October 26, 1943 and placed under Kwantung Army control on Oct 30ᵗʰ. With its headquarters in Mukden the 3ʳᵈ Area Army was to defend south and west Manchuria. General Naosaburō Okabe was commander from Oct 29ᵗʰ until Aug 25, 1944 and General Jun Ushiroku until it was deactivated in Mukden on August 18, 1945.

Subordinate armies / duty dates:
4ᵗʰ Army from Oct 30, 1943 until May 30, 1945 (to the Kwantung Army)
6ᵗʰ Army from Oct 30, 1943 until Jan 25, 1945 (to the China Expeditionary Army)
44ᵗʰ Army from May 30, 1945 until Aug 18, 1945
30ᵗʰ Army from Jul 30, 1945 until Aug 18, 1945

Service History:
1945: On Aug 9ᵗʰ the Red Army invaded Manchuria. The 3ʳᵈ Area Army commander General Ushiroku, tried desperately to protect the 1,000,000 Japanese citizens living in the region ○ On Aug 14ᵗʰ ignoring his standing orders to withdraw to the Tunghua Redoubt near the Korean border, General Ushiroku began concentrating his troops to the north and south of Mukden. The lightning advance of the Red Army forced him to

reconsider in favor of the Kwantung Army's original plan but confusion set in. Puyi's Manchukuo National Army, fighting under 3rd Area Army control, mutinied at that moment putting an end to any hope of saving the situation ○ The 3rd Area Army was deactivated in Mukden on August 18th ○

<u>Major Units</u>: See division / brigade page for order of battle
108th Division Hirosaki 1937 祐 *Suke* – Jehol	221
136th Division Manchuria 1945 不抜 *Hubatu* – Penchihu	230
79th Independent Mixed Brigade 1945 丈夫 *Masurao* – Antung	265
130th Independent Mixed Brigade 1945 奮闘 *Hunto* – Mukden	276
134th Independent Mixed Brigade 1945 奮励 *Hunrei* – Linchiang	277
1st Independent Armored Brigade 1944 迫 *Sako* – Mukden	279

<u>Units under control of the 3rd Area Army</u>: Mukden 強 *Kyou* 9331

3rd Area Army Headquarters	9338 (1,361)
54th Signal Regiment	37809 (1,913)
171st Anti-Aircraft Regiment	3112 (1,791)
22nd Field Anti-Aircraft Unit Command	13100 (42) 13103
85th Field Anti-Aircraft Battalion	13104 (521)
88th Field Anti-Aircraft Battalion	13105 (521)
90th Field Anti-Aircraft Battalion	13106 / 14005 (527)
91st Field Anti-Aircraft Battalion	13114 (527)
92nd Field Anti-Aircraft Battalion	13116 (527)
100th Field Anti-Aircraft Battalion	14008 (527)
65th Independent Field Anti-Aircraft Battalion	14009 (161)
26th Anti-Aircraft Regiment	2687 (1,644)
1st Field Anti-Aircraft Searchlight Battalion	1224 (453)
6th Field Anti-Aircraft Searchlight Battalion	14036 / 13129 (431)
7th Field Anti-Aircraft Searchlight Battalion	14038 (431)
14th Ind. Field Anti-Aircraft Searchlight Company	14039 (186)
68th Field Machine Cannon Company	13118 (105)
69th Field Machine Cannon Company	13119 (105)
70th Field Machine Cannon Company	13130 (105)
71st Field Machine Cannon Company	13121 (105)
72nd Field Machine Cannon Company	13122 (105)
73rd Field Machine Cannon Company	13123 (105)
74th Field Machine Cannon Company	13124 (105)
75th Field Machine Cannon Company	13125 (105)
76th Field Machine Cannon Company	13126 (105)
77th Field Machine Cannon Company	13127 (105)
85th Field Machine Cannon Company	15655 (105)
61st Fortress Heavy Artillery Company	3111 (247)
610th Specially Established Guard Battalion	unknown (420)
615th Specially Established Guard Company	unknown (126)
616th Specially Established Guard Company	unknown (126)
617th Specially Established Guard Company	unknown (126)
618th Specially Established Guard Company	unknown (126)
649th Specially Established Guard Company	unknown (126)

3rd Area Army: continued   強 *Kyou*
650th Specially Established Guard Company   unknown (126)
611th Specially Established Engineer Unit   unknown (930)
612th Specially Established Engineer Unit   unknown (930)
Fushin Guard Unit Headquarters   13108 (30)
602nd Specially Established Guard Company   2692 (126)
603rd Specially Established Engineer Unit   3157 (930)
Penchihu Guard Unit Command   13107 (30)
603rd Specially Established Guard Company   2693 (126)
606th Specially Established Guard Company   2696 (126)
604th Specially Established Engineer Unit   3158 (930)
Anshan Guard Unit Command   13109 (30)
601st Specially Established Guard Company   2691 (126)
605th Specially Established Engineer Unit   3160 (930)
Kwantung Army 1st Specially Est. Guard HQ   3402 (440)
1st Specially Established Guard Battalion   37402 (1,400)
2nd Specially Established Guard Battalion   37402 (1,400)
3rd Specially Established Guard Battalion   37402 (1,400)
4th Specially Established Guard Battalion   37402 (1,400)
5th Specially Established Guard Battalion   37402 (1,400)
6th Specially Established Guard Battalion   37402 (1,400)
7th Specially Established Guard Battalion   37402 (1,400)
8th Specially Established Guard Battalion   37402 (1,400)
9th Specially Established Guard Battalion   37402 (1,400)
10th Specially Established Guard Battalion   37402 (1,400)
1st Kwantung Specially Est. Guard Signal Unit   37402 (300)
1st Kwantung Specially Est. Guard Work Unit   37402 (1,030)
1st Kwantung Specially Est. Training Work Unit   37402 (500)
11th Raiding Unit   37810 (3,789)
651st Specially Established Guard Battalion   3161 (550)
611th Specially Established Guard Battalion   unknown (420)
612th Specially Established Guard Battalion   unknown (420)
613th Specially Established Guard Battalion   unknown (420)
614th Specially Established Guard Battalion   unknown (420)
615th Specially Established Guard Battalion   unknown (420)
616th Specially Established Guard Battalion   unknown (420)
608th Specially Established Guard Company   unknown (126)
609th Specially Established Guard Company   unknown (126)
610th Specially Established Guard Company   unknown (126)
607th Specially Established Engineer Unit   3169 (930)
652nd Specially Established Guard Battalion   3162 (550)
653rd Specially Established Guard Battalion   3163 (550)
606th Specially Established Guard Battalion   2605 (420)
607th Specially Established Guard Battalion   unknown (420)
608th Specially Established Guard Battalion   unknown (420)
611th Specially Established Guard Company   unknown (126)

3rd Area Army: continued

612th Specially Established Guard Company	unknown (126)
613th Specially Established Guard Company	unknown (126)
602nd Specially Established Engineer Unit	3154 (930)
606th Specially Established Engineer Unit	3168 (930)
609th Specially Established Engineer Unit	unknown (930)
610th Specially Established Engineer Unit	unknown (930)
901st Temporary Independent Infantry Battalion	13140
3rd Area Army Judiciary Corp	unknown
7th Kwantung Army Prison Office	満 986 (9)
81st Independent Motor Transport Battalion	unknown
34th Construction Duty Company	3302
89th Line of Communications Hospital	6004
3rd Area Army Field Horse Replacement Depot	2654

South Central Manchuria

30th Army 敏 *Bin*

The 30th Army was activated on July 28, 1945 and placed under the 3rd Area Army's control on July 30th. Its mission was to construct fortifications along the south central Manchuria border and provide security for the region. The 30th Army's headquarters were in Yenchi from July 28th until Aug 9th, Meihokou until Aug 12th and Hsinking until it was deactivated. Lt Gen Shōjirō Īda was 30th Army commander from July 25th until deactivation in Hailing on August 18th.

Service History:
1945: On Aug 9th the Red Army invaded Manchuria ○ The 30th Army was deployed to the west of the 1st Area Army but saw little action before the surrender on Aug 15th ○

Major Units: See division / brigade page for order of battle

39th Division Hiroshima 1939 藤 *Fuji* – Hailung	208
125th Division Hiroshima 1945 英機 *Eiki* – Tunghua	226-7
138th Division Manchuria 1945 不動 *Hudō* – Fushun	231
148th Division Manchuria 1945 富嶽 *Hūgaku* – Changechun	235-6

Units under control of the 30th Army: Meihokou	敏 *Bin*
30th Army Headquarters	25301 (466)
1st Heavy Artillery Regiment	7703 (1,201)
19th Heavy Artillery Regiment	No # (1,208)
7th Independent Heavy Artillery Battalion	No # (616)
21st Independent Field Heavy Artillery Battalion	unknown
27th Independent Mortar Battalion	3111 (648)
116th Independent Motor Transport Battalion	37814 (680)
53rd Independent Transport Battalion	3759 (1,028)
42nd Field Road Construction Unit	9750 (304)

30th Army: continued   敏 *Bin*

Unit	Number
2nd Engineer Unit Headquarters	3880 (42)
601st Specially Established Guard Battalion	3166 (420)
604th Specially Established Guard Battalion	1254 (420)
601st Specially Established Guard Engineer Unit	3153 (930)
609th Specially Established Guard Battalion	No # (420)
638th Specially Established Guard Company	No # (126)
639th Specially Established Guard Company	No # (126)
640th Specially Established Guard Company	No # (126)
642nd Specially Established Guard Company	No # (126)
40th Independent Engineer Regiment, 2nd Coy.	1486
46th Line of Communications Sector Command	4620 (203)
46th Sector Transport Unit	4620
46th Line of Communications Guard Company	4622 (1,035)
88th Land Duty Company	4017 (511)
41st Sea Duty Company	4011 (511)
80th Construction Duty Company	14040 (511)
30th Army Motor Vehicle Depot	unknown
36th Kwantung Army Hospital	unknown (50)

West Manchuria

44th Army 遠征 *Ensei* 14000

The 44h Army was activated in Liaoyuan on May 30, 1945, from former Kwantung Defense Army personnel. With headquarters in Liaoyuan on May 30th it was placed under 3rd Area Army control to defend western Manchuria. On August 13th its headquarters moved to Mukden. Lt Gen Yoshio Hongō was 44h Army commander from May 30th until it was deactivated in Chengchiatum on August 18th.

Service History:

1945: On Aug 9th the Red Army spearhead for the invasion of western Manchuria, the 6th Guards Tank Army bypassed and isolated the 107th Division, which continued to fight a guerilla war until it was ordered to surrender. The 44th Army was the only 3rd Area Army unit to engage in major combat ○

Major Units: See division / brigade page for order of battle

Unit	Page
63rd Division Utsunomiya 1943 陣 *Jin* – Tungliao	212
107th Division Hirosaki 1944 凪 *Nagi* – Wuchakou	220-1
117th Division North China 1944 弘 *Hiroshi* – Taonan	222-3
9th Independent Armored Brigade 1945 奮迅 *Hunjin* – Ssupingchien	282

Units under control of the 44th Army: Liaoyuan   遠征 *Ensei* 14000

Unit	Number	
44th Army Headquarters	14001 (183)	
17th Field Medium Artillery Regiment	1013 (1,776)	
30th Field Medium Artillery Regiment	14063 (1,252)	
29th Independent Rapid Firing Gun Battalion	14062	anti-tank

44th Army: continued

14th Independent Field Artillery Battalion	14023 (528)
6th Independent Heavy Artillery Company	14066 (180)
31st Signal Regiment	12968 (1,746)
46th Independent Transport Battalion	30868
2nd Raiding Unit	13944 (866)
605th Specially Established Guard Company	2695 (126)
607th Specially Established Guard Company	2697 (126)
619th Specially Established Guard Company	No # (126)
643rd Specially Established Guard Company	No # (126)
644th Specially Established Guard Company	No # (126)
648th Specially Established Guard Company	No # (126)
75th Line of Communications Duty Company	1387 (511)
112th Independent Motor Transport Battalion	14068 (680)
73rd Independent Transport Company	6766 (398)
47th Field Road Construction Unit	3619 (304)
40th Construction Duty Company	4640 (511)
55th Casualty Clearing Platoon	8205 (54)
19th Field Ordinance Depot	2636 (2,032)
19th Field Motor Vehicle Depot	2641 (2,213)
19th Field Freight Depot	2646 (1,966)
Baicheng (31st Kanto) Army Hospital	11167 (113)
82nd Kanto Army Hospital	11168 (50)
88th Kanto Army Hospital	11179 (50)

Type 96 15cm howitzers towed by Type 92 Model B diesel 5 ton prime movers (author)

Korean Peninsula

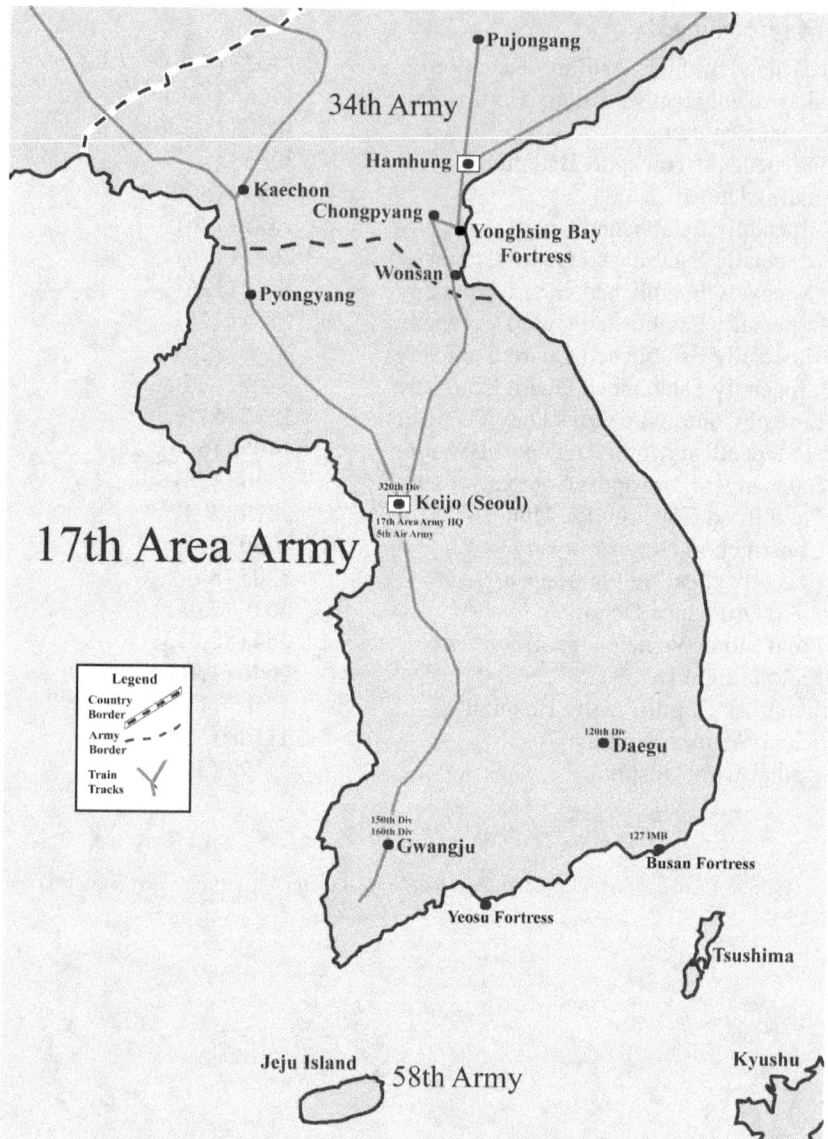

17th Area Army / Korea Army District 築 *Kizuka*

The 17th Area Army was activated on Jan 22, 1945, from former Korea Army personnel. Headquarters in Seoul, on Feb 6th it was placed under Imperial Headquarters direct control with a mandate to defend the Korean peninsula. IGHQ placed special emphasis on protecting the rail system, Japan's lifeline from China and Manchuria to the sea port in Pusan, as well as the northern Korean railway and key areas along the Tumen River. General Seishirō Itagaki commanded the 17th Area Army from Feb 6, 1945 until April

7th and Lt Gen Yoshio Kōzuki until September 12th. With the Soviet invasion on Aug 9th the 17th Area Army headquarters moved to Pyongyang and on the 10th the area army was placed under Kwantung Army direction. The 17th Area Army was deactivated in Pyongyang on September 12, 1945.

Note: Korea was also called Chosen by the Japanese.

Subordinate army / duty dates:
58th Army from April 8, 1945, until the war ended

Service History:
1905: A Japanese garrison remained in Korea after the Russo-Japanese War ○
1910: Japan annexed Korea, ostensibly to suppress nationalism and protect Korea's border with Russia ○
1915: On Dec 24th the 19th and 20th Divisions were created in Korea, the only front line units there until 1943 ○
1943: On Jan 6th the 20th Division sailed for Wewak. This was the first large-scale troop movement from Korea ○ On May 14th the 30th Div was raised and activated in Pyongyang ○ In Nov the 19th Division was sent to the Philippines ○
1944: In May the 30th Div was sent to the Philippines ○ On May 27th the 49th Div was raised and activated in Seoul, it was sent to Burma a month later ○ With the war going badly an invasion of Japan had to be considered, the only troops in Korea at the time were training units for the 19th, 20th and 30th Depot Divisions ○
1945: Feb 6th, homeland defense districts reorganize ○ On Feb 11th the 17th Area Army was activated to defend Korea. Its mission included securing the railway line extending the length of the peninsula, the north Korean railway, certain key sectors along the Tumen River and overseeing the Korean Army Administrative Districts ○ Feb 28th, the 150th and 160th Div were activated in Cholla Pukto and Cholla Nambdo to secure the southern coastline ○ Mar 12th, *Ketsu-go* announced, in it Korea is the 7th Area ○ On Mar 31st the 58th Army was activated in Seoul ○ On Apr 8th the 58th Army made subordinate to the 17th Area Army. It was deployed to Cheju Island at the end of April to create an Iwo Jima like fortress ○ On May 30th the Kwantung Army was given control over operations in north Korea but the 17th Area Army maintained administrative control. In southern Korea the 17th Area Army maintained operational and administrative control. The changes were to free up the area army for planning and constructing defenses in central and southern Korea. The 17th Area Army was ordered to only engage Soviet forces that threatened Wonsan. The Kwantung Army took control of the 79th Division, 101st I.M.B., Rajin and Yunghsing Bay Fortress garrisons in the north ○ In May the 17th Area Army had an estimated strength was 170,000 men ○ On June 15th a briefing and map maneuvers were held for staff operations officers ○ June 25th with Okinawa lost IGHQ assumed the Allies would secure a base for the invasion of Japan next, Korea was considered a logical choice. With just four and a half divisions Korean defenses were inadequate against either the U.S. or Russia ○ By June 30th the 5th Air Army had transferred to Korea to provide support for the Korean mainland and Cheju Is. ○ On July 13th the 34th Army dug in on the Korean-Soviet border. Some of its units could be sent to defend Seoul if needed ○ Aug 9th, the Soviets invaded Manchuria ○ Aug 10th effective 0600, the 17th Area Army was placed under Kwantung Army control ○ Aug 15th Korea surrendered, except in the Ranam and Kyongsong Districts where fighting continued until Aug 19th owing to disrupted communications ○ The 17th Area Army was deactivated on Sept 12th ○

Major Units: See division / brigade page for order of battle
120th Div. Zentsuji 1944 邁進 *Maishin* – Daegu		224
150th Division Himeji 1945 護朝 *Gocho* – Cholla Namdo		236-7
160th Division Pyongyang 1945 護鮮 *Gosen* – Cholla Namdo		240-1
320th Division Keijo 1945 宣武 *Sanbu* – Seoul		251
127th Independent Mixed Brigade 1945 壯図 *Souzu* – Pusan		275

Units under control of the 17th Area Army: Keijo 築 *Kizuka*

Unit	Code	Location
17th Area Army Headquarters	12701 (235)	Seoul
39th Independent Mixed Regiment	29120 (3,442)	Mokpo
40th Independent Mixed Regiment	29121 (2,528)	
10th Independent Field Artillery Regiment	29123 (1,862)	
12th Tank Regiment	1408 (1,071)	
151st Anti-Aircraft Regiment	7420 (2,577)	
152nd Anti-Aircraft Regiment	7421 (1,891)	
41st Independent Anti-Aircraft Battalion	7422	
42nd Independent Anti-Aircraft Battalion	7441 (832)	
46th Independent Anti-Aircraft Battalion	7404 (669)	
30th Trench Mortar Battalion	29126 (1,407)	
31st Trench Mortar Battalion	29127 (1,407)	
20th Independent Machine Cannon Company	7406 (144)	
21st Independent Machine Cannon Company	7407 (144)	
5th Signal Unit Headquarters	17792 (154)	
4th Signal Regiment	7252 (1,099)	
116th Wire Company	12387 (310)	
117th Wire Company	12388 (310)	
82nd Independent Radio Platoon	9452	
94th Independent Radio Platoon	2544 (59)	
133rd Independent Radio Platoon	17794 (57)	
134th Independent Radio Platoon	17795 (57)	
135th Independent Radio Platoon	17796 (57)	
136th Independent Radio Platoon	17797 (57)	
137th Independent Radio Platoon	17798 (57)	
138th Independent Radio Platoon	17799 (57)	
86th Independent Signal Labor Unit	29135 (302)	
87th Independent Signal Labor Unit	29136 (302)	
88th Independent Signal Labor Unit	29137 (310)	
89th Independent Signal Labor Unit	29138 (302)	
90th Independent Signal Labor Unit	29139 (302)	
Pusan Fortress Headquarters	6335 (168)	
Pusan Fortress Heavy Artillery Regiment	7400 (999)	
41st Guard Headquarters	7411	
41st Guard Battalion	10288 (637)	
459th Specially Established Guard Battalion	7484 (550)	
415th Specially Established Guard Battalion	7452 (420)	
406th Specially Established Engineer Unit	7448 (930)	
407th Specially Established Engineer Unit	7449 (930)	

17ᵗʰ Area Army: continued

Yeosu Fortress Headquarters	6336 (82)	
Yeosu Fortress Heavy Artillery Regiment	7401 (317)	
416ᵗʰ Specially Established Guard Battalion	7486 (420)	
464ᵗʰ Specially Established Guard Battalion	7476 (550)	
408ᵗʰ Specially Established Guard Battalion	7472 (420)	
414ᵗʰ Specially Established Guard Battalion	7438 (420)	
411ᵗʰ Specially Established Guard Company	7442 (5)	
71ˢᵗ Korean Artillery Battalion, Rajin Battery	7402 (590)	
43ʳᵈ (Korean) Police Battalion	No #	
12ᵗʰ Engineers Unit Headquarters	12704 (32)	
125ᵗʰ Independent Engineer Battalion	29128 (871)	
128ᵗʰ Independent Engineer Battalion	29131 (891)	
129ᵗʰ Independent Engineer Battalion	29132 (891)	
130ᵗʰ Independent Engineer Battalion	29133 (891)	
131ˢᵗ Independent Engineer Battalion	29134 (891)	
37ᵗʰ Air Intelligence (Radar) Unit	7440	Pyongyang
62ⁿᵈ Line of Comm. Sector Unit Command	7023 (411)	
12ᵗʰ Field Transport Headquarters	7562 (156)	
65ᵗʰ Independent Motor Transport Battalion	3633 (808)	
70ᵗʰ Independent Motor Transport Battalion	5075 (808)	
82ⁿᵈ Independent Motor Transport Battalion	7572 (1,145)	
63ʳᵈ Independent Transport Company	7002 (353)	
64ᵗʰ Independent Transport Company	7003 (503)	
72ⁿᵈ Independent Transport Company	6765 (307)	
74ᵗʰ Independent Transport Company	6767 (307)	
36ᵗʰ Field Duty Unit	12760 (860)	
36ᵗʰ Field Duty Unit Headquarters	12761 (17)	
166ᵗʰ Land Duty Company	12762 (511)	
167ᵗʰ Land Duty Company	12763 (511)	
168ᵗʰ Land Duty Company	12764 (511)	
169ᵗʰ Land Duty Company	12765 (511)	
170ᵗʰ Land Duty Company	12766 (511)	
171ˢᵗ Land Duty Company	12767 (511)	
172ⁿᵈ Land Duty Company	12768 (511)	
37ᵗʰ Field Duty Unit	12770 (762)	
37ᵗʰ Field Duty Unit Headquarters	12771 (17)	
173ʳᵈ Land Duty Company	12772 (511)	
174ᵗʰ Land Duty Company	12773 (511)	
175ᵗʰ Land Duty Company	12774 (511)	
176ᵗʰ Land Duty Company	12775 (511)	
177ᵗʰ Land Duty Company	12776 (511)	
178ᵗʰ Land Duty Company	12777 (511)	
179ᵗʰ Land Duty Company	12778 (511)	
10ᵗʰ Field Service Unit	No #	
10ᵗʰ Field Service Unit Headquarters	4641 (17)	

17th Area Army: continued   築 *Kizuka*

210th Land Duty Company	29141 (500)
211th Land Duty Company	29142 (500)
212th Land Duty Company	29143 (500)
213th Land Duty Company	29144 (500)
214th Land Duty Company	29145 (500)
139th Specially Established Sea Duty Company	19789 (61+)
140th Specially Established Sea Duty Company	19790 (61+)
141st Specially Established Sea Duty Company	19791 (61+)
41st Construction Duty Company	3027 (511)
59th Construction Duty Company	7043 (511)
109th Specially Est. Construction Duty Company	5050 (61+)
71st Line of Communications Hospital	1365 (541)
16th Army Veterinary Quarantine Depot	8207 (137)

Note: A Specially Established Sea Duty Company had an authorized strength of 61 officers and men + an additional +/- 604 local or foreign conscripted laborers.

Cheju Island

58th Army 砦 Toride 12702

The 58th Army was activated in Seoul, Korea on March 31, 1945 and placed under 17th Area Army control on Apr 8th. It was Cheju Island's garrison under Lt Gen Sadashige Nagatsu from April 7th until it was deactivated on August 18, 1945.

Service History:

1945: On Apr 15th the 58th Army was activated. Its order of battle included the 96th and 111th Divisions, 108th I.M.B. and various support and service units from other areas. Because of Cheju Island's strategic significance the 58th Army's mission was to turn it into an impenetrable fortress ○ In early April the not yet fully equipped, newly mobilized 96th Division arrived ○ In early April the 96th Div commander, Lt Gen Iinuma, given interim control over the Reisui Fortress Garrison and part of the 30th Depot Div. worked to construct defenses around the island ○ Mid-April, the 108th Independent Mixed Brigade arrived and was placed under the 96th Division's control ○ End of April the 54th Army's headquarters arrived and Lt Gen Nagatsu took over control of preparations on Cheju ○ Apr-May, the steady troop build up continued until the 54th Army reached its planned strength ○ The 36th Shipping Engineer Regt's. 300-ton transports and schooners provided service to and from the mainland. In May the Regt. strained to keep up but between delivering weapons, supplies and troops there was a backlog of construction material. Deliveries scheduled for March were still dockside in May. Four transports from the 1st Sea Transport Unit and 60 motorized schooners from the 13th, 14th and 15th Sea Transport Battalions were to assist ○ At the end of May the 111th Div was the only fully operational force on Cheju, the 96th Div and the 108th I.M.B. were only partly equipped and trained ○ In mid-June the 121st Div. from Taejon and in late June the 6th Ind Field Artillery Regt from Kunsan arrived. The 58th Army's strength was 3 and 1/2 divisions. The 121st Div became a mobile striking force for the eastern part of the island ○ On July 13th the Army General Staff told the 17th Area Army to ready one reinforced division for shipment to Cheju in case of an enemy landing ○ On Aug 13th the 120th Div on the mainland was ready and scheduled to ship. Although Korea had a manpower shortage the division was needed on Cheju ○ End of July, enemy bombs had sunk more than half the powered schooners and all the large transport ships. Efforts to raise and transport units to Cheju continued until the war ended, these included 2 mortar btns, a tank company, a heavy artillery company and 2 anti-aircraft companies ○ The Cheju garrison constructed 137 caves and an airfield with the intention of defending the island to the last man, but the war ended before the 58th Army saw any action ○

Major Units: See division / brigade page for order of battle

Unit	Page
96th Division Fukuoka 1945 玄 Gen	220
111th Division Zentsuji 1944 市 Ichi	221-2
121st Division Zentsuji 1945 栄光 Eiko	224-5
108th Independent Mixed Brigade 1945 翠 Sui	269

Units under control of the 58th Army: Cheju Island 砦 Toride 12702

Unit	Code (Strength)	Notes
58th Army Headquarters	21703 (365)	
12th Artillery Headquarters	29122 (126)	
6th Independent Field Artillery Regiment	15152 (1,700)	
20th Independent Mountain Artillery Regiment	29124 (2,977)	
15th Field Medium Artillery Regiment	8550 (1,116)	
29th Trench Mortar Battalion	29125 (1,350)	
23rd Independent Mortar Battalion	3667 (650)	
1st Rocket Gun Battalion	12382 (844)	
32nd Independent Rapid Firing Gun Battalion	15151 (480)	anti-tank
11th Signal Regiment	5303 (832)	
126th Independent Engineer Battalion	29129 (808)	
127th Independent Engineer Battalion	29130 (509)	
64th Line of Communications Hospital	7863 (359)	
14th Independent Tank Company	26001	active 8/15/'45
405th Specially Established Guard Company	8823 (126)	
408th Specially Established Engineer Unit	7450 (930)	
65th Independent Transport Company	7004 (398)	
1st Independent Well Drilling Platoon	7517 (45)	
2nd Independent Well Drilling Platoon	7518 (46)	
3rd Independent Well Drilling Platoon	7519 (46)	
1st Specially Established Duty Unit Headquarters	12731 (413)	
4th Specially Established Duty Company	12732 (662)	
5th Specially Established Duty Company	12733 (660)	
6th Specially Established Duty Company	12734 (662)	
7th Specially Established Duty Company	12735 (659)	
8th Specially Established Duty Company	12736 (660)	
9th Specially Established Duty Company	12737 (640)	
10th Specially Established Duty Company	12738 (660)	
11th Specially Established Duty Company	12739 (657)	
12th Specially Established Duty Company	12740 (611)	
13th Specially Established Duty Company	12741 (659)	

Korean Army District:
Recruiting and Training

On Feb 6, 1945, the Divisional Districts in Japan and Korea were placed under local Area Army headquarters control. In Korea the 17th Area Army took over the Korea Army District and its Divisional and Administrative Districts. 17th Area Army commanders recieved the equivalent post in the divisional district organization as they held in the Area Army. On April 10th the 19th Depot Division became Ranam Divisional District, 20th Depot Division became Seoul Divisional District and the 30th Depot Division became Pyongyang Divisional District. The 150th Division was organized by the 20th Depot Division and the 160th Division by the 30th Depot Division, organizing and equipping the two divisions took until the end of May.

Korea Army District	朝鮮 Chosen
Korea Army District Headquarters	6315 (596)
Rajin Army Transport Control Section	No # (93)
Korean Army Training Unit	206 (64)
Pusan Army Transport Control Section	No # (245)
Pusan Army Military Affairs Department	No # (83)
Pusan Commissariat	6392 (443)
Daejeon Army Military Affairs Department	No # (94)
Chuncheon Army Military Affairs Department	No # (88)
Cheongju Army Military Affairs Department	No # (90)
15th Fld Hvy. Artillery Regiment Replacement Unit	207 (194)
Masan Hvy. Artillery Regiment Replacement Unit	201 (756)
Army Medical Materials Depot 1st Branch	29751
38th Field Duty Unit	12780
38th Field Duty Unit Headquarters	12781 (17)
180th Land Duty Company	12782 (388)
181st Land Duty Company	12783 (391)
182nd Land Duty Company	12784 (325)
183rd Land Duty Company	12785 (391)
77th Sea Duty Company	12786 (511)
78th Sea Duty Company	12787 (511)
79th Sea Duty Company	12788 (511)
39th Field Duty Unit	12790
39th Field Duty Unit Headquarters	12791 (17)
184th Land Duty Company	12792 (511)
185th Land Duty Company	12793 (511)
186th Land Duty Company	12794 (511)
187th Land Duty Company	12795 (511)
188th Land Duty Company	12796 (511)
189th Land Duty Company	12797 (511)
Korean Army District Extraordinary Court-martial	No #
Korean Army District Extraordinary Judiciary	No #
Korean Army Temporary Veterinary Hospital	12752
Incheon Army Arms Manufacturing Depot	No # (9,959)
Pyongyang Army Ordnance Re-supply Depot	6382 (48)

Unit	Barracks # (Personnel)
Korean Army Freight Unit	No #
Pusan Army Hospital	6367 (197)
Wonsan Army Hospital	6375
Yeosu Army Hospital	6370 (23)
Korean Army District Quarantine Section	No #
451st Specially Established Guard Battalion	8810 (550)
452nd Specially Established Guard Battalion	7453 (550)
461st Specially Established Guard Battalion	7416 (550)
402nd Specially Established Guard Battalion	8830 (420)
403rd Specially Established Guard Battalion	8832 (420)
405th Specially Established Guard Battalion	7412 (420)
408th Specially Established Guard Company	7487 (126)
401st Specially Established Engineer Unit	7443 (930)
409th Specially Established Engineer Unit	7453 (930)
410th Specially Established Engineer Unit	7455 (930)
12th Field Horse Replacement Depot	7489 / 29003

Korean Army District Headquarters　　　　　　　　東北 6315 (596)

Ranam Divisional District:

Ranam Divisional District Headquarters　Ranam　　　朝鮮 32820 (106)

Recruiting and home defense units
19th Depot Division – Ranam Divisional District

Unit	Location	Barracks # (Personnel)
19th Depot Division Headquarters	Ranam	Chosen
73rd Infantry Regiment Repl. Unit	Ranam	朝鮮 2
75th Infantry Regiment Repl. Unit	Hoeryong	朝鮮 3
76th Infantry Regiment Repl. Unit	Ranam	朝鮮 4
25th Mtn. Arty. Regt. Repl. Unit	Ranam	朝鮮 8?
Reorganized on Feb 6, 1945		*Chosen*
Ranam 1st Infantry Replacement Unit	Ranam	202 / 32821 (1,933)
Ranam 2nd Infantry Replacement Unit	Ranam	243 / 32822 (1,933)
Ranam Artillery Replacement Unit	Ranan	208 / 32823 (573)
Ranam Engineer Replacement Unit	Ranam	210 / 32824 (705)
Ranam Signal Replacement Unit	Ranam	211 / 津 32825 (345)
Ranam Transport Replacement Unit	Ranam	212 / 津 32826 (659)

Major units supplied by the Ranam Divisional District include:
19th Div.

Ranam Regimental District: Kankyohokudo Administrative District

Ranam Regimental District HQ　　　　　　　　　朝鮮 6331 (25)

Ranam District:　　　　　　　　　　　　　　　朝鮮 *Chosen*

Unit	Barracks # (Personnel)
141st Garrison Battalion	7612 (573)
142nd Garrison Battalion	7613 (573)
143rd Garrison Battalion	7614 (573)

Ranam District: continued   朝鮮 *Chosen*

144th Garrison Battalion	7615 (573)
145th Garrison Battalion	7616 (573)
Ranam Army Hospital	6380 (370)
Rajin Army Hospital	6373
Hoeryong Army Hospital	6379 (148)
Hamhung Army Hospital	6374 (44)

Pyongyang Divisional District:

Pyongyang Divisional District HQ   Pyongyang   朝 6319 (251)

Recruiting and home defense units
30th Depot Division / Pyongyang Divisional District:

Unit	Location	Barracks # (Personnel)
30th Depot Division Headquarters	Pyongyang	*Chosen*
41st Infantry Regt Replacement Unit	Fukuyama	朝鮮 42
74th Infantry Regt Replacement Unit	Hamhung	朝鮮 43
77th Infantry Regt Replacement Unit	Pyongyang	朝鮮 44
30th Cavalry Regt Replacement Unit	Pyongyang	朝鮮 46
30th Field Arty. Regt Repl. Unit	Pyongyang	朝鮮 47
30th Engineer Regt Repl Unit	Pyongyang	朝鮮 48
30th Div Signal Unit Repl Unit	Pyongyang	朝鮮 47
30th Transport Regt Repl Unit	Pyongyang	朝鮮 50
Reorganized on Feb 6, 1945		*Chosen*
Pyongyang 1st Infantry Repl. Unit	Pyongyang	242 (1,933) 41st Inf. R.
Pyongyang 2nd Inf. Repl Unit	Pyongyang	244 (1,933) 77th Inf. R.
Pyongyang Artillery Repl Unit	Pyongyang	247 (573) 30th Art. R.
Pyongyang Engineer Repl Unit	Pyongyang	248 (705) 30th Eng. R.
Pyongyang Signal Replacement Unit	Pyongyang	249 (345) 30th Sig Unit
Pyongyang Transport Repl. Unit	Pyongyang	250 (659) 30th Trans U.

Major units supplied by the Pyongyang Divisional District include:
30th Div, 160th Div.

Sinuiju Regimental District: Heianhokudo Admin District

   Sinuiju Regimental Headquarters   朝 6333 (25)

Pyongyang District: 朝 *Asa*

Haeju Military Affairs Department	No # (90)
150th Garrison Battalion	7621 (573)
151st Garrison Battalion	7622 (573)
152nd Garrison Battalion	7623 (573)
153rd Garrison Battalion	7624 (573)
154th Garrison Battalion	7625 (573)
Pyongyang 1st Army Hospital	6377 (111)

Pyongyang District: continued

Pyongyang 2nd Army Hospital	6378 (111)
407th Specially Established Guard Battalion	7413 (420)
453rd Specially Established Guard Battalion	7414 (550)
454th Specially Established Guard Battalion	7415 (550)
409th Specially Established Guard Company	7488 (126)
410th Specially Established Guard Company	7439 (126)
402nd Specially Established Engineer Unit	7444 (930)
412th Specially Established Engineer Unit	7457 (930)
413th Specially Established Engineer Unit	7458 (930)

Haeju Regimental District: Okaido Administrative District

Haeju Regimental District Headquarters	朝 6334 (25)

Seoul Divisional District:

Seoul Divisional District HQ	Seoul	京 6320 (252)

Recruiting and home defense units
20th Depot Division / Seoul Divisional District:

Unit	Location	Barracks # (Personnel)
20th Depot Division Headquarters	Seoul	Chosen
78th Infantry Regt Replacement Unit	Seoul	朝鮮 22
79th Infantry Regt Replacement Unit	Seoul	朝鮮 23
80th Infantry Regt Replacement Unit	Taikyu	朝鮮 24
20th Cavalry Regt Replacement Unit	Seoul	朝鮮 25
26th Field Arty Regt Repl. Unit	Seoul	朝鮮 26
20th Engineer Regt Repl. Unit	Seoul	朝鮮 27
20th Div. Signal Unit Repl Unit	Seoul	朝鮮 29
20th Transport Regt Repl. Unit	Seoul	朝鮮 30
Reorganized on Feb 6, 1945		*Chosen*
Seoul 1st Infantry Replacement Unit	Seoul	朝鮮 222 (3,202)
Seoul 2nd Infantry Replacement Unit	Seoul	朝鮮 223 (3,202)
Seoul 3rd Infantry Replacement Unit	Seoul	朝鮮 224 (3,202)
Seoul Artillery Replacement Unit	Seoul	朝鮮 226 (573)
Seoul Engineer Replacement Unit	Seoul	朝鮮 227 (705)
Seoul Signal Replacement Unit	Seoul	朝鮮 229 (345)
Seoul Transport Replacement Unit	Seoul	朝鮮 230 (659)

Major units supplied by the Seoul Divisional District include:
20th Div, 49th Div, 150th Div.

Chuncheon Regimental District: Eharado Administrative District

Chunechon Regimental District Headquarters	朝 6328 (25)

Seoul Regimental District: Keikido Administrative District
Seoul District   京 *Sō*

Seoul District: continued   京 Sō

Unit	Barracks # (Personnel)
Seoul Military Affairs Department	No # (136)
Seoul Army Jail	No # (13)
Seoul Sector Command	6329 (31)
146th Garrison Battalion	7617 (573)
147th Garrison Battalion	7618 (573)
148th Garrison Battalion	7619 (573)
149th Garrison Battalion	7620 (573)
Seoul Army Hospital	6366 (460)
Kunsan Army Hospital	6372 (40)
455th Specially Established Guard Battalion	7477 (550)
456th Specially Established Guard Battalion	7478 (550)
457th Specially Established Guard Battalion	7479 (550)
458th Specially Established Guard Battalion	7480 (550)
410th Specially Established Guard Battalion	7474 (420)
413th Specially Established Guard Battalion	7437 (420)
403rd Specially Established Engineer Unit	7445 (930)
411th Specially Established Engineer Unit	7456 (930)

Chonju Regimental District: Chuseihokudo Administrative District

Chonju Regimental District Headquarters   朝 6326 (25)

Daejeon Regimental District: Chuseinando Administrative District

Daejeon Regimental District Headquarters   朝 6324 (25)

Daegu Divisional District:

Daegu Divisional District Headquarters   朝鮮 6318

Recruiting and home defense units
Newly Created / Daegu Divisional District:

Unit	Location	Barracks # (Personnel)
Daegu 1st Infantry Replacement Unit		215 (1,933)
Daegu 2nd Infantry Replacement Unit		216 (1,933)
Daegu Artillery Replacement Unit		217 (573)
Daegu Engineer Replacement Unit		218 (705)
Daegu Signals Replacement Unit		219 (345)
Daegu Transport Replacement Unit		220 (659)

Daegu Regimental District: Keishohokudo Administrative District

Daegu District: 朝鮮 *Chosen*

Unit	Barracks # (Personnel)
Daegu Military Affairs Department	No # (103)
Daegu Sector Command	6323 (25)
155th Garrison Battalion	15067 (573)
156th Garrison Battalion	15068 (573)
157th Garrison Battalion	15069 (573)

Daegu Regimental District: continued

Unit	Barracks # (Personnel)
158th Garrison Battalion	7059 (573)
Daegu Army Hospital	6368 (72)
463rd Specially Established Garrison Battalion	7475 (550)
409th Specially Established Garrison Battalion	7473 (420)
402nd Specially Established Garrison Company	8820 (126)
404th Specially Established Engineer Unit	7446 (930)

Busan Regimental District: Keishonando Admin District

Busan Regimental District Headquarters   朝 6322 (25)

Gwangju Divisional District

Gwangju Divisional District HQ   Gwangju   朝鮮 6316 (202)

Recruiting and home defense units

Newly Created / Gwangju Divisional District

Unit	Location	Barracks # (Personnel)
Gwangju 1st Infantry Repl. Unit	Gwangju	朝鮮 232 (1,933)
Gwangju 2nd Infantry Repl. Unit	Gwangju	朝鮮 233 (1,933)
Gwangju Artillery Replacement Unit	Gwangju	朝鮮 234 (573)
Gwangju Engineer Replacement Unit	Gwangju	朝鮮 235 (705)
Gwangju Signal Replacement Unit	Gwangju	朝鮮 236 (345)
Gwangju Transport Repl. Unit	Gwangju	朝鮮 237 (659)

Cheonju Regimental District: Zenrahokudo Admin District

Cheonju Regimental District Headquarters   朝 6327 (25)

Gwangju Regimental District: Zenranando Admin District

Gwangju District: 朝鮮 *Chosen*

Unit	Barracks # (Personnel)
Gwangju Military Affairs Department	No # (135)
Gwangju Sector Command	6325 (25)
Chonju Military Affairs Department	No # (47)
159th Garrison Battalion	7060 (573)
160th Garrison Battalion	7061 (573)
405th Specially Established Engineer Unit	7447 (930)
Gwangju Army Hospital	6369 (204)
Chonju Army Hospital	6371 (204)

Korea Army Air Units

5th Air Army 隼 *Hayabusa*

The 5th Air Army Headquarters was activated in Nanking on February 10, 1944, from former 3rd Air Division personnel. Lt Gen Takuma Shimoyama was its commander from Feb 14th until the war ended. 5th Air Army headquarters were located in Nanking from Feb 14th and joined the China Expeditionary Army on the 15th, transferred to Air General Army on May 15, 1945, and relocated to Seoul, Korea June 30th where it remained until the war ended.

Service History:
1944: On Feb 10th the 5th Air Army HQ was activated in Nanking ○ Feb 15th attached to the China Expeditionary Army to support operation Ichi-go but was at half authorized strength. Fifty replacement planes were scheduled to arrive each month, pilots were harder to find ○ Apr 17th, Ichi-go, opening the Beijing-Hankou rail corridor, began. 5th Air Army supplied reconnaissance and bombing support and the 9th Air Regiment was charged with protecting the Pawangcheng Bridge ○ On Apr 29th the 2nd Air Bgde arrived from Manchuria, HQs went to Hsinhsiang Field, 6th Air Regt to Anyang and the 48th Air Regt to Nanking ○ On Apr 29th twenty-six B-24's damaged the Pawangcheng Bridge. Japanese fighters and bombers attacked U.S. airbases in Honan and Shensi ○ On May 6th forty-five U.S. fighters and bombers attacked Wuhan inflicting heavy damage ○ On May 18th the 5th Air Army's Command Post moved to Hankou. The 2nd Air Bgde was to providing direct air support for the 23rd Army. 5th Air Army was assigned to the 11th Army's Hunan-Kwangsi operation ○ May 27th, the Hunan-Kwangsi operation began but was confined to a narrow corridor along the banks of the Yangtze River, which made the troops vulnerable to air attacks. Airfield repairs and delayed fuel shipments kept fighter units from using advanced air bases and long distance flying limited the number of flights ○ Wuhan and Pailochi served as the main hubs for Hunan-Kwangsi air operations, during the course of which 5th Air Army losses rose and the number of replacement planes and aircrew diminished ○ On June 15th B-29's from Chengtu bombed Moji and Yawata in Japan ○ On June 18th the 11th Army occupied Changsha despite continuous rain ○ On June 26th the 11th Army occupied Hengyang Airfield ○ On June 28th the assault on Hengyang began but was suspended July 2nd ○ On Aug 8th Hengyang was captured ○ Aug 17th, to cover *Ichi-go* losses the 22nd, 29th and 60th Air Regts were sent to the 5th Air Army for one month. The 22nd Air Regt from the 1st Air Army was the best fighter unit in the Army ○ On Nov 9th the 11th Army and 5th Air Army attacked Guilin ○ Nov 10th, the 13th Div. entered Liuchow. *Ichi-go*'s first objectives, Liuchow and Guilin, were taken the same day ○
1945: Jan 3rd, the 2nd Air Brigade's 6th and 44th Air Regts and the 54th Ind. Air Squadron remained on the front lines while other 5th Air Army air units were withdrawn to reorganize ○ Jan. 20th, control over the Canton-Hankou railway was established and the 23rd Army destroyed U.S. airbases in the Suichuan-Kanhsien district ○ In Jan following the fall of the Philippines and Okinawa the 5th Air Army found it impossible to replace its losses ○ US air bases were established in the Philippines and Okinawa to bomb Mainland China. The 5th Air Army temporarily moved its planes to safety rather than waste them to no effect ○ End of January, front line Air Army units concentrated mostly in Wuhan-Hankou to train intensively as compensation for shrinking numbers ○ In the Canton area the 2nd Air Bgde became responsible for airfield repairs and fortification ○ By Jan 26th the Canton-Hankou railway has been secured and the

Suichuan-Kanhsien airfields neutralized ○ Feb 8th marked the end of *Ichi-go* ○ On Feb 26th the 13th Air Division was activated in Nanking ○ Mar 6th, the 13th Air Div joined the 5th Air Army ○ In May Nanning was lost to the Chinese resulting in the Manchuria-Indochina rail corridor (*Ichi-go's* objective) collapsing ○ On May 15th the 5th Air Army transferred from the China Expeditionary Army to Air General Army for redeployment to Seoul, Korea. Airfields based north of Lunghai Railway in China remained with the 5th Air Army to be used as rear bases for training. The 13th Air Division was to take control of air units south of the Lunghai Railway ○ By June 30th the 5th Air Army was in Korea. About 120 planes were sent and about 60 remained in China. Units sent to Korea included the 5th Air Army headquarters, 1st and 2nd Air Brigades and their ground units ○ Korea was short of airfields so the 5th Air Army and 2nd Air Army in Manchuria shared the following airfields in Manchuria; Hsingcheng, Hsiungyuehoheng, Suchung, Chou-Shuitsu and Houchiatun. Although expedient the situation created congestion and hampered air operations ○

Units under control of the 5th Air Army: Seoul	隼 *Hayabusa*	
5th Air army Headquarters	2371 (398)	Seoul
5th Air Army Headquarters Signal Section	2371 (109)	
105th Secondary Air Training Brigade Headquarters	2389 (36)	China
14th Flight Education Unit	15301 (395)	
18th Flight Education Unit	15305 (395)	
28th Flight Education Unit	17303 (395)	
5th Advanced Flight Training Unit	16635 (449)	
19th Advanced Flight Training Unit	17327 (449)	
3rd Air Sector Command	9863 (56)	
43rd Air Sector Command	17321 (44)	
44th Air Sector Command	16643 (44)	Kimpo
48th Air Sector Command	17328 (44)	Busan
54th Air Sector Command	17329 (44)	
55th Air Sector Command	17330 (44)	
3rd Air Route Department	9453 (549)	
18th Airfield Battalion	9147 (461)	
128th Airfield Battalion	17314 (372)	
159th Airfield Battalion	16659 (372)	
160th Airfield Battalion	16660 (372)	
161st Airfield Battalion	16661 (372)	
167th Airfield Battalion	17322 (372)	
182nd Airfield Battalion	16656 (372)	Sachon
183rd Airfield Battalion	16657 (372)	
185th Airfield Battalion	17325 (372)	
196th Airfield Battalion	11666 (372)	
197th Airfield Battalion	16667 (372)	
198th Airfield Battalion	16668 (372)	
199th Airfield Battalion	16669 (372)	
200th Airfield Battalion	16672 (372)	
202nd Airfield Battalion	19374 (372)	
203rd Airfield Battalion	19375 (372)	Tamyang

204th Airfield Battalion	19376 (372)	
206th Airfield Battalion	19377 (372)	
207th Airfield Battalion	8327 (372)	
208th Airfield Battalion	19378 (372)	
221st Airfield Battalion	16693 (372)	
222nd Airfield Battalion	19381 (372)	
223rd Airfield Battalion	19382 (372)	Ulsan
224th Airfield Battalion	19383 (372)	
225th Airfield Battalion	19384 (372)	Kaiuntai-Pusan
226th Airfield Battalion	19385 (372)	
6th Field Airfield Construction Headquarters	2402 (28)	
7th Field Airfield Construction Headquarters	19089 (27)	
155th Field Airfield Construction Unit	18419 (175)	
156th Field Airfield Construction Unit	18420 (175)	
157th Field Airfield Construction Unit	18421 (175)	
161st Field Airfield Construction Unit	6684 (356)	
164th Field Airfield Construction Unit	5784 (356)	
165th Field Airfield Construction Unit	5786 (356)	
166th Field Airfield Construction Unit	14182 (356)	
167th Field Airfield Construction Unit	14183 (356)	
5th Air Signals Headquarters	19549 (93)	Nangjin
4th Air Signal Regiment	8366 (1,706)	
14th Air Signal Regiment	18483 (1,495)	
15th Air Signal Regiment	9876 (1,699)	
23rd Air Signal Regiment	17332 (1,084)	
24th Air Signal Regiment	21200 (1,488)	
5th Fixed Air Signal Unit	9896 (296)	
3rd Wireless Radio Unit	18951 (212)	
8th Wireless Radio Unit	18956 (212)	
10th Wireless Radio Unit	16658 (212)	
51st Wireless Radio Unit	17316 (196)	
52nd Wireless Radio Unit	17317 (196)	
53rd Wireless Radio Unit	17318 (196)	
54th Wireless Radio Unit	17319 (196)	
55th Wireless Radio Unit	19153 (209)	
56th Wireless Radio Unit	19154 (209)	
57th Wireless Radio Unit	8337 (209)	
58th Wireless Radio Unit	8338 (209)	
76th Wireless Radio Unit	19563 (209)	
7th Special Air Signal Unit	9647 (259)	
5th Air Intelligence Regiment	17320 (2,560)	
6th Air Intelligence Regiment	9877 (2,560)	
22nd Air Intelligence Regiment	17333 (1,684)	Seoul
4th Meteorological Regiment	9880 (2,229)	Ulsan
8th Field Air Repair Depot	8331 (1,741)	
15th Field Air Repair Depot	9885 (3,247)	

23rd Field Air Repair Depot   9321 (1,088)
24th Field Air Repair Depot   17308 (1,879)
26th Field Air Repair Depot   17334 (1,484)
120th Independent Maint. Unit (Ki-43, Oscar)   18985 (172)
138th Independent Maint. Unit (Ki-46, Dinah)   19010 (172)
141st Independent Maintenance Unit (Ki-51, Sonia)   19013 (172)
152nd Independent Maintenance Unit (Ki-43)   17335 (233)
153rd Independent Maintenance Unit (Ki-43)   17336 (233)
156th Independent Maintenance Unit (Ki-43)   8346 (233)
166th Independent Maint. Unit (Ki-84, Frank)   17337 (233)   Kaiuntai-Busan
167th Independent Maintenance Unit (Ki-84)   17338 (233)   Kumchon
168th Independent Maintenance Unit (Ki-84)   17339 (233)
171st Independent Maintenance Unit (Ki-84)   19056 (233)   Daegu
172nd Independent Maintenance Unit (Ki-84)   19057 (233)
173rd Independent Maintenance Unit (Ki-84)   19058 (233)
174th Independent Maintenance Unit (Ki-84)   19059 (233)
180th Independent Maintenance Unit (Ki-84)   19065 (233)
181st Independent Maintenance Unit (Ki-84)   19066 (233)
191st Independent Maintenance Unit (Ki-102B)   19076 (347)
187th Independent Maintenance Unit (Ki-102B)   19072 (336)
303rd Independent Maintenance Unit (Ki-21, Sally)   19083 (275)
304th Independent Maintenance Unit (Ki-21)   19084 (275)
308th Independent Maintenance Unit (Ki-46)   17340 (167)
316th Independent Maintenance Unit (unknown)   21910 (233)
15th Field Air Freight Depot   No # (2,214)
64th Line of Comm. Motor Transport Company   9829 (170)

1st Air Brigade: Chinju   隼魁 *Hayabusa Sakigake*

1st Air Brigade Headquarters   2373   Chinju
 • 22nd Air Regiment (fighter)   18913 (323)   Sachon
 • 25th Air Regiment (fighter)   2387   Sachon
 • 85th Air Regiment (fighter)   8385   Sachon

2nd Air Brigade: Daegu   朝鮮 *Chosen*

2nd Air Brigade Headquarters   9101   Daegu
 • 6th Air Regiment (fighter)   9102/81   Daegu
 • 44th Air Regiment (recon) minus 1 squadron   2376

8th Air Brigade: Pyongyang   隼魁 *Hayabusa Sakigake*

8th Air Brigade Headquarters   9141   Pyongyang
 • 16th Air Regiment (light bomber)   9142   Ulsan

3rd Air Brigade: Nanking   隼 *Hayabusa* 2374

3rd Air Brigade Headquarters   2375 (26)   Nanking

3rd Air Brigade: continued   隼 *Hayabusa*
- 48th Air Regiment   16618
- 81st Air Regiment, an element (recon)   2380   Nanching

3rd Air Brigade: Activated on March 30, 1935. With the Shanghai Expeditionary Army from Sept 11, 1937 until Dec 7th, Central China Area Army until Feb 14, 1938, Central China Expeditionary Army until Aug 2nd, Air Corps until Apr 28, 1939, Central China Expeditionary Army until Sept 23rd, China Expeditionary Army until Nov 6th, 3rd Air Group until Apr 15, 1942, 3rd Air Division until July 10th, China Expeditionary Army until Jan 30, 1943, 7th Air Div until Jan 15, 1945 and 5th Air Army but remained in China until the war ended.

53rd Air Division: Seoul 1945   宙 *Chū*

53rd Air Division Headquarters	503 (318)	Seoul
2nd Advanced Flight Training Unit (air crew)	521 (391)	Suwon
12th Advanced Flight Training Unit (air crew)	526 (391)	Kunsan
23rd Advanced Flight Training Unit (air crew)	527 (394)	Kunsan
25th Advanced Flight Training Unit (air crew)	529 (479)	Sentoku
11th Secondary Flight Training Unit (air crew)	534 (344)	Yonpo
19th Secondary Flight Training Unit	535 (344)	
30th Secondary Flight Training Unit (advanced)	536 (349)	Daejon
41st Secondary Flight Training Unit (advanced)	539 (364)	Suwon
9th Flight Training Unit (pilot training)	543 (1,114)	Daejon
1st Air Training Unit	570 (1,058)	
14th Secondary Flight Training Unit	580 (1,015)	

53rd Air Division: Activated in Seoul, Korea on Feb 13, 1945 from 103rd Air Training Brigade troops. It had headquarters in Seoul and was attached to the 5th Air Army from Feb 13th until Apr 8th and Air General Army until the war ended.

Ki-48 "Lily" bomber overhead (author)

End: Armies in Japan, Manchuria and the territories

Chapter 3

Divisions and Brigades: Japan and the Territories

Over a period of 77 years the army created 168 infantry divisions plus 3 Imperial Guard, 4 armored and 4 anti-aircraft divisions. The first twenty mobilized between 1888 and 1915 and were permanent, except the 13th, 15th, 17th and 18th, which were temporary for wartime and eventually deactivated on May 1, 1925 to save money. Between 1868 and 1938 there were never more than twenty divisions.

An infantry division was formed around a group of 3 or 4 infantry regiments supported by a permanent coterie of reconnaissance, engineer and artillery units. Transport, signal, ordinance, medical, veterinary and other service units kept it self-sufficient in the field. Divisions were classified in three different ways: A type: strengthened, added firepower and/or personnel: B type: standard and C type: light, equipped for garrison and security work. Some divisions were formed around independent infantry battalions instead of regiments. These retained the two infantry brigade structure dropped by divisions with regiments. 154 divisions were in service at the time Japan surrendered.

Infantry Brigades Transition to Infantry Groups:
Originally all divisions in the Imperial Army were *square* with two permanent infantry brigades of two infantry regiments each. Study devoted to the optimal regimental strength for a division was concluded in 1936 and the triangular format of three regiments in an infantry group gained general acceptance. Divisions activated Apr 4, 1938 and after were all triangular. Square divisions became triangular as follows:

From Square to Triangular Divisions: Regt. & date dropped (new division or bgde).
1st Division: 3rd Infantry Regiment Jul 16, 1940 (3rd to 28th Div)
2nd Division: 30th Infantry Regiment Jul 10, 1940 (30th to 28th Div)
3rd Division: 18th Infantry Regiment Jul 31, 1941 (18th to 29th Div)
4th Division: 70th Infantry Regiment Mar 9, 1940 (70th to 25th Div)
5th Division: 41st Infantry Regiment Dec 1, 1942 (41st to Kawamura Det)
6th Division: 47th Infantry Regiment Nov 30, 1940 (47th to 48th Div)
7th Division: 25th Infantry Regiment Jul 19, 1941 (25th to Karafuto MB)
8th Division: 32nd Infantry Regiment Oct 1, 1939 (32nd to 24th Div)
9th Division: 36th Infantry Regiment Mar 9, 1940 (36th to 28th Div)
10th Division: 40th Infantry Regiment Jul 30, 1940 (40th to 25th Div)
11th Division: 22nd Infantry Regiment Oct 2, 1939 (22nd to 24th Div)
12th Division: 14th Infantry Regiment Aug 1, 1940 (14th to 25th Div)
13th Division: 58th Infantry Regiment Mar 22, 1943 (58th to 31st Div)
14th Division: 50th Infantry Regiment Jul 30, 1940 (50th to 29th Div)
16th Division: 38th Infantry Regiment Jul 22, 1941 (38th to 29th Div)
18th Division: 124th Infantry Regiment Apr 30, 1943 (124th to 31st Div)
19th Division: 74th Infantry Regiment Nov 1, 1942 (74th to 30th Div)
20th Division: 77th Infantry Regiment Jul 27, 1941 (77th to 30th Div)
104th Division: 170th Infantry Regiment Jan 13, 1941 (170th to 21st I.M.B.)
106th Division: deactivated 113th, 125th, 145th, 147th Infantry Regiments Mar 9, 1940 (113th to 56th Div, 125th to 88th Div, 145th & 147th to 46th Div)
110th Division: 140th Infantry Regiment Apr 16, 1942 (140th to 71st Div)
116th Division: 138th Infantry Regiment Dec 25, 1942 (138th I.R. to 31st Div)
Karafuto Mixed Brigade: deactivated Sakhalin 1945 (25th I.R., 125th I.R. to 88th Div)

New divisions and brigades activated around dropped regiments:
Karafuto Mixed Brigade: Activated Sakhalin Jul 22, 1941 (25th I.R., 125th I.R.)
24th Division: Activated Manchuria Oct 6, 1939 (22nd I.R. & 32nd I.R)
25th Division: Activated Manchuria Jul 10, 1940 (14th I.R., 40th I.R. & 70th I.R.)
28th Division: Activated Manchuria Aug 1, 1940 (3rd I.R., 30th I.R. & 36th I.R.)
29th Division: Activated Manchuria on Jul 22, 1941 (18th I.R., 38th I.R. & 50th I.R.)
21st I.M.B.: Activated Hanoi, Indochina June 26, 1941 (170th I.R.)
30th Division: Activated Pyongyang May 14, 1943 (41st I.R., 74th I.R. & 77th I.R.)
31st Division: Activated in Bangkok Mar 22, 1943 (58th I.R., 124th I.R. & 138th I.R.)
46th Division: Activated in Kumamoto May 14, 1943 (145th I.R. & 147th I.R.)
48th Division: Activated Hainan Is, China Nov 30, 1940 (47th I.R.)
56th Division: Activated Kurume Jul 10, 1940 (113th I.R.)
71st Division: Activated Manchuria Apr 16, 1942 (140th I.R.)
88th Division: Activated Sakhalin Feb 28, 1945 (25th I.R. & 125th I.R.) from Karafuto

Divisional Infantry Group Headquarters:
The headquarters of an infantry group or brigade coordinated and executed the operations of infantry regiments and their supporting units. Infantry group headquarters never had a signal section, which rendered them incapable of direct control over subordinate units, instead they relied on divisional or regimental signal assets to communicate for them. If a detachment needed headquarters, infantry group headquarters could be separated from the division without directly affecting operations.

To replace its infantry group headquarters some divisions had an Assistant Division

Commander who served as the infantry group's leader from within the division's headquarters. This came with the added advantage of a shorter chain of command.

The last infantry group headquarters activated was the 94th Division's (in Vol 2), which assembled in Kuala Lumpur, Malaya on Oct 14, 1944, all the divisions raised subsequently lacked them.

Independent Brigades:

Independent mixed brigades (I.M.B.) were the most numerous, having an infantry component of one or two regiments or three to six independent battalions supported by signal, artillery and engineer elements. There were 116 independent mixed brigades in addition to two ind. brigades, fourteen independent infantry brigades, nine independent armored brigades, one airborne, one mobile and four amphibious brigades.

As Japan's military influence expanded rapidly independent brigades, combat capable as they were, helped fill rear-area security vacuums economically and, in so doing, kept the army fluid and adaptable.

On Conscription and Replacement Personnel:

Conscription into the Army:

All Japanese males between 17 and 40 years of age, except criminals and those with disabilities, were liable for service in the Imperial Armed Forces. In peacetime, enlistment was for a two-year period but wartime service (beginning in 1937 for those in China and 1942 for all others) became a three-year obligation, one year of training and two in the field. After 1942 soldiers who were stranded overseas often served for 5 or more years. In Korea conscription began in 1944 and on Formosa in 1945 but the nationals of both were mostly conscripted as laborers.

The War Ministry's Soldiers Affairs Bureau handled conscription through army districts, divisional districts, regimental districts and recruiting districts (in descending order), with most of the administrative work being done at the regimental district level.

The Japanese military began the year on December 1. Every Japanese male turning 19 the following year had to report his residence, occupation, education, physical health, etc, before the end of November. The results were sent to the regimental district commander for collating and arrive at the War Ministry by Feb 10. Quota for each divisional district were decided and those taking the conscription exam notified in writing by their city or ward administration. The exam formed the basis for order of induction, assignment to a branch of service and, if qualified, for officer/NCO training. Qualified regular conscripts received the results of their examination with a unit assignment, branch of service and a time and place to report.

Army Officer Selection, the Most Promising:

There were two classifications for officers in the Imperial Army, regular or reserve and three ways to obtain a commission. They could graduate from a Military Academy, take reserve officer candidate courses after serving in the ranks or at a technical institution or move up from warrant officer or NCO. Officer candidates served two to six months in a unit before receiving their commission. Potential reserve officers were chosen from new recruits during the conscription exam and served at least two months before becoming reserve officer/NCO candidates. At this point they were graded either *A* suitable as an officer or *B* suitable for an NCO.

Depot Divisions / Divisional Districts
留守 Rusu: The Division's Home Duty Unit:
The Army kept depot divisions (*rusu shidan*) staffed by reservists at the division's home station. Entrusted with home duty affairs these units trained recruits, tended to returning personnel, tended to active duty personnel records, issued KIA allowances, etc.

補充 Hojū: Replacement Units:
A depot division commonly had one replacement unit for each division's three infantry regiments. Recruits for these were drawn from a regiment's home station district. There was also a replacement unit for each division's reconnaissance, artillery, engineer, transport and signal units. Replacement troops for these were drawn from all over the divisional district.

師管 Depot Divisions:
With the exception of Imperial Guard Divisions and the Korean 19th and 20th Divisions, which recruited from all over Japan, depot divisions recruited and trained within their home districts. It was the function of every depot division to raise and activate new units as directed by the Minister of War. They organized and trained everything from new divisions to small independent units. As war progressed depot divisions raised increasing numbers of units, for which they were obliged to perform home duty affairs as long as those units remained in the field.

In 1915 the Korean 19th and 20th Divisions were organized. To fill the ranks troops were enlisted from all over Japan as the divisions' home stations were in two army districts in Korea. Korean nationals weren't conscripted into the Japanese army until late in the war.

The Home Stations of Units Activated Outside Japan:
The Minister of War decided the new home station for units activated outside Japan. Personnel in these units often found their new home station had no connection to their permanent residence but their records were forwarded and maintained there anyway.

Home Designations:
While the location of a unit's training barracks was its Home Station, a barracks was designated according to army district: North 北, East 東, Central 中, etc, and a number: East 3 Unit, North 5 Unit, etc. East 3 Unit refers to specific barracks under the activating Depot Division, which was responsible for replacement personnel and home duty affairs. The designation followed a unit throughout its service. Regardless of which unit it was its barracks designation was forever attached to every unit that passed through it.

Army District Units and Replacements (Independent Units):
Barracks existed outside the depot division system to house army district units. These were the independent units that served directly under an army headquarters in the field. Like their divisional counterparts they trained and activated units and replacement units drawn from within their army district. Demands for specialty units kept training depots too busy for administering them so unit home stations were often transferred elsewhere.

1940 Territorial Recruiting Reorganization:
In 1925, to save money, four of Japan's 18 divisions were abolished and the 14 divisional districts reorganized. Each district had a permanent division ready at all times. In 1940 six army districts were organized: Northern Army Administrative

District, Eastern Army District, Central Army District, Mid Central Army District, Western Army District, Shikoku Army District and two territories: Korean Army District and Formosan Army District. In 1941 District armies were organized in each of the army districts and placed under the General Defense Headquarters. Under the new rules, for most part, regimental district boundaries followed prefecture boundaries and a regiment's home station was named after the town its barracks were in.

With the active duty divisions becoming triangular, the depot divisions were also made triangular in 1940-41.

1925 to 1940 District Designation	1941 to Feb 1945 Divisional Districts	Final Jurisdiction
2nd Imp. Guard Dep. Div.	Tokyo Divisional Distinct	12th Area Army
2nd Depot Division	Sendai Divisional Distinct	11th Area Army
3rd Depot Division	Nagoya Divisional Distinct	54th Army, 13AA
4th Depot Division	Osaka Divisional Distinct	15th Area Army
5th Depot Division	Hiroshima Divisional Distinct	59th Army, 15AA
6th Depot Division	Kumamoto Divisional Distinct	57th Army, 16AA
7th Depot Division	Asahikawa Divisional District	5th Area Army
20th Depot Division	Seoul Divisional Distinct	17th Area Army
30th Depot Division	Pyongyang Divisional District	17th Area Army
51st Depot Division	Utsunomiya Div. Distinct	12th Area Army
52nd Depot Division	Kanazawa Divisional Distinct	13th Area Army
53rd Depot Division	Kyoto Divisional Distinct	15th Area Army
54th Depot Division	Nagano Divisional Distinct	12th Area Army
55th Depot Division	Zentsuji Divisional Distinct	55th Army 15AA
56th Depot Division	Kurume Divisional Distinct	56th Army, 16AA
57th Depot Division	Hirosaki Divisional Distinct	50th Army, 11AA

Divisions

In this chapter space was a consideration so the major unit profiles are generally limited to raw data; on the plus side searching through details is made easier.
Divisions are arranged with service units under headquarters followed by infantry, recon, fire support and transport. There is no good reason for this except the author felt it made them easier to read, whether or not that's actually true. In contrast brigade components are generally presented in descending order by code number.
Division/brigade format:
Left side column: Unit name.
Right side column: Top code name. Below code number and (personnel authorized)
Dates and Places:
Activation place and date, home station, square to triangular details, parent army and join date, detachments formed by spinning off units or parts of units, deactivation date.
Note: A date without a year means it took place in the last year shown.
Service History:
Location with a date is always a battle.
Classifying Japanese Army Divisions:
甲 A: (*A* type) Strengthened; augmented firepower and/or personnel.
乙 B: (*B* type) Standard.
丙 C: (*C* type) Security/garrison, lighter in composition.
Mojifu (Code name): Above every unit's list of code numbers is the organization's kanji code name, shown with its correct romaji pronunciation.
Manchu: 満州, used by units whose code numbers originated in the Kwantung Army.
Note: D. P. & Water Supply Unit = Disease Prevention and Water Supply Units

Chapter 3

Imperial Guard

1st Imperial Guards Division Tokyo 1943 　　隅 *Gū* (15,297)

Konoe 1st Division Headquarters　　　　No # (81)
Konoe 1st Division Signal Unit　　　　東部 82 (383)
Konoe 1st Infantry Brigade
　• Konoe 1st Infantry Regiment　　　　東部 2 (2,862)
　• Konoe 2nd Infantry Regiment　　　　東部 3 (2,862)
Konoe 2nd Infantry Brigade
　• Konoe 6th Infantry Regiment　　　　東部 7 (2,862)
　• Konoe 7th Infantry Regiment　　　　東部 8 (2,862)
• Konoe 1st Cavalry Regiment　　　　　 東部 4 (754)
• Konoe 1st Field Artillery Regiment　　東部 13 (1,027)
• Konoe 1st Machine Cannon Battalion　東部 20 (942)　　activ. 8/31/44
• Konoe 1st Engineer Regiment　　　　　東部 81 (745)
• Konoe 1st Transport Unit　　　　　　　東部 17

<u>1st Imperial Guards Division</u>: Activated in Tokyo May 14, 1943. Home station: Tokyo. Eastern District Army from May 24, 1943 until Feb 6, 1945 and Tobu Army District in Tokyo until the war ended. Deactivated in Tokyo on Sept 10, 1945.
<u>Service History</u>: Japan: Tokyo. (東部 "Tobu" barracks designations, elements of this division were never given the usual code names and numbers)

3rd Imperial Guards Division Tokyo 1944　　範 *Han* 3820 (13,762)

Konoe 3rd Division Headquarters　　　　3821 (358) deactivated 10/10/45
Konoe 3rd Division Signal Unit　　　　　3830 (239) deactivated 10/10/45
Konoe 3rd Division Ordinance Duty Unit　3836 (81)
Konoe 3rd Division Medical Unit　　　　 3832 (529)
Konoe 3rd Division 1st Field Hospital　　3833 (242)
Konoe 3rd Division 4th Field Hospital　　3834 (242)
Konoe 3rd Division Anti-Gas Unit　　　　3835 (85)
Konoe 3rd Division Veterinary Unit　　　3837 (52)
Konoe Infantry Group Headquarters　　　3823 (80)　　deactivated 2/6/45
　• Konoe 8th Infantry Regiment (Tokyo)　3824 (3,092)
　• Konoe 9th Infantry Regiment (Kōhu)　3825 (3,092)
　• Konoe 10th Infantry Regiment Sakura) 3826 (3,092)
• Konoe 3rd Cavalry Regiment　　　　　 3827 (480)
• Konoe 3rd Field Artillery Regiment　　 3828 (1,116)
• Konoe 3rd Engineer Regiment　　　　　3829 (961)
• Konoe 3rd Transport Regiment　　　　 3831 (749)

<u>3rd Imperial Guards Division</u>: (A type) Activated Tokyo April 4, 1944. Home station: Tokyo. With the Eastern District Army from July 6th until Feb 6, 1945, 12th Area Army until April 8th and 52nd Army in Joto until it was deactivated in Togane on Sept 9th.
<u>Service History</u>: Japan:

Regular Infantry Divisions

7ᵗʰ Division Sapporo 1888　　　　　　　熊 *Kuma* 9241 (17,782)

7ᵗʰ Division Headquarters	9200 (217)
7ᵗʰ Division Signal Unit	9221 (226)
7ʰ Division Ordinance Duty Unit	9225 (112)
7ᵗʰ Division Medical Unit	9227 (650)
7ᵗʰ Division 1ˢᵗ Field Hospital	9231 (293)
7ᵗʰ Division 2ⁿᵈ Field Hospital	9232 (293)
7ᵗʰ Division 3ʳᵈ Field Hospital	9233 (293)
7ᵗʰ Division 4ᵗʰ Field Hospital	9234 (300)
7ᵗʰ Division D. P. & Water Supply Unit	9236 (239)
7ᵗʰ Division Veterinary Unit	9235 (123)
7ᵗʰ Division Infantry Group	
• 26ᵗʰ Infantry Regiment (Asahikawa)	9203 (1,827)
• 27ᵗʰ Infantry Regiment (Asahikawa)	9207 (3,102)
• 28ᵗʰ Infantry Regiment (Asahikawa)	9208 (3,102) Ichiki Detachment
• 7ᵗʰ Cavalry Regiment	9212 (527)
• 7ᵗʰ Mountain Artillery Regiment	9216 (2,206)
• 7ᵗʰ Engineer Regiment	9218 (783)
• 7ᵗʰ Transportation Regiment	9223 (816)

<u>7ᵗʰ Division</u>: (A type) Activated in Sapporo May 12, 1896. Home station: Asahikawa. Lost the 25ᵗʰ Inf Regt becoming triangular Oct 17, 1940. With Imperial HQ from Nov 17, 1937 until Feb 14,1938, Kwantung Army until Aug 23, 1940, Imperial HQ until Dec 2, 1941, Northern District Army until Feb 11, 1943, Northern Army until Mar 16, 1944 and 5ᵗʰ Area Army in Obihiro until it was deactivated sometime between Sept 15ᵗʰ and 22ⁿᵈ 1945.

Note: Ichiki Detachment, 28ᵗʰ Inf Regt Guadalcanal: Tenaru River Aug 18 1942.

<u>Service History</u>: Manchuria: garrison. Japan: Asahikawa and Obihiro garrison.

9ᵗʰ Division Kanazawa 1898　　　　　　武 *Take* 1573 (14,203)

9ᵗʰ Division Headquarters	1515 (286)
9ᵗʰ Division Signal Unit	1560 (209)
9ᵗʰ Division Ordinance Duty Unit	1568 (81)
9ᵗʰ Division 1ˢᵗ Field Hospital	1582 (196)
9ᵗʰ Division 2ⁿᵈ Field Hospital	1586 (196)
9ᵗʰ Division 4ᵗʰ Field Hospital	1595 (294)
9ᵗʰ Division D. P. & Water Supply Unit	1519 (136)
9ᵗʰ Division Infantry Group	
• 7ᵗʰ Infantry Regiment (Kanazawa)	1524 (2,641)
• 19ᵗʰ Infantry Regiment (Tsuruga)	1528 (2,641)
• 35ᵗʰ Infantry Regiment (Toyama)	1533 (2,641)
• 9ᵗʰ Cavalry Regiment	1513　　deactivated 11/11/44

9th Division continued
- 9th Mountain Artillery Regiment   1546 (2,511)
- 9th Engineer Regiment   1559 (949)
- 9th Transport Regiment   1564 (1,014)

9th Division: (A type) Activated in Kanazawa Oct 1, 1898. Home station: Kanazawa. Lost the 36th Regiment became triangular Mar 9, 1940. With the Shanghai Expeditionary Army from Sept 11, 1937 until Feb 14, 1938, Central China Expeditionary Army until Aug 22nd, 11th Army until June 6, 1939, Imperial HQ until Mar. 28, 1940, Eastern District Army until Sept 27, 1940, 3rd Army until June 26, 1944, 32nd Army until Jan 10, 1945 and 10th Area Army in Formosa until the war ended.

2nd Expeditionary Unit (Mortlok Is): Detached from the 9th Div. on Feb 21, 1944.

Service History: China: 1st Shanghai Jan 28 1932, 2nd Shanghai Sept 27 1937, Nanking Dec 9 1937, Xuzhou Mar 24 1938, Wuhan June 24 1938, Yichang May 31 1940. Okinawa: Ozata garrison. Formosa: Taipei garrison.

11th Division Zentsuji 1898   錦 *Nishiki* 2491 (17,253)

11th Division Headquarters	2410 (383)
11th Division Signal Unit	2481 (230)
11th Division Ordinance Duty Unit	2483 (112)
11th Division Medical Unit	2484 (1,109)
11th Division Field Hospital	2486 (277)
11th Division D. P. & Water Supply Unit	1203 (239)
11th Division Anti-Gas Unit	2482 (227)
11th Division Veterinary Unit	2487 (119)
11th Division Guerilla Unit	unknown (540)
11th Infantry Group Headquarters	unknown (79) deactiv. 5/1/43
• 12th Infantry Regiment (Marugame)	2425 (3,272)
• 43rd Infantry Regiment (Tokushima)	2435 (2,882)
• 44th Infantry Regiment (Kochi)	2445 (2,854)
• 11th Cavalry Regiment	2455 (1,048)
• 11th Mountain Artillery Regiment	2465 (2,613)
• 11th Engineer Regiment	2475 (644)
• 11th Transport Regiment	2485 (3,600)

11th Division: (A type) Activated in Zentsuji on October 1, 1898. Home station: Zentsuji. Lost the 22nd Inf Regt, became triangular Oct 2, 1939. With the Shanghai Expeditionary Army from Aug 15, 1937 until Dec 7th, 5th Army until Feb 15, 1938, Imperial HQ until Sept 28th, Kwantung Army until Nov 21st, 3rd Army until May 19, 1939, 5th Army until March 31, 1945, 15th Army (but did not ship to Burma) until April 8th and (in transit to) the 55th Army in Kochi, Japan where it was deactivated on September 12th.

6th Expeditionary Unit (Guam): Detached from the 11th, 12th and 1st Div on Feb 21, 1944.

Service History: China: 1st Shanghai Jan 28 1932, 2nd Shanghai Aug 23 1937.

12th Division Kurume 1898 　　　　　　　　　剣 *Ken* 8712 (12,747)

12th Division Headquarters 　　　　　　　　8713 (306)
12th Division Signal Unit 　　　　　　　　　8748 (217)
12th Division Ordinance Duty Unit 　　　　 8754 (81)
12th Division Medical Unit 　　　　　　　　21114 (500)
12th Division 1st Field Hospital 　　　　　　8768
12th Division 2nd Field Hospital 　　　　　 21113 (200)
12th Division D. P. & Water Supply Unit 　 1204 (194)
12th Division Anti-Gas Unit 　　　　　　　　8714 (187)
12th Division Veterinary Unit 　　　　　　 8789 (48)
12th Infantry Group Headquarters 　　　　 unknown (79)　deactiv. 5/1/43
　• 24th Infantry Regiment (Fukuoka) 　　 8703 (2,615)
　• 46th Infantry Regiment (Omura) 　　　 8705 (2,615)
　• 48th Infantry Regiment (Kurume) 　　　8707 (2,615)
• 24th Field Artillery Regiment 　　　　　　8722 (2,284)
• 12th Cavalry Regiment 　　　　　　　　　満州449 　deactiv. 11/21/44
• 18th Engineer Regiment 　　　　　　　　 8745 (595)
• 18th Transport Regiment 　　　　　　　　 8751 (749)

<u>12th Division</u>: (A type) Activated in Kurume October 1, 1898. Home station: Kurume. Lost the 14th Inf Regt becoming triangular Aug 1, 1940. With the Kwantung Army from July 7, 1937 until Jan 13, 1938, 3rd Army until Dec 22, 1944 and 10th Area Army in Tainan, Formosa until the war ended.
4th Expeditionary Unit (Yap Is): Detached from the 1st and 12th Div Feb 21st 1944.
6th Expeditionary Unit (Guam): Detached from the 11th, 12th and 1st Div Feb 21st 1944.
<u>Service History</u>: Manchuria: Hsinchu garrison. Formosa: Tainan.

24th Division Harbin 1939 　　　　　　　　山 *Yama* 3472 (16,215)

24th Division Headquarters 　　　　　　　　3430 (213)
24th Division Signal Unit 　　　　　　　　　3482 (275)
24th Division Ordinance Duty Unit 　　　　 3484 (64)
24th Division 1st Field Hospital 　　　　　　3486 (193)
24th Division 2nd Field Hospital 　　　　　 3487 (193)
24th Division D. P. & Water Supply Unit 　 1207 (165)
24th Division Anti-Gas Unit 　　　　　　　 3477 (208)
24th Division Veterinary Unit 　　　　　　 3490 (43)
24th Division Infantry Group
　• 22nd Infantry Regiment (Matsuyama) 　3474 (2,876)
　• 32nd Infantry Regiment (Yamagata) 　 3475 (2,876)
　• 89th Infantry Regiment (Asahikawa) 　 3476 (2,876)
• 24th Cavalry Regiment 　　　　　　　　　 3478 (449)
• 42nd Field Artillery Regiment 　　　　　　3480 (2,234)
• 24th Engineer Regiment 　　　　　　　　 3481 (912)
• 24th Transport Regiment 　　　　　　　　 3483 (1,014)

<u>24th Division</u>: (A type) Activated in Harbin, Manchuria on Oct 6, 1939. Home station:

Kumamoto. With the 5th Army from Oct 7th until July 5, 1944, 31st Army until Aug 21st and 32nd Army, destroyed on Okinawa by June 23, 1945.
1st Expeditionary Unit (Saipan): Detached from the 25th, 24th and 10th Div Feb 21, 1944.
7th Expeditionary Unit (Mereyon Is.): Detached from the 24th Div Feb 21, 1944.
9th Expeditionary Unit (Saipan): 24th Inf Group HQ detached Apr 4, 1944.
<u>Service History</u>: Formosa: Okinawa April 23 1945.

25th Division Tonei 1940   国 *Kuni* 4930 (22,314)

25th Division Headquarters	4901 (383)
25th Division Signal Unit	4909 (236)
25th Division Ordinance Duty Unit	4912 (112)
25th Division Medical Unit	4934 (1,109)
25th Division Field Hospital	4935 (227)
25th Division D. P. & Water Supply Unit	1208 (239)
25th Division Anti-Gas Unit	4911 (227)
25th Division Veterinary Unit	4913 (119)
25th Infantry Group Headquarters	4702 (?)
• 14th Infantry Regiment (Kokura)	4903 (4,299)
• 40th Infantry Regiment (Tottori)	4904 (4,334)
• 70th Infantry Regiment (Shinoyama)	4905 (4,362)
• 75th Cavalry Regiment (Sakai)	4906 (1,048)
• 15th Mountain Artillery Regiment	4907 (3,659)
• 25th Engineer Regiment	4908 (644)
• 25th Transport Regiment	4910 (3,573)

<u>25th</u> Division: (A type) Activated in Mutanjiang, Manchuria July 10, 1940, from 14th Inf Regt (12th Div) and 40th Inf Regt (10th Div) personnel and additional small units. Home station: Osaka. With the Kwantung Army from July 29,1940 until Oct 22nd, 5th Army until Sept 19, 1941, 20th Army until Sept 27, 1944, 5th Army until Mar 15, 1945 and 16th Area Army in Kobayashi, Miyazaki Japan until it was deactivated in Miyakonojo on October 19th.
1st Expeditionary Unit (Saipan): Detached from 25th, 24th and 10th Div. Feb 21, 1944.
<u>Service History</u>: Manchuria: Mutanjiang. Japan: Miyazaki, in transit to Kobayashi.

28th Division Tokyo 1940   豊 *Toyo* 5614 (19,713)

28th Division Headquarters	5611 (250)
28th Division Signal Unit	5653 (240)
28th Division Ordinance Repair Unit	5661 (10)
28th Division 2nd Field Hospital	5676 (287)
28th Division 3rd Field Hospital	5681 (287)
28th Division 4th Field Hospital	5683 (294)
28th Division D. P. & Water Supply Unit	1209 (250)
28th Division Anti-Gas Unit	5634 (10)

28th Division continued   豊 *Toyo*

28th Division Infantry Group
- 3rd Infantry Regiment (Tokyo)   5620 (2,500)
- 30th Infantry Regiment (Niigata)   5623 (2,500)
- 36th Infantry Regiment (Fukui)   5629 (3,100)
• 28th Mountain Artillery Regiment   5647 (2,200)
• 28th Cavalry Regiment   5640 (530)
• 28th Engineering Regiment   5649 (750)
• 28th Transportation Regiment   5656 (500)

<u>28th Division</u>: (A type) Activated in Hsinking, Manchuria Aug 1, 1940. Home station: Tokyo. With the Kwantung Army until July 4, 1942, 1st Area Army until Feb 10, 1944, 3rd Area Army until June 26th, Imperial Headquarters until June 30th, 32nd Army until June 24, 1945 and 10th Area Army on Miyako Jima until the war ended.
Attached: 25th and 26th Rapid Firing Gun Companies (118 men ea.)
<u>Service History</u>: Manchuria: Harbin garrison. Japan: Ryukyu Island garrison.

39th Division Hiroshima 1939   藤 *Fuji* 6860

39th Division Headquarters   6861 (275)
39th Division Signal Unit   6870 (219)
39th Division Ordinance Duty Unit   6872 (95)
39th Division Field Hospital   6873 (352)
39th Division Veterinary Unit   6876 (45)
39th Division Infantry Group
- 231st Infantry Regiment (Hiroshima)   6864 (3,427)
- 232nd Infantry Regiment (Hamada)   6865 (3,427)
- 233rd Infantry Regiment (Yamaguchi)   6866 (3,427)
• 39th Field Artillery Regiment   6868 (932)
• 39th Engineer Regiment   6869 (901)
• 39th Transport Regiment   6871 (501)

<u>39th Division</u>: (C type) Activated in Hiroshima June 30, 1939. Home station: Hiroshima. With the 11th Army from Oct. 2nd until April 15, 1944, Wuhan Garrison Army until July 17th, 34th Army until May 30, 1945, Kwantung Army until July 30th and 30th Army south of Hailung, Manchuria until it was deactivated on August 18, 1945.
<u>Service History</u>: China: Yichang May 4 1940, Hupei Nov 25 1940, South Henan Jan 30 1941, Chungyuan May 5 1941, Changde Nov 2 1943, Laohokau Mar 21 1945. Manchuria: Siping garrison/fortification construction.

42nd Division Sendai 1943   勲 *Isao* 11900 (14,963)

42nd Division Headquarters   11901 (461)
42nd Division Signal Unit   11909 (239)
42nd Division Ordinance Duty Unit   11911 (81)
42nd Division Medical Unit   28787 (699)

42nd Division continued

42nd Division 1st Field Hospital	11913 (241)	
42nd Division 2nd Field Hospital	11914 (208)	
42nd Division 4th Field Hospital	11915 (247)	
42nd Division D. P. & Water Supply Unit	11917 (239)	
42nd Division Veterinary Unit	28788 (119)	
42nd Division Infantry Group	11902	deact. 4/12/44
• 129th Infantry Regiment (see note)	11903 (2,881)	
• 130th Infantry Regiment (Sendai)	11904 (2,881)	
• 158th Infantry Regiment (Yamagata)	11905 (2,881)	
• 12th Field Artillery Regiment	28786 (1,800)	
• 42nd Engineer Regiment	11908 (961)	
• 42nd Transport Regiment	11910 (1,840)	
• 5th Independent Tank Company	12605 (124)	to 5th A.A. 7/6/45
• 6th Independent Tank Company	12606 (124)	

42nd Division: (C type) Activated in Sendai May 14, 1943, from former 62nd Ind Inf Group personnel. Home station: Sendai. With the Eastern District Army from June 1st until Feb 1, 1944, Northern Army until Mar 16th, 27th Army until Jan 22, 1945 and 5th Area Army on Wakkanai in the Kurile Islands until it was deactivated Sept 17, 1945.
Note: 129th Inf Regt home station was in Aizuwakamatsu City.
42nd Infantry Group Headquarters became the 43rd I.M.B. on Apr 12, 1944.
Service History: Japan: Wakkanai Island garrison.

44th Division Osaka 1944   橘 *Tachibana* 14150 (13,373)

44th Division Headquarters	14151 (359)	
44th Division Signal Unit	14159 (226)	
44th Division Ordinance Duty Unit	14180 (810	
44th Division Medical Unit	14161 (491)	
44th Division 1st Field Hospital	14162 (195)	
44th Division 4th Field Hospital	14163 (200)	
44th Division Anti Gas Unit	14179 (79)	
44th Division Veterinary Unit	14181 (41)	
44th Division Machine Cannon Unit	14156 (413)	
44th Infantry Group Headquarters	14152	deact. 2/6/45
• 92nd Infantry Regiment (Osaka)	14153 (3,091)	
• 93rd Infantry Regiment (Osaka)	14154 (3,091)	
• 94th Infantry Regiment (Wakayama)	14155 (3,091)	
• 44th Field Artillery Regiment	14157 (1,089)	
• 44th Engineer Regiment	14158 (932)	
• 44th Transport Regiment	14160 (755)	

44th Division: (C type) Activated in Osaka April 4, 1944, from 4th Depot Division personnel. Home station: Osaka. With the Central district Army until Feb 6, 1945, 12th Area Army until Apr 8th and 51st Army in Osaka until deact. in Hokoda Sept 20th
Service History: Japan: Takahagi garrison.

50th Division Taiwan 1944   蓬 *Hō* 19700 (12,063)

50th Division Headquarters	19710 (130)	
50th Division Signal Unit	19707 (167)	
50th Division Ordinance Duty Unit	19709 (80)	activated 9/22/44
50th Division Medical Unit	19711 (465)	activated 9/22/44
50th Division 1st Field Hospital	19712 (206)	activated 9/22/44
50th Division 4th Field Hospital	19713 (211)	activated 9/22/44

50th Division Infantry Group
- 301st Infantry Regiment (Taipei)   19701 (2,620)
- 302nd Infantry Regiment (Tainan)   19702 (2,620)
- 303rd Infantry Regiment (Fengshan)   19703 (2,620)
- 50th Cavalry Regiment   19704 (356)
- 50th Mountain Artillery Regiment   19705 (1,490)
- 50th Engineer Regiment   19706 (422)
- 50th Transport Regiment   19708 (351)

<u>50th Division</u>: (C type) Activated in Taipei, Formosa May 3, 1944, from 48th Depot Division troops. Home station: Taipei. With the Formosa Army (called the 10th Area Army from Sept. 22nd) in Tainan from May 3rd until it was deactivated Sept 1, 1945.
<u>Service History</u>: Formosa: Pingtung garrison.

57th Division Hirosaki 1940   奥 *Oku* 7225 (16,904)

57th Division Headquarters	7200 (407)	
57th Division Signal Unit	7230 (226)	
57th Division Ordinance Duty Unit	7240 (133)	
57th Division Medical Unit	unknown	
57th Division 2nd Field Hospital	7244 (278)	
57th Division Veterinary Unit	7249 (119)	
57th Infantry Group Headquarters	7210	

- 52nd Infantry Regiment (Hirosaki)   7202 (3,788)
- 117th Infantry Regiment (Akita)   7217 (3,780)
- 132nd Infantry Regiment (Yamagata)   7232 (3,784)
- 57th Cavalry Regiment   7215   to 136th IMB
- 57th Field Artillery Regiment   7221 (2,102)
- 57th Engineer Regiment   7227 (878)
- 57th Transportation Regiment   7235 (1,822)

<u>57th Division</u>: (B type) Activated in Hirosaki July 10, 1940, from 8th Depot Div troops. Home station: Hirosaki. With Imperial Headquarters from Aug 1st until Dec 2nd, Northern District Army until Aug 1, 1941, 3rd Army (as part of "Kwantung Army special maneuvers") until Dec 3rd, 4th Army in Heilongjiang until Mar 31, 1945, 36th Army until May 10th and 16th Area Army in Sasaguri, Fukuoka. Deactivated 10/5/45. 11th Expeditionary Unit (Kurile Is): 57th Infantry Group HQ detached Apr. 4, 1944.
<u>Service History</u>: Manchuria: Garrison. Japan: Fukuoka but was in transit to 1st General Army when the war ended.

59th Division North China 1942   衣 *Koromo* 2350 (13,799)

59th Division Headquarters	2351 (186)
59th Division Signal Unit	4299 (398)
59th Division Field Hospital	2311 (349)
59th Division Veterinary Unit	4297 (44)
53rd Infantry Brigade Headquarters	4291 (117)
• 41st Independent Infantry Battalion	4292 (1,324)
• 42nd Independent Infantry Battalion	4293 (1,324)
• 43rd Independent Infantry Battalion	4294 (1,324)
• 44th Independent Infantry Battalion	4295 (1,324)
54th Infantry Brigade Headquarters	2353 (117)
• 45th Independent Infantry Battalion	4296 (1,324)
• 109th Independent Infantry Battalion	3040 (1,324)
• 110th Independent Infantry Battalion	3041 (1,324)
• 111th Independent Infantry Battalion	3042 (1,324)
• 59th Division Mortar Unit	1496 (577)
• 59th Division Engineer Unit	4298 (901)
• 59th Division Transport Unit	2354 (508)

<u>59th Division</u>: (C type) Activated in Shandong, North China Feb 2, 1942, from former 10th I.M.B. personnel. Home station: Kanko, north Korea. With the 12th Army from Apr 10th, until Aug 26, 1944, North China Area Army until Mar 30, 1945, 43rd Army until May 30th, Kwantung Army until Jul 18th and 34th Army until it was deactivated in Kanko, North Korea on August 18, 1945. Inherited the 10th I.M.B.s code name.
Note: Involved in the *Kanto Incident* on Dec 27, 1942, a mutiny over alcohol.
<u>Service History</u>: China: Taihang Mtns Apr 27 1943. Korea: Border guard USSR/Korea.

62nd Division Kyoto 1943   石 *Ishi* 1881 (13,637)

62nd Division Headquarters	1882 (183)	
62nd Division Signal Unit	3599 (330)	
62nd Division Field Hospital	5325 (357)	
62nd Division Veterinary Unit	4297 (45)	
63rd Infantry Brigade Headquarters	3591 (117)	
• 11th Independent Infantry Battalion	3592 (1,233)	
• 12th Independent Infantry Battalion	3593 (1,233)	
• 13th Independent Infantry Battalion	3594 (1,233)	
• 14th Independent Infantry Battalion	3595 (1,233)	
64th Infantry Brigade Headquarters	4281 (117)	
• 15th Independent Infantry Battalion	3596 (1,233)	
• 21st Independent Infantry Battalion	4282 (1,233)	
• 22nd Independent Infantry Battalion	4283 (1,233)	
• 23rd Independent Infantry Battalion	4284 (1,233)	Yamamoto Unit
• 62nd Division Engineer Unit	3598 (177)	
• 62nd Division Transport Unit	3597 (502)	

<u>62nd Division</u>: (C type) Activated in Taiyuan, Shanxi Prov, China May 1, 1943, from former 4th I.M.B. (became 63rd I. Bgde) and 6th I.M.B. (became 64th I. Bgde) personnel. Home station: Kyoto. With the 1st Army until Mar 15, 1944, 12th Army until July 4th, Imperial HQ until Jul 24th and 32nd Army on Okinawa, destroyed before June 24, 1945.

<u>Service History</u>: China: Formosa: Okinawa Apr 1 1945.

63rd Division Utsunomiya 1943   陣 *Jin* 2990 (13,640)

63rd Division Headquarters	2991 (275)
63rd Division Communications Unit	2999 (398)
63rd Division Field Hospital	2932 (357)
63rd Division Veterinary Unit	4288 (45)
66th Infantry Brigade Headquarters	1884 (156)
• 24th Independent Infantry Battalion	4285 (1,283)
• 25^h Independent Infantry Battalion	4286 (1,283)
• 77th Independent Infantry Battalion	2992 (1,283)
• 78^h Independent Infantry Battalion	2993 (1,283)
67th Infantry Brigade Headquarters	1886 (156)
• 79th Independent Infantry Battalion	2994 (1,283)
• 80^h Independent Infantry Battalion	2995 (1,283)
• 81st Independent Infantry Battalion	2996 (1,283)
• 137^h Independent Infantry Battalion	1924 (1,283)
• 63rd Division Mortar Unit	1497 (577)
• 63rd Division Engineer Unit	2998 (901)
• 63rd Division Transport Unit	2997 (502)

<u>63rd Division</u>: (C type) Activated in Beijing, North China May 1, 1943, from former 6th I.M.B. and 15th I.M.B. personnel. Home station: Utsunomiya. Served with the North China Area Army until May 30, 1945, Kwantung Army until June 15th and 44th Army Tungliao, Manchuria until it was deactivated on August 18, 1945. Inherited the 15th I.M.B.s code name.

<u>Service History</u>: China: Luoyang Apr 17 1944. Manchuria: Tungliao Aug 9 1945.

66th Division Taiwan 1944   敢 *Kan* 1795 (11,678)

66th Division Headquarters	1785 (162)
66th Division Signal Unit	1783 (330)
66th Division Ordinance Duty Unit	12466 (80)
66th Division Medical Unit	10273 (699)
66th Division 1st Field Hospital	10274 (206)
66th Division 2nd Field Hospital	21112 (330)
66th Division Veterinary Unit	21115 (45)
66th Division Infantry Group	
• 249th Taiwan Infantry Regiment	7167 (2,306)
• 304th Taiwan Infantry Regiment	1786 (3,055)

66th Division continued
- 305th Taiwan Infantry Regiment — 1787 (3,055)
- 66th Division Rapid Firing Gun Unit — 10170 (480)
- 66th Division Trench Mortar Unit — 1788 (833)
- 66th Division Engineer Unit — 1789 (173)
- 66th Division Transport Unit — 1793 (298)

<u>66th Division</u>: (C type) Activated in Taipei, Formosa July 12, 1944, from former 46th I.M.B. personnel. Home station: Formosa. Served with the Formosa Army until Sept 22, 1944 and 10th Area Army on Formosa until the war ended.
Service History: Taiwan: Keelung.

71st Division Asahikawa 1942 — 命 *Mikoto* 4355 (13,572)

Unit	Code
71st Division Headquarters	13250 / 4321 (150)
71st Division Signal Unit	13271 / 4326 (150)
71st Division Ordinance Duty Unit	13291 / 4394 (100)
71st Division 1st Field Hospital	13295 (196)
71st Division D. P. & Water Supply Unit	1285 / 4397 (200)
71st Division Anti-Gas Unit	13297 / 4391 (200)
71st Division Veterinary Unit	13298 / 4398 (100)
71st Infantry Group Headquarters	4355 to Pagan Is.
• 87th Infantry Regiment (Asahikawa)	13285 / 4322 (2,000)
• 88th Infantry Regiment (Asahikawa)	13272 / 4323 (2,000)
• 140th Infantry Regiment (Asahikawa)	13299 / 3909 (2,000)
• 71st Cavalry Regiment	4392 detached 1/23/45
• 71st Mountain Artillery Regiment	13282 / 4324 (1,800)
• 71st Engineer Regiment	13273 (500)
• 71st Transport Regiment	13293 / 4393 (200)

<u>71st Division</u>: (C type) Activated in Hunchun, Manchuria Apr 16, 1942, from former Hunchan Garrison Unit, 108th Inf Bgde and 140th Inf Regt personnel. Home station: Asahikawa. With the Kwantung Army from May 16th until July 4th, 2nd Army until Oct 30, 1943, 3rd Army until July 24, 1944, Kwantung Army until Jan 23, 1945 and 10th Area Army in Tainan, Formosa until the war ended.
5th Expeditionary Unit (to Pagan Is.): Detached from the 71st Div on Feb 21, 1944.
Service History: Manchuria: Sanchiang border garrison. Formosa: garrison.

72nd Division Sendai 1944 — 伝 *Den* 3370 (13,671)

Unit	Code
72nd Division Headquarters	3371 (357)
72nd Division Signal Unit	3379 (239)
72nd Division Ordinance Duty Unit	3385 (81)
72nd Division Medical Unit	3381 (529)
72nd Division 1st Field Hospital	3382 (242)
72nd Division 4th Field Hospital	3383 (242)
72nd Division Anti-Gas Unit	3384 (85) activated 2/6/45

72nd Division continued   伝 Den

72nd Division Veterinary Unit	3386 (52)	
72nd Infantry Group Headquarters	3372 (68)	activated 2/6/45
• 134th Infantry Regiment (Sendai)	3373 (3,092)	
• 152nd Infantry Regiment (Yamagata)	3374 (3,092)	
• 155th Infantry Regiment (Wakamatsu)	3375 (3,092)	
• 72nd Division Rapid Firing Gun Unit	3376 (480)	
• 72nd Field Artillery Regiment	3377 (1,116)	
• 72nd Engineer Regiment	3378 (961)	
• 72nd Transport Regiment	3380 (749)	

<u>72nd Division</u>: (C type) Activated in Sendai July 6, 1944, from 2nd Depot Division personnel. Home station: Sendai. With the Eastern District Army from Apr. 6th until Feb 6, 1945 and 11th Area Army in Fukushima until it was deactivated Sept 12, 1945. <u>Service History</u>: Japan: Fukushima.

73rd Division Hiroshima 1944   怒 Ikari 14300 (13,764)

73rd Division Headquarters	14301 (358)	
73rd Division Signal Unit	14309 (239)	
73rd Division Ordinance Duty Unit	14315 (81)	
73rd Division Medical Unit	14311 (529)	
73rd Division 1st Field Hospital	14312 (242)	
73rd Division 4th Field Hospital	14313 (242)	
73rd Division Anti-Gas Unit	14314 (85)	
73rd Division Veterinary Unit	14316 (52)	
73rd Infantry Group Headquarters	14302	deactivated 2/6/45
• 196th Infantry Regiment (Nagoya)	14303 (3,092)	
• 197th Infantry Regiment (Shizuoka)	14304 (3,092)	
• 198th Infantry Regiment (Gifu)	14305 (3,092)	
• 73rd Division Machine Cannon Unit	14306 (480)	
• 73rd Field Artillery Regiment	14307 (1,116)	
• 73rd Engineer Regiment	14308 (961)	
• 73rd Transport Regiment	14310 (749)	

<u>73rd Division</u>: (C type) Activated Nagoya July 6, 1944, from 3rd Depot Division personnel. Home station: Nagoya. With the Central District Army until Feb 6, 1945 and 13th Area Army in Toyohashi and deactivated in Okazaki on September 18th. <u>Service History</u>: Japan: Suruga Bay, later Toyohashi.

77th Division Asahikawa 1944   稔 Nen 9252 (14,774)

77th Division Headquarters	9254 (357)
77th Division Signal Unit	9270 (239)
77th Division Ordinance Duty Unit	15578 (81)
77th Division Medical Unit	9274 (529)
77th Division 1st Field Hospital	9276 (242)

77th Division continue

77th Division 4th Field Hospital	9278 (242)
77th Division Anti Gas Unit	15577 (85)
77th Division Veterinary Unit	15579 (52)
77th Infantry Group Headquarters	9256 deactivated 2/28/45
• 98th Infantry Regiment (Asahikawa)	9258 (3,054)
• 99th Infantry Regiment (Asahikawa)	9260 (3,054)
• 100th Infantry Regiment (Asahikawa)	9262 (3,054)
• 77th Cavalry Regiment	9264 (672)
• 77th Division Rapid Firing Gun Unit	9266 (480)
• 77th Mountain Artillery Regiment	9268 (2,307)
• 77th Engineer Regiment	9269 (961)
• 77th Transport Regiment	9272 (738)
• 75th Independent Engineer Battalion	unknown

77th Division: (C type) Activated Asahikawa on Mar 27, 1944, from 7th Depot Division personnel. Home station: Asahikawa. With the 5th Area Army from Apr 1st until May 8, 1945 and 16th Area Army in Kajiki until it was deactivated in Sakurajima on Oct 15th.
Service History: Japan: Yufutsu, later Asahikawa, later Kajiki.

79th Division Korea 1945   奏 *Sō* 21150

79th Division Headquarters	21151 (302)
79th Division Signal Unit	21161 (237)
79th Division Ordinance Duty Unit	21164 (81)
79th Division Medical Unit	21166 (529)
79th Division 1st Field Hospital	21167 (242)
79th Division 2nd Field Hospital	21168 (242)
79th Division 4th Field Hospital	21169 (242)
79th Division Anti-Gas Unit	21163 (85)
79th Division Veterinary Unit	21165 (52)
79th Division Infantry Group	
• 289th Infantry Regiment (Ranam)	21152 (3,544)
• 290th Infantry Regiment (Hoeryong)	21153 (3,544)
• 291st Infantry Regiment (Ranam)	21154 (3,544)
• 79th Cavalry Regiment	21156 (672)
• 79th Mountain Artillery Regiment	21158 (2,496)
• 79th Engineer Regiment	21160 (961)
• 79th Transport Regiment	21162 (1,003)

79th Division: (C type) Activated in Seoul, Korea Feb 6, 1945, from 19th Depot Division personnel. Home station: Seoul. With the 17th Area Army from Feb 18th until May 30th and 3rd Army in Tumen, eastern Manchuria. Deactivated in Ranam, Korea.
Service History: Korea: Manchuria: Tumen Aug 9 1945.

81st Division Utsunomiya 1942   納 *Nou* (19,428)

81st Division Headquarters	2881 (357)	
81st Division Signal Unit	2883 (239)	
81st Division Ordinance Duty Unit	2885 (81)	
81st Division Medical Unit	2886 (529)	
81st Division Motorized Medical Unit	2886 (170)	
81st Division 1st Field Hospital	2887 (242)	
81st Division 4th Field Hospital	2888 (242)	
81st Division Anti-Gas Unit	2890 (85)	
81st Division Veterinary Unit	2889 (52)	
81st Infantry Group Headquarters	2885 (93)	deactivated 2/6/45
• 171st Infantry Regiment (Utsunomiya)	2876 (4,579)	
• 172nd Infantry Regiment (Mito)	2877 (4,579)	
• 173rd Infantry Regiment (Takasaki)	2878 (4,579)	
• 81st Division Rapid Firing Gun Unit	2879 (480)	
• 81st Field Artillery Regiment	2880 (2,641)	
• 81st Engineer Regiment	2882 (961)	
• 81st Transport Regiment	2884 (748)	

<u>81st Division</u>: (C type) Activated in Utsunomiya, Japan Apr 4, 1944, from 51st Depot Division personnel. Home station: Utsunomiya. With the 36th Army in Ibaraki from July 21st. Deactivated in Ichioka between September 7th and 10th.
<u>Service History</u>: Japan: Yuki-cho, Ibaraki Pref. reserve division/agricultural duty.

84th Division Himeji 1944   突 *Totsu* 10130 (13,784)

84th Division Headquarters	10131 (357)	
84th Division Signal Unit	10139 (226)	
84th Division Ordinance Duty Unit	10145 (81)	
84th Division Medical Unit	10141 (529)	
84th Division 1st Field Hospital	10142 (242)	
84th Division 4th Field Hospital	10143 (242)	
84th Division Anti-Gas Unit	10144 (85)	
84th Division Veterinary Unit	10146 (52)	
84th Infantry Group Headquarters	10132 (92)	deactivated 7/6/45
• 199th Infantry Regiment (Himeji)	10133 (3,092)	
• 200th Infantry Regiment (Himeji)	10134 (3,092)	
• 201st Infantry Regiment (Himeji)	10135 (3,092)	
• 84th Division Rapid Firing Gun Unit	10136 (480)	
• 84th Field Artillery Regiment	10137 (1,116)	
• 84th Engineer Regiment	10138 (961)	
• 84th Transport Regiment	10140 (749)	

<u>84th Division</u>: (C type) Activated in Himeji July 6, 1944, from 56th Depot Division personnel. Home station: Himeji. Served with the Central District Army until Feb 6, 1945, 15th Area Army until April 8th and 53rd Army in Matsuda, Kanagawa. Deactivated in Fujisawa on Aug 30th.
<u>Service History</u>: Japan: Matsuda.

86th Division Kurume 1944　　　　　　　　積 *Seki* (13,418)

86th Division Headquarters	15100 (357)
86th Division Signal Unit	15108 (239)
86th Division Ordinance Duty Unit	15115 (81)
86th Division Medical Unit	15110 (529)
86th Division 1st Field Hospital	15111 (242)
86th Division 4th Field Hospital	15112 (242)
86th Division Anti-Gas Unit	15113 (85)
86th Division Veterinary Unit	15114 (52)
86th Infantry Group Headquarters	15101　　deactivated 2/6/45
• 187th Infantry Regiment (Fukuoka)	15102 (3,092)
• 188th Infantry Regiment (Ōmura)	15103 (3,092)
• 189th Infantry Regiment (Kurume)	15104 (3,092)
• 86th Division Machine Cannon Unit	15105 (480)
• 86th Field Artillery Regiment	15106 (1,734)
• 86th Engineer Regiment	15107 (961)
• 86th Transport Regiment	15109 (738)
Attached Infantry Unit	
• 364th Infantry Regiment	28245 (3,207)
• 765th Independent Infantry Battalion	28365 (897)
• 766th Independent Infantry Battalion	28366 (897)
• 767th Independent Infantry Battalion	28367 (897)

86th Division: (C type) Activated in Kurume, Japan Apr 4, 1944, from 56th Depot Division personnel. Home station: Kurume. With the Western District Army from July 6th until Feb 6, 1945, 16th Area Army until April 8th and 57th Army in Shibushi, Kagoshima where it was deactivated on September 28th.
Service History: Japan: Shibushi garrison.

88th Division Asahikawa 1945　　　　　　　要 *Kaname* 2222 (20,388)

88th Division Headquarters	22951 (798)
88th Division Signal Unit	22955 (226)
88th Division Ordinance Duty Unit	22957 (112)
88th Division Medical Unit	22958 (1,004)
88th Division 1st Field Hospital	22960 (246)
88th Division 4th Field Hospital	22961 (247)
88th Division D. P. & Water Supply Unit	22962 (129) planned, not activ.
88th Division Veterinary Unit	22959 (77)
88th Division Infantry Group	
• 25th Infantry Regiment (Sapporo)	2221 (2,836)
• 125th Infantry Regiment (Asahikawa)	2232 (3,507)
• 306th Infantry Regiment (Asahikawa)	22952 (4,952)
• 88th Mountain Artillery Regiment	22953 (1,832)
• 88th Engineer Regiment	22954 (1,152)
• 88th Transport Regiment	22956 (2,000)

88th Division: (C type) Activated on Sakhalin Is. Feb 28, 1945, from former Karafuto Mixed Brigade personnel (same code name). Home station: Asahikawa. With the 5th Area Army in Toyohara from Mar 26th until it was deactivated on Sept 28, 1945.
Service History: Sakhalin Is.: Esutoru Aug 9 1945.

89th Division Asahikawa 1945	摧 *Sai* 9256 (14,500)
89th Division Headquarters	23001 (777)
89th Division Signal Unit	23003 (226)
89th Division Ordinance Duty Unit	23006 (112)
89th Division Medical Unit	23009 (1,004)
89th Division 3rd Bgde Chishima Hospital	12649 (123)
3rd Mixed Brigade Headquarters	12644 (294)
3rd Brigade Signal Unit	12647 (278)
3rd Brigade Ordinance Duty Unit	12648 (154)
• 294th Independent Infantry Battalion	12694 (985)
• 295th Independent Infantry Battalion	12695 (985)
• 296th Independent Infantry Battalion	12696 (985)
• 297th Independent Infantry Battalion	12697 (985)
• 419th Independent Infantry Battalion	12698 (985)
• 420th Independent Infantry Battalion	12699 (985)
• 3rd Brigade Artillery Unit	12645 (735)
• 3rd Brigade Labor Unit	12646 (267)
4th Mixed Brigade Headquarters	12609 (298)
4th Brigade Signal Unit	12628 (226)
• 421st Independent Infantry Battalion	12623 (814)
• 422nd Independent Infantry Battalion	12624 (814)
• 423rd Independent Infantry Battalion	12625 (814)
• 424th Independent Infantry Battalion	12626 (814)
• 460th Independent Infantry Battalion	23011 (983)
• 461st Independent Infantry Battalion	23013 (983)
• 4th Brigade Artillery Unit	12627 (464)
• 4th Brigade Labor Unit	12629 (157)

89th Division: (C type) Activated in Sapporo on February 28, 1945, from former 43rd I.M.B. (3rd Mixed Bgde) and 69th I.M.B. plus 460th and 461st Ind Btns. Home station: Asahikawa. With the 5th Area Army on Etorofu from Mar 26th until the war ended, with elements of the 3rd Mixed Bgde on Iturup and 4th Mixed Bgde on Shikotan. The 89th Division was deactivated on Sept 17, 1945.
Service History: Japan: Shikotan, the Kurile Islands Sept 1 1945.

91st Division Asahikawa 1944	先 *Saki* 12600 (19,510)
91st Division Headquarters	12640 (477)
91st Division Signal Unit	12666 (328)
91st Division Ordinance Duty Unit	12668 (200)
91st Division 1st Field Hospital	12669 (285)

91st Division continued

91st Division Air Defense Unit	12664 (840)
73rd Infantry Brigade Headquarters	12673 (90)
73rd Infantry Brigade Signal Unit	12671 (233)
73rd Infantry Brigade Labor Unit	12672 (157)
• 282nd Independent Infantry Battalion	12682 (858)
• 283rd Independent Infantry Battalion	12683 (858)
• 284th Independent Infantry Battalion	12684 (858)
• 285th Independent Infantry Battalion	12685 (858)
• 286th Independent Infantry Battalion	12686 (858)
• 287th Independent Infantry Battalion	12687 (858)
74th Infantry Brigade Headquarters	12674 (90)
74th Infantry Brigade Signal Unit	12675 (233)
74th Infantry Brigade Labor Unit	12676 (157)
• 288th Independent Infantry Battalion	12688 (858)
• 289th Independent Infantry Battalion	12689 (858)
• 290th Independent Infantry Battalion	12690 (858) detached to 5th A.A.
• 291st Independent Infantry Battalion	12691 (858)
• 292nd Independent Infantry Battalion	12692 (858)
• 293rd Independent Infantry Battalion	12693 (858)
• 11th Tank Regiment	12084 (561) Shumushu Island
• 2nd Independent Tank Company	12084 (94)
• 91st Division Machine Cannon Unit	12661 (419)
• 91st Division 1st Artillery Unit	12662 (961)
• 91st Division 2nd Artillery Unit	12663 (480)
• 91st Division Engineer Unit	12665 (785)
• 91st Division Transport Unit	12667 (284)

91st Division: (C type) Activated in the Kurile Islands April 12, 1944, from 1st Chishima Garrison Unit personnel. Home station: Asahikawa. With the 27th Army until Jan. 22, 1945 and 5th Area Army on Shumushu I. until it was deactivated between Sept 11 and 24, 1945.
Service History: Japan: Shumushu Aug 18 1945.

93rd Division Kanazawa 1944　　　　　　　決 *Ketsu* 6660 (21,516)

93rd Division Headquarters	6661 (359)
93rd Division Signal Unit	6670 (239)
93rd Division Ordinance Duty Unit	6678 (81)
93rd Division Medical Unit	6672 (529)
93rd Division 1st Field Hospital	6673 (242)
93rd Division 4th Field Hospital	6676 (242)
93rd Division Anti-Gas Unit	6677 (85)
93rd Division Veterinary Unit	6679 (52)
93rd Infantry Group Headquarters	6662　　　deactivated 2/ 6/45
• 202nd Infantry Regiment (Toyama)	6663 (4,541)

- 203rd Infantry Regiment (Kanazawa) — 6664 (4,541)
- 204th Infantry Regiment (Toyama) — 6665 (4,541)
- 93rd Cavalry Regiment — 6666 (672)
- 93rd Division Rapid Firing Gun Unit — 6667 (480)
- 93rd Mountain Artillery Regiment — 6668 (3,791)
- 93rd Engineer Regiment — 6669 (961)
- 93rd Transport Regiment — 6671 (749)

93rd Division: (C type) Activated in Kanazawa July 6, 1944, from 52nd Depot Division personnel. Home station: Kanazawa. With the 36th Army in Matsudo, Chiba Prefecture from July 21st until it was deactivated in Machioji between September 11th and 24th.
Service History: Japan: Matsudo reserve division.

96th Division Fukuoka 1945   玄 Gen 22001

- 96th Division Headquarters — 22002 (250)
- 96th Division Signal Unit — 22008 (204)
- 96th Division Field Hospital — 22009 (306)
- 96th Division Infantry Group
  - 292nd Infantry Regiment (Fukuoka) — 22003 (2,432)
  - 293rd Infantry Regiment (Ōmura) — 22004 (2,432)
  - 294th Infantry Regiment (Ōmura) — 22005 (2,432)
- 96th Division Trench Mortar Unit — 22006 (577)
- 96th Division Engineer Unit — 22007 (426)

96th Division: (C type) Activated in Keijo (Seoul), Korea Feb. 6, 1945, from 20th and 30th Depot Division personnel. Home station: Fukuoka, Japan. With the 58th Army from Apr 8th until it was deactivated on August 18, 1945.
Service History: Korea: Jeju Island defense force.

107th Division Hirosaki 1944   凪 Nagi 20000/20099 (16,877)

- 107th Division Headquarters — 20050 (581)
- 107th Division Signal Unit — 20021 (239)
- 107th Division Ordinance Duty Unit — 13959 (112)   activated 5/1/45
- 107th Division Medical Unit — 20040 (1,109)   activ. 8/10/45
- 107th Division 1st Field Hospital — unknown (232)   activ. 8/10/45
- 107th Division 4th Field Hospital — unknown (236)   activ. 8/10/45
- 107th Division Anti-Gas Unit — unknown (187)   activ. 8/10/45
- 107th Division D. P. & Water Supply Unit — 20027 (238)
- 107th Division Veterinary Unit — 12062 (119)   activated 5/5/45
- 107th Division Raiding Unit — 20011 (1,130)   activated 7/10/45
- 107th Division Infantry Group
  - 90th Infantry Regiment (Hirosaki) — 20008 (3,654)
  - 177th Infantry Regiment (Hirosaki) — 20001 (3,596)
  - 178th Infantry Regiment (Aomori) — 20002 (3,478)
- 107th Cavalry Regiment — 20007 (603)

107th Division continued
- 107th Field Artillery Regiment   20006 (2,809)
- 107th Engineer Regiment   20003 (961)
- 107th Transport Regiment   20020 (1,014)

107th Division: (C type) Activated in Arshaan, Manchuria May 16, 1944, from former Arshaan Garrison Unit and 7th Ind. Mixed Regt troops. Home station: Hirosaki. With the 3rd Area Army from June 13th until May 30, 1945 and 44th Army in western Manchuria until the war ended. Surrendered in the Jalaid Banner Mtns on Aug 27, 1945.
Service History: Manchuria: Hailar Aug 9 1945.

108th Division Hirosaki 1937   祐 *Yū* 14050 (14,651)

108th Division Headquarters	14055 (143)
108th Division Signal Unit	20120 (207)
108th Division Ordinance Duty Unit	20150 (112)
108th Division Medical Unit	20140 (1,109)
108th Division 1st Field Hospital	20170 (232)
108th Division 4th Field Hospital	20180 (236)
108th Division D. P. & Water Supply Unit	20160 (239)
108th Division Veterinary Unit	20161 (125)
108th Division Anti-Gas Unit	20130 (187)
108th Division Raiding Battalion	20550 (1,130)
108th Division Infantry Group	
• 240th Infantry Regiment (Hirosaki)	20560 (3,453)
• 241st Infantry Regiment (Akita)	20570 (3,453)
• 242nd Infantry Regiment (Akita)	20580 (3,453)
• 171st Cavalry Regiment	20590 (529)
• 108th Field Artillery Regiment	20100 (1,923)
• 108th Engineer Regiment	20110 (288)
• 108th Transport Regiment	20030 (1,014)

108th Division: (C type) Activated in Hirosaki Aug 26, 1937, from former 8th Depot Division personnel. Home station: Hirosaki. With the 2nd Army from Aug 31st until Mar 30, 1938 and 1st Army until it was deactivated in Japan on February 21, 1940.
Note: Reactivated in Chengde, Manchuria July 12, 1944, from former 9th Ind Garrison Unit troops. Home station: Hirosaki. With the Kwantung Defense Army from Aug 5th until May 30, 1945, 44th Army until July 15th and 3rd Area Army in Jinzhou. Deactivated in Chengde on August 19, 1945.
Service History 1937-40: China: Linfen Aug 1937.
Service History 1944-5: Manchuria: Jinzhou garrison.

111th Division Zentsuji 1944   市 *Ichi* 13050 (12,000)

111th Division Headquarters	13055 (183)
111th Division Signal Unit	13057 (207)
111th Division Ordinance Duty Unit	12956 (112)

111th Division continued   市 *Ichi*

111th Division Medical Unit   12957 (1,109)
111th Division 1st Field Hospital   12958 (277)
111th Division 4th Field Hospital   12959 (284)
111th Division D. P. & Water Supply Unit   12961 (239)
111th Division Veterinary Unit   12960 (119)
111th Division Infantry Group
- 243rd Infantry Regiment (Tokushima)   13051 (3,482)
- 244th Infantry Regiment (Kochi)   13052 (3,475)
- 245th Infantry Regiment (Marugame)   13053 (3,453)
- 111th Field Artillery Unit   13054 (617)
- 111th Engineer Unit   13056 (288)
- 111th Transport Regiment   13058 (1,014)

111th Division: (C type) Activated in Manchuria on July 12, 1944, from former 9th Independent Garrison Unit troops. Home station: Zentsuji, Japan. With the 20th Army from Aug 5th until Sept 27th, 3rd Army until Mar 31, 1945, 17th Area Army until May 1st and 58th Army Cheju Island, Korea until it was deactivated on August 18, 1945.

Service History: Manchuria: East Manchuria garrison. Korea: Cheju Island garrison.

112th Division Kureme 1944   公 *Kimi* 13150 (14,566)

112th Division Headquarters   13180 (143)
112th Division Signal Unit   20315/13115 (207)
112th Division Ordinance Duty Unit   20362/12962 (112)
112th Division Medical Unit   20374 (699)
112th Division 1st Field Hospital   20376 (242)
112th Division 4th Field Hospital   20378 (247)
112th Division Veterinary Unit   20366/12966 (125)
112th Division Anti-Gas Unit   unknown   activated Aug '45
112th Division Raiding Battalion   20355 (1,130)
112th Division Infantry Group
- 246th Infantry Regiment (Fukuoka)   20320/13120 (3,476)
- 247th Infantry Regiment (Ōmura)   20325/13125 (3,476)
- 248th Infantry Regiment (Kureme)   20328/13128 (3,453)
- 112th Field Artillery Regiment   20336/13136 (1,923)
- 112th Engineer Unit   20331/13131 (288)
- 112th Transport Regiment   20317/13117 (1,014)

112th Division: (C type) Activated in Hunchun, Manchuria July 10, 1944, from former 28th Depot Division and 9th Ind. Garrison Unit personnel. Home station: Kureme. With the 3rd Army from Aug 5th until it was deactivated in Yenchi on August 18, 1945.

Service History: Manchuria: Hunchun garrison, Eastern Manchuria Aug 9 1945.

117th Division North China 1944   弘 *Hiroshi* 1466 (11,891)

117th Division Headquarters   3140 (175)

117th Division continued

117th Division Signal Unit	1471 (329)
117th Division Field Hospital	15631 (352)
117th Division Veterinary Unit	15632 (45)
87th Infantry Brigade	15621
87th Infantry Brigade Headquarters	15622 (50)
• 203rd Independent Infantry Battalion	1467 (1,233)
• 204th Independent Infantry Battalion	1468 (1,233)
• 205th Independent Infantry Battalion	1469 (1,233)
• 206th Independent Infantry Battalion	1470 (1,233)
88th Infantry Brigade	15623
88th Infantry Brigade Headquarters	15624 (50)
• 388th Independent Infantry Battalion	15625 (1,233)
• 389th Independent Infantry Battalion	15626 (1,233)
• 390th Independent Infantry Battalion	15627 (1,233)
• 391st Independent Infantry Battalion	15628 (1,233)
• 117th Mortar Unit	1499 (577)
• 117th Engineer Unit	15629 (901)
• 117th Transport Unit	15630 (867)

117th Division: (C type) Activated in Xinxiang, China July 10, 1944, from former 4th Ind Inf Bgde personnel (became 87th Inf Bgde). Home station: Unknown. With the 12th Army from July 17th until May 30, 1945 and 44th Army in Taonan, Manchuria. Ended the war in Hsinking and was deactivated in Wangyehmia on August 19, 1945.
Service History: China: Henan. Manchuria: Taonan garrison, Liaoyuan.

119th Division Tokyo 1944   宰 *Sai* 20400

119th Division Headquarters	20411 (144)
119th Division Signal Unit	20416 (239)
119th Division Ordinance Duty Unit	12994 (112)
119th Division Medical Unit	20491 / 12995 (1,109)
119th Division 1st Field Hospital	20492 / 12996 (277)
119th Division 2nd Field Hospital	20493 / 12997 (277)
119th Division 4th Field Hospital	20494 / 12998 (283)
119th Division D. P. & Water Supply Unit	12999 (239)
119th Division Anti-Gas Unit	20460 (187)
119th Division Veterinary Unit	20458 (119)
119th Division Raiding Battalion	20413 (1,130)
20th Infantry Brigade	
• 253rd Infantry Regiment (Tokyo)	20462 (3,851)
• 254th Infantry Regiment (Tokyo)	20481 (3,851)
• 255th Infantry Regiment (Ichikawa)	20415 (3,851)
• 119th Cavalry Regiment	20496 (603)
• 119th Field Artillery Regiment	20418 (2,913)
• 119th Engineer Regiment	20495 (938)
• 119th Transport Regiment	20498 (1,022

119th Division: (C type) Activated in Heilongjiang, Manchuria Oct 11, 1944, from former 8th Border Garrison Unit and 23rd Div personnel. Home station: Tokyo. With the 6th Army from Oct 11th until Jan 25, 1945, 3rd Area Army until May 30th and 4th Army in Hailar where it was deactivated on August 16, 1945. HQ designated 6th Army HQ for security purposes after the 6th Army HQ was sent to Hangchow, China.
Service History: Manchuria: Hailar Aug 9 1945.

120th Division Zentsuji 1944　　　　　　　　邁進 *Maishin* 13950 (12,000)

120th Division Headquarters	13955 (156)
120th Division Signal Unit	13957 (207)
120th Division Ordinance Duty Unit	No # (112)
120th Division Medical Unit	21073 (700)
120th Division Field Hospital	21074 (280)
120th Division Veterinary Unit	No # (119)
120th Division Infantry Group	
• 259th Infantry Regiment (Marugame)	13951 (3,409)
• 260th Infantry Regiment (Tokushima)	13952 (3,409)
• 261st Infantry Regiment (Kochi)	13953 (3,409)
•120th Division Artillery Unit	13954 (617)
• 120th Division Engineer Unit	13956 (288)
• 120th Transport Regiment	13958 (749)

120th Division: (C type) Activated Dongning, Manchuria Nov 21, 1944, from a 12th Div cadre and 4th Border Unit personnel Home station: Zentsuji. With the 3rd Army until Mar 31st and 17th Area Army in Pyongyang Korea. Deactivated near Pyongyang on Aug 17, 1945.
Service History: Korea: Pyongyang garrison.

121st Division Zentsuji 1945　　　　　　　　栄光 *Eikō* 13960 (13,000)

121st Division Headquarters	13961 / 364 (155)
121st Division Signal Unit	13967 / 624 (239)
121st Division Ordinance Duty Unit	13969 / 701 (112)
121st Division Medical Unit	13912 (560)
121st Division 1st Field Hospital	13913 (227)
121st Division 2nd Field Hospital	13914 (227)
121st Division 4th Field Hospital	13915 (227)　　never mobilized
121st Division D. P. & Water Supply Unit	13916 (239)
121st Division Anti-Gas Unit	13911 (187)
121st Division Veterinary Unit	13970 / 406 (119)
121st Division Infantry Group	
• 262nd Infantry Regiment (Marugame)	13962 / 97 (3,410)
• 263rd Infantry Regiment (Tokushima)	13963 / 177 (3,410)
• 264th Infantry Regiment (Kochi)	13964 / 674 (3,410)
• 121st Division Field Artillery Unit	13965 / 379 (1,923)
• 121st Division Engineer Unit	13966 / 204 (960)

121st Division continued
- 121st Division Transport Unit   13968 / 974 (1,014)

121st Division: (C type) Activated in Manchuria Jan 16, 1945, from the 3rd Cavalry Bgde, and 28th Div personnel. Home station: Zentsuji. With the 3rd Army until Mar 31st and 58th Army on Jeju Is., Korea where it was deactivated on August 18th.
Service History: Korea: Jeju Island garrison.

122nd Division Tokyo 1945   舞鶴 *Maitsuru* (14,752)

122nd Division Headquarters	12061 (155)
122nd Division Signal Unit	12067 (239)
122nd Division Ordinance Duty Unit	12069 (112)
122nd Division Medical Unit	13918 (476)
122nd Division 1st Field Hospital	13919 (304)
122nd Division 2nd Field Hospital	13920 (304)
122nd Division 4th Field Hospital	13921 (301)
122nd Division D. P. & Water Supply Unit	13922 (254)
122nd Division Anti-Gas Unit	13917 (227) activated 8/10/45
122nd Division Veterinary Unit	12070 (119)
122nd Division Raiding Battalion	13923 (1,130) activated 7/10/45

122nd Division Infantry Group
- 265th Infantry Regiment (Tokyo)   12062 (3,410)
- 266th Infantry Regiment (Kofu)   12063 (3,410)
- 267th Infantry Regiment (Sakura)   12064 (3,410)
- 122nd Field Artillery Regiment   12065 (1,923)
- 122nd Engineer Regiment   12066 (960)
- 122nd Transport Regiment   12068 (1,014)

122nd Division: (C type) Activated in Mudanjiang, Manchuria Jan 16, 1945, from 11th Division remnants. Home station: Tokyo. With the 1st Area Army in Mudanjiang from Feb 26th, it was deactivated on August 17th.
Service History: Manchuria: Mudanjiang, Ningan garrison.

123rd Division Nagoya 1945   松風 *Mazukaze* (14,752)

123rd Division Headquarters	15201 (155)
123rd Division Signal Unit	15207 (239)
123rd Division Ordinance Duty Unit	15209 (112)
123rd Division Medical Unit	15212 (560) activated 8/10/45
123rd Division 1st Field Hospital	15213 (277) activated 8/10/45
123rd Division 2nd Field Hospital	15214 (277) activated 8/10/45
123rd Division 4th Field Hospital	15215 (277) activated 8/10/45
123rd Division D. P. & Water Supply Unit	15216 (239) activated 8/10/45
123rd Division Anti-Gas Unit	15211 (157) activated 8/10/45
123rd Division Veterinary Unit	15210 (119)
123rd Division Raiding Battalion	15295 (1,130) activated 8/10/45

123rd Division continued   松風 *Mazukaze*

123rd Division Infantry Group
- 268th Infantry Regiment (Nagoya)   15202 (3,410)
- 269th Infantry Regiment (Tsu)   15203 (3,410)
- 270th Infantry Regiment (Gifu)   15204 (3,410)
- 123rd Field Artillery Regiment   15205 (1,923)
- 123rd Engineer Regiment   15206 (960)
- 123rd Transport Regiment   15208 (1,014)

123rd Division: (C type) Activated in Sunwu, Manchuria Jan 16, 1945, from 73rd I.M.B. personnel. Home station: Nagoya. With the 4th Army south of Aigun from Feb 26th, it was deactivated on August 18th.

Service History: Manchuria: Sunwa Aug 9 1945.

124th Division Sendai 1945   遠謀 *Enbou* 15230 (14,442)

124th Division Headquarters   15231 (117)
124th Division Signal Unit   15227 (207)
124th Division Ordinance Duty Unit   13941 (112) activated 8/10/45
124th Division Medical Unit   15218 (560) activated 8/10/45
124th Division 1st Field Hospital   15219 (277) activated 8/10/45
124th Division 4th Field Hospital   15220 (277) activated 8/10/45
124th Division D. P. & Water Supply Unit   15221 (239) activated 8/10/45
124th Division Anti-Gas Unit   15217 (157) activated 8/10/45
124th Division Veterinary Unit   15229 (119)
124th Division Raiding Battalion   15232 (1,130) activated 7/10/45
124th Division Infantry Group
- 271st Infantry Regiment (Sendai)   15222 (3,410)
- 272nd Infantry Regiment (see note)   15223 (3,410)
- 273rd Infantry Regiment (Yamagata)   15224 (3,410)
- 116th Field Artillery Regiment   15225 (1,923)
- 124th Engineer Regiment   15226 (288)
- 124th Transport Regiment   15228 (882)

124th Division: (C type) Activated in Suiyang, Manchuria Jan 16, 1945, from former 111th Div personnel. Home station: Sendai. With the 3rd Army from Feb 26th until May 30th and 5th Army in Suiyang, Muling. It was deactivated on August 18th.

Note: 272nd Inf. Regt. is affiliated with Aizuwakamatsu City.

Service History: Manchuria: Suiyang garrison, Muling Aug 12 1945.

125th Division Hiroshima 1945   英機 *Eiki* 15240

125th Division Headquarters   15241 (117)
125th Division Signal Unit   15242 (207)
125th Division Ordinance Duty Unit   13992
125th Division Field Hospital   unknown
125th Division Veterinary Unit   37808 (119)

125th Division continued

125th Division Raiding Unit	15249 (1,130)
125th Division Infantry Group	
• 275th Infantry Regiment (Yamaguchi)	15236 (3,410)
• 276th Infantry Regiment (Hamada)	3780 (3,410) activated 7/10/45
• 388th Infantry Regiment (Manchuria)	unknown (3,410)
• 125th Field Artillery Regiment	37804 (1,923) activated 7/10/45
• 125th Engineer Regiment	15239 (964)
• 125th Transport Regiment	15258 (1,180)

125th Division: (C type) Activated in Shenwutun, Manchuria Jan 16, 1945 from former 57th Div and 13th Border Guard Unit personnel. Home station: Hiroshima. With the 4th Army from Feb 26th until April 20th, 3rd Area Army until Aug 9th and 30th Army in Tunghua until it was deactivated on August 18th.
Service History: Manchuria: Tunghua garrison.

126h Division Kumamoto 1945 — 英断 *Eidan* 15250 (16,613)

126th Division Headquarters	15251 (117)
126th Division Signal Unit	15256 (207) activated 7/10/45
126th Division Ordinance Duty Unit	13993 (112) activated 5/5/45
126th Division Medical Unit	unknown (660) activ.8/10/45
126th Division 1st Field Hospital	unknown (274) activ.8/10/45
126th Division 4th Field Hospital	unknown (274)
126th Division D. P. & Water Supply Unit	unknown (239)
126th Division Anti-Gas Unit	unknown (157) activ. 8/10/45
126th Division Veterinary Unit	unknown (119) activ. 7/10/45
126th Division Raiding Battalion	15259 (1,130) activated 7/10/45
126th Division Infantry Group	
• 277th Infantry Regiment (Miyakonojo)	15252 (3,410)
• 278th Infantry Regiment (Kumamoto)	15253 (3,410)
• 279th Infantry Regiment (Kagoshima)	15260 (3,410) activated 7/10/45
• 126th Field Artillery Regiment	15254 (1,923) activated 7/10/45
• 126th Engineer Regiment	15255 (288) activated 7/10/45
• 126th Transport Regiment	15257 (882) activated 7/10/45

126th Division: (C type) Activated in Linkou, Manchuria Jan 16, 1945, from former 12th Border Guard Unit personnel. Home station: Kumamoto, Japan. With the 5th Army from Feb 26th in Linkow, Pamientung, Yehho and northeast of Lishunchen, it was deactivated on August 18th.
Service History: Manchuria: Mutanchiang Aug 12 1945.

127h Division Utsunomiya 1945 — 英邁 *Eimai* 15270 (12,498)

127th Division Headquarters	15271 (117)
127th Division Signal Unit	15272 (207)
127th Division Ordinance Duty Unit	13994 (112) activated 5/5/45

127ʰ Division continued   英邁 *Eimai*

127th Division Medical Unit	unknown (400)	activ. 8/10/45
127th Division 1st Field Hospital	unknown (304)	activ. 8/10/45
127th Division 4th Field Hospital	unknown (311)	activ. 8/10/45
127th Division D. P. & Water Supply Unit	unknown (254)	activ. 8/10/45
127th Division Anti-Gas Unit	unknown (187)	activ. 8/10/45
127th Division Veterinary Unit	15274 (119)	
127th Division Raiding Battalion	15276 (1,130)	activ. 8/10/45
127th Division Infantry Group		
• 280th Infantry Regiment (Utsunomiya)	15265 (3,410)	
• 281st Infantry Regiment (Mito)	15266 (3,410)	
• 282nd Infantry Regiment (Takasaki)	15267 (3,410) activated 7/10/45	
• 127th Field Artillery Regiment	15268 (1,923) activated 7/10/45	
• 127th Engineer Unit	15269 (288)	
• 127th Transport Unit	15273 (882)	

127ᵗʰ Division: (C type) Activated in Manchuria Mar 20, 1945, from former 9th Border Guard Unit personnel. Home station: Utsunomiya. With the 3rd Army in building defenses Hunchun and Jilin from Feb 26th. Deactivated in Hunchun on Aug 18th.
Service History: Manchuria: Tumen Aug 9 1945.

128th Division Kanazawa 1945   英武 *Eibu* 15280 (12,498)

128th Division Headquarters	15281 (117)
128th Division Signal Unit	15287 (207)
128th Division Ordinance Duty Unit	15289/13995 (112) activ. 5/1/45
128th Division 1st Field Hospital	unknown activated 8/10/45
128th Division 4th Field Hospital	unknown activated 8/10/45
128th Division D. P. & Water Supply Unit	unknown activated 8/10/45
128th Division Anti-Gas Unit	unknown activated 8/10/45
128th Division Veterinary Unit	15290 (119)
128th Division Raiding Battalion	15291 (1,130)
128th Division Infantry Group	
• 283rd Infantry Regiment (Kanazawa)	15282 (3,410)
• 284th Infantry Regiment (Toyama)	15283 (3,410)
• 285th Infantry Regiment (Toyama)	15284/3696 (3,410) act. 7/10/45
• 128th Field Artillery Regiment	15285 (1,923)
• 128th Engineer Unit	15286 (288)
• 128th Transport Unit	15288 (882)

128ᵗʰ Division: (C type) Activated in Manchuria Jan 16, 1945, from former 120th Div and 2nd and 11th Border Guard Unit troops. Home station: Kanazawa, Japan. With the 3rd Army in Tungning, Manchuria from Feb 26th until it was deactivated on Aug 18th.
Service History: Manchuria: Dongning Aug 9 1945.

134th Division Manchuria 1945　　　　　勾玉 *Magatama* 25262 (14,056)

134th Division Headquarters	25263 (240)
134th Division Signal Unit	25271 (239)
134th Division Ordinance Duty Unit	25273 (112)
135th Division Medical Unit	unknown (400)　activ. 8/10/45
135th Division 1st Field Hospital	unknown (304)　activ. 8/10/45
135th Division 4th Field Hospital	unknown (311)　activ. 8/10/45
135th Division D. P. & Water Supply Unit	unknown (254)　activ. 8/10/45
134th Division Veterinary Unit	25277 (119)
134th Division Anti-Gas Unit	25267　(187)　activ. 8/10/45
134th Division Raiding Battalion	25268 (1,130)
134th Division Infantry Group	
• 365th Infantry Regiment (Manchuria)	25264 (3,409)
• 366th Infantry Regiment (Manchuria)	25265 (3,409)
• 367th Infantry Regiment (Manchuria)	25266 (3,409)
• 134th Field Artillery Regiment	25269 (1,923)
• 134th Engineer Regiment	25270 (964)
• 134th Transport Regiment	25272 (1,180)

134th Division: (C type) Activated in Manchuria July 10, 1945, from former 14th Border Guard Unit, Fujin Garrison Unit and 78th I.M.B. personnel. Home station: Unknown. With the 1st Area Army in Fangcheng from Jul 10th. Deactivated in Chiamusa Aug 18th. Note: Inherited the 78th I.M.B.s code name.
Service History: Manchuria: Chiamussu

135th Division Manchuria 1945　　　　　真心 *Magokoro* 25251 (14,228)

135th Division Headquarters	25252 (240)
135th Division Signal Unit	25260 (239)
135th Division Ordinance Duty Unit	25262 (112)
135th Division Medical Unit	25263 (1,109)　activated 8/10/45
135th Division 1st Field Hospital	25264 (232)
135th Division 4th Field Hospital	25265 (236)
135th Division D. P. & Water Supply Unit	25267 (239)　activated 8/10/45
135th Division Anti-Gas Unit	25256 (187)　activated 8/10/45
135th Division Veterinary Unit	25266 (119)
135th Division Raiding Battalion	25257 (1,130)
135th Division Infantry Group	
• 368th Infantry Regiment (Manchuria)	25253 (3,409)
• 369th Infantry Regiment (Manchuria)	25254 (3,409)
• 370th Infantry Regiment (Manchuria)	25255 (3,409)
• 135th Field Artillery Regiment	25258 (1,923)
• 135th Engineer Regiment	25259 (964)
• 135th Transport Regiment	25261 (1,180)

135th Division: (C type) Activated in Tungan, Manchuria July 10, 1945, from former 2nd, 4th Border Guard, 46th L.o.C. Guard personnel and the 77th I.M.B. Home station:

Tungan. With the 5th Army in Yehho Manchuria from Jul 10th. Deactivated in Tungan on Aug18th.
Note: Inherited the 77th I.M.B. Mojifu (code name).
Service History: Manchuria: Pamientung, Tungan.

136th Division Manchuria 1945   不抜 *Hubatu* 37220

136th Division Headquarters	37217 (240)
136th Division Signal Unit	37232 (239)
136th Division Ordinance Duty Unit	37233 (112)
136th Division Medical Unit	37231 (1,109) activated 8/10/45
136th Division 1st Field Hospital	37228 (232) activated 8/10/45
136th Division 4th Field Hospital	37229 (236) activated 8/10/45
136th Division D. P. & Water Supply Unit	37231 (239) activated 8/10/45
136th Division Veterinary Unit	37230 (119) activated 8/10/45
136th Division Anti-Gas Unit	unknown (187) activ. 8/10/45
136th Division Raiding Battalion	37228 (1,130)
136th Division Infantry Group	
• 371st Infantry Regiment (Manchuria)	37221 (3,409)
• 372nd Infantry Regiment (Manchuria)	37222 (3,409)
• 373rd Infantry Regiment (Manchuria)	37223 (3,409)
• 136th Cavalry Regiment	37227 (?)
• 136th Field Artillery Regiment	37225 (1,923)
• 136th Engineer Regiment	37224 (964)
• 136th Transport Regiment	37226 (1,180)

137th Division: (C type) Activated in Hamhung, Korea July 10, 1945, from former 79th Div personnel and other units in Hamhung. Home station: Hamhung. With the 34th Army in Hamgyong then Pyongyang, deactivated in the Pyongyang area Aug 25th.
Service History: Korea: Pyongyang.

137th Division Manchuria 1945   扶翼 *Huyoku*

137th Division Headquarters	37237 (240)
137th Division Signal Unit	37246 (239)
137th Division Ordinance Duty Unit	37247 (112)
137th Division Medical Unit	37248 (1,109) activated 8/10/45
137th Division 1st Field Hospital	37249 (232) activated 8/10/45
137th Division 4th Field Hospital	37250 (236) activated 8/10/45
137th Division D. P. & Water Supply Unit	37252 (239) activated 8/10/45
137th Division Veterinary Unit	37251 (119)
137th Division Anti-Gas Unit	37241 (187)
137th Division Raider Battalion	37242 (1,130)
137th Division Infantry Group	
• 374th Infantry Regiment (Ranam)	37238 (3,409)

137th Division continued
- 375th Infantry Regiment (Ranam)　　　37239 (3,409)
- 376th Infantry Regiment (Hoeryong)　　37240 (3,409)
- 137th Field Artillery Regiment　　37243 (1,923)
- 137th Engineer Regiment　　37244 (964)
- 137th Transport Regiment　　37245 (1,180)

137th Division: (C type) Activated in Hamhung, Korea July 10, 1945, from former 79th Div personnel and other units in Hamhung. Home station: Hamhung. With the 34th Army in Hamgyong then Pyongyang, deactivated in the Pyongyang area Aug 25th.
Service History: Korea: Pyongyang.

138th Division Manchuria 1945　　　不動 *Hudō*

138th Division Headquarters　　　37257 (240)
138th Division Signal Unit　　　37266 (239)
138th Division Ordinance Duty Unit　　37267 (112)
138th Division Medical Unit　　37268 (1,109)　activated 8/10/45
138th Division 1st Field Hospital　　37269 (232)　activated 8/10/45
138th Division 4th Field Hospital　　37270 (236)　activated 8/10/45
138th Division D. P. & Water Supply Unit　37272 (239)　activated 8/10/45
138th Division Veterinary Unit　　37273 (119)
138th Division Anti-Gas Unit　　37261 (187)　activated 8/10/45
138th Division Raiding Battalion　　37262 (1,130)
138th Division Infantry Group
- 377th Infantry Regiment (Manchuria)　37258 (3,409)
- 378th Infantry Regiment (Manchuria)　37259 (3,409)
- 379th Infantry Regiment (Manchuria)　37260 (3,409)
- 138th Field Artillery Regiment　　37263 (1,923)
- 138th Engineer Regiment　　37264 (963)
- 138th Transport Regiment　　37265 (1,180)

138th Division: (C type) Activated in Panshih, Manchuria July 10, 1945, from units in Hsinking. Home station: Panshih. With the 30th Army in Fushin from July 10th. It was deactivated in Hailung on August 25th.
Service History: Manchuria: Penshih

139th Division Manchuria 1945　　　不屈 *Hukutsu* 37310

139th Division Headquarters　　　37301 (240)
139th Division Signal Unit　　　37316 (239)
139th Division Ordinance Duty Unit　　37310 (112)
139th Division Medical Unit　　37311 (1,109)　activated 8/10/45
139th Division 1st Field Hospital　　37312 (232)　activated 8/10/45
139th Division 4th Field Hospital　　37313 (236)　activated 8/10/45

139th Division Manchuria 1945　　　　　　不屈 *Hukutsu* 37310

139th Division Headquarters	37301 (240)	
139th Division Signal Unit	37316 (239)	
139th Division Ordinance Duty Unit	37310 (112)	
139th Division Medical Unit	37311 (1,109)	activated 8/10/45
139th Division 1st Field Hospital	37312 (232)	activated 8/10/45
139th Division 4th Field Hospital	37313 (236)	activated 8/10/45
139th Division D. P. & Water Supply Unit	37315 (239)	activated 8/10/45
139th Division Anti-Gas Unit	37305 (1870	activated 8/10/45
139th Division Veterinary Unit	37314 (119)	
139th Division Raiding Battalion	37306 (1,130)	
139th Division Infantry Group		
• 380th Infantry Regiment (Manchuria)	37302 (3,409)	
• 381st Infantry Regiment (Manchuria)	37303 (3,409)	
• 382nd Infantry Regiment (Manchuria)	37304 (3,409)	
• 139th Field Artillery Regiment	37307 (1,923)	
• 139th Engineer Regiment	37308 (964)	
• 139th Transport Regiment	37309 (1,180)	

<u>139th Division</u>: (C type) Activated in Tunhua, Manchuria July 10, 1945, from former 77th, 79th and 80th L. of C. Guard Unit personnel. Home station: Tunhua. From Jul 10th it was with the 1st Area Army in Tunhua where it was deactivated on August 18th.
<u>Service History</u>: Manchuria: Tunhua, Lake Chingpo area.

140th Division Tokyo 1945　　　　　　護東 *Gotō* 22051 (13,641)

140th Division Headquarters	22052 (293)	
140th Division Signal Unit	22058 (235)	
140th Division Ordinance Duty Unit	22060 (108)	
140th Division Field Hospital	22061 (201)	activated 6/4/45
140th Division Infantry Group		
• 401st Infantry Regiment (Tokyo)	22053 (3,841)	
• 402nd Infantry Regiment (Kofu)	22054 (3,841)	
• 403rd Infantry Regiment (Sakura)	22055 (3,841)	
• 404th Infantry Regiment (Mizonokuchi)	22056 (3,207)	
• 140th Division Rapid Firing Gun Unit	22057 (480)	
• 140th Division Artillery Unit	36363 (502)	activated 5/23/45
• 140th Division Transport Unit	22059 (360)	

<u>140th Division</u>: (Coastal type) Activated in Tokyo on Feb 28, 1945. Home station: Tokyo. With the 53rd Army in Fujisawa from Apr 8th, deactivated in Kamakura on Aug 30th.
<u>Service History</u>: Japan: Fujisawa coastal defense.

142ⁿᵈ Division Sendai 1945   護仙 *Gosen* 22201 (13,537)

142ⁿᵈ Division Headquarters	22202 (293)
142ⁿᵈ Division Signal Unit	22208 (235)
142ⁿᵈ Division Ordinance Duty Unit	22210 (108) activated 5/10/45
142ⁿᵈ Division Field Hospital	22212 (201) activated 6/25/45

142ⁿᵈ Division Infantry Group
- 405ᵗʰ Infantry Regiment (Sendai)   22203 (3,102)
- 406ᵗʰ Infantry Regiment (Yamagata)   22204 (3,102)
- 407ᵗʰ Infantry Regiment (see note)   22205 (3,102)
- 408ᵗʰ Infantry Regiment (Sendai)   22206 (2,935) activated 5/10/45
- 142ⁿᵈ Division Rapid Firing Gun Unit   22207 (403)
- 142ⁿᵈ Division Field Artillery Unit   22211 (684)   activated 6/30/45
- 142ⁿᵈ Division Transport Unit   22209 (360)

<u>142ⁿᵈ Division</u>: (Coastal type) Activated in Sendai Apr 9, 1945. Home station: Sendai. With the 11ᵗʰ Area Army in Yoshioka, Miyagi from Apr 9ᵗʰ until it was deactivated in Yoshioka on September 12ᵗʰ. Note: 407ᵗʰ Inf Regt's home station is Aizuwakamatsu.
<u>Service History</u>: Japan: Sendai Bay, Ishinomaki Bay coastal defense.

143ʳᵈ Division Nagoya 1945   護古 *Goko* 22251 (13,185)

143ʳᵈ Division Headquarters	22252 (324)
143ʳᵈ Division Signal Unit	22258 (235)
143ʳᵈ Division Ordinance Duty Unit	22260 (108) activated 5/5/45
143ʳᵈ Division Field Hospital	22261 (201) activated 6/14/45

143ʳᵈ Division Infantry Group
- 409ᵗʰ Infantry Regiment (Nagoya)   22253 (3,102)
- 410ᵗʰ Infantry Regiment (Shizuoka)   22254 (3,102)
- 411ᵗʰ Infantry Regiment (Gifu)   22255 (3,102)
- 412ᵗʰ Infantry Regiment (Tsu)   22256 (2,935)   activated 5/5/45
- 143ʳᵈ Division Rapid Firing Gun Unit   22257 (403)   activated 5/5/45
- 143ʳᵈ Division Artillery Unit   21733 (692)   activated 6/30/45
- 143ʳᵈ Division Transport Unit   22259 (360)

<u>143ʳᵈ Division</u>: (Coastal type) Activated in Nagoya Apr 6, 1945. Home station: Nagoya. With the 13ᵗʰ Area Army from Apr 8ᵗʰ until June 19ᵗʰ and 54ᵗʰ Army in Kiga, Shizuoka Prefecture until it was deactivated in Hamamatsu on September 10ᵗʰ.
<u>Service History</u>: Japan: Kiga.

144ᵗʰ Division Osaka 1945   護阪 *Gohan* 22301 (13,342)

44ᵗʰ Division Headquarters	22302 (293)
144ᵗʰ Division Signal Unit	22308 (237)
144ᵗʰ Division Ordinance Duty Unit	22310 (108)
144ᵗʰ Division Field Hospital	unknown (201) activated 6/4/45

144ᵗʰ Division Infantry Group

144th Division continued   護阪 *Gohan*
- 413th Infantry Regiment (Osaka)   22303 (3,102)
- 414th Infantry Regiment (Wakayama)   22304 (3,102)
- 415th Infantry Regiment (Osaka)   22305 (3,102)
- 416th Infantry Regiment (Wakayama)   22306 (2,935)
- 144th Division Rapid Firing Gun Unit   22307 (403)
- 144th Division Artillery Unit   28281 (510)   activated 5/23/45
- 144th Division Transport Unit   22309 (360)

144th Division: (Coastal type) Activated in Osaka Feb 28, 1945. Home station: Osaka. With the 15th Area Army in Wakayama from April 8th until it was deactivated there on September 7th.
Service History: Japan: Wakayama coastal defense.

145th Division Hiroshima 1945   護州 *Goshū* 22351 (15,631)

145th Division Headquarters   22352 (293)
145th Division Signal Unit   22358 (235)
145th Division Ordinance Duty Unit   22360 (108)
145th Division Field Hospital   22361 (201)
145th Division Infantry Group
- 417th Infantry Regiment (Hiroshima)   22353 (3,841)
- 418th Infantry Regiment (Hamada)   22354 (3,841)
- 419th Infantry Regiment (Yamaguchi)   22355 (3,841)
- 420th Infantry Regiment (Hiroshima)   22356 (3,207)
- 145th Division Rapid Firing Gun Unit   22357 (480)
- 145th Division Rocket Gun Unit   28357 (692)   activated 6/30/45
- 145th Division Transport Unit   22359 (360)

145th Division: (Coastal type) Activated in Hiroshima on Feb. 28, 1945. Home station: Hiroshima. With the 16th Area Army from April 8th until June 19th and 56th Army in Ashiya, Fukuoka Prefecture until it was deactivated in Wakamatsu Sept 24th.
Service History: Japan: Ashiya coastal defense.

146th Division Kumamoto 1945   護南 *Gonan* 22401 (13,641)

146th Division Headquarters   22402 (293)
146th Division Signal Unit   22408 (237)
146th Division Ordinance Duty Unit   22410 (108)
146th Division Field Hospital   22419 (201)   activated 6/4/45
146th Division Infantry Group
- 421st Infantry Regiment (Kumamoto)   22403 (3,841)
- 422nd Infantry Regiment (Miyakonojo)   22404 (3,841)
- 423rd Infantry Regiment (Kagoshima)   22405 (3,841)
- 424th Infantry Regiment (Kumamoto)   22406 (3,207)
- 146th Division Rapid Firing Gun Unit   42325 (480)

146th Division continued

- 146th Division Artillery Unit   22407 (508)   activated 5/23/45
- 146th Division Transport Unit   22409 (360)

<u>146th Division</u>: (Coastal type) Activated Kumamoto February 28, 1945. Home station: Kumamoto. With the 57th Army from April 8th until June 19th and 40th Army in Oguchi, Kagoshima until it was deactivated in Oguchi on September 27th.

<u>Service History</u>: Japan: Kagoshima coastal defense.

147th Division Asahikawa 1945   護北 *Gohoku* 22451 (13,641)

147th Division Headquarters   22452 (294)
147th Division Signal Unit   22458 (235)
147th Division Ordinance Duty Unit   22460 (108)
147th Division Field Hospital   22461 (201)   activated 6/4/45
147th Division Infantry Group
- 425th Infantry Regiment (Asahikawa)   22453 (3,841)
- 426th Infantry Regiment (Asahikawa)   22454 (3,841)
- 427th Infantry Regiment (Asahikawa)   22455 (3,841)
- 428th Infantry Regiment (Asahikawa)   22456 (3,207)
- 147th Division Rapid Firing Gun Unit   22457 (480)
- 147th Division Artillery Unit   36364 (502)   activated 5/23/45
- 40th Trench Mortar Battalion   22463 (?)
- 147th Division Engineer Unit   22464 (?)
- 147th Division Transport Unit   22459 (360)

<u>147th Division</u>: (Coastal type) Activated Asahikawa February 28, 1945. Home station: Asahikawa. With the 5th Area Army from Apr 8th until May 1st and 52nd Army in Mobara, Chiba Prefecture until it was deactivated in Mobara on September 20th.

<u>Service History</u>: Japan: Mobaru coastal defense.

148th Division Manchuria 1945   富嶽 *Hūgaku* 37321

148th Division Headquarters   37322 (240)
148th Division Signal Unit   37331 (239)
148th Division Ordinance Duty Unit   37332 (112)
148th Division Medical Unit   37333 (1,109) activated 8/10/45
148th Division 1st Field Hospital   37334 (232)   activated 8/10/45
148th Division 4th Field Hospital   37335 (236)   activated 8/10/45
148th Division D. P. & Water Supply Unit   37337 (239)   activated 8/10/45
148th Division Anti-Gas Unit   37326 (187)   activated 8/10/45
148th Division Veterinary Unit   37336 (119)
148th Division Raiding Battalion   37327 (1,130)
148th Division Infantry Group
- 383rd Infantry Regiment (Manchuria)   37323 (3,609)

148th Division continued   富嶽 *Hūgaku*

- 384th Infantry Regiment (Manchuria)   37324 (3,609)
- 385th Infantry Regiment (Manchuria)   37325 (3,609)
- 148th Field Artillery Regiment   37328 (1,923)
- 148th Engineer Regiment   37329 (964)
- 148th Transport Regiment   37330 (1,180)

148th Division: (C type) Activated in Hsinking, Manchuria July 10, 1945, from former 101st Guard HQ and 62nd L. of C. Guard personnel. Home station: Hsinking. With the 30th Army in Hsinking from July 30th until it was deactivated on September 12th.
Service History: Manchuria: Hsinking garrison/construction duty.

149th Division Manchuria 1945   不撓 *Hutō* 37350

149th Division Headquarters	37341 (240)
149th Division Signal Unit	37348 (239)
149th Division Ordinance Duty Unit	37350 (112)
149th Division Medical Unit	unknown (1,109) activ. 8/10/45
149th Division 1st Field Hospital	unknown (232) activ. 8/10/45
149th Division 4th Field Hospital	unknown (236) activ. 8/10/45
149th Division Anti-Gas Unit	unknown (187) activ. 8/10/45
149th Division D. P. & Water Supply Unit	unknown activated 8/10/45
149th Division Veterinary Unit	37351 (119)
149th Division Raiding Battalion	37345 (1,130)

149th Division Infantry Group
- 274h Infantry Regiment (Hiroshima)   37342 (3,410)
- 386th Infantry Regiment (Manchuria)   37343 (3,409)
- 387th Infantry Regiment (Manchuria)   37344 (3,409)
- 149th Artillery Regiment   37346 (1,923)
- 149th Engineer Regiment   37347 (964)
- 149th Transport Regiment   37349 (1,180)

149th Division: (C type) Activated in Tsitsihar, Manchuria July 10, 1945, from former 74th L. of C. Guard personnel. Home station: Tsitsihar. With the 4th Army in Tsitsihar from July 10th and Harbin from Aug. 11th, deactivated in Tsitsihar on August 18th.
Service History: Manchuria: Tsitsihar, Peian Aug 9 1945.

150th Division Himeji 1945   護朝 *Gosen* 22501 (13,641)

150th Division Headquarters	22502 (293)
150th Division Signal Unit	22508 (237)
150th Division Ordinance Duty Unit	22510 (108)
150th Division Field Hospital	22511 (201) activated 6/4/45
150th Division Rocket Gun Unit	22512/28246 (692) act. 8/10/45
150th Division Anti-Gas Unit	unknown (187) activ. 8/10/45
150th Division Infantry Group	

150th Division continued
- 429th Infantry Regiment (Himeji)   22503 (3,102)
- 430th Infantry Regiment (Himeji)   22504 (3,102)
- 431st Infantry Regiment (Himeji)   22505 (3,107)
- 432nd Infantry Regiment (Himeji)   22506 (2,935)
- 150th Division Rapid Firing Gun Unit   22507 (403)
- 150th Division Artillery Unit   28246 (692)
- 150th Division Transport Unit   22509 (360)

150th Division: (Coastal type) Activated Seoul, Korea February 28, 1945. Home station: Himeji. With the 17th Area Army in Jeongeup from Apr 8th until it was deactivated in SW Korea on August 18th.
Service History: Korea: North and South Jeolla Provinces coastal defense.

151st Division Utsunomiya 1945   護宇 *Gou* 22551 (13,290)

151st Division Headquarters   22552 (292)
151st Division Signal Unit   22553 (235)
151st Division Ordinance Duty Unit   22555 (108)   activated 5/10/45
151st Division Field Hospital   22561 (201)   activated 6/14/45
151st Division Rocket Gun Unit   36362 (684)   activated 6/30/45
151st Division Infantry Group
- 433rd Infantry Regiment (Utsunomiya)   22556 (3,841)
- 434th Infantry Regiment (Mito)   22557 (3,841)
- 435th Infantry Regiment (Takasaki)   22558 (3,841)
- 436th Infantry Regiment (Utsunomiya)   22559 (3,207)
- 151st Division Rapid Firing Gun Unit   22560 (480)   activated 5/5/45
- 151st Division Artillery Unit   36362 (684)
- 151st Division Transport Unit   22554 (360)

151st Division: (Coastal type) Activated in Utsunomiya April 25, 1945. Home station: Utsunomiya. With the 51st Army in Mito, Ibaraki Prefecture from Apr 8th until it was deactivated in Ota, Japan on September 9th.
Service History: Japan: Ibaraki Prefecture coastal defense.

152nd Division Kanazawa 1945   護沢 *Gotaku* 22601 (13,641)

152nd Division Headquarters   22602 (293)
152nd Division Signal Unit   22608 (237)
152nd Division Ordinance Duty Unit   22610 (108)
152nd Division Field Hospital   22615 (201)   activated 6/4/45
152nd Division Infantry Group
- 437th Infantry Regiment (Toyama)   22603 (3,841)
- 438th Infantry Regiment (Kanazawa)   22604 (3,841)
- 439th Infantry Regiment (Kanazawa)   22605 (3,841)
- 440th Infantry Regiment (Toyama)   22606 (3,207)

152nd Division continued   護沢 *Gotaku*

- 152nd Division Rapid Firing Gun Unit   22607 (480)
- 152nd Division Artillery Unit   36365 (502)   activated 5/25/45
- 37th Trench Mortar Battalion   22613
- 152nd Division Transport Unit   22609 (360)
- 76th Independent Engineer Battalion   22614

<u>152nd Division</u>: (Coastal type) Activated in Kanazawa on February 28, 1945. Home station: Kanazawa. With the 52nd Army in Chōshi from Apr 8th until it was deactivated in Sakura on Sept 9th.

<u>Service History</u>: Japan: Chōshi, Chiba.

153rd Division Kyoto 1945   護京 *Gokyo* 22651 (13,641)

153rd Division Headquarters   22652 (324)
153rd Division Signal Unit   22658 (237)   activated 5/10/45
153rd Division Ordinance Duty Unit   22660 (108)   activated 5/10/45
153rd Division Field Hospital   22661 (201)   activated 6/24/45
153rd Division Infantry Group
 • 441st Infantry Regiment (Tsuruga)   22653 (3,102)
 • 442nd Infantry Regiment (Kyoto)   22654 (3,102)
 • 443rd Infantry Regiment (Tsuruga)   22455 (3,102) activated 4/28/45
 • 444th Infantry Regiment (Kyoto)   22656 (2,935) activated 5/10/45
- 153rd Division Rapid Firing Gun Unit   22657 (403)   activated 5/10/45
- 153rd Division Field Artillery Unit   21734 (508)   activated 7/28/45
- 153rd Division Transport Unit   22659 (360)   activated 5/10/45

<u>153rd Division</u>: (Coastal type) Activated Kyoto Apr 8, 1945. Home station: Kyoto. With the 13th Area Army in Ujiyamada, Mie Prefecture from Apr 8th where it was deactivated on September 16th.

<u>Service History</u>: Japan: Ise-shima, Atsumi Peninsula coastal defense.

154th Division Hiroshima 1945   護路 *Goro* 22701 (16,524)

154th Division Headquarters   22702 (293)
154th Division Signal Unit   22708 (237)
154th Division Ordinance Duty Unit   22710 (108)
154th Division Field Hospital   22711 (201)
154th Division Infantry Group
 • 445th Infantry Regiment (Tottori)   22703 (3,841)
 • 446th Infantry Regiment (Tottori)   22704 (3,841)
 • 447th Infantry Regiment (Okayama)   22705 (3,841)
 • 448th Infantry Regiment (Okayama)   22706 (3,207)
- 154th Division Rapid Firing Gun Unit   22707 (480)
- 154th Division Artillery Unit   28356/36356 (510) act 05/23/45
- 154th Division Transport Unit   22709 (360)

154th Division: (Coastal type) Activated in Hiroshima February 28, 1945. Home station: Hiroshima. With the 57th Army in Tsuma, Miyazaki Prefecture from Apr 8th where it was deactivated on September 28th.
Service History: Japan: Miyazaki Prefecture coastal defense.

155th Division Zentsuji 1945	護土 *Godo* 22751 (13,641)	
155th Division Headquarters	22752 (293)	
155th Division Signal Unit	22758 (237)	
155th Division Ordinance Duty Unit	22760 (108)	
155th Division Field Hospital	22761 (201)	activated 6/4/45
155th Division Infantry Group		
• 449th Infantry Regiment (Marugame)	22753 (3,841)	
• 450th Infantry Regiment (Tokushima)	22754 (3,841)	
• 451st Infantry Regiment (Kochi)	22755 (3,841)	
• 452nd Infantry Regiment (Marugame)	22756 (3,207)	
• 155th Division Rapid Firing Gun Unit	22757 (480)	
• 155th Division Artillery Unit	23307 (508)	activated 5/23/45
• 155th Division Transport Unit	22759 (360)	

155th Division: (Coastal type) Activated Zentsuji Feb 28, 1945. Home station: Zentsuji. With the 55th Army in Kami, Kochi Prefecture from Apr 8th until it was deactivated on September 13th.
Service History: Japan: Kochi Prefecture coastal defense.

156th Division Kureme 1945	護西 *Gosei* 22801 (13,041)	
156th Division Headquarters	22802 (275)	
158th Division Signal Unit	22808 (235)	
156th Division Ordinance Duty Unit	22810 (108)	
156th Division Field Hospital	22811 (208)	activated 6/4/45
156th Division Infantry Group		
• 453rd Infantry Regiment (Fukuoka)	22803 (3,850)	
• 454th Infantry Regiment (Ōmura)	22804 (3,850)	
• 455th Infantry Regiment (Kureme)	22805 (3,850)	
• 456th Infantry Regiment (Kureme)	22806 (3,207)	
• 156th Division Rapid Firing Gun Unit	22807 (480)	
• 156th Division Artillery Unit	22812 (508)	activated 5/31/45
• 156th Division Transport Unit	22809 (360)	

156th Division: (Coastal type) Activated Kurume Feb 28, 1945. Home station: Kurume. With the 57th Army in Miyazaki, Apr 8th until it was deactivated in Honjo Sept 28th.
Service History: Japan: Miyazaki area coastal defense.

157th Division Hirosake 1945	護弘 *Goko* 22851 (13,576)
157th Division Headquarters	22852 (293)

157th Division continued   護弘 *Goko*

157th Division Signal Unit	22864 (235)	
157th Division Ordinance Duty Unit	22868 (108)	activated 5/10/45
157th Division Field Hospital	22870 (201)	activated 6/18/45
157th Division Infantry Group		
• 457th Infantry Regiment (Hirosaki)	22857 (3,841)	
• 458th Infantry Regiment (Akita)	22858 (3,841)	
• 459th Infantry Regiment (Akita)	22859 (3,841)	
• 460th Infantry Regiment (Hirosaki)	22860 (3,207)	activated 5/10/45
• 157th Division Rapid Firing Gun Unit	22862 (480)	activated 5/10/45
• 157th Division Artillery Unit	22869 (684)	activated 7/20/45
• 157th Division Transport Unit	22866 (360)	

<u>157th Division</u>: (Coastal type) Activated Hirosaki Apr 10, 1945. Home station: Hirosaki. With the 11th Area Army in Sanbongi, Miyagi from Apr 8th until June 19th and 50th Army in Aomori Prefecture until it was deactivated in Sanbongi on September 12th.
<u>Service History</u>: Japan: Aomori Prefecture coastal defense.

158th Division Manchuria 1945   不滅 *Humetsu* 37370

158th Division Headquarters	37361 (260)
158th Division Signal Unit	37369 (239)
158th Division Ordinance Duty Unit	37371 (112)
158th Division Medical Unit	37372 (1,109)
158th Division 1st Field Hospital	37373 (232)
158th Division 4th Field Hospital	37374 (236)
158th Division D. P. & Water Supply Unit	37375 (239)
158th Division Anti-Gas Unit	37366 (187)
158th Division Veterinary Unit	37376 (119)
158th Division Raiding Battalion	37365 (1,130)
158th Division Infantry Group	
• 389th Infantry Regiment (Manchuria)	37362 (3,407)
• 390th Infantry Regiment (Manchuria)	37363 (3,407)
• 391st Infantry Regiment (Manchuria)	37364 (3,407)
• 158th Field Artillery Regiment	37367 (1,923)
• 158th Engineer Regiment	37368 (964)
• 158th Division Transport Unit	37370 (1,180)

The Kwantung Army prepared to mobilize the 158th Division in Manchuria beginning on Aug 10, 1945 but the war ended Aug 15th before mobilization was completed.

160th Division Pyongyang 1945   護鮮 *Gosen* 22901 (13,641)

160th Division Headquarters	22902 (293)
160th Division Signal Unit	22908 (237)
160th Division Ordinance Duty Unit	22910 (108)

Chapter 3

160th Division continued

160th Division Field Hospital	22912 (201)	activated 6/4/45
160th Division Rocket Gun Unit	28280 (692)	activated 8/10/45

160th Division Infantry Group
- 461st Infantry Regiment (Hiroshima) — 22903 (3,102)
- 462nd Infantry Regiment (Hamada) — 22904 (3,102)
- 463rd Infantry Regiment (Yamaguchi) — 22905 (3,102)
- 464th Infantry Regiment (Tottori) — 22906 (2,935)
- 160th Division Rapid Firing Gun Unit — 22907 (403)
- 160th Division Transport Unit — 22909 (360)

160th Division: (Coastal type) Activated in Pyongyang Feb 28, 1945. Home station: Hiroshima. With the 17th Area Army in Gunsan, Korea from Apr 8th until it was deactivated in SW Korea on August 18th.
Service History: Korea: North Jeolla coastal defense.

201st Division Tokyo 1945   武蔵 *Musasi* 14240 (18,295)

201st Division Headquarters	14241 (477)	deact. 10/10/45
201st Division Signal Unit	14250 (300)	
201st Division Ordinance Duty Unit	14252 (112)	
201st Division Medical Unit	24416 (1,109)	never mobilized
201st Division 1st Field Hospital	24417 (277)	never mobilized
201st Division 2nd Field Hospital	24418 (277)	never mobilized
201st Division 4th Field Hospital	14256 (277)	
201st Division Anti Gas Unit	24414 (186)	never mobilized
201st Division Veterinary Unit	24419 (119)	never mobilized

201st Division Infantry Group
- 501st Infantry Regiment (Tokyo) — 14242 (4,368)
- 502nd Infantry Regiment (Kofu) — 14243 (4,368)
- 503rd Infantry Regiment (Sakura) — 14244 (4,368)
- 201st Field Artillery Regiment — 14257 (2,135)
- 201st Trench Mortar Regiment — 14246 (1,643)
- 201st Division Rapid Firing Gun Unit — 14247 (483)
- 201st Trench Machine Cannon Unit — 14248 (340)
- 201st Division Engineer Unit — 14249 (999)
- 201st Division Transport Unit — 14251 (431)

201st Division: (Mobile type) Activated in Tokyo April 2, 1945. Home station: Tokyo. With the 36th Army in Tokyo from May 10th until it was deactivated Aug 30th.
Service History: Japan: Kantō area mobile reserve.

202nd Division Sendai 1945   青葉 *Aoba* 30401 (20,322)

202nd Division Headquarters	30402 (477)	deact. 10/10/45
202nd Division Signal Unit	30410 (300)	

202nd Division continued　　　　　　　　　青葉 *Aoba*

202nd Division Ordinance Duty Unit	30412 (112)	activated 7/20/45
202nd Division Medical Unit	21416 (1,109)	never mobilized
202nd Division 1st Field Hospital	21417 (277)	never mobilized
202nd Division 2nd Field Hospital	21418 (277)	never mobilized
202nd Division 4th Field Hospital	30416 (277)	activated 6/4/45
202nd Division Anti Gas Unit	21414 (186)	never mobilized
202nd Division Veterinary Unit	21419 (119)	never mobilized
202nd Division Infantry Group		
• 504th Infantry Regiment (Sendai)	30403 (4,368)	
• 505th Infantry Regiment (Fukushima)	30404 (4,368)	
• 506th Infantry Regiment (Yamagata)	30405 (4,368)	
• 202nd Mountain Artillery Regiment	22871 (2,496)	
• 202nd Trench Mortar Regiment	30406 (1,643)	
• 202nd Division Rapid Firing Gun Unit	30407 (483)	
• 202nd Division Mountain Artillery Unit	30408 (340)	
• 202nd Division Engineer Unit	30409 (999)	
• 202nd Division Transport Unit	30411 (431)	

202nd Division: (Mobile type) Activated in Sendai April 2, 1945. Home station: Sendai. With the 36th Army in Maebashi, Gunma from May 10th until it was deactivated in Maebashi between September 14th and 20th.

Service History: Japan: Kantō area mobile reserve.

205th Division Hiroshima 1945　　　　　安芸 *Aki* 15053 (21,967)

205th Division Headquarters	15054 (477)	
205th Division Signal Unit	15062 (300)	
205th Division Ordinance Duty Unit	15064 (112)	activated 7/20/45
205th Division Medical Unit	15062 (1,109)	never mobilized
205th Division 1st Field Hospital	15074 (277)	never mobilized
205th Division 2nd Field Hospital	15075 (277)	never mobilized
205th Division 4th Field Hospital	15076 (277)	activated 6/4/45
205th Division Anti Gas Unit	28202 (186)	never mobilized
205th Division Veterinary Unit	15077 (119)	never mobilized
205th Division Infantry Group		
• 507th Infantry Regiment (Yamaguchi)	15055 (4,368)	
• 508th Infantry Regiment (Tottori)	15056 (4,368)	
• 509th Infantry Regiment (Okayama)	15057 (4,368)	
• 205th Field Artillery Regiment	15050 (2,135)	
• 205th Trench Mortar Regiment	15058 (1,643)	
• 205th Division Rapid Firing Gun Unit	15059 (483)	
• 205th Division Machine Cannon Unit	15060 (340)	
• 205th Division Engineer Unit	15061 (999)	
• 205th Division Transport Unit	15063 (431)	

205th Division: (Mobile type) Activated in Hiroshima on April 2, 1945. Home station: Hiroshima. With the 55th Army in Kōchi from May 10th until deactivated Sept 20th.
Service History: Japan: Kōchi mobile reserve.

206th Division Kumamoto 1945　　　　　　　阿蘇 *Aso* 32401 (23,426)

206th Division Headquarters	32402 (477)	
206th Division Signal Unit	32410 (300)	
206th Division Ordinance Duty Unit	32412 (112)	activated 7/20/45
206th Division Medical Unit	32413 (1,109)	never mobilized
206th Division 1st Field Hospital	32414 (277)	never mobilized
206th Division 4th Field Hospital	32416 (277)	activated 6/4/45
206th Division Anti Gas Unit	32418 (186)	never mobilized
206th Division Veterinary Unit	32415 (119)	never mobilized
206th Division Infantry Group		
• 510th Infantry Regiment (Kumamoto)	32403 (4,368)	
• 511th Infantry Regiment (Miyakonojo)	32404 (4,368)	
• 512th Infantry Regiment (Kagoshima)	32405 (4,368)	
• 206th Mountain Artillery Regiment	14350 (2,496)	
• 206th Division Trench Mortar Regiment	32406 (1,643)	
• 206th Division Rapid Firing Gun Unit	32407 (483)	
• 206th Division Machine Cannon Unit	32408 (340)	
• 206th Division Engineer Unit	32409 (999)	
• 206th Division Transport Unit	32411 (431)	

206th Division: (Mobile type) Activated in Kumamoto, April 2, 1945. Home station: Kumamoto. With the 16th Area Army in southern Kyoto from May 10th until it was deactivated in Hitoyoshi on September 27th.
Service History: Japan: Western Kagoshima mobile reserve.

209th Division Kanazawa 1945　　　　　　　加越 *Kaetsu* 21610 (19,941)

209th Division Headquarters	21611 (407)	deact. 10/10/45
209th Division Signal Unit	21619 (300)	
209th Division Ordinance Duty Unit	21621 (112)	activated 7/20/45
209th Division Medical Unit	21627 (1,109)	never mobilized
209th Division 1st Field Hospital	21622 (277)	never mobilized
209th Division 2nd Field Hospital	21623 (277)	never mobilized
209th Division 4th Field Hospital	21625 (277)	activated 6/4/45
209th Division Anti Gas Unit	21626 (186)	never mobilized
209th Division Veterinary Unit	21628 (119)	never mobilized
209th Division Infantry Group		
• 513th Infantry Regiment (Kanazawa)	21612 (4,278)	
• 514th Infantry Regiment (Toyama)	21613 (4,278)	
• 515th Infantry Regiment (Kanazawa)	21614 (4,278)	
• 209th Mountain Artillery Regiment	21612? (2,496)	

209th Division continued   加越 Kaetsu
- 209th Trench Mortar Regiment   21615 (1,454)
- 209th Division Rapid Firing Gun Unit   21616 (403)
- 209th Division Machine Cannon Unit   21617 (340)
- 209th Division Engineer Unit   21618 (999)
- 209th Division Transport Unit   21620 (431)

209th Division: (Mobile type) Activated in Kanazawa on April 2, 1945. Home station: Kanazawa. With the 36th Army in Ishikawa Prefecture from May 10th until it was deactivated in Aisawa on September 5th.
Service History: Japan: Ishikawa, Toyama, Gifu mobile reserve.

212th Division Kureme 1945   菊池 *Kikuchi* 32601 (22,290)

212th Division Headquarters	32602 (477)	
212th Division Signal Unit	32611 (300)	
212th Division Ordinance Duty Unit	32613 (112)	activated 7/20/45
212th Division Medical Unit	32615 (1,109)	never mobilized
212th Division 1st Field Hospital	32616 (277)	never mobilized
212th Division 2nd Field Hospital	32617 (277)	never mobilized
212th Division 4th Field Hospital	32618 (277)	activated 6/4/45
212th Division Anti Gas Unit	32614 (186)	never mobilized
212th Division Veterinary Unit	32619 (119)	never mobilized

212th Division Infantry Group
- 516th Infantry Regiment (Kureme)   32603 (4,368)
- 517th Infantry Regiment (Fukuoka)   32604 (4,368)
- 518th Infantry Regiment (Omura)   32605 (4,368)
- 212th Ind. Mountain Artillery Regiment   32606 (2,496)
- 212th Trench Mortar Regiment   32607 (1,643)
- 212th Division Rapid Firing Gun Unit   32608 (483)
- 212th Division Machine Cannon Unit   32609 (340)
- 212th Division Engineer Unit   32610 (999)
- 212th Division Transport Unit   32612 (431)

212th Division: (Mobile type) Activated Kurume April 2, 1945. Home station: Kurume. With the 57th Army in south Kyushu from May 10th until it was deactivated in Miyakonojo on Sept 28th. Although mobile the 212th Div was assigned to coastal defense.
Service History: Japan: Miyazaki, Kurume coastal defense.

214th Division Utsunomiya 1945   常盤 *Tokiwa* (20,001)

214th Division Headquarters	30851 (477)	deactiv. 10/10/45
214th Division Signal Unit	30863 (300)	
214th Division Ordinance Duty Unit	30861 (112)	activated 7/16/45
214th Division Medical Unit	27503 (1,109)	never mobilized

214th Division continued

Unit	Code	Status
214th Division 1st Field Hospital	30852 (277)	never mobilized
214th Division 2nd Field Hospital	30853 (277)	never mobilized
214th Division 4th Field Hospital	30854 (277)	activated 6/19/45
214th Division Anti-Gas Unit	27501 (187)	never mobilized
214th Division Veterinary Unit	30855 (119)	never mobilized
214th Division Infantry Group		
• 519th Infantry Regiment (Utsunomiya)	30856 (4,368)	activated 6/10/45
• 520th Infantry Regiment (Mito)	30857 (4,368)	activated 6/10/45
• 521st Infantry Regiment (Takasaki)	30858 (4,368)	activated 6/10/45
• 214th Field Artillery Regiment	36371 (2,135)	activated 5/10/45
• 214th Trench Mortar Regiment	30859 (1,643)	activated 6/10/45
• 214th Division Machine Cannon Unit	30866 (340)	activated 6/10/45
• 214th Division Rapid Firing Gun Unit	30867 (483)	activated 6/10/45
• 214th Division Engineer Unit	30862 (999)	activated 5/10/45
• 214th Division Transport Unit	30864 (438)	activated 6/10/45

<u>214th Division</u>: (Mobile type) Activated in Utsunomiya April 4, 1945. Home station: Utsunomiya. With the 36th Army in Tochigi Prefecture from May 10th until it was deactivated in Utsunomiya between September 4th and 8th.

<u>Service History</u>: Japan: Tochigi Prefecture mobile reserve.

216th Division Kyoto 1945   比叡 *Hiei* 10252 (20,693)

Unit	Code	Status
216th Division Headquarters	10252 (477)	activated 4/2/45
216th Division Signal Unit	10260 (300)	
216th Division Ordinance Duty Unit	10262 (112)	activated 7/20/45
216th Division Medical Unit	10263 (1109)	never mobilized
216th Division 1st Field Hospital	10264 (277)	never mobilized
216th Division 2nd Field Hospital	10267 (277)	never mobilized
216th Division 4th Field Hospital	10268 (277)	activated 6/4/45
216th Division Anti Gas Unit	unknown (186)	never mobilized
216th Division Veterinary Unit	10269 (119)	never mobilized
216th Division Infantry Group		
• 522nd Infantry Regiment (Kyoto)	10253 (4,368)	
• 523rd Infantry Regiment (Tsuruga)	10254 (4,368)	
• 524th Infantry Regiment (Himeji)	10255 (4,368)	
• 216th Field Artillery Regiment	24305 (2,135)	
• 216th Trench Mortar Regiment	10256 (1,643)	
• 216th Division Rapid Firing gun Unit	10257 (483)	
• 216th Division Machine Cannon Unit	10258 (340)	
• 216th Division Engineer Unit	10259 (999)	
• 216th Division Transport Unit	10261 (431)	

<u>216th Division</u>: (Mobile type) Activated in Kyoto June 10, 1945. Home station: Kyoto. With the 16th Area Army in Fukuoka until it was deactivated in Kureme on Sept 19th.

<u>Service History</u>: Japan: Kurume / Kumamoto mobile reserve.

221st Division Nagano 1945   天龍 *Tenryū* 27677 (484)

221st Division Headquarters	27678 (542)	activated 7/10/45
221st Division Signal Unit	27684 (253)	never mobilized
221st Division Ordinance Duty Unit	27686 (113)	never mobilized
221st Division Medical Unit	27682 (529)	never mobilized
221st Division 1st Field Hospital	27688 (278)	never mobilized
221st Division 2nd Field Hospital	27689 (278)	never mobilized
221st Division Veterinary Unit	27682 (119)	never mobilized
221st Division Infantry Group		
• 316th Infantry Regiment (see note)	27679 (3,314)	never mobilized
• 317th Infantry Regiment (Matsumoto)	27680 (3,314)	never mobilized
• 318th Infantry Regiment (Shibata)	27681 (3,314)	never mobilized
• 221st Division Trench Mortar Unit	27682 (757)	never mobilized
• 221st Division Engineer Unit	27683 (875)	never mobilized
• 221st Division Transport Unit	27685 (461)	never mobilized

221st Division: (Mobile type) Mobilizing in Nagano May 23, 1945. Home station: Nagano. Attached to the 51st Army in Kashima, Ibaraki Prefecture from June 19th until it was deactivated in Matabe on October 10, 1945.
Service History: Japan:

222nd Division Hirosaki 1945   八甲 *Hakko* 27380 (12,433)

222nd Division Headquarters	27381 (466)	activated 6/10/45
222nd Division Signal Unit	27379 (255)	activated 7/30/45
222nd Division Ordinance Duty Unit	27386 (113)	never mobilized
222nd Division Medical Unit	27386 (529)	never mobilized
222nd Division 1st Field Hospital	27388 (278)	never mobilized
222nd Division 2nd Field Hospital	27389 (278)	never mobilized
222nd Division Veterinary Unit	27447 (119)	never mobilized
216th Division Infantry Group		
• 307th Infantry Regiment (Hirosaki)	27374 (3,232)	activated 7/30/45
• 308th Infantry Regiment (Akita)	27375 (3,232)	activated 7/30/45
• 309th Infantry Regiment (Yamagata)	27376 (3,232)	activated 7/25/45
• 222nd Division Trench Mortar Unit	27377 (754)	activated 7/25/45
• 222nd Division Engineer Unit	27378 (886)	activated 7/30/45
• 222nd Division Transport Unit	27382 (467)	activated 7/25/45

222nd Division: (Mobile type) Activated in Hirosaki May 23, 1945. Home station: Hirosaki. With the 11th Area Army in Hasedō, Yamagata Prefecture until it was deactivated in Hirosaki on September 12, 1945.
Service History: Japan: Hasedō, Yamagata mobile reserve.

224th Division Hiroshima 1945   赤穂 *Akao* 28328 (12,843)

224th Division Headquarters	28329 (531)
224th Division Signal Unit	28335 (254)

224th Division continued

224th Division Ordinance Duty Unit	28337 (113)	activated 7/31/45
224th Division Medical Unit	28338 (529)	activated 7/31/45
224th Division 1st Field Hospital	28339 (278)	activated 7/31/45
224th Division 2nd Field Hospital	28340 (278)	activated 7/31/45
224th Division Veterinary Unit	28341 (119)	activated 7/31/45

224th Division Infantry Group
- 340th Infantry Regiment (Hiroshima)   28330 (3,311)
- 341st Infantry Regiment (Tottori)   28331 (3,311)
- 342nd Infantry Regiment (Okayama)   28332 (3,311)
- 224th Division Trench Mortar Unit   28333 (752)
- 224th Division Engineer Unit   28334 (885)
- 224th Division Transport Unit   28336 (483)

<u>224th Division</u>: (Mobile type) Activated in Hiroshima May 23, 1945. Home station: Hiroshima. With the 54th Army in Omaezaki, deactivated in Hiroshima on Sept 6th.
<u>Service History</u>: Japan: Omaezaki, Hamamatsu (On Aug 6th some elements still in Hiroshima training, were destroyed by the atomic bomb)

225th Division Osaka 1945   金剛 *Kongō* 28256 (12,401)

225th Division Headquarters	28257 (536)	
225th Division Signal Unit	28263 (254)	
225th Division Ordinance Duty Unit	28265 (113)	never mobilized
225th Division Medical Unit	28266 (529)	never mobilized
225th Division 1st Field Hospital	28267 (278)	never mobilized
225th Division 2nd Field Hospital	28268 (278)	never mobilized
225th Division Veterinary Unit	28269 (119)	never mobilized

225th Division Infantry Group
- 343rd Infantry Regiment (Osaka)   28258 (3,311)
- 344th Infantry Regiment (Osaka)   28259 (3,311)
- 345th Infantry Regiment (Himeji)   28260 (3,311)
- 225th Division Trench Mortar Unit   28261 (752)
- 225th Division Engineer Unit   28262 (885)
- 225th Division Transport Unit   28264 (483)

<u>225th Division</u>: (Mobile type) Activated in Osaka June 20, 1945. Home station: Osaka. With the 15th Area Army in Kobe, Hyōgo Pref where it was deactivated on Sept 8th.
<u>Service History</u>: Japan: Hyōgo mobile reserve.

229th Division Kanazawa 1945   北越 *Hokuetsu* 21740 (12,818)

229th Division Headquarters	21741 (545)	
229th Division Signal Unit	21747 (254)	
229th Division Ordinance Duty Unit	21749 (113)	never mobilized
229th Division Medical Unit	21750 (529)	never mobilized

229th Division continued   北越 *Hokuetsu*

229th Division 1st Field Hospital	21751 (278)	never mobilized
229th Division 2nd Field Hospital	21752 (278)	never mobilized
229th Division Veterinary Unit	21753 (119)	never mobilized
229th Division Infantry Group		
• 334th Infantry Regiment (Kanazawa)	21742 (3,304)	
• 335th Infantry Regiment (Toyama)	21743 (3,304)	
• 336th Infantry Regiment (Toyama)	21744 (3,304)	
• 229th Division Trench Mortar Unit	21745 (754)	
• 229th Division Engineer Unit	21746 (886)	
• 229th Division Transport Unit	21748 (469)	

<u>229th Division</u>: (Mobile type) Activated in Kanazawa June 10, 1945. Home station: Kanazawa. With the 13th Area Army in Iida, Nagano Prefecture where it was deactivated on September 11th.
<u>Service History</u>: Japan: Iida, Nagano mobile reserve.

230th Division Tokyo 1945   総武 *Sōbu* 27691 (12,830)

230th Division Headquarters	27692 (542)	
230th Division Signal Unit	27698 (253)	
230th Division Ordinance Duty Unit	27700 (113)	never mobilized
230th Division Medical Unit	27701 (529)	never mobilized
230th Division 1st Field Hospital	27702 (278)	never mobilized
230th Division 2nd Field Hospital	27703 (278)	never mobilized
230th Division Veterinary Unit	27704 (119)	never mobilized
230th Division Infantry Group		
• 319th Infantry Regiment (Tokyo)	27693 (3,313)	
• 320th Infantry Regiment (Kofu)	27694 (3,313)	
• 321st Infantry Regiment (Sakura)	27695 (3,313)	
• 230th Division Trench Mortar Unit	27696 (757)	
• 230th Division Engineer Unit	27697 (879)	
• 230th Division Transport Unit	27699 (461)	

<u>230th Division</u>: (Mobile type) Activated in Tokyo May 23, 1945. Home station: Tokyo. With the 59th Army in Okayama. Deactivated in Saijo on Sept 20th.
<u>Service History</u>: Japan: Okayama mobile reserve.

231st Division Hiroshima 1945   大國 *Okuni* 28342 (12,843)

231st Division Headquarters	28343 (536)	
231st Division Signal Unit	28349 (254)	
231st Division Ordinance Duty Unit	28351 (113)	activated 7/20/45
231st Division Medical Unit	28352 (529)	activated 7/20/45
231st Division 1st Field Hospital	28353 (278)	activated 7/20/45
231st Division 2nd Field Hospital	28354 (278)	activated 7/20/45

231st Division continue

231st Division Veterinary Unit	28355 (119) activated 7/20/45
231st Division Infantry Group	
• 346th Infantry Regiment (Hiroshima)	28344 (3,311)
• 347th Infantry Regiment (Hamada)	28345 (3,311)
• 348th Infantry Regiment (Yamaguchi)	28346 (3,311)
• 231st Division Trench Mortar Unit	28347 (752)
• 231st Division Engineer Unit	28348 (885)
• 231st Division Transport Unit	28360 (483)

231st Division: (Mobile type) Activated in Hiroshima May 23, 1945. Home station: Hiroshima. With the 59th Army in Yamaguchi, deactivated in Nagi on Sept 26th.
Service History: Japan: Yamaguchi mobile reserve.

234th Division Tokyo 1945   利根 *Tone* 27705 (12,830)

234th Division Headquarters	27706 (542)	
234th Division Signal Unit	27712 (253)	
234th Division Ordinance Duty Unit	27714 (113)	never mobilized
234th Division Medical Unit	27712 (529)	never mobilized
234th Division 1st Field Hospital	27716 (278)	never mobilized
234th Division 2nd Field Hospital	27717 (278)	never mobilized
234th Division Veterinary Unit	27712 (119)	never mobilized
234th Division Infantry Group		
• 322nd Infantry Regiment (Mizonokuchi)	27707 (3,311)	
• 323rd Infantry Regiment (Kashiwa)	27708 (3,311)	
• 324th Infantry Regiment (Kohu)	27709 (3,311)	
• 234th Division Trench Mortar Unit	27710 (757)	
• 234th Division Engineer Unit	27711 (879)	
• 234th Division Transport Unit	27713 (1,161)	

234th Division: (Mobile type) Activated in Tokyo May 23, 1945. Home station: Tokyo. With the 52nd Army in Yokaichiba, Chiba until it was deactivated in Yokaichiba Oct 10th.
Service History: Japan: Chiba mobile reserve.

303rd Division Nagoya 1945   高師 *Takashi* 21770 (11,905)

303rd Division Headquarters	21771 (466)
303rd Division Signal Unit	21777 (280)
303rd Division Field Hospital	21779 (278)
303rd Division Infantry Group	
• 337th Infantry Regiment (Nagoya)	21772 (3,026)
• 338th Infantry Regiment (Gifu)	21773 (3,026)
• 339th Infantry Regiment (Tsu)	21774 (3,026)

303rd Division continued 高師 *Takashi*
- 303rd Division Rocket Gun Unit   21775 (692)
- 303rd Division Engineer Unit   21776 (806)
- 303rd Division Transport Company   21778 (300)

<u>303rd Division</u>: (Coastal type) Activated Nagoya May 23, 1945. Home station: Nagoya. With the 40th Army in Kagoshima until it was deactivated in Iizuka on September 18th.

<u>Service History</u>: Japan: Kagoshima coastal defense.

308th Division Hirosaki 1945   岩木 *Yuwaki* 27410 (11,031)

308th Division Headquarters   27411 (466)   activated 6/10/45
308th Division Signal Unit   27417 (253)
308th Division Field Hospital   27419 (232)
308th Division Infantry Group
- 310th Infantry Regiment (Hirosaki)   27412 (2,915)
- 311th Infantry Regiment (Hirosaki)   27413 (2,915)
- 312th Infantry Regiment (Akita)   27414 (2,915)
- 308th Division Rocket Gun Unit   27415 (684)
- 308th Division Engineer Unit   27416 (806)
- 308th Division Transport Company   27418 (300)

<u>308th Division</u>: (Mobile type) Activated in Hirosaki July 20, 1945. Home station: Hirosaki. With the 50th Army in Shimokita, Aomori Prefecture where it was deactivated on Sept 5, 1945.

<u>Service History</u>: Japan: Shimokita

312th Division Kureme 1945   千歳 *Chitose* 32620 (11,023)

312th Division Headquarters   32621 (466)
312th Division Signal Unit   32627 (280)
312th Division Field Hospital   32629 (231)
312th Division Infantry Group
- 358th Infantry Regiment (Fukuoka)   32622 (3,043)
- 359th Infantry Regiment (Kurume)   32623 (3,043)
- 360th Infantry Regiment (Omura)   32624 (3,043)
- 312th Division Rocket Gun Regiment   32625 (692)
- 312th Division Engineer Unit   32626 (806)
- 312th Division Transport Company   32628 (300)

<u>312th Division</u>: (Coastal type) Activated Kurume May 23, 1945. Home station: Kurume. With the 56th Army in Imari, Saga Prefecture where it was deactivated on Sept 21st.

<u>Service History</u>: Japan: Imari, Saga coastal defense.

316th Division Kyoto 1945　　　　　　　　山城 *Yamashiro* 28225

316th Division Headquarters	28226 (464)	activated 7/10/45
316th Division Signal Unit	28232 (280)	
316th Division Ordinance Duty Unit	28235	never mobilized
316th Division Medical Unit	28236	never mobilized
316th Division Field Hospital	28234 (278)	
316th Division Veterinary Unit	28239	never mobilized
316th Division Infantry Group		
• 349th Infantry Regiment (Kyoto)	28227 (2,883)	
• 350th Infantry Regiment (Tsuruya)	28228 (2,883)	
• 351st Infantry Regiment (Tsuruya)	28229 (2,883)	
• 316th Division Rocket Gun Unit	28230 (692)	
• 316th Division Engineer Unit	28231 (805)	
• 316th Division Motor Transport Company	28233 (398)	

316th Division: (Coastal type) Activated in Kyoto Aug 15, 1945. Home station: Kyoto. With the 53rd Army in Kōzu, Kanagawa Prefecture. Deactivated in Kōzu on Aug 30th.
Service History: Japan: Kōzu coastal defense.

320th Division Keijo 1945　　　　　　　　宣武 *Senbu* 29100 (11,847)

320th Division Headquarters	29101 (370)
320th Division Signal Unit	29107 (280)
320th Division Field Hospital	29109 (275)
320th Division Infantry Group	
• 361st Infantry Regiment (Korea)	29102 (3,042)
• 362nd Infantry Regiment (Korea)	29103 (3,042)
• 363rd Infantry Regiment (Korea)	29104 (3,042)
• 320th Division Rocket Gun Unit	29105 (692)
• 320th Division Engineer Unit	29106 (806)
• 320th Division Transport Company	29108 (300)

320th Division: (Coastal type) Activated in Seoul on May 23, 1945. Home station: Seoul. With the 17th Area Army in Seoul Korea. Deactivated near Pyongyang 8/18/45.
Service History: Japan: Seoul coastal defense.

321st Division Tokyo 1945　　　　　　　　磯 *Iso* 27719 (11,607)

321st Division Headquarters	27720 (470)
321sr Division Signal Unit	27726 (280)
321st Division Field Hospital	27728 (241)
321st Division Infantry Group	
• 325th Infantry Regiment (Kashiwa)	27721 (3,042)
• 326th Infantry Regiment (Kofu)	27722 (3,042)
• 327th Infantry Regiment (Sakura)	27723 (3,042)
• 321st Division Artillery Unit	27724 (502)
• 321st Division Engineer Unit	27725 (800)

321st Division continued   磯 *Iso*
- 321st Division Transport Company   27727 (183)

<u>321st Division</u>: (Coastal type) Activated in the Izu Islands May 23, 1945, from former 65th I.M.B troops. Home station: Tokyo. With the 12th Area Army on Oshima, the Izu Is. Deactivated between Sept 27 and Oct 11 1945. Took the 65th I.M.B.s code name.
<u>Service History</u>: Japan: Oshima Island coastal defense.

322nd Division Sendai 1945   磐梯 *Bandai* 27420 (11,520)

322nd Division Headquarters   27421 (538)
332nd Division Signal Unit   27427 (253)
332nd Division Field Hospital   27429 (232)
322nd Division Infantry Group
- 313th Infantry Regiment (Sendai)   27422 (2,915)
- 314th Infantry Regiment (Wakamatsu)   27423 (2,915)
- 315th Infantry Regiment (Yamagata)   27424 (2,915)
- 322nd Division Artillery Unit   27425 (508)
- 322nd Division Engineer Unit   27426 (806)
- 322nd Division Transport Company   27428 (300)

<u>322nd Division</u>: (Coastal type) Activated in Sendai Jul 10, 1945. Home station: Sendai. With the 11th Area Army in Iwanuma, Miyagi Prefecture until it was deactivated on September 6, 1945.
<u>Service History</u>: Japan: Iwanuma coastal defense.

344th Division Zentsuji 1945   剣山 *Kenzan* 28270 (11,566)

344th Division Headquarters   28271 (464)
344th Division Signal Unit   28277 (280)
344th Division Field Hospital   28279 (278)
344th Division Infantry Group
- 352nd Infantry Regiment (Marugame)   28272 (2,883)
- 353rd Infantry Regiment (Kōchi)   28273 (2,883)
- 354th Infantry Regiment (Kōchi)   28274 (2,883)
- 344th Division Rocket Gun Unit   28275 (692)
- 344th Division Engineer Unit   28276 (805)
- 344th Division Transport Company   28278 (398)

<u>344th Division</u>: (Coastal type) Activated Zentsuji May 23, 1945. Home station: Zentsuji. With 55th Army in Shukuge, Kochi Prefecture where it was deactivated on Sept 10th.
<u>Service History</u>: Japan: Kochi Prefecture coastal defense

351st Division Utsunomiya 1945   赤城 *Akagi* 27729 (11,145)

351st Division Headquarters   27730 (470)   activated 6/10/45
351st Division Signal Unit   27736 (280)

351st Division continued

351st Division Field Hospital	27738 (241)
351st Division Infantry Group	
• 328th Infantry Regiment (Utsunomiya)	27731 (3,042)
• 329th Infantry Regiment (Mito)	27732 (3,042)
• 330th Infantry Regiment (Takasaki)	27733 (3,042)
• 351st Division Rocket Gun Unit	27734 (684)
• 351st Division Engineer Unit	27735 (800)
• 351st Division Transport Company	27737 (299)

351st Division: (Coastal type) Activated in Utsunomiya June 26, 1945. Home station: Utsunomiya. With the 56th Army in Koga, deactivated in Fukuoka on Sept 18th.
Service History: Japan: Koga, Fukuoka coastal defense

354th Division Tokyo 1945   武甲 *Bukō* 27739 (11,905)

354th Division Headquarters	27740 (470)
354th Division Signal Unit	27746 (280)
354th Division Field Hospital	27748 (241)
354th Division Infantry Group	
• 331st Infantry Regiment (Mizonokuchi)	27741 (3,042)
• 332nd Infantry Regiment (Kohu)	27742 (3,042)
• 333rd Infantry Regiment (Sakura)	27743 (3,042)
• 354th Division Rocket Gun Unit	27744 (684)
• 354th Division Engineer Unit	27745 (800)
• 354th Division Transport Company	27747 (299)

354th Division: (Coastal type) Activated in Tokyo May 23, 1945. Home station: Tokyo. With the Tokyo Bay Army in Maruyama until deactivation in Tateyama Aug 30th.
Service History: Japan: Maruyama Cho in Tokyo.

355th Division Himeji 1945   那智 *Nashi* 28297 (11,566)

355th Division Headquarters	28298 (464)	
355th Division Signal Unit	28304 (280)	activ incomplete
355th Division Field Hospital	28306 (278)	activ incomplete
355th Division Infantry Group		
• 355th Infantry Regiment (Himeji)	28299 (2,883)	activ incomplete
• 356th Infantry Regiment (Osaka)	28300 (2,883)	activ incomplete
• 357th Infantry Regiment (Osaka)	28301 (2,883)	activ incomplete
• 355th Division Rocket Gun Unit	28302 (692)	activ incomplete
• 355th Division Engineer Unit	28303 (805)	activ incomplete
• 355th Division Transport Unit	28305 (398)	activ incomplete

355th Division: (Coastal type) Activated in Himeji July 9, 1945. Home station: Himeji. With the 54th Army until it was deactivated in Fukue on Sept 8th.
Service History: Japan: coastal defense, in transit when the war ended.

Armoured Divisions

1ˢᵗ Armored Division Fukuoka 1942 — 拓 *Taku* 12070 (10,729)

1ˢᵗ Tank Division Headquarters	12080 (201)
1ˢᵗ Tank Division Maintenance Unit	12082 (778)
1ˢᵗ Tank Brigade Headquarters	126 満州 deactivated 10/11/44
• 1ˢᵗ Tank Regiment (Fukuoka)	12071 (1,071)
• 3ʳᵈ Tank Regiment	12075/満152 (1,071)
• 5ᵗʰ Tank Regiment (Fukuoka)	12083 (1,071)
• 1ˢᵗ Mechanized Infantry Regiment	12072 (3,029)
• 1ˢᵗ Tank Division Rapid Firing Gun Unit	12073 (444)
• 1ˢᵗ Mechanized Artillery Regiment	12078 (1,506)
• 1ˢᵗ Tank Engineer Regiment	12081 (1,149)
• 1ˢᵗ Tank Division Transport Regiment	12085 (764)
• 1ˢᵗ Tank Division Air Defense Unit	呂12079 (1,014)

1ˢᵗ Armored Division: Activated in Manchuria June 24, 1942. Home station: Fukuoka. With the 1ˢᵗ Mechanized Army from July 4ᵗʰ until Oct 30, 1943, 1ˢᵗ Area Army until Mar 15, 1945 and 36ᵗʰ Army in Sano, Tochigi until it was deactivated on Sept 11ᵗʰ.
Service History: Japan: Tochigi mobile reserve.

4ᵗʰ Armored Division Osaka 1944 — 鋼 *Hagane* 12375 (5,961)

4ᵗʰ Armored Division Headquarters	12369 (165)
4ᵗʰ Armored Division Signal Unit	12372 (189)
4ᵗʰ Armored Division Maintenance Unit	12373 (530)
• 28ᵗʰ Tank Regiment (Tsudanuma)	12370 (1,198)
• 29ᵗʰ Tank Regiment (Tsudanuma)	12371 (1,198)
• 30ᵗʰ Tank Regiment (Tsudanuma)	12950 (1,198)
• 4ᵗʰ Armored Division Transport Unit	12374 (767)
• 4ᵗʰ Armored Div. Machine Cannon Unit	12337 (716) activated 4/6/45

4ᵗʰ Armored Division: Activated in Osaka July 6, 1942. Home station: Osaka. With the 36ᵗʰ Army in Sakura, Chiba Prefecture until it was deactivated on October 10ᵗʰ.
Service History: Japan: Sakura mobile reserve.

Chapter 3

Anti Aircraft Artillery Divisions

1st Anti Aircraft Division Tokyo 1944　　　　晴 *Hare* 1050 (31,855)

1st A.A. Division Headquarters	1900 (805)	Tokyo
1st A.A. Div HQ Signal Section	1900 (143)	
6th Anti-Aircraft Brigade Headquarters	unknown	activated 7/9/45
111th Anti Aircraft Regiment (Tokyo)	1902 (3,584)	
112th Anti Aircraft Regiment (Tokyo)	1903 (3,563)	
113th Anti Aircraft Regiment (Yokosuka)	4100 (3,607)	
114th Anti Aircraft Regiment (Ishikawa)	1904 (3,435)	
115th Anti Aircraft Regiment (Ishikawa)	1901 (3,435)	
116th Anti Aircraft Regiment (Ishikawa)	1991 (3,603)	
117th Anti Aircraft Regiment (Yokosuka)	4101 (2,913)	
118th Anti Aircraft Regiment (Tokyo)	1992 (1,688)	
119th Anti Aircraft Regiment (Ishikawa)	1993 (1,702)	
1st Independent Anti Aircraft Battalion	1993 (922)	
2nd Independent Anti Aircraft Battalion	1954 (753)	
3rd Independent Anti Aircraft Battalion	1953 (417)	
4th Independent Anti Aircraft Battalion	1955 (753)	
44th Independent Anti Aircraft Battalion	28203 (528)	
49th Independent Anti Aircraft Battalion	1065 (528)	
50th Independent Anti Aircraft Battalion	unknown (528)	
48th Independent Anti Aircraft Company	1059 (162)	
49th Independent Anti Aircraft Company	1060 (162)	
50th Independent Anti Aircraft Company	1061 (162)	
51st Independent Anti Aircraft Company	1062 (162)	
95th Field Anti Aircraft Battalion	1958 (584)	
96th Field Anti Aircraft Battalion	1959 (521)	
1st Searchlight Regiment	1952 (1,937)	
1st Independent Searchlight Battalion	1051 (431)	
1st Machine Cannon Battalion	1951 (459)	
4th Machine Cannon Battalion	1956 (861)	
1st Independent Machine Cannon Battalion	1052 (451)	
1st Independent Machine Cannon Company	1053 (138)	
2nd Ind. Machine Cannon Company	1054 (138)	
13th Ind. Machine Cannon Company	1055 (138)	
14th Ind. Machine Cannon Company	1056 (138)	
15th Ind. Machine Cannon Company	1057 (138)	
16th Ind. Machine Cannon Company	1058 (138)	
34th Ind. Machine Cannon Company	1066 (138)	
1st Strategic Balloon Unit	1920 (503)	

<u>1st Anti-Aircraft Division</u>: Activated in Tokyo December 22, 1944, from former Eastern Army Anti Aircraft Group personnel. Home station: Tokyo. With the Eastern District Army until Feb.6, 1945 and 12th Area Army in Tokyo. Deactivated on Oct 9th.
<u>Service History</u>: Japan: Tokyo air defense.

2ⁿᵈ Anti-Aircraft Division Nagoya 1945 　　　逐 *Chiku* 21630 (10,812)

2ⁿᵈ A.A. Division Headquarters	21631 (776)	Nagoya
124ᵗʰ Anti Aircraft Regiment (Nagoya)	4102 (3,413)	
125ᵗʰ Anti Aircraft Regiment (Nagoya)	4103 (3,475)	
123ʳᵈ Anti Aircraft Regiment, 9ᵗʰ Coy.	4168 (167)	
5ᵗʰ Independent Rapid Firing Gun Battalion	21602 (672)	
12ᵗʰ Independent Anti Aircraft Battalion	7611 (753)	
47ᵗʰ Independent Anti Aircraft Battalion	1063 (669)	
97ᵗʰ Field Anti Aircraft Battalion	12468 (521)	
52ⁿᵈ Independent Anti Aircraft Company	21627 (162)	
53ʳᵈ Independent Anti Aircraft Company	21628 (162)	
54ᵗʰ Independent Anti Aircraft Company	21629 (162)	
12ᵗʰ Machine Cannon Battalion	4118 (861)	
106ᵗʰ Machine Cannon Battalion	12453 (340)	
23ʳᵈ Ind. Machine Cannon Company	21633 (144)	
24ᵗʰ Ind. Machine Cannon Company	21634 (144)	
25ᵗʰ Ind. Machine Cannon Company	21635 (144)	
42ⁿᵈ Ind. Machine Cannon Company	21605 (144)	
43ʳᵈ Ind. Machine Cannon Company	21606 (144)	
44ᵗʰ Ind. Machine Cannon Company	21607 (144)	
11ᵗʰ Searchlight Regiment	4108 (596)	

<u>2ⁿᵈ Anti-Aircraft Division</u>: Activated in Nagoya May 6, 1945, from former Nagoya Anti Aircraft Group personnel. Home station: Nagoya. With the 13ᵗʰ Area Army in Nagoya where it was deactivated on September 19ᵗʰ.
<u>Service History</u>: Japan: Nagoya air defense.

3ʳᵈ Anti-Aircraft Division Osaka 1945 　　　炸 *Saku* 12409 (11,667)

3ʳᵈ A.A. Division Headquarters	12410 (776)	Osaka
121ˢᵗ Anti Aircraft Regiment (Osaka)	7650 (3,487)	
122ⁿᵈ Anti Aircraft Regiment (Osaka)	7651 (3,459)	
123ʳᵈ Anti Aircraft Regiment (Osaka)	4168 (1,523)	
11ᵗʰ Independent Anti Aircraft Battalion	4107 (1,143)	
13ᵗʰ Independent Anti Aircraft Battalion	4116 (255)	
22ⁿᵈ Independent Anti Aircraft Battalion	8077 (753)	
45ᵗʰ Independent Anti Aircraft Battalion	28204 (699)	
57ᵗʰ Independent Anti Aircraft Company	28205 (162)	
58ᵗʰ Independent Anti Aircraft Company	28206 (162)	
11ᵗʰ Machine Cannon Battalion	4117 (861)	
47ᵗʰ Ind. Machine Cannon Company	28211 (144)	
48ᵗʰ Ind. Machine Cannon Company	28212 (144)	
49ᵗʰ Ind. Machine Cannon Company	28213 (144)	
50ᵗʰ Ind. Machine Cannon Company	28214 (144)	
51ˢᵗ Ind. Machine Cannon Company	28215 (144)	

3rd Anti-Aircraft Division: Activated in Osaka Apr 28, 1945, from former Central Anti Aircraft Group personnel. Home station: Osaka. It was identical to the Central Anti Aircraft Group but with reinforcements and additional responsibilities. With the 15th Area Army in Osaka from May 6th until it was deactivated on Sept 11th.
Service History: Japan: Osaka air defense.

4th Anti-Aircraft Division Kokura 1945	彗 *Sui* (14,759)	
4th A.A. Division Headquarters	8060 (780)	Takarabe
4th Anti Aircraft Brigade Headquarters	8004 (162)	
131st Anti Aircraft Regiment (Kokura)	8061 (3,575)	
132nd Anti Aircraft Regiment (Kokura)	8062 (3,225)	
133rd Anti Aircraft Regiment (Kokura)	8063 (1,520)	
134th Anti Aircraft Regiment (Kokura)	8064 (1,508)	
136th Anti Aircraft Regiment (Kokura)	8001 (2,002)	
98th Field Anti Aircraft Battalion	12469 (521)	
21st Independent Anti Aircraft Battalion	8076 (753)	
23rd Independent Anti Aircraft Battalion	8075 (255)	
24th Independent Anti Aircraft Battalion	8078 (753)	
43rd Independent Anti Aircraft Battalion	8043 (528)	
55th Independent Anti Aircraft Company	8045 (162)	
56th Independent Anti Aircraft Company	8046 (162)	
5th Machine Cannon Battalion	unknown	
21st Machine Cannon Battalion	8088 (718)	
11th Ind. Machine Cannon Company	8010 (138)	
12th Ind. Machine Cannon Company	8044 (138)	
26th Ind. Machine Cannon Company	8019 (138)	
27th Ind. Machine Cannon Company	8047 (138)	
28th Ind. Machine Cannon Company	8048 (138)	
31st Ind. Machine Cannon Company	8091 (144)	
32nd Ind. Machine Cannon Company	8092 (144)	
33rd Ind. Machine Cannon Company	8093 (144)	
21st Ind. Searchlight Battalion	8079 (638)	
21st Strategic Balloon Unit	8069 (132)	

4th Anti-Aircraft Division: Activated Apr 28, 1945, from former Western Anti Aircraft Group personnel. Home station: Kokura. It was identical to the Western Anti Aircraft Group but with reinforcements and additional responsibilities. With the 16th Area Army in Kokura from May 6th until June when it was placed under the 57th Army and its HQ moved to Takarabe. Deactivated in Kokura on Sept 24th.
Service History: Japan: Kokura air defense.

End of Divisions

Brigades

Work being done on a pontoon bridge in China ca. 1941 (author)

Independent Mixed Brigades:
The powerful independent mixed brigades were most numerous (I.M.B.), the infantry component was typically one or two regiments or three to six independent battalions with signal, artillery and engineer units in support. There were 116 I.M.B. in addition to 14 infantry, 9 armored, 1 airborne, 1 mobile and 4 amphibious brigades.

43rd Independent Mixed Brigade 1944　　　奇 *Kuoi* 12643

43rd Brigade Headquarters	12644 (294)
• 294th Independent Infantry Battalion	12694 (985)
• 295th Independent Infantry Battalion	12695 (983)
• 296th Independent Infantry Battalion	12696 (983)
• 297th Independent Infantry Battalion	12697 (983)
• 419th Independent Infantry Battalion	12698 (983)　activated 7/29/44
• 420th Independent Infantry Battalion	12699 (983)　activated 7/29/44
• 43rd Brigade Artillery Unit	12645 (738)
• 43rd Brigade Engineer Unit	12646 (267)
• 43rd Brigade Signal Unit	12647 (278)
• 43rd Brigade Ordinance Duty Unit	12648 (154)

43rd I.M.B.: Activated on Iturup Is., the Kuriles April 12, 1944, from former the 42nd Inf Group HQ, 3rd Chishima Garrison Unit and Iturup District Garrison Unit personnel. Home station: Sendai. With the 5th Area Army from Jan 22, 1945, until Feb 28th when it was deactivated to establish the 3rd Mixed Brigade, 89th Division.
Service History: Kurile Islands:

44th Independent Mixed Brigade 1944　　　球 *Kyu* (4,694)

44th Brigade Headquarters	18800 (60)
• 2nd Mixed Infantry Regiment	7071 (2,046)　deact. 9/22/44
• 1st Infantry Battalion	7071
• 2nd Infantry Battalion	7071
• 3rd Infantry Battalion	7071
• 2nd Regiment Artillery Unit	7071
• 2nd Regiment Anti Tank Unit	7071
• 15th Independent Mixed Regiment	7836 (2,180)
• 1st Infantry Battalion	7836
• 2nd Infantry Battalion	7836
• 3rd Infantry Battalion	7836
• 15th Regiment Engineer Unit	7836
• 15th Regiment Anti Tank Unit	7836
• 44th Brigade Artillery Unit	7072 (369)
• 44th Brigade Engineer Unit	7073 (173)

44th I.M.B.: Activated in Japan May 3, 1944, in part from former Nakagusuku Bay Fortress Unit troops. The Toyama Maru was sunk June 29th drowning entire units. The Bgde rebuilt on Okinawa, the 15th I.M.R. joined in mid-July. The 272nd and 273rd I.I.B. from 45th I.M.B., 23rd Shipping Engineer Regt and 7th Heavy Artillery Regt were attached later. With the 32nd Army on Okinawa, destroyed by June 23, 1945.
Service History: Japan: Okinawa April 1 1945.

45th Independent Mixed Brigade 1944　　　球 *Kyu* (2,964)

45th Independent Mixed Brigade continued   球 *Kyu*

45th Brigade Headquarters	18801 (59)	
• 271st Independent Infantry Battalion	6467 (683)	activated 7/12/44
• 272nd Independent Infantry Battalion	14212 (683)	activated 7/12/44
• 273rd Independent Infantry Battalion	14213 (683)	activated 7/12/44
• 298th Independent Infantry Battalion	6461 (683)	
• 299th Independent Infantry Battalion	6462 (683)	
• 300th Independent Infantry Battalion	6463 (683)	
• 301st Independent Infantry Battalion	6464 (683)	
• 45th Brigade Engineer Unit	6465 (173)	
• 45th Brigade Signal Unit	6466	

<u>45th I.M.B.</u>: Activated in Japan May 3, 1944, from former Funauki Fortress Unit personnel. The Toyama Maru was sunk June 29th drowning some units. Rebuilt on Ishigaki. Home station: Marugame. With the 32nd Army from May 3rd until June 24, 1945 and 10th Area Army on Ishigaki Island until the war ended. The 272nd and 273rd Ind Infantry Battalions were attached to the 44th I.M.B. and destroyed on Okinawa.
<u>Service History</u>: Japan: Okinawa April 1 1945.

46th Independent Mixed Brigade 1944   敢 *Kan*

46th Brigade Headquarters	1785
• 304th Taiwan Infantry Regiment	1786
• 305th Taiwan Infantry Regiment	1787
• 46th Brigade Artillery Unit	1788
• 46th Brigade Engineer Unit	1789
• 46th Brigade Signal Unit	1783

<u>46th I.M.B.</u>: Activated May 22, 1944. Home station: Unknown. Part of the 46th I.M.B. was sunk sailing from Japan to Formosa. With the Formosa Army from May until July 12th when it was deactivated to form the 66th Division
<u>Service History</u>: Formosa:

59th Independent Mixed Brigade 1944   碧 *Heki* 12940 (3,500)

59th Brigade Headquarters	12945 (150)
• 393rd Independent Infantry Battalion	12941 (600)
• 394th Independent Infantry Battalion	12942 (600)
• 395th Independent Infantry Battalion	12943 (600)
• 396th Independent Infantry Battalion	12944 (600)
• 59th Brigade Artillery Unit	12946 (400)
• 59th Brigade Engineer Unit	12947 (280)
• 59th Brigade Signal Unit	12948 (200)

<u>59th I.M.B.</u>: Activated in Manchuria July 12, 1944, from former 9th Ind Garrison Unit personnel. Home station: Kanazawa. With the 32nd Army, Miyakojima, Okinawa Prefecture and 10th Area Army (after the loss of Okinawa) until the war ended.

59th I.M.B.: continued
Service History: Japan: Miyakojima Island garrison.

60th Independent Mixed Brigade 1944   駒 *Koma* 13066 (3,500)

60th Brigade Headquarters	13065 (150)
• 397th Independent Infantry Battalion	13061 (600)
• 398th Independent Infantry Battalion	13062 (600)
• 399th Independent Infantry Battalion	13063 (600)
• 400th Independent Infantry Battalion	13064 (600)
• 60th Brigade Artillery Unit	13067 (400)
• 60th Brigade Engineer Unit	13068 (280)
• 60th Brigade Signal Unit	13069 (200)

60th I.M.B.: Activated in Manchuria July 12, 1944, from former 9th Ind Garrison Unit personnel. Home station: Utsunomiya. With the 32nd Army on Miyakojima, Okinawa Prefecture and 10th Area Army (after the loss of Okinawa) until the war ended.
Service History: Japan: Miyakojima Island garrison.

64th Independent Mixed Brigade 1944   球 *Kyu* (7,643)

64th Brigade Headquarters	7165 (104)	
• 21st Independent Mixed Regiment	7156 (2,230)	
• 22nd Independent Mixed Regiment	7166 (2,250)	
• 6th Medium Artillery Regiment	2740 (997)	detached
• 79th Field Anti Aircraft Battalion	2172 (521)	
• 80th Field Anti Aircraft Battalion	2173 (521)	
• 81st Field Anti Aircraft Battalion	12425 (521)	
• 103rd Machine Cannon Battalion	2177 (340)	
• 104th Machine Cannon Battalion	12427 (340)	
• 105th Machine Cannon Battalion	12526 (340)	

64th I.M.B.: Activated in Hiroshima, Japan on Jul 12, 1944. Home station: Yamaguchi. Amami Shima Detachment with the 32nd Army until June 20, 1945 and 57th Army until the war ended. The Amami Detachment was transferred to the 57th Army after Okinawa was lost.
Service History: Japan: Tokunoshima Island garrison (Satsunan Islands, Ryukyus).

65th Independent Mixed Brigade: With the Tokyo Bay Army Corps until it was deactivated on May 23, 1945 to form the 321st Division.

66th Independent Mixed Brigade 1944   境 *Saki* (4,321)

66th Brigade Headquarters	12377 (218)
• 18th Independent Mixed Regiment	7069 (2,230)
• 427th Independent Infantry Battalion	10288 (564)
• 66th Brigade Field Hospital	12437 (121)

66th Independent Mixed Brigade continued   境 *Saki*

Nijima Detachment:	7835 (388)	
22nd Ind. Mountain Artillery Battalion	2891 (415)	
27th Ind. Rapid Firing Gun Company	2488 (145)	anti tank
5th Independent Machinegun Battalion	12399 (334)	
100th Ind. Fld. Hvy. Art. Battalion, 3rd Co.	unknown (138)	
15th Specially Est. Guard Company	7892 (126)	Niijima
16th Specially Est. Guard Company	7893 (126)	Kamitsu-shima
17th Specially Est. Guard Company	7894 (126)	Miyake-shima

<u>66th I.M.B.</u>: Activated in Niijima, Izu Islands July 12, 1944, from former Niijima Detachment personnel. Home station: Unknown. With the Eastern District Army until Feb 6, 1945 and 12th Area Army on Niijima until it was deactivated on Oct 24th.
<u>Service History</u>: Japan: Island garrison Niijima

67th Independent Mixed Brigade 1944   浦 *Ura* (8,227)

67th Brigade Headquarters	12378 (241)	
• 425th Independent Infantry Battalion	10276 (564)	
• 426th Independent Infantry Battalion	10277 (564)	
• 668th Independent Infantry Battalion	14232 (898)	from 65th I.M.B.
• 669th Independent Infantry Battalion	2235 (898)	fr 65th I.M.B. new #
• 67th Brigade Field Hospital	12438 (121)	
• 100th Indep. Heavy Artillery Battalion	13359 (462)	
• 1st Mobile Ordinance Repair Unit	12364 (237)	
Hachijojima Detachment:		
Hachijojima Detachment Headquarters	7834 (1,452)	
• 16th Independent Mixed Regiment	6064 (2,180)	
16th Independent Machinegun Battalion	15574 (334)	
15th Indep. Rapid Firing Gun Battalion	12379 (403)	
24th Indep. Rapid Firing Gun Company	14795 (145)	
12th Independent Field Artillery Battalion	14207 (415)	
23rd Indep. Mountain Artillery Battalion	2872 (415)	
52nd Indep. Field Anti-Aircraft Company	2175 (161)	
63rd Independent Engineer Battalion	2893 (894)	
5th Specially Established Guard Battalion	2169 (463)	Hachijo-shima
219th Ind. Motor Transport Company	2856 (183)	
112th Land Duty Company 262	9749 (511)	
50th Field Machine Cannon Company	1971 (105)	
4th Heavy Artillery Company	13366 (168)	
41st Specially Est. Machine Cannon Co.	2183 (85)	
42nd Specially Est. Machine Cannon Co.	2184 (85)	

<u>67th I.M.B.</u>: Activated on Hachijojima July 12, 1944, from former Hachijojima Detach personnel. Home station: Yokosuka. With the Eastern District Army until Feb 6, 1945 and 12th Area Army in the Izu Islands until deactivation in Hachijo prior to Dec 1st.
<u>Service History</u>: Japan: Hachijojima Island garrison, Tokyo City jurisdiction

69th Independent Mixed Brigade 1944   憲 *Ken* 12608

69th Brigade Headquarters	12609 (229)
• 421st Independent Infantry Battalion	12623 (814)
• 422nd Independent Infantry Battalion	12624 (814)
• 423rd Independent Infantry Battalion	12625 (814)
• 424th Independent Infantry Battalion	12626 (814)
• 69th Brigade Mountain Artillery Unit	12627 (464)
• 69th Brigade Engineer Unit	12629 (157)
• 69th Brigade Signal Unit	12628 (226)

69th I.M.B.: Activated south Kurile Islands on July 29, 1944, from former 8th Ind Mixed Regt personnel. Home station: Asahikawa. With the 27th Army until Jan 22, 1945 and 5th Area Army until Feb 21, 1945. Deactivated on Feb 28th to establish the 4th Mixed Brigade, 89th Division.
Service History: Japan: Island garrison South Kuriles.

73rd Independent Mixed Brigade 1944   赫 *Kaku*

73rd Brigade Headquarters	13171 (188)
• 445th Independent Infantry Battalion	13172 (708)
• 446th Independent Infantry Battalion	13173 (708)
• 447th Independent Infantry Battalion	13174 (708)
• 448th Independent Infantry Battalion	13175 (708)
• 449th Independent Infantry Battalion	13176 (708)
• 73rd Brigade Artillery Unit	13177 (739)
• 73rd Brigade Engineer Unit	13178 (288)
• 73rd Brigade Signal Unit	13179 (207)

73rd I.M.B.: Activated in Manchuria Oct 11, 1944, from 1st Div personnel. Home station: Osaka. With the 4th Army until Jan 16, 1945 when it was deactivated to establish the 123rd Division in Sunwa, Manchuria.
Service History: Manchuria: Sunwu garrison

75th Independent Mixed Brigade 1945   興 *Kyō* 12850

75th Brigade Headquarters	12851 (187)
• 560th Independent Infantry Battalion	12852 (809)
• 561st Independent Infantry Battalion	12853 (809)
• 562nd Independent Infantry Battalion	12854 (809)
• 563rd Independent Infantry Battalion	12855 (809)
• 564th Independent Infantry Battalion	12856 (809)
• 12th Heavy Artillery Regiment	12857 (603)
• 75th Brigade Engineer Unit	12858 (249)

75th I.M.B.: Activated on Formosa January 4, 1945, from former Hokoto Fortress Unit personnel. Home station: Marugame. With the 10th Area Army in the Hokoto (Pescadores) Islands until the war ended.

75th I.M.B continued
Service History: Formosa: Hokoto Island garrison.

76th Independent Mixed Brigade 1945   律 *Ritsu* 12860

76th Brigade Headquarters   12861 (189)
  • 565th Independent Infantry Battalion 12862 (809)
  • 566th Independent Infantry Battalion 12863 (809)
  • 567th Independent Infantry Battalion 21119 (809)   activated 3/10/45
• 13th Heavy Artillery Regiment   12865 (945)
• 76th Brigade Engineer Unit   12864 (249)

76th I.M.B.: Activated on Hoping Island, Formosa Jan 4, 1945, from former Keelung Fortress Unit personnel. Home station: Hiroshima. With the 10th Area Army in the Keelung area until the war ended.
Service History: Formosa: Hoping Island garrison.

77th Independent Mixed Brigade 1945   真心 *Magokoro* 25251

77th Brigade Headquarters   25252 / 満州343 (352)
  • 568th Independent Infantry Battalion 25253 / 満州813 (1,329)
  • 569th Independent Infantry Battalion 25254 / 満州807 (1,329)
  • 570th Independent Infantry Battalion 25255 / 満州312 (1,329)
  • 571st Independent Infantry Battalion 25256 / 満州367 (1,329)
  • 572nd Independent Infantry Battalion 25257 / 満州626 (1,329)
• 77th Brigade Artillery Unit   25258 / 満州636 (587)
• 77th Brigade Engineer Unit   25259 / 満州819 (587)
• 77th Brigade Signal Unit   25260 / 満州228 (226)
• 77th Brigade Transport Unit   25261 / 満州820 (540)

77th I.M.B.: Activated in Tonei, Manchuria on Jan. 16, 1945, from former 3rd Cavalry Brigade personnel. Home station: Fukuoka. With the 5th Army until it was deactivated in Tungan on Jul 10th to establish the 135th Division, which took the 77th I.M.B.s code name.
Service History: Manchuria:

78th Independent Mixed Brigade 1945   勾玉 *Magatama* 25262

78th Brigade Headquarters   25263 / 満州134 (88)
  • 573rd Independent Infantry Battalion 25264 / 満州853 (708)
  • 574th Independent Infantry Battalion 25265 / 満州728 (708)
  • 575th Independent Infantry Battalion 25266 / 満州291 (708)
  • 576th Independent Infantry Battalion 25267 / 満州432 (708)
  • 577th Independent Infantry Battalion 25268 / 満州831 (708)
• 78th Brigade Artillery Unit   25269 / 満州824 (332)
• 78th Brigade Engineer Unit   25270 / 満州773 (288)

78th Independent Mixed Brigade continued

- 78th Brigade Signal Unit — 25271 / 満州445 (207)
- 78th Brigade Transport Unit — 25272 / 満州973 (608)

<u>78th I.M.B.</u>: Activated in Manchuria on Jan 16, 1945, from former 7th Ind Garrison Unit personnel. Home station: Hirosaki. With the 1st Area Army until it was deactivated July 10th to establish the 134th Division, which took the 78th I.M.B.s code name.
<u>Service History</u>: Manchuria:

79th Independent Mixed Brigade 1945 — 丈夫 *Masurao* 25273

- 79th Brigade Headquarters — 25274 (168)
  - 578th Independent Infantry Battalion — 25275 (819)
  - 579th Independent Infantry Battalion — 25276 (819)
  - 580th Independent Infantry Battalion — 25277 (819)
  - 581st Independent Infantry Battalion — 25278 (819)
  - 582nd Independent Infantry Battalion — 25279 (819)
- 79th Brigade Artillery Unit — 25280 (577)
- 79th Brigade Engineer Unit — 25281 (288)
- 79th Brigade Signal Unit — 25282 (202)
- 79th Brigade Raiding Battalion — 37815 (1,130) activated 7/10/45
- 79th Brigade Transport Unit — 25283 (608)

<u>79th I.M.B.</u>: Activated in Manchuria Jan. 16, 1945. Home station: Nagoya. With the 1st Area Army until May 30th and 3rd Area Army in Antung until deactivated on Aug 18th.
<u>Service History</u>: Manchuria:

80th Independent Mixed Brigade 1945 — 鋭鋒 *Eihō* 25284

- 80th Brigade Headquarters — 25285 / 満州703 (168)
  - 583rd Independent Infantry Battalion — 25286 / 満州18 (819)
  - 584th Independent Infantry Battalion — 25287 / 満州558 (819)
  - 585th Independent Infantry Battalion — 25288 / 満州559 (819)
  - 586th Independent Infantry Battalion — 25289 / 満州283 (819)
  - 587th Independent Infantry Battalion — 25290 / 満州700 (819)
- 80th Brigade Artillery Unit — 25291 / 満州737 (577)
- 80th Brigade Engineer Unit — 25292 / 満州97 (288)
- 80th Brigade Signal Unit — 25293 / 満州226 (207)
- 80th Brigade Transport Unit — 25294 / 満州744 (608)
- 80th Brigade Raiding Battalion — unknown (1,130) activ. 7/10/45

<u>80th I.M.B.</u>: Activated in Manchuria Jan 16, 1945, from 8th Border Garrison Unit personnel. Home station: Osaka. With the 3rd Area Army from Jan 16th until May 30th and 4th Army in Hailer until it was deactivated on Aug 18th. On Aug 9th the 80th I.M.B. repulsed a Russian tank brigade that attacked Hailar.
<u>Service History</u>: Manchuria: Hailar August 9, 1945.

95th Independent Mixed Brigade 1945   俊 *Shun* 7274

95th Brigade Headquarters   7275 (271)
- 651st Independent Infantry Battalion   7281 (898)
- 652nd Independent Infantry Battalion   7282 (898)
- 653rd Independent Infantry Battalion   7283 (898)
- 654th Independent Infantry Battalion   7284 (898)
- 33rd Ind. Heavy Artillery Battalion   13362 (584)   activated 2/22/45
- 95th Brigade Engineer Unit   7285 (249)

95th I.M.B.: Activated in Hirosaki, Japan on March 8, 1945. Home station: Hirosaki. With the 11th Area Army from Feb 18th until June 19th and 50th Army in Hachinohe, Aomori Prefecture until it was deactivated on September 5th.
Service History: Japan:

96th Independent Mixed Brigade 1945   幡 *Hata* 14223 (5,600)

96th Brigade Headquarters   14224 (271)
- 655th Independent Infantry Battalion   14225 (898)
- 656th Independent Infantry Battalion   14226 (898)
- 657th Independent Infantry Battalion   14227 (898)
- 658th Independent Infantry Battalion   14228 (898)
- 659th Independent Infantry Battalion   14229 (898)
- 660th Independent Infantry Battalion   14230 (898)
- 96th Brigade Engineer Unit   14231 (249)

96th I.M.B.: Activated in Tokyo on Feb 6, 1945, from former 3rd Imperial Guard Infantry Group personnel. Home station: Tokyo. With the 12th Area Army from Feb 18th until June 19th and Tokyo Bay Army Corps in Tateyama where it was deactivated on Aug 31st.
Service History: Japan:

97th Independent Mixed Brigade 1945   東明 *Tomei* 5780 (3,101)

97th Brigade Headquarters   5781 (271)   deactivated 9/21/45
- 661st Independent Infantry Battalion   5782 (898)
- 662nd Independent Infantry Battalion   5783 (898)
- 663rd Independent Infantry Battalion   5784 (898)
- 38th Ind. Heavy Artillery Battalion   4152 (406)   deactivated 5/5/45
- 97th Brigade Engineer Unit   14178 (249)

97th I.M.B.: Activated in Nagoya Mar 5, 1945. Home station: Nagoya. With the 13th Area Army from Feb 18th until June 19th and 54th Army in Toyohashi where it was deactivated on September 7th.
Service History: Japan:

98th Independent Mixed Brigade 1945   堅志 *Kenshi* (5,427)

98th Independent Mixed Brigade continued

98th Brigade Headquarters	7062 (272)
• 664th Independent Infantry Battalion	7063 (898)
• 665th Independent Infantry Battalion	7064 (898)
• 666th Independent Infantry Battalion	7065 (898)
• 667th Independent Infantry Battalion	7066 (898)
• 98th Brigade Engineer Unit	7067 (249)
• 15th Heavy Artillery Regiment	13560 (929)

98th I.M.B.: Activated in Kumamoto, Kyushu Feb 6, 1945. Home station: Kumamoto. With the 16th Area Army from Feb 18th to April 8th and 57th Army in Kumamoto. Deactivated in Kaya on September 19th.
Service History: Japan:

100th Independent Mixed Brigade 1945　　　磐石 *Banjaku*

100th Brigade Headquarters	21111 (116)
• 30th Independent Mixed Regiment	12870 (2,419)
• 51st Garrison Battalion	10287 (637)
• 16th Heavy Artillery Regiment	4522 (710)

100th I.M.B.: Activated in Takao, Formosa on Feb 17, 1945, from former Takao Fortress Unit personnel. Home station: Formosa. With the 10th Area Army in Kaohsiung for the duration of the war.
Service History: Formosa: Kaohsiung garrison.

101st Independent Mixed Brigade 1945　　　達 *Tatsu* 12604 (5,696)

101st Brigade Headquarters	12603 (332)
• 456th Independent Infantry Battalion	12657 (982)
• 457th Independent Infantry Battalion	12658 (982)
• 458th Independent Infantry Battalion	12659 (982)
• 459th Independent Infantry Battalion	12660 (982)
• 101st Brigade Artillery Unit	12661 (737)
• 101st Brigade Engineer Unit	12617 (267)
• 101st Brigade Signal Unit	12618 (278)
• 101st Brigade Ordinance Duty Unit	12619 (154)

101st I.M.B.: Activated in Kitami, Hokkaido on Feb 28, 1945, from former 31st and 32nd Guard Unit troops. Home station: Asahikawa. With the 5th Area Army in Tomakomai Hokkaido from Mar 26th until it was deactivated between September 12th and 17th.
Service History: Japan:

102nd Independent Mixed Brigade 1945　　　八幡 *Hachiman* 12880

102nd Brigade Headquarters	12881 (92)
• 464th Independent Infantry Battalion	12884 (869)

102ⁿᵈ Independent Mixed Brigade continued　　八幡 *Hachiman*
- 465ᵗʰ Independent Infantry Battalion　　12885 (869)
- 466ᵗʰ Independent Infantry Battalion　　12886 (869)
- 467ᵗʰ Independent Infantry Battalion　　12887 (869)
- 102ⁿᵈ Brigade 1ˢᵗ Artillery Unit　　12888 (160)
- 102ⁿᵈ Brigade 2ⁿᵈ Artillery Unit　　12889 (160)
- 102ⁿᵈ Brigade Signal Unit　　12890 (144)

102ⁿᵈ I.M.B.: Activated in Hualien Harbor, Formosa on Feb 17, 1945. Home station: Kumamoto. With the 10ᵗʰ Area Army in Hualien Port until the war ended.
Service History: Taiwan: Hualien garrison.

103ʳᵈ **Independent Mixed Brigade** 1945　　破竹 *Hatuku* 21100
103ʳᵈ Brigade Headquarters　　21101 (92)
- 468ᵗʰ Independent Infantry Battalion　　21102 (809)
- 469ᵗʰ Independent Infantry Battalion　　21103 (809)
- 470ᵗʰ Independent Infantry Battalion　　21104 (809)
- 103ʳᵈ Brigade Reconnaissance Unit　　21105 (722)
- 103ʳᵈ Brigade Artillery Unit　　21106 (1,054)
- 103ʳᵈ Brigade Ordinance Duty Unit　　21107 (112)
- 103ʳᵈ Brigade Signal Unit　　21108 (144)
- 103ʳᵈ Brigade Transport Unit　　21109 (690)

103ʳᵈ I.M.B.: Activated in Takao, Formosa Feb 17, 1945, from former 19ᵗʰ Division personnel. Home station: Fukuoka. With the 10ᵗʰ Area Army in Takao for the diration.
Service History: Formosa: Takao.

107ᵗʰ **Independent Mixed Brigade** 1945　　堡 *Hō* (6,042)
107ᵗʰ Brigade Headquarters　　2700 (288)
- 636ᵗʰ Independent Infantry Battalion　　2701 (805)
- 637ᵗʰ Independent Infantry Battalion　　2702 (805)
- 638ᵗʰ Independent Infantry Battalion　　2703 (805)
- 639ᵗʰ Independent Infantry Battalion　　2704 (805)
- 640ᵗʰ Independent Infantry Battalion　　2705 (805)
- 641ˢᵗ Independent Infantry Battalion　　2706 (805)
- 107ᵗʰ Brigade Artillery Unit　　2707 (572)
- 107ᵗʰ Brigade Engineer Unit　　2708 (178)
- 107ᵗʰ Brigade Signal Unit　　2709 (175)

107ᵗʰ I.M.B.: Activated in Kurume on Mar 16, 1945. Home station: Kureme. With the 16ᵗʰ Area Army in Fukue, Yamaguchi Prefecture from Mar 10ᵗʰ. Deactivated in Fukue on October 15ᵗʰ.
Service History: Japan:

108th Independent Mixed Brigade 1945   翠 *Sui* 12479 (6,042)

  108th Brigade Headquarters   12411 (287)
- 642nd Independent Infantry Battalion   12481 (805)
- 643rd Independent Infantry Battalion   12482 (805)
- 644th Independent Infantry Battalion   12483 (805)
- 645th Independent Infantry Battalion   12484 (805)
- 646th Independent Infantry Battalion   12485 (805)
- 647th Independent Infantry Battalion   12486 (805)
- 108th Brigade Artillery Unit   12487 (592)
- 108th Brigade Engineer Unit   12488 (178)
- 108th Brigade Signal Unit   12489 (175)

108th I.M.B.: Activated in Kyōto, Japan Mar 16, 1945. Home station: Maizuru. With the 17th Area Army from March 10th until April 8th and 58th Army on Jeju Island, Korea.
Service History: Korea: Jeju Island garrison.

109th Independent Mixed Brigade 1945   剣閃 *Kensen* 13581 (5,630)

  109th Brigade Headquarters   13570 (37)
- 678th Independent Infantry Battalion   13571 (590)
- 679th Independent Infantry Battalion   13572 (590)
- 680th Independent Infantry Battalion   13573 (590)
- 681st Independent Infantry Battalion   13574 (705)
- 682nd Independent Infantry Battalion   13575 (705)
- 683rd Independent Infantry Battalion   13576 (705)
- 684th Independent Infantry Battalion   13577 (705)
- 26th Independent Field Artillery Battalion   13562 (492)
- 109th Brigade Engineer Unit   13578 (188)
- 109th Brigade Signal Unit   13579 (162)
- 109th Brigade Medical Unit   13581 (70)

Attached
- 55th Specially Est. Machine Cannon Unit   12543 (85)
- 203rd Specially Est. Guard Battalion   7088 (420)

109th I.M.B.: Activated on Tanegashima, May 14, 1945. Home station: Tanegashima. With the 57th Army on Tanegashima, Ōsumi Is., where it was deactivated on Oct 15th.
Service History: Japan:

112th Independent Mixed Brigade 1945   雷神 *Raijin* 21137

  112th Brigade Headquarters   21134
- 32nd Independent Mixed Regiment   12882
- 33rd Independent Mixed Regiment   21116
- 42nd Independent Mixed Regiment   5307
- 648th Independent Infantry Battalion   21122 (878)

112ᵗʰ I.M.B.: Activated in Yilan, Formosa April 9, 1945. Home station: Unknown. With the 10ᵗʰ Area Army in Yilan County, Formosa until the war ended.
Service History: Formosa: Yilan garrison.

113ᵗʰ Independent Mixed Brigade 1945   瑞光 *Zuiko* 27430 (6,058)

113ᵗʰ Brigade Headquarters	27431 (224)
• 685ᵗʰ Independent Infantry Battalion	27432 (897)
• 686ᵗʰ Independent Infantry Battalion	27433 (897)
• 687ᵗʰ Independent Infantry Battalion	27434 (897)
• 688ᵗʰ Independent Infantry Battalion	27435 (897)
• 689ᵗʰ Independent Infantry Battalion	27436 (897)
• 113ᵗʰ Brigade Artillery Unit	27437 (553)
• 113ᵗʰ Brigade Engineer Unit	27438 (572)
• 113ᵗʰ Brigade Signal Unit	27439 (224)

113ᵗʰ I.M.B.: Activated in Sendai, Miyagi Prefecture July 5, 1945. Home station: Wakamatsu. Attached to the 11ᵗʰ Area Army in Fukushima from June 19ᵗʰ until it was deactivated in Taira on September 5ᵗʰ.
Service History: Japan:

114ᵗʰ Independent Mixed Brigade 1945   房 *Bō* 27749 (6,915)

114ᵗʰ Brigade Headquarters	27750 (225) activated 6/6/45
• 690ᵗʰ Independent Infantry Battalion	27751 (895)
• 691ˢᵗ Independent Infantry Battalion	27752 (895)
• 692ⁿᵈ Independent Infantry Battalion	27753 (895)
• 693ʳᵈ Independent Infantry Battalion	27754 (895)
• 694ᵗʰ Independent Infantry Battalion	27755 (895)
• 695ᵗʰ Independent Infantry Battalion	27756 (895)
• 114ᵗʰ Brigade Artillery Unit	27757 (545)
• 114ᵗʰ Brigade Engineer Unit	27758 (565)
• 114ᵗʰ Brigade Signal Unit	27759 (224)

114ᵗʰ I.M.B.: Activated in Nagano on July 30, 1945. Home station: Nagano. With the Tokyo Bay Army Corps in Yokosuka until it was deactivated in Matsuyama Aug 30ᵗʰ.
Service History: Japan:

115ᵗʰ Independent Mixed Brigade 1945   建 *Ken* 27760 (6,779)

115ᵗʰ Brigade Headquarters	27761 (225)
• 696ᵗʰ Independent Infantry Battalion	27762 (895)
• 697ᵗʰ Independent Infantry Battalion	27763 (895)
• 698ᵗʰ Independent Infantry Battalion	27764 (895)
• 699ᵗʰ Independent Infantry Battalion	27765 (895)
• 700ᵗʰ Independent Infantry Battalion	27766 (895)

115th Independent Mixed Brigade continued
- 701st Independent Infantry Battalion   27767 (895)
- 115th Brigade Artillery Unit   27768 (545)
- 115th Brigade Engineer Unit   27769 (565)
- 115th Brigade Signal Unit   27770 (224)

115th I.M.B.: Activated in Utsunomiya, Tochigi Prefecture July 25, 1945. Home station: Utsunomiya. With the 51st Army in Kashima, Ibaraki from July 25th until it was deactivated on September 9th.
Service History: Japan:

116th Independent Mixed Brigade 1945   建 *Ken* 27771 (6,222)

116th Brigade Headquarters   27772 (225)
- 702nd Independent Infantry Battalion   27773 (895)
- 703rd Independent Infantry Battalion   27774 (895)
- 704th Independent Infantry Battalion   27775 (895)
- 705th Independent Infantry Battalion   27776 (895)
- 706th Independent Infantry Battalion   27777 (895)
- 116th Brigade Artillery Unit   27778 (545)
- 116th Brigade Engineer Unit   27779 (565)
- 116th Brigade Signal Unit   27780 (224)

116th I.M.B.: Activated in Utsunomiya on July 10, 1945. Home station: Utsunomiya. With the 51st Army in Tamatsukuri, Ibaraki Prefecture from June 23rd until it was deactivated on October 10th.
Service History: Japan:

117th Independent Mixed Brigade 1945   東部 *Tobū* 27781 (7,198)

117th Brigade Headquarters   27782 (225)
- 707th Independent Infantry Battalion   27783 (895)
- 708th Independent Infantry Battalion   27784 (895)
- 709th Independent Infantry Battalion   27785 (895)
- 710th Independent Infantry Battalion   27786 (895)
- 711th Independent Infantry Battalion   27787 (895)
- 712th Independent Infantry Battalion   27788 (895)
- 117th Brigade Artillery Unit   27789 (814)
- 117th Brigade Engineer Unit   27790 (565)
- 117th Brigade Signal Unit   27791 (224)

117th I.M.B.: Activated in Tokyo on May 23, 1945. Home station: Tokyo. With the 53rd Army in Kumazu, Kanagawa Prefecture from June 23rd. Deactivated there Aug 20th.
Service History: Japan:

118th Independent Mixed Brigade 1945   堅塁 *Kenrui* 27792 (6,494)

118th Brigade Headquarters   13518 (225)
- 713th Independent Infantry Battalion   27793 (895)
- 714th Independent Infantry Battalion   27794 (895)
- 715th Independent Infantry Battalion   27795 (895)
- 716th Independent Infantry Battalion   27796 (895)
- 717th Independent Infantry Battalion   27797 (895)
- 18th Medium Artillery Regiment   2738 (642)   renamed 5/23/45
- 118th Brigade Artillery Unit   27798 (814)
- 118th Brigade Engineer Unit   27799 (565)
- 118th Brigade Signal Unit   27800 (224)

118th I.M.B.: Activated in Saganoseki on June 25, 1945, from former Hoyo Fortress Unit personnel. Home station: Ariake. With the 16th Area Army in Saganoseki, Ōita Prefecture from June 23rd until it was deactivated in Seheki on September 20th.
Service History: Japan:

119th Independent Mixed Brigade 1945   東旭 *Tokyoku* 21780 (6,073)

119th Brigade Headquarters   21781 (225)   activated 6/10/45
- 718th Independent Infantry Battalion   21782 (897)
- 719th Independent Infantry Battalion   21783 (897)
- 720th Independent Infantry Battalion   21784 (897)
- 721st Independent Infantry Battalion   21785 (897)
- 722nd Independent Infantry Battalion   21786 (897)
- 119th Brigade Artillery Unit   21787 (551)
- 119th Brigade Engineer Unit   21788 (572)
- 119th Brigade Signal Unit   21789 (224)

119th I.M.B.: Activated in Nagoya, Aichi on July 26, 1945. Home station: Shizuoka. With the 54th Army in Hamaoka from June 19th until it was deactivated in Shimizu on Sept 9th.
Service History: Japan: Shizuoka coastal defense.

120th Independent Mixed Brigade 1945   東天 *Joten* 21810 (6,326)

120th Brigade Headquarters   21811 (225) activated 6/10/45
- 723rd Independent Infantry Battalion   21812 (897)
- 724th Independent Infantry Battalion   21813 (897)
- 725th Independent Infantry Battalion   21814 (897)
- 726th Independent Infantry Battalion   21815 (897)
- 727th Independent Infantry Battalion   21816 (897)
- 120th Brigade Artillery Unit   21817 (820)
- 120th Brigade Engineer Unit   21818 (572)
- 120th Brigade Signal Unit   21819 (224)

120th I.M.B.: Activated in Nagoya, Aichi on July 26, 1945. Home station: Shizuoka. With the 54th Army in Shimizu from June 19th until it was deactivated in Omaezaki on September 10th.
Service History: Japan:

121st Independent Mixed Brigade 1945   菊水 *Kikusui* (6,051)

121st Brigade Headquarters	28236 (216)
• 728th Independent Infantry Battalion	28237 (897)
• 729th Independent Infantry Battalion	28238 (897)
• 730th Independent Infantry Battalion	28239 (897)
• 731st Independent Infantry Battalion	28240 (897)
• 732nd Independent Infantry Battalion	28241 (897)
• 121st Brigade Artillery Unit	28242 (551)
• 121st Brigade Engineer Unit	28243 (574)
• 121st Brigade Signal Unit	28244 (225)

121st I.M.B.: Activated in Zentsuji May 23, 1945. Home station: Tokushima. With the 55th Army in Tokushima from June 23rd. It was deactivated there on Sept 16th.
Service History: Japan:

122nd Independent Mixed Brigade 1945   堅城 *Kenjō* 13501 (6,719)

122nd Brigade Headquarters	13510 (225)
• 733rd Independent Infantry Battalion	28282 (897)
• 734th Independent Infantry Battalion	28283 (897)
• 735th Independent Infantry Battalion	28284 (897)
• 736th Independent Infantry Battalion	28285 (897)
• 737th Independent Infantry Battalion	28286 (897)
• 17th Medium Artillery Regiment	2739 (387)
• 122nd Brigade Artillery Unit	28287 (823)
• 122nd Brigade Engineer Unit	28288 (574)
• 122nd Brigade Signal Unit	28289 (225)

122nd I.M.B.: Activated in Nagasaki June 10, 1945, from former Nagasaki Fortress Unit personnel. Home station: Nagasaki. With the 16th Area Army in Nagasaki from June 23rd, where it was deactivated on September 18th.
Service History: Japan:

123rd Independent Mixed Brigade 1945   紀伊 *Kii* 28308 (6,948)

123rd Brigade Headquarters	28309 (216)
• 738th Independent Infantry Battalion	28310 (897)
• 739th Independent Infantry Battalion	28311 (897)
• 740th Independent Infantry Battalion	28312 (897)
• 741st Independent Infantry Battalion	28313 (897)

123rd Independent Mixed Brigade continued　　紀伊 *Kii*
- • 742nd Independent Infantry Battalion　　28314 (897)
- • 743rd Independent Infantry Battalion　　28315 (897)
- 123rd Brigade Artillery Unit　　28316 (551)
- 123rd Brigade Engineer Unit　　28317 (574)
- 123rd Brigade Signal Unit　　28318 (225)

<u>123rd I.M.B.</u>: Activated in Ōsaka July 10, 1945. Home station: Wakayama. Attached to the 15th Area Army in Gobō from June 19th where it was deactivated on Sept 8th.
<u>Service History</u>: Japan:

124th Independent Mixed Brigade 1945　　鬼城 *Keijo* 28358 (6,311)

124th Brigade Headquarters　　28359 (216)
- • 744th Independent Infantry Battalion　　28360 (897)
- • 745th Independent Infantry Battalion　　28361 (897)
- • 746th Independent Infantry Battalion　　28362 (897)
- • 747th Independent Infantry Battalion　　28363 (897)
- • 748th Independent Infantry Battalion　　28364 (897)
- 124th Brigade Artillery Unit　　28368 (823)
- 124th Brigade Engineer Unit　　28369 (574)
- 124th Brigade Signal Unit　　28370 (225)

<u>124th I.M.B.</u>: Activated in Hiroshima Aug. 3, 1945. Home station: Okayama. Attached to the 59th Army in Yamaguchi from June 19th, deactivated in Shimonoseki Sept 6th.
<u>Service History</u>: Japan:

125th Independent Mixed Brigade 1945　　敬天 *Keiten* (7,144)

125th Brigade Headquarters　　42326 (225)
- • 749th Independent Infantry Battalion　　42327 (897)
- • 750th Independent Infantry Battalion　　42328 (897)
- • 751st Independent Infantry Battalion　　42329 (897)
- • 752nd Independent Infantry Battalion　　42330 (897)
- • 753rd Independent Infantry Battalion　　42331 (897)
- • 754th Independent Infantry Battalion　　42332 (897)
- 125th Brigade Artillery Unit　　42333 (551)
- 125th Brigade Engineer Unit　　42334 (572)
- 125th Brigade Signal Unit　　42335 (224)
- 125th Brigade Medical Unit　　42336 (190)

<u>125th I.M.B.</u>: Activated in Ibusuki on May 23, 1945, from former 3rd Amphibious Brigade personnel. Home station: Kagoshima. With the 40th Army in Ibusuki, Kagoshima from June 19th. It was deactivated in Chiran on October 14th.
<u>Service History</u>: Japan:

126th Independent Mixed Brigade 1945   敬忠 *Keichū* (6,281)

126th Brigade Headquarters	42337 (180)
• 755th Independent Infantry Battalion	42338 (897)
• 756th Independent Infantry Battalion	42339 (897)
• 757th Independent Infantry Battalion	42340 (897)
• 758th Independent Infantry Battalion	42341 (897)
• 759th Independent Infantry Battalion	42342 (897)
• 126th Brigade Artillery Unit	42343 (820)
• 126th Brigade Engineer Unit	42344 (572)
• 126th Brigade Signal Unit	42345 (224)

126th I.M.B.: Activated in Kumamoto on May 23, 1945. Home station: Kumamoto. With the 16th Area Army in Amakusa from June 23rd. Deactivated in Sendai Oct 8th.
Service History: Japan:

127th Independent Mixed Brigade 1945   壮図 *Souto* 29110

127th Brigade Headquarters	29111 (225)
• 760th Independent Infantry Battalion	29112 (897)
• 761st Independent Infantry Battalion	29113 (897)
• 762nd Independent Infantry Battalion	29114 (897)
• 763rd Independent Infantry Battalion	29115 (897)
• 764th Independent Infantry Battalion	29116 (897)
• 127th Brigade Artillery Unit	29117 (820)
• 127th Brigade Engineer Unit	29118 (572)
• 127th Brigade Signal Unit	29119 (224)

127th I.M.B.: Activated in Seoul, Korea on May 23, 1945. Home station: Seoul. With the 17th Area Army in Pusan from June 19th until deactivated in SE Korea Aug 15th.
Service Record: Korea: Pusan garrison.

129th Independent Mixed Brigade 1945   高嶺 *Takane*

129th Brigade Headquarters	12637 (165)
• 807th Independent Infantry Battalion	12639 (800)
• 808th Independent Infantry Battalion	12677 (800)
• 809th Independent Infantry Battalion	12678 (800)
• 129th Brigade Rapid Firing Gun Unit	13606 (150)
• 129th Brigade Artillery Unit	13607 (650)
• 129th Brigade Ordinance Duty Unit	13609 (80)
• 129th Brigade Signal Unit	13608 (170)
• 129th Brigade Labor Unit	12679 (157)
• 129th Brigade Field Hospital	13610 (150)

129th I.M.B.: Activated on Urrup, Kuriles July 16, 1945, from former 1st Kurile Islands Group Headquarters (57th Inf. Group HQ) and local units. Home station: Sapporo.

129th I.M.B.: continued
With the 5th Area Army on Urrup from July 15th until it was deactivated on Sept 1st.
Service History: Japan: Urrup garrison.

130th Independent Mixed Brigade 1945   奮闘 *Hunto* 37501

130th Brigade Headquarters 7502 (233)
- 775th Independent Infantry Battalion 37503 (718)
- 776th Independent Infantry Battalion 37504 (718)
- 777th Independent Infantry Battalion 37505 (718)
- 778th Independent Infantry Battalion 37506 (718)
- 130th Brigade Artillery Unit 37507 (577)
- 130th Brigade Engineer Unit 37508 (288)
- 130th Brigade Signal Unit 37509 (207)
- 130th Brigade Raiding Unit 37510 (1,130)
- 130th Brigade Transport Unit 37511 (608)

130th I.M.B.: Activated in Fushin, Manchuria July 10, 1945, from units in Fushin. Home station: Fushin. With 3rd Area Army in Mukden until it was deactivated in Benxi on August 18th.
Service History: Manchuria: Fushin garrison.

131st Independent Mixed Brigade 1945   奮進 *Hunshin*

131st Brigade Headquarters 37512 (233)
- 779th Independent Infantry Battalion 37513 (718)
- 780th Independent Infantry Battalion 37514 (718)
- 781st Independent Infantry Battalion 37515 (718)
- 782nd Independent Infantry Battalion 37516 (718)
- 131st Brigade Raiding Battalion 37517 (1,130)
- 131st Brigade Artillery Unit 37518 (577)
- 131st Brigade Engineer Unit 37519 (288)
- 131st Brigade Transport Unit 37520 (608)
- 131st Brigade Signal Unit 37521 (207)

131st I.M.B.: Activated in Harbin, Manchuria July 10, 1945, from former 103rd Guard Unit personnel. Home station: Harbin. With the 4th Army in Harbin from July 10th until it was deactivated on August 18th.
Service History: Manchuria: Harbin garrison.

132nd Independent Mixed Brigade 1945   奮戦 *Hunshen* 37530

132nd Brigade Headquarters 37523/37522 (233)
- 783rd Independent Infantry Battalion 37524 (718)
- 784th Independent Infantry Battalion 37525 (718)
- 785th Independent Infantry Battalion 37526 (718)
- 786th Independent Infantry Battalion 37527 (718)

132nd Independent Mixed Brigade continued

- 132nd Brigade Raiding Battalion 37528 (1,130)
- 132nd Brigade Artillery Unit 37529 (577)
- 132nd Brigade Engineer Unit 37531 (288)
- 132nd Brigade Transport Unit 37533 (608)
- 132nd Brigade Signal Unit 37532 (207)

<u>132nd I.M.B.</u>: Activated in Tungning, Manchuria July 10, 1945, from 1st, 2nd and 11th Border Guard personnel. Home station: Tungning. With the 3rd Army in Tungning from July 30th until it was deactivated on August 18th.
<u>Service History</u>: Manchuria: Dongning Aug 9 1945.

133rd Independent Mixed Brigade 1945   福寿 *Hukuju* 37535

133rd Brigade Headquarters 37534 (233)
- 787th Independent Infantry Battalion 37535 (718)
- 788th Independent Infantry Battalion 37536 (718)
- 789th Independent Infantry Battalion 37537 (718)
- 790th Independent Infantry Battalion 37538 (718)
- 133rd Brigade Raiding Battalion 37539 (1,130)
- 133rd Brigade Artillery Unit 37540 (577)
- 133rd Brigade Engineer Unit 37541 (288)
- 133rd Brigade Signal Unit 37542 (207)
- 133rd Brigade Transport Unit 37543 (608)

<u>133rd I.M.B.</u>: Activated in Seoul, Korea on July 10, 1945. Home station: Pyonyang. With the 34th Army from July 10th in Wŏnsan where it was deactivated Aug 15th.
<u>Service History</u>: Korea: Wŏnsan garrison.

134th Independent Mixed Brigade 1945   奮励 *Hunrei* 37551

134th Brigade Headquarters 37552 (233)
- 791st Independent Infantry Battalion 37553 (718)
- 792nd Independent Infantry Battalion 37554 (718)
- 793rd Independent Infantry Battalion 37555 (718)
- 794th Independent Infantry Battalion 37556 (718)
- 134th Brigade Raiding Unit 37557 (1,130)
- 134th Brigade Artillery Unit 37558 (577)
- 134th Brigade Engineer Unit 37559 (288)
- 134th Brigade Signal Unit 37560 (207)
- 134th Brigade Transport Unit 37561 (608)

<u>134th I.M.B.</u>: Activated in Linkou, Manchuria on 10 July 1945, from units in Mukden and Chinhsien. Home station: Chinhsien. With the 3rd Area Army in Chengde, Manchuria until it was deactivated on August 18th.
<u>Service History</u>: Manchuria: Chengde garrison.

135th Independent Mixed Brigade 1945   不朽 *Hukyū* 37570

135th Brigade Headquarters   37562 (233)
- 795th Independent Infantry Battalion   37563 (718)
- 796th Independent Infantry Battalion   37564 (718)
- 797th Independent Infantry Battalion   37565 (718)
- 798th Independent Infantry Battalion   37566 (718)
- 135th Brigade Raiding Battalion   37567 (1,130)
- 135th Brigade Artillery Unit   37568 (577)
- 135th Brigade Engineer Unit   37569 (288)
- 135th Brigade Signal Unit   37571 (207)
- 135th Brigade Transport Unit   37572 (608)

135th I.M.B.: Activated in Aigun, Manchuria July 10, 1945, from former 5th, 6th and 7th Border Garrison Unit personnel. Home station: Heiho. With the 4th Army in Aigun until it was deactivated on Aug 18th.
Service History: Manchuria: Aigun Aug 9 1945.

136th Independent Mixed Brigade 1945   奮躍 *Hunyaku* 37580

136th Brigade Headquarters   7573 (233)
- 799th Independent Infantry Battalion   37574 (718)
- 800th Independent Infantry Battalion   37575 (718)
- 801st Independent Infantry Battalion   37576 (718)
- 802nd Independent Infantry Battalion   37577 (718)
- 136th Brigade Raiding Battalion   37578 (1,130)
- 136th Brigade Artillery Unit   37579 (577)
- 136th Brigade Transport Unit   37581 (608)
- 136th Brigade Signal Unit   37582 (207)

57th Cavalry Regiment   7215   from 57th Division

136th I.M.B.: Activated in Manchuria July 10, 1945, from former 5th, 6th and 7th Border Garrison Unit personnel. Home station: Nencheng. With the 4th Army in Payen, Manchuria until it was deactivated on August 18th.
Service History: Manchuria: Payen Aug 9 1945.

Cavalry Brigade

3rd Cavalry Brigade 1937　　　　　　　　　花 *Hana* 5001

3rd Cavalry Brigade Headquarters	5022
• 23rd Cavalry Regiment	5012
• 24th Cavalry Regiment	5014
• 3rd Cavalry Brigade Artillery Regiment	5018
• 3rd Cavalry Brigade Transport Unit	5025
• 3rd Cavalry Brigade Signal Unit	5013
• 3rd Cavalry Brigade Medical Unit	5027
• 3rd Cavalry Brigade Veterinary Unit	5029

3rd Cavalry Brigade: First activated April 1, 1909 then deactivated on July 7, 1937. Reactivated July 16, 1941. Home station: Hirosaki. With the 5th Army from July 7th until it was deactivated again on January 16, 1945 to establish the 77th I.M.B.
Service History: Manchuria:

Independent Armored Brigades

1st Independent Armored Brigade 1945　　　迫 *Sako* 13040 (3,113)

1st Armored Brigade Headquarters	13047 (80)
• 34th Tank Regiment	13041 (670)
• 35th Tank Regiment	13042 (670)
• 1st Armored Brigade Mobile Infantry Unit	13043 (592)
• 1st Armored Bgde Machine Cannon Unit	13044 (536)
• 1st Armored Brigade Engineer Unit	13045 (359)
• 1st Armored Brigade Maintenance Unit	13046 (289)

1st I.A.B.: Activated in northeast China Oct 11, 1944, from 2nd Armored Div personnel. Home Station: Osaka. With the 1st Area Army from Oct 11th until May 30, 1945 and 3rd Area Army in Mukden, Manchuria. Deactivated in Chengchiatum on Aug 18th
Service History: Manchuria: Mukden mobile reserve.

2nd Independent Armored Brigade 1945　　　顕 *Ken* (2,973)

2nd Armored Brigade Headquarters	12327 (70) deactivated 10/10/45
2nd Armored Brigade HQ Signal Section	12327 (139)
• 2nd Tank Regiment	12385 (1,157)
• 41st Tank Regiment	12328 (598)
• 2nd Armored Brigade Machine Cannon Unit	12329 (441)
• 2nd Armored Brigade Maintenance Unit	12330 (202)
• 2nd Armored Brigade Transport Unit	12331 (377)

2nd I.A.B.: Activated in Arima on April 6, 1945. Home station: Tsudanuma. With the

53rd Army in Odawara, Kanagawa Prefecture from Apr 8th until it was deactivated in Arima-mura on August 30th.
Service History: Japan:

3rd Independent Armored Brigade 1945   徹 *Tetu* (3,504)

3rd Armored Brigade Headquarters	12332 (70) deactivated 10/10/45
3rd Armored Brigade HQ Signal Section	12332 (139)
• 33rd Tank Regiment	12969 (1,200)
• 36th Tank Regiment	12333 (1,200)
• 3rd Armored Brigade Machine Cannon Unit	12334 (441)
• 3rd Armored Brigade Maintenance Unit	12335 (202)
• 3rd Armored Brigade Transport Unit	12336 (377)

3rd I.A.B.: Activated in Sarashina, Chiba April 6, 1945. Home station: Tsudanuma. Served with the 52nd Army in Chiba from Apr 8th until it was deactivated on Sept 7th.
Service History: Japan:

4th Independent Armored Brigade 1945   鑿 *Saku* 12499 (3,041)

4th Armored Brigade Headquarters	12491 (70)
4th Armored Brigade HQ Signal Section	12491 (139)
• 19th Tank Regiment	12449 (1,200)
• 42nd Tank Regiment	12492 (612)
• 4th Armored Brigade Machine Cannon Unit	12493 (441)
• 4th Armored Brigade Maintenance Unit	12494 (202)
• 4th Armored Brigade Transport Unit	12495 (377)

4th I.A.B.: Activated in Fukumaru, Japan April 6, 1945. Home station: Osaka. With the 16th Area Army from Apr 8th until the 21st and 56th Army in Fukumaru, Fukuoka until it was deactivated on October 5th.
Service History: Japan:

5th Independent Armored Brigade 1945   躍 *Yaku* (3,104)

5th Armored Brigade Headquarters	12580 (70)
5th Armored Brigade HQ Signal Section	12580 (139)
• 18th Tank Regiment	12532 (1,200) activated 8/28/44
• 43rd Tank Regiment	12549 (612)
• 5th Armored Brigade Machine Cannon Unit	12547 (440)
• 5th Armored Brigade Maintenance Unit	12574 (202)
• 5th Armored Brigade Transport Unit	12576 (377)

5th I.A.B.: Activated in Yinozaki, Fukuoka on April 6, 1945. Home station: Kurume. With the 57th Army in Honjo, Kagoshima from Apr 8th until it was deactivated in Yuinozaki on Sept 18th.
Service History: Japan:

6th Independent Armored Brigade 1945   闘 *Tō* (3,692)

6th Armored Brigade Headquarters   12590 (70)
6th Armored Brigade HQ Signal Section   12590 (139)
   • 37th Tank Regiment   12577 (1,200)
   • 40th Tank Regiment   12533 (1,200) activated 8/28/44
• 6th Armored Brigade Machine Cannon Unit   12548 (441)
• 6th Armored Brigade Maintenance Unit   12575 (202)
• 6th Armored Brigade Transport Unit   12578 (377)

<u>6th I.A.B.</u>: Activated in Okubo on April 6, 1945. Home station: Kurume. With the 57th Army in Kirishima, Kagoshima from Apr 8th until it was deactivated in Okubo on Sept 20th.
<u>Service History</u>: Japan:

7th Independent Armored Brigade 1945   琢 *Taku* (3,618)

7th Armored Brigade Headquarters   21404 (70) deactivated 10/10/45
   • 38th Tank Regiment   21405 (1,200)
   • 39th Tank Regiment   21415 (1,200)
• 7th Armored Brigade Machine Cannon Unit   21406 (441)
• 7th Armored Brigade Maintenance Unit   21407 (202)
• 7th Armored Brigade Transport Unit   21408 (377)

<u>7th I.A.B.</u>: Activated in Shimonaka on April 6, 1945. Home station: Hirosaki. With the 51st Army in Mito, Ibaraki from Apr 8th until deactivated in Shimonaka on Sept 7th.
<u>Service History</u>: Japan:

8th Independent Armored Brigade 1945   鋭敏 *Eibin* 12051 (3,805)

8th Armored Brigade Headquarters   12052 (70)   deactivated 9/22/45
   • 23rd Tank Regiment   12053 (1,041)
   • 24th Tank Regiment   12054 (675)
• 8th Armored Brigade Mobile Infantry Unit   12055 (828)
• 8th Armored Bgde Machine Cannon Unit   12056 (569)
• 8th Armored Brigade Engineer Unit   12057 (405)
• 8th Armored Brigade Maintenance Unit   12058 (292)
• 8th Armored Brigade Signal Unit   12059 (168)
• 8th Armored Brigade Transport Unit   12060 (292)   activated 5/9/45

<u>8th I.A.B.</u>: Activated in Japan on May 1, 1945, from former Armored Training Brigade personnel. Home station: Fukuoka. With the 13th Area Army in Aichi from Apr 28th until it was deactivated in Mikkanichi on September 8, 1945.
<u>Service History</u>: Japan:

Tank Training Brigade 1942

Unit	満州 Manshu	Barracks #	
Tank Training Brigade Headquarters	550	中部 9	
23rd Tank Regiment	530	中部 9	9/13/41
24th Tank Regiment	552	中部 9	11/21/41
Tank Training Brigade Infantry Unit	259	中部 85	
Tank Training Brigade Artillery Unit	401	中部 52	
Tank Training Brigade Engineer Unit	755	中部 15	
Tank Training Brigade Signal Unit	278	中部 88	
Tank Training Brigade Maint. Unit	282	中部 9	

Tank Training Brigade: Activated in North China on June 24, 1942 and attached to the 1st Mechanized Army in Siping, Manchuria on Jul 4th, Kwantung Army Oct 30, 1943 and deactivated Apr 28, 1945, became the 8th Ind. Armored Brigade on May 1st.
Service History: Training tank crews in Manchuria

9th Independent Armored Brigade 1945   奮迅 Hunjin 37606

9th Armored Brigade Headquarters	37605 (66)
• 51st Tank Regiment	37603 (876)
• 52nd Tank Regiment	37604 (876)

9th I.A.B.: Activated in Manchuria July 10, 1945, from former Heiriku Army Tank School personnel. Home station: Unknown. With the 44th Army in Ssupingchien, Manchuria until it was deactivated in Taonan on August 18, 1945.
Service History: Manchuria: Mukden.

Air Raiding Brigade (Paratroops and Glider Troops)

Created under Army Regulation Kō No.93, Dec. 1, 1941

1st Raiding Brigade 1944   帥 Sui, attach 6th Air A. 5/2/45

1st Infantry Raiding Brigade Headquarters	9944	2/30/41 to 8/31/45
• 1st Infantry Raiding Regiment	9945 (894)	11/30/44 to 8/26/45
• 2nd Infantry Raiding Regiment	9946 (894)	11/30/44 to 8/31/45
• 1st Raiding Tank Unit	19049 (465)	
• 1st Raiding Maintenance Unit	19051 (340)	
101st Airfield Company	19043 (174)	
102nd Airfield Company	19152 (179)	
103rd Airfield Company	19053 (179)	

1st Air Raiding Group: Activated between Dec 1, 1941 and Nov 30, 1944. Home station: Takanabe. With the 1st Air Army until Oct 22, 1944, Raiding Group HQ and the Air Raiding Group joined the 4th Air Army Nov. 28th in P.I., 3rd and 4th Air Raiding Regts arrived in Manila by Nov 11th, raided Burauen, Maj Gen Rikichi became commander of Kembu Army Group Jan 6, 1945. Sailed for the Philippines in early Dec losing

1st Air Raiding Brigade continued
men to attacks during the voyage. 1st Air Raiding Group HQ left Japan Dec 27th and landed on Clark Field Jan 8, 1945. U.S. Intelligence estimated each Air Raiding Regt had about 35 transport planes (Intelligence Bulletin Apr 7, 1945).
The 1st Inf Raiding Bgde remained in Japan with the 6th Air Army and took part in Yontan, Okinawa raid. Note: Activated in 1943 the 5th Air Raiding Regt was converted to the 2nd Glider Infantry Regt in Nov or Dec 1944.
Service History: Sumatra: Palembang Feb 14 1942. Philippines: Burauen Airfields Dec 6 1944, Clark Field Jan 25 1945. Okinawa: Yontan Field May 25 1945

Amphibious Brigades

3rd Amphibious Brigade 1943   轟 *Todoroki* (5,366)

3rd Amphibious Brigade Headquarters	12631 (120)
• 1st Amphibious Battalion	12632 (1,036)
• 2nd Amphibious Battalion	12633 (1,036)
• 3rd Amphibious Battalion	12634 (1,036)
• 3rd Amphib Bgde Machine Cannon Unit	12504 (76)
• 3rd Amphibious Brigade Tank Unit	12635 (66)
• 3rd Amphibious Brigade Engineer Unit	15590 (243)
• 3rd Amphibious Brigade Signal Unit	15591 (139)
• 3rd Amphibious Brigade Medical Unit	15592 (190)
• 3rd Amphibious Brigade Transport Unit	6155 (1,542)

3rd Amphibious Brigade: Activated in Kagoshima November 16, 1943, from former 1st Chishima Garrison Unit personnel. Home station: Asahikawa. With the Northern Army from Nov 16th until Mar 22, 1944, 27th Army until Jan 22, 1945, 5th Area Army until May 1st and 57th Army until it was deactivated on May 22nd and 23rd to form the 125th I.M.B. and 57th Shipping Engineer Regiment.
Service History: Japan:

4th Amphibious Brigade 1943   攘 *Harai* 15582 (5,366)

4th Amphibious Brigade Headquarters	15583 (120)
• 1st Amphibious Battalion	15584 (1,036)
• 2nd Amphibious Battalion	15585 (1,036)
• 3rd Amphibious Battalion	15586 (1,036)
• 4th Amphib. Bgde. Machine Cannon Unit	12505 (76)
• 4th Amphibious Brigade Tank Unit	12636 (66)
• 4th Amphibious Brigade Engineer Unit	15587 (243)
• 4th Amphibious Brigade Signal Unit	15588 (139)
• 4th Amphibious Brigade Medical Unit	15589 (190)
• 4th Amphibious Brigade Transport Unit	6156 (1,359) Aomori

4th Amphibious Brigade: Activated in the Kurile Islands Nov 16, 1943, from former 7th Infantry Group HQ personnel. Home station: Asahikawa. With the 27th Army from 4th

Amphibious Brigade continued
Mar 16th until Jan 22, 1945, 5th Area Army until June 1st. and 36th Army until it was deactivated in Saitama between September 7th and 15th.
Service History: Japan: mobile reserve.

Mobile Brigade

1st Mobile Brigade 1945   速 *Soku*

1st Mobile Brigade Headquarters   25221 満州835 (91)
1st Mobile Regiment   25222 満州750 (2,256)
2nd Mobile Regiment   25223 満州502 (2,256)
3rd Mobile Regiment   25224 満州752 (2,256)

1st Mobile Brigade: Activated in Manchuria March 1, 1944. Picked, elite troops (2nd Mobile Regt entirely officers and NCO). Home station: Osaka. Designed as a mobile striking force to take on special missions behind enemy lines. With the 3rd Army in Shihliping from June 13th. It was deactivated in Kirin, Manchuria on Aug 18, 1945.
Service History: Manchuria

Guard Brigades (Tokyo)

1st Guard Brigade 1945   幡 *Hata*

1st Brigade Headquarters   2122 (82)
• 1st Guard Infantry Battalion   3361 (639)
• 2nd Guard Infantry Battalion   3362 (639)
• 3rd Guard Infantry Battalion   4848 (639)
• 4th Guard Infantry Battalion   4849 (639)
• 5th Guard Infantry Battalion   6682 (639)
• 6th Guard Infantry Battalion   6683 (639)
• 1st Brigade Signal Unit   2119 (163)

1st Guard Brigade: Activated in Tokyo Feb 6, 1945. Home station: Tokyo. With the 12th Area Army until June 23rd and Tokyo Defense Army. Deactivated on September 3rd.

2nd Guard Brigade 1945   幡 *Hata*

2nd Brigade Headquarters   2118 (82)
• 7th Guard Infantry Battalion   7626 (639)
• 8th Guard Infantry Battalion   7627 (639)
• 9th Guard Infantry Battalion   7628 (639)
• 10th Guard Infantry Battalion   7629 (639)
• 11th Guard Infantry Battalion   6479 (639)

- 12th Guard Infantry Battalion　　　　6480 (639)
- 2nd Brigade Signal Unit　　　　　　12472 (163)

<u>2nd Guard Brigade</u>: Activated in Tokyo Feb 6, 1945. Home station: Tokyo. With the 12th Area Army until June 23rd and Tokyo Defense Army until it was deactivated on September 3rd.

3rd Guard Brigade 1945　　　　　　　幡 *Hata*

3rd Brigade Headquarters　　　　　　14234 (82)
- 13th Guard Infantry Battalion　　　　15070 (639)
- 14th Guard Infantry Battalion　　　　15071 (639)
- 15th Guard Infantry Battalion　　　　15072 (639)
- 16th Guard Infantry Battalion　　　　9776 (639)
- 17th Guard Infantry Battalion　　　　9777 (639)
- 18th Guard Infantry Battalion　　　　7068 (639)
- 3rd Brigade Signal Unit　　　　　　13563 (169)

<u>3rd Guard Brigade</u>: Activated in Tokyo Feb 6, 1945. Home station: Mizonokuchi. With the 12th Area Army until June 23rd and Tokyo Defense Army until it was deactivated on September 3rd.

Fortress Units

Tokyo Bay Fortress Unit 1908　　　　房 *Bou*

Tokyo Bay Fortress Headquarters　　　　13300 (203)
Tokyo Bay Fortress Artillery Regiment　　2112 (603)
1st Tokyo Bay Fortress Artillery Unit　　　13367 (603)
2nd Tokyo Bay Fortress Artillery Unit　　　13368 (483)
1st Tokyo Bay Fortress Engineer Unit　　　4104 (264)
2nd Tokyo Bay Fortress Engineer Unit　　　4105 (264)
Tokyo Bay Fortress Signal Unit　　　　　2121 (473)

<u>Tokyo Bay Fortress</u>: Activated by Tokyo Bay Dec 21, 1908 completed mobilizing Nov 8, 1941. With the Eastern District Army until Feb 6, 1945 and 12th Area Army until June 19th when it became the Tokyo Bay Fortress Group to provide security for Tokyo Bay.

Tsushima Fortress Garrison 1924　　　睦 *Mutsumi*

Tsushima Fortress Headquarters　　　　No #
Tsushima Fortress Hvy Artillery Regiment　2736
1st Tsushima Fortress Infantry Battalion　　2730
2nd Tsushima Fortress Infantry Battalion　　2731

Tsushima Fortress Garrison continued	睦 *Mutsumi*
3rd Tsushima Fortress Infantry Battalion	2732
4th Tsushima Fortress Infantry Battalion	15134
5th Tsushima Fortress Infantry Battalion	15135
6th Tsushima Fortress Infantry Battalion	15136

<u>Tsushima Fortress</u>: Activated in Tsushima, Western Japan on Feb 4, 1924. With the Army General Staff from July 7, 1937 until Aug 2nd, Western District Army until Feb 6, 1945 and 16th Area Army until the war ended.

<u>Other fortress garrisons</u>: Amami Ōshima Fortress, Chichijima Fortress, Eikō Bay Fortress, Funauki Fortress, Fusan Fortress, Hoyo Fortress, Iki Fortress, Kitachishima Fortress, Kojima Fortress, Maizuru Fortress, Mototaka Fortress, Nagasaki Fortress, Nakagusuku Bay Fortress, Rashin Fortress, Reisui Fortress, Ryojun Fortress, Shimonoseki Fortress, Soya Fortress, Takao Fortress, Tsugaru Fortress, Yura Fortress.

Locale Defense Unit

Muroran Guard Unit 1945	達 *Tatsu*
Muroran Defense Unit Headquarters	9580 (38)
8th Independent Guard Unit	12638 (1,085)
141st Anti-Aircraft Regiment	9557 (1,791)
2nd Company, 26th Infantry Regiment	9203
355th Specially Established Guard Battalion	unknown (550)

<u>Muroran Guard Unit</u>: Activated in Muroran, Hokkaido on Mar 19, 1945. It was assigned to defend the Muroran Iron and Steel Works under 5th Area Army control. The U.S. bombarded the factory grounds on July 15, 1945 (4 battleships, 2 cruisers and 8 destroyers fired 300 to 400 shells). The 33rd Guard Battalion became the 8th Independent Guard Unit on Feb 28, 1945.

End of Brigades

Chapter 4

The Rules and Regulations for Unit Codes

Beginning on September 1, 1937, Imperial Headquarters ordered overseas forces to become known by their commanders' surnames in order to conceal common unit names and deployed strengths. Mixed battle group identification would become vague, based on size they were to be called *Shitai*, *Heidan* or *Butai*, with *Tai* being a company sized unit or smaller. Regular forces in Japan continued with their "street" identities until July 10, 1940 when *Detailed Rules for Army Peacetime Formation* were enacted and they too were assigned code names.

On Sept 10, 1940 the army adopted *1941 Detailed Rules for Army Mobilization Plan*, in part to rid itself of the consequences of replacing one unit commander's name with another. Army and division commanders in Japan, Korea, Formosa and Manchuria were assigned kanji names of one or two characters called *Mojifu*. These major units were also assigned a block of sequential code numbers called *tsusho bango*. Commanders attached the unit's kanji name to one number for each sub-unit under his command. Together the code kanji and number were called a unit's *Tsushogo*, its secret identity, which is how it wasto be known in the field for security purposes.

On Nov 14, 1940 the *Rules on Code Names for Units in Manchuria* came into use as a means of concealing the transition. Under the new rules the prefix (満州) *Manshū* was adopted for use by all units activated in Manchuria. Many units ended up with two code numbers, a two or three digit one for Manchuria and another for elsewhere.

Prolonged fighting in China made it necessary to introduce controls for mobilizing, alternating and deactivating units in each area.

Matters on the Code Names of Units in China allowed for certain kanji code names and numbers to be distributed to each army in China. Commanders with subordinate

divisions and independent brigades in turn affixed them to units requiring them.
To maintain coherence units were organized one after another under the parent unit's kanji code name, this was carried out according to already prescribed rules or by an independent army order. Service/support units used their major unit's code name.
In 1941, following the initial *Tsushogo* distribution, Mobilization Administrators were assigned to each organizing body, these functionaries were responsible for issuing code numbers to new units in the process of being activated.
In the Pacific war against America *Tsushogo* eventually proved insufficient. On Feb 26, 1944, *Matters on the Code Names of Units that are Subordinate to, or Commanded by, the Southern Army* came into use. Units were ordered to stop using their original designations and begin using newly issued code kanji associated with areas they were stationed in.
In the autumn of 1944 *Detailed Rules of Delegated Martial Order in the Southern Area* was published. These rules gave army commanders the power to issue their own code kanji names to new units being activated in their areas. This effectively did away with the old system of assignment, based on Nov 1940 detailed rules or by an army order, in the field.
On Apr 20, 1945 the *Army Units War Time Code Name Rules* were overhauled. To conceal information in China and the southern areas army commanders could select a different code kanji to identify any unit for outward communication. In Japan the use of the same number by two or more units with different code names was abolished to prevent mistakes. All the rules regarding code numbers that had been made up to this point were collected and printed in one document. The army replacement system in Japan was reformed and numbers under 9999 that had already been issued were omitted from reuse to avoid confusion.
In lists where the 41st Army's subordinate unit code numbers remained unknown, or perhaps unreported late in the war but added after, they were designated 41A.
The early practice of naming units after their commanders' didn't entirely go away. Detachments naturally continued with the system. Battalions and companies, which were part of the permanent establishment of a division, brigade or regiment, were also identified by their commanders' name with the suffix *Butai* or *Tai*, which means unit. Chapter 2, Article 6 of *Rules on the War Time Code Names of Army Units* provided a rule for that.
Many code numbers have become orphaned or lost for reasons that include being merged with other units, deactivated before 1945 and destroyed or lost documents.
For local communications four-digit code numbers were sometimes abbreviated to their last two digits.
Example: 21st Division units (討 *Utsu*) all begin with 42, HQ being 4231. In local communications it might be referred to as 31, 62nd I.R. as 34, 21st Engr. Regt as 38.

Rules on the Wartime Code Names of Army Units: (See Note p. 291)
Chapter 1. General rules:
Article 1. This rule, is based on Article 41 (and others) of the *Army Mobilization Plan Order*, and provides the necessary protocols for code-naming army units.
Article 2. Code names are mainly used to conceal the strength, formation, arm of service, duty, use and the common name of army units.
Chapter 2. The Formation of Code Names:

Article 3. A unit's code name is usually a code number crowned with the ideographic sign of its parent corps.

Article 4. The code number and the ideographic sign crowning it shall be proper to the corps. A corps of lower rank will not use the code number of higher rank corps.

Article 5. The code name of a unit that has no proper ideographic sign, and that is placed into an order of battle under the control of an Area Army or Army shall have its code number crowned with the ideographic sign of the Area Army or Army concerned.

Before joining an order of battle and before the unit is taken into the formation of an Area Army or Army, the unit's code number will be crowned with the ideographic sign of its Mobilization Administrator. The ideographic code names of Army Districts (incl. Divisional Districts) shall crown the code numbers where the unit is located.

Article 6. The name of every regiment, battalion or company within a unit will be the surname of its commander. Companies contained within a regiment will omit the name of its battalion (commander) from references.

Article 7. The code name of a unit that does not use a code name in the usual manner and specially established units will use their common names, except those whose code names are shown in the annexed lists.

Article 8. Specially provided code names are shown in the annexed lists No. 1 and No. 2.

Chapter 3. Use of Code Names:

Article 9. Wartime army units, except those shown in Article 10 will use the code names provided under these rules.

Article 10. The common names of units will only be used as follows:

Military registers

The register of names in Wartime

The register of names concerning military men in their homes

The register of names concerning levies

Sick bed journals

The register of names concerning patients in hospital

Medical diagnoses

Certificates of recognition

Certificates of fact

Documents concerning personal affairs as follows:
- Enlisted soldiers service records
- Register of names concerning promotion by selection
- Register of names concerning candidates
- The standings of cadets
- Career details
- Staff lists
- Appointments and dismissals concerning ranks, postings and services
- Documents concerning pensions, conferment of rank and decorations
- Documents of results
- Documents concerning photographs presented to the Imperial House
- Register of names dedicated to the Yasakuni Shrine
- Secret military documents and top-secret articles

Article 11. Units stationed in Manchuria (including units in Kwantung) will prefix 満州 *Manshū* to their names for outside communication instead of using their proper (unit) ideographic sign.

Article 12. Units in the China Expeditionary Army and units subordinate to the commander of the Southern Expeditionary Army, including those under their command as well as those commanded provisionally in areas of operation, shall use the ideographic signs decided by China Expeditionary Army or Southern Expeditionary Army commanders instead of their proper (unit) signs for outward communication.

Article 13. When a unit that has its own code name (under homeland peacetime mobilization) is mobilized (reorganized for war), it shall give up its code name for the one provided under the rules at the time it completes mobilization.

Chapter 4. The Allotment of Code Numbers:

Article 14. The number for a unit, except specially appointed numbers, will usually be assigned by its mobilizing administrator without waiting for orders to sanction it. For this purpose units will be allotted a number from the code numbers shown in Annexed List No. 2.

Article 15. When a mobilization administrator is not allotted any code numbers in accordance with the above rules, an administrator of superior rank who is allotted code numbers will assign one of these to the newly mobilized unit.

Chapter 5. Miscellaneous Rules:

Article 16. The Army District commander or the Army commander (in foreign lands, a mobilization administrator of high rank) may decide the code name of a unit to which the provisions cannot be applied, he must use the provisions as much as possible. In this case the administrator will report the circumstances to the Army Minister and the Chief of the General Staff, and inform the units concerned as soon as possible.

Article 17. Commanders of the Kwantung Army, China Expeditionary Army and the Southern Expeditionary Army will provide detailed reports on code names and numbers.

Article 18. The armies and divisions to whom code numbers have been allotted will compile a list of code numbers and the units they were distributed to.

Article 19. The divisions with distributed code numbers are listed on Annexed Paper No. 4. The commanders of units to which code numbers were allotted, as prescribed in the preceding paragraphs, may select the necessary articles in the present provisions (to the minimum necessary) copy them and distribute them to his subordinate units (the units should be above the grade of brigade headquarters or of the same grade).

Article 20. Each unit shall, if necessary, make its code name known to public offices in its district with which it has close relations.

When code names are used in mail, by telegraph and so on, they shall be used with the name of the district it is sent from (e.g., dispatched in North China or from Burma, etc.) in the case of overseas units and the name of the location (e.g., Tokyo-to or Osaka Prefecture, etc.) in he case of homeland communication.

Article 21. The code names of units are to be used on the 'list of the date of completion of organization' and on the list of districts in charge of home affairs (replacement affairs) which the administration of mobilization reports in accordance with Articles 499 and 502 of the *(1941) Detailed Rules of the Order of Military Mobilization Plan*. In addition, whenever the mobilization is concluded or code numbers are changed, a report will be made to the War Minister and the Chief of the General Staff by telegraph, the units concerned will be informed as well.

Chapter 4

Charter documents on the rules for code naming army units:
1 - July 10, 1940, *Detailed Rules of Army Peacetime Formation*
2 - September 10, 1940, 1941 *Detailed Rules for Army Mobilization Plan*
3 - November 14, 1940, *The Rules on Code Names of Units in Manchuria*
4 - October 9, 1942, *Matters on the Code Names of Units in China*
5 - 1942, *Main Points for the Reformation of Military Preparedness*
6 - February 26, 1944, *Matters on the Code Names of Units that are Subordinate or Commanded by the Southern (Expeditionary) Army*
7 - Autumn 1944, *Detailed Rules of Delegated Martial Order in the Southern Area*

Note: The *Rules on the Wartime Code Names of Army Units* (JACAR code C12121215800, document pages 10 to 19) is reworded to provide clarity where the original document appears to be lacking it. Every effort has been made to adhere to the original meaning of its chapters and articles.

Type 92 heavy machine gun and crew (author)

Index of Sequential Unit Code Numbers
for Japan and the Territories

"On account of insufficient materials, completeness may not be expected."
1st Demobilization Bureau, Dec. 26, 1945

Terms and Abbreviations:
Code names as written are the proper translation of kanji associated with the organization they appear with. This is noteworthy because a single kanji may have a number of pronunciations and meanings. The Romaji (English sounds) are as found in JACAR.
Field Medium Artillery Units are written as 'Field "Heavy" Artillery' Units in Japanese. Because they were armed with mid-range 75mm cannon, 105mm howitzers and were relatively mobile the U.S. practice of referring to them as "Medium" has been adoptd here. In translating unit types the Japanese has been respected as much as possible to preserve flavor and meaning.
'Specially Established' doesn't mean "special" in a western sense (Special Forces) but rather is a lesser class of unit usually raised to fill a pressing need.
Abbreviations found in the text: Sp. = Special, Est. = Established, Co., Coy = Company, Btn = Battalion, HQ = Headquarters, Ind. = Independent, Maint. = Maintenance, L.of C./L.o.C. = Line of Communications (rear area units)
Some units have no page number. These may be incomplete entries due to space, ghost units (existed but are now unverifiable) or a mistake by the author. In any case it was decided to leave the entry for the sake of a later point of reference.

Japanese/English - Numbers Conversion Table

0	1	2	3	4	5	6	7	8	9	10
〇	一	二	三	四	五	六	七	八	九	十

Chapter 4

Abbreviations (in parentheses) Identifying Parent Organization(s):
Army (A) preceded by a number is an army; (2A) is 2nd Army
Area Army (AA)
General Army (GA)
Air General Army (AGA)
Imperial General Headquarters (GHQ)
Air Army (AirA)
Air Division (AirDiv)
Burma Area Army (BAA)
China Expeditionary Army (CA)
Continental Railway (CRR)
Japan (homeland) Railway (RR)
Kembu Army Group, the Philippines (KeG)
Mongolia Garrison Army (MGA)
Army Shipping Corps, Japan (SC)
Southern Army Shipping (SoS)
Southern Army Railway (SRR)
6th Air Division under the 18th Army in New Guinea (6AirDiv 18A)
Southern Expeditionary Army (SA)
Tokyo Bay Army (TBC)
Tokyo Defense Army (TDA)
I.M.B. = Independent Mixed Brigade
I.I.G.B. = Independent Infantry Garrison/Guard Battalion

<u>Japan's Army Districts</u>:
North (*Hokubu* 北部) Army District (HoB)
Northeast (*Tohoku* 東北) Army District (ToH)
East (*Tobu* 東部) Army Distinct (ToB)
East Sea (*Tokai* 東海) Army District (ToK)
Central (*Chubu* 中部) Army District (ChB)
Central Country (*Chugoku* 中国) Army District (ChG)
Shikoku (*Shikoku* 四国) Army District (Shikoku)
West (*Seibu* 西部) Army District (SeB)
Korea (*Chosen* 朝鮮) Divisional District (KoD)
Formosa (*Wan* 湾) Army District (FoD)
Kwantung Army (滿州, 滿, 德) also called the *Kantō* Army. Some units have the 2 or 3 digit code #s issued in Manchuria in addition to the standard Tsushogo code. (KA)

Code numbers:
DN • Distributed Numbers: An activating unit was assigned a code # from a (DN) block of #'s. Units listed twice may indicate a detached element, different units that were issued the same number or a unit converted to another type or joined another organization and kept its its original number.
As war progressed certain independent mixed brigades were converted to divisions. At the time, in some cases, they also received new code names and numbers while retaining their formal names; those units may also be listed twice.
DN • Apr 1945 distribution: From blocks of numbers distributed in April 1945
DN • not distributed: Does **<u>not</u>** mean numbers in this block were never used.

0	1	2	3	4	5	6	7	8	9	10
〇	一	二	三	四	五	六	七	八	九	十

Code # - Kanji Code - Formal Unit Name - (Affiliation) - Page No.

2-3 東部 Konoe 1st Infantry Brigade, 1st Guards Division (ToB) - 203
4 東部 Konoe 1st Cavalry Regiment, 1st Guards Division (ToB) - 203
7-8 東部 Konoe 2nd Infantry Brigade, 1st Guards Division (ToB) - 203
13 東部 Konoe 1st Field Artillery Regiment, 1st Guards Division (ToB) - 203
20 東部 Konoe 1st Mountain Artillery Battalion, 1st Guards Division (ToB) - 203
30 徳 Kwantung Army Military Police Headquarters (KA) - 153
31/9913 台湾 8th Air Regiment (8AirDiv, 10AA) - 44
32 台湾 14th Air Regiment (8AirDiv, 10AA) - N/A
34 台湾 4th Air Brigade Headquarters (Formosa) - N/A
35 台湾 104th Ind. Secondary Air Training Brigade HQ (8AirDiv, 10AA) - 45
41 誠 23rd Independent Air Squadron (8AirDiv 10AA) - 44
42 誠 20th Secondary Air Training Unit (8AirDiv, 10AA) - 45
43 誠 21st Secondary Air Training Unit (8AirDiv, 10AA) - 45
44 誠 22nd Secondary Air Training Unit (8AirDiv, 10AA) - 45
70 北部 20th Air Brigade Headquarters, 1st Air Div (5AA) - N/A
71 達 Maizuru Fortress Heavy Artillery Regiment (15AA) - 96
71 達 Tsugaru Fortress Heavy Artillery Regiment (5AA) - 52
72 北部 54th Flying Regiment (1AirDiv 5AA) - 56
75 中部 Yura Fortress Headquarters (15AA) - 96
75 中部 5th Heavy Artillery Regiment (15AA) - 96
81 東部 Konoe 1st Engineer Regiment, 1st Guards Division (ToB) - 203
81/9102 朝鮮 6th Air Regiment (5AirA) - 195
82 東部 Konoe 1st Division Signal Unit, 1st Guards Division (ToB) - 203
86 線 16th Railway Regiment (RR) - 139
87 線 17th Railway Regiment (RR) - 139
91/5686 達 24th Anti-Aircraft Regiment (5AA) - 51
91 線 Railway Training Group Headquarters (RR) - 139
100 北部 27th Army Headquarters (5AA) - became 15th Area Army HQ
100 中部 Army Airfield Construction Training Department (2AirTrainingBde) - 130
113 中部 105th Air Training Regiment/5th Air Training Unit (ChB) - N/A
114 満州 Shinkyo (now Changchun) 2nd Army Hospital (KA) - 155
115 東部 17th Air Brigade Headquarters (ToB) - N/A
121 中部 18th Air Brigade Headquarters (ChB) - N/A
122 西部 19th Air Brigade Headquarters (SeB) - N/A
126 満州 (拓) 1st Armored Brigade (3AA) - 278
128 西部 Western District Army Artillery Command (16AA)
137 満州 and 21086 岩 Dongning (66th Kanto) 2nd Army Hospital (3A)
145 中部 Maizuru Fortress Headquarters (15AA) - 96
200/1046 北部 1st Air Division Headquarters (5AA) - 56
201 朝鮮 Masan Heavy Artillery Regiment Replacement Unit (KoD) - 186
202 / 32821 朝鮮 Ranam 1st Infantry Replacement Unit (KoD) - 187
205 築 23rd Independent Engineer Battalion (17AA) - N/A
206 朝鮮 Korean Army Training Unit (KoD) - 186

207 朝鮮 15th Field Heavy Artillery Regiment Replacement Unit (KoD) - 186
208 / 32823 朝鮮 Ranam Artillery Replacement Unit (KoD) - 187
210 / 32824 朝鮮 Ranam Engineer Replacement Unit (KoD) - 187
211 / 32825 朝鮮 Ranam Signals Replacement Unit (KoD) - 187
212 / 32826 朝鮮 Ranam Transport Replacement Unit (KoD) - 187
215 朝鮮 Taegu 1st Infantry Replacement Unit (KoD) - N/A
216 朝鮮 Taegu 2nd Infantry Replacement Unit (KoD) - N/A
217 朝鮮 Taegu Artillery Replacement Unit (KoD) - N/A
218 朝鮮 Taegu Engineer Replacement Unit (KoD) - N/A
219 朝鮮 Taegu Signals Replacement Unit (KoD) - N/A
220 朝鮮 Taegu Transport Replacement Unit (KoD) - N/A
222 朝鮮 Seoul 1st Infantry Replacement Unit (KoD) - 189
223 朝鮮 Seoul 2nd Infantry Replacement Unit (KoD) - 189
224 朝鮮 Seoul 3rd Infantry Replacement Unit (KoD) - 189
226 朝鮮 Seoul Artillery Replacement Unit (KoD) - 189
227 朝鮮 Seoul Engineer Replacement Unit (KoD) - 189
229 朝鮮 Seoul Signals Replacement Unit (KoD) - 189
230 朝鮮 Seoul Transport Replacement Unit (KoD) - 189
232 朝鮮 Guanzhou 1st Infantry Replacement Unit (KoD) - 191
233 朝鮮 Guanzhou 2nd Infantry Replacement Unit (KoD) - 191
234 朝鮮 Guanzhou Artillery Replacement Unit (KoD) - 191
235 朝鮮 Guanzhou Engineer Replacement Unit (KoD) - 191
236 朝鮮 Guanzhou Signals Replacement Unit (KoD) - 191
237 朝鮮 Guanzhou Transport Replacement Unit (KoD) - 191
242 朝鮮 Pyongyang 1st Infantry Replacement Unit (KoD) - 188
243 朝鮮 Ranam 2nd Infantry Replacement Unit (KoD) - 187
244 朝鮮 Pyongyang 2nd Infantry Replacement Unit (KoD) - 188
247 朝鮮 Pyongyang Artillery Replacement Unit (KoD) - 188
248 朝鮮 Pyongyang Engineer Replacement Unit (KoD) - 188
249 朝鮮 Pyongyang Signals Replacement Unit (KoD) - 188
250 朝鮮 Pyongyang Transport Replacement Unit (KoD) - 188
251 西部 59th Air Regiment (SeB) - N/A
252/18437 東部 116th Airfield Battalion (ToB) - 134
277 滿州 104th Guard Headquarters (4A) - 159
308 滿州 201st Airfield Battalion (2AirA, KA) - 163
358 滿州 / 1226 城 1st Engineer Unit Headquarters (5A) - 172
372 滿州 / 26853 光 84th Kanto Army Hospital (4A) - 159
392 滿州 Ajō Army Hospital (KA) - 155
449 滿州 12th Cavalry Regiment, 12th Division (10AA) - 206
467 滿州 Tungning 1st Army Hospital (3A) - 171
497 先 91st Division (5AA) - 218
500 師 Air General Army Headquarters (AGA) - 127
501 空 51st Air Division Headquarters (AGA) - 129
502 紺 52nd Air Division Headquarters (AGA) - 130
503 宙 53rd Air Division Headquarters, air division omitted (AGA) - 196
512 師 2nd Air Training Brigade Headquarters (AGA) - 130
513 紺 3rd Air Training Brigade Headquarters (52AirDiv, AGA) - 130

0	1	2	3	4	5	6	7	8	9	10
〇	一	二	三	四	五	六	七	八	九	十

514 空 4th Air Training Brigade Headquarters (51Air Div AGA) - 129
520 紺 1st Advanced Flight Training Unit (52AirDiv AGA) - 130
521 宙 2nd Advanced Flight Training Unit (53AirDiv 5AirA) - 196
522 誠 3rd Advanced Flight Training Squadron (8AirDiv 10AA) - 45
523 空 8th Advanced Flight Training Unit (51AirDiv AGA) - 129
524 空 10th Advanced Flight Training Unit (51AirDiv AGA) - 129
525 空 11th Advanced Flight Training Unit (51AirDiv AGA) - 129
526 宙 12th Advanced Flight Training Unit (53AirDiv 5AirA) - 196
527 宙 23rd Advanced Flight Training Unit (53AirDiv 5AirA) - 196
529 宙 25th Advanced Flight Training Unit (53AirDiv 5AirA) - 196
530 空 1st Secondary Flight Training Unit (51AirDiv AGA) - 129
531 紺 4th Secondary Flight Training Unit (52AirDiv AGA) - 130
533 空 10th Secondary Flight Training Unit (51AirDiv AGA) - 129
534 宙 11th Secondary Flight Training Unit (53AirDiv 5AirA) - 196
535 宙 19th Secondary Flight Training Unit (53AirDiv 5AirA) - 196
536 宙 30th Secondary Flight Training Unit (53AirDiv 5AirA) - 196
537 紺 39th Secondary Flight Training Unit (52AirDiv AGA) - 130
538 空 40th Secondary Air Training Unit (51AirDiv AGA) - 129
539 宙 41st Secondary Flight Training Unit (53AirDiv AGA) - 196
540 紺 Part of 6th Advanced Flight Training Unit (52AirDiv AGA) - 130
540 空 Part of 6th Advanced Flight Training Unit (51AirDiv AGA) - 129
543 宙 9th Flight Training Unit (53AirDiv 5AirA) - 196
550 師 7th Air Signals Regiment (1AirA AGA) - 131
551 師 31st Air Signals Regiment (2nd Air Training Bgde AGA) - 130
552 師 1st Air Intelligence Regiment (2nd Air Training Bgde AGA) - 130
554 師 1st Air Navigation Regiment (2nd Air Training Bgde AGA) - 130
555 師 1st Meteorological Regiment (2nd Air Training Bgde AGA) - 130
560 紺 Tokorozawa Secondary Flight Training Unit (52AirDiv AGA) - 130
561 紺 Tachikawa Secondary Flight Training Unit (52AirDiv AGA) - 130
562 紺 Hachinohe Secondary Flight Training Unit (52AirDiv AGA) - 130
563 空 1st Gifu Flight Training Unit (51AirDiv AGA) - 129
563 紺 24th Advanced Flight Training Unit (52AirDiv AGA) - 130
564 空 2nd Gifu Flight Training Unit (51AirDiv AGA) - 130
565 空 Nara Flight Training Unit (51AirDiv AGA) - 130
570 宙 1st Air Training Unit (53AirDiv 5AirA) - 196
571 空 3rd Flight Training Unit (51AirDiv AGA) - 129
573 空 5th Flight Training Unit (51AirDiv AGA) - 129
574 空 6th Flight Training Unit (51Air Div AGA) - 129
575 空 7th Flight Training Unit (51AirDiv AGA) - 129
576 空 8th Flight Training Unit (51AirDiv AGA) - 129
577 空 9th Flight Training Unit (51AirDiv AGA) - 129
579 師 13th Flight Training Unit (2nd Air Training Bgde AGA) - 130
580 宙 14th Secondary Flight Training Unit (53AirDiv 5AirA) - 196
581 師 1st Army Air Education Unit (2nd Air Training Bgde AGA) - 130

767 満州 / 8365 羽 3rd Air Intelligence Regiment (2AirA) - 162
800 満州 / 8212 羽 2nd Air Army Headquarters (2AirA) - 162
815 満州 Kwantung Army Intendance Dept Training Unit (KA) - N/A
875 満州 Shinkyo (now Changchun) 1st Army Hospital (KA) - 155
986 満州 7th Kwantung Army Prison Office - N/A
996 満州 and 8362 羽 2nd Air Signal Regiment (2AirA KA) - 162
DN • 1000-49 Tokyo Divisional District
1000 風 Special Air Control Group (Air Command, 6AirA, AGA) - N/A
1013 遠征 17th Field Medium Artillery Regiment (44A 3AA) - 178
1014 宗 10th Field Medium Artillery Regiment (56A 16AA) - 116
1020 断 5th Artillery Intelligence Regiment (53A 12AA) - 73
1022 城 8th Independent Heavy Artillery Battalion (5A 1AA) - 172
1023 睦 9th Independent Heavy Artillery Battalion (16AA) - 113
1027 達 23rd Independent Field Anti-Aircraft Company (5AA) - 51
1040 天翔 10th Air Division Headquarters (10AirDiv 1AirA) - 134
1041 天鷲 11th Air Division Headquarters (11AirDiv AGA) - 129
1042 風天 12th Air Division Headquarters (12AirDiv 6AirA) - 138
1045 鏑 1st Air Division, # not a unit (5AA) - 56
1046 鏑 1st Air Division Headquarters (5AA) - 56
DN • 1050-99 東部 *Tobu* Army District
DN • 1050–99, 晴 *Hare*, 1st Anti-Aircraft Division, Apr. 1945 distribution
1050-62 晴 1st Anti-Aircraft Division (12AA) - 255
1063 逐 2nd Anti-Aircraft Division (13AA) - 256
1063 逐 47th Independent Anti-Aircraft Battalion, 2nd AAA Div (13AA) - 256
1064 進 48th Independent Anti-Aircraft Battalion (11AA) - 61
1065 晴 49th Independent Anti-Aircraft Battalion, 1st AAA Div (12AA) - 255
1099 晴 1st Anti-Aircraft Division (12AA) - 255
DN • 1100-49 薩 *Satsu*, Kumamoto Divisional District
DN • 1200-99 徳 *Toku*, Kwantung (Kantō) Army
1203 錦 11th Div. Disease Pretension and Water Purification Unit (55A) - 205
1204 剣 12th Div. Disease Pretension and Water Purification Unit (10AA) - 206
1207 山 24th Div. Disease Prevention and Water Purification Unit (32A) - 206
1208 国 25th Div. Disease Prevention and Water Purification Unit (16AA) - 207
1209 豊 28th Div. Disease Prevention and Water Purification Unit (32A) - 207
1210 建 7th Artillery Headquarters (51A) - 71
1211 捷 8th Artillery Headquarters (52A) - 72
1214 満州 2nd Heavy Artillery Regiment (3A) - 170
1215 満州 3rd Heavy Artillery Regiment (3A) - 170
1219 城 5th Independent Heavy Artillery Battalion (5A) - 172
1221 球 1st Independent Survey Company (32A) - 39
1221 宗 1st Artillery Intelligence Regiment (56A) - 116
1224 強 1st Field Anti-Aircraft Searchlight Battalion (3AA) - 175
1226 城 / 358満 1st Engineer Unit Headquarters (5A) - 172
1230 路 3rd Railway Command (CRR) - 165
1231 / 34101 路 3rd Railway Regiment (CRR) - 166
1233 路 172nd Railway Station Command (CRR) - 166
1234 路 173rd Railway Station Command (CRR) - 166

0	1	2	3	4	5	6	7	8	9	10
〇	一	二	三	四	五	六	七	八	九	十

1235 路 174th Railway Station Command (CRR) - 166
1238 / 34102 路 4th Railway Regiment (CRR) - 165
1395 路 104th Railway Station Command (CRR) - 166
1241 徳 3rd Specially Est. Railway Bridge Construction Unit (CRR) - 165
1242 路 6th Specially Established Railway Construction Duty Unit (CRR) - 165
1253 鋭 603rd Specially Established Guard Battalion (1AA) - 169
1254 敏 604th Specially Established Guard Battalion (30A) - 178
1259 路 10th Independent Railway Battalion (CRR) - 165
1261 城 1st Independent Heavy Artillery Company (5A) - 172
1266 路 11th Independent Railway Battalion (CRR) - 165
1267 路 12th Independent Railway Battalion (CRR) - 165
1270 鋒 3rd Railway Engineer Unit -
1271 鋒 3rd Engineer Unit Headquarters (57A) - 118
1286 路 15th Independent Railway Battalion (CRR) - 165
1290 / 25296 徳 Kwantung Army Field Veterinary Depot (KA) - 154
DN • 1300-99 仙 *Sen,* Sendai Divisional District
1350 敏 45th Independent Transport Battalion (2AirA) - 163
1354 – 6 東北 Sendai Dist. 1st to 3rd Specially Est. Garrison Units (11AA) - 65
1358 – 61 東北 Sendai Dist. 4th to 7th Specially Est. Garrison Units (11AA) - 65
1365 築 71st Line of Communications Hospital (17AA) - 184
1367 - 79 東北 Sendai Dist. 8th to 18th Specially Est. Garrison Units (11AA) - 65
1383 – 6 東北 Sendai Dist. 19th Specially Est. Garrison Units (11AA) - 65
1386 城 75th Line of Communications Guard Unit (5A) - 173
1387 遠征 75th Line of Communications Duty Company (44A) - 179
1390 東北 Sendai Dist. 23rd Specially Established Garrison Unit (11AA) - 65
1394 路 103rd Railway Station Command (CRR) - 165
1395 路 104th Railway Station Command (CRR) - 165
DN • 1400-99 甲 *Ko,* North China Area Army
1408 築 12th Tank Regiment (17AA) - 182
1418 満 /13081 鋭 114th Independent Motor Transport Btn (1AA) - 168
1437 中部 4th Independent Artillery Regiment (15 AA) - 96
1441 鋭 1st Area Army (KA) - 168
1448 鋭 1st Area Army Headquarters (KA) - 168
DN • 1440-45 甲 *Ko,* not used - North China Area Army
DN •1446 甲 *Ko,* not used - North China Area Army
1466-99 弘 117th Division (44A) - 222
1469 弘 205th Independent Infantry Battalion, 117th Div (44A) - 223
1484 展 11th Independent Field Artillery Battalion (#$A) - 156
1486 敏 40th Independent Engineer Regiment, 2nd Coy (30A) - 178
1496 衣 59th Division Mortar Unit (34A) - 211
1497 陣 63rd Division Mortar Unit (44A) - 212
DN • 1500-99 澤 *Sawa,* Kanazawa Divisional District
1513- 95 武 9th Division (10AA) - 204
DN • 1600-99 Not Distributed

1616 球 32nd Army Headquarters (10AA) - 38
1620 満州 2nd Air Signal Unit -
1622 隼 China Expeditionary Army 1st Air Training Unit (5AirA) - N/A
DN • 1700-99 湾 *Wan,* Formosa (Taiwan) Army
1743 湾 305th Independent Motor Transport Company (10AA) - 32
1746 湾 308th Independent Motor Transport Company (10AA) - 32
1761 湾 111th Specially Established Land Duty Company (10AA) - 32
1762 湾 112th Specially Established Land Duty Company (10AA) - 32
1763 湾 113th Specially Established Land Duty Company (10AA) - 32
1764 湾 114th Specially Established Land Duty Company (10AA) - 32
1765 湾 115th Specially Established Land Duty Company (10AA) - 32
1766 湾 116th Specially Established Land Duty Company (10AA) - 32
1767 湾 117th Specially Established Land Duty Company (10AA) - 32
1769 湾 112th Specially Established Sea Duty Company (10AA) - 32
1770 湾 113th Specially Established Sea Duty Company (10AA) - 32
1771 湾 114th Specially Established Sea Duty Company (10AA) - 32
1772 湾 115th Specially Established Sea Duty Company (10AA) - 32
1773 湾 116th Specially Established Sea Duty Company (10AA) - 32
1774 湾 117th Specially Established Sea Duty Company (10AA) - 33
1777 湾 106th Specially Est. Construction Duty Company (10AA) - 33
1783 敢 46th I.M.B. Signal Unit (10AA) later 66th Div (10AA) - 259 / 212
1785-9 敢 46th Independent Mixed Brigade, later 66th Div (10AA) - 260 / 212
1785-9 敢 66th Division (10AA) - 212
1793 敢 66th Division Transport Unit (10AA) - 213
1791 湾 10th Area Army Signal Unit (10AA) - 31
1795 敢 66th Division, division's code number (10AA) - 212
1796 湾 7th Independent Machinegun Battalion (10AA) - 31
1797 湾 8th Independent Machinegun Battalion (10AA) - 31
1798 湾 16th Independent Rapid Firing Gun Battalion (10AA) - 31
DN • 1800-99 甲 *Ko,* North China Area Army
1881 石 62nd Division, not a unit (32A) - 211
1882 石 62nd Division Headquarters (32A) - 211
1884-86 陣 63rd Division (44A) - 212
1893 城 18th Independent Engineer Regiment (5A) - 172
1894 光 29th Independent Engineer Regiment (4A) - 159
DN • 1900-99 東部 *Tobu* Army District
1900-59 晴 1st Anti-Aircraft Division (12AA) - 255
1920 晴 1st Strategic Balloon Unit, 1st Anti-Aircraft Division (12AA) - 255
1924 陣 137h Independent Infantry Battalion, 63rd Div (44A) - 212
1926 鏑 21st Field Airfield Construction Unit (1AirDiv) - 56
1950 東 32nd Air Intelligence Unit (AGA) - 127
DN • 1960-69 not used *Tobu* Army District
DN • 1960 – 1969 東部 *Tobu* Army District, not distributed
1971 浦 67th Independent Mixed Brigade (12AA) - 262
DN • 1972 – 1984 東部 *Tobu* Army District, not distributed
DN • 1986 – 1989 東部 *Tobu* Army District, not distributed
DN • 2000-99 Imperial Palace District

0	1	2	3	4	5	6	7	8	9	10
〇	一	二	三	四	五	六	七	八	九	十

2004 路 169th Railway Station Command (CRR) - 166
2005 路 170th Railway Station Command (CRR) - 166
2017 路 207th Railway Station Command (CRR) - 166
DN • 2100-99 東部 *Tobu* Army District
2112-3 房 1st and 2nd Tokyo Bay Fortress Artillery Regts (TBAC) - 74 / 285
2116 幡 1st Fortification Construction Duty Company (12AA) - 69
2117 幡 2nd Fortification Construction Duty Company (12AA) - 69
2118 幡 2nd Guard Brigade Headquarters (TDA) - 284
2119 幡 1st Guard Brigade Signal Unit (TDA) - 284
2121 房 Tokyo Bay Fortress Signal Unit (TBAC) - 74, 285
2122 幡 1st Guard Brigade Headquarters (TDA) - 284
2161 東部 1th Specially Established Engineer Unit, Tokyo (ToB) - 78
2162 東部 2nd Specially Established Engineer Unit, Tokyo (ToB) - 78
2163 東部 3rd Specially Established Engineer Unit, Tokyo (ToB) - 78
2163 靖 22nd Independent Machine Cannon Company (6AirA) - 137
2164 東部 4th Specially Established Engineer Unit, Tokyo (ToB) - 78
2165 東部 5th Specially Established Engineer Unit, Chiba (ToB) - 80
2166 東部 6th Specially Established Engineer Unit, Tokyo (ToB) - 78
2167 東部 7th Specially Established Engineer Unit, Yokohama (ToB) - 79
2168 東部 8th Specially Established Engineer Unit, Yokohama (ToB) - 79
2169 浦 5th Sp. Est. Garrison Battalion, 67th I.M.B. Hachijojima (12AA) - 262
2172 球 79th Field Anti-Aircraft Battalion, attached 64 IMB (57A) - 261
2173 球 80th Field Anti-Aircraft Battalion, attached 64 IMB (57A) - 261
2174-96 浦 67th Independent Mixed Brigade, Hachijojima Det. (12AA) - 262
2177 球 103rd Machine Cannon Battalion, attached 64 IMB (57A) - 261
2181 湾 56th Field Machine Cannon Company (10AA) - 32
2182 湾 57th Field Machine Cannon Company (10AA) - 32
2183 浦 41st Specially Est. Machine Cannon Co., 67th I.M.B. (12AA) - 262
2184 浦 42nd Specially Est. Machine Cannon Co., 67th I.M.B. (12AA) - 262
DN • 2200-99 松 *Mutu,* Asahikawa Divisional District
2200 要 356th Specially Established Guard Battalion, Hakodate (5AA) - 52, 55
2206 睦 119th Line of Communications Hospital (16AA) - 114
2210 要 351st Specially Established Guard Battalion, Karafuto (5AA) - 54
2211 要 352nd Specially Established Guard Battalion, Karafuto (5AA) - 53
2212 要 353rd Specially Established Guard Battalion, Karafuto (5AA) - 53
2213 要 301st Specially Established Guard Company, Karafuto (5AA) - 54
2214 要 302nd Specially Established Guard Company, Karafuto (5AA) - 52, 54
2215 要 303rd Specially Established Guard Company, Karafuto (5AA) - 54
2216 要 304th Specially Established Guard Company, Karafuto (5AA) - 54
2217 要 305th Specially Established Guard Company, Karafuto (5AA) - 53
2218 要 306th Specially Established Guard Company, Karafuto (5AA) - 53
2219 要 307th Specially Established Guard Company, Karafuto (5AA) - 52, 54
2221 要 25th Infantry Regiment, Karafuto Mixed Brigade and 88th Div (5AA) - 217
2222 要 88th Division (division #, not a unit) (5AA) - 217

2225 要 Karafuto Mixed Brigade Artillery Unit, Became 88th Div (5AA) - 217
2227 要 Karafuto Mixed Brigade Engineer Unit, Became 88th Div (5AA) - 217
2229 要 Karafuto Mixed Brigade Signal Unit, Became 88th Div (5AA) - 217
2231 要 Karafuto Mixed Brigade Transport Unit, Became 88th Div (5AA) - 217
2232 要 125th Infantry Regiment, Karafuto Mixed Brigade and 88th Div (5AA) - 217
2233 要 Karafuto Mixed Brigade Medical Unit, Became 88th Div (5AA) - 217
2235 浦 669th Independent Infantry Battalion, 67th I.M.B. (12AA) - 262
2260 要 308th Specially Established Guard Company, Karafuto (5AA) - 54
2261 達 309th Specially Established Guard Company (5AA) - 52
2262 達 310th Specially Established Guard Company (5AA) - 52
2269 達 311th Specially Established Guard Company Asahikawa (5AA) - 54
2270 達 312th Specially Established Guard Company Asahikawa (5AA) - 54
2274 達 313th Specially Established Guard Company Asahikawa (5AA) - 54
2275 達 354th Specially Established Guard Company, Asahikawa (NAD) - 54
2276 達 355th Specially Established Guard Company, Asahikawa (NAD) - 54
2277 達 314th Specially Established Guard Company, Hakkodate (NAD) - 55
2278 達 315th Specially Established Guard Company Kushiro (5AA) - 56
2283 / 15570 達 331st Specially Established Guard Company, Kushiro (HoB) - 56
2284 達 316th Specially Established Guard Company Kushiro (5AA) - 56
2285 達 317th Specially Established Guard Company, Kushiro (5AA) - 56
2286 達 318th Specially Established Guard Company, Kushiro (5AA) - 56
2288 達 320th Specially Established Guard Company, Kushiro (5AA) - 55
2289 達 321st Specially Established Guard Company, Sapporo (5AA) - 55
2291 宰 322nd Specially Established Guard Company (5AA) - 54
2292 宰 323rd Specially Established Guard Company (5AA) - 54
2299 宰 324th Specially Established Garrison Company (5AA) - 54
DN • 2300-49 栄 *Sakae*, China Expeditionary Army
DN • 2350-60 甲 *Ko*, North China Area Army
DN • 2361-99 Not Distributed
2371 隼 5th Air Army Headquarters, Korea (17AA) - 193
2373 隼魁 1st Air Brigade Headquarters (5AirA) - 195
2374 隼 3rd Air Brigade # not a unit (5AirA) - 195
2375 隼 3rd Air Brigade Headquarters (5AirA) - 195
2376 朝鮮 44th Air Regiment (5AirA) - 195
2378 靖 60th Air Regiment (6AirA) - 135
2380 隼魁 81st Air Regiment, an element (3rd Air Brigade 5AirA) - 196
2384 天風 83rd Independent Air Squadron (12AirDiv 6AirA) - N/A
2388 隼 105th Secondary Air Training Brigade, # not a unit (5AirA) - N/A
2389 隼 105th Secondary Air Training Brigade Headquarters (5AirA) - 193
DN • 2400-99 四國 *Shikoku* Army District
2402 隼 6th Field Airfield Construction Headquarters (5AirA) - 194
2406 燕 25th Field Airfield Construction Unit (1AirA) - 133
2407 燕 26th Field Airfield Construction Unit (1AirA) - 133
2408 靖 27th Field Airfield Construction Unit (6AirA) - 137
2409 靖 28th Field Airfield Construction Unit (6AirA) - 137
2410 錦 11th Division Headquarters (55A) - 205
2425 錦 12th Infantry Regiment, 11th Div (55A) - 205

0	1	2	3	4	5	6	7	8	9	10
〇	一	二	三	四	五	六	七	八	九	十

2481-91 錦 11th Division (55A) - 205
2487 錦 11th Division Veterinary Unit, 11th Div (55A) - 205
2488 幡 27th Ind. Rapid Firing Gun Company, 66th IMB Niijima (12AA) - 262
2527 球 27th Signal Regiment, 5th Company (32A) - 39
2531 路 2nd Bridge Construction Battalion (CRR) - 165
2544 築 94th Independent Radio Platoon (17AA) - 182
DN • 2550-99 Not Distributed
2569 球 19th Air Sector Command (32A) - 42
2571 羽 2nd Air Army 1st Education Unit (2AirA) - 163
DN • 2600-99 德 *Toku*, Kwantung (Kantō) Army
2600 光 74th Line of Communications Duty Company (4A) - 159
2602 光 76th Line of Communications Duty Company (4A) - 159
2603 岩 77th Line of Communications Guard Unit (3A) - 171
2604 鋭 605th Specially Established Guard Battalion (1AA) - 169
2605 強 606th Specially Established Guard Battalion (3AA) - 176
2608 城 80th Line of Communications Duty Company (5A) - 173
2609 幡 11th Tractor Company (56A) - 116
2610 鋒 12th Tractor Company (57A) - 118
2611 幡 13th Tractor Company (12AA) - 69
2612 幡 14th Tractor Company (12AA) - 69
2614 / 15502 德 64th Independent Motor Transport Battalion (KA) - 155
2618 幡 17th Field Service Unit Headquarters (12AA) - 69
2619 幡 25th Bridging Materials Company (12AA) - 69
2620 幡 6th Field Construction Unit Headquarters (12AA) - 69
2622 睦 8th Field Fixed (?) Headquarters (16AA) -
2623 城 19th Line of Communications Medical Unit Headquarters (5A) - 173
2630 光 11th Army Veterinary Quarantine Depot (4A) - 159
2631 城 20th Veterinary Quarantine Depot (5A) - 173
2632 岩 15th Field Ordinance Depot (3A) - 171
2633 満 / 93000 鋭 16th Field Ordinance Depot (1AA) - 169
2634 城 17th Field Ordinance Depot (5A) - 173
2635 光 18th Field Ordinance Depot (4A) - 159
2636 遠征 19th Field Ordinance Depot (44A) - 179
2637 岩 20th Field Ordinance Depot (3A) - 171
2638 岩 16th Field Motor Transport Depot (3A) - 171
2639 城 17th Field Motor Vehicle Depot (5A) - 173
2640 光 18th Field Motor Vehicle Depot (4A) - 159
2641 遠征 19th Field Motor Vehicle Depot (44A) - 179
2642 岩 20th Field Motor Transport Depot (3A) - 171
2643 岩 16th Field Freight Depot (3A) - 171
2644 城 17th Field Freight Depot (5A) - 173
2645 光 18th Field Freight Depot (4A) - 159
2646 遠征 19th Field Freight Depot (44A) - 179
2647 岩 20th Field Freight Depot (3A) - 171

2648 / 15504 滿州 Kwantung Army Field Ordinance Depot (KA) - 154
2650 路 Kwantung Army Field Railway Depot (CRR) - 165
2651 徳 Kwantung Army Field Freight Depot (KA) - 154
2654 強 3rd Area Army Field Horse Replacement Depot (3AA) - 177
2687 強 26th Anti-Aircraft Regiment (3AA) - 175
2691 強 601st Specially Established Guard Company (3AA) - 176
2692 強 602nd Specially Established Guard Company (3AA) - 176
2693 強 603rd Specially Established Guard Company (3AA) - 176
2694 光 604th Specially Established Guard Company (4A) - 159
2695 遠征 605th Specially Established Guard Company (44A) - 179
2696 強 606th Specially Established Guard Company (3AA) - 176
2697 遠征 607th Specially Established Guard Company (44A) - 179
DN • 2700-99 西部 *Seibu* Army District
2700-9 堡 107th Independent Mixed Brigade (16AA) - 268
2730 睦 1st Tsushima Fortress Infantry Battalion (16AA) - 114, 285
2731 睦 2nd Tsushima Fortress Infantry Battalion (16AA) - 114, 285
2732 睦 3rd Tsushima Fortress Infantry Battalion (16AA) - 115, 285
2735 宗 Shimonoseki Heavy Artillery Regiment (56A) - 117
2736 睦 Tsushima Fortress Heavy Artillery Regiment (16AA) - 114, 285
2737 宗 Iki Fortress Heavy Artillery Regiment (56A) - 117
2738 堅塁 18th Medium Artillery Regiment, 118th IMB (16AA) - 271
2739 堅城 17th Medium Artillery Regiment, 122nd IMB (16AA) - 272
2740 球 6th Medium Artillery Regiment, 64th I.M.B. (57A) - 260
2740 球 6th Medium Artillery Regt. Amami Oshima Det. (57A) - 119
2741 宗 254th Specially Established Garrison Battalion (ChG, 56A) - 108, 117
2742 西部 255th Specially Established Garrison Battalion, Fukuoka (56A) - 121
2743 西部 256th Specially Established Garrison Battalion, Fukuoka (56A) - 121
2744 剣閃 257th Specially Est. Garrison Battalion, Fukuoka (56A) - 121, 124
2745 宗 1st Iki Fortress Infantry Battalion (56A) - 117
2746 宗 2nd Iki Fortress Infantry Battalion (56A) - 117
2747 宗 3rd Iki Fortress Infantry Battalion (56A) - 117
2748 宗 4th Iki Fortress Infantry Battalion (56A) - 117
2749 宗 5th Iki Fortress Infantry Battalion (56A) - 117
2750 宗 6th Iki Fortress Infantry Battalion (56A) - 117
2761 中国 201st Specially Est. Engineer Unit, Yamaguchi (ChG, 56A) - 108, 117
2762 西部 202nd Specially Established Engineer Unit, Fukuoka (56A) - 121
2763 宗 203rd Specially Established Engineer Unit, Fukuoka (56A) - 121
2764 西部 204th Specially Established Engineer Unit, Fukuoka (56A) - 121
2774 球 6th Fortification Construction Duty Company, Okinawa (32A) - 39
2775 球 7th Fortification Construction Duty Company, Okinawa (32A) - 39
2776 球 8th Fortification Construction Duty Company, Miyako Jima (10AA) - 40
2776 球 8th Fortification Construction Duty Coy, 1 platoon, Ishigaki (10AA) - 41
2781 西部 Nagasaki Army Hospital, Nagasaki Army District (SeB) - 122
2784 中国 205th Specially Established Engineer Unit, Hiroshima (ChG) - 106
2785 中国 206th Specially Established Engineer Unit, Hōfu City (ChG) - 108
2786 山陽 207th Specially Established Engineer Unit, Shimonoseki (59A) - 104
2787 西部 208th Specially Established Engineer Unit, Fukuoka (SeB) - 121

0	1	2	3	4	5	6	7	8	9	10
〇	一	二	三	四	五	六	七	八	九	十

2788 西部 209th Specially Established Engineer Unit, Fukuoka (SeB) - 121
2789 西部 210th Specially Established Engineer Unit, Fukuoka (SeB) - 121
2790 西部 211th Specially Established Engineer Unit, Saga (SeB) - 121
2791 西 212th Specially Established Engineer Unit, Kumamoto (Nishi) - 123
2792-3 西 213th and 214th Specially Est. Engineer Unit, Miyazaki (Nishi) - 124
2794 西 215th Specially Established Engineer Unit, Kagoshima (Nishi) - 124
2795 西 216th Specially Established Engineer Unit, Kagoshima (Nishi) - 124
2796 西 217th Specially Established Engineer Unit, Kagoshima (Nishi) - 124
DN • 2800-99 丸 *Maru*, Utsunomiya Divisional District
2829 陽 8th Self-Propelled Artillery Battalion (40A) - 115
2871 東部 13th Specially Established Garrison Company, Maebashi (ToB) - 77
2872 浦 23rd Ind. Mountain Artillery Battalion, 67th I.M.B. (12AA) - 262
2881-90 納 81st Division (36A) - 215-6
2891 境 22nd Independent Mountain Artillery Battalion, 66th I.M.B. (12AA) - 262
DN • 2900-99 甲 *Ko,* North China Area Army
2940 暁 General Shipping Command Headquarters, Ujina (SC) - 143
2942 暁 13th Shipping Group Headquarters (SC) - 147
2943 暁 1st Shipping Headquarters (SC) - 143
2947 暁 14th Shipping Group Headquarters (SC) - 147
2950 暁 15th Shipping Group Headquarters (SC) - 147
2951 暁 16th Shipping Group Headquarters (SC) - 147
2952 暁 11th Shipping Headquarters (32A) - 42
2953 暁 1st Shipping Artillery Regiment (SC) - 144
2959 暁 Shipping Fixed Signal Regiment (SC) - 146
2990-99 陣 63rd Division (44A) - 212
DN • 3000-99 *Yō,* Tokyo Divisional District
3027 築 41st Construction Duty Company (17AA) - 184
3028 羽 42nd Construction Duty Company (2AirA) - 163
3039 / 3339 岩 2nd Independent Heavy Artillery Company (3A) - 170
DN • 3100-99 德 *Toku,* Kwantung (Kantō) Army
3100 監 Kwantung Army Inspectorate General of Supply HQ (KA) - 153
3102 捷 11th Independent Heavy Artillery Battalion (52A) - 72
3103 建 12th Independent Heavy Artillery Battalion (51A) - 71
3104 断 13th Independent Heavy Artillery Battalion (53A) - 73
3107 / 21764 颯 13th Trench Mortar Battalion (54A) - 86
3108 / 21765 颯 14th Trench Mortar Battalion (54A) - 86
3109 球 23rd Field Medium Artillery Regiment (32A) - 39
3111 敏 27th Independent Mortar Battalion (30A) - 177
3111 強 61st Fortress Heavy Artillery Company (3AA) - 175
3112 強 171st Anti-Aircraft Regiment (3AA) - 175
3140 弘 117th Division Headquarters (44A) - 222
3150 光 10th Independent Field Artillery Battalion (4A) - 158
3153 敏 601st Specially Established Engineer Unit (30A) - 178
3154 強 602nd Specially Established Engineer Unit (3AA) - 177

3155 展 15th Trench Mortar Battalion (34A) - 156
3156 断 16th Trench Mortar Battalion (53A) - 73
3157 強 603rd Specially Established Engineer Unit (3AA) - 176
3158 強 604th Specially Established Engineer Unit (3AA) - 176
3160 強 605th Specially Established Engineer Unit (3AA) - 176
3161 強 651st Specially Established Guard Battalion (3AA) - 176
3162 強 652nd Specially Established Guard Battalion (3AA) - 176
3163 強 653rd Specially Established Guard Battalion (3AA) - 176
3164 光 654th Specially Established Guard Battalion (4A) - 159
3165 鋭 655th Specially Established Guard Battalion (1AA) - 169
3166 敏 601st Specially Established Guard Battalion (30A) - 177
3167 光 602nd Specially Established Guard Battalion (4A) - 159
3168 強 606th Specially Established Engineer Unit (3AA) - 177
3169 強 607th Specially Established Engineer Unit (3AA) - 176
DN • 3200-99 張 *Hari,* Nagoya Divisional District
3226 捷 24th Independent Rapid Firing Gun Battalion (52A) - 72
3323 球 19th Independent Machinegun Battalion, Ishigaki Island (32A) - 40
3226 捷 24th Independent Rapid Firing Gun Battalion (52A) - 72
DN • 3300-99 仙 *Sen,* Sendai Divisional District
3302 強 34th Construction Duty Company (3AA) - 177
3308 羽 70th Land Duty Company (2AirA) - 163
3310 幡 3rd Garrison Headquarters, Nigata (12AA) - 68
3311 東部 2nd Specially Established Garrison Battalion, Niigata (12AA) - 68
3312 東部 3rd Specially Established Garrison Battalion, Niigata (12AA) - 68
3313 東部 21st Specially Established Garrison Company, Niigata (12AA) - 68
3314 東部 22nd Specially Established Garrison Company, Niigata (12AA) - 68
3315 進 63rd Specially Established Garrison Battalion, Sendai (11AA) - 65
3316 進 30th Specially Established Garrison Company, Sendai (11AA) - 61
3317 進 31st Specially Established Garrison Company, Sendai (11AA) - 61
3318 進 32nd Specially Established Garrison Company, Fukushima (11AA) - 61
3319 進 33rd Specially Established Garrison Company, Fukushima (11AA) - 61
3320 進 34th Specially Established Garrison Company, Fukushima (11AA) - 61
3323 球 19th Independent Machinegun Battalion, Ishigaki Jima (10AA) - 40
3325 富士 21st Independent Machinegun Battalion (36A) - 70
3339 / 3039 岩 2nd Independent Heavy Artillery Company (3A) - 170
3333-58 東北 1st to 26th Specially Est. Garrison Unit, Fukushima (ToH) - 65-6
3359 燕 159th Field Airfield Construction Unit (1AirA) - 134
3360 磯 669th Ind. Infantry Battalion, 65th IMB became 321st Div (TBC) - 250
3361 幡 1st Garrison Infantry Battalion, 1st Guard Brigade (TDA) - 284
3362 幡 2nd Garrison Infantry Battalion, 1st Guard Brigade (TDA) - 284
3364 捷 67th Independent Engineer Battalion (52A) - 72
3364- 69 東北 Yamagata 1st to 6th Specially Est. Guard Units (ToH) - 66
3370-86 伝 72nd Division (11AA) - 213-4
3390-99 東北 7th to 16th Specially Est. Guard Units, Yamagata (ToH) - 66
DN • 3400-99 薩 *Satsu,* Kumamoto Divisional District
3402 強 Kwantung Army 1st Specially Est. Garrison HQ (3AA) - 176
3430-87 山 24th Division (32A) - 206

0	1	2	3	4	5	6	7	8	9	10
〇	一	二	三	四	五	六	七	八	九	十

3492 / 21099 城 20th Heavy Artillery Regiment (5A) - 172
DN • 3500-49 甲 *Ko*, North China Area Army
DN • 3550-75 丸 *Maru*, Utsunomiya Divisional District
DN • 3576-99 Not Distributed
3577-79 石 62nd Division, not used
3590-99 石 62nd Division (32A) - 211
DN • 3600-99 徳 *Toku* Kwantung (Kantō) Army
3600 岩 3rd Army Headquarters (1AA) - 170
3604 幡 66th Independent Motor Transport Battalion (12AA) - 68
3609 捷 2nd Artillery Intelligence Regiment (52A) - 72
3611 岩 46th Field Road Construction Unit (3A) - 171
3618 富士 6th Signal Regiment (36A) - 70
3619 遠征 47th Field Road Construction Unit (44A) - 179
3620 幡 67th Independent Motor Transport Battalion (12AA) - 68
3633 築 65th Independent Motor Transport Battalion (17AA) - 183
3646 睦 9th Field Transport Headquarters (16AA) - 114
3655 徳 120th Specially Established Land Duty Company (KA) - 154
3656 徳 121st Specially Established Land Duty Company (KA) - 154
3666 球 1st Independent Mortar Regiment (32A) - 39
3667 砦 23rd Independent Mortar Battalion (58A) - 185
3692 岩 3rd Army (1AA) - 170
3696/15284 英武 285th Infantry Regiment, 128th Div. (3A) - 228
DN • 3700-99 張 *Hari*, Nagoya Divisional District
3752 岩 52nd Independent Transport Battalion (3A) - 170
3755 城 47th Casualty Clearing Platoon (5A) - 173
3759 敏 53rd Independent Transport Battalion (30A) - 177
3763 光 49th Casualty Clearing Platoon (4A) - 159
3765 断 2nd Field Medium Artillery Regiment (53A) - 73
3769 幡 11th Field Medium Artillery Regiment (TDA) - 74
3774 満州 16th Field Anti-Aircraft Unit Headquarters (KA) - 154
3780 英機 276th Infantry Regiment, 125th Div. (30A) - 227
3794 幡 52nd Field Medium Artillery Regiment (12AA) - 68
DN • 3800-99 蔵 *Zō*, Tokyo Divisional District
3820-37 範 3rd Guards Division (52A) - 203
3857 線 175th Railroad Station Headquarters (RR) - 140
3858 路 176th Railway Station Command (CRR) – 166
3862 幡 8th Field Transport Headquarters (12AA) - 68
3870 鋒 1st Artillery Headquarters (57A) - 118
3872 捷 19th Field Duty Headquarters (52A) - 72
3872 捷 1st/19th Field Duty Unit (52A) - 72
3873 断 20th Field Duty Headquarters (53A) - 73
3874 湾 214th Independent Motor Transport Company (10AA) - 32
3877 湾 213th Independent Motor Transport Company (10AA) - 32
3880 敏 2nd Engineer Unit Headquarters (30A) - 177

DN • 3900-99 Nagano District
3909 命 140th Infantry Regiment, 71st Div (10AA) - 213
3963 光 28th Bridging Materials Company (4A) - 159
3989 德 277th Independent Motor Transport Company (KA) - 154
DN • 4000-49 中部 *Chubu* Army District
4000 / 33998 路 119th Railway Station Command (CRR) - 166
4003 路 116th Railway Station Command (CRR) - 166
4011 敏 41st Sea Duty Company (30A) - 178
4012 鋭 42nd Sea Duty Company (1AA) - 169
4017 敏 88th Land Duty Company (30A) - 178
4018 羽 89th Land Duty Company (2AirA) - 163
4019 羽 90th Land Duty Company (2AirA) - 163
DN • 4050-99 攝 *Setu*, Osaka Divisional District
DN • 4100-55 中部 *Chubu* Army District
4100-1 晴 1st Anti-Aircraft Division (12AA) - 255
4102-3 逐 124th and 125th Anti-Aircraft Regiments, 2nd A.A. Div (13AA) - 256
4104 房 1st Tokyo Bay Fortress Engineer Unit (TB) - 74, 285
4105 房 2nd Tokyo Bay Fortress Engineer Unit (TB) - 74, 285
4107-17 炸 3rd Anti-Aircraft Division (15AA) - 256
4108 逐 11th Searchlight Regiment, 2nd Anti Aircraft Division (13AA) - 256
4117 中部 11th Garrison Headquarters, Kobe District (ChB) - 102
4118 逐 12th Machine Cannon Battalion 2nd Anti Aircraft Division (13AA) - 256
4120 中部 155th Specially Established Garrison Battalion, Osaka (ChB) - 100
4121 東海 104th Specially Established Garrison Company, Tsu (ToK) - 92
4122 東海 105th Specially Established Garrison Company, Tsu (ToK) - 92
4123 中部 151st Specially Established Garrison Battalion, Kobe (ChB) - 102
4124 中部 152nd Specially Established Garrison Battalion, Kobe (ChB) - 102
4125 中部 153rd Specially Established Garrison Battalion, Kobe (ChB) - 102
4126 中部 154th Specially Established Garrison Battalion, Kobe (ChB) - 102
4128 中部 156th Specially Established Garrison Battalion, Osaka (ChB) - 100
4129 中部 157th Specially Established Garrison Battalion, Osaka (ChB) - 100
4130 中部 158th Specially Established Garrison Battalion, Osaka (ChB) - 100
4131 中部 159th Specially Established Garrison Battalion, Osaka (ChB) - 100
4132 中部 160th Specially Established Garrison Battalion, Kyoto (ChB) - 98
4134 東海 162nd Specially Established Garrison Battalion, Nagoya (ToK) - 89
4135 東海 163rd Specially Established Garrison Battalion, Gifu (ToK) - 89
4136 東海 164th Specially Established Garrison Battalion, Nagoya (ToK) - 89
4137 楠 106th Specially Established Garrison Company, Wakayama (ChB) - 97
4138 東海 107th Specially Established Garrison Company, Shizuoka (ToK) - 91
4139 東海 108th Specially Established Garrison Company, Shizuoka (ToK) - 91
4140 東海 109th Specially Established Garrison Company, Tsu (ToK) - 92
4141 中部 110th Specially Established Garrison Company, Otsu (ChB) - 99
4142 中部 101st Specially Established Engineer Unit, Osaka (ChB) - 100
4143 中部 102nd Specially Established Engineer Unit, Osaka (ChB) - 100
4144 中部 103rd Specially Established Engineer Unit, Osaka (ChB) - 101
4145 東海 104th Specially Established Engineer Unit, Gifu (ToK) - 89
4146 東海 105th Specially Established Engineer Unit, Nagoya (ToK) - 89

0	1	2	3	4	5	6	7	8	9	10
〇	一	二	三	四	五	六	七	八	九	十

4147 東海 106th Specially Established Engineer Unit, Nagoya (ToK) - 89
4148 中部 107th Specially Established Engineer Unit, Kobe (ChB) - 102
4149 中部 108th Specially Established Engineer Unit, Kobe (ChB) - 102
4150 楠 Yura Fortress Heavy Artillery Regiment (15AA) - 96
4151 颯 37th Independent Heavy Artillery Battalion (54A) - 86
4152 東明 38th Independent Heavy Artillery Battalion (13AA) - 85   both units 4152
4152 球 7th Medium Artillery Regiment, attached 44 IMB (32A) - 38
4153 偕 39th Independent Heavy Artillery Battalion (55A) - 109
4154 球 8th Medium Artillery Regiment, Ishigaki, Ryukyus (10AA) - 40
4154 偕 5th Independent Heavy Artillery Company (55A) - 109
DN • 4156-99 Not Distributed
4164 幡 3rd Fortification Construction Duty Company (12AA) - 69
4166 楠 Central District Anti-Aircraft Headquarters (15AA) - 96
4167 秀 Nagoya Anti-Aircraft Artillery Headquarters (13AA) - 85
4168 逐 123rd Anti-Aircraft Regiment, 9th Co, 2nd Anti Aircraft Div (13AA) - 255
4168 炸 123rd Anti-Aircraft Regiment, 3rd Anti Aircraft Div (15AA) - 255
4173 球 Funauki (船浮) Army Hospital, Ishigaki Jima (10AA) - 41
4175 中部 11th Guard Battalion (ToB) - N/A
4176 楠 111th Specially Established Garrison Company, Wakayama (ChB) - 97
4177 東海 109th Specially Established Engineer Unit, Shizuoka (ToK) - 90
4178 東海 110th Specially Established Engineer Unit, Nagoya (ToK) - 89
4179 東海 111th Specially Established Engineer Unit, Nagoya (ToK) - 89
4180 東海 112th Specially Established Engineer Unit, Gifu (ToK) - 90
4181 中部 113th Specially Established Engineer Unit, Otsu (ChB) - 99
4182 東海 114th Specially Established Engineer Unit, Tsu (ToK) - 91
4184 中部 116th Specially Established Engineer Unit, Kobe (ChB) - 102
4183 中部 115th Specially Established Engineer Unit, Osaka (ChB) - 101
4184 中部 116th Specially Established Engineer Unit, Kobe (ChB) - 102
4185 中部 117th Specially Established Engineer Unit, Kobe (ChB) - 102
4186 中部 118th Specially Established Engineer Unit, Osaka (ChB) - 101
DN • 4200-99 甲 *Ko*, North China Area Army
4215 光 57th Reconnaissance Regiment (4A) - N/A
4280 石 64th Infantry Brigade, 62nd Division (32A) - 211
4280-9 秋 6th Independent Mixed Brigade (became the 62nd Div) - *In Vol 2*
4281-97 石 62nd Division (32A) - 211
4285-88 陣 63rd Division (44A) - 212
4290-98 衣 59th Division (34A) - 211
DN • 4300-4499 満州 Kantō Army
4321- 26 命 71st Division (10AA) - 213
4329/26709 岩 Tungning Heavy Artillery Regiment (3A) - 170
4338 師 6th Air Transport Unit (AGA) - N/A
4350 路 5th Railway Command (CRR) - 165
4351 路 19th Railway Regiment (CRR) - 165
4352 路 20th Railway Regiment (CRR) - 165

4353 路 17th Independent Railway Battalion (CRR) - 165
4354 路 18th Independent Railway Battalion (CRR) - 165
4355 路 19th Independent Railway Battalion (CRR) - 165
4356 路 20th Independent Railway Battalion (CRR) - 165
4357 路 21st Independent Railway Battalion (CRR) - 165
4362 / 5091 睦 7th Signal Regiment (16AA) - 113
4370 路 1st Armored Train Unit (CRR) - 165
4371 路 2nd Armored Train Unit (CRR) - 165
4374 / 15539 德 2nd Kwantung Army Duty Unit - 155
4387 展 Mutanchiang Heavy Artillery Regiment (34A) - 156
4391-98 命 71st Division (10AA) - 213
4410 光 1st Construction Unit (4A) - 159
4455 光 4th Army Headquarters (KA) - 158
4464 宗 68th Independent Motor Transport Battalion (56A) - 116
4475 光 4th Army (KA) - 158
DN • 4500-99 湾 *Wan*, Formosa (Taiwan) Army
4500 暁 7th Shipping Transport Headquarters, Okinawa Branch - 41
4512 湾 Keelung Island Fortress Heavy Artillery Regiment (10AA) - 33
4522 磐石 16th Heavy Artillery Regiment, 100th I.M.B. (10AA) - 267
4550 湾 161st Field Anti-Aircraft Regiment (10AA) - 31
4570 湾 10th Area Army Air Intelligence Unit (10AA) - 31
4586 湾 551st Specially Established Garrison Battalion (10AA) - 35
4587 湾 162nd Field Anti-Aircraft Regiment (10AA) - 32
4591 湾 561st Specially Established Garrison Battalion (10AA) - 35
4593 湾 566th Specially Established Garrison Battalion (10AA) - 35
4596 湾 562nd Specially Established Garrison Battalion (10AA) - 35
4597 湾 563rd Specially Established Garrison Battalion (10AA) - 35
4598 湾 564th Specially Established Garrison Battalion (10AA) - 35
4599 湾 565th Specially Established Garrison Battalion (10AA) - 35
DN • 4600-99 澤 *Sawa*, Kanazawa Divisional District
4600 湾 4th Independent Rapid Firing Gun Battalion (10AA) - 31
4618 幡 24th Bridging Materials Company (12AA) - 69
4619 幡 24th Bridging Materials Company (12AA) - 69
4620 敏 46th Line of Communications Sector Command (30A) - 178
4620 德 46th Sector Transport Unit (30A) - 178
4620 德 46th Line of Communications Duty Unit (5A) - 173
4621 光 46th Line of Communications Guard Unit (4A) - 159
4622 德 46th Line of Communications Guard Company (30A) - 178
4631 岩 13th Line of Communications Medical Unit Headquarters (3A) - 171
4636 路 107th Railway Station Command (CRR) - 165
4639 幡 39th Construction Duty Company (12AA) - 69
4640 遠征 40th Construction Duty Company (44A) - 179
4641 統 10th Field Service Unit Headquarters (17AA) - 183
4647 – 12th Field Well Drilling Company (unknown) - N/A
4648 – 13th Field Well Drilling Company (unknown) - N/A
4649 球 14th Field Well Drilling Company, attached 62 Div (32A) - 38
DN • 4700-99 陸 *Riku*, Hirosaki Divisional District

0	1	2	3	4	5	6	7	8	9	10
〇	一	二	三	四	五	六	七	八	九	十

4756 東海 101st Specially Established Garrison Company, Shizuoka (ToK) - 91
DN • 4800-99 丸 Maru, Utsunomiya Divisional District
4818 建 45th Line of Communications Sector Command (51A) - 71
4818 建 45th Line of Communications Duty Unit (51A) - 71
4818 建 45th Line of Communications Guard Unit (51A) - 71
4825 路 105th Railway Station Command (CRR) - 165
4826 暁 30th Field Anchorage Headquarters (SC) - 146
4831 球 71st Land Duty Company, Amami Oshima Detach. (57A) - 119
4832 球 72nd Land Duty Company (32A) - 39
4838 城 3rd Field Fortification Unit (5A) - 172
4840 光 34th Field Road Construction Unit (4A) - 159
4847 磯 670th Ind. Infantry Battalion, 65th IMB became 321st Div. (TBA)
4848 幡 3rd Guard Infantry Battalion, 1st Guard Brigade (TDA) - 284
4849 幡 4th Guard Infantry Battalion, 1st Guard Brigade (TDA) - 284
4850 燕 160th Field Airfield Construction Unit (1AirA) - 134
DN • 4900-49 攝 Setu, Osaka Divisional District
4901-35 国 25th Division (16AA) - 207
DN • 4950-99 Not Distributed
DN • 5000-99 徳 Toku, Kwantung (Kantō) Army
5001 花 3rd Cavalry Brigade, brigade #, not a unit became 135th Div (5A) - 279
5012-29 花 3rd Cavalry Brigade became 77th I.M.B. then 135th Div (5A) - 279
5033 城 5th Army Headquarters (1AA) - 172
5046 徳 122nd Specially Established Land Duty Company (KA) - 154
5047 徳 123rd Specially Established Land Duty Company (KA) - 154
5050 築 109th Specially Established Construction Duty Company (17AA) - 184
5071 鋒 7th Field Transport Headquarters (57A) - 118
5075 築 70th Independent Motor Transport Battalion (17AA) - 183
5087 城 5th Army (1AA) - 172
5091 / 4362 睦 7th Signal Regiment (16AA) - 113
DN • 5100-99 中国 Chugoku Army District
5122 羽 2nd Air Special Signal Unit (2AirA) - 162
5124 宗 60th Line of Communications Sector Command (56A) - 116
5124 宗 60th Line of Communications Duty Unit (56A) - 116
5124 宗 60th Line of Communications Guard Unit (56A) - 116
DN • 5200-99 陸 Riku, Hirosaki Divisional District
5204 鋒 4th Field Construction Command (57A) - 118
5220 進 33rd Guard Headquarters (11AA) - 61
5225 進 325th Specially Established Garrison Company, Morioka (11AA) - 61
5226 進 326th Specially Established Garrison Company, Yamagata (11AA) - 61
5232 俊 332nd Specially Established Garrison Company, Aomori (50A) - 62
5233 俊 333rd Specially Established Garrison Company, Morioka (50A) - 62
5234 進 324th Specially Established Garrison Company, Morioka (11AA) - 61
5245 城 45th Field Road Construction Unit (5A) - 172
5247 球 17th Independent Machinegun Battalion, attached 24 Div (32A) - 38

Chapter 4

5248 球 18th Independent Machinegun Battalion, Miyako, Ryukyus (10AA) - 40
5265 湾 64th Independent Engineer Battalion (10AA) - 32
DN • 5300-49 張 *Hari*, Nagoya Divisional District
DN • 5305-6 戊 not used Mongolia Garrison Army
5303 砦 64th Line of Communications Hospital (58A) - 185
5307 雷神 42nd Independent Mixed Regiment, 112th IMB (10AA) - 269
5307 湾 25th Tank Regiment (10AA) - 32   both units are 5307
5530 睦 50th Field Road Construction Unit (16AA) - 114
DN • 5600-5749 蔵 *Zō*, Tokyo Divisional District
5611-83 豊 28th Division, Miyako Jima, Ryukyus (10AA) - 207
5629 豊 36th Infantry Regiment, 28th Div. detached, Daito Jima (10AA) - 207
5657 展 107th Specially Established Construction Duty Company (34A) - 156
5681 豊 28th Division, 3rd Field Hospital, Ishigaki Jima (10AA) - 40
5686 達 24th Anti Aircraft Regiment (5AA) - 51
5700 断 151st Line of Communications Sector Command (53A) - 73
5700 断 151st District Transport Unit (53A) - 73
5700 断 151st Line of Communications Duty Unit (53A) - 73
5700 断 151st Line of Communications Guard Unit (53A) - 73
5704 幡 44th Independent Motor Transport Battalion (12AA) - 68
5706 磯 246th Ind. Motor Transport Company, 65th I.M.B. became 321st Div - 250
5721 路 111th Railway Station Command (CRR) - 165
5722 路 112th Railway Station Command (CRR) - 165
5723 路 113th Railway Station Command (CRR) - 166
5727 鋒 44th Construction Duty Company (57A) - 118
5728 鋒 45th Construction Duty Company (57A) - 118
5729 光 46th Construction Duty Company (4A) - 159
5731/6531 岩 84th Land Duty Company (3A) - 171
5735 湾 1st Field Fortification Unit (10AA) - 32
5737 岩 15th Veterinary Quarantine Depot (3A) - 171
5746 中部 101st Specially Established Guard Company (53A) - 73
5747 東海 102nd Specially Established Guard Company, Shizuoka (ToK) - 91
5748 東海 103rd Specially Established Guard Company, Shizuoka (54A) - 91
DN • 5750-99 中部 *Chubu* Army District
5753 球 27th Field Disease Prevention and Water Supply Unit, Okinawa (32A) - 38
5768 湾 21st Sea Raiding Base Battalion (10AA) - 33
5769 湾 22nd Sea Raiding Base Battalion (10AA) - 33
5770 岩 77th Line of Communications Duty Company (3A) - 171
5780-4 東明 97th Independent Mixed Brigade (54A) - 266
5784 東明 663rd Independent Infantry Battalion, 97th I.M.B. (54A) - 266
5784 隼 164th Field Airfield Construction Unit (5AirA) - 194
5786 隼 165th Field Airfield Construction Unit (5AirA) - 194
DN • 5800-99 蔵 *Zō*, Tokyo Divisional District
5803 路 2nd Railway Regiment (CRR) - 165
5807 路 2nd Railway Materials Depot (CRR) - 165   both units share 5807
5807 球 83rd Land Duty Company (32A) - 39
5808 路 3rd Railway Materials Depot (CRR) - 165
5864 鋒 34th Independent Motor Transport Battalion (57A) - 118

0	1	2	3	4	5	6	7	8	9	10
〇	一	二	三	四	五	六	七	八	九	十

5879 球 215th Independent Motor Transport Company (32A) - 39
5896 球 49th Line of Communications Sector Command (32A) - 39
5897 捷 150th Line of Communications Sector Command (52A) - 72
5897 捷 150th Sector Transport Unit (52A) - 72
5897 捷 150th Line of Communications Duty Unit (52A) - 72
5897 捷 150th Line of Communications Guard Unit (52A) - 72
DN • 5900-49 滿州 Kantō Army
DN • 5950-99 Not Distributed
DN • 6000-49 中部 Chubu Army District
6004 強 89th Line of Communications Hospital (3AA) - 177
6021 光 27th Bridging Materials Company (4A) - 159
DN • 6050-99 攝 Setu, Osaka Divisional District
6052 幡 47th Independent Motor Transport Battalion (12AA) - 68
6058 球 259th Independent Motor Transport Company (32A) - 39
6064 浦 16th Independent Mixed Regiment, att. 67th I.M.B. (12AA) - 262
6071 球 Miyako Jima Army Hospital, Miyako, Ryukyus (10AA) - 40
6090 球 3rd Independent Machinegun Battalion, attached 24 Div (32A) - 38
6140 暁 Field Shipping Main Depot (SC) - 145
6147 暁 5th Shipping Engineer Regiment (32A) - 41
6151 暁 27th Shipping Engineer Regiment (SC) - 146
6155 轟 3rd Amphibious Brigade Transport Unit (57A) - 283
6155 暁 57th Shipping Engineer Regiment (SC) - 146
6156 払 4th Amphibious Brigade Transport Unit (5AA) - 283
DN • 6157-99 四國 Shikoku Army District
6160 暁 5th Shipping Transport Headquarters (SC) - 146
6163 暁 51st Hospital Shipping Medical Section (SC) - 147
6165 暁 53rd Hospital Shipping Medical Section (SC) - 148
6167 暁 1st Shipping Training Section Headquarters (SC) - 143
6167 暁 Shipping Training Department (SC) - 143
6168 暁 1st Shipping Transport Command (SC) - 146
6174 暁 6th Shipping Engineer Regiment (SC) - 146
6175 暁 58th Shipping Engineer Regiment (SC) - 143
6177 暁 Shipping Medical Unit Headquarters (SC) - 147
6178 暁 1st Shipping Machine Cannon Regiment (SC) - 144
6179 暁 2nd Shipping Machine Cannon Regiment (SC) - 144
6180 暁 Shipping Artillery Group Headquarters (SC) - 143
6182 暁 Military Shipping Detention Depot (SC) - 148
6183 暁 3rd Shipping Group Headquarters - (SC) - N/A
6186 暁 6th Debarkation Unit (SC) - 147
6193 暁 6th Sea Transport Battalion (SC) - 146
6195 暁 4th Field Shipping Depot (SC) - 147
6196 暁 9th Field Shipping Depot (SC) - 145
6197 暁 10th Field Shipping Depot (SC) - 145
6198 暁 11th Field Shipping Depot (SC) - 145

DN • 6200-99 洛 *Raku*, Kyoto Divisional District
6250 球 5th Ind. Rapid Firing Gun Battalion, Miyako Jima (10AA) - 40
6261 德 57th Independent Transport Battalion (KA) - 154
6262 德 58th Independent Transport Battalion (KA) - 154
DN • 6300-49 德 *Toku*, Kwantung (Kantō) Army
6315 朝 Korea Army Divisional District Headquarters (KoD) - 186
6316 朝 Gwangju Divisional District Headquarters (KoD) - 191
6318 朝鮮 Daegu Divisional District Headquarters (KoD) - 190
6319 朝 Pyongyang Divisional District Headquarters (KoD) - 188
6320 京 Seoul Divisional District Headquarters (KoD) - 189
6322 朝 Busan Sector Command (KoD) - 191
6323 朝鮮 Daegu Sector Command (KoD) - 190
6324 朝 Daejeon Sector Command (KoD) - 190
6325 朝鮮 Guangju Sector Command (KoD) - 191
6326 朝 Chonju Sector Command (KoD) - 190
6327 朝 Cheongju Sector Command (KoD) - 191
6328 朝 Chunchon Sector Command (KoD) - 189
6329 京 Seoul Sector Command (KoD) - 190
6330 朝 Hamhung Sector Command (KoD) - N/A
6331 朝 Ranam Sector Command (KoD) - 187
6332 朝 Pyongyang Sector Command (KoD) - N/A
6333 朝 Sinuiju Sector Command (KoD) - 188
6334 朝 Haeju Sector Command (KoD) - 189
6335 築 Pusan (Busan) Fortress Headquarters (17AA) - 182
6336 築 Yeosu Fortress Headquarters (17AA) - 183
6337 岩 Rajin Fortress Headquarters (3A) - 170
DN • 6350-99 Not Distributed
6350 師 12th Air Transport Squadron (AGA) - N/A
6366 京 Seoul Army Hospital (KoD) - 190
6367 朝 Pusan Army Hospital (KoD) - 187
6368 朝鮮 Daegu Army Hospital (KoD) - 191
6369 朝鮮 Gwangju Army Hospital (KoD) - 191
6370 朝 Yeosu Army Hospital (KoD) - 187
6371 朝鮮 Chonju Army Hospital (KoD) - 191
6372 京 Kunsan Army Hospital (KoD) - 190
6373 朝 Rajin Army Hospital (KoD) - 188
6374 朝 Hamhung Army Hospital (KoD) - 188
6375 朝鮮 Wonsan Army Hospital (KoD) - 187
6377 朝 Pyongyang 1st Army Hospital (KoD) - 188
6378 朝 Pyongyang 2nd Army Hospital (KoD) - 189
6379 朝 Hoeryong Army Hospital (KoD) - 188
6380 朝 Ranam Army Hospital (KoD) - 188
6382 朝 Pyongyang Army Ordnance Re-supply Depot (KoD) - 186
6392 朝 Pusan Commissariat (KoD) - 186
DN • 6400-99 四國 *Shikoku* Army District
6403 球 3rd Independent Rapid Firing Gun Battalion, attached 24 Div (32A) - 38
6415 幡 31st Bridging Materials Company (12AA) - 69

0	1	2	3	4	5	6	7	8	9	10
〇	一	二	三	四	五	六	七	八	九	十

6416 鋭 32nd Bridge Building Materials Company (1AA) - 168
6420 睦 56th Independent Motor Transport Battalion (16AA) - 114
6427 路 152nd Railway Station Command (RR/CRR) - 166
6428 / 34008 路 153rd Railway Station Command (CRR) - 166
6432 路 155th Railway Station Command (CRR) - 166
6443 球 109th Land Duty Company, Miyako, Ryukyus (10AA) - 40
6460 智 228th Specially Est. Garrison Company, Kochi (Shikoku) - 111
6461-7 球 45th Independent Mixed Brigade (10AA) - 260
6466 智 229th Specially Est. Garrison Company, Kochi (Shikoku) - 111
6477 暁 28th Sea Raiding Base Battalion (32A) - 42
6478 鋭 80th Independent Transport Company (1AA) - 168
6479 幡 11th Guard Infantry Battalion, 2nd Guard Brigade (TDA) - 284
6480 幡 12th Guard Infantry Battalion, 2nd Guard Brigade (TDA) - 285
6481 羽 170th Field Airfield Construction Unit (2AirA) - 163
6482 偕 6th Independent Mountain Artillery Regiment (55A) - 109
6483 偕 37th Trench Mortar Battalion (55A) - 109
6484 偕 79th Independent Engineer Battalion (55A) - 109
6485-96 四国 1st to 12th Specially Est. Garrison Units, Takamatsu (Shikoku) - 110
6510-28 四国 1st to 19th Specially Est. Garrison Units, Matsuyama (Shikoku) - 111
DN • 6500-49 徳 *Toku*, Kwantung (Kantō) Army
6523 球 1st Field Medium Artillery Regiment, minus 1st Battalion (32A) - 38
6523 球 1st Field Medium Artillery Regiment, 1st Btn. Miyako Jima (10AA) - 40
6531/5731 84th Land Duty Company (3A) - 171
6540-51 四国 1st to 10th Specially Est. Garrison Units, Tokushima (Shikoku) - 110-1
DN • 6550-99 洛 *Raku*, Kyoto Divisional District
6560-69 四国 1st Specially Established Garrison Unit, Kochi (Shikoku) - 111-2
DN • 6600-99 澤 *Sawa*, Kanazawa Divisional District
6601 球 16th Field Well Drilling Company, Miyako, Ryukyus (10AA) - 40
6611 師 11th Flying Transport Squadron (AGA) - N/A
6611 東海 23rd Specially Established Garrison Company, Toyama (ToK) - 88
6612 東海 24th Specially Established Garrison Company, Toyama (ToK) - 88
6614 東海 27th Specially Established Garrison Company, Kanazawa (ToK) - 87
6660-79 決 93rd Division (36A) - 219
6682 幡 5th Guard Infantry Battalion, 1st Guard Brigade, (TDA) - 284
6683 幡 6th Guard Infantry Battalion, 1st Guard Brigade, (TDA) - 284
6684 隼 161st Field Airfield Construction Unit (5AirA) - 194
DN • 6700-99 黒 *Kuro*, Kurume Divisional District
6711 鋒 65th Line of Communications Sector Command (57A) - 118
6712 鋒 65th Line of Communications Guard Unit (57A) - 118
6713 鋒 65th Line of Communications Duty Unit (57A) - 118
6750 幡 7th Independent Rapid Firing Gun Battalion (12th AA) - 68
6752 岩 69th Independent Motor Transport Company (3A) - 170
6753 城 70th Independent Transport Company (5A) - 172
6754 城 71st Independent Transport Company (5A) - 173

6765 築 72nd Independent Transport Company (17AA) - 183
6766 遠征 73rd Independent Transport Company (44A) - 179
6767 築 74th Independent Transport Company (17AA) - 183
6775 暁 53rd Hospital Shipping Medical Section (SC) - 148
6777 暁 55th Hospital Shipping Medical Section (SC) - 148
6779 暁 56th Hospital Shipping Medical Section (SC) - 148
6790 西部 202nd Specially Established Guard Battalion, Nagasaki (16AA) - 115
6791 西部 201st Specially Established Guard Company, Saga (56A) - 117
6792 西部 202nd Specially Established Guard Company, Saga (56A) - 121
6793 西部 203rd Specially Established Guard Company, Fukuoka (SeB) - 121
6796 西部 252nd Specially Established Guard Battalion, Fukuoka (SeB) - 121
6797 西部 213th Specially Established Guard Company, Fukuoka (SeB) - 121
6798 西部 214th Specially Established Guard Company, Fukuoka (SeB) - 121
6799 西部 215th Specially Established Guard Company, Fukuoka (SeB) - 121
DN • 6800-19 仙 *Sen*, Sendai Divisional District
DN • 6820-39 丸 *Maru*, Utsunomiya Divisional District
DN • 6840-55 攝 *Setu*, Osaka Divisional District
DN • 6860-79 Hiroshima Divisional District
6860-76 藤 39th Division (30A) - 208
DN • 6880-6905 四國 *Shikoku* Divisional District
6903 路 129th Railway Station Command (CRR) - 166
DN • 6910-49 越 *Etsu*, Nagano Divisional District
6916 鋒 13th Field Construction Command (57A) - 118
6917 岩 95th Land Duty Company (3A) - 171
6946 鋒 99th Line of Communications Hospital (57A) - 118
DN • 6950-99 Not Distributed
DN • 7000-99 薩 *Satsu*, Kumamoto Divisional District
7000 城 64th Independent Transport Battalion (5A) - 172
7002 築 63rd Independent Transport Company (17AA) - 183
7003 築 64th Independent Transport Company (17AA) - 183
7004 砦 65th Independent Transport Company (58A) - 185
7014 / 7104 幡 53rd Independent Motor Transport Battalion (12AA) - 68
7023 築 62nd Line of Communications Sector Unit Command (17AA) - 183
7030 球 284th Ind. Motor Transport Company, Miyako Jima (10AA) - 40
7030 球 284th Ind. Motor Transport Co., 1 platoon Ishigaki Jima (10AA) - 41
7034 路 148th Railway Station Command (SRR/CRR) - 166
7035 / 34006 線 149th Railroad Station Headquarters (RR/CRR) - 166
7037 甲 145th Railway Station Command (CRR) - N/A
7038 路 146th Railway Station Command (CRR) - 166
7039 德 62nd Line of Communications Duty Company (KA) - 154
7041 岩 79th Line of Communications Duty Company (3A) - 171
7043 満州 59th Construction Duty Company (KA) - 184
7051 湾 8th Field Well Drilling Company (10AA) - 32
7052 湾 9th Field Well Drilling Company (10AA) - 32
7057 靖 172nd Field Airfield Construction Unit (6AirA) - 137
7059 朝鮮 158th Garrison Battalion (KoD) - 191
7060 朝鮮 159th Garrison Battalion, Gwangju (KoD) - 191

0	1	2	3	4	5	6	7	8	9	10
〇	一	二	三	四	五	六	七	八	九	十

7061 朝鮮 160th Garrison Battalion (Korean Div. District) - 191
7062-7 堅志 98th Independent Mixed Brigade (57A) - 266-7
7068 幡 18th Guard Infantry Battalion, 3rd Guard Brigade, (TDA) - 285
7069 境 18th Independent Mixed Regiment, 66th I.M.B. (12AA) - 261
7070 睦 59th Line of Communications Sector Command (16AA) - 114
7071-3 球 44th Independent Mixed Brigade (32A) - 259
7074 鋒 23rd Independent Mixed Regiment (57A) - 118
7075 剣軍 220th Specially Est. Garrison Company, Amami Det. (57A) - 119
7076 剣軍 221st Specially Est. Garrison Company, Amami Det. (57A) - 119
7077 剣軍 222nd Specially Est. Garrison Company, Amami Det. (57A) - 119
7078 球 223rd Specially Est. Garrison Company, attached 62 Div (32A) - 38
7079 球 224th Specially Est. Garrison Company, attached 62 Div (32A) - 38
7080 球 225th Specially Established Garrison Company, Daito (10AA) - 41
7081 球 226th Specially Established Garrison Company, Ishigaki (10AA) - 40
7082 球 227th Specially Established Garrison Company, Ishigaki (10AA) - 40
7088 鋒 203rd Sp. Est. Garrison Battalion, attached 109th I.M.B. (57A) - 268
7089 鋒 204th Specially Established Garrison Company (57A) - 119
7090 鋒 205th Specially Established Garrison Company (57A) - 119
7091 陽 206th Specially Established Garrison Company, Kagoshima (SeB) - 115
7092 鋒 207th Specially Established Garrison Company, Kagoshima (57A) - 119
7093 鋒 208th Specially Established Garrison Company, Kagoshima (57A) - 119
7094 球 209th Specially Established Garrison Company, Ishigaki (10AA) - 40
7095 球 210th Specially Established Garrison Company, Ishigaki (10AA) - 40
7096 球 211th Specially Est. Garrison Company, Daito Jima Det. (32A) - 41
7097 宗 21st Security Battalion (56A) - 117
DN • 7100-99 中国 *Chugoku* Army District
7102 鋭 29th Bridging Materials Company (1AA) - 168
7104 / 7014 幡 53rd Independent Motor Transport Battalion (12AA) - 68
7111 徳 137th Railway Station Headquarters (KA/CRR) - 166
7113 / 34004 路 139th Railway Station Command (CRR) - 166
7116 路 142nd Railway Station Command (CRR) - 166
7117 路 143rd Railway Station Command (CRR) - 166
7140 暁 14th Hospital Shipping Medical Section (SC) - 147
7141 暁 15th Hospital Shipping Medical Section (SC) - N/A
7156 球 21st Independent Mixed Regiment, 64th I.M.B. (57A) - 261
7159 樟 201st Specially Established Guard Battalion, Matsue (15AA, ChG) - 97, 107
7161 中国 251st Specially Est. Garrison Battalion, Hiroshima (59A, ChG) - 104, 106
7162 中国 212th Specially Est. Guard Company, Yamaguchi (59A, ChG) - 104, 108
7163 中国 21st Guard Company (59A) - 104
7164 西部 22nd Specially Est. Garrison Company, Fukuoka (SeB) - 121
7165 球 64th Brigade Headquarters, 64th I.M.B. (57A) - 261
7166 球 22nd Independent Mixed Regiment, 64th I.M.B. (57A) - 261
7167 敢 249th Taiwan Infantry Regiment, 66th Division (10AA) - 212
7170 睦 59th Sector Transport Unit (16AA) - 114

7170 陸 59th Line of Communications Guard Unit (16AA) - 114
7171 陸 59th Line of Communications Duty Unit (16AA) - 114
7181 岩 43rd Independent Mixed Regiment (3A) - 170
7181 路 188th Railway Station Command (CRR) - 166
7183 路 186th Railway Station Command (CRR) - 166
7185 路 189th Railway Station Command (CRR) - 166
7200 奥 57th Division Headquarters, 57th Division (16AA) - 210
7202 奥 52nd Infantry Regiment, 57th Div (16AA) - 210
7210 奥 57th Division Infantry Group Headquarters, 57th Div. (16AA) - 210
7210 北部 1st Kurile, 57th Infantry Group HQ, became 129th I.M.B. HQ (5AA) - 275
7215 奮躍 57th Cavalry Regiment, 136th IMB (4A) - 278
7215 奥 57th Cavalry Regiment, 57th Division (16AA) - 210
7217 奥 117th Infantry Regiment, 57th Division (16AA) - 210
7221-49 奥 57th Division (16AA) - 210
7252 築 4th Signal Regiment (17AA) - 182
7261 師 11th Underground Construction Unit (AirGA) - 127
7262 燕 162nd Field Airfield Construction Unit (1AirA) - 134
7263 靖 163rd Field Airfield Construction Unit (6AirA) - 137
7274-85 俊 95th Independent Mixed Brigade (50A) - 266
DN • 7300-49 栄 *Sakae*, China Expeditionary Army
DN • 7350-79 洛 *Raku*, Kyoto Divisional District
DN • 7380-99 越 *Etsu*, Nagano Divisional District
DN • 7400-49 朝鮮 *Chosen* Army (Korean Army)
7400 築 Pusan Fortress Heavy Artillery Regiment (17AA) - 182
7401 築 Yeosu Fortress Heavy Artillery Regiment (17AA) - 183
7402 築 71st Korean Artillery Battalion, Rajin Bty (17AA) - 183
7402 岩 Rajin Fortress Artillery Unit (3A) - 170
7403 展 Yunghsing Bay Fortress Artillery Unit (34A) - 156
7403 展 Yunghsing Bay Fortress Garrison / 642 Guard Battalion (34A) - 156
7404 築 46th Independent Anti-Aircraft Battalion (17AA) - 182
7405 築 462nd Guard Battalion (17AA) - N/A
7406 築 20th Independent Machine Cannon Company (17AA) - 182
7407 築 21st Independent Machine Cannon Company (17AA) - 182
7411 築 41st Guard Headquarters (17AA) - 182
7412 砦 405th Specially Established Guard Battalion (KoD) - 187
7413 築 407th Specially Established Guard Battalion (KoD) - 189
7414 築 453rd Specially Established Guard Battalion (KoD) - 189
7415 築 454th Specially Established Guard Battalion (KoD) - 189
7416 朝 461st Specially Established Guard Battalion (KoD) - 187
7420 築 151st Anti Aircraft Regiment (17AA) - 182
7421 築 152nd Anti Aircraft Regiment (17AA) - 182
7422 築 41st Independent Anti Aircraft Battalion (17AA) - 182
7437 楠 35th Air Intelligence Unit (AGA) - 127
7437 朝鮮 413th Specially Established Guard Battalion (KoD) - 190
7438 築 414th Specially Established Guard Battalion (17AA) - 183
7439 朝 410th Specially Established Guard Company (KoD) - 189
7440 築 37th Air Intelligence (Radar) Unit (AirGA, 17AA) - 127, 183

0	1	2	3	4	5	6	7	8	9	10
〇	一	二	三	四	五	六	七	八	九	十

7441 築 42nd Independent Anti-Aircraft Battalion (17AA) - 182
7442 朝 411th Specially Established Guard Company (17AA) - 183
7443 朝 401st Specially Established Engineer Unit (KoD) - 187
7444 朝 402nd Specially Established Engineer Unit (KoD) - 189
7445 朝鮮 403rd Specially Established Engineer Unit (KoD) - 190
7446 朝鮮 404th Specially Established Engineer Unit (KoD) - 191
7447 朝鮮 405th Specially Established Engineer Unit (KoD) - 191
7448 築 406th Specially Established Engineer Unit (17AA) - 182
7449 築 407th Specially Established Engineer Unit (17AA) - 182
DN • 7450-99 South Jeolla Divisional District (Korea)
7450 砦 408th Specially Established Engineer Unit (58A) - 185
7452 築 415th Specially Established Garrison Battalion (17AA) - 182
7453 朝 452nd Specially Established Garrison Battalion (KoD) - 187
7453 朝 409th Specially Established Engineer Unit (KoD) - 187
7455 朝 410th Specially Established Engineer Unit (KoD) - 187
7456 朝 411th Specially Established Engineer Unit (KoD) - 190
7457 朝 412th Specially Established Engineer Unit (KoD) - 189
7458 朝 413th Specially Established Engineer Unit (KoD) - 189
7472 築 408th Specially Established Garrison Battalion (17AA) - 183
7473 朝鮮 409th Specially Established Garrison Battalion (KoD) - 191
7474 朝鮮 410th Specially Established Garrison Battalion (KoD) - 190
7475 朝鮮 463rd Specially Established Garrison Battalion (KoD) - 191
7476 朝鮮 464th Specially Established Garrison Battalion (17AA) - 183
7477 朝鮮 455th Specially Established Garrison Battalion (KoD) - 190
7478 朝鮮 456th Specially Established Garrison Battalion (KoD) - 190
7479 朝鮮 457th Specially Established Garrison Battalion (KoD) - 190
7480 朝鮮 458th Specially Established Garrison Battalion (KoD) - 190
7481 岩 101st Independent Mixed Regiment (3A) - 170
7482 朝 404th Specially Established Garrison Battalion - N/A
7483 朝 406th Specially Established Garrison Battalion - N/A
7482 展 462nd Specially Established Garrison Battalion (34A) - 156
7484 朝 459th Specially Established Garrison Battalion (17AA) - 182
7486 朝 416th Specially Established Garrison Battalion (17AA) - 183
7487 朝 408th Specially Established Garrison Company (KoD) - 187
7488 朝 409th Specially Established Garrison Company (KoD) - 189
7489 / 29003 朝 12th Field Horse Replacement Depot (KoD) - 187
DN • 7500-99 德 *Toku*, Kwantung (Kantō) Army
7517 砦 1st Independent Well Drilling Platoon (58A) - 185
7518 砦 2nd Independent Well Drilling Platoon (58A) - 185
7519 砦 3rd Independent Well Drilling Platoon (58A) - 185
7533 達 1st Tsugaru Infantry Unit (5AA) - 52
7534 達 2nd Tsugaru Infantry Unit (5AA) - 52
7551 徳 1st Kanto Army Hospital (KA) - 155
7554 路 Kwantung Army 1st Railway Station Headquarters (CRR) - 165

7562 築 12ᵗʰ Field Transport Headquarters (17AA) - 183
7566 徳 11ᵗʰ Fixed Signals Unit (KA) - 153
7572 築 82ⁿᵈ Independent Motor Transport Battalion (17AA) - 183
7573 奮躍 136ᵗʰ Brigade Headquarters, 136ᵗʰ I.M.B. (4A) - 278
7574 睦 84ᵗʰ Independent Motor Transport Battalion (16AA) - 114
7580 徳 Kwantung Army Fixed Signal Unit Headquarters (KA) - 153
7583 徳 14ᵗʰ Fixed Signals Unit (KA) - 153
7584 徳 13ᵗʰ Fixed Signals Unit (KA) - 153
7585 徳 12ᵗʰ Fixed Signals Unit (KA) - 153
7586 徳 11ᵗʰ Fixed Signals Unit (KA) - 153
7588 徳 18ᵗʰ Signal Regiment (KA) - 154
7589 鋭 17ᵗʰ Signals Regiment (1AA) - 168
7590 建 8ᵗʰ Signal Regiment (51A) - 71
7593 路 209ᵗʰ Railway Station Command (CRR) - 166
7594 路 210ᵗʰ Railway Station Command (CRR) - 166
7595 路 211ᵗʰ Railway Station Command (CRR) - 166
7596 路 212ᵗʰ Railway Station Command (CRR) - 166
DN • 7600-99 中部 *Chubu* Army District
7611 逐 12ᵗʰ Independent Anti-Aircraft Battalion, 2ⁿᵈ AAA Div (13AA) - 256
7612-4 朝鮮 141ˢᵗ to 143ʳᵈ Garrison Battalions (KoD) - 187
7615 朝鮮 144ᵗʰ Garrison Battalion (KoD) - 188
7616 朝鮮 145ᵗʰ Garrison Battalion (KoD) - 188
7617-20 京 146ᵗʰ to 149ᵗʰ Garrison Battalions - 190
7621-5 朝 150ᵗʰ to 154ᵗʰ Garrison Battalions (KoD) - 188
7626-9 幡 2ⁿᵈ Guard Brigade (TDA) - 284
7635 中部 161ˢᵗ Specially Established Garrison Battalion, Kyoto (ChB) - 98
7635-47 中部 1ᵗʰ to 13ᵗʰ Specially Established Garrison Units, Kyoto (ChB) - 98
7648 中部 22ⁿᵈ Specially Established Garrison Unit, Kyoto (ChB) - 98
7650 炸 121ˢᵗ Anti-Aircraft Regiment, 3ʳᵈ AAA Div (15AA) - 256
7651 炸 122ⁿᵈ Anti-Aircraft Regiment, 3ʳᵈ AAA Div (15AA) - 256
7652-59 中部 14ᵗʰ to 21ˢᵗ Specially Established Garrison Units, Kyoto (ChB) - 98
7650-1 炸 3ʳᵈ Anti-Aircraft Division (15AA) - 256
7660-75 中部 1ˢᵗ to 16ᵗʰ Specially Established Garrison Units, Otsu (ChB) - 98-9
7676-89 中部 1ˢᵗ to 14ᵗʰ Specially Established Garrison Units, Fukui (ChB) - 99
7690-99 中部 1ˢᵗ 10ᵗʰ Specially Established Garrison Units, Osaka (ChB) - 100
DN • 7700-99 丸 *Maru*, Utsunomiya Divisional District
7703 満州 1ˢᵗ Heavy Artillery Regiment (30A) - 177
DN • 7800-99 蔵 *Zō*, Tokyo Divisional District
7807 球 83ʳᵈ Land Duty Company (32A) - 39
7834 Hachijojima Detachment Headquarters Deactivated 7/12/44 (12AA) - 261
7835 境 Niijima Detachment, 66ᵗʰ I.M.B. (12AA) - 261
7836 球 15ᵗʰ Independent Mixed Regiment, 44ᵗʰ IMB (32A) - 259
7848 城 64ᵗʰ Land Duty Company (5A) - 172
7849 徳 65ᵗʰ Land Duty Company (KA) - 154
7851 岩 32ⁿᵈ Construction Duty Company (3A) - 171
7852 宗 33ʳᵈ Construction Duty Company (56A) - 117
7855 東部 55ᵗʰ Specially Established Garrison Battalion, Tokyo (ToB) - 78

0	1	2	3	4	5	6	7	8	9	10
〇	一	二	三	四	五	六	七	八	九	十

7856 東部 56th Specially Established Garrison Battalion, Tokyo (ToB) - 78
7857 東部 57th Specially Established Garrison Battalion, Tokyo (ToB) - 78
7858 東部 58th Specially Established Garrison Battalion, Tokyo (ToB) - 78
7863 砦 64th Line of Communications Hospital (58A) - 185
7864 幡 65th Line of Communications Hospital (12AA) - 68
7868 岩 9th Patient Transport Unit Headquarters (3A) - 171
7870 岩 36th Casualty Clearing Platoon (3A) - 171
7874 東部 59th Specially Established Garrison Battalion, Tokyo (ToB) - 78
7875 東部 60th Specially Established Garrison Battalion, Tokyo (ToB) - 78
7876 東部 61st Specially Established Garrison Battalion, Tokyo (ToB) - 78
7877 東部 62nd Specially Established Garrison Battalion, Tokyo (ToB) - 78
7878 東部 25th Specially Established Garrison Company, Urawa (ToB) - 80
7879 東部 26th Specially Established Garrison Company, Chiba (ToB) - 80
7886 磯 1st Sp. Est. Garrison Btn., 65th I.M.B. became 321st Div. (TBA) - 251
7887 東部 51st Specially Est. Garrison Battalion, Yokohama (ToB) - 79
7888 東部 52nd Specially Est. Garrison Battalion, Yokohama (ToB) - 79
7889 東部 53rd Specially Est. Garrison Battalion, Yokohama (ToB) - 79
7890 東部 54th Specially Est. Garrison Battalion, Yokohama (ToB) - 79
7891 東部 14th Specially Est. Garrison Company, Yokohama (ToB) - 79
7892 境 15th Specially Est. Garrison Company, 66th I.M.B. Niijima (12AA) - 262
7893 境 16th Specially Est. Garrison Company, 66th I.M.B. Niijima (12AA) - 262
7894 境 17th Specially Est. Garrison Company, 66th I.M.B. Niijima (12AA) - 262
7897 東部 28th Specially Established Garrison Company, Chiba (ToB) - 80
7898 東部 29th Specially Established Garrison Company, Chiba (ToB) - 80
DN • 7900-29 Not Distributed
DN • 7930-49 仙 *Sen*, Sendai Divisional District
DN • 7950-60 Not Distributed
DN • 7961-99 栄 *Sakae*, China Expeditionary Army
DN • 8000-99 西部 *Seibu* Army District
8001 彗 136th Anti-Aircraft Regiment 4th AAA Div (16AA) - 257
8004 彗 4th Anti-Aircraft Brigade Headquarters 4th AAA Div (16AA) - 257
78010 彗 11th Independent Machine Cannon Company 4th AAA Div (16AA) - 257
8011 路 124th Railway Station Command (CRR) - 166
8019 彗 26th Independent Machine Cannon Company 4th AAA Div (16AA) - 257
8020 靖 30th Independent Machine Cannon Company (6th Air A) - 137
8043 彗 43rd Independent Machine Cannon Battalion 4th AAA Div (16AA) - 257
8044 彗 12th Independent Machine Cannon Company 4th AAA Div (16AA) - 257
8047 彗 27th Independent Machine Cannon Company 4th AAA Div (16AA) - 257
8048 彗 28th Independent Machine Cannon Company 4th AAA Div (16AA) - 257
8049 靖 29th Independent Machine Cannon Company (6th Air A) - 137
8060-78 彗 4th Anti-Aircraft Division (16AA) - 257
8074 師 36th Air Intelligence Unit (AGA) - 127
8077 炸 22nd Independent Anti-Aircraft Battalion 3rd AAA Div (15AA) - 256
8078 彗 24th Independent Anti-Aircraft Battalion 4th AAA Div (16AA) - 257

Chapter 4

8079 彗 21st Ind. Anti-Aircraft Searchlight Battalion, 4th AAA Div (16AA) - 257
8088 彗 21st Machine Cannon Battalion, 4th AAA Div (16AA) - 257
8091 彗 31st Independent Machine Cannon Company 4th AAA Div (16AA) - 257
8092 彗 32nd Independent Machine Cannon Company 4th AAA Div (16AA) - 257
8093 彗 33rd Independent Machine Cannon Company 4th AAA Div (16AA) - 257
DN • 8100-20 Not Distributed
DN • 8121-49 栄 *Sakae*, China Expeditionary Army
8124 幡 3rd Motor Transport Unit (12AA) - 68
DN • 8150-59 Not Distributed
8150 達 5th Area Army Headquarters (GHQ) - 51
8151 東方 1st General Army Headquarters (GHQ) - 59
8152 西方 2nd General Army Headquarters (GHQ) - 94
DN • 8160-99 栄 *Sakae*, China Expeditionary Army
DN • 8200-99 洛 *Raku*, Kyoto Divisional District
8204 岩 97th Line of Communications Hospital (3A) - 171
8205 遠征 55th Casualty Clearing Platoon (44A) - 179
8207 築 16th Army Veterinary Quarantine Depot (17AA) - 184
8210 路 123rd Railway Station Command (CRR) - 166
8213 / 10054 栄 126th Railway Station Command (CRR) - 165
8221 湾 91st Land Duty Company (10AA) - 32
8222 城 92nd Land Duty Company (5A) - 172
8230 幡 2nd Field Construction Unit Headquarters (12AA) - 68
8244 靖 245th Airfield Battalion (6AirA) - 136
DN • 8300-49 朝鮮 *Chosen* Army (Korea)
DN • 8300-49 朝鮮 *Chosen* Army (Korea)
8301 燕 1st Air Regiment (1AirA) - 131
8304 羽 241st Airfield Battalion (2AirA) - 161
8306 靖 247th Airfield Battalion (6AirA) - 136
8311 燕 11th Flying Regiment (1AirA) - 131
8312/800 羽 2nd Air Army Headquarters (KA) - 162
8316 靖 7th Field Air Repair Depot (6AirA) - 136
8316 靖 7th Field Air Repair Depot, 2nd Ind. Maintenance Unit (6AirA) - 136
8320 燕 12th Air Brigade Headquarters (1AirA) - 131
8327 隼 207th Airfield Battalion (5AirA) - 194
8331 羽 8th Field Air Repair Depot (2AirA) - 163
8331 隼 8th Field Air Repair Depot (5AirA) - 194
8335 羽 215th Airfield Battalion (2AirA) - 163
8336 羽 36th Airfield Battalion (2AirA) - 162
8337 隼 57th Wireless Radio Unit (5AirA) - 194
8338 隼 58th Wireless Radio Unit (5AirA) - 194
8339 誠 Sei 26th Air Regiment (8AirDiv 10AA) - 44
8341 羽 9th Field Air Repair Depot (2AirA) - 163
8342 羽 242nd Airfield Battalion (2AirA) - 163
8343 羽 243rd Airfield Battalion (2AirA) - 163
8346 隼 156th Independent Maintenance Unit (5AirA) - 195
8349 誠 3rd Airfield Company (8AirDiv 10AA) - 45
DN • 8350-99 西部 *Seibu* Army District

0	1	2	3	4	5	6	7	8	9	10
〇	一	二	三	四	五	六	七	八	九	十

8355 / 8356 羽 10th Field Air Repair Depot (2AirA) - 163
8358 羽 201st Airfield Battalion (2AirA) - 163
8360 球 205th Airfield Battalion, Miyako Jima, Ryukyus (10AA) - 40
8362 洋 / 996 満州 2nd Air Signal Regiment (2AirA) - 162
8365 羽 3rd Air Intelligence Regiment (2AirA) - 162
8366 隼魁 4th Air Signal Regiment (5AirA) - 194
8367 羽 11th Field Air Repair Depot (2AirA) - 163
8370 天翔 70th Air Regiment (10AirDiv 1AirA) - 134
8371 羽 71st Airfield Battalion (2AirA) - 163
8372 羽 12th Field Air Repair Depot (2AirA) - 163
8385 隼魁 85th Air Regiment, 1st Air Brigade (5AirA) - 195
8388 羽 88th Airfield Battalion (2AirA) - 163
8391 羽 7th Field Air Freight Depot (2AirA) - 163
8392 羽 8th Field Air Freight Depot (2AirA) - 163
8393 羽 9th Field Air Freight Depot (2AirA) - 163
8394 靖 10th Field Air Freight Depot (6AirA) - 138
8395 羽 11th Field Air Freight Depot (2AirA) - 163
8396 靖 12th Field Air Freight Depot (6AirA) - N/A
8398 羽 2nd Meteorological Regiment (2AirA) - 162
DN • 8400-49 四國 *Shikoku* Divisional District
DN • 8450-8549 Not Distributed
DN • 8550-99 South Jeolla Divisional District (Korea)
8550 砦 15th Field Medium Artillery Regiment (58A) - 185
8648 達 280th Independent Infantry Battalion (5AA) - 52
DN • 8700-99 黒 *Kuro*, Kurume Divisional District
8703-89 劍 12th Division (10AA) - 206
8737 建 9th Field Medium Artillery Regiment (51A) - 71
DN • 8800-49 Not Distributed
8801 靖 176th Field Airfield Construction Unit (6AirA) - 137
8810 朝 451st Specially Established Guard Battalion (KoD) - 187
8812 朝鮮 401st Specially Established Guard Battalion (KoD) - N/A
8820 朝鮮 402nd Specially Established Guard Company (KoD) - 191
8823 砦 405th Specially Established Guard Company (58A) - 185
8830 朝 402nd Specially Established Guard Battalion (KoD) - 187
8832 朝 403rd Specially Established Guard Battalion (KoD) - 187
DN • 8850-99 漢 *Kan*, Keijo Divisional District Seoul, Korea
8866 睦 16th Field Duty Headquarters (16AA) - 114
8876 山陽 103rd Specially Established Land Duty Company (59A) - 104
8884 球 101st Specially Est. Sea Duty Company Daito Jima (10AA) - 41
8885 球 102nd Specially Established Sea Duty Company (32A) - 39
8886 球 103rd Specially Established Sea Company (32A) - 39
8887 球 104th Specially Established Sea Company (32A) - 39
8888 幡 105th Specially Est. Sea Duty Company, att. 321st Div (12AA) - 68
DN • 8940-53 湾 *Wan*, Formosa (Taiwan) Army

DN • 8954-64 Not Distributed
DN • 8965-99 栄 *Sakae*, China Expeditionary Army
DN • 9000-20 薩 *Satsu*, Kumamoto Divisional District
DN • 9021-49 Gifu Air Division
DN • 9050-99 湾 *Wan*, Formosa (Taiwan) Army
9053-71 西 1st to 19th Specially Est. Garrison Units, Kagoshima (Nishi) - 124-5
DN • 9100-49 薩 *Satsu*, Kumamoto Divisional District
9101 朝鮮 2nd Air Brigade Headquarters (5AirA) - 195
9102 朝鮮 6th Air Regiment, 2nd Air Brigade (5AirA) - 195
9104 威 65th Air Regiment (6AirA) - 135
9105 羽 2nd Air Sector Command (2AirA) - 162
9107 羽 30th Airfield Battalion (2AirA) - 162
9115 威 6th Air Brigade Headquarters (6AirA) - 135
9116 羽 16th Airfield Battalion (2AirA) - 162
9121 威 7th Air Brigade Headquarters (6AirA) - 138
9122 誠 12th Air Regiment (8AirDiv 10AA) - 44
9123 誠 27th Air Regiment (8AirDiv 10AA) - 44
9129 羽 93rd Airfield Battalion (2AirA) - 163
9132 燕 74th Air Regiment (1AirA) - 131
9141 隼魁 8th Air Brigade Headquarters (5AirA) - 195
9142 隼魁 16th Air Regiment, 8th Air Brigade (5AirA) - 195
9143 鏑 32nd Air Regiment (1AirDiv 5AA) - 56
9145 誠 58th Air Regiment (8AirDiv 10AA) - 44
9147 隼 18th Airfield Battalion (5AirA) - 193
9149 羽 53rd Airfield Battalion (2AirA) - 163
DN • 9150-99 Gifu Air Division
9150 靖 66th Air Regiment (6AirA) - 135
9160 燕 28th Independent Air Unit (1AirA) - 131
9162 羽 81st Independent Air Squadron (2AirA) - 162
9163 誠 29th Air Regiment (8AirDiv 10AA) - 43
9164 羽 39th Airfield Battalion (2AirA) - 162
9171 靖 66th Independent Air Squadron (6AirA) - 136
9173 球 56th Airfield Battalion (32A) - 42
9180 誠 71st Independent Air Squadron (8AirDiv 10AA) - 44
9191 羽 67th Airfield Battalion (2AirA) - 163
9192 球 69th Airfield Battalion (10AA) - 41
9193 羽 79th Airfield Battalion (2AirA) - 163
9199 羽 29th Airfield Battalion (2AirA) - 162
DN • 9200-99 松 *Mutu*, Asahikawa Divisional District
9200-36 熊 7th Division (5AA) - 204
9241 熊 7th Division, as a whole, not a unit (5AA) - 204
9252-78 稔 77th Division (16AA) - 214
9256 攉 89th Division, as a whole, not a unit (5AA) - 218
9259 暁 53rd Field Anchorage Headquarters (SC) - 146
DN • 9300-49 Gifu Air Division
9321 隼 23rd Field Aircraft Repair Depot (5AirA) - 195
9331 強 3rd Area Army (KA) - 175

```
0    1    2    3    4    5    6    7    8    9    10
〇   一   二   三   四   五   六   七   八   九   十
```

9338 強 3rd Area Army Headquarters (KA) - 175
DN • 9350-99 徳 *Toku*, Kwantung (Kantō) Army
9350 師 12th Air Transport Squadron (AGA) - N/A
9354 鋭 6th Division, 21st River Crossing Materials Company (1AA) - 168
DN • 9400-20 Not Distributed
9421 暁 9th Shipping Engineer Regiment (32A) - 41
9452 築 82nd Independent Radio Platoon (17AA) - 182
9453 隼 3rd Air Route Department (5AirA) - 193
9482 監 193rd Line of Communications Hospital (KA) - 155
9484 展 179th Line of Communications Hospital (34A) - 157
DN • 9500-49 松 *Mutu*, Asahikawa Divisional District
9503 達 Soya Fortress Heavy Artillery Regiment (5AA) - 52
9506 達 Soya Fortress Headquarters (5AA) - 52
9507 達 Soya Army Hospital (5AA) - 52
9531 達 3rd Soya Fortress Infantry Unit (5AA) - 52
9532 達 4th Soya Fortress Infantry Unit (5AA) - 52
9533 達 1st Soya Fortress Infantry Unit (5AA) - 52
9534 達 2nd Soya Fortress Infantry Unit (5AA) - 52
DN • 9550-99 北部 *Hokubu* Army District
9557 達 141st Anti-Aircraft Regiment, Muroran Guard Unit (5AA) - 286
9562 達 31st Independent Anti-Aircraft Battalion (5AA) - 52
9566 進 34th Independent Anti-Aircraft Company (11AA) - 61
9574 達 5th Area Army Air Intelligence Unit (5AA) - 51
9580 達 Muroran Defense Unit Headquarters (5AA) - 286
DN • 9600-99 Gifu Air Division
9601 誠 9th Air Brigade Headquarters (8AirDiv 10AA) - 43
9602 誠 24th Air Regiment (8AirDiv 10AA) - 44
9604 誠 61st Air Regiment (8AirDiv 10AA) - 44
9626 羽 40th Airfield Battalion (2AirA) - 162
9628 羽 97th Airfield Battalion (2AirA) - 163
9640 誠 10th Air Regiment (8AirDiv 10AA) - 43
9647 隼 7th Special Air Signal Unit (5AirA) - 194
DN • 9700-49 黒 *Kuro*, Kurume Divisional District
9700 球 5th Artillery Command (32A) - 38
9730 線 160th Railroad Station Command (CRR) - 166
9731 路 156th Railway Station Command (CRR) - 166
9734 路 159th Railway Station Command (CRR) - 166
9749 浦 112th Land Duty Company, attached 67th IMB (12AA) - 262
DN • 9750-99 西部 *Seibu* Army District
9750 敏 42nd Field Road Construction Unit (30A) - 177
9756 線 191st Railroad Station Command (RR) - 141
9758 線 194th Railway Station Command (CRR) - 166
9760 西部 Amami Oshima Detachment - 119
9760 球 Daito Island Detachment Headquarters - 41

9764 西部 253rd Specially Est. Garrison Battalion, Nagasaki (SeB) - 122
9765 西部 216th Specially Est. Garrison Company (16AA, SeB) - 115, 122
9766 西部 217th Specially Est. Garrison Company (16AA, SeB) - 115, 122
9767 西部 218th Specially Est. Garrison Company, Nagasaki (SeB) - 122
9768 西部 219th Specially Est. Garrison Company, (56A, SeB) - 117, 122
9776 幡 16th Guard Infantry Battalion, 3rd Guard Brigade (TDA) - 285
9777 幡 17th Guard Infantry Battalion, 3rd Guard Brigade (TDA) - 285
9790 暁 30th Sea Raiding Base Battalion (SC) - 145
DN • 9800-49 東部 *Tobu* Army District
9829 隼 64th L. o. C. Motor Transport Company (5AirA) - 195
9831 城 25th Field Motor Vehicle Depot (5A) - 173
9832 城 25th Field Freight Depot (5A) - 173
DN • 9850-99 栄 *Sakae*, China Expeditionary Army
9863 隼 3rd Air Sector Command (5AirA) - 193
9876 隼 15th Air Signal Regiment (5AirA) - 194
9877 隼 6th Air Intelligence Regiment (5AirA) - 194
9880 隼 4th Meteorological Regiment (5AirA) - 194
9885 隼 15th Field Aircraft Repair Depot (5AirA) - 194
9896 隼魁 5th Fixed Air Signal Unit (5AirA) - 194
9899 達 5th Area Army Intelligence Unit (5AA) - 51
DN • 9900-99 Gifu Air Division
9906 燕 14th Air Regiment (6AirA) - 135
9908 師 62nd Air Regiment (30th Fighter Brigade, 6AirA) - N/A
9910 誠 47th Independent Air Squadron (8AirDiv 10AA) - 43
9911 誠 48th Independent Air Squadron (8AirDiv 10AA) - 43
9912 誠 49th Independent Air Squadron (8AirDiv 10AA) - 43
9913 誠 8th Air Regiment (8AirDiv 10AA) - 44
9914 誠 50th Air Regiment (8AirDiv 10AA) - 44
9916 誠 38th Air Sector Command (8AirDiv 10AA) - 45
9930 天鷲 163rd Airfield Battalion (11th Air Div AGA) - 129
9944 帥 1st Infantry (Air) Raiding Brigade Headquarters (6AirA) - 138 /282
9945 帥 1st Infantry Raiding Regiment (6AirA) - 138, 282
9946 帥 2nd Infantry Raiding Regiment (6AirA) - 138, 282
9987 師 7th Air Transport Command (AGA) - N/A
DN • 10000-15, 星 *Hoshi*, 68th Brigade
DN • 10016-99, 洛 *Raku*, Kyoto Divisional District
10054 路 156th Railway Station Command (CRR) - 166
DN • 10100-99, 兵 *Hei*, 54th Division
10130-46 突 84th Division (53A) - 216
10158 球 2nd Field Fortification Construction Unit (32A) - 39
10170 敢 66th Division Rapid Firing Gun Unit (10AA) - 213
10172 暁 26th Sea Raiding Base Battalion (32A) - 42
10173 暁 27th Sea Raiding Base Battalion (32A) - 42
DN • 10200-99, 洛 *Raku*, Kyoto Divisional District
10252-69 比叡 216th Division (16AA) - 245
10265 燕 168th Field Airfield Construction Unit (1AirA) - 134
10266 燕 169th Field Airfield Construction Unit (1AirA) - 134

0	1	2	3	4	5	6	7	8	9	10
〇	一	二	三	四	五	六	七	八	九	十

10273-4 敢 66th Division (10AA) - 212
10275 - 25th Sea Raiding Base Battalion - N/A
10276-7 浦 425th and 426th Ind. Inf. Battalion 67th I.M.B. (12AA) - 262
10279 球 66th Independent Engineer Battalion (32A) - 39
10287 磐石 51st Garrison Battalion, 100th I.M.B. (10AA) - 267
10288 境 427th Independent Infantry Battalion, 66th I.M.B. (12AA) - 260
10288 築 41st Guard Battalion (17AA) - 182
10290 球 4th Independent Machinegun Battalion, attached 62 Div (32A) - 38
DN • 10300-499, 威 *i* Southern Expeditionary Army, April 1945 distribution
DN • 10500-49, Not Distributed
DN • 10600 – 10699, 尚武 *Shobu*, 14th Area Army, Apr. 1945 distribution
10652 誠 22nd Air Brigade Headquarters (8AirDiv 10AA) - 44
10654 靖 45th Air Regiment (1AirA) - 131
DN • 10700-99, 林 *Hayashi*, 15th Army, Apr. 1945 distribution
DN • 10800-99, 治 *Osamu*, 16th Army, Apr. 1945 distribution
10800 湾 10th Area Army Field Ordinance Depot (10AA) - 31
DN • 10900-99, 富 *Tomi*, 25th Army, Apr. 1945 distribution
DN • 11000-49, 灘 *Nada*, 37th Army, Apr. 1945 distribution
DN • 11050-11149, 司 *Tsukasa*, 3rd Air Army, Apr. 1945 distribution
11050 誠 21st Air Regiment (8AirDiv 10AA) - 44
11071 誠 204th Air Regiment (8AirDiv 10AA) - 44
DN • 11150-99, 遠征 *Sizume*, 44th Army, Apr. 1945 distribution
11167 遠征 Baicheng (31st Kanto) Army Hospital (44A) - 179
11168 遠征 82nd Kanto Army Hospital (44A) - 179
11170 山陽 122nd Specially Established Sea Duty Company (59A) - 104
11171 – 123rd Specially Established Sea Duty Company (unknown) - N/A
11175 – 127th Specially Established Sea Duty Company (unknown) - N/A
11179 遠征 88th Kanto Army Hospital (44A) - 179
DN • 11200-99, 剛 *Go*, 8th Area Army, Apr. 1945 distribution
DN • 11300-99, 沖 *Oki*, 17th Army, Apr. 1945 distribution
DN • 11400-99, 猛 *Mo*, 18th Army, Apr. 1945 distribution
11610 羽 15th Air Brigade Headquarters, Anshan Ironworks (2AirA) - 162
11612 羽 14th Air Sector Command (2AirA) - 162
11614 靖 12th Independent Air Unit (6AirA) - 136
11618 羽 45th Airfield Battalion (2AirA) - 162
11636 羽 28th Air Sector Command (2AirA) - 162
DN • 11700-99, 林 *Hayashi*, 15th Army
11703 誠 13th Air Regiment (8AirDiv 10AA) - 44
DN • 11800 – 99, 襲 *Shu*, 7th Air Division
DN • 11900-29, 勲 *Isao*, 42nd Division
11900-17 勲 42nd Division (5AA) - 208
DN • 11930-49, 誉 *Homare*, 43rd Division
DN • 11950-59, Not Distributed
DN • 11960-89, 静 *Sei*, 46th Division

DN • 11990-12014, 弾 *Dan*, 47th Division
DN • 12015-19, Not Distributed
DN • 12020-49, 緑 *Midori*, Heijo Divisional District (Korea)
DN • 12050-69, 徳 *Toku*, Kwantung (Kantō) Army, Apr. 1945 distribution
12051-60 鋭敏 8th Independent Armored Brigade (13AA) - 281
12061-70 舞鶴 122nd Division (1AA) - 225
12062 凪 107th Division Veterinary Unit (44A) - 220
DN • 12071-89, 拓 *Taku*, 1st Armored Division
12070-85 拓 "1st Armored Division (36A) - 253
12083 拓 5th (Light) Tank Regiment, 1st Armored Div. (36A) - 253
12084 先 11th Tank Regiment, 91st Division (5AA) - 219
DN • 12090-109, 撃 *Geki*, 2nd Armored Division
12102 球 27th Tank Regiment, minus 3rd Company attached 62 Div (32A) - 38
12102 撃 27th Tank Regiment, 3rd Company, Miyako Jima (10AA) - 40
DN • 12110-99, 桜 *Sakura*, 20th Army, Apr. 1945 distribution
DN • 12200-99, 森 *Mori*, Burma Area Army, Apr. 1945 distribution
DN • 12300-99, 東部 *Tobu* Army District, Apr. 1945 distribution
12300 進 11th Area Army Headquarters (1st GA) - 60
12301 幡 8th Field Medium Artillery Regiment (TDA) - 74
12302 湾 16th Field Medium Artillery Regiment, Chiayi City (10AA) - N/A
12303 幡 19th Field Medium Artillery Regiment (TDA) - 74
12304 達 15th Independent Mortar Battalion (5AA) - 51
12305 達 16th Independent Mortar Battalion (5AA) - 51
12307 建 3rd Artillery Intelligence Regiment (51A) - 71
12308 秀 4th Artillery Intelligence Regiment (13AA) - 85
12311 幡 2nd Artillery Headquarters (TDA) - 74
12315 幡 25th Independent Engineer Regiment (TDA) - 74
12325 幡 6th Engineer Unit Headquarters (TDA) - 74
12326 幡 7th Engineer Unit Headquarters (TDA) - 74
12327-31 顕 2nd Independent Armored Brigade (53A) - 279
12332-6 徹 3rd Independent Armored Brigade (52A) - 280
12345 幡 12th Area Army Headquarters (1GA) - 68
12357 偕 45th Tank Regiment (55A) - 109
12358 捷 48th Independent Tank Regiment (52A) - 72
12359 師 12th Underground Construction Unit (AGA) - 127
12360 師 16th Underground Construction Unit (AGA) - 127
12364-79 浦 67th Independent Mixed Brigade (12AA) - 262
12364 浦 1st Mobile Ordinance Repair Unit, attached 67th IMB (12AA) - 261
12365 球 2nd Ordinance Duty Unit (32A) - 38
12365 球 2nd Mobile Ordinance Repair Unit, Miyako, Ryukyus (10AA) - 40
12369-75 鋼 4th Armored Division (36A) - 253
12376 磯 65th Independent Mixed Brigade HQ, became 321st Div. (TBA) - N/A
12377 境 66th Independent Mixed Brigade Headquarters (12AA) - 262
12378 浦 67th Independent Mixed Brigade Headquarters (12AA) - 262
12379 浦 15th Independent Rapid Firing Gun Battalion, 67th I.M.B (12AA) - 262
12380 房 6th Field Medium Artillery Battalion, minus 1 battery (TBAC) - 74
12380 房 6th Field Medium Artillery Btn., 1 Battery att. 321st Div. (12AA) - 68

0	1	2	3	4	5	6	7	8	9	10
〇	一	二	三	四	五	六	七	八	九	十

12381 捷 7th Field Medium Artillery Battalion (52A) - 72
12382 砦 1st Rocket Launcher Battalion (58A) - 185
12383 鋒 2nd Rocket Launcher Battalion (57A) - 118
12385 顕 2nd Independent Armored Brigade (53A) - 278
12387 築 116th Wire Company (17AA) - 182
12388 築 117th Wire Company (17AA) - 182
12389 偕 118th Independent Wire Company (55A) - 109
12394 岩 1st Independent Trench Mortar Company (3A) - 170
12396 球 3rd Independent Trench Mortar Company (32A) - 39
12397 球 4th Independent Trench Mortar Company (32A) - 39
12398 球 5th Independent Trench Mortar Company (32A) - 39
12399 境 5th Independent Machinegun Battalion, 66th I.M.B. (12AA) - 262
DN • 12400-99, 中部 Chubu Army District, Apr. 1945 distribution
12400 達 18th Independent Mortar Battalion (5AA) - 51
12401 達 19th Independent Mortar Battalion (5AA) - 51
12402 鋒 6th Artillery Intelligence Regiment (57A) - 118
12409-10 炸 3rd Anti-Aircraft Division (15AA) - 255
12411-89 翠 108th Independent Mixed Brigade (58A) - 269
12425 球 81st Field Anti-Aircraft Battalion, attached 64 IMB (57A) - 261
12426 湾 82nd Field Anti-Aircraft Battalion (10AA) - 32
12427 球 104th Machine Cannon Battalion, attached 64 IMB (57A) - 261
12428 湾 58th Field Machine Cannon Company (10AA) - 32
12429 湾 59th Field Machine Cannon Company (10AA) - 32
12430 湾 60th Field Machine Cannon Company (10AA) - 32
12431 湾 61st Field Machine Cannon Company (10AA) - 32
12432 達 62nd Field Machine Cannon Company (5AA) - 51
12435 偕 22nd Independent Mortar Battalion (55A) - 109
12436 磯 65th I.M.B. Field Hospital, 65th I.M.B., later the 321st Div. (TBA) - N/A
12437 境 66th Independent Mixed Brigade Field Hospital (12AA) - 260
12438 浦 67th Independent Mixed Brigade Field Hospital (12AA) - 261
12439 球 6th Independent Trench Mortar Company (32A) - 39
12440 球 7th Independent Trench Mortar Company (32A) - N/A
12441 球 8th Independent Trench Mortar Company (32A) - N/A
12442 球 9th Independent Trench Mortar Company (32A) - N/A
12443 球 10th Independent Trench Mortar Company (32A) - N/A
12444 球 47th Specially Established Machine Cannon Unit, Miyako Is. (10AA) - 40
12445 球 48th Specially Established Machine Cannon Unit, Ishigaki Is. (10AA) - 40
12446 球 49th Specially Established Machine Cannon Unit, Daito Is. (10AA) - 41
12447 球 50th Specially Established Machine Cannon Unit, Daito Is. (10AA) - 41
12449 鑿 4th Independent Armored Brigade (53A) - 279
12453 逐 2nd Anti-Aircraft Division (13AA) - 255
12466 敢 66th Division Ordinance Duty Unit (12AA) - 212
12468 逐 97th Field Anti-Aircraft Battalion, 2nd AAA Div (13AA) - 255
12469 彗 98th Field Anti-Aircraft Battalion, 4th AAA Div (16AA) - 256

12472 幡 2nd Guard Brigade Signal Unit (TDA) - 285
12475 偕 55th Army Headquarters (15AA) - 109
12476 楠 10th Engineer Unit Headquarters (15AA) - 96
12477 師 14th Underground Construction Unit (AGA) - 127
12478 師 17th Underground Construction Unit (AGA) - 127
12480 秀 13th Area Army Headquarters (1st GA) - 85
12490 楠 15th Area Army Headquarters (2nd GA) - 96
12491-5 鑿 4th Independent Armored Brigade (56A) - 280
12499 鑿 4th Independent Armored Brigade, not a unit (56A) - 280
DN • 12500-99, 西部 *Seibu* Army District, Apr. 1945 distribution
12504 轟 3rd Amphib. Bgde Machine Cannon Unit, later 61st I.M.C. Co. (40A) - 282
12504 陽 61st Independent Machine Cannon Company (40A) - 115
12504 轟 3rd Amphibious Bgde Machine Cannon Unit (57A) - 283
12505 払 4th Amphibious Bgde Machine Cannon Unit (5AA) - 283
12518 球 32nd Army Ordinance Duty Unit, Okinawa (32A) - 38
12524 湾 83rd Field Anti Aircraft Battalion (10AA) - 32
12526 球 105th Machine Cannon Battalion, attached 64 IMB (57A) - 261
12530 達 66th Field Machine Cannon Company (5AA) - 52
12531 達 67th Field Machine Cannon Company (5AA) - 51
12532 躍 18th Tank Regiment, 5th Independent Armored Brigade (57A) - 280
12533 闘 40th Tank Regiment, 6th Independent Armored Brigade (57A) - 281
12538 球 113th Independent Radio Platoon (32A) - 39
12539 球 114th Independent Radio Platoon (32A) - 39
12540 球 115th Independent Radio Platoon (32A) - 39
12541 球 116th Independent Radio Platoon (32A) - 39
12543 剣閃 55th Specially Est. Machine Cannon Unit, att. 109th I.M.B. (57A) - 269
12544 湾 56th Specially Established Machine Cannon Unit (10AA) - 32
12545 球 21st Field Anti Aircraft Headquarters (32A) - 39
12546 宗 46th Independent Tank Regiment (56A) - 116
12547-9 躍 5th Independent Armored Brigade (57A) - 279
12548 闘 6th Independent Tank Brigade (57A) - 281
12551 西部 151st Land Duty Company (SeB) - N/A
12552 西部 152nd Land Duty Company (SeB) - N/A
12553 西部 153rd Land Duty Company (SeB) - N/A
12554-7 西部 154th to 157th Land Duty Company (SeB) - N/A
12561-8 西部 158th to 165th Land Duty Company (SeB) - N/A
12569 暁 35th Field Duty Unit Headquarters (SC) - 145
12570 暁 67th Sea Duty Company (SC) - 145
12571 暁 68th Sea Duty Company (SC) - 145
12572 暁 69th Sea Duty Company (SC) - 145
12573 暁 70th Sea Duty Company (SC) - 145
12574-6 躍 5th Independent Armored Brigade (57A) - 280
12575-8 闘 6th Independent Armored Brigade (57A) - 281
12580 躍 5th Independent Armored Brigade (57A) - 280
12581 鋒 13th Field Medium Artillery Regiment (57A) - 118
12582 颯 53rd Field Medium Artillery Regiment (54A) - 86
12583 鋒 54th Field Medium Artillery Regiment (57A) - 118

0	1	2	3	4	5	6	7	8	9	10
〇	一	二	三	四	五	六	七	八	九	十

12588 陽 44th Independent Heavy Artillery Battalion (40A) - 115
12590 闘 6th Independent Armored Brigade (57A) - 281
DN • 12600-99, 達 *Tatsu*, 5th Area Army, Apr. 1945 distribution
12600 先 91st Division, not a unit (5AA) - 218
12603-4 達 101st Independent Mixed Brigade (5AA) - 267
12605-6 勲 42nd Division Tank Companies (5AA) - 209
12608-28 憲 69th Independent Mixed Brigade, later 89th Div (5AA) - 263
12608-99 摧 89th Division (5AA) - 218
12612 達 25th Signal Regiment (5AA) - 51
12613 達 5th Area Army Signal Unit (5AA) - 51
12614 達 22nd Tank Regiment (5AA) - 51
12616 幡 30th Signal Regiment (12AA) - 68
12617-9 達 101st Independent Mixed Brigade (5AA) - 267
12623-6 摧 89th Division (5AA) - 218
12631-5 轟 3rd Amphibious Brigade, later 125th IMB (40A) - 283
12635 陽 13th Independent Tank Company (40A) - 115
12636 払 4th Amphibious Brigade Tank Unit (5AA) - 283
12637-79 高嶺 129th Independent Mixed Brigade (5AA) - 275
12638 達 8th Independent Guard Unit, Muroran Guard Unit (5AA) - 286
12640 先 91st Division Headquarters (5AA) - 218
12643-8 奇 43rd Independent Mixed Brigade, later 89th Div (5AA) - 259
12643-9 摧 89th Division (5AA) - 218
12657-61 達 101st Independent Mixed Brigade (5AA) - 267
12666-93 先 91st Division (5AA) - 218-9
12690 達 290th Independent Infantry Battalion, Nemuro Defense Unit (5AA) - 52
12694-9 奇 43rd Independent Mixed Brigade, later 89th Div (5AA) - 259
12694-9 摧 89th Division (5AA) - 218
DN •12700-99, 朝鮮 *Chosen* Army District (Korea)
12701 築 17th Area Army Headquarters (KA) - 182
12702 砦 58th Army (17AA) - 185
12703 砦 58th Army Headquarters (17AA) - 185
12704 築 12th Engineer Unit Headquarters (17AA) - 183
12731 砦 1st Specially Established Duty Unit Headquarters (58A) - 185
12732 砦 4th Specially Established Duty Company (58A) - 185
12733 砦 5th Specially Established Duty Company (58A) - 185
12734 砦 6th Specially Established Duty Company (58A) - 185
12735 砦 7th Specially Established Duty Company (58A) - 185
12736 砦 8th Specially Established Duty Company (58A) - 185
12737 砦 9th Specially Established Duty Company (58A) - 185
12738 砦 10th Specially Established Duty Company (58A) - 185
12739 砦 11th Specially Established Duty Company (58A) - 185
12740 砦 12th Specially Established Duty Company (58A) - 185
12741 砦 13th Specially Established Duty Company (58A) - 185
12752 朝 Korean Army District Temporary Veterinary Hospital (KoD) - 186

12753 暁 71st Sea Duty Company (SC) - 145
12754 暁 72nd Sea Duty Company (SC) - 145
12755 暁 73rd Sea Duty Company (SC) - 146
12756 暁 74th Sea Duty Company (SC) -146
12757 暁 75th Sea Duty Company (SC) - 146
12758 暁 76th Sea Duty Company (SC) - 146
12760 築 36th Field Duty Unit (17AA) - 183
12761 築 36th Field Duty Unit Headquarters (17AA) - 183
12762 築 166th Land Duty Company (17AA) - 183
12763 築 167th Land Duty Company (17AA) - 183
12764 築 168th Land Duty Company (17AA) - 183
12765 築 169th Land Duty Company (17AA) - 183
12766 築 170th Land Duty Company (17AA) - 183
12767 築 171st Land Duty Company (17AA) - 183
12768 築 172nd Land Duty Company (17AA) - 183
12770 築 37th Field Duty Unit (17AA) - 183
12771 築 37th Field Duty Unit Headquarters (17AA) - 183
12772 築 173rd Land Duty Company (17AA) - 183
12773 築 174th Land Duty Company (17AA) - 183
12774 築 175th Land Duty Company (17AA) - 183
12775 築 176th Land Duty Company (17AA) - 183
12776 築 177th Land Duty Company (17AA) - 183
12777 築 178th Land Duty Company (17AA) - 183
12778 築 179th Land Duty Company (17AA) - 183
12780 築 38th Field Duty Unit (17AA) - 186
12781 築 38th Field Duty Unit Headquarters (17AA) - 186
12782 築 180th Land Duty Company (17AA) - 186
12783 築 181st Land Duty Company (17AA) - 186
12784 築 182nd Land Duty Company (17AA) - 186
12785 築 183rd Land Duty Company (17AA) - 186
12786 築 77th Sea Duty Company (17AA) - 186
12787 築 78th Sea Duty Company (17AA) - 186
12788 築 79th Sea Duty Company (17AA) - 186
12790 築 39th Field Duty Unit (17AA) - 186
12791 築 39th Field Duty Unit Headquarters (17AA) - 186
12792 築 184th Land Duty Company (17AA) - 186
12793 築 185th Land Duty Company (17AA) - 186
12794 築 186th Land Duty Company (17AA) - 186
12795 築 187th Land Duty Company (17AA) - 186
12796 築 188th Land Duty Company (17AA) - 186
12797 築 189th Land Duty Company (17AA) - 186
DN • 12800-99, 湾 *Wan*, 10th Area Army, Apr. 1945 distribution (Taiwan)
12800 湾 Formosa Army Ordinance Depot (10AA) - 31
12805 湾 Formosa Army Freight Depot (10AA) - 31
12806 湾 10th Area Army Freight Depot (10AA) - 31
12826 /13826 湾 50th Field Duty Headquarters Unit (10AA) - 33
12831 湾 1st Takasago Raiding Unit (10AA) - 31

0	1	2	3	4	5	6	7	8	9	10
〇	一	二	三	四	五	六	七	八	九	十

12832 湾 2nd Takasago Raiding Unit (10AA) - 31
12850-8 興 75th Independent Mixed Brigade (10AA) - 263
12860-5 律 76th Independent Mixed Brigade (10AA) - 264
12870 磐石 30th Independent Mixed Regiment, 100th I.M.B. (10AA) - 267
12871 湾 86th Field Machine Cannon Company (10AA) - 32
12872 湾 87th Field Machine Cannon Company (10AA) - 32
12873 湾 88th Field Machine Cannon Company (10AA) - 32
12874 湾 89th Field Machine Cannon Company (10AA) - 32
12875 湾 10th Raiding Unit Headquarters (10AA) - 31
12876 湾 90th Field Machine Cannon Company (10AA) - 32
12877 湾 34th Signal Regiment (10AA) - 31
12880-90 八幡 102nd Independent Mixed Brigade (10AA) - 267-8
12882 雷神 32nd Independent Infantry Regiment, 112th I.M.B. (10AA) - 269
12883 湾 42nd Independent Engineer Battalion (10AA) - 32
12892 湾 10th Area Army Sector Headquarters (10AA) - 31
12893 湾 354th Independent Motor Transport Company (10AA) - 32
12896 湾 6th Independent Railway Regiment (10AA) - 32
12898 湾 91st Field Machine Cannon Company (10AA) - 32
DN • 12900-99, 徳 *Toku*, Kwantung (Kantō) Army, Apr. 1945 distribution
12906 鏑 6th Air Special Signal Unit (1AirDiv 5AA) - 56
12909 威 106th Independent Wire Company (32A) - 39
12918 球 100th Independent Radio Platoon (32A) - 39
12938 偕 37th Signal Regiment (55A) - 109
12940-8 碧 59th Independent Mixed Brigade (32A) - 260
12950 鋼 30th Tank Regiment, 4th Armored Division (36A) - 254
12956-61 市 111th Division (58A) - 221-2
12962/20362 公 112th Division Ordinance Duty Unit (3A) - 222
12966/20366 公 112th Division Veterinary Unit (3A) - 222
12968 遠征 31st Signal Regiment (44A) - 179
12969 徹 3rd Independent Armored Brigade (52A) - 280
12973 球 126th Independent Wire Company (32A) - 39
12974 球 127th Independent Wire Company (32A) - 39
12994 宰 119th Division Ordinance Duty Unit (4A) - 223
12995 - 132nd Independent Wire Platoon -
12995 / 20491 宰 119th Division Medical Unit (4A) - 223
12996-9 宰 119th Division (4A) - 223
DN • 13000-99, 鋭 *Ei*, 1st Area Army, Apr. 1945 distribution
13000 鋭 12th Independent Engineer Regiment (1AA) - 168
13001 幡 27th Independent Engineer Regiment (TDA) - 74
13002-9 東北 Fukin Brigade (ToH 11AA) - N/A
13011 鋭 Mudanjiang (8th Kanto) 1st Army Hospital (1AA) - 169
13012 鋭 Jiamusi 1st (38th Kanto) Army Hospital (1AA) - 169
13013 鋭 Ning'an (62nd Kanto) Army Hospital (1AA) - 169
13014 鋭 69th Kanto Army Hospital (1AA) - 169

Chapter 4

13015 鋭 Suifenhe (76th Kanto) Army Hospital (1AA) - 169
13016 鋭 Hsinking (7th Kanto) 1st Army Hospital (1AA) - 169
13017 鋭 Hōsei (72nd Kanto) Army Hospital (1AA) - 169
13018 鋭 Boli (78th Kanto) Army Hospital (1AA) - 169
13020 鋭 76th Kanto Army Hospital (1AA) - 169
13021 鋭 Jiamusi 2nd (90th Kanto) Army Hospital (1AA) - 169
13022 鋭 60th Kanto Army Hospital (1AA) - 169
13023 鋭 Xingshan (91st Kanto) Army Hospital (1AA) - 169
13024 鋭 Fujin 92nd Kanto Army Hospital (1AA) - 169
13025 鋭 104th Guard Headquarters (4A) - 159
13027 鋭 103rd Guard Headquarters (4A) - 169
13028 鋭 Kwantung Army 2nd Field Horse Remount Depot (1AA) - 169
13040-7 迫 1st Independent Armored Brigade (3AA) - 279
13050-8 市 111th Division (58A) - 221
13061-9 駒 60th Independent Mixed Brigade (32A) - 261
13080 城 9th Guerilla Unit (5A) - 172
13081 鋭 114th Independent Motor Transport Battalion (1AA) - 168
13085 鋭 Mishan Army Hospital (1AA) - 169
DN • 13100-99, 強 *Kyou*, 3rd Area Army, Apr. 1945 distribution
13100 強 22nd Field Anti-Aircraft Unit Command (3AA) - 175
13104 強 85th Field Anti-Aircraft Battalion (3AA) - 175
13105 強 88th Field Anti-Aircraft Battalion (3AA) - 175
13106 / 14005 強 90th Field Anti-Aircraft Battalion (3AA) - 175
13107 強 Penchihu Guard Unit Headquarters (3AA) - 176
13108 強 Fushin Guard Unit Headquarters (3AA) - 176
13109 強 Anshan Guard Unit Headquarters (3AA) - 176
13112 光 102nd Guard Headquarters (4A) - 159
13114 強 91st Field Anti-Aircraft Battalion (3AA) - 175
13115/20315 公 112th Division Signal Unit (3A) - 222
13116 強 92nd Field Anti-Aircraft Battalion (3AA) - 175
13117/20317 公 112th Transport Regiment, 112th Div. (3A) - 222
13118 強 68th Field Machine Cannon Company (3AA) - 175
13119 強 69th Field Machine Cannon Company (3AA) - 175
13120 / 20320 公 246th Infantry Regiment, 112th Div. (3A) - 222
13121 強 71st Field Machine Cannon Company (3AA) - 175
13122 強 72nd Field Machine Cannon Company (3AA) - 175
13123 強 73rd Field Machine Cannon Company (3AA) - 175
13124 強 74th Field Machine Cannon Company (3AA) - 175
13125/20325 公 247th Infantry Regiment, 112th Div. (3A) - 222
13125 強 75th Field Machine Cannon Company (3AA) - 175
13126 強 76th Field Machine Cannon Company (3AA) - 175
13127 強 77th Field Machine Cannon Company (3AA) - 175
13128/20328 公 248th Infantry Regiment, 112th Div. (3A) - 222
13129 / 14036 強 6th Field Anti-Aircraft Searchlight Battalion (3AA) - 175
13130 強 70th Field Machine Cannon Company (3AA) - 175
13131/20331 公 112th Engineer Unit, 112th Div. (3A) - 222
13133 光 Jimmu Temple (39th Kanto) Army Hospital (4A) - 160

0	1	2	3	4	5	6	7	8	9	10
○	一	二	三	四	五	六	七	八	九	十

13136/20336 公 112th Field Artillery Regiment, 112th Div. (3A) - 222
13137 光 Songo (87th Kanto) 2nd Army Hospital (4A) - 159
13140 強 901st Temporary Independent Infantry Battalion (3AA) - 177
13150 公 112th Division, division #, not a unit (3A) - 222
13171-9 赫 73rd Independent Mixed Brigade (4A) - 263
13180 公 112th Division Headquarters (3A) - 222
DN • 13200-49, 徳 *Toku*, Kwantung (Kantō) Army
13222 球 22nd Independent Rapid Firing Gun Company (32A) - 39
13223 球 23rd Independent Rapid Firing Gun Company (32A) - 39
DN • 13250-99, Not Distributed
13250-98 命 71st Division (10AA) - 213
DN • 13300-99, 東部 *Tobu* Army District, Apr. 1945 distribution
13300 房 Tokyo Bay Fortress Headquarters (12AA) - 74, 285
13301-7 not used, Tobu Army District (ToB)
13308 東部 64th Specially Established Garrison Battalion, Tokyo (ToB) - 78
13309 東部 65th Specially Established Garrison Battalion, Tokyo (ToB) - 78
13310 東部 66th Specially Established Garrison Battalion, Tokyo (ToB) - 78
13311 東部 67th Specially Established Garrison Battalion, Tokyo (ToB) - 78
13312 東部 68th Specially Established Garrison Battalion, Tokyo (ToB) - 78
13313 東部 69th Specially Established Garrison Battalion, Tokyo (ToB) - 78
13314 東北 9th Specially Established Engineer Unit, Hirosaki (ToH) - N/A
13315 東北 10th Specially Established Engineer Unit, Hirosaki (ToH) - N/A
13316 東北 11th Specially Established Engineer Unit, Morioka (ToH) - 63
13317 東北 12th Specially Established Engineer Unit, Sendai (ToH) - 65
13318 東北 13th Specially Established Engineer Unit, Sendai (ToH) - 65
13319 東部 14th Specially Established Engineer Unit, Utsunomiya (ToB) - 76
13320 東部 15th Specially Established Engineer Unit, Utsunomiya (ToB) - 76
13321 東部 16th Specially Established Engineer Unit, Mito (ToB) - 75
13322 東部 17th Specially Established Engineer Unit, Mito (ToB) - 75
13323 東部 18th Specially Established Engineer Unit, Maebashi (ToB) - 77
13324 東部 19th Specially Established Engineer Unit, Urawa (ToB) - 80
13325 東部 20th Specially Established Engineer Unit, Chiba (ToB) - 80
13326 東部 21st Specially Established Engineer Unit, Chiba (ToB) - 80
13327 東部 22nd Specially Established Engineer Unit, Chiba (ToB) - 80
13328 東部 23rd Specially Established Engineer Unit, Tokyo (ToB) - 78
13329 東部 24th Specially Established Engineer Unit, Urawa (ToB) - 80
13330 東部 25th Specially Established Engineer Unit, Tokyo (ToB) - 78
13331 東部 26th Specially Established Engineer Unit, Tokyo (ToB) - 78
13332 東部 27th Specially Established Engineer Unit, Yokohama (ToB) - 79
13333 捷 52nd Army Headquarters (12AA) - 71
13334 燕 3rd Independent Machine Cannon Company (1AirA) - 133
13335 燕 4th Independent Machine Cannon Company (1AirA) - 133
13336 燕 5th Independent Machine Cannon Company (1AirA) - 133
13337 燕 6th Independent Machine Cannon Company (1AirA) - 133

13338 燕 17th Independent Machine Cannon Company (1AirA) - 133
13339 進 18th Independent Machine Cannon Company (11AA) - 61
13340 進 19th Independent Machine Cannon Company (11AA) - 61
13341 捷 35th Independent Machine Cannon Company (52A) - 72
13342 捷 36th Independent Machine Cannon Company (52A) - 72
13343 建 37th Independent Machine Cannon Company (51A) - 71
13344 燕 38th Independent Machine Cannon Company (1AirA) - 133
13345 燕 39th Independent Machine Cannon Company (1AirA) - 133
13346 燕 40th Independent Machine Cannon Company (1AirA) - 133
13347 燕 41st Independent Machine Cannon Company (1AirA) - 133
13348-50 not used, Tobu Army District
13351 線 1st Independent Railway Battalion (RR) - 141
13352 線 2nd Independent Railway Battalion (RR) - 140
13353 線 3rd Independent Railroad Battalion (RR) - 140
13354 線 4th Independent Railroad Battalion (RR) - 140
13355 線 5th Independent Railroad Battalion (RR) - 141
13356 線 6th Independent Railroad Battalion (RR) - 141
13357 線 7th Independent Railroad Battalion (RR) - 141
13358 線 8th Independent Railway Battalion (RR) - 140
13359 浦 67th Independent Mixed Brigade (12AA) - 261
13360 湾 31st Field Disease Prevention and Water Supply Dept. (10AA) - 31
13361 捷 14th Heavy Artillery Regiment (52A) - 72
13362 俊 33rd Independent Heavy Artillery Battalion, 95th IMB (50A) - 266
13363 進 34th Independent Heavy Artillery Battalion (11AA) - 60
13364 建 35th Independent Heavy Artillery Battalion (51A) - 71
13365 断 36th Independent Heavy Artillery Battalion (53A) - 73
13366 浦 4th Heavy Artillery Company, 67th I.M.B. (12AA) - 262
13367 幡 1st Tokyo Bay Fortress Artillery Unit (TB) - 74, 285
13368 幡 2nd Tokyo Bay Fortress Artillery Unit (TB) - 74, 285
13369 幡 26th Field Medium Artillery Regiment (12AA) - 68
13370 捷 27th Field Medium Artillery Regiment (52A) - 72
13373 捷 39th Signal Regiment (52A) - 72
13374 秀 40th Signal Regiment (13AA) - 85
13378 睦 3rd Signal Unit Headquarters (16AA) - 113
13379 陽 43rd Signal Regiment (40A) - 115
13380-99 not used (ToB)
DN • 13400-99, 中部 *Chubu* Army District, Apr. 1945 distribution
13400-25 中部 11th to 35th Specially Est. Garrison Units, Osaka (ChB) - 100-1
13430-42 中部 1st to 13th Specially Est. Garrison Units, Nara (ChB) - 101
13443-53 中部 2nd to 11th Specially Est. Garrison Units, Wakayama (ChB) - 101-2
13454-94 中部 1st to 41st Specially Est. Garrison Units, Kobe (ChB) - 102-3
DN • 13500-99, 西部 *Seibu* Army District, Apr. 1945 distribution
13500 睦 16th Area Army Headquarters (2GA) - 113
13501 堅城 122nd Independent Mixed Brigade, not a unit (16AA) - 273
13505 宗 29th Field Medium Artillery Regiment (56A) - 116
13510 堅城 122nd Independent Mixed Brigade Headquarters (16AA) - 273
13511 睦 11th Engineer Unit Headquarters (16AA) - 114

0	1	2	3	4	5	6	7	8	9	10
〇	一	二	三	四	五	六	七	八	九	十

13512 睦 52nd Signal Regiment (16AA) - 113
13513 秀 53rd Signal Regiment (13 AA) - 85
13514 睦 5th Short Wave Signal Company (16AA) - 113
13515 師 15th Underground Construction Unit (AGA) - 127
13518 堅塁 118th Independent Mixed Brigade (16AA) - 271
13540 宗 31st Field Duty Unit Command (56A) - 116
13541 宗 137th Land Duty Unit (56A) - 116
13542 宗 138th Land Duty Unit (56A) - 116
13543 宗 139th Land Duty Unit (56A) - 116
13544 宗 140th Land Duty Unit (56A) - 116
13545 宗 141st Land Duty Unit (56A) - 116
13546 宗 142nd Land Duty Unit (56A) - 116
13547 宗 143rd Land Duty Unit (56A) - 117
13548 鋒 32nd Field Construction Command (57A) - 118
13549 鋒 144th Land Duty Company (57A) - 118
13550 鋒 145th Land Duty Company (57A) - 118
13551 鋒 146th Land Duty Company (57A) - 118
13552 鋒 147th Land Duty Company (57A) - 118
13553 鋒 148th Land Duty Company (57A) - 118
13554 鋒 149th Land Duty Company (57A) - 118
13555 鋒 150th Land Duty Company (57A) - 118
13556 鋒 41st Signals Regiment (57A) - 118
13557 宗 44th Signal Regiment (56A) - 116
13560 堅志 98th Independent Mixed Brigade (57A) - 266
13561 鋒 40th Independent Heavy Artillery Battalion (57A) - 118
13563 幡 3rd Guard Brigade Signal Unit (TDA) - 285
13570-79 剣閃 109th Independent Mixed Brigade (57A) - 269
13580 宗 56th Army Headquarters (16AA) - 116
13581 剣閃 109th Independent Mixed Brigade, not a unit (57A) - 268
13590 鋒 57th Army Headquarters (16AA) - 118
DN • 13600-99, 達 *Tatsu*, 5th Area Army, Apr. 1945 distribution
13606-10 高嶺 129th Independent Mixed Brigade (5AA) - 275
13611 達 41st Independent Mixed Regiment (5AA) - 51
13631 陽 301st Specially Established Engineer Unit, Karafuto (HoB) - 54
13632 陽 302nd Specially Established Engineer Unit, Karafuto (HoB) - 54
13633 陽 303rd Specially Established Engineer Unit, Karafuto (HoB) - 53
13634 達 304th Specially Established Engineer Unit, Asahikawa (5AA) - 54
13635 達 305th Specially Established Engineer Unit (5AA) - 52
13636 北部 306th Specially Established Engineer Unit, Nemuro (5AA) - 52, 56
13637 達 307th Specially Established Engineer Unit, Kushiro (5AA) - 55
13638 達 308th Specially Established Engineer Unit, Sapporo (5AA) - 54
13639 達 309th Specially Established Engineer Unit, Sapporo (5AA) - 55
13640 達 310th Specially Established Engineer Unit, Sapporo (5AA) - 55
DN • 13700-99, 朝鮮 *Chosen* Army District (Korea)

13742 幡 151st Independent Radio Platoon (12AA) - 68
13743 幡 152nd Independent Radio Platoon (12AA) - 68
DN • 13800-99, 湾 *Wan*, 10th Area Army, Apr. 1945 distribution (Taiwan)
13800-4 湾 500th to 504th Specially Est. Motor Transport Unit (10AA) - 34
13810-24 湾 500th to 514th Specially Est. Guard Transport Unit (10AA) - 34
13825 湾 50th Field Transport Headquarters (10AA) - 34
13826 / 12826 湾 50th Field Duty Headquarters Unit (10AA) - 32, 34
13827 湾 22nd Line of Communications Veterinary Depot (10AA) - 33
13830-4 湾 500th to 504th Specially Est. Guard Land Duty Unit (10AA) - 34
13840-5 湾 500th to 505th Specially Est. Guard Sea Duty Unit (10AA) - 34-5
13850 湾 500th /Specially Established Casualty Transport Unit (10AA) - 33
13851 湾 501st Specially Established Casualty Transport Unit (10AA) - 33
13861-3 湾 504th to 506th Specially Est. Garrison Battalion (10AA) - 35
13864 湾 535th Specially Established Garrison Battalion (10AA) - 35
13865 湾 536th Specially Established Garrison Battalion (10AA) - 35
13866 湾 519th Specially Established Garrison Company (10AA) - 35
13867 湾 509th Specially Established Garrison Battalion (10AA) - 35
13868 湾 520th Specially Established Garrison Company (10AA) - 35
13869 湾 507th Specially Established Garrison Battalion (10AA) - 35
13870 湾 510th Specially Established Garrison Battalion (10AA) - 35
13871 湾 511th Specially Established Garrison Battalion (10AA) - 35
13872 湾 508th Specially Established Garrison Battalion (10AA) - 35
13873 湾 512th Specially Established Garrison Battalion (10AA) - 35
13874-8 湾 537th to 540th Specially Established Garrison Battalion (10AA) - 35
13879 湾 522nd Specially Established Garrison Company (10AA) - 35
13880 湾 523rd Specially Established Garrison Company (10AA) - 35
13882 湾 521st Specially Established Garrison Company (10AA) - 35
13883 湾 524th Specially Established Garrison Company (10AA) - 35
13886 湾 504th Specially Established Garrison Company (10AA) - 35
13887-91 湾 513th to 517th Specially Established Garrison Battalion (10AA) - 35
DN • 13900-99, 徳 *Toku*, Kwantung (Kantō) Army, Apr. 1945 distribution
13903 徳 Kwantung Army Construction Headquarters (KA) - 154
13904 徳 1st Kwantung Army Construction Unit (KA) - 154
13905 徳 2nd Kwantung Army Construction Unit (KA) - 154
13906 徳 3rd Kwantung Army Construction Unit (KA) - 154
13907 徳 Kwantung Army Construction Engineer Unit (KA) - 154
13908 徳 Kwantung Army Construction Materials Depot (KA) - 154
13909 徳 Kwantung Army Construction Inspectorate (KA) - 154
13911-69 栄光 121st Division (58A) - 224
13918-23 舞鶴 122nd Division (1AA) - 225
13923 徳 Kwantung Army NCO Officer Candidate Intendance Unit (KA) - 153
13924 徳 Kwantung Army NCO Officer Candidate Medical Unit (KA) - 153
13925 徳 Kwantung Army NCO Officer Candidate Veterinary Unit (KA) - 153
13928 光 42nd Signal Regiment (4A) - 159
13929 – 132nd Independent Wire Company - N/A
13930 – 133rd Independent Wire Company - N/A
13931 – 134th Independent Wire Company - N/A

0	1	2	3	4	5	6	7	8	9	10
〇	一	二	三	四	五	六	七	八	九	十

13933 幡 136th Independent Wire Company (12AA) - 68
13941 遠謀 124th Division Ordinance Duty Unit (5A) - 226
13944 遠征 2nd Raiding Unit (44A) - 179
13946 徳 Kwantung Army Education Section (KA) - 153
13948 城 46th Signal Regiment (5A) - 172
13949 徳 Kwantung Army Survey Department (KA) - 153
13951-8 邁進 120th Division (17AA) - 224
13959 凪 107th Division Ordinance Duty Unit (44A) - 220
13960 栄光 121st Division (division number, not a unit) (58A) - 224
13971 監 Kwantung Army 3rd Duty Unit (KA) - 155
13972 監 Kwantung Army 4th Duty Unit (KA) - 155
13980 徳 Kwantung Army 1st NCO Officer Candidate Infantry Unit (KA) - 153
13981 徳 Kwantung Army 2nd NCO Officer Candidate Infantry Unit (KA) - 153
13983 徳 Kwantung Army NCO Officer Candidate Cavalry Unit (KA) - 153
13984 徳 Kwantung Army NCO Officer Candidate Artillery (KA) - 153
13985 徳 Kwantung Army NCO Officer Candidate Anti-Aircraft Unit (KA) - 153
13986 徳 Kwantung Army NCO Officer Candidate Engineer Unit (KA) - 153
13987 徳 Kwantung Army NCO Officer Candidate Transport Unit (KA) - 153
13988 徳 Kwantung Army Signals Training Unit (KA) - 153
13989 徳 Kwantung Army Pigeon Breeding Plant (KA) -
13990 徳 Kwantung Army Dog Training Unit (KA) -
13992 英機 125th Division Ordinance Duty Unit (30A) - 226
13993 英断 126th Division Ordinance Duty Unit (30A) - 227
13994 英邁 127th Division Ordinance Duty Unit (3A) - 227
13995/15289 英武 128th Division Ordinance Duty Unit (3A) - 228
13997 徳 1st Independent Meteorological Company (KA) - 154
13998 徳 Kwantung Army Technical Department (KA) - N/A
13999 徳 Kwantung Army Maintenance Training Corps (KA) - N/A
DN • 14000-99, 遠征 *Sizume*, 44th Army, Apr. 1945 distribution
14000 遠征 44th Army (3AA) - 178
14001 遠征 44th Army Headquarters (3AA) - 178
14005 / 13106 強 90th Field Anti-Aircraft Battalion (3AA) - 175
14008 強 100th Field Anti-Aircraft Battalion (3AA) - 175
14009 強 65th Independent Field Anti-Aircraft Battalion (3AA) - 175
14012 北部 2nd Ind. Garrison Btn, 1st Kurile Grp became 129th I.M.B. (5AA) - 275
14014 北部 4th Ind. Garrison Battalion, 1st Kurile Group (5AA) - 275
14021 北部 29th Ind. Garrison Battalion, 1st Kurile Group (5AA) - 275
14023 遠征 14th Independent Field Artillery Battalion (44A) - 179
14036 / 13129 強 6th Field Searchlight Battalion (3AA) - 175
14038 強 7th Field Searchlight Battalion (3AA) - 175
14039 強 14th Independent Field Searchlight Company (3AA) - 175
14040 敏 80th Construction Duty Company (30A) - 178
14050 祐 108th Division, division #, not a unit (3AA) - 221
14055 祐 108th Division Headquarters (3AA) - 221

14056 展 56th Signal Regiment (34A) - 156
14062 遠征 29th Independent Rapid Firing Gun Battalion (44A) - 178
14063 遠征 30th Field Medium Artillery Regiment (44A) - 178
14066 遠征 6th Independent Heavy Artillery Company (44A) - 179
14068 遠征 112th Independent Motor Transport Battalion (44A) - 179
DN • 14100-49, 緑 Midori, Heijo Divisional District (Korea)
DN • 14150-14199 攝 Setu, Osaka Divisional District
14100 靖 177th Field Airfield Construction Unit (6AirA) - 137
14150-81 橘 44th Division (51A) - 209
14164 湾 23rd Sea Raiding Base Battalion (10AA) - 33
14165 湾 24th Sea Raiding Base Battalion (10AA) - 33
14172 楠 35th Trench Mortar Battalion (15AA) - 96
14173 宗 71st Independent Engineer Battalion (56A) - 116
14178 東明 97th I.M.B. Engineer Unit (54A) - 266
14182 隼 166th Field Airfield Construction Unit (5AirA) - 194
14183 隼 167th Field Airfield Construction Unit (5AirA) - 194
DN • 14200-99, 蔵 Zō, Tokyo Divisional District
14201 達 23rd Independent Machinegun Battalion (5AA) - 51
14202 湾 24th Independent Machinegun Battalion (10AA) - 31
14203 富士 62nd Independent Engineer Battalion (36A) - 70
14204 富士 27th Independent Rapid Firing Gun Battalion (36A) - 70
14205 富士 62nd Independent Engineer Battalion (36A) - 70
14206 磯 27th Independent Mixed Regiment, 65th I.M.B. deactivated (TBA) - 261
14207-32 浦 67th Independent Mixed Brigade 12AA) - 262
14211 / 2600 光 74th Line of Communications Duty Company (4A) - 159
14212 球 272nd Independent Infantry Battalions, det. 45 IMB (32A) - 38, 260
14213 球 273rd Independent Infantry Battalions, det. 45 IMB (32A) - 38, 260
14223-31 幡 96th Independent Mixed Brigade (TBA) - 266
14232 磯 668th Ind. Infantry Battalion, 65th I.M.B. to 67th I.M.B. (TBA) - 262
14234 幡 3rd Guard Brigade Headquarters (TDA) - 285
14235 鋒 28th Independent Field Artillery Battalion (57A) - 118
14236 燕 158th Field Airfield Construction Unit (1AirA) - 134
14237 幡 3rd Independent Heavy Artillery Regiment (12AA) - 68
14240-56 武蔵 201st Division (36A) - 241
14262 偕 149th Line of Communications Duty Company (55A) - 109
DN • 14300-49, 張 Hari, Nagoya Divisional District
14300-16 怒 73rd Division (13AA) - 214
14318 陽 28th Field Medium Artillery Regiment (40A) - 115
14320 秀 70th Independent Engineer Battalion (13AA) - 85
DN • 14350-99, 薩 Satsu, Kumamoto Divisional District
14350 阿蘇 206th Division (16AA) - 243
14353-69 西 1st to 17th Specially Established Garrison Units, Kumamoto (SeB) - 123
14370-86 西 1st to 17th Specially Established Garrison Units, Oita (SeB) - 123-4
14387-99 西 1st to 13th Specially Established Garrison Units, Miyazaki (SeB) - 124
DN • 14400-99, 徳 Toku, Kwantung (Kantō) Army
14400 達 13th Independent Rapid Firing Gun Company (5AA) - 51
14401 達 14th Independent Rapid Firing Gun Company (5AA) - 51

0	1	2	3	4	5	6	7	8	9	10
〇	一	二	三	四	五	六	七	八	九	十

14457 達 17th Independent Rapid Firing Gun Company (5AA) - 51
DN • 14500-99, Not Distributed
DN • 14600-799, 徳 *Toku*, Kwantung (Kantō) Army
14602 湾 29th Independent Rapid Firing Gun Company (10AA) - 31
14603 湾 30th Independent Rapid Firing Gun Company (10AA) - 31
14605 湾 5th Field Artillery Battalion (10AA) - 31
14721 達 31st Independent Rapid Firing Gun Company (5AA) - 51
14739 球 32nd Independent Rapid Firing Gun Battalion, att. 62nd Div. (32A) - 38
14795 浦 67th Independent Mixed Brigade (12AA) - 262
14798 豊 25th Rapid Firing Gun Company, 28th Div (10AA) - 207-8
14799 豊 26th Rapid Firing Gun Company, 28th Div (10AA) - 207-8
14957 展 127th Specially Established Land Duty Company (34A) - 157
DN • 14800-99, Not Distributed
DN • 14900-49, Not Distributed
DN • 14950-99, 徳 *Toku*, Kwantung (Kantō) Army
15050-64 安芸 205th Division (55A) - 242
15052 鋒 72nd Independent Engineer Battalion (57A) - 118
15066 睦 29th Sea Raiding Base Battalion (32A) - 42
15072 幡 15th Guard Infantry Battalion, 3rd Guard Brigade (TDA) - 285
15073 羽 171st Field Airfield Construction Unit (2AirA) - 163
15074-77 安芸 205th Division (55A) - 242
15078 線 185th Railroad Station Headquarters, Hiroshima (RR) - 140
15079 線 132nd Railroad Station Headquarters, Nagoya (RR) - 140
15080 線 140th Railroad Station Headquarters, Osaka (RR) - 140
DN • 15100-49, 黒 *Kuro*, Kurume Divisional District
15100-14 積 86th Division (57A) - 217
15116 陽 9th Independent Field Artillery Regiment (40A) - 115
15117 睦 18th Independent Mountain Artillery Regiment (16AA) - 113
15118 陽 24th Trench Mortar Battalion (40A) - 115
15119 鋒 26th Trench Mortar Battalion (57A) - 118
15120 宗 27th Trench Mortar Battalion (56A) - 116
15121 宗 119th Independent Engineer Battalion (56A) - 116
15122 鋒 121st Independent Engineer Battalion (57A) - 118
15123 睦 123rd Independent Engineer Battalion (16AA) - 114
15124-8 睦 56th to 60th Independent Signal Labor Units (16AA) - 114
15129-30 睦 66th and 67th Independent Signal Labor Units (16AA) - 114
15134 睦 4th Tsushima Fortress Infantry Battalion (16AA) - 115, 286
15135 睦 5th Tsushima Fortress Infantry Battalions (16AA) - 115, 286
15136 睦 6th Tsushima Fortress Infantry Battalions (16AA) - 115, 286
15137 宗 7th Iki Fortress Infantry Battalion (56A) - 117
15138 宗 8th Iki Fortress Infantry Battalion (56A) - 117
15139 宗 9th Iki Fortress Infantry Battalion (56A) - 117
15140 睦 27th Sea Transport Battalion (16AA) - 114
15143-9 西部 1st to 7th Specially Est. Garrison Units, Fukuoka (SeB) - 120

DN • 15150-99, 漢 *Kan*, Keijo Divisional District, Korea
15150 靖 175th Field Airfield Construction Unit (6AirA) - N/A
15151 砦 32nd Independent Rapid Firing Gun Battalion (58A) - 185
15152 砦 6th Independent Field Artillery Regiment (58A) - 185
DN • 15200-99, 徳 *Toku*, Kwantung (Kantō) Army, Apr. 1945 distribution
15201-16 松風 123rd Division (4A) - 225-6
15217-32 遠謀 124th Division (5A) - 226
15236-49 英機 125th Division (30A) - 226-7
15250-60 英断 126h Division (5A) - 227
15265-76 英邁 127th Division (3A) - 227-8
15280-91 英武 128th Division (3A) - 228
15295 松風 123rd Division Raiding Battalion, 123rd Division (4A) - 225
DN • 15300-49, Not Distributed
15301 隼 14th Air Education Unit (5AirA) - 193
15305 隼 18th Air Education Unit (5AirA) - 193
15306 鏑 12th Field Airfield Construction Unit (1AirDiv 5AA) - 56
15310 師 5th Air Regiment (20th Fighter Group, AGA) - 129
15312 羽 101st Independent Air Training Brigade Headquarters (2AirA) - 162
15324 燕 20th Field Airfield Construction Headquarters (1AirA) - 133
DN • 15351-99, Not Distributed
15351 誠 17th Air Regiment (8AirDiv 10AA) - 44
15352 誠 19th Air Regiment (8AirDiv 10AA) - 44
15353 羽 23rd Secondary Air Training Unit (2AirA) - 162
15354 羽 24th Secondary Air Training Unit (2AirA) - 162
15385 球 29th Field Airfield Construction Unit (32A) - 42
15386 靖 30th Field Airfield Construction Unit (6AirA) - 137
15392 球 128th Field Airfield Construction Unit, Ishigaki Is. (10AA) - 41
15393 球 129th Field Airfield Construction Unit, Miyako Is. (10AA) - 40
15394 燕 130th Field Airfield Construction Unit (1AirA) - 133
15395 燕 131st Field Airfield Construction Unit (1AirA) - 133
15396 燕 132nd Field Airfield Construction Unit (1AirA) - 133
15397 誠 133rd Field Airfield Construction Unit (8AirDiv 10AA) - 45
DN • 15400-99, 眞 *Shin*, 4th Air Army
DN • 15500, Not Distributed
15500 徳 Kwantung Army Field Motor Transport Depot (KA) - 154
DN • 15501-49, 監 Kantō Supply Inspectorate Department
15501 監 Kwantung Army Inspectorate General of Supply, not a unit (KA) - 153
15502 / 2614 徳 64th Independent Transport Battalion (KA) - 155
15503 徳 Kwantung Army Ordnance Manufacturing Depot (KA) - 154
15504 / 2648 徳 Kwantung Army Field Ordinance Depot (KA) - 154
15505 徳 Kwantung Army Ordinance Replacement Depot (KA) - 154
15507 徳 Kwantung Army Field Freight Harbin Branch Depot (KA) - 154
15508 徳 Kwantung Army Field Clothing Depot (KA) - 154
15509 徳 Kwantung Army Field Provisions Depot (KA) - 154
15510 徳 Kwantung Army Field Munitions Depot (KA) - 154
15511 徳 Kwantung Army Medical Stores Depot (KA) - 154
15512 徳 Kwantung Army Veterinary Stores Depot (KA) - 154

0	1	2	3	4	5	6	7	8	9	10
〇	一	二	三	四	五	六	七	八	九	十

15513 徳 Kwantung Army Horse Remount Depot (KA) - 154
15514 徳 1st Field Horse Remount Depot (KA) - 154
15516 監 Port Arthur Army Hospital (KA) - 155
15517 監 Lushun (21st Kanto) Army Hospital (KA) - 155
15518 監 Dalien Army Hospital (KA) - 155
15519 監 Jinzhou (6th Kanto) Army Hospital (KA) - 155
15520 監 Ryujuton 51st Kanto Army Hospital (KA) - 155
15521 監 Yingkou (52nd Kanto) Army Hospital (KA) - 155
15522 監 Haicheng (55th Kanto) Army Hospital (KA) - 155
15523 監 Liaoyang (39th Kanto) 1st Army Hospital (KA) - 155
15524 監 Liaoyang (58th Kanto) 2nd Army Hospital (KA) - 155
15525 監 Fengtian (3rd Kanto) Army Hospital (KA) - 155
15526 監 Tieling (4th Kanto) Army Hospital (KA) - 155
15527 監 Siping (33rd Kanto) Army Hospital (KA) - 155
15528 監 Gōngzhǔlǐng (27th Kanto) Army Hospital (KA) - 155
15529 監 Hsinking (5th Kanto) 1st Army Hospital (KA) - 155
15530 監 Hsinking (7th Kanto) 2nd Army Hospital (1AA) - 155
15531 監 Harbin (56th Kanto) 1st Army Hospital (KA) - 155
15532 監 Harbin (57th Kanto) 2nd Army Hospital (KA) - 155
15533 監 Mukden (39th Kanto) Army Hospital (KA) - 155
15534 監 Xingcheng (2nd Kanto) Army Hospital (KA) - 155
15535 監 Xingcheng (61st Kanto) 2nd Army Hospital (KA) - 155
15536 監 Jinzhou (54th Kanto) Army Hospital (KA) - 155
15538 監 Kwantung Army 1st Duty Unit (KA) - 155
15539 / 4374 監 Kwantung Army 2nd Duty Unit (KA) - 155
15540 監 Kwantung Army 5th Duty Unit (KA) - 155
15541 監 Kwantung Army 6th Duty Unit (KA) - 155
15542 監 Kwantung Army 7th Duty Unit (KA) - 155
15543 監 Kwantung Army 8th Duty Unit (KA) - 155
15544 監 Kwantung Army 9th Duty Unit (KA) - 155
15545 監 Kwantung Army 10th Duty Unit (KA) - 155
15546 徳 Kwantung Army 1st Independent Duty Company (KA) - 155
15547 徳 Kwantung Army 2nd Independent Duty Company (KA) - 155
15548 徳 Kwantung Army 3rd Independent Duty Company (KA) - 155
DN • 15550-99, 松 *Mutu*, Asahikawa Divisional District
15562 達 375th Specially Established Garrison Battalion, Sapporo (HoB) - 54
15563 達 357th Specially Established Guard Battalion, Karafuto (5AA) - 52
15564 北部 302nd Specially Established Garrison Battalion, Kushiro (5AA) - 52, 56
15565 達 327th Specially Established Guard Company (5AA) - 52
15569 達 330th Specially Established Garrison Company, Sapporo (5AA) - 52, 55
15570 / 2283 北部 331st Specially Est. Garrison Company, Kushiro (5AA) - 52, 56
15573 俊 15th Independent Machinegun Battalion (50th A) - 62
15574 浦 67th Independent Mixed Brigade (12AA) - 262
15575 進 21st Independent Rapid Firing Gun Battalion (11th AA) - 61

15576 球 22nd Independent Rapid Firing Gun Battalion (32A) - 39
15577-9 稔 77th Division (16AA) - 214-5
15580 燕 174th Field Airfield Construction Unit (1AirA) - 134
15582-9 払 4th Amphibious Brigade (5AA) - 283
DN • 15600-799, 甲 *Ko*, North China Area Army, Apr. 1945 distribution
15621-32 弘 117th Division (44A) - 222-3
15621 弘 87th Infantry Brigade, brigade code # 117th Div (44A) - 223
15623 弘 88th Infantry Brigade, brigade code # 117th Div (44A) - 223
15655 強 85th Field Machine Cannon Company (3AA) - 175
15763 路 80th Railway Regiment, 1st Battalion (CRR) - 165
DN • 15800-16299, 威 *i*, Southern Expeditionary Army, Apr. 1945 distribution
16275 湾 25th Sea Raiding Base Battalion (10AA) - 33
DN • 16300-99, 輝 *Kagayaku*, 2nd Area Army, Apr. 1945 distribution
DN • 16400-99, 勢 *Ikioi*, 2nd Army, April 1945 distribution
DN • 16500-99, 翔 *Kakeru*, 9th Air Division
16500 誠 24th Independent Flying Squadron (8AirDiv) - 44
DN • 16600-99, 羽 *Hane*, 2nd Air Army, Apr. 1945 distribution
16607 羽 10th Airfield Battalion (2AirA) - 162
16608 羽 8th Air Signal Regiment (2AirA) - 162
16609 羽 9th Airfield Battalion (2AirA) - 162
16610 師 15th Independent Air Group Headquarters (2AirA) - 162
16613 羽 2nd Air Army 1st Training Unit (2AirA) - 163
16614 羽 54th Airfield Battalion (2AirA) - 163
16616 羽 26th Secondary Air Training Unit (2AirA) - 162   both units are 16616
16616 羽 11th Airfield Battalion (2AirA) - 162
16617 羽 13th Airfield Battalion (2AirA) - 162
16618 隼魁 48th Air Regiment, 3rd Air Brigade (5AirA) - 196
16621 燕 21st Wireless Radio Unit (1AirA) - 131
16622 羽 22nd Wireless Radio Unit (2AirA) - 162
16626 誠 26th Wireless Radio Unit (8AirDiv, 10AA) - 45
16627 羽 27th Wireless Radio Unit (2AirA) - 162
16628 羽 28th Wireless Radio Unit (2AirA) - 162
16629 羽 29th Wireless Radio Unit (2AirA) - 162
16632 羽 212th Airfield Battalion (2AirA) - 163
16633 羽 213th Airfield Battalion (2AirA) - 163
16634 羽 4th Advanced Air Training Unit (2AirA) - 162
16635 隼 5th Advanced Air Training Unit (5AirA) - 193
16638 天翔 140th Airfield Battalion (10AirDiv, 1AirA) - 134
16639 天翔 141st Airfield Battalion (10AirDiv, 1AirA) - 134
16640 燕 4th Air Signal Headquarters (1AirA) - 131
16641 靖 49th Air Sector Command (6AirA) - 136
16642 羽 42nd Secondary Air Training Unit (2AirA) - 162
16643 隼 44th Air Sector Command (5AirA) - 193
16644 球 44th Airfield Battalion (32A) - 42
16647 靖 45th Air Sector Command (6AirA) - 136
16650 球 50th Airfield Battalion (32A) - 42
16655 靖 181st Airfield Battalion (6AirA) - 136

0	1	2	3	4	5	6	7	8	9	10
〇	一	二	三	四	五	六	七	八	九	十

16656 隼 182nd Airfield Battalion (5AirA) - 193
16657 隼 183rd Airfield Battalion (5AirA) - 193
16658 隼 10th Wireless Radio Unit (5AirA) - 194
16659 隼 159th Airfield Battalion (5AirA) - 183
16660 隼 160th Airfield Battalion (5AirA) - 193
16661 隼 161st Airfield Battalion (5AirA) - 193
16662 羽 11th Air Intelligence Regiment (2AirA) - 162
16663 羽 13th Advanced Air Training Unit (2AirA) - 162
16664 羽 22nd Advanced Air Training Unit (2AirA) - 162
16666 羽 196th Airfield Battalion (5AirA) - 193
16667 隼 197th Airfield Battalion (5AirA) - 193
16668 隼 198th Airfield Battalion (5AirA) - 193
16669 隼 199th Airfield Battalion (5AirA) - 193
16670 羽 240th Airfield Battalion (2AirA) - 163
16672 隼 200th Airfield Battalion (5AirA) - 193
16674 羽 214th Airfield Battalion (2AirA) - 163
16676 羽 216th Airfield Battalion (2AirA) - 163
16677 羽 57th Air Sector Headquarters Unit (2AirA) - 162
16678 羽 58th Air Sector Headquarters Unit (2AirA) - 162
16680 羽 Kantō (Kwantung) Army Air Depot (2AirA) - 163
16682 羽 25th Independent Squadron (2AirA) - 162
16683 誠 41st Independent Air Squadron (8AirDiv 10AA) - 44
16684 羽 2nd Air Army Temporary Airfield Construction Unit (2AirA) - 162
16693 隼 221st Airfield Battalion (3AirDiv later 5AirA) - 194
16694 羽 2nd Air Army Temporary Signal Training Unit (2AirA) - 162
16696 羽 17th Air Intelligence Unit (2AirA) - 162
DN • 16700-99, 暁 *Akatsuki*, Army Shipping Corps Headquarters
16700 暁 16th Shipping Engineer Regiment (SC) - 143
16706 暁 1st Mobile Transport Unit Headquarters (SC) - 144
16707 暁 1st High Speed Transport Battalion (SC) - 145
16708 暁 1st Sea Pursuit Battalion (SC) - 145
16709 暁 9th Shipping Engineer Replacement Unit (SC) - 145
16710 暁 Shipping Signal Replacement Unit (SC) - 145
16711 暁 Mobile Transport Replacement Unit (SC) - 145
16712 暁 Sea Pursuit Battalion Replacement Unit (SC) - 145
16718 暁 1st Shipping Signal Battalion (SC) - 147
16719 暁 2nd Shipping Signal Battalion (SC) - 146
16721 暁 58th Anchorage Headquarters - N/A
16722 暁 59th Anchorage Headquarters (SC) - 145
16723 暁 60th Anchorage Headquarters (SC) - 145
16726 暁 2nd Mobile Transport Company (SC) - 144
16727 暁 3rd Mobile Transport Company (SC) - 144
16728 暁 4th Mobile Transport Company (SC) - 144
16729 暁 5th Mobile Transport Company (SC) - 144

16730 暁 6th Mobile Transport Company (SC) - 144
16731 暁 7th Mobile Transport Company (SC) - 144
16734 暁 10thMobile Transport Company (SC) - 144
16735 暁 11th Mobile Transport Company (SC) - 144
16739 暁 15th Mobile Transport Company (SC) - 144
16740 暁 22nd Shipping Engineer Regiment (SC) - 147
16741 暁 23rd Shipping Engineer Regiment, minus 3rd Coy (32A) - 38
16744 暁 26th Shipping Engineer Regiment minus 3rd Coy (10AA) - 41
16744 睦 26th Shipping Engineer Regt, 3rd Coy, Amami Oshima (57A) - 119
16751 暁 1st Independent Sea Transport Company (SC) - 147
16752 暁 3rd Independent Sea Transport Company (SC) - N/A
16753 暁 4th Independent Sea Transport Company, 85 men (SC) - N/A
16754 暁 5th Independent Sea Transport Company, 84 men (SC) - N/A
16757 暁 28th Shipping Engineer Regiment (10AA) - 41
16759 湾 30th Shipping Engineer Regiment (10AA) - 41
16760 暁 31st Shipping Engineer Regiment (SC) - 147
16761 暁 2nd Mobile Transport Unit Headquarters (SC) - 144
16762 湾 16th Mobile Transport Company (SC) - N/A
16766 暁 20th Mobile Transport Company (SC) - N/A
16767 暁 21st Mobile Transport Company (SC) - 144
16768 暁 22nd Mobile Transport Company (SC) - 144
16769 暁 23rd Mobile Transport Company (SC) - 144
16770 暁 24th Mobile Transport Company (SC) - 144
16771 暁 25th Mobile Transport Company (SC) - 144
16772 暁 26th Mobile Transport Company (SC) - 144
16773 暁 27th Mobile Transport Company (SC) - 144
16774 暁 28th Mobile Transport Company (SC) - 144
16775 暁 29th Mobile Transport Company (SC) - 145
16776 暁 30th Mobile Transport Company (SC) - 144
16777 球 1st Sea Raiding Squadron (32A) - 41
16778 球 2nd Sea Raiding Squadron (32A) - 41
16779 球 3rd Sea Raiding Squadron (32A) - 41
16780 球 4th Sea Raiding Squadron, Miyako Is. (10AA) - 40
16781 球 5th Sea Raiding Squadron (32A) - 41
16788 湾 1st Sea Raiding Base Unit (32A) - 42
16789 暁 2nd Sea Raiding Base Battalion (32A) - 42
16790 暁 3rd Sea Raiding Base Battalion (32A) - 42
16791 湾 14th Sea Raiding Base Unit (10AA) - 33, 40
16798 暁 11th Sea Transport Battalion (32A) - 39
DN • 16800-99, 策 *Saku*, 28th Army, Apr. 1945 distribution
DN • 16900-99, 定 *Tei*, 29th Army, Apr. 1945 distribution
DN • 17000-99, 信 *Sin*, 38th Army, Apr. 1945 distribution
17051 展 115th Independent Motor Transport Battalion (34A) - 156
DN • 17100-99, 義 *Gi*, 39th Army, Apr. 1945 distribution
DN • 17200-99, 秀嶺 *Shurei*, 43rd Army, Apr. 1945 distribution
DN • 17300-99, 隼 *Hayabusa*, 5th Air Army
17303 隼 28th Flight Education Unit (5AirA) - 193

0	1	2	3	4	5	6	7	8	9	10
〇	一	二	三	四	五	六	七	八	九	十

17308 隼 24th Field Aircraft Repair Depot (5AirA) - 195
17310 隼 110th Independent Air Training Headquarters (5AirA) - N/A
17314 隼 128th Airfield Battalion (5AirA) - 193
17316 隼 51st Wireless Radio Unit (5AirA) - 194
17317 隼 52nd Wireless Radio Unit (5AirA) - 194
17318 隼 53rd Wireless Radio Unit (5AirA) - 194
17319 隼 54th Wireless Radio Unit (5AirA) - 194
17320 隼 5th Air Intelligence Regiment (5AirA) - 194
17321 隼 43rd Air Sector Command (5AirA) - 193
17322 隼 167th Airfield Battalion (5AirA) - 193
17325 隼 185th Airfield Battalion (5AirA) - 193
17327 隼 19th Advanced Flight Training Unit (5AirA) - 193
17328 隼 48th Air Sector Command (5AirA) - 193
17329 隼 54th Air Sector Command (5AirA) - 193
17330 隼 55th Air Sector Command (5AirA) - 193
17332 隼 23rd Air Signal Regiment (5AirA) - 194
17333 隼 22nd Air Intelligence Regiment (5AirA) - 194
17334 隼 26th Field Air Repair Depot (5AirA) - 195
17335 隼 152nd Independent Maintenance Unit (5AirA) - 195
17336 隼 153rd Independent Maintenance Unit (5AirA) - 195
17337 隼 166th Independent Maintenance Unit (5AirA) - 195
17338 隼 167th Independent Maintenance Unit (5AirA) - 195
17339 隼 168th Independent Maintenance Unit (5AirA) - 195
17340 隼 308th Independent Maintenance Unit (5AirA) - 195
17379 靖 210th Airfield Battalion (6AirA) - 136
17380 靖 211th Airfield Battalion (6AirA) - 136
DN • 17400-49, 北部 Hokubu, 27th Army
17406 達 6th Independent Machinegun Battalion (5AA) - 51
17421 / 21076 城 31st Independent Rapid Firing Gun Unit (5A) - 172
DN • 17450-99, Not Distributed
DN • 17500-99, 備 Sonae, 31st Army, Apr. 1945 distribution
DN • 17600-99, 尚武 Shobu, 14th Area Army, Apr. 1945 distribution
DN • 17700-899, 統 Tou, 6th Area Army, Apr. 1945 distribution
17792 築 5th Signal Unit Headquarters (17AA) - 182
17794 統 133rd Independent Radio Platoon (17AA) - 182
17795 築 134th Independent Radio Platoon (17AA) - 182
17796 築 135th Independent Radio Platoon (17AA) - 182
17797 築 136th Independent Radio Platoon (17AA) - 182
17798 築 137th Independent Radio Platoon (17AA) - 182
17799 築 138th Independent Radio Platoon (17AA) - 182
DN • 17900-99, Not Distributed
DN • 18000-99, 展 Ten, 34th Army, Apr. 1945 distribution
18000 展 34th Army Headquarters (KA) - 156
DN • 18100-99, 富士 Fuji, 36th Army, Apr. 1945 distribution

18100 富士 36th Army Headquarters (12AA) - 70
DN • 18200-99, 尚 Shou, 35th Army, Apr. 1945 distribution
DN • 18300-99, 膽 Tan, 109th Division
DN • 18400-99, Not Distributed
18405 燕 141st Field Airfield Construction Unit (1AirA) - 134
18406 靖 142nd Field Airfield Construction Unit (6AirA) - 137
18410 誠 146th Field Airfield Const.Unit (8AirDiv 10AA) - 45
18411 燕 147th Field Airfield Construction Unit (1AirA) - 134
18412 燕 148th Field Airfield Construction Unit (1AirA) - 134
18413 燕 149th Field Airfield Construction Unit (1AirA) - 134
18414 燕 150th Field Airfield Construction Unit (1AirA) - 134
18415 靖 151st Field Airfield Construction Unit (6AirA) - 137
18416 靖 152nd Field Airfield Construction Unit (6AirA) - 137
18417 靖 153rd Field Airfield Construction Unit (6AirA) - 137
18418 靖 154th Field Airfield Construction Unit (6AirA) - 137
18419 隼 155th Field Airfield Construction Unit (5AirA) - 194
18420 隼 156th Field Airfield Construction Unit (5AirA) - 194
18421 隼 157th Field Airfield Construction Unit (5AirA) - 194
18422 燕 16th Air Brigade Headquarters (1AirA) - 131
18423 威 21st Air Brigade Headquarters (6AirA) - 138
18423 空 8th Primary Flight Training Unit (51AirDiv AGA) - 129
18424 燕 51st Air Regiment (1AirA) - 131
18425 燕 52nd Air Regiment (1AirA) - 131
18426 天翔 53rd Flying Regiment (10AirDiv 1AirA) - 134
18427 天鷲 55th Flying Regiment (11AirDiv AGA) - 129
18428 天鷲 56th Flying Regiment (11AirDiv AGA) - 129
18429 天風 71st Flying Regiment (12AirDiv 6AirA) - 138
18430 靖 72nd Flying Regiment (21st Air Bgde 6AirA) - 138
18431 靖 73rd Flying Regiment (21st Air Bgde 6AirA) - 138
18432 空 7th Primary Flight Training Unit (51AirDiv AGA) - 129
18435 鏑 27th Air Sector Command (1AirDiv 5AA) - 56
18436 燕 95th Airfield Battalion (1AirA) - 132
18437 天翔 116th Airfield Battalion (10AirDiv 1AirA) - 134
18457 誠 138th Airfield Battalion (8AirDiv 10AA) - 45
18458 誠 139th Airfield Battalion (8AirDiv 10AA) - 45
18459 靖 142nd Airfield Battalion (6AirA) - 136
18460 天鷲 143rd Airfield Battalion (11AirDiv AGA) - 129
18461 燕 144th Airfield Battalion (1AirA) - 132
18462 靖 145th Airfield Battalion (6AirA) - 136
18463 靖 146th Airfield Battalion (6AirA) - 136
18464 靖 55th Airfield Company (6AirA) - 136
18465 燕 56th Airfield Company (1AirA) - 132
18466 靖 57th Airfield Company (6AirA) - 136
18467 燕 58th Airfield Company (1AirA) - 132
18468 誠 59th Airfield Company (8AirDiv 10AA) - 45
18469 誠 60th Airfield Company (8AirDiv 10AA) - 45
18470 誠 61st Airfield Company (8AirDiv 10AA) - 45

0	1	2	3	4	5	6	7	8	9	10
〇	一	二	三	四	五	六	七	八	九	十

18471 誠 62nd Airfield Company (8AirDiv 10AA) - 45
18472 誠 63rd Airfield Company (8AirDiv 10AA) - 45
18473 誠 64th Airfield Company (8AirDiv 10AA) - 45
18474 天翔 65th Airfield Company (10AirDiv 1AirA) - 134
18478 燕 71st Airfield Company (1AirA) - 132
18479 燕 72nd Airfield Company (1AirA) - 132
18480 誠 73rd Airfield Company (8AirDiv 10AA) - 45
18481 達 74th Airfield Company (8AirDiv 10AA) - 45
18482 球 75th Airfield Company, Amami Jima Det. (57A) - 119
18483 隼 14th Air Signal Regiment (5AirA) - 194
18495 誠 156th Airfield Battalion (8AirDiv 10AA) - 45
18496 誠 157th Airfield Battalion (8AirDiv 10AA) - 45
18497 誠 158th Airfield Battalion (8AirDiv 10AA) - 45
18498 靖 162nd Airfield Battalion (6AirA) - 136
18499 誠 16th Air Signal Regiment (8AirDiv 10AA) - 45
DN • 18500-99, 岡 *Oka*, 7th Area Army, Apr. 1945 distribution
DN • 18600-99, 昆 *Kon*, 33rd Army, April 1945 distribution
DN • 18700-49, 狼 *Rō*, 49th Division
DN • 18750-99, Not Distributed
DN • 18800-99, 球 *Kyu*, 32nd Army, April 1945 distribution
18800 球 44th Independent Mixed Brigade Headquarters (32A) - 259
18801 球 45th Independent Mixed Brigade Headquarters (32A) - 260
18803 球 Okinawa Army Hospital, Okinawa (32A) - 39
18804 球 100th Independent Heavy Artillery Battalion (32A) - 39
18809 球 14th Independent Machinegun Battalion, attached 62 Div (32A) - 38
18810 球 20th Field Well Drilling Company, Okinawa (32A) - 39
18811 球 32nd Army Field Freight Depot, Okinawa (32A) - 38
18812 球 32nd Army Field Ordinance Depot, Okinawa (32A) - 38
18813 球 3rd Raiding Unit, Kunigami Det. Daito Island (32A) - 41
18814 球 4th Raiding Unit, Kunigami Det. Daito Island (32A) - 41
18815 球 501st Specially Established Guard Engineer Unit, Okinawa (32A) - 39
18816 球 502nd Specially Established Guard Engineer Unit, Okinawa (32A) - 39
18817 球 503rd Specially Established Guard Engineer Unit, Okinawa (32A) - 39
18818 球 504th Specially Established Guard Engineer Unit, Okinawa (32A) - 39
18819 球 505th Specially Established Guard Engineer Unit, Miyako Is. (10AA) - 40
18820 球 506th Specially Established Guard Engineer Unit, Ishigaki Is. (10AA) - 40
18830 球 36th Signal Regiment, Amami Jima Det. (31A) - 39
18830 球 36th Signal Regt, one wire and one radio pltn, Amami Oshima (57A) - 119
DN • 18900-1, 誠 *Makoto*, 8th Air Division
18900 誠 8th Air Division, number for all 'Sei' Kamikaze units (8AirDiv 10AA) - 44
18901 誠 8th Air Division Headquarters (8AirDiv 10AA) - 43
DN • 18902-49, Not Distributed
18903 誠 62nd Wireless Radio Unit (8AirDiv 10AA) - 45
18904 師 8th Air Transport Command (AGA) - N/A

18905 師 13th Air Transport Squadron (AGA) - N/A
18906 師 14th Air Transport Squadron (AGA) - N/A
18907 師 15th Air Transport Squadron (AGA) - N/A
18913 隼 22nd Air Regiment (5AirA) - 195
18918 師 Central Air Traffic Control Department (AGA) - 127
18919 靖 100th Air Brigade Headquarters (6AirA) - 135
18920 靖 101st Air Regiment (100th Air Bgde, 6AirA) - 135
18921 靖 102nd Air Regiment (100th Air Bgde, 6AirA) - 135
18922 靖 103rd Air Regiment (100th Air Bgde, 6AirA) - 135
18923 羽 104th Air Regiment (2AirA) - 162
18924 靖 106th Air Regiment (6AirA) - 135
18925 靖 107th Air Regiment (6AirA) - 135
18926 靖 1st Independent Air Squadron (206th Ind. Air Unit 6AirA) - 136
18927 燕 17th Air Sector Command (1AirA) - 132
18928 誠 39th Air Sector Command (8AirDiv 10AA) - 45
18929 燕 40th Air Sector Command (1AirA) - 132
18930 靖 41st Air Sector Command (6AirA) - 136
18931 天鷲 61st Airfield Battalion (11AirDiv AGA) - 129
18932 天鷲 62nd Airfield Battalion (11AirDiv AGA) - 129
18933 天風 64th Airfield Battalion (12AirDiv 6AirA) - 138
18934 天風 65th Airfield Battalion (12AirDiv 6AirA) - 138
18935 燕 66th Airfield Battalion (1AirA) - 132
18936 燕 74th Airfield Battalion (1AirA) - 132
18937 誠 112th Airfield Battalion (8AirDiv 10AA) - 45
18938 燕 164th Airfield Battalion (1AirA) - 132
18939 燕 165th Airfield Battalion (1AirA) - 132
18940 燕 166th Airfield Battalion (1AirA) - 132
18941 燕 169th Airfield Battalion (1AirA) - 132
18942 燕 170th Airfield Battalion (1AirA) - 132
18943 靖 171st Airfield Battalion (6AirA) - 136
18944 靖 172nd Airfield Battalion (6AirA) - 136
18945 靖 173rd Airfield Battalion (6AirA) - 136
18946 靖 174th Airfield Battalion (6AirA) - 136
18947 燕 175th Airfield Battalion (1AirA) - 132
18948 燕 176th Airfield Battalion (1AirA) - 132
18949 燕 177th Airfield Battalion (1AirA) - 132
DN • 18950-9049, Not Distributed
18950 鏑 178th Airfield Battalion (1AirDiv 5AA) - 56
18951 隼 3rd Wireless Radio Unit (5AirA) - 194
18952 燕 4th Wireless Radio Unit (1AirA) - 131
18954 靖 6th Wireless Radio Unit (6AirA) - 137
18955 誠 7th Wireless Radio Unit (8AirDiv 10AA) - 45
18956 隼 8th Wireless Radio Unit (5AirA) - 194
18959 師 101st Independent Maintenance Unit (AGA) - 128
18960 師 102nd Independent Maintenance Unit (AGA) - 127
18961 師 103rd Independent Maintenance Unit (AGA) - 127
18962 師 104th Independent Maintenance Unit (AGA) - 127

0	1	2	3	4	5	6	7	8	9	10
〇	一	二	三	四	五	六	七	八	九	十

18963 師 105th Independent Maintenance Unit (AGA) - 128
18964 師 106th Independent Maintenance Unit (AGA) - 128
18965 師 23rd Air Brigade Headquarters, 20th Fighter Group (AGA) - 128
18966 誠 25th Independent Air Brigade Headquarters (8AirDiv 10AA) - 44
18967 誠 3rd Air Regiment (1AirA) - 131
18968 隼 20th Air Regiment (8AirDiv 10AA) - 44
18969 誠 67th Air Regiment (8AirDiv 10AA) - 44
18972 師 107th Independent Maintenance Unit (AGA) - 128
18973 師 108th Independent Maintenance Unit (AGA) - 128
18974 師 109th Independent Maintenance Unit (AGA) - 128
18975 師 110th Independent Maintenance Unit (AGA) - 128
18976 師 111th Independent Maintenance Unit (AGA) - 128
18977 師 112th Independent Maintenance Unit (AGA) - 128
18978 誠 113th Independent Maintenance Unit (8AirDiv 10AA) - 45
18979 師 114th Independent Maintenance Unit (AGA) - 128
18980 誠 115th Independent Maintenance Unit (8AirDiv 10AA) - 45
18981 師 116th Independent Maintenance Unit (AGA) - 128
18982 師 117th Independent Maintenance Unit (AGA) - N/A
18983 誠 118th Independent Maintenance Unit (32A, 8AirDiv 10AA) - 42, 45
18984 鏑 119th Independent Maintenance Unit (1AirDiv 5AA) - 57
18985 隼 120th Independent Maintenance Unit (5AirA) - 195
18986 師 121st Independent Maintenance Unit (AGA) - 128
18987 師 122nd Independent Maintenance Unit (AGA) - 128
18988 師 123rd Independent Maintenance Unit (AGA) - 128
18989 師 124th Independent Maintenance Unit (AGA) - 128
18990 誠 125th Independent Maintenance Unit (8AirDiv 10AA) - 45
18991 師 126th Independent Maintenance Unit (AGA) - 128
18992 師 127th Independent Maintenance Unit (AGA) - 128
18993 師 128th Independent Maintenance Unit (AGA) - 128
18999 燕 16th Independent Air Unit (1AirA) - 131
19001 師 129th Independent Maintenance Unit (AGA) - 128
19002 師 130th Independent Maintenance Unit (AGA) - 128
19003 師 131st Independent Maintenance Unit (AGA) - 128
19004 師 132nd Independent Maintenance Unit (AGA) - 128
19005 師 133rd Independent Maintenance Unit (AGA) - 128
19006 師 134th Independent Maintenance Unit (8AirDiv 10AA) - 45
19007 師 135th Independent Maintenance Unit (AGA) - 128
19008 師 136th Independent Maintenance Unit (AGA) - 128
19009 師 137th Independent Maintenance Unit (AGA) - 128
19010 隼 138th Independent Maintenance Unit (5AirA) - 195
19011 鏑 139th Independent Maintenance Unit (1AirDiv 5AA) - 57
19012 師 140th Independent Maintenance Unit (AGA) - 128
19013 隼 141st Independent Maintenance Unit (5AirA) - 195
19014 誠 142nd Independent Maintenance Unit (8AirDiv 10AA) - 45

Chapter 4

19015 師 143rd Independent Maintenance Unit (AGA) - 128
19016 師 144th Independent Maintenance Unit (AGA) - 128
19017 湾 145th Independent Maintenance Unit (8AirDiv 10AA) - 46
19018 師 146th Independent Maintenance Unit (AGA) - 128
19019 師 147th Independent Maintenance Unit (AGA) - 128
19020 師 148th Independent Maintenance Unit (AGA) - 128
19021 誠 149th Independent Maintenance Unit (8AirDiv 10AA) - 46
19022 鏑 150th Independent Maintenance Unit (1AirDiv 5AA) - 57
19023 誠 5th Field Air Repair Depot, Formosa (8AirDiv 10AA) - 45
19024 誠 5th Field Air Freight Depot, Formosa (8AirDiv 10AA) - 45
19025 師 30th Fighter Group Headquarters (6AirA) - N/A
19026 天翔 23rd Air Regiment (10AirDiv, 1AirA) - 134
19027 靖 110th Air Regiment (6AirA) - 135
19028 靖 200th Air Regiment (6AirA) - 136
19029 靖 2nd Independent Air Unit (20FG AGA) - 129
19030 靖 3rd Independent Air Unit (6AirA) - 135
19031 師 4th Independent Air Unit (AGA) - 127
19032 誠 187th Airfield Battalion (8AirDiv 10AA) - 45
19033 誠 188th Airfield Battalion (8AirDiv 10AA) - 45
19034 燕 189th Airfield Battalion (1AirA) - 132
19035 燕 190th Airfield Battalion (1AirA) - 132
19036 天風 193rd Airfield Battalion (12AirDiv, 6AirA) - 138
19037 天風 194th Airfield Battalion (12AirDiv, 6AirA) - 138
19043 帥 101st Airfield Company, 1st Raiding Brigade (6AirA) - 138, 282
19049 帥 1st Raiding Tank Unit, 1st Raiding Brigade (6AirA) - 138, 282
DN • 19050, 昭 *Akira*, 55th Air Division
DN • 19051-99, 昭 *Akira*, 55th Air Division
19051 帥 1st Raiding Maintenance Unit, 1st Raiding Brigade (6AirA) - 138, 282
19053 帥 103rd Airfield Company, 1st Raiding Brigade (6AirA) - 138, 282
19054 靖 169th Independent Maintenance Unit (6AirA) - 136
19055 靖 170th Independent Maintenance Unit (6AirA) - 137
19056 隼 171st Independent Maintenance Unit (5AirA) - 195
19057 隼 172nd Independent Maintenance Unit (5AirA) - 195
19058 隼 173rd Independent Maintenance Unit (5AirA) - 195
19059 隼 174th Independent Maintenance Unit (5AirA) - 195
19060 靖 175th Independent Maintenance Unit (6AirA) - 137
19061 燕 176th Independent Maintenance Unit (1AirA) - 133
19062 燕 177th Independent Maintenance Unit (1AirA) - 133
19063 燕 178th Independent Maintenance Unit (1AirA) - 133
19064 燕 179th Independent Maintenance Unit (1AirA) - 133
19065 隼 180th Independent Maintenance Unit (5AirA) - 195
19066 隼 181st Independent Maintenance Unit (5AirA) - 195
19067 師 182nd Independent Maintenance Unit (AGA) - N/A
19068 燕 183rd Independent Maintenance Unit (1AirA) - 133
19069 燕 184th Independent Maintenance Unit (1AirA) - 133
19070 燕 185th Independent Maintenance Unit (1AirA) - 133
19071 燕 186th Independent Maintenance Unit (1AirA) - 133

0	1	2	3	4	5	6	7	8	9	10
〇	一	二	三	四	五	六	七	八	九	十

19072 隼 187th Independent Maintenance Unit (5AirA) - 195
19073 燕 188th Independent Maintenance Unit (1AirA) - 133
19074 靖 189th Independent Maintenance Unit (6tAirA) - 137
19075 燕 190th Independent Maintenance Unit (1AirA) - 133
19076 隼 191st Independent Maintenance Unit (5AirA) - 195
19077 燕 197th Independent Maintenance Unit (1AirA) - 133
19078 燕 198th Independent Maintenance Unit (1AirA) - 133
19079 靖 199th Independent Maintenance Unit (6AirA) - 137
19080 靖 200th Independent Maintenance Unit (6AirA) - 137
19081 燕 301st Independent Maintenance Unit (1AirA) - 133
19082 燕 302nd Independent Maintenance Unit (1AirA) - 133
19083 隼 303rd Independent Maintenance Unit (5AirA) - 195
19084 隼 304th Independent Maintenance Unit (5AirA) - 195
19085 靖 305th Independent Maintenance Unit (6AirA) - 137
19086 燕 306th Independent Maintenance Unit (1AirA) - 133
19087 燕 310th Independent Maintenance Unit (1AirA) - 133
19088 燕 311th Independent Maintenance Unit (1AirA) - 133
19089 隼 7th Field Airfield Construction Headquarters (5AirA) - 194
19093 東海 4th Underground Construction Unit (ToK) -
19098 東海 9th Underground Construction Unit (ToK) -
DN • 19100-49, 誠 *Makoto*, 8th Air Division
19101 誠 42nd Air Sector Command (8AirDiv 10AA) - 45
19102 誠 105th Flying Regiment (8AirDiv 10AA) - 44
19103 誠 108th Flying Regiment (8AirDiv 10AA) - 43
19104 誠 42nd Independent Air Squadron (8AirDiv10AA) - 44
19107 誠 46th Independent Air Squadron (8AirDiv 10AA) - 43
19108 誠 43rd Independent Air Squadron (8AirDiv 10AA) - 44
19113 誠 52nd Air Sector Command (8AirDiv 10AA) - 45
19114 誠 53rd Air Sector Command (8AirDiv 10AA) - 45
19115 誠 151st Independent Maintenance Unit (8AirDiv 10AA) - 46
19116 誠 158th Independent Maintenance Unit (8AirDiv 10AA) - 46
19117 誠 159th Independent Maintenance Unit (8AirDiv 10AA) - 46
19118 誠 192nd Independent Maintenance Unit(8AirDiv 10AA) - 46
19119 誠 193rd Independent Maintenance Unit (8AirDiv 10AA) - 46
19120 誠 307th Independent Maintenance Unit (8AirDiv 10AA) - 46
19122 誠 Makoto Air Replacement Unit (8AirDiv 10AA) - 45
19152 鷲 102nd Airfield Company, 1st Raiding Brigade (6AirA) - 138, 282
19153 隼 55th Wireless Radio Unit (5AirA) - 194
19154 隼 56th Wireless Radio Unit (5AirA) - 194
19156 燕 2nd Air Special Signal Unit (1AirA) - 131
19157 誠 8th Air Special Signal Unit (8AirDiv 10AA) - 45
19158 靖 9th Special Air Signal Unit (6AirA) - 137
19159 誠 21st Air Signal Unit (8AirDiv 10AA, 6AirA) - 45, 137
19160 師 8th Air Navigational Aid Unit (AGA) - 127

Chapter 4

19161 誠 9th Air Intelligence Unit (8AirDiv 10AA) - 45
19162 靖 154th Independent Maintenance Unit (6AirA) - 136
19163 燕 155th Independent Maintenance Unit (1AirA) - 132
19164 燕 160th Independent Maintenance Unit (1AirA) - 132
19167 燕 195th Independent Maintenance Unit (1AirA) - 133
19168 燕 196th Independent Maintenance Unit (1AirA) - 133
19185 燕 13th Air Signal Regiment (1AirA) - 131
19186 靖 18th Air Signal Regiment (6AirA) - 137
19187 燕 1st Wireless Radio Unit (1AirA) - 131
19188 燕 2nd Wireless Radio Unit (1AirA) - 131
19189 / 122 靖 13th Wireless Radio Unit (AGA) - 137
19190 天翔 18th Flying Regiment (10AirDiv 1AirA) - 134
19191 天翔 3rd Airfield Battalion (10Air Div 1AirA) - 134
19192 天翔 6th Airfield Battalion (10Air Div 1AirA) - 134
19193 天翔 7th Airfield Battalion (10Air Div 1AirA) - 134
19194 天翔 43rd Airfield Battalion (10Air Div 1AirA) - 134
19195 天翔 244th Airfield Battalion (10Air Div 1AirA) - 134
19196 天鷲 246th Flying Regiment (11Air Div AGA) - 129
19197 天鷲 42nd Airfield Battalion (11Air Div AGA) - 129
19198 天鷲 246th Airfield Battalion (11Air Div AGA) - 129
DN • 19250-349, 鏑 *Cabra*, 1st Air Division
19250 鏑 6th Field Air Repair Depot (1AirDiv 5AA) - 56
19251 鏑 6th Field Air Freight Depot (1AirDiv 5AA) - 56
19252 鏑 21st Air Sector Command (1AirDiv 5AA) - 56
19253 鏑 1st Fixed Signal Unit (1AirDiv 5AA) - 56
19254 鏑 11th Wireless Radio Unit (1AirDiv 5AA) - 56
19255 鏑 12th Wireless Radio Unit (1AirDiv 5AA) - 56
19257 鏑 2nd Airfield Battalion (1AirDiv 5AA) - 56
19266 鏑 21st Field Airfield Construction Unit (1AirDiv 5AA) - 56
19270 鏑 20th Air Brigade Headquarters (1AirDiv 5AA) - 56
19272 鏑 54th Air Regiment (1AirDiv 5AA) - 56
19274 鏑 1st Airfield Battalion (1AirDiv 5AA) - 56
19275 鏑 10th Air Signal Regiment (1AirDiv 5AA) - 56
19276 鏑 20th Air Intelligence Unit (1AirDiv 5AA) - 56
19277 鏑 20th Air Navigation Aid Unit (1AirDiv 5AA) - 56
19320 鏑 73rd Airfield Battalion (1AirDiv 5AA) - 56
19335 鏑 20th Air Sector Command (1AirDiv 5AA) - 56
19336 鏑 49th Airfield Battalion (1AirDiv 5AA) - 56
19337 鏑 55th Airfield Battalion (1AirDiv 5AA) - 56
19338 鏑 63rd Airfield Battalion (1AirDiv 5AA) - 56
19342 鏑 38th Flying Regiment (1AirDiv 5AA) - 56
19345 鏑 77th Airfield Battalion (1AirDiv 5AA) - 56
19346 鏑 80th Airfield Battalion (1AirDiv 5AA) - 56
19347 鏑 83rd Airfield Battalion (1AirDiv 5AA) - 56
19349 鏑 11th Field Meteorological Unit (1AirDiv, 5AA) - 56
DN • 19350-449, 空 *Kyoku*, 51st Air (Training) Division
19350 天翔 46th Air Sector Command (10AirDiv, 1AirA) - 134

0	1	2	3	4	5	6	7	8	9	10
〇	一	二	三	四	五	六	七	八	九	十

19351 天鷲 47th Air Sector Command (11AirDiv AGA) - 129
19352 靖 191st Airfield Battalion (6AirA) - 136
19353 靖 192nd Airfield Battalion (6AirA) - 136
19354 靖 195th Airfield Battalion (6AirA) - 136
19359 靖 60th Air Sector Command (6AirA) - 136
19360 靖 61st Air Sector Command (6AirA) - 136
19361 靖 249th Airfield Battalion (6AirA) - 136
19362 靖 250th Airfield Battalion (6AirA) - 136
19363 靖 251st Airfield Battalion (6AirA) - 136
19364 燕 252nd Airfield Battalion (1AirA) - 132
19365 燕 253rd Airfield Battalion (1AirA) - 132
19366 靖 254th Airfield Battalion (6AirA) - 136
19368 靖 312th Independent Maintenance Unit (6AirA) - 137
19369 靖 313th Independent Maintenance Unit (6AirA) - 137
19370 燕 314th Independent Maintenance Unit (1AirA) - 133
19373 天風 51st Air Sector Command (12AirDiv 6AirA) - 138
19374 隼 202nd Airfield Battalion (5AirA) - 193
19375 隼 203rd Airfield Battalion (5AirA) - 193
19376 隼 204th Airfield Battalion (5AirA) - 194
19376 靖 255th Airfield Battalion (6AirA) - 136
19377 隼 206th Airfield Battalion (5AirA) - 194
19378 隼 208th Airfield Battalion (5AirA) - 194
19381 隼 222nd Airfield Battalion (5AirA) - 194
19382 隼 223rd Airfield Battalion (5AirA) - 194
19383 隼 224th Airfield Battalion (5AirA) - 194
19384 隼 225th Airfield Battalion (5AirA) - 194
19385 隼 226th Airfield Battalion (5AirA) - 194
19386 靖 227th Airfield Battalion (6AirA) - 136
19387 靖 228th Airfield Battalion (6AirA) - 136
19388 靖 229th Airfield Battalion (6AirA) - 136
19389 靖 230th Airfield Battalion (6AirA) - 136
19390 靖 231st Airfield Battalion (6AirA) - 136
19391 靖 157th Independent Maintenance Unit (6AirA) - 136
19392 靖 163rd Independent Maintenance Unit (6AirA) - 136
19393 燕 164th Independent Maintenance Unit (1AirA) - 132
19394 燕 165th Independent Maintenance Unit (1AirA) - 132
19395 燕 309th Independent Maintenance Unit (1AirA) - 133
DN • 19450-99, Not Distributed
DN • 19500, 靖 *Yasu*, 6th Air Army Headquarters
19500 靖 6th Air Army Headquarters (6AirA) - 135
19501 師 18th Underground Construction Unit (AGA) - 127
19502 師 19th Underground Construction Unit (AGA) - 127
19503 師 20th Underground Construction Unit (AGA) - 127
DN • 19501-699, Not Distributed

19529 天鷲 82nd Independent Air Squadron (11AirDiv 6AirA) -
19530 天風 83rd Independent Air Squadron (12AirDiv 6AirA) -
19531 燕 232nd Airfield Battalion (1AirA) - 132
19532 燕 233rd Airfield Battalion (1AirA) - 132
19533 燕 234th Airfield Battalion (1AirA) - 132
19534 天風 235th Airfield Battalion (12AirDiv 6AirA) - 138
19535 天風 236th Airfield Battalion (12AirDiv 6AirA) - 138
19536 燕 237th Airfield Battalion (1AirA) - 132
19537 燕 238th Airfield Battalion (1AirA) - 132
19538 燕 239th Airfield Battalion (1AirA) - 132
19539 燕 76th Airfield Company (1AirA) - 132
19540 燕 77th Airfield Company (1AirA) - 132
19541 燕 78th Airfield Company (1AirA) - 132
19542 燕 79th Airfield Company (1AirA) - 132
19543 燕 80th Airfield Company (1AirA) - 132
19544 燕 81st Airfield Company (1AirA) - 132
19545 燕 82nd Airfield Company (1AirA) - 132
19546 靖 83rd Airfield Company (6AirA) - 136
19547 靖 84th Airfield Company (6AirA) - 136
19548 靖 1st Air Signals Headquarters (6AirA) - 137
19549 隼 5th Air Signals Headquarters (5AirA) - 194
19550 燕 63rd Wireless Radio Unit (1AirA) - 131
19551 燕 64th Wireless Radio Unit (1AirA) - 131
19552 燕 65th Wireless Radio Unit (1AirA) - 131
19553 燕 66th Wireless Radio Unit (1AirA) - 132
19554 燕 67th Wireless Radio Unit (1AirA) - 132
19555 靖 68th Wireless Radio Unit (6AirA) - 137
19556 靖 69th Wireless Radio Unit (6AirA) - 137
19557 靖 70th Wireless Radio Unit (6AirA) - 137
19558 靖 71st Wireless Radio Unit (6AirA) - 137
19559 靖 72nd Wireless Radio Unit (6AirA) - 137
19560 靖 73rd Wireless Radio Unit (6AirA) - 137
19561 靖 74th Wireless Radio Unit (6AirA) - 137
19562 靖 75th Wireless Radio Unit (6AirA) - 137
19563 隼 76th Wireless Radio Unit (5AirA) - 194
19564 球 32nd Army Air Intelligence Unit: Miyako, Ishigaki, Daito (10AA) - 38, 40
19565 誠 10th Field Meteorology Unit, minus 3rd Company (8AirDiv 10AA) - 45
19565 誠 10th Field Meteorology Unit, 3rd Company (32A) - 42
DN • 19700, 蓬 Hō, 50th Division
19700 蓬 50th Division, Div # not a unit - 210
DN •19701-49, 湾 Wan, Formosa (Taiwan) Army
19701-13 蓬 50th Division (10AA) - 210
DN • 19750-899, 暁 Akatsuki, Army Shipping Corps Headquarters
19759 湾 20th Sea Raiding Squadron (10AA) - 33, 41
19760 湾 21st Sea Raiding Squadron (10AA) - 33
19761 湾 22nd Sea Raiding Squadron (10AA) - 33
19762 湾 23rd Sea Raiding Squadron (10AA) - 33

0	1	2	3	4	5	6	7	8	9	10
〇	一	二	三	四	五	六	七	八	九	十

19763 湾 24th Sea Raiding Squadron (10AA) - 33
19764 湾 25th Sea Raiding Squadron (10AA) - 33
19765 球 26th Sea Raiding Squadron (32A) - 41
19766 球 27th Sea Raiding Squadron (32A) - 41
19767 球 28th Sea Raiding Squadron (32A) - 41
19768 球 29th Sea Raiding Squadron (32A) - 41
19769 暁 30th Sea Raiding Squadron (32A) - 41
19772 暁 4th Sea Raiding Base Unit Headquarters (10AA) - 33
19773 暁 5th Sea Raiding Base Unit Headquarters (32A) - 42
19775 暁 5th Shipping Signal Battalion (SC) - 145
19776 暁 Shipping Intelligence Regiment (SC) - 144
19781 暁 131st Specially Established Sea Duty Company (SC) - 147
19782 暁 132nd Specially Established Sea Duty Company (SC) - 146
19783 暁 133rd Specially Established Sea Duty Company (SC) - 146
19784 暁 134th Specially Established Sea Duty Company (SC) - 146
19785 暁 135th Specially Established Sea Duty Company (SC) - 146
19786 暁 136th Specially Established Sea Duty Company (SC) - 146
19787 暁 137th Specially Established Sea Duty Company (10AA) - 33
19788 暁 138th Specially Established Sea Duty Company (10AA) - 33
19789 築 139th Specially Established Sea Duty Company (17AA) - 184
19790 築 140th Specially Established Sea Duty Company (17AA) - 184
19791 築 141st Specially Established Sea Duty Company (17AA) - 184
19802 暁 152nd Specially Established Sea Duty Company (SC) - 147
19803 暁 153rd Specially Established Sea Duty Company (SC) - 147
19804 暁 154th Specially Established Sea Duty Company (SC) - 147
19805 暁 155th Specially Established Sea Duty Company (SC) - 147
19808 暁 7th Field Shipping Depot (10AA) - 33
19812 暁 35th Shipping Engineer Regiment (SC) - 146
19813 暁 36th Shipping Engineer Regiment (SC) - 146
19814 暁 12th Sea Transport Battalion (SC) - 144
19815 暁 13th Sea Transport Battalion (SC) - 144
19816 暁 14th Sea Transport Battalion (SC) - 144
19817 湾 15th Sea Transport Battalion (10AA) - 33
19818 暁 16th Sea Transport Battalion (SC) - 144
19819 暁 17th Sea Transport Battalion (SC) - 144
19820 暁 18th Sea Transport Battalion (SC) - 144
19822 暁 37th Shipping Engineer Regiment (SC) - 147
19823 暁 38th Shipping Engineer Regiment (SC) - 147
19824 暁 39th Shipping Engineer Regiment (SC) - 147
19825 暁 40th Shipping Engineer Regiment (SC) - 147
19826 暁 41st Shipping Engineer Regiment (SC) - 147
19827 暁 42nd Shipping Engineer Regiment (SC) - 147
19828 暁 43rd Shipping Engineer Regiment (SC) - 147
19829 暁 44th Shipping Engineer Regiment (SC) - 147

19830 暁 54th Shipping Engineer Regiment (SC) - 143
19831 暁 46th Shipping Engineer Regiment (SC) - 147
19832 暁 47th Shipping Engineer Regiment (SC) - 147
19833 暁 19th Sea Transport Battalion (SC) - 144
19834 暁 20th Sea Transport Battalion (SC) - 144
19835 暁 6th Shipping Signal Battalion (SC) - 145
19836 暁 7th Shipping Signal Battalion (SC) - 145
19837 暁 48th Shipping Engineer Regiment (SC) - 143
19838 暁 49th Shipping Engineer Regiment (SC) - 143
19839 暁 50th Shipping Engineer Regiment (SC) - 143
19846 睦 31st Sea Raiding Squadron (16AA) - 114
19847 睦 32nd Sea Raiding Squadron (16AA) - 114
19848 睦 33rd Sea Raiding Squadron (16AA) - 114
19849 睦 34th Sea Raiding Squadron (16AA) - 114
19850 睦 35th Sea Raiding Squadron (16AA) - 114
19851 睦 36th Sea Raiding Squadron (16AA) - 114
19852 睦 37th Sea Raiding Squadron (16AA) - 114
19853 睦 38th Sea Raiding Squadron (16AA) - 114
19854 楠 39th Sea Raiding Squadron (15AA) - 96
19855 楠 40th Sea Raiding Squadron (15AA) - 96
19856 暁 41st Sea Raiding Squadron (SC) - 143
19857 暁 42nd Sea Raiding Squadron (SC) - 143
19858 暁 43rd Sea Raiding Squadron (SC) - 143
19859 暁 44th Sea Raiding Squadron (SC) - 143
19860 暁 45th Sea Raiding Squadron (SC) - 143
19861 暁 46th Sea Raiding Squadron (SC) - 143
19862 暁 47th Sea Raiding Squadron (SC) - 143
19863 暁 48th Sea Raiding Squadron (SC) - 143
19864 暁 49th Sea Raiding Squadron (15AA) - 143
19865 暁 50th Sea Raiding Squadron (15AA) - 144
19866 睦 1st Sea Raiding Maintenance Unit (16AA) - 114
19867 睦 2nd Sea Raiding Maintenance Unit (16AA) - 114
19868 睦 3rd Sea Raiding Maintenance Unit (16AA) - 114
19869 睦 4th Sea Raiding Maintenance Unit (16AA) - 114
19870 睦 5th Sea Raiding Maintenance Unit (16AA) - 114
19871 睦 6th Sea Raiding Maintenance Unit (16AA) - 114
19872 睦 7th Sea Raiding Maintenance Unit (16AA) - 114
19873 睦 8th Sea Raiding Maintenance Unit (16AA) - 114
19874 楠 9th Sea Raiding Maintenance Unit (15AA) - 96
19875 楠 10th Sea Raiding Maintenance Unit (15AA) - 97
19876 楠 11th Sea Raiding Maintenance Unit (SC) - 144
19877 楠 12th Sea Raiding Maintenance Unit (SC) - 144
19878 楠 13th Sea Raiding Maintenance Unit (SC) - 144
19879 楠 14th Sea Raiding Maintenance Unit (SC) - 144
19880 楠 15th Sea Raiding Maintenance Unit (SC) - 144
19881 楠 16th Sea Raiding Maintenance Unit (SC) - 144
19882 楠 17th Sea Raiding Maintenance Unit (SC) - 144

0	1	2	3	4	5	6	7	8	9	10
〇	一	二	三	四	五	六	七	八	九	十

19883 楠 18th Sea Raiding Maintenance Unit (SC) - 144
19884 楠 19th Sea Raiding Maintenance Unit (SC) - 144
19885 楠 20th Sea Raiding Maintenance Unit (SC) - 144
19886 暁 200th Land Duty Company (SC) - 145
19887 暁 201st Land Duty Company (SC) - 145
19888 暁 202nd Land Duty Company (SC) - 145
19889 暁 203rd Land Duty Company (SC) - 145
19890 暁 204th Land Duty Company (SC) - 145
19891 暁 205th Land Duty Company (SC) - 145
19892 暁 206th Land Duty Company (SC) - 145
19893 暁 207th Land Duty Company (SC) - 145
19894 暁 208th Land Duty Company (SC) - 145
19895 暁 209th Land Duty Company (SC) - 145
DN • 19900-99, 昭 *Akira*, 55th Air (Training) Division
DN • 20000-99, 凪 *Nagi*, 107th Division
20000-27 凪 107th Division (44A) - 220-1
20030 祐 108th Division Transport Regiment (3AA) - 221
20040 凪 107th Division Medical Unit (44A) - 220
DN • 20100-99, 祐 *Yū*, 108th Division
20110-80 祐 108th Division (3AA) - 221
DN • 20200-99, Not Distributed
DN • 20300-99, 公 *Kimi*, 112th Division
20315-78 公 112th Division (3A) - 222
DN • 20400-99, 宰 *Sai*, 119th Division
20400-98 宰 119th Division (4A) - 223
DN • 20500-49, 凪 *Nagi*, 107th Division
DN • 20550-9, 祐 *Yū*, 108th Division
20550-90 祐 108th Division (3AA) - 221
DN • 20600-49, Not Distributed
DN • 20650-99, 公 *Kimi*, 112th Division
DN • 20700-49, 宰 *Sai*, 119th Division
20702 光 Load Carrying Camel Unit (4A) - 158
DN • 20750-99, 陸 *Riku*, Hirosaki Divisional District
DN • 20750-99, 陸 *Riku*, Hirosaki Divisional District
20750-63 東北 1st to 14th Specially Established Garrison Units, Aomori (ToH) - 63
20717 / 26817 光 17th Mortar Battalion (4A) - 158
20764-80 東北 1st to 17th Specially Est. Garrison Units, Morioka (ToH) - 63-4
20781-92 東北 1st to 12th Specially Established Garrison Units, Akita (ToH) - 64
DN • 20800-49, 張 *Hari*, Nagoya Divisional District
20800 秀 152nd Line of Communications Unit Headquarters (13AA) - 85
20801 秀 152nd Line of Communications Duty Company (13AA) - 85
DN • 20850-99, 攝 *Setu*, Osaka Divisional District
DN • 20900-49, 黒 *Kuro*, Kureme Divisional District
20902 – 80th Independent Engineer Battalion - N/A

20903 靖 173rd Field Airfield Construction Unit (6AirA) - 137
20904-24 西部 8th to 28th Specially Est. Garrison Units, Fukuoka (SeB) - 120-1
20925-34 西部 1st to 10th Specially Established Garrison Units, Saga (SeB) - 121
20935-49 西部 1st to 15th Specially Established Garrison Units, Nagasaki (SeB) - 122
DN • 20950-99, 松 Mutu, Asahikawa Divisional District
DN • 21000-49, Not Distributed
DN • 21050-99, 城 Shiro, 5th Army, April 1945 distribution
21073 邁進 120th Division Medical Unit (17AA) - 24
21074 邁進 120th Division Field Hospital (17AA) - 224
21076 / 17421 31st Independent Rapid Firing Gun Unit (5A) - 172
21077 城 Mudanjiang (37th Kanto) 2nd Army Hospital (5A) - 173
21079 岩 Pingyang (Kanto) Army Hospital (3A) - 171
21080 岩 Hailar (23rd Kanto) 1st Army Hospital (3A) - 171
21081 鋭 Port Arthur (24th Kanto) 1st Army Hospital (1AA) - 169
21082 鋭 Linkou (25th Kanto) Army Hospital (1AA) - 169
21083 城 Hulin (32nd Kanto) Army Hospital (5A) - 173
21084 城 Hutou (68th Kanto) Army Hospital (5A) - 173
21085 鋭 Mamorukami Army Hospital (1AA) - 169
21085 岩 Baoqing (74th Kanto) Army Hospital (3A) - 171
21086 岩 Tungning (66th Kanto) 2nd Army Hospital (3A) - 171
21087 城 Suiyang (34th Kanto) Army Hospital (5A) - 173
21088 城 73rd Kanto Army Hospital (5A) - 173
21089 城 Bamiantongzhen (80th Kanto) Army Hospital (5A) - 173
21092 城 Baodong (78th Kanto) Army Hospital (1AA) - 169
21092 城 Xingshu (78th Kanto) Army Hospital (5A) - 173
21093 城 Jixi (79th Kanto) Army Hospital (5A) - 173
21094 城 Mudanjiang (63rd Kanto) 3rd Army Hospital (5A) - 173
21099 / 3492 城 20th Heavy Artillery Regiment (5A) - 172
DN • 21100-49, Not Distributed
21100-9 破竹 103rd Independent Mixed Brigade (10AA) - 268
21111 磐石 100th Independent Mixed Brigade Headquarters (10AA) - 267
21112 敢 2nd Field Hospital, 66th Div (10AA) - 212
21113 劍 2nd Field Hospital, 12th Div (10AA) - 206
21114 劍 Medical Unit, 12th Div (10AA) - 206
21115 敢 Veterinary Unit, 66th Div (10AA) - 212
21116 雷神 33rd Independent Infantry Regiment, 112th I.M.B. (10AA) - 269
21117 湾 92nd Field Machine Cannon Company (10AA) - 32
21118 湾 93rd Field Machine Cannon Company (10AA) - 32
21119 律 567th Independent Infantry Battalion, 76th I.M.B. (10AA) - 264
21122 雷神 648th Independent Infantry Battalion, 112th I.M.B. (10AA) - 269
21123 湾 Taipei Army Hospital (10AA) - 33
21124 湾 Keelung Island Army Hospital (10AA) - 33
21125 湾 Tainan Army Hospital (10AA) - 33
21126 湾 Kaohsiung Army Hospital (10AA) - 33
21127 湾 Pingtung Army Hospital (10AA) - 33
21128 湾 Penghu Island Army Hospital (10AA) - 33
21129 湾 Hualien Army Hospital (10AA) - 33

0	1	2	3	4	5	6	7	8	9	10
〇	一	二	三	四	五	六	七	八	九	十

21130 湾 Taitung Army Hospital (10AA) - 33
21131 湾 Taichung Army Hospital (10AA) - 33
21132 湾 Chiayi Army Hospital (10AA) - 33
21133 湾 222nd Line of Communications Hospital (10AA) - 33
21134 雷神 112th Independent Mixed Brigade Headquarters (10AA) - 269
21136 湾 Formosa Provisional Epidemic Prevention Department (10AA) - 31
21138 湾 221st Line of Communications Hospital (10AA) - 33
21141 湾 10th Area Army Motor Vehicle Depot (10AA) - 31
DN • 21150-99, 奏 *So*, 79th Division
21150-69 奏 79th Division (3A) - 215
DN • 21200-99, 靖 *Yasu*, 6th Air Army, April 1945 distribution
21200 隼 24th Air Signal Regiment (5AirA) - 194
21201 靖 206th Independent Air Unit Headquarters (6AirA) - 135
21202 靖 7th Air Regiment (6AirA) - 135
21203 靖 98th Air Regiment (6AirA) - 135
21204 天風 19th Independent Air Squadron (12AirDiv 6AirA) - 138
21205 靖 19th Air Signal Regiment (6AirA) - 137
DN • 21300-49, 陽 *Yo*, 40th Army, April 1945 distribution
21300 陽 40th Army Headquarters (16AA) - 115
21301 湾 33rd Signal Regiment (10AA) - 31
DN • 21350-400, Not Distributed
DN • 21401-600, 東北 *Tohoku* Army District
21401 進 38th Signals Regiment (11AA) - 61
21402 楠 45th Signal Regiment (15AA) - 96
21405-15 琢 7th Independent Armored Brigade (51A) - 281
21409 進 44th Independent Tank Regiment (11AA) - 61
21410 建 51st Army Headquarters (51A) - 71
21411 偕 47th Tank Regiment (55A) - 109
21412 進 8th Engineers Headquarters (11AA) - 61
21413 俊 50th Army Headquarters (11AA) - 62
21441 – 512th Land Duty Company - N/A
21442 進 17th Field Transport Headquarters (11AA) - 61
21446 東北 7th Field Horse Replacement Depot (11AA) - 61
21497 東部 501st Construction Duty Company (ToB) - N/A
21498 西部 502nd Construction Duty Company (SeB) - N/A
DN • 21601-800, 東海 *Tokai* Army District, Apr. 1945 distribution
21601 断 53rd Army Headquarters (12AA) - 73
21602-35 逐 2nd Anti-Aircraft Division (13AA) - 256
21603 秀 9th Engineer Unit Headquarters (13AA) - 85
21604 師 13th Underground Construction Unit (AGA) - 127
21608 燕 45th Independent Machine Cannon Company (1AirA) - 133
21609 燕 46th Independent Machine Cannon Company (1AirA) - 133
21610-28 加越 209th Division (36A) - 243-4
21637 師 2nd Ultra Short Wave Signal Company (AGA) - 127

21640 颯 54th Army (13AA) - 86
21641 颯 54th Army Headquarters (13AA) - 86
21642 颯 3rd Artillery Headquarters (54A) - 86
21643 陽 4th Artillery Headquarters (40A) - 115
21646 秀 19th Field Transport Headquarters (13AA) - 85
21703 砦 58th Army Headquarters (58A) - 185
21709 東部 509th Construction Duty Company (ToB) - N/A
21710 東部 510th Construction Duty Company (ToB) - N/A
21711 東部 511th Construction Duty Company (ToB) - N/A
21712 西部 512th Construction Duty Company (SeB) - N/A
21733 護古 143rd Division Artillery Unit (54A) - 233
21733 秀 9th Field Horse Remount Depot (13AA) - 85
21734 護京 153rd Division Field Artillery Unit (13AA) - 238
21735 陽 104th Independent Engineer Battalion (40A) - 115
21736 颯 105th Independent Engineer Battalion (54A) - 86
21737 颯 106th Independent Engineer Battalion (54A) - 86
21738 颯 107th Independent Engineer Battalion (54A) - 86
21739 秀 108th Independent Engineer Battalion (13 AA) - 85
21740-53 北越 229th Division (13AA) - 247-8
21763 宗 12th Trench Mortar Battalion (56A) - 116
21764 / 3107 秀 13th Trench Mortar Battalion (54A) - 86
21765 / 3108 秀 14th Trench Mortar Battalion (54A) - 86
21766 秀 15th Trench Mortar Battalion (13 AA) - 85
21767 颯 33rd Independent Artillery Battalion (54A) - 86
21768 颯 34th Independent Artillery Battalion (54A) - 86
21769 秀 15th Independent Mountain Artillery Regiment (13AA) - 85
21770-9 高師 303rd Division (40A) - 249-50
21780-9 東旭 119th Independent Mixed Brigade (54A) - 272
21790 鋒 5th Self-propelled Artillery Battalion (57A) - 118
21791 秀 6th Self-Propelled Artillery Battalion (13AA) - 85
21793 宗 19th Field Medium Artillery Battalion (56A) - 116
21794 陽 20th Field Medium Artillery Battalion (40A) - 115
21795 秀 24th Sea Transport Battalion (13AA) - 85
DN • 21801-900, 紺 *Kon*, 52nd Air (Training) Division
21810-9 東天 120th Independent Mixed Brigade (54A) - 272
Note: The following air units share same #'s as the 120th IMB
21813 燕 62nd Air Sector Command (1AirA) - 132
21814 燕 256th Airfield Battalion (1AirA) - 132
21815 燕 257th Airfield Battalion (1AirA) - 132
21816 燕 258th Airfield Battalion (1AirA) - 132
21817 燕 315th Independent Maintenance Unit (1AirA) - 133
21910 隼 316th Independent Maintenance Unit (5AirA) - 195
DN • 21901-2000, 宙 *Chu*, 53rd Air (Training) Division
DN • 22001-50, 漢 *Kan*, Keijo Divisional District (Korea)
22001-9 玄 96th Division (58A) - 220
DN • 22051-100, 護東 *Gotō*, 140th Division, April 1945 distribution
22051-61 護東 140th Division (53A) - 232

0	1	2	3	4	5	6	7	8	9	10
〇	一	二	三	四	五	六	七	八	九	十

DN • 22101-200, 隼魁 *Hayabusa Sakigake*, 13th Air Division
DN • 22201-50, 護仙 *Gosen*, 142nd Division
22201-12 護仙 142nd Division (11AA) - 233
DN • 22251-300, 護古 *Goko*, 143rd Division
22251-61 護古 143rd Division (54A) - 233
DN • 22301-50, 護阪 *Gohan*, 144th Division
22301-10 護阪 144th Division (15AA) - 233-4
22351-400, 護州 *Gosyu*, 145th Division
22351-61 護州 145th Division (56A) - 234
DN • 22401-50, 護南 *Gonan*, 146th Division
22401-19 護南 146th Division (40A) - 234-5
DN • 22451-500, 護北 *Gohoku*, 147th Division
22451-64 護北 147th Division (52A) - 235
22462 富士 8th Independent Mountain Artillery Regiment (36A) - 70
22463 捷 40th Trench Mortar Battalion (52A) - 72
22464 断 74th Independent Engineer Battalion (53A) - 73
DN • 22501-50, 護朝 *Gosen*, 150th Division
22501-12 護朝 150th Division (17AA) - 236-7
DN • 22551-600, 護宇 *Gou*, 151st Division
22551-61 護宇 151st Division (51A) - 237
DN • 22601-50, 護沢 *Gotaku*, 152nd Division
22601-15 護沢 152nd Division (52A) - 237-8
22612 加越 209th Division 209th Mountain Artillery Regiment (36A) - 243
22612 東部 9th Independent Mountain Artillery Regiment (12AA) - 75
DN • 22651-700, 護京 *Gokyo*, 153rd Division
22651-61 護京 153rd Division (13AA) - 238
DN • 22701-50, 護路 *Goro*, 154th Division
22701-11 護路 154th Division (55A) - 238
DN • 22751-800, 護土 *Godo*, 155th Division
22751-61 護土 155th Division (55A) - 239
DN • 22801-50, 護西 *Gosei*, 156th Division
22801-12 護西 156th Division (57A) - 239
DN • 22851-900, 護弘 *Goko*, 157th Division
22851-70 護弘 157th Division (50A) - 239-40
22871 青葉 202nd Mountain Artillery Regiment, 202nd Division (36A) - 242
DN • 22901-50, 護鮮 *Gosen*, 160th Division
22901-12 護鮮 160th Division (17AA) - 240-1
DN • 22951-3050, 達 *Tatsu*, 5th Area Army
22951-61 要 88th Division (5AA) - 217
23001-13 摧 89th Division (5AA) - 218
DN • 23051-200, 登 *Nobori*, 13th Army, April 1945 distribution
23011 達 460th Independent Infantry Battalion, Nemuro Defense Unit (5AA) - 52
DN • 23201-300, 乙 *Otsu*, 1st Army, Apr. 1945 distribution
DN • 23301-400, 仁 *Hito*, 12th Army, Apr. 1945 distribution

23307 護土 155th Division Artillery Unit (55A) - 239
DN • 23401-500, 戊 *Bo*, Mongolia Garrison Army
DN • 23501-600, 波 *Nami*, 23rd Army, April 1945 distribution
DN • 23601-5000, Not Distributed
24305 比叡 216th Field Artillery Regiment, 216th Division (16AA) - 245
24414 武蔵 201st Division Anti-Gas Unit (36A) - 241
24416 武蔵 201st Division Medical Unit (36A) - 241
24417 武蔵 201st Division 1st Field Hospital (36A) - 241
24418 武蔵 201st Division 2nd Field Hospital (36A) - 241
24419 武蔵 201st Division Veterinary Unit (36A) - 241
DN • 25001-100, 東方 *Toho*, 1st General Army, April 1945 distribution
DN • 25101-200, 西方 *Seiho*, 2nd General Army, April 1945 distribution
DN • 25201-400, 徳 *Toku*, Kwantung (Kantō) Army, April 1945 distribution
25201 to 25206 徳 Kwantung Army Water Purification Headquarters (KA) - 153
25207 徳 Kwantung Army Horse Convalescence Depot (KA) - 154
25208 徳 Kwantung Army Accounting Department (KA) - 153
25211/25212 徳 Kwantung Army Siping Fuel Depot (KA) - 154
25221 速 1st Mobile Brigade Headquarters (KA) - 284
25222 速 1st Mobile Regiment, 1st Mobile Brigade (KA) - 284
25223 速 2nd Mobile Regiment, 1st Mobile Brigade (KA) - 284
25224 速 3rd Mobile Regiment, 1st Mobile Brigade (KA) - 284
25231 徳 Kwantung Chemical Department Training Unit (KA) - 153
25233 徳 Kwantung Army Special Intelligence Service (KA) - 154
25241 徳 Kwantung Army Intelligence Department (KA) - 153
25242 徳 Kwantung Army Special Intelligence Unit (KA) - 153
25244 徳 Kwantung Army Signal Intelligence Unit (KA) - 153
25251-61 真心 77th Independent Mixed Brigade, became the 135th Div (5A) - 264
25251-67 真心 135th Division (5A) - 229
25262-72 勾玉 78th Ind. Mixed Brigade, became the 134th Div (1AA) - 264-5
25262-77 勾玉 134th Division (1AA) - 229
25273-83 丈夫 79th Independent Mixed Brigade (3AA) - 265
25285-93 鋭鋒 80th Independent Mixed Brigade (4A) - 265
25296 / 1290 徳 Kwantung Army Field Veterinary Depot (KA) - 154
25301 敏 30th Army Headquarters (30A) - 177
DN • 25401-700, 栄 *Sakae*, China Expeditionary Army, April 1945 distribution
DN • 25701-900, 威 *i*, Southern Expeditionary Army, April 1945 distribution
DN • 25901-6000, 森 *Mori*, Burma Area Army, April 1945 distribution
DN • 26001-100, 達 *Tatsu*, 5th Area Army, April 1945 distribution
26001 砦 14th Independent Tank Company (58A) - 185
DN • 26101-200, 進 *Sunuma*, 11th Area Army, April 1945 distribution
DN • 26201-300, 幡 *Hata*, 12th Area Army, April 1945 distribution
DN • 26301-400, 秀 *Syo*, 13th Area Army, April 1945 distribution
DN • 26401-500, 楠 *Kusunoki*, 15th Area Army, April 1945 distribution
DN • 26501-600, 睦 *Mutu*, 16th Area Army, April 1945 distribution
DN • 26601-700, 築 *Kizuka*, 17th Area Army, April 1945 distribution
DN • 26701-800, 岩 *Iwa*, 3rd Army, April 1945 distribution
26709 / 4329 岩 Tungning Heavy Artillery Regiment (3A) - 170

0	1	2	3	4	5	6	7	8	9	10
〇	一	二	三	四	五	六	七	八	九	十

26711 岩 Hunchun Army Hospital (3A) - 171
26712 岩 Yanji (28th Kanto) Army Hospital (3A) - 171
26714 岩 Lao Heishan (30th Kanto) Army Hospital (3A) - 171
26717 岩 Tungning 3rd Army Hospital (3A) - 171
26718 岩 64th Kanto Army Hospital (3A) - 171
26721 / 3680 岩 55th Signal Regiment (3A) - 170
26722 岩 1st Independent Motor Transport Company (3A) - 170
DN • 26801-900, 光 *Hikari*, 4th Army, April 1945 distribution
26817 / 20717 光 17th Mortar Battalion (4A) - 158
26830 光 30th Independent Rapid Firing Gun Battalion (4A) - 158
26850 光 Songo (35th Kanto) 1st Army Hospital (4A) - 159
26851 光 Heihe (83rd Kanto) Army Hospital (4A) - 159
26852 光 Bei'an (85th Kanto) Army Hospital (4A) - 159
26853 光 Aigun (84th Kanto) Army Hospital (4A) - 159
26854 光 Qiqihar (9th Kanto) Army Hospital (4A) - 159
26855 光 Hailar (26th Kanto) 2nd Army Hospital (4A) - 159
26856 光 Fularji (81st Kanto) Army Hospital (4A) - 159
26857 光 Nenjiang (86th Kanto) Army Hospital (4A) - 160
26858 光 免渡洵 (89th Kanto) Army Hospital (4A) - 160
26898 光 12th Raiding Unit (4A) - 159
DN • 26901-7000, 守 *Mamoru*, 6th Army, April 1945 distribution
DN • 27001-200, 呂 *Ro*, 11th Army, April 1945 distribution
DN • 27201-500, 東北 *Tohoku* Army District units, April 1945 distribution
27379-89 八甲 222nd Division (11AA) - 246
27383 偕 31st Independent Field Artillery Battalion (55A) - 109
27384 楠 32nd Independent Artillery Battalion (15AA) - 96
27385 進 12th Independent Mountain Artillery Regiment (11AA) - 60
27390 睦 1st Independent Signal Labor Unit (16AA) - 113
27391 睦 2nd Independent Signal Labor Unit (16AA) - 114
27392 睦 3rd Independent Signal Labor Unit (16AA) - 114
27393 進 4th Independent Signal Labor Unit (11AA) - 61
27394 進 5th Independent Signal Labor Unit (11AA) - 61
27395 進 6th Independent Signal Labor Unit (11AA) - 61
27396 進 7th Independent Signal Labor Unit (11AA) - 61
27397 進 8th Independent Signal Labor Unit (11AA) - 61
27398 進 9th Independent Signal Labor Unit (11AA) - 61
27399 進 10th Independent Signal Labor Unit (11AA) - 61
27400 偕 10th Artillery Headquarters (55A) - 109
27401 暁 21st Sea Transport Battalion (5AA) - 51
27402 俊 24th Independent Trench Mortar Battalion (50A) - 62
27403 鋒 82nd Independent Engineer Battalion (57A) - 118
27404 幡 83rd Independent Engineer Battalion (TDA) - 74
27405 俊 84th Independent Engineer Battalion (50A) - 62
27406 進 85th Independent Engineer Battalion (11AA) - 61

27407 進 86th Independent Engineer Battalion (11AA) - 61
27408 進 87th Independent Engineer Battalion, deactivated (11AA) - N/A
27409 富士 88th Independent Engineer Battalion (36A) - 70
27410-9 岩木 308th Division (50A) - 250
27420-9 磐梯 322nd Division (11AA) - 252
27430-9 瑞光 113th Independent Mixed Brigade (11AA) - 270
27444 俊 1st Trench Mortar Battalion (50A) - 62
27445 進 2nd Trench Mortar Battalion (11AA) - 61
27446 進 3rd Trench Mortar Battalion (11AA) - 61
27447 八甲 222nd Division Veterinary Unit (11AA) - 252
27448 颯 48th Signal Regiment (54A) - 86
27449 俊 49th Signals Regiment (50A) - 62
27500 俊 50th Army (11AA) - 62
27570 岩 113th Independent Motor Transport Battalion (3A) - 170
DN • 27501-800, 東部 *Tobu* Army District, Apr. 1945 distribution
27659 東部 503rd Construction Duty Company (ToB 12AA) - N/A
27660 東部 504th Construction Duty Company (ToB 12AA) - N/A
27661 東部 505th Construction Duty Company (ToB 12AA) - N/A
27662 東部 506th Construction Duty Company (ToB 12AA) - N/A
27663 東部 507th Construction Duty Company (ToB 12AA) - N/A
27664 東部 508th Construction Duty Company (ToB 12AA) - N/A
27677-89 天龍 221st Division (51A) - 246
27691-704 総武 230th Division (59A) - 248
27705-17 利根 234th Division (52A) - 249
27719-28 磯 321st Division (12AA) - 251-2
27722 磯 326th Infantry Regiment, 321st Div. (12AA) - 251
27729-38 赤城 351st Division (56A) - 252-3
27739-48 武甲 354th Division (TBA) - 253
27749-9 房 114th Independent Mixed Brigade (TBA) - 270
27760-70 建 115th Independent Mixed Brigade (12AA) - 270-1
27771-80 建 116th Independent Mixed Brigade (12AA) - 271
27781-91 東部 117th Independent Mixed Brigade (12AA) - 271
27792-800 堅塁 118th Independent Mixed Brigade (16AA) - 272
DN • 27801-100, 東海 *Tokai* Army District, April 1945 distribution
27820 秀 36th Independent Signal Labor Unit (13 AA) - 85
27821 秀 37th Independent Signal Labor Unit (13 AA) - 85
27822 秀 38th Independent Signal Labor Unit (13 AA) - 85
27823 秀 39th Independent Signal Labor Unit (13 AA) - 85
27824 秀 40th Independent Signal Labor Unit (13 AA) - 85
27825 秀 41st Independent Signal Labor Unit (13 AA) - 85
27826 秀 42nd Independent Signal Labor Unit (13 AA) - 85
27827 秀 43rd Independent Signal Labor Unit (13 AA) - 85
27828 秀 44th Independent Signal Labor Unit (13 AA) - 85
27829 秀 45th Independent Signal Labor Unit (13 AA) - 85
DN • 28101-400, 中部 *Chubu* Army District, April 1945 distribution
28147 中部 583rd Land Duty Company (ChB 15AA) - N/A
28148 中部 584th Land Duty Company (ChB 15AA) - N/A

0	1	2	3	4	5	6	7	8	9	10
〇	一	二	三	四	五	六	七	八	九	十

28149 中部 585th Land Duty Company (ChB 15AA) - N/A
28150 中部 586th Land Duty Company (ChB 15AA) - N/A
28151 中部 587th Land Duty Company (ChB 15AA) - N/A
28152 中部 588th Land Duty Company (ChB 15AA) - N/A
28153 中部 589th Land Duty Company (ChB 15AA) - N/A
28154 中部 590th Land Duty Company (ChB 15AA) - N/A
28174 中部 513th Construction Duty Company (ChB 15AA) - N/A
28175 中部 514th Construction Duty Company (ChB 15AA) - N/A
28176 中部 515th Construction Duty Company (ChB 15AA) - N/A
28177 中部 516th Construction Duty Company (ChB 15AA) - N/A
28203 晴 44th Independent Anti-Aircraft Battalion, 1st AAA Div (12AA) - 255
28204-15 炸 3rd Anti-Aircraft Division (15AA) - 256
28207 靖 7th Independent Machine Cannon Company (6AirA) - 137
28208 靖 8th Independent Machine Cannon Company (6AirA) - 137
28209 靖 9th Independent Machine Cannon Company (6AirA) - 137
28210 靖 10th Independent Machine Cannon Company (6AirA) - 137
28211 炸 47th Independent Mobile Anti-Aircraft Battery, 3rd AAA Div. (15AA) - 256
28212 炸 48th Independent Mobile Anti-Aircraft Battery, 3rd AAA Div. (15AA) - 256
28213 炸 49th Independent Mobile Anti-Aircraft Battery, 3rd AAA Div. (15AA) - 256
28214 炸 50th Independent Mobile Anti-Aircraft Battery, 3rd AAA Div. (15AA) - 256
28215 炸 51st Independent Mobile Anti-Aircraft Battery, 3rd AAA Div. (15AA) - 256
28216 靖 52nd Independent Machine Cannon Company (6AirA) - 138
28217 靖 53rd Independent Machine Cannon Company (6AirA) - 138
28218 靖 54th Independent Machine Cannon Company (6AirA) - 138
28219 燕 55th Independent Machine Cannon Company (1AirA) - 133
28220 燕 56th Independent Machine Cannon Company (1AirA) - 133
28221 燕 57th Independent Machine Cannon Company (1AirA) - 133
28222 燕 58th Independent Machine Cannon Company (1AirA) - 133
28223 燕 59th Independent Machine Cannon Company (1AirA) - 133
28224 燕 60th Independent Machine Cannon Company (1AirA) - 133
28225-35 山城 316th Division (56A) - 251
28236-44 菊水 121st Independent Mixed Brigade (55A) - 273
28245 積 86th Division (57A) - 217
28246 護朝 150th Division Rocket Gun Unit, (17AA) - 236
28247 偕 16th Trench Mortar Battalion (55A) - 109
28248 楠 19th Trench Mortar Battalion (15AA) - 96
28249 鋒 7th Self-Propelled Artillery Regiment (57A) - 118
28250 偕 109th Independent Engineer Battalion (55A) - 109
28251 偕 110th Independent Engineer Battalion (55A) - 109
28252 偕 111th Independent Engineer Battalion (55A) - 109
28253 楠 46th Independent Signal Labor Unit (15AA) - 96
28254 楠 47th Independent Signal Labor Unit (15AA) - 96
28255 楠 48th Independent Signal Labor Unit (15AA) - 96
28256-64 金剛 225th Division (15AA) - 247

28270-9 剣山 344th Division (55A) - 252
28280 護鮮 160th Division Rocket Gun Unit (17AA) - 241
28281 護阪 144th Division Artillery Unit (15AA) - 234
28282-9 堅城 122nd Independent Mixed Brigade (16AA) - 273
28290 楠 16th Independent Mountain Artillery Regiment (15AA) - 96
28291 秀 22nd Trench Mortar Battalion (13AA) - 85
28292 陽 8th Self-Propelled Artillery Battalion (40A) - 115
28293 楠 112th Independent Engineer Battalion (15AA) - 96
28294 楠 113th Independent Engineer Regiment (15AA) - 96
28295 楠 49th Independent Signal Labor Unit (15AA) - 96
28296 楠 50th Independent Signal Labor Unit (15AA) - 96
28297-306 那智 355th Division (54A) - 253
28308-18 紀伊 123rd Independent Mixed Brigade (15AA) - 273-4
28319 楠 38th Independent Mixed Regiment (15AA) - 96
28320 富士 17th Independent Mountain Artillery Regiment (36A) - 70
28321 陽 21st Trench Mortar Battalion (40A) - 115
28322 偕 9th Mortar Battalion (55A) - 109
28323 楠 114th Independent Engineer Regiment (15AA) - 96
28324 秀 115th Independent Engineer Battalion (13AA) - 85
28325 楠 51st Independent Signal Labor Unit (15AA) - 96
28326 楠 52nd Independent Signal Labor Unit (15AA) - 96
28327 楠 25th Sea Transport Battalion (15AA) - 97
28328-40 赤穂 224th Division (54A) - 246-8
28341 偕 18th Trench Mortar Battalion (55A) - 109
28342-60 大國 231st Division (59A) - 248-9
28356 and 36356 護路 154th Division Artillery Unit (57A) - 238
28357 護州 145th Division Artillery Unit (56A) - 234
28358-70 鬼城 124th Independent Mixed Brigade (59A) - 274
28365-7 積 86th Division 765th to 767th Infantry Battalions (57A) - 217
28372 鋒 20th Trench Mortar Battalion (57A) - 118
28373 幡 10th Self-Propelled Artillery Battalion (12AA) - 68
28374 幡 116th Independent Engineer Battalion (TDA) - 74
28375 幡 117th Independent Engineer Battalion (12AA) - 68
28376 幡 118th Independent Engineer Battalion (12AA) - 68
28377 楠 53rd Independent Signal Labor Unit (15AA) - 96
28378 楠 54th Independent Signal Labor Unit (15AA) - 96
28379 楠 55th Independent Signal Labor Unit (15AA) - 96
28380 楠 26th Sea Transport Battalion (15AA) - 97
28381 偕 17th Trench Mortar Battalion (55A) - 109
28382 富士 23rd Trench Mortar Battalion (36A) - 70
28383 富士 32nd Trench Mortar Battalion (36A) - 70
28384 偕 25th Independent Mortar Battalion (55A) - 109
28385 偕 26th Independent Mortar Battalion (55A) - 109
28386 楠 3rd Short Wave Signal Company (15AA) - 96
28387 秀 4th Short Wave Signal Company (13AA) - 85
28388 鋒 43rd Independent Heavy Artillery Battalion (57A) - 118
DN • 28401-700, 西部 *Seibu* Army District, April 1945 distribution

0	1	2	3	4	5	6	7	8	9	10
〇	一	二	三	四	五	六	七	八	九	十

28401 宗 6th Artillery Headquarters (56A) - 116
28471 暁 517th Construction Duty Company (SC) - 145
28484 西部 10th Field Horse Replacement Depot (SeB) - N/A
DN • 28701-9000, 北部 *Hokubu* Army District, April 1945 distribution
28714 北部 11th Field Horse Replacement Depot (5AA) - 52
28734 築 84th Independent Signal Labor Unit (17AA) - N/A
28775 暁 29th Sea Transport Battalion (5AA) - 51, 144
28776 達 76th Independent Signal Labor Unit (5AA) - 51
28777 達 77th Independent Signal Labor Unit (5AA) - 51
28778 達 78th Independent Signal Labor Unit (5AA) - 51
28779 達 79th Independent Signal Labor Unit (5AA) - 51
28780 達 80th Independent Signal Labor Unit (5AA) - 52
28781 達 81st Independent Signal Labor Unit (5AA) - 52
28782 達 82nd Independent Signal Labor Unit (5AA) - 52
28783 達 83rd Independent Signal Labor Unit (5AA) - 52
28784 達 84th Independent Signal Labor Unit (5AA) - 52
28785 達 85th Independent Signal Labor Unit (5AA) - 52
28786 勲 42nd Field Artillery Regiment, 42nd Division (5AA) - 209
28787 勲 42nd Division Medical Unit, 42nd Division (5AA) - 208
28788 勲 42nd Division Veterinary Unit, 42nd Division (5AA) - 209
28789 達 649th Independent Infantry Battalion, Soya (5AA) - 52
28790 達 Nemuro Defense Unit Headquarters (5AA) - 52
28791 達 33rd Independent Rapid Firing Gun Battalion (5AA) - 51
28792 達 67th Independent Anti-Aircraft Battalion (5AA) - 51
28793 達 68th Independent Anti-Aircraft Battalion (5AA) - 51
28794 達 66th Independent Field Anti-Aircraft Company (5AA) - 51
28795 達 67th Independent Field Anti-Aircraft Company (5AA) - 51
28796 達 5th Anti Aircraft Unit Headquarters (5AA) - 51
28797 達 19th Independent Field Searchlight Company (5AA) - 51
28798 達 36th Independent Field Artillery Battalion (5AA) - 52
28799 達 37th Independent Field Artillery Battalion (5AA) - 51
28800 達 7th Independent Heavy Artillery Company (5AA) - 51
28801 達 8th Independent Heavy Artillery Company (5AA) - 51
DN • 29001-100, Not Distributed
29003 / 7489 朝 12th Field Horse Replacement Depot (KoD) - 187
DN • 29101-300, 朝鮮 *Chosen* Army, April 1945 distribution (Korea)
29100-9 宣武 320th Division (17AA) - 251
29110-9 壯図 127th Independent Mixed Brigade (17AA) - 275
29120 築 39th Independent Mixed Regiment (17AA) - 182
29121 築 40th Independent Mixed Regiment (17AA) - 182
29122 砦 12th Artillery Headquarters (58A) - 185
29123 光 10th Independent Field Artillery Regiment (17AA) - 182
29124 砦 20th Independent Mountain Artillery Regiment (58A) - 185
29125 砦 29th Trench Mortar Battalion (58A) - 185

29126 築 30th Trench Mortar Battalion (17AA) - 182
29127 築 31st Trench Mortar Battalion (17AA) - 182
29128 築 125th Independent Engineer Battalion (17AA) - 183
29129 砦 126th Independent Engineer Battalion (58A) - 185
29130 砦 127th Independent Engineer Battalion (58A) - 185
29131 築 128th Independent Engineer Battalion (17AA) - 183
29132 築 129th Independent Engineer Battalion (17AA) - 183
29133 築 130th Independent Engineer Battalion (17AA) - 183
29134 築 131st Independent Engineer Battalion (17AA) - 183
29135 築 86th Independent Signal Labor Unit (17AA) - 182
29136 築 87th Independent Signal Labor Unit (17AA) - 182
29137 築 88th Independent Signal Labor Unit (17AA) - 182
29138 築 89th Independent Signal Labor Unit (17AA) - 182
29139 築 90th Independent Signal Labor Unit (17AA) - 182
29140 睦 30th Sea Transport Battalion (16AA) - 114
29141 築 210th Land Duty Company (17AA) - 183
29142 築 211th Land Duty Company (17AA) - 184
29143 築 212th Land Duty Company (17AA) - 184
29144 築 213th Land Duty Company (17AA) - 184
29145 築 214th Land Duty Company (17AA) - 184
29146 楠 215th Land Duty Company (15AA) - 97
29147 楠 216th Land Duty Company (15AA) - 97
29148 楠 217th Land Duty Company (15AA) - 97
29149 楠 218th Land Duty Company (15AA) - 97
29150 楠 219th Land Duty Company (15AA) - 97
DN • 29301-600, 湾 *Wan*, Formosa Army District, April 1945 distribution
DN • 29601-900 臣 *Shin*, Minister of the Army
29651 風 Air Command Headquarters (Air Command 6AirA) - N/A
29652 風 Aviation Work Depot (Air Command 6AirA) - N/A
29653 風 Aviation Examination Department (Air Command 6AirA) - N/A
29654 風 Meteorological Department (Air Command 6AirA) - N/A
29661 風 1st Aeronautical Engineering Laboratory (Army Air Commd 6AirA) - N/A
29662 風 2nd Aeronautical Engineering Laboratory (Army Air Commd 6AirA) - N/A
29663 風 3rd Aeronautical Engineering Laboratory (Army Air Commd 6AirA) - N/A
29664 風 4th Aeronautical Engineering Laboratory (Army Air Commd 6AirA) - N/A
29665 風 5th Aeronautical Engineering Laboratory (Army Air Commd 6AirA) - N/A
29666 風 6th Aeronautical Engineering Laboratory (Army Air Commd 6AirA) - N/A
29667 風 7th Aeronautical Engineering Laboratory (Army Air Commd 6AirA) - N/A
29668 風 8th Aeronautical Engineering Laboratory (Army Air Commd 6AirA) - N/A
29669 風 Various Technologies Laboratory (Air Command 6AirA) - N/A
29751 – Army Medical Materials Depot 1st Branch (KoD) - 186
DN • 29901-0000 道 *Dō*, Inspector General of Military Training
DN • 30001-100, 燕 *Tsubame*, 1st Air Army, April 1945 distribution
30001 燕 1st Air Army Headquarters (AGA) - 131
DN • 30101-200, 松 *Mutu*, Asahikawa Divisional District
30101-4 北部 1st to 4th Specially Est. Garrison Units, Asahikawa (HoB) - 54
30105-12 北部 1st to 8th Specially Est. Garrison Units, Sapporo (HoB) - 54-5

0	1	2	3	4	5	6	7	8	9	10
〇	一	二	三	四	五	六	七	八	九	十

30113-17 北部 1st to 5th Specially Est. Garrison Units, Hakodate (HoB) - 55
30118-25 北部 1st to 8th Specially Est. Garrison Units, Kushiro (HoB) - 55-6
30126-33 陽 1st 8th Specially Established Garrison Units, Karafuto (HoB) - 53-4
DN • 30201-400, 陸 *Riku*, Hirosaki Divisional District
30203 進 69th Line of Communications Sector Command (11AA) - 61
30204 進 69th Line of Communications Duty Unit (11AA) - 61
DN • 30401-600, 仙 *Sen*, Sendai Divisional District
30401-16 青葉 202nd Division (36A) - 241-2
DN • 30601-800, 蔵 *Zō*, Tokyo Divisional District
30601-26 東部 1st to 26th Specially Est. Garrison Units, Chiba (ToB) - 80-1
30641-60 東部 1st to 20th Specially Est. Garrison Units, Tokyo (ToB) - 78-9
30681-97 東部 1st to 17th Specially Est. Garrison Units, Urawa (ToB) - 80
30721-46 東部 1st to 26th Specially Est. Garrison Units, Yokohama (ToB) - 79-80
30761-72 東部 1st to 12th Specially Est. Garrison Units, Kōfu (ToB) - 81
DN • 30801-1000, 丸 *Maru*, Utsunomiya Divisional District
30801-19 東部 1st to 19th Specially Est. Garrison Units, Mito (ToB) - 75-6
30820-33 東部 1st to 14th Specially Est. Garrison Units, Utsunomiya (ToB) - 76
30834-50 東部 1st to 17th Specially Est. Garrison Units, Maebashi (ToB) - 76-7
30851-67 常盤 214th Division (36A) - 244-5
30868 滿州 46th Independent Transport Battalion (44A) - 179
DN • 31001-200, 越 *Etsu*, Nagano Divisional District
31001-22 東部 1st to 22nd Specially Est. Garrison Units, Nagano (ToB) - 82-3
31101-22 東部 1st to 22nd Specially Est. Garrison Units, Niigata (ToB) - 83
DN • 31201-400, 澤 *Sawa*, Kanazawa Divisional District
31201-12 東海 1st to 12th Specially Est. Garrison Units, Kanazawa (ToK) - 87
31213-24 東海 1st to 12th Specially Est. Garrison Units, Toyama (ToK) - 88
DN • 31401-600, 張 *Hari*, Nagoya Divisional District
31401-26 東海 1st to 26th Specially Est. Garrison Units, Nagoya (ToK) - 89
31431-56 東海 1st to 26th Specially Est. Garrison Unit, Shizuoka (ToK) - 90-1
31461-82 東海 1st to 22nd Specially Est. Garrison Units, Gifu (ToK) - 90
31501-26 東海 1st to 26th Specially Established Garrison Units, Tsu (ToK) - 91
DN • 31601-800, 洛 *Raku*, Kyoto Divisional District
DN • 31801-32000, 攝 *Setu*, Osaka Divisional District
DN • 32001-200, 中国 *Chugoku* Divisional District
32001-26 中国 1st to 26th Specially Est. Garrison Units, Okayama (ChG) - 105
32027-36 中国 1st to 10th Specially Est. Garrison Unit, Tottori (ChG) - 105-6
32037-62 中国 1st to 26th Specially Est. Garrison Units, Hiroshima (ChG) - 106
32063-80 中国 1st 18th Specially Est.Garrison Units, Matsue (ChG) - 107
32081-106 中国 1st to 26th Specially Est. Garrison Units, Yamaguchi (ChG) - 107-8
32200 山陽 59th Army Headquarters (59A) - 104
DN • 32201-400, 四國 *Shikoku* Divisional District
32325-27 四国 13th to 15th Sp. Est. Garrison Units, Takamatsu (Shikoku) - 110
32330 四国 20th Specially Established Garrison Unit, Matsuyama (Shikoku) - 111
32335 四国 11th Specially Established Garrison Unit, Kochi (Shikoku) - 112

32336 四国 12th Specially Established Garrison Unit, Kochi (Shikoku) - 112
DN • 32401-600, 薩 *Satsu*, Kumamoto Divisional District
32401-16 阿蘇 206th Division (16AA) - 243
32420 線 144th Railroad Station Headquarters, Moji (RR) - 141
DN • 32601-800, 黒 *Kuro*, Kureme Divisional District
32601-19 菊池 212th Division (57A) - 244
32620-9 千歳 312th Division (56A) - 250
DN • 32801-3000, 津 *Shin*, Ranam Divisional District, Korea
32820 津 Ranam Divisional District Headquarters (KoD) - 187
32821 / 202 津 Ranam 1st Infantry Replacement Unit (KoD) - 187
32822 / 243 津 Ranam 2nd Infantry Replacement Unit (KoD) - 187
32823 / 208 津 Ranam Artillery Replacement Unit (KoD) - 187
32824 / 210 津 Ranam Engineer Replacement Unit (KoD) - 187
32825 / 211 津 Ranam Signals Replacement Unit (KoD) - 187
32826 / 212 津 Ranam Transport Replacement Unit (KoD) - 187
DN • 33001-200, 緑 *Midori*, Heijo (Pyongyang) Divisional District, Korea
DN • 33201-400, 漢 *Kan*, Keijo (Seoul) Divisional District, Korea
DN • 33401-600, 邱 *Kyū*, Taikyu (Taegu) Divisional District, Korea
DN • 33601-800, 木 *Moku*, Koshu (Gongju) Divisional District, Korea
DN • 33801-900, Not Distributed
DN • 33901-50, 隅 *Gū*, 1st Imperial Guard Division
DN • 33951-34100, 線 *Sen*, Homeland Rail Road Headquarters
DN • 33801-900, Not Distributed
DN • 33901-50, 隅 *Gū*, 1st Imperial Guard Division
DN • 33951-34100, 線 *Sen*, Homeland Rail Road Headquarters
33951 線 1st Independent Railroad Engineer Unit, Moji (RR) - 141
33952 線 2nd Independent Railroad Engineer Unit, Moji (RR) - 141
33953 線 3rd Independent Railroad Engineer Unit, Moji (RR) - 141
33954 線 4th Independent Railroad Engineer Unit, Shikoku (RR) - 141
33955 線 5th Independent Railroad Engineer Unit, Osaka (RR) - 140
33956 線 6th Independent Railroad Engineer Unit, Nagoya (RR) - 140
33957 線 7th Independent Railroad Engineer Unit, Nagoya (RR) - 140
33958 線 8th Independent Railroad Engineer Unit, Tokyo (RR) - 140
33959 線 9th Independent Railroad Engineer Unit, Moji (RR) - 141
33960 線 10th Independent Railroad Engineer Unit, Hiroshima (RR) - 140
33961 線 11th Independent Railroad Engineer Unit, Osaka (RR) - 140
33962 線 12th Independent Railroad Engineer Unit, Moji (RR) - 141
33963 線 13th Independent Railroad Engineer Unit, Tokyo (RR) - 140
33964 線 14th Independent Railroad Engineer Unit, Sendai (RR) - 141
33965 線 15th Independent Railroad Engineer Unit, Sapporo (RR) - 141
33966 線 16th Independent Railroad Engineer Unit, Tokyo (RR) - 140
33967 線 17th Independent Railroad Engineer Unit, Moji (RR) - 141
33968 線 18th Independent Railroad Engineer Unit, Hiroshima (RR) - 140
33969 線 19th Independent Railroad Engineer Unit, Tokyo (RR) - 140
33970 線 20th Independent Railroad Engineer Unit, Nagoya (RR) - 140
33971 線 21st Independent Railroad Engineer Unit, Niigata (RR) - 141
33972 線 22nd Independent Railroad Engineer Unit, Sapporo (RR) - 141

0	1	2	3	4	5	6	7	8	9	10
○	一	二	三	四	五	六	七	八	九	十

33973 線 23rd Independent Railroad Engineer Unit, Sapporo (RR) - 141
33974 線 24th Independent Railroad Engineer Unit, Tokyo (RR) - 140
33975-90 線 25th to 40th Independent Railroad Engineer Unit - N/A
33992 線 171st Railroad Station Headquarters, Oita (RR) - 141
33993 線 175th Railroad Station Headquarters, Tokyo (RR) - 140
33997 線 103rd Railroad Station Headquarters, Sendai (RR/CRR) - 141, 166
33998 線 119th Railroad Station Headquarters, Tokyo (RR/CRR) - 140, 166
33999 線 122nd Railroad Station Headquarters, Osaka (RR) - 140
34000 線 127th Railroad Station Headquarters, Tokyo (RR) - 140
34001 線 128th Railroad Station Headquarters, Nagoya (RR/CRR) - 140, 166
34002 線 177th Railroad Station Headquarters, Niigata (RR) - 141
34003 線 134th Railroad Station Headquarters, Nagoya (RR/CRR) - 140, 166
34004 / 7113 線 139th Railroad Station HQ, Hiroshima (RR/CRR) - 140, 166
34006 / 7035 線 149th Railroad Station Headquarters, Osaka (RR/CRR) - 141/166
34007 線 150th Railroad Station Headquarters, Shikoku (RR) - 141
34008 / 6428 線 153rd Railroad Station Headquarters, Shikoku (RR/CRR) - 141, 166
34010 線 165th Railroad Station Headquarters, Niigata (RR) - 141
34011 線 166th Railroad Station Headquarters, Sendai (RR) - 141
DN • 34101-200, 路 Michi, Continental Railway Headquarters
34101 / 1231 徳 3rd Railroad Regiment (CRR) - 166
34102 / 1238 徳 4th Railroad Regiment (CRR) - 165
34111 路 22nd Independent Railway Battalion (CRR) - 165
34112 路 23rd Independent Railway Battalion (CRR) - 165
DN • 34201-400, 師 Sui, Air General Army, April 1945 distribution
34200 路 Continental Railway Headquarters (CRR) - 165
34200 徳 Kwantung Army Railway Headquarters (KA) - 155
34201 師 Army Air Transport Office (AGA) - N/A
34202 師 Tachikawa Army Air Depot (AGA) - N/A
34203 師 Kamigahara Army Air Depot (AGA) - 128
34204 師 Osaka Army Air Depot (AGA) - 128
34205 師 Tachiarai Army Air Depot (AGA) - 128
34206 師 Utsunomiya Army Air Depot (AGA) - 128
34207 師 Pyongyang Army Air Depot (AGA) - 128
34208 師 Tokyo Army Air Freight Depot (AGA) - 128
34209 師 Osaka Army Air Freight Depot (AGA) - 128
34212 天風 47th Air Regiment (12AirDiv 6AirA) - 138
34213 師 244th Air Regiment, 30th Fighter Brigade (6AirA) - N/A
34214 師 17th Independent Air Squadron, 30th Fighter Bgde (6AirA) - N/A
34217 師 1st Electric Wave Induction Unit (AGA) - 127
34217 師 111th Air Regiment (23rd Air Bgde, AGA) - 129
34218 師 112th Air Regiment (23rd Air Bgde, AGA) - 129
34219 師 1st Independent Air Unit (AGA) - 127
34220 師 20th Fighter Group Headquarters (AGA) - 128
34221 燕 26th Air Brigade Headquarters (1AirA) - 131

34222 靖 27th Air Brigade Headquarters (6AirA) - 135
34224 師 1st Photographic Work Unit (AGA) - 127
DN • 34401-500, 羽 *Hane*, 2nd Air Army, April 1945 distribution
DN • 34501-600, 司 *Tsukasa*, 3rd Air Army, April 1945 distribution
DN • 34601-700, 鷲 *Washi*, 2nd Air Division
DN • 34701-800, 高 *Taka*, 5th Air Division
DN • 34801-900, 天鷲 *Amawashi*, 11th Air Division
DN • 34901-5000, 天翔 *Tensho*, 10th Air Division
DN • 35001-100, 天風 *Tenpu*, 12th Air Division
35001 天風 4th Air Regiment (12AirDiv 6AirA) - 138
35002 師 59th Air Regiment, 30th Fighter Brigade (6AirA) - N/A
35003 天風 4th Airfield Battalion (12AirDiv 6AirA) - 138
35004 天風 248th Airfield Battalion (12AirDiv 6AirA) - 138
DN • 35101-200, 暁 *Akatsuki*, Army Shipping Corps Headquarters
DN • 35201-37200, 東部 *Tobu* Army District
36356 / 28356 護路 154th Division Artillery Unit (57A) - 238
36362 護宇 151st Division Artillery Unit (51A) - 237
36363 護東 140th Division Artillery Unit (53A) - 232
36364 護北 147th Division Artillery Unit (52A) - 235
36365 護沢 152nd Division Artillery Unit (52A) - 238
36366 断 36th Independent Mixed Regiment (53A) - 73
36367 断 37th Independent Mixed Regiment (53A) - 73
36368 断 11th Artillery Headquarters (53A) - 73
36369 幡 8th Independent Field Artillery Regiment (12AA) - 68
36371 捷 14th Independent Mountain Artillery Regiment (52A) - 72
36372 鋒 4th Trench Mortar Battalion (57A) - 118
36373 治 5th Trench Mortar Battalion, att. 321st Div. (12AA) - 68
36374 房 6th Trench Mortar Battalion (TBAC) - 74
36375 富士 7th Trench Mortar Battalion (36A) - 70
36376 富士 8th Trench Mortar Battalion (36A) - 70
36377 富士 9th Trench Mortar Battalion (36A) - 70
36378 富士 10th Trench Mortar Battalion (36A) - 70
36379 富士 11th Trench Mortar Battalion (36A) - 70
36380 宗 1st Self-Propelled Artillery Battalion (56A) - 116
36381 幡 2nd Self-Propelled Artillery Battalion (12AA) - 68
36382 幡 3rd Self-Propelled Artillery Battalion (12AA) - 68
36383 幡 4th Self-Propelled Artillery Battalion (12AA) - 68
36384 建 16th Field Medium Artillery Battalion (51A) - 71
36385 偕 17th Independent Heavy Artillery Battalion (55A) - 109
36386 捷 18th Field Medium Artillery Battalion (52A) - 72
36387 秀 41st Independent Heavy Artillery Battalion (13AA) - 85
36389 捷 42nd Independent Heavy Artillery Battalion (52A) - 72
36390 睦 89th Independent Engineer Battalion (16AA) - 114
36391 宗 90th Independent Engineer Battalion (56A) - 116
36392 建 91st Independent Engineer Battalion (51A) - 71
36393 建 92nd Independent Engineer Battalion (51A) - 71
36394 建 93rd Independent Engineer Battalion (51A) - 71

0	1	2	3	4	5	6	7	8	9	10
○	一	二	三	四	五	六	七	八	九	十

36395 捷 94th Independent Engineer Battalion (52A) - 72
36396 捷 95th Independent Engineer Battalion (52A) - 72
36397 捷 96th Independent Engineer Battalion (52A) - 72
36398 捷 97th Independent Engineer Battalion (52A) - 72
36399 断 98th Independent Engineer Battalion (53A) - 73
36400 断 99th Independent Engineer Battalion (53A) - 73
36401 房 100th Independent Engineer Battalion (TBAC) - 74
36402 富士 101st Independent Engineer Battalion (36A) - 70
36403 富士 102nd Independent Engineer Battalion (36A) - 70
36404 幡 103rd Independent Engineer Battalion (12AA) - 68
36405 幡 1st Signal Unit Headquarters (12AA) - 68
36406 幡 2nd Signal Unit Headquarters (12AA) - 68
36407 断 50th Signals Regiment (53A) - 73
36408 幡 51st Signals Regiment (12AA) - 68
36409 幡 1st Short Wave Signal Company (12AA) - 68
36410 睦 11th Independent Signal Labor Unit (16AA) - 114
36411 睦 12th Independent Signal Labor Unit (16AA) - 114
36412 to 36334 幡 12th to 35th Independent Signal Labor Units (12AA) - 68
36435 幡 22nd Sea Transport Battalion (12AA) - 69
36436 楠 23rd Sea Transport Battalion (15AA) - 97
36437 幡 190th Land Duty Company (12AA) - 69
36438 幡 191st Land Duty Company (12AA) - 69
36439 幡 192nd Land Duty Company (12AA) - 69
36440 幡 193rd Land Duty Company (12AA) - 69
36441 幡 194th Land Duty Company (12AA) - 69
36442 秀 195th Land Duty Company (13AA) - 85
36443 秀 196th Land Duty Company (13AA) - 85
36444 秀 197th Land Duty Company (13AA) - 85
36445 秀 198th Land Duty Company (13AA) - 85
36446 秀 199th Land Duty Company (13AA) - 85
36455 東部 1st Electric Company (ToB) - N/A
36456 秀 2nd Electric Company (13AA) - 85
36457 中部 3rd Electric Company (ChB) - N/A
36458 西部 4th Electric Company (SeB) - N/A
36670 建 13th Independent Mountain Artillery Regiment (51A) - 71
DN • 37201-38200, 徳 *Toku*, Kwantung (Kantō) Army
37220-33 不抜 136th Division (3AA) - 230
37237-52 扶翼 137th Division (34A) - 230-1
37257-73 不動 138th Division (30A) - 231
37301-16 不屈 139th Division (1A) - 231-2
37321-37 富嶽 148th Division (30A) - 235-6
37341-51 不撓 149th Division (4A) - 236
37361-76 不滅 158th Division (KA) - 240
37401 徳 57th Signal Regiment (KA) - 154

Chapter 4

37402 強 1st Kwantung Specially Established Guard Headquarters (3AA) - 176
37402 強 1st to 10th Specially Established Guard Battalions (3AA) - 176
37402 強 1st Kwantung Specially Established Guard Signal Unit (3AA) - 176
37402 強 1st Kwantung Specially Established Guard Work Unit (3AA) - 176
37501-11 奮闘 130th Independent Mixed Brigade (3AA) - 276
37512-21 奮進 131st Independent Mixed Brigade (4A) - 276
37522-32 奮戦 132nd Independent Mixed Brigade (3A) - 276-7
37533-43 福寿 133rd Independent Mixed Brigade (34A) - 277
37551-61 奮励 134th Independent Mixed Brigade (3AA) - 277
37562-72 不朽 135th Independent Mixed Brigade (4A) - 278
37573-82 奮躍 136th Independent Mixed Brigade (4A) - 278
37603-6 奮迅 9th Independent Armored Brigade (44A) - 282
37606 徳 Kwantung Army Signal Headquarters (KA) - 153
37607 徳 Kwantung Army 1st Signal Unit (KA) - 153
37608 徳 Kwantung Army 2nd Signal Unit (KA) - 153
37609 徳 Kwantung Army 3rd Signal Unit (KA) - 153
37802 英機 275th Infantry Regiment, 125th Div. (30A) - 227
37804 英機 125th Field Artillery Regiment, 125th Div. (30A) - 227
37808 英機 125th Division Veterinary Unit, 125th Div. (30A) - 226
37809 強 54th Signal Regiment (3AA) - 175
37810 強 11th Raiding Unit (3AA) - 176
37814 敏 116th Independent Motor Transport Battalion (30A) - 177
37815 丈夫 79th Independent Mixed Brigade (3AA) - 265
DN • 38201-400, Air Army Board
DN • 38401-500, 房 *Bou*, Tokyo Bay Army Corps
DN • 38501-40000, Not Distributed
42325 護南 146th Division Rapid Firing Gun Unit (40A) - 234
42326-36 敬天 125th Independent Mixed Brigade (40A) - 274
42337-45 敬忠 126th Independent Mixed Brigade (16AA) - 275
42346 睦 433rd Independent Infantry Battalion (16AA) - 113
42347 睦 434th Independent Infantry Battalion (16AA) - 113
42348 睦 435th Independent Infantry Battalion (16AA) - 113
42349 鋒 19th Independent Mountain Artillery Regiment (57A) - 118
42350 陽 25th Trench Mortar Battalion (40A) - 115
42351 鋒 28th Trench Mortar Battalion (57A) - 118
42352 鋒 120th Independent Engineer Battalion (57A) - 118
42353 陽 122nd Independent Engineer Battalion (40A) - 115
42354 睦 124th Independent Engineer Battalion (16AA) - 114
42355-9 睦 61st to 65th Independent Signal Labor Units (16AA) - 114
42360-4 睦 71st to 75th Independent Signal Labor Units (16AA) - 114
42365 睦 28th Sea Transport Battalion (16AA) - 114

End of code numbers for Japan and the Territories

Appendix

By November 1945 the Imperial Japanese Army had ceased to exist

Chart 1: Imperial Army ca. August 1945

Organization	Code Name	Posting
Imperial General HQ	*Never had a code name*	Tokyo
General Armies:		
Kwantung Army	*Toku* 徳4570	Hsinking, Manchuria
China Expeditionary Army	*Sakae* 栄1490	Nanking, China
Southern Army	*i* 威1160	Saigon, Vietnam
1st General Army	*Toho* 東方8151	Tokyo, Japan
2nd General Army	*Seiho* 西方8152	Honshu, Japan
General Air Army	*Sui* 師500	Tokyo, Japan
Area Armies:		
1st Area Army	*Ei* 鋭1448	Mutanchiang, Manchuria
2nd Area Army	*Kagayaku* 輝16300	Manado, Celebese
3rd Area Army	*Kyou* 強9331	Mukden, Manchuria
5th Area Army	*Tatsu* 達8150	Sapporo, Japan
6th Area Army	*Tou* 統17700	Hankou, China
7th Area Army	*Oka* 岡1615	Singapore
8th Area Army	*Go* 剛7960	Rabaul, New Britain Is.
10th Area Army	*Wan* 湾 No #	Taipei Formosa
11th Area Army	*Sunuma* 進12300	Sendai, Japan
12th Area Army	*Hata* 幡12345	Tokyo, Japan

Organization	Code Name	Posting
13th Area Army	Syo 秀 12480	Nagoya, Japan
14th Area Army	Shobu 尚武 1600	Manila, Philippines
15th Area Army	Kusunoki 楠 12490	Osaka, Japan
16th Area Army	Mutu 睦 13500	Fukuoka, Japan
17th Area Army	Kizuka 築 12701	Seoul, Korea
18th Area Army	Gi 義 7970	Bangkok, Thailand
North China A. A.	Ko 甲 1400	Beijing, China
Burma Area Army	Mori 森 7900	Moulmein Burma

Armies:

1st Army	Otsu 乙 3500	Tiayuan, North China
2nd Army	Ikioi 勢 16400	Macassar Is.
3rd Army	Iwa 岩 3600	Yenchi, Manchuria
4th Army	Hikari 光 4455	Tsitsihar, Manchuria
5th Army	Shiro 城 5033	Yehho, Manchuria
6th Army	Mamoru 守 1305	Nanking, China
11th Army	Ro 呂 5500	Hankou, China
12th Army	Hito 仁 4221	Chengchow, China
13th Army	Nobori 登 7331	Shanghai, China
14th Army	Shobu 尚武 1600	14th Area Army
15th Army	Hayashi 林 1611	Rangoon, Burma
16th Army	Osamu 治 1602	Batavia, Java
17th Army	Oki 沖 9811	Buin, Solomon Is.
18th Army	Mo 猛 7910	Madang, New Guinea
19th Army	Ken 堅 9450	Batavia, Java
20th Army	Sakura 桜 7907	Hankow, China
23rd Army	Nami 波 8111	Canton, China
25th Army	Tomi 富 8990	De Kock, Sumatra
27th Army	Hokubu 北部 100	Kurile Islands, Japan
28th Army	Saku 策 9410	Paung, Burma
29th Army	Tei 定 9411	Taiping, Malaya
30th Army	Bin 敏 25301	Meihokou, Manchuria
31st Army	Sonae 備 7920	Truk Island
32nd Army	Kyu 球 1616	Okinawa, Japan
33rd Army	Kon 昆 7901	Bilin, Burma
34th Army	Ten 展 (Robu 呂武)	Hamhung, Korea
35th Army	Shou 尚 18200	Cebu Island
36th Army	Fuji 富士 18100	Urawa, Japan
37th Army	Nada 灘 9801	Sangpong, Borneo
38th Army	Sin 信 7950	Saigon, Vietnam
39th Army	Gi 義 7970	Thailand
40th Army	Yo 陽 21300	Kagoshima
41st Army	Sugi 杉 4732	South of Manila P.I.
43rd Army	Shurei 秀嶺 12700	Shangtung, China
44h Army	Sizume 遠征 14001	Liaoyuan, Manchuria
50th Army	Shun 俊 21413	Aomori, Japan

Organization	Code Name	Posting
51st Army	*Ken* 建21410	Mito, Japan
52nd Army	*Sho* 捷13333	Susui, Japan
53rd Army	*Dan* 断21601	Tamagawa, Japan
54th Army	*Satsu* 颯21641	Shinshiromachi, Japan
55th Army	*Kai* 偕12475	Kochi, Japan
56th Army	*Shuu* 宗13580	Iizuka, Japan
57th Army	*Hou* 鋒13590	Takanabe, Japan
58th Army	*Toride* 砦21703	Cheju Island, Korea
59th Army	*Sanyo* 山陽32200	Hiroshima, Japan
Mongolia Garrison	*Bo* 戊5301	Wanchuan, Inner Mongolia
Tokyo Def. Army	*Hata* 幡 No number	Tokyo, Japan
Tokyo Bay Corps	*Bou* 房13300	Tateyama, Japan
Air Armies:		
1st Air Army	*Tsubame* 燕30001	Tokyo, Japan
2nd Air Army	*Hane* 羽8212	Hsinking, Manchuria
3rd Air Army	*Tsukasa* 司9813	Singapore
4th Air Army	*Shin* 眞15300	Manila, Philippines
5th Air Army	*Hayabusa* 隼2371	Seoul, Korea
6th Air Army	*Yasu* 靖19500	Fukuoka, Japan
13th Air Division	*Hayabusa Sakigake* 隼魁	Nanching, China
6th Air Division	*Yō* 洋	18th Army, New Guinea
Shipping and Rail:		
Shipping Command	*Akatsuki* 暁2940	Ujina, Japan
1st R.R. Command	*Sen* 線	Tokyo, Japan
Continental R.R.	*Michi* 路	Hsinking, Manchuria
Manchuria	*Manshu* 満州	Hsinking, Manchuria

Chain of command: A General Army controlled several Area Armies, which in turn controlled several Field or Garrison Armies. For a time the 13th Army was a defacto Area Army with the 6th Army its subordinate.

Japanese field armies were more or less the size of a U.S. army corps.

Chart 2: Army Activations and Movement from 1940 to 1945

In July 1937 the Marco Polo Bridge Incident precipitated the 2nd Sino-Japanese War (the China Incident). As fighting in China continued relations with the West deteriorated, diplomacy finally breaking down in 1941.

Vichy France agreed to allow Japan to occupy southern French Indochina, which threatened Allied interests in the region. The West retaliated in July. America, Britain and Holland placed an oil embargo on Japan, who could produce no more than 10% of its yearly consumption domestically and had less than one year's supply in reserve.

As Japan was already at war, and with an oil crisis looming, the speedy annexation of the British and Dutch East Indies, which together produced 50 million barrels a year, was the obvious next move.

In the months before Pearl Harbor Japan allied itself with Thailand and finalized plans for south Asia and the Pacific. Hope was that a swift victory would force the Allies to sue for peace and allow Japan to keep possession of her gains. Dec 8th was X-Day, the start date for the invasions of Hong Kong, Malaysia, Java and the Philippines.

Six months later, on June 7th, Japan's remarkable string of victories ended in the defeat at Midway.

Legend: **Bold is a** new army, *Italic* is an event and date.

1940:
1. Imperial General Headquarters:
1a. under direct control: Korean Army, Formosa Army, 1st Shipping Transport HQ became **Shipping Transport HQ** *June 7th*, **South China Area Army** *from July 25th*, **22nd Army** *from Jul 25th* and *deactivated Nov 19th*, **Indochina Army** *active Sept 5th*
2. Kwantung Army:
2a. under direct control: 3rd Army, 4th Army, 5th Army, 6th Army
3. China Expeditionary Army:
3a. under direct control: 11th Army, 13th Army, 21st Army *became Soouth China Area Army Feb 9th*
3b. North China Area Army: 1st Army, 12th Army, Mongolia Garrison Army
3c. **South China Area Army** *activated Feb 9th under I.G.HQ control from Jul 25th:* **22nd Army** *joined Feb 9th transferred with South China Area Army Jul 25th*

1941:
1. Imperial General Headquarters:
1a. under direct control: Korean Army, Formosa Army, Northern Area Army, **23rd Army** *joined Jul 5th, to China Exp. Army Aug 15th*, **25th Army** *joined Jul 5th, to Southern Army Nov 15th*, **South Seas Detachment** *joined Nov 16th*
1b. South China Area Army: Indochina Area Army
1c. Shipping Transport Command
2. Kwantung Army:
2a. under direct control: 3rd Army, 4th Army, 5th Army, 6th Army, **20th Army** *joined Sept 19th*, **Kwantung Defense Army** *joined July 12th*
3. China Expeditionary Army:
3a. under direct control: 23rd Army *from Aug 12th*, 3rd Air Corps *deactivated Nov 8th*, 1st Air Brigade *activated Nov 8th*
3b. North China Area Army: 1st Army, 12th Army, Mongolia Garrison Army
4. **Southern Expeditionary Army**: *activated on Nov 5th*
4a. under direct control: **14th Army** *joined Nov 6th*, **15th Army** *joined Nov 6th*,

1941: continued

16th Army *joined Nov 6th*, 25th Army *from Nov 15th*, 3rd Air Corps *joined Nov 15th*, 5th Air Corps *joined Nov 15th*, 1st Air Corps

5. **General Defense Army**: *activated Jul 12th*

5a. under direct control: Northern Army District, Eastern Army District, Central Army District, Western Army District

1942:

1. Imperial General Headquarters:

1a. under direct command: Korea Army, Formosa Army, 14th Army *IGHQ shared command w/Southern Army until June 29th*, **17th Army** *activated May 18th to 8th AA Nov 15th*, South Seas Detachment *to 17th Army May 20th*, **Gov. Gen. of Hong Kong Dept.** *joined Jan 28th*, **North Seas Detachment** *joined May 5th deactivated Oct 24th*, **Ichiki Detachment** *active May 5th to 17th Army Aug 10th*, 1st Flying Corps *deactivated June 6th*, 1st Air Army *joined Aug 10th*

1b. **8th Area Army** *activated Nov 15th*: 17th Army *joined Nov 15th*, **18th Army** *active Nov 16th*

1c. General Defense Army: Northern Army District, Eastern Army District, Central Army District, Western Army District

1d. Shipping Transport Headquarters: *deactivated Jul 14th*, **Shipping Command** *activated Jul 14th*

2. Kwantung Army:

2a. under direct control: Kwantung Defense Army, **Mechanized Army** *joined Jul 4th*, Kwantung Air Corps *dissolved June 10th*, **2nd Air Army** *joined June 10th*

2b. **1st Area Army**, 3rd Army, 5th Army and 20th Armies, **2nd Army** *all joined Jul 4th*

2c. **2nd Area Army** *joined Jul 4th*: 4th Army, 6th Army

3. China Expeditionary Army:

3a. under direct control: 11th Army, 13th Army, 23rd Army, 1st Air Group *dissolved Jul 10th*, **3rd Air Division** *activated Jul 10th*

3b. North China Area Army: 1st Army, 12th Army, Mongolia Garrison Army

4. Southern Expeditionary Army:

4a. under direct control: 14th Army *shared command w/I.G.HQ until June 29th*, 15th Army, 16th Army, 25th Army, **Borneo Defense Army HQ** *active from Apr 20th*, **Indochina Garrison Army** *active Nov 10th*, 3rd Air Corps *deactivated Jul 7th*, 5th Air Corps *deactivated Jul 7th*, **22nd Air Brigade** *active Mar 20th sent to 14th Army on Jul 15th*, **3rd Air Army** *activated Jul 10th*

1943:

1. Imperial General Headquarters:

1a. under direct command: Korea Army, Formosa Army, 14th Army, Governor General of Hong Kong Dept., North Seas Detachment *became the North Area Army on Feb. 5th*, 1st Air Army

1b. 8th Area Army: 17th Army, 18th Army, 4th Air Army *joined the 8th AA on Jul 28th*

1c. 2nd Area Army *from Oct. 30th*, 2nd Army *joined 2nd AA on Oct.30th*

1d. General Defense Army: **Northern Defense Army** *activated Feb 5th*, Northern District Army *deactivated Feb 5th*, Eastern District Army, Central District Army, Western District Army

1e. Shipping Command

2. Kwantung Army:

1942: continued

2a. under direct control: Kwantung Defense Army, Mechanized Army *deactivated on Oct 30th,* 2nd Air Army

2b. 1st Area Army: 2nd Army *to 2nd Area Army Oct 30th,* 3rd Army, 5th Army, 20th Army

2c. 2nd Area Army *to Imp HQ Oct 30th:* 4th Army *to 3rd Area Army Oct 30th,* 6th Army *to 3rd Area Army Oct 30th*

2d. **3rd Area Army** *joined Oct 30th:* 4th Army, 6th Army

3. China Expeditionary Army:

3a. under direct control: 11th Army, 13th Army, 23rd Army, 3rd Air Division

3b. North China Area Army: 1st Army, 12th Army, Mongolia Garrison Army

4. Southern Expeditionary Army:

4a. under direct control: 16th Army, 25th Army, Borneo Defense Army, **19th Army** *activated Jan 7th joined 2nd AA on Oct 30th,* **Thailand Garrison Army** *activated Jan 4th,* Indochina Garrison Army *joined the Southern Army Dec 10th,* 3rd Air Army

4b. **Burma Area Army** *joined Mar 27th:* 15th Army

4c. 2nd Area Army *from Oct 30th:* 19th Army *from Oct 30th*

1944:

1. Imperial General Headquarters:

1a. under direct command: Korea Army, Formosa Army *until Mar 20th,* 14th Army *shared command w/Southern Army, removed Apr 15th,* **32nd Army** *created Mar 22nd to the West District Army May 10th.* **31st Army** *created Feb 25th,* **Ogasawara Army Group** *from June 26th,* Governor of Hong Kong Dept. *to 6th Area Army on Dec 11th,* **36th Army** *activated Jul 15th, I.G.HQ to Gen Def Command Oct 27th,* 1st Air Army *until Mar 27th,* 10th Area Army *from Oct 25th*

1b. 2nd Area Army *to Southern Army Mar 27th:* 19th Army, 2nd Army

1c. 8th Area Army: 17th Army, 18th Army *to 2nd Area Army Mar 25th and to Southern Army June 20th,* 4th Air Army *to 2nd Area Army Mar 25th, to Southern Ex. Army Apr 15th*

1d. **5th Area Army** *created Mar 6th:* **27th Army** *activated Mar 6th*

1e. **10th Area Army** *created Sept 9th*

1f. General Defense Army: Northern Defense Army *became the* **5th Area Army** *under I.G.HQ from Mar 6th,* 36th Army *to 12th Area Army Feb '45,* Eastern District Army, Central District Army, Western District Army, **6th Air Army** *from Dec 25th*

1g. Shipping Command

2. Kwantung Army:

2a. under direct control: Kwantung Defense Army, 2nd Air Army

2b. 1st Area Army: 2nd Army, 3rd Army, 5th Army, 20th Army *until Sept 27th*

2c. 3rd Area Army: 4th Army, 6th Army

3. China Expeditionary Army:

3a. under direct control: 11th Army *until Aug 26th,* 13th Army, 23rd Army *until Aug 26th,* **34th Army** *until Jul 17th* 3rd Air Division *until Feb 15th,* **5th Air Army** *from Feb. 15th*

3b. North China Area Army: 1st Army, 12th Army, Mongolia Garrison Army

3c. **6th Area Army** *from Aug 26th:* 34th Army *from Aug 26th,* 20th Army *from Oct 19th,* 23rd Army *from Aug 26th*

4. Southern Expeditionary Army:

4a. under direct control: 14th Army *shared command w/I.G.HQ until Apr 15th,* Borneo Defense Army *became the* **37th Army** *on Oct 12th,* Thailand Garrison Army *became*

1944: continued

the **39th Army** *on Dec 10th*, French Indochina Garrison Army *became the* **38th Army** *on Dec 26th*, 3rd Air Army

4b. **14th Area Army** *created from 14th Army on Aug 4th*: **34th Army** *created Aug 4th*

4c. **7th Area Army** *created Mar 27th*, 16th Army *from Mar 27th*, 25th Army *from Mar 27th*, 29th Army *from Mar 27th*

4d. Burma Area Army: 15th Army, **28th Army** *from Jan 15th*, **33rd Army** *from Apr 11th*

4e. 2nd Area Army *from Mar 27th*, 19th Army, 2nd Army

1945:

1. Imperial General Headquarters:

1a. under direct control: Korea Army *became* **17th Area Army** *on Feb 6th to Kw. Army*, 31st Army, Ogasawara Army Group, 1st Air Army *until Apr 8th*

1b. General Defense Army *became* **1st General Army** *on Apr 8th*: Eastern District Army *became* **12th Area Army** *Feb 6th*, Central District Army *became the* **15th Area Army** *Feb 6th*, Western District Army *became the* **16th Area Army** *Feb 6th*, 6th Air Army *joined* **Air General Army** *Apr 8th*

1c. 5th Area Army: 27th Army *until Jan 22nd HQ became the* **15th Area Army HQ**

1d. 10th Area Army: 32nd Army, 40th Army *until Jan 16th and 16th Area Army on May 20th*

1e. 8th Area Army *abandoned in Rabaul on June 17th*: 17th Army, 18th Army *until June 17th transferred to the Southern Expeditionary Army.*

1f. Shipping Command:

2. Kwantung Army: *reorganized May 30th*

2a. under direct control: 4th Army *from May 30th*, 6th Army *to China Exp. Army Jan 25th*, Kwantung Defense Army *became the* **44th Army** *May 30th*, **34th Army** *created June 18th*, 2nd Air Army *to Air General Army on May 15th*

2b. **17th Area Army** *was Korea Army until Feb 6th, joined Kwantung Army Aug 10th*: **58th Army** *created Apr 8th*

2c. 1st Area Army *reorg. May 30th*: 3rd Army *from May 30th*, 5th Army *from May 30th*

2d. 3rd Area Army *reorg. May 30th*: 30th Army *from Jul 30th*, 44th Army *from May 30th*

3. China Expeditionary Army:

3a. under direct control: 13th Army, 6th Army *from Jan 25th*, 23rd Army *from Mar 10th*, 5th Air Army *to Kwantung Army on May 16th*

3b. North China Area Army: 1st Army, 12th Army, Mongolia Defense Army, 43rd Army *from Mar 22nd*

3c. 6th Area Army: 11th Army, 20th Army, 23rd Army *to China Expeditionary Army Mar 10th*, 34th Army *to Kwantung Army on June 18th*, Gov. Gen. of Hong Kong *to 23rd Army Mar 10th*

4. Southern Expeditionary Army:

4a. under direct control: 37th Army, 2nd Army *under the Southern Army from June 13th*, 39th Army *became the* **18th Area Army** *on Jul 15th*, 38th Army, 18th Army *after June 17th*, 3rd Air Army, 4th Air Army *deactivated Feb 17th*

4b. Burma Area Army: 15th Army, 28th Army, 33rd Army

4c. 7th Area Army: 16th Army, 25th Army, 29th Army

4d. 14th Area Army: 35th Army, **41st Army** *from Apr 20th*

4e. 2nd Area Army *deactivated June 13th*: 2nd Army *to the Southern Army*, 19th Army *deactivated Feb 28th*.

<u>1945</u>: continued
4f. **18th Area Army** *was the 39th Army until Jul 15th:* 15th Army *from Jul 15th*
5. **1st General Army** *created Apr 8th:*
5a. **11th Area Army** *created Feb 6th:* **50th Army** *created Feb 6th*
5b. **12th Area Army** *created Feb 6th:* 36th Army *attached Feb 6th*, **51st Army** *created Apr 8th,* **52nd Army** *created Apr 8th,* **53rd Army** *created Apr 8th,* **Tokyo Bay Army Corps** *created June 19th,* **Tokyo Defense Army** *created June 23rd*
5c. **13th Area Army** *created Feb 6th:* **54th Army** *created June 19th*
6. **2nd General Army** *created Apr 8th:*
6a. **15th Area Army** *created Feb 6th:* **55th Army** *created Apr 8th,* **59th Army** *created June 15th*
6b. **16th Area Army** *created Feb 6th:* 40th Army *joined May 20th,* **56th Army** *created Apr 21st,* **57th Army** *created Apr 8th*
7. **Air General Army**: *created Apr. 8th*
7a. under direct control: , 1st Air Army *from Apr 8th,* 2nd Air Army *from May 15th,* 5th Air Army *from May 15th,* 6th Air Army *from Apr 8th*

Bibliography

Books

Anonymous. August 24, 2015. *A Dictionary of Military Terms and Expressions*: Sagwan Press

ATIS. 1947. (Allied Translator and Interpreter Section), Supreme Commander for the Allied Powers. *Report on surrendered Japanese personnel in U.S.S.R. territories*. CARL Digital Library EBook

ATIS. 1945. *Restoration of Captured Documents. ATIS Publication No. 10*: Allied Translator and Interpreter Section South West Pacific Area. CARL Digital Library EBook

ATIS. 1944 *The Exploitation of Japanese Documents*: Allied Translator and Interpreter Section, South West Pacific Area, Publication No. 6 CARL Digital Library EBook

Bullard, Steven (translator). 2007. *Japanese army operations in the South Pacific area, New Britain and Papua campaigns, 1942-43*: A.W.M. EBook

Bullard, Steven and Tamura Keiko (eds.). 2004. *From a hostile shore: Australia and Japan at war in New Guinea*. Canberra, ACT: Aust. War Memorial EBook

Frank, Richard B. 1990. *Guadalcanal: the definitive account of the landmark battle*. Penguin Random House

General Headquarters, Military Intelligence Section, General Staff. *Final progress of demobilization of the Japanese Armed Forces, December 31, 1946*: CARL Digital Library EBook. (PDF in four parts)

General Headquarters, South West Pacific Area, Military Intelligence Section, General Staff.1945. *Periodic Summary of Enemy Trends, No. 29*. CARL Digital Library EBook

Kai, Shunichiro. 1991. 日本陸海軍部隊要覧 *(Nihon Riku Kai Gun Butai Yoran)*: Shinpu Shobo

McNaughton, James C. 2006. *Nisei Linguists, Japanese Americans in the Intelligence Service during World War II*: Dept. of the Army, Washington D.C. (Chapter 3. EBook https://history.army.mil/books/Recent/Nisei/Ch3.pdf)

Military Intelligence Division. War Dept. 1945. *Guide to Maps of the Far East, Special Series N0. 31*. War Dept: CARL Digital Library EBook

Military Intelligence Division. 1945. *Japanese Recruiting and Replacement System*. War Department: CARL Digital Library EBook (PDF in two parts)

Military Intelligence Service. 1942. *Japanese Ground and Air Forces, Information Bulletin No. 14, MID 461*. War Department, Washington D.C.: CARL Digital Library EBook

Pacific Unit M.I.D. 1943. *Applied Tactics Japanese Army, Translation of Japanese Manual, Revised 1938*. War Department, Washington D.C.: CARL Digital Library EBook (PDF in six parts)

Pinyol, Joan. 2016. *The Rising Sun in Arms - Order of Battle of the Imperial Japanese Armed Forces, 1937- 1945*: Self-published 2nd Edition

Remmelink, Willem (translator). 2016. *Invasion of the Dutch East Indies*. Compiled by the War Office of the National Defense College of Japan 1967. Corts Foundation/Leiden University Press, 2015

Sledge, E.B. 1981. *With the Old Breed*: Presidio Press, a Division of Random House

U.S. War Dept. 1944. *Japanese military dictionary*: *Japanese-English*
United States. War Dept. 1944. *Handbook on Japanese military forces*. Washington: U.S. Govt. Print. Off.

The Japanese Monographs: Commissioned by the Historical Section, G-2, GHQ, FE. CA. Two-DVD disc set by LRA 2014, purchased from the late Jim Lansdale. The initial proposal for the Monograph series came from US Government *Instruction No. 126, Institution for War Records Investigation*. Begun in November 1945, Japan's Demobilization Bureau coordinated the project. Owing to essential missing operational records such as original orders, unit journals and plans the Japanese ranking and staff Army and Navy officers involved reconstructed missing details from personal papers and memory. Aside from a patriotic softening of adverse events, these accounts (which include many unedited translations) are believed to be substantially accurate.

Note: Monographs marked * are available as downloads from: http://ibiblio.org/hyperwar/Japan/Monos/

Monograph number – Title and details:

1 – Philippines Operations Record, Phase 1, Invasion of the Philippines, November 6, 1941 – June 30, 1942, unedited translation, 243 pages, unaccredited, undated

3 – Philippines Operations Record, Phase 2, Subjugation of islands, guerrillas and insurgents, the Philippines as a logistics base, December 1942 – June 1944, 56 pages by Col. Yasuji Okada, October 1946

4 – Philippines Operations Record, Phase III, 14th Area Army plans for defense, July 1944 – November 1944, 50 pages by Col. Shujiro Kobayashi and Col. Ryoichiro Aojima, October 1946

6 – Philippines Operations Record, 35th Army's defense of Leyte, June 1944 – August 1945, 171 pages by Maj. Masataka Iwano, Maj. Gen. Yoshihara Tomochika, editors Ryoichiro Aoshima and Rigai Watanabe, October 1946

7 – Philippines Operations Record, defensive preparations and U.S. invasion of Leyte, January – August 1945, 222 pages by Maj. Masataka Iwano and Col. Ryoichiro Aoshima, October 1946

8 – Philippines Operations Record, Shimbu Army Group in Southern Luzon, December 1944 – August 1945, 36 pages by Maj. Masataka Iwano and Col. Ryoichiro Aoshima, October 1946

9 – Philippines Operations Record, Shimbu Army Group defense of Clark Field, December 1944 – August 1945, 31 pages by Col. Yasuji Okada, November 1946

12*– Philippines Air Operations Record, 4th Air Army operations in Leyte, Luzon and Mindoro, August 1944–February 1945, 119 pages by Col. Matsumae, former 4th Air Army staff officer, Oct. 1946

13 – North of Australia Operations Record, 2nd Area Army, 1943 – 1945, 108 pages, unedited translation, unaccredited, July 1946

14 – Second Area Army Operations in the Western New Guinea Area (battle summary), May 1944 – January 1945, 18 pages, unedited translation, unaccredited, undated

15 – Outline of the Battle for Morotai (32nd Division), 15 September – 13 May 1945, 19 pages, unedited translation, unaccredited, undated

16*– Ambon (Amboina) and Timor Invasion Operations, January – February

1942, edited reproduced, 23 pages by Lt. Col. Tozuka Susumu based on diary notes, then expanded by Lt. Col. Kengoro Tanaka et al. January 31, 1953

17*– Homeland Operations Record, 1941 – 1945, 246 pages, rewritten and reproduced with the assistance of Susumu Nishimura: Monograph 17 by Maj. Gen. Yoshihide Kato et al., later compiled into one with Homeland Operations Monographs No. 18: Vol. II, 19: Vol. III, and No. 20; 16th Area Army, undated.

21 – Homeland Operations Record, Volume IV, Fifth Area Army, late 1943 – 1945, 50 pages, edited reproduced by Lt. Col. Risaburo Taguma from memory and documents in his possession, July 30, 1952

22 – Seventeenth Area Army Operations, 1941 – 1945, 46 pages by Lt. Col. Matsushige Ishibashi and Maj. Fusakichi Fueda, rewritten and reproduced by Col. Muraji Yano, July 23, 1956

23 – Air Defense of the Homeland, 1944 – 1945, 91 pages by Maj. Takejiro Shiba, rewritten by former Japanese officers Toshikazu Ohmae, Ryosuke Nomura and Tadao Shudo, June 5, 1956

24*– History of the Southern Army, 1941 – 1945, 159 pages, rewritten by the 1st Demobilization Bureau, July 1946

25 – French Indo-China Area Operations Record, 1940 – 1945, 40 pages by Lt. Col. Tateki Sakai with assistance from Lt. Col. Sakuji Ishimaru, Lt. Col. Kakuo Yamamoto, Lt. Col. Wasatatsu Shirai and Lt. Col. Isamu Hashizume, September 17, 1952

26 – Borneo Operations, 1941 – 1945, 98 pages by Col. Itsu Ogawa assisted by Lt. Col. Masashi Ino, rewritten and corrected incorporating extensive research by the Foreign Histories Division, Nov 20, 1957

27 – Jolo Island Invasion Operations Record, Dec. 1941, 3 pages by Col. Tsuneo Yano, edited, undated

28 – Tarakan Invasion Operations Record, Jan. 1942, 6 pages by Col. Tsuneo Yano, edited, Mar 4, 1952

29 – Balikpapan Invasion Operations Record, January 1942, 8 pages by Col. Tsuneo Yano, edited, March 31, 1953

30 – Bandjermasin Invasion Operations Record, February 1942, 7 pages by Col. Tsuneo Yano, edited April 21, 1953

31*– Southern Area Air Operations Record, 1941 – 1945, 37 pages, unedited translation, unaccredited, undated

32*– Southeast Area Air Operations Record, November 1942 - April 1944, 39 pages, unedited translation by Lt. Col. Koji Tanaka, undated

34 – Southeast Area Operations Record, Volume I, 17th Army on Guadalcanal, May 1942 – January 1943, 162 pages, unedited translation by Lt. Col. Norikuni Sadashima and Lt. Gen. Haruo Konuma, Sept. 1946

35 – Southeast Area Operations Record, Volume II, 17th Army's withdrawal from Guadalcanal, February 1943 – August 1945, 172 pages, unedited translation by Lt. Col. Norikuni Sadashima, Lt. Gen. Haruo Konuma, Lt. Col. Shiro Hara, Col. Toshihara Kamiya, Lt. Col. Matsuichi Iino and Maj. Isamu Tanaka, September 1946

37 – Southeast Area Ops Record 18th Army Ops, Vol. I, January 1942 – June 1943, 195 pages by Col. Shigeru Sugiyama, rewritten and reproduced by Lt. Col. Kengoro Tanaka, October 14, 1953

38 – Southeast Area Ops Record 18th Army Ops, Vol. II, June 1943 – February 1944, 212 pages, unedited translation, 1st Demobilization Bureau, unaccredited, September 1946

39 – Southeast Area Ops Record 18th Army Ops, Vol. III, Mar 1944 – August 1944, 191 pages, unedited translation, 1st Demobilization Bureau, unaccredited, September 1946

40 – Southeast Area Ops Record 18th Army Ops, Volume IV, Sept 1944 – June 1945, 321 pages, unedited translation, 1st Demobilization Bureau, unaccredited, October 1946

44 – History of the Eighth Area Army, November 1942 – August 1945, 114 pages, unedited translation by Maj. Gen. Kazuo Tanikawa, undated

45*– History of Imperial General Headquarters, Army Section, 1941 – 1945, 382 pages, unaccredited Nov 1946, corrected and rewritten by Col. Takushiro Hattori assisted by former general officers, May 11, 1959

54 – Malay Operations Record, November 1941 – March 1942, 104 pages, unedited translation by Col. Sugita, Lt. Col. Kunitake and Lt. Col. Hashizune, September 1946

58 – Burma Operations Record Phase II, early 1943 – summer 1944, 76 pages, unedited translation by Col. Fusa, Lt. Col. Minoru Kawachi and Col. Shigemoto Kobayashi, undated

66*– The Invasion of the Netherlands East Indies, November 1941 – March 1942, 59 pages by Col. Akimitsu Oda, read by Maj. Gen. Takashima and Lt. Col Yamashita. Owing to a number of inaccuracies and omissions it was rewritten later, April 10, 1958

67 – Palembang and Bangka Islands Operations Record, January – February 1942, 16 pages based on memories and personal papers by Lt. Col. Minoru Miyako, Col. Yoshimitsu Ake and Col. Seiichi Kume, April 28, 1953

76*– Air Operations in the China Area, July 1937 – August 1945, 220 pages by Maj. Takejiro Shiba based on documents from Co. Genichi Yamamoto, Col. Hiroshi Saso, Lt. Col. Hirokichi Mizuo and Maj. En Komatsu, rewritten and corrected by the Japanese Research division, December 10, 1956

78 – The Kwantung Army in the Manchurian Campaign, 1941 – 1945, 45 pages, unedited translation. Kwantung Army information is based on personal papers of Lt. Col. Ishiwatari and memories of Maj. Komuratani, Lt. Col. Mizumachi, Maj. Iwano and returnees from Korea and Manchuria. U.S.S.R. based on information contributed by Maj. Shishikura former I.G.HQ staff officer

130 – China Area Ops Record - 6th Area Army Operations, July 1944 – August 1945, 126 pages by Mr. Jiso Yamaguchi based on memories of Maj. Gen. Renya Mutaguchi, Lt. Col. Bun Hirai, Lt. Col. Iwaichi Fujiwara, et al., October 10, 1952. Edited, revised with assistance from Gen. Kawabe, Lt. Gen. Sato, Maj. Gen. HJayashi, et al., October 10, 1957

132*– Burma Ops Record 28th Army Ops Akyab Area, Nov 1943 – Sept 1945, 212 pages by Col. Aiichi Okamura (formerly 28th Army, written while interned in Burma), reviewed by Lt. Gen. Shozo Sakurai. Rewritten and corrected by Maj. Nizo Yamaguchi in employ of 1st Demob. Bureau, August 29, 1952

134*– Burma Operations Record, 15th Army Operations in Imphal Area and Withdrawal to Northern Burma, January 1943 – January 1945, 191 pages rewritten and revised, October 10, 1957

135 – Okinawa Operations Record, March – June 1945, 265 pages unedited translation by Lt. Col. Katsushiro Mizumachi, August 1946

138*– Japanese Preparations for Operations in Manchuria, January 1943 – August 1945, 190 pages based on war time notes and diaries of Lt. Col. Prince Tsunenori Takeda and prepared by Lt. Col. Katsushiro Mizumachi translated into English in 1951, final edit with assistance from Co. Muraji Yano, Lt. Col. Ko Takahashi and Lt. Col. Kengoro Tanaka, November 1953

143 – Southeast Area Operations Record Part I, January – May 1942, 19 pages, unedited translation, unaccredited, 2nd Demobilization Board (IJN), January 1950

148 – Burma Area Operations Record 33rd Army Operations, April 1944 – August 1945, 234 pages by Fumi Yamaguchi, reference materials from Maj. Hiroshi Kibini and Col. Tsuji's diary, August 1950, revised edition 1960

151 – Air Operations Record Against Soviet Russia, June 1941 – September 1945, 65 pages by Lt. Col. Katsuo Sato from memory, personal papers and available unit records, edited and corrected, March 3, 1952

154*– Record of Operations Against Soviet Russia, Eastern Front, August 1945, 364 pages by Lt. Col. Genichiro Arinuma, Maj. Kyoji Takasugi, 1st Area Army page 26 by Col. Hiroshi Matsumoto, 3rd Army page 60 by Lt. Col. Naotomo Hosokawa, 79th Division (and 112th Div.) page 110 by Col. Takaharu Shinabe, 127th Division page 139 by Maj. Masao Sakai, 5th Army page 148 by Col. Akiji Kashiwada, 124th Division page 225 by Col. Toyoharu Iwasaki, 126th Division page 246 by Col Masashi Tanaka, 135th Division page 274 by Col. Toshisuke Inouye, 132nd I.M.B. page 331 by Maj. Gen. Goichi Onitake. Edited, April 6, 1954

162 – 7th Area Army's Southwest Area Operations Record, April 1944 – August 1945, 186 pages by Col. Yutaka Imaoka based on fragmentary data and personal recollections, unedited translation, February 1951

164 – Railway Operations Record (overseas and homeland) 1941 – 1945, 209 pages by Lt. Col. Shigeru Kubota from memoranda and memory, unedited translation, March 1951

165 – Java Operations Record Part II, early 1944 - August 1945, 16th Army, 27 pages by Lt. Col. Shizuo Miyamoto from memory and fragmentary reports, unedited translation, April 1951

167 – Malay Operations Record, January 1944 – August 1945, 29th Army, 52 pages by Lt. Gen. Masuzo Fujimura and Lt. Gen. Naokazu Kawahara, unedited translation, May 1951

177 –Thailand Operations Record, 1941 – 1945, 39th Army and 18th Area Army, 37 pages by Col. Konishi Takeo with assistance from Lt. Col. Hachiro Tokunaga, rewritten November 30, 1953

180*–South China Area Operations Record, 1937 – 1941, 21st Army and South China Area Army, 139 pages by the Reports and Statistical Section of the Demobilization Bureau and from documents in the possession of Lt. Col. Heizo Ishiwari with fragments from other sources, maps supplied by the editor with assistance from Lt. Col. Tadao Shudo, rewritten, March 9, 1956

185 – 25th Army, Sumatra Operations Record, March 1942 - August 1945, 18 pages

from the memories and personal papers of Lt. Col. Eiji Yamaguchi, Lt. Col. Sakai Omura and Maj. Takuji Kuramasu, June 19,1953

JACAR: Japan Center for Asian Historical Records

The *Japan Center for Asian Historical Records* (*JACAR*) is the portal used for the majority of primary source material relating to Imperial Japanese Army code names and numbers (*Tsushogo*). Documents, for the most part, are in the Japanese language and require recognizable kanji phrasing (or a reference number) to search them out. Recently, the Center has incorporated an auxiliary English home page and search facility. A number of relevant documents in English have been preserved from MacArthur's time, JACAR reference numbers will provide quick access for any who care to explore further.

JACAR documents are held in either: A: *National Archives of Japan*. B: *Diplomatic Archives of the Ministry of Foreign Affairs*. C: *National Institute for Defense Studies of the Ministry of Defense*. All document reference numbers accessed through JACAR are preceded by one of the three letters denoting the institution that holds the document.

        Wrong entry 17850   Correct entry 17650

Japanese army lists all have inaccuracies, in this example, the *11th Independent Machinegun Battalion* appears twice under different code numbers in the same list; 部隊通称番號一覧表 No. 1 Repatriation Bureau, Nov. 11, 1946, JACAR Ref. Code: C12121106600 (most accurate list I know of). Where possible the code numbers here have been checked and verified against at least two independently produced lists. Also note there are thousands of legitimate unidentified unit numbers.

Army Lists in English:
List 1:
JACAR Ref. C15011165100 End of October 1945. Field Marshal MacArthur's Headquarters submission *Japanese Imperial army units compilation table* (original record). *List 1*. National Institute for Defense Studies.
List 1, Download: 350 files (Total: 65.8 MB)
    Cover: C15011165100
    Inside Cover (English) C15011165200
    Index C15011165300
    Last file: Shipping Units: C15011200000
List 2:
JACAR Ref. C15011231900. End of October 1945. Field Marshal MacArthur's Headquarters submission, *Japanese Imperial army units survey compilation table* (original record) *List 2*. National Institute for Defense Studies.
List 2 Download: 103 files (Total: 45.7 MB)
    Cover: C15011231800
    Inside Cover (English): C15011232000
    Index: C15011232100
    Last file: Various Army Training Units: C15011242100
List 3:

JACAR Ref. C15011242300. End of October 1945. Field Marshal MacArthur's Headquarters submission *Japanese Imperial army units survey compilation table* (original record) *List 3*. National Institute for Defense Studies.
List 3 Download: 88 files (Total: 22.5 MB)
    Cover: C15011242300
    Inside Cover (English): C15011242400
    Index: C15011242500
    Last file: Kwantung Army Misc. Units C15011251000

List 4:
JACAR Ref.C15011251200. End of October 1945. Field Marshal MacArthur's Headquarters submission *Japanese Imperial army units survey compilation table* (original record) *List 4*. National Institute for Defense Studies.
List 4 Download: 27 files (Total: 79.5 MB)
    Cover: C15011251200
    Inside Cover (English): C15011251300
    Index (Army Districts): C15011251400
    Last file: Shipping Units: C15011253800

List 5:
JACAR Ref.C15011254000. End of October 1945. Field Marshal MacArthur's Headquarters submission *Japanese Imperial army units survey compilation table* (original record) *List 5*. National Institute for Defense Studies.
List 5 Download: 19 files (Total: 16.2 MB)
    Cover: C15011254000
    Inside Cover (English): C15011254100
    Index (Homeland Defense Units): C15011254200
    Last file: Hokubu Units: C15011255800

Air Force:
JACAR Ref.C15011256100. End of October 1945. Field Marshal MacArthur's Headquarters submission *Japanese Imperial Army Units Survey Compilation Table* (original record). List in 4 parts. Japanese Army Ministry. National Institute for Defense Studies)
Download: 6 files (Total: 24.8 MB)
    Cover: C15011256000
    List 1: Air Unit HQs and Flying Units: C15011256100
    List 2 (1 of 2): Air Service HQs and Units: C15011256200
    List 2 (2 of 2): Air Service HQs and Units cont.: C15011256300
    List 3: Air Army Ground Units: C15011256400
    List 4: Air Army HQs Training Units, etc.: C15011256500

Other Primary Source Documents from JACAR in English:
JACAR Ref. C12121215800. November 11, 1945. (Document in Japanese and English, P. 10) *Rules on the War Time Code Names of Army Units* and (P. 16) *Summarized History of Code Names*. National Institute for Defense Studies. 19 pages. Japanese Army Department. 19 files (Total: 88.0 MB)

JACAR Ref. C15011200300. *Japanese Army Ministry List 2 No.1 Table No.2 Part 1 (ground units, etc.)*. End of October 1945. Field Marshal MacArthur's Headquarters submission. *Survey table of the Japanese Imperial Army units, Compilation table (original record) List 2- (1) Japanese Army Ministry*. National Institute for Defense

Studies. 315 files (Total: 50.7 MB)
JACAR Ref. C15011256800. *Abbreviations.* Field Marshal MacArthur's Headquarters submission *Japanese Imperial Army units survey table compilation table (original record) Japanese Army.* National Institute for Defense Studies. 2 of 5 files (Total: 8.3 MB)
JACAR Ref. C15011256900. *(1) General explanation about survey table as a whole.* National Institute for Defense Studies. 3 of 5 files
JACAR Ref. C15011257000. Field Marshal MacArthur's Headquarters submission. November 2, 1945. *(2) Japanese Imp. Army units unit types list.* National Institute for Def. Studies. 4 of 5 files
JACAR Ref. C15011257100. Field Marshal MacArthur's Headquarters submission *(3) Japanese Imperial Army Units alias and number list General explanation.* National Institute for Defense Studies. 5 of 5

Army Lists in Japanese:
部隊通称番号一覧表 *1001 to 38500* (Translation: *Unit Tsushogo Catalog 1001 to 38500)* 昭和21年11月11日 (Repatriation Bureau. November 11, 1946) 5 files (Total: 31.8 MB)
A list of sequential code numbers and units in abbreviated Japanese form (独 = 独立 Independent) some knowledge of Japanese will be needed to read them. Largest and most accurate of all the unit lists.
JACAR. Ref. C12121106500. National Institute for Defense Studies. Cover. 1 page
JACAR. Ref. C12121106600. National Institute for Defense Studies. Part 1.
    50 pages
JACAR. Ref. C12121106700. National Institute for Defense Studies. Part 2.
    50 pages
JACAR. Ref. C12121106800. National Institute for Defense Studies. Part 3.
    50 pages
JACAR. Ref. C12121106900. National Institute for Defense Studies. Part 4.
    18 pages

陸軍部隊調表 (Army Unit Survey List) Oct. 28, 1945, Prepared by the Army Ministry. These lists are by unit type.
Major Units List:
JACAR. Ref. C12121087200. National Institute for Defense Studies. Cover. 1 page
JACAR. Ref. C12121087300. National Institute for Defense Studies. Inside
    cover 1 page
JACAR. Ref. C12121087400. National Institute for Defense Studies. Contents.
    1 page
JACAR. Ref. C12121087500. National Institute for Defense Studies. Segment 1
    Index, list. 50 pages
JACAR. Ref. C12121087600. National Institute for Defense Studies.
    Segment 2. List. 50 pages
JACAR. Ref. C12121087700. National Institute for Defense Studies. Segment
    3. List. 9 pages
Independent Units List:

JACAR. Ref. C12121087800. National Institute for Defense Studies. List 2, segment 1. 51 pages
JACAR. Ref. C12121087900. National Institute for Defense Studies. List 2, segment 2. 52 pages
Manchuria Units List:
JACAR. Ref. C12121088000. National Institute for Defense Studies. List 3. 46 pages
Air Units List:
JACAR. Ref. C12121088100. National Institute for Defense Studies. List 4, segment 1. 37 pages
JACAR. Ref. C12121088200. National Institute for Defense Studies. List 4 segment 2. 4 pages
北方鮮満部隊編成補充担任部隊一覧表. April 1947. Supplementary units organized for North Korea and Manchuria
JACAR. Ref. C1501004480. Cover. 2 pages
JACAR. Ref. C13010270000. Notes. 1 page
JACAR Ref. C13010269900. Manchuria (Kanto) Army direct control. 8 pages
JACAR Ref. C13010270200. 1st Area Army direct control. 3 pages
JACAR Ref. C13010270300. 3rd Army. 4 pages
JACAR Ref. C13010270400. 5th Army. 3 pages
JACAR Ref. C13010270500. 3rd Area Army direct control. 5 pages
JACAR Ref. C13010270600. 30th Army. 3 pages
JACAR Ref. C13010270700. 44th Army. 3 pages
JACAR Ref. C13010270800. 4th Army. 5 pages
JACAR Ref. C13010270900. 17th Area Army and 34th Army. 3 pages
JACAR Ref. C13010271000. Korea Army District. 3 pages
JACAR Ref. C13010271100. 5th Area Army direct control. 5 pages

Records Used for Most Unit Personnel Totals: (In Japanese)
Cover Pages:
JACAR Ref. C12120965900. (National Institute for Defense Studies). 兵籍異動通報綴 (*Military Register; Personnel Assignment Reports Binder*). 2 files (Total: 235.1 Kbytes)
JACAR Ref. C12120966000. February 1947. (National Institute for Defense Studies). 兵籍異動通報 (*Military Register; Personnel Assignment Reports*)
General Armies:
JACAR Ref. C12120966200 to JACAR Ref. C12120967000. July 1940 to 1945. *Kwantung Army organization; number of persons*. (National Institute for Defense Studies). 9 files (Total: 26.4 MB)
JACAR Ref. C12120968000 to JACAR Ref. C12120968200. July 1940 to 1945. *Kwantung Army organization; number of persons*. 3 files (Total: 13.0 MB)
JACAR Ref. C12120968400 to JACAR Ref. C12120969500. June 1937 to 1945. *China Expeditionary Army organization; number of persons*. 12 files (Total: 40.3 MB)
JACAR Ref. C12120971400 to JACAR Ref. C12120972400. July 1941 to 1945. *Southern Expeditionary Army organization; number of persons*. 11 files (Total: 33.8 MB)

JACAR Ref. C12121034100 to JACAR Ref. C12121036200. *1st and 2nd General Army organization; number of persons.* 22 files (Total: 11.7 MB)

Area Armies:

JACAR Ref. C12120972600 to JACAR Ref. C12120973700. June 1937 to 1945. *Burma Area Army organization; number of persons.* 12 files (Total: 39.5 MB)

JACAR Ref. C12120969700 to JACAR Ref. C12120970600. January 1937 to 1945. *North China Area Army organization; number of persons.* 10 files (Total: 22.8 MB)

JACAR Ref. C12120974200 to JACAR Ref. C12120974700. July 1940 to 1945. *1st Area Army organization; number of persons.* 6 files (Total: 17.2 MB)

Note: 2nd Area Army demobilized. File missing

JACAR Ref. C12120974900 to JACAR Ref. C12120975900. *3rd Area Army organization; number of persons.* 11 files (Total: 25.9 MB)

JACAR Ref. C12120976100 to JACAR Ref. C12120977400. August 1941 to 1945. *5th Area Army organization; number of persons.* 14 files (Total: 47.7 MB)

JACAR Ref. C12120977600 to JACAR Ref. C12120978900. June 1938 to 1945. *6th Area Army organization; number of persons.* 14 files (Total: 37.3 MB)

JACAR Ref. C12120979100 to JACAR Ref. C12120979500. 1941 to 1945. *7th Area Army organization; number of persons.* 5 files (Total: 10.9 MB)

JACAR Ref. C12120979700 to JACAR Ref. C12120980600. July 1938 to 1945. *8th Area Army organization; number of persons.* 10 files (Total: 26.4 MB)

JACAR Ref. C12120980800 to JACAR Ref. C12120982800. July 1941 to 1945. *10th Area Army organization; number of persons.* 21 files (Total: 55.0 MB)

JACAR Ref. C12120983000 to JACAR Ref. C12120983700. January 1944 to 1945. *11th Area Army organization; number of persons.* 8 files (Total: 17.5 MB)

JACAR Ref. C12120983900 to JACAR Ref. C12120985000. July 1941 to 1945. *12th Area Army organization; number of persons.* 12 files (Total: 40.2 MB)

JACAR Ref. C12120985200 to JACAR Ref. C12120985800. June 1938 to 1945. *13th Area Army organization; number of persons.* 7 files (Total: 22.7 MB)

JACAR Ref. C12120986000 to JACAR Ref. C12120987700. *14th Area Army organization; number of persons.* 18 files (Total: 61.3 MB)

JACAR Ref. C12120987900 to JACAR Ref. C12120988400. *15th Area Army organization; number of persons.* 6 files (Total: 15.9 MB)

JACAR Ref. C12120988600 to JACAR Ref. C12120990300. *16th Area Army organization; number of persons.* 18 files (Total: 43.9 MB)

JACAR Ref. C12120990500 to JACAR Ref. C12120991300. *17th Area Army organization; number of persons.* 9 files (Total: 24.4 MB)

JACAR Ref. C12120991500 to JACAR Ref. C12120991800. *18th Area Army organization; number of persons.* 4 files (Total: 9.2 MB)

Armies:

JACAR Ref. C12120970800 to JACAR Ref. C12120971200. February 10, 1938 to 1945. *Mongolia Garrison Army organization; number of persons.* 5 files (Total: 7.4 MB)

JACAR Ref. C12120992000 to JACAR Ref. C12120992600. *1st Army organization; number of persons.* 7 files (Total: 11.8 MB)

JACAR Ref. C12120992800 to JACAR Ref. C12120994000. *2nd Army organization; number of persons.* 13 files (Total: 42.0 MB)

JACAR Ref. C12120994200 to JACAR Ref. C12120995000. *3rd Army organization; number of persons.* 9 files (Total: 22.4 MB)
JACAR Ref. C12120995200 to JACAR Ref. C12120996200. *4th Army organization; number of persons.* 11 files (Total: 25.9 MB)
JACAR Ref. C12120996400 to JACAR Ref. C12120997000. *5th Army organization; number of persons.* 7 files (Total: 16.9 MB)
JACAR Ref. C12120997200 to JACAR Ref. C12120997900. *6th Army organization; number of persons.* 8 files (Total: 15.2 MB)
JACAR Ref. C12120998100 to JACAR Ref. C12120998700. *11th Army organization; number of persons.* 7 files (Total: 22.8 MB)
JACAR Ref. C12120998900 to JACAR Ref. C12121000000. *12th Army organization; number of persons.* 12 files (Total: 20.5 MB)
JACAR Ref. C12121000200 to JACAR Ref. C12121001500. *13th Army organization; number of persons.* 14 files (Total: 36.8 MB)
Note: 14th Army organization; number of persons. File missing
JACAR Ref. C12121001700 to JACAR Ref. C12121002100. *15th Army organization; number of persons.* 5 files (Total: 8.3 MB)
JACAR Ref. C12121002300 to JACAR Ref. C12121002700. *16th Army organization; number of persons.* 5 files (Total: 7.2 MB)
JACAR Ref. C12121002900 to JACAR Ref. C12121003300. *17th Army organization; number of persons.* 5 files (Total: 8.1 MB)
JACAR Ref. C12121003500 to JACAR Ref. C12121004200. *18th Army organization; number of persons.* 8 files (Total: 29.4 MB)
Note: 19th Army organization; number of persons. File missing
JACAR Ref. C12121004400 to JACAR Ref. C12121005400. *20th Army organization; number of persons.* 11 files (Total: 22.0 MB)
JACAR Ref. C12121005600 to JACAR Ref. C12121007000. *23rd Army organization; number of persons.* 15 files (Total: 31.9 MB)
JACAR Ref. C12121007200 to JACAR Ref. C12121007700. *25th Army organization; number of persons.* 6 files (Total: 14.6 MB)
JACAR Ref. C12121007900 to JACAR Ref. C12121008300. *28th Army organization; number of persons.* 5 files (Total: 12.6 MB)
JACAR Ref. C12121008500 to JACAR Ref. C12121009200. *29th Army organization; number of persons.* 8 files (Total: 18.1 MB)
JACAR Ref. C12121010100 to JACAR Ref. C12121011100. *31st Army organization; number of persons.* 11 files (Total: 25.2 MB)
JACAR Ref. C12121011300 to JACAR Ref. C12121012300. *32nd Army organization; number of persons.* 11 files (Total: 34.8 MB)
JACAR Ref. C12121012500 to JACAR Ref. C12121012800. *33rd Army organization; number of persons.* 4 files (Total: 9.2 MB)
JACAR Ref. C12121013000 to JACAR Ref. C12121013400. *34th Army organization; number of persons.* 5 files (Total: 10.7 MB)
JACAR Ref. C12121013600 to JACAR Ref. C12121014300. *35th Army organization; number of persons.* 8 files (Total: 20.4 MB)
JACAR Ref. C12121014500 to JACAR Ref. C12121015500. *36th Army organization; number of persons.* 11 files (Total: 23.3 MB)
JACAR Ref. C12121015700 to JACAR Ref. C12121016100. *37th Army*

organization; number of persons. 5 files (Total: 9.5 MB)
JACAR Ref. C12121016300 to JACAR Ref. C12121017000. *38th Army organization; number of persons.* 8 files (Total: 17.8 MB)
Note: 39th Army, Thailand. File missing
JACAR Ref. C12121017200 to JACAR Ref. C12121017600. *40th Army organization; number of persons.* 5 files (Total: 9.5 MB)
JACAR Ref. C12121017800 to JACAR Ref. C12121018200. *41st Army organization; number of persons.* 5 files (Total: 15.8 MB)
JACAR Ref. C12121018400 to JACAR Ref. C12121019200. *43rd Army organization; number of persons.* 9 files (Total: 15.2 MB)
JACAR Ref. C12120967200 to JACAR Ref. C12120967800. July 1939 to 1945. *44th Army organization; number of persons.* 7 files (Total: 19.0 MB)
JACAR Ref. C12121019400 to JACAR Ref. C12121019800. *50th Army organization; number of persons.* 5 files (Total: 6.8 MB)
Note: 51st Army Organization; Mito, Japan. File missing
JACAR Ref. C12121020900 to JACAR Ref. C12121021500. *52nd Army organization; number of persons.* 7 files (Total: 14.6 MB)
JACAR Ref. C12121021700 to JACAR Ref. C12121022300. *53rd Army organization; number of persons.* 7 files (Total: 13.7 MB)
JACAR Ref. C12121022500 to JACAR Ref. C12121023200. *54th Army organization; number of persons.* 8 files (Total: 13.1 MB)
JACAR Ref. C12121023400 to JACAR Ref. C12121024000. *55th Army organization; number of persons.* 7 files (Total: 16.0 MB)
JACAR Ref. C12121024200 to JACAR Ref. C12121024800. *56th Army organization; number of persons.* 7 files (Total: 16.4 MB)
JACAR Ref. C12121025000 to JACAR Ref. C12121025800. *57th Army organization; number of persons.* 9 files (Total: 21.2 MB)
JACAR Ref. C12121026000 to JACAR Ref. C12121026500. *58th Army organization; number of persons.* 6 files (Total: 13.6 MB)
JACAR Ref. C12121026700 to JACAR Ref. C12121027100. *59th Army organization; number of persons.* 5 files (Total: 5.8 MB)
JACAR Ref. C12121027300 to JACAR Ref. C12121028900. *Air Army attached units organization; number of persons.* 17 files (Total: 38.7 MB)

Air Armies:
JACAR Ref. C12121029100 to JACAR Ref. C12121029600. *1st Air Army organization; number of persons.* 6 files (Total: 20.3 MB)
JACAR Ref. C12121029800 to JACAR Ref. C12121030000. *2nd Air Army organization; number of persons.* 3 files (Total: 15.6 MB)
JACAR Ref. C12121030200 to JACAR Ref. C12121031400. *3rd Air Army organization; number of persons.* 13 files (Total: 40.1 MB)
JACAR Ref. C12121031600 to JACAR Ref. C12121032000. *4th Air Army organization; number of persons.* 5 files (Total: 17.8 MB)
JACAR Ref. C12121032200 to JACAR Ref. C12121032600. *5th Air Army organization; number of persons.* 5 files (Total: 27.3 MB)
JACAR Ref. C12121032800 to JACAR Ref. C12121033200. *6th Air Army organization; number of persons.* 5 files (Total: 19.2 MB)
JACAR Ref. C12121033400 to JACAR Ref. C12121033500. *5th Area Army, 1st Air*

Division organization; number of persons. 2 files (Total: 6.2 MB)
JACAR Ref. C12121033700 to JACAR Ref. C12121033900. *10th Area Army, 8th Air Division organization; number of persons.* 3 files (Total: 13.4 MB)
JACAR Ref. C12121050000 to JACAR Ref. C12121050100. *Miscellaneous air units; number of persons.* 6 files (Total: 5.2 MB)

Homeland:
JACAR Ref. C12121036400 to JACAR Ref. C12121036700 *Hokubu and Asahikawa organization; number of persons.* 4 files (Total: 7.2 MB)
JACAR Ref. C12121036900 to JACAR Ref. C12121037300. *Tohoku organization; number of persons.* 5 files (Total: 10.9 MB)
JACAR Ref. C12121037500 to JACAR Ref. C12121038200. *Tobu organization; number of persons.* 8 files (Total: 27.2 MB)
JACAR Ref. C12121038400 to JACAR Ref. C12121038800. *Tokai organization; number of persons.* 5 files (Total: 13.7 MB)
JACAR Ref. C12121039000 to JACAR Ref. C12121039400. *Chubu organization; number of persons.* 5 files (Total: 18.5 MB)
JACAR Ref. C12121039600 to JACAR Ref. C12121039700. *Chugoku organization; number of persons.* 2 files (Total: 6.1 MB)
JACAR Ref. C12121039900 to JACAR Ref. C12121040000. *Shikoku organization; number of persons.* 2 files (Total: 4.7 MB)
JACAR Ref. C12121040200 to JACAR Ref. C12121040800. *Seibu organization; number of persons.* 7 files (Total: 21.7 MB)

Articles:
Bradsher, Dr. Greg (Senior Archivist). December 19, 2017. *The beginnings of the United States Army's Japanese language training: From the Presidio of San Francisco to Camp Savage, Minnesota 1941-1942*: National Archives at College Park. Blog entry
Bradsher, Dr. Greg (Senior Archivist, NARA). August 10, 2012. *From Rabaul to Stack 190: The travels of a famous Japanese Army publication.* National Archives and Records Administration at College Park. Blog entry
Tanaka, Professor Hiromi (Keiko Tamura translator). Undated. *AWM 82 Captured Japanese documents*: Australian War Museum: Australian-Japanese Research Project, Online article
Takizawa, Akira. 2004-2019. *Taki's home page.* http://www3.plala.or.jp/takihome/

Illustrations and Photographs:
Cover:
Design and artwork: Roderick Grigor hereafter identified as (author)
Volume 1:
Chapter 1: Pages 1 to 10
Page 10: Sea Duty Co. unloading Daihatsu China (author)
Chapter 2: Pages 11 to 18
Page 11 Manchuria Incident medal (author)
Page 12 (1) Philippines diary. (2) Additional diary photo (author)
Page 13 (1) Document binding. (2) Asia button, (3) China Incident medal (author)
Page 14 (1) Pen case. (2) Soldier's China service memorabilia (author)

Page 15 (1) Inf. parade in Kanazawa 1920s (anon. photo). (2) Superior Private photo taken in China (anon. photo)
Page 16 (1) Type 98 machine cannon (Taki's Type 98 machine cannon page). (2) Type 98 machine cannon (Handbook on Japanese military forces)
Page 17 (7) Photos of Japanese army dog tags (author)
Page 18 (1) Reconnoitering enemy positions. (2) Soldiers marching (author)
Chapter 3: Pages 19 to 196
Page 29 Hirohito: Caption: 1940 Emperor review of the troops (author)
Page 46 (1) USO style show performer. (2) USO style show audience (author)
Page 57 Foraging for hay (author)
Page 83 Division's infantry on parade (author)
Page 92 Army parade: (1) Hirohito on white horse (2) Infantry in review (author)
Page 125 Division's cavalry on parade (author)
Page 148 Winter patrol in Manchuria (author)
Page 179 Type 96 howitzers towed by Model B tractors (author)
Page 196 Ki-48 Lily bomber overhead (author)
Chapter 4: Pages 197 to 286
Page 258 Pontoon Bridge in China ca. 1941 (author)
Chapter 5: Pages 287 to 375
Page 291 Heavy machine gun and crew (author)
Appendix and Bibliography: Pages 376 to 397

About the author:
Toronto born Roderick Grigor graduated from the Ontario College of Art in 1981. He became an award winning professional illustrator, producing work for advertising, packaging, newspapers and magazines. In the mid 1990s high-end illustration became a casualty of inexpensive digital image manipulation and soon Grigor turned to super-realism fine art painting. He has several solo art shows to his credit.
A lifelong fascination with military and Japanese history has over years transformed the artist into a serious student and collector of WW2 Japanese military history books and artifacts. In 2014 he took on the idea of creating a comprehensive overview of the Imperial Army in WW2. Original English and Japanese source material forms the basis for an unprecedented look into the long-vanquished Imperial Japanese Army.